FOR REFERENCE

SPIRITS, FAIRIES, GNOMES, AND GOBLINS

AN ENCYCLOPEDIA OF THE LITTLE PEOPLE

SPIRITS, FAIRIES, GNOMES, AND GOBLINS

AN ENCYCLOPEDIA OF THE LITTLE PEOPLE

Carol Rose

ABC-CLIO

Santa Barbara, California
Denver, Colorado
Oxford, England

All illustrations appearing in this work, except those listed below, are from the private collection of the author Carol Rose. Illustration sources are as follows: pp. 33 and 136, *The Complete Adventures of Snugglepot and Cuddlepie* by May Gibbs. London: Angus Robertson, 1946; pp. 54, 116, 215, and 288, *Folklore of the Isle of Man* by M. Killip, illustrated by Norman Sayle. London: B. T. Batsford Ltd., 1975; p. 138, *Lancashire Ghosts* by Kathleen Eyre. Yorkshire, England: Dalesman Publishing Company Ltd., 1979; p. 57, *Welsh Legends and Fairy Folklore* by D. Parry-Jones, illustrated by Ivor Owen. London: B. T. Batsford Ltd., 1953; pp. 85 and 302, *English Legends* by Henry Bett, illustrated by Eric Fraser. London: B. T. Batsford Ltd., 1950; pp. 114, 236, 258, 314, and 346, *Who is Santa Claus?* by Robin Crichton, illustrated by Margaret Nisbet. Edinburgh, Scotland: Canongate Publishing, 1987; p. 238, *The Awakening* by John Galsworthy, illustrated by R. H. Sauter. London: Heinemann. Reproduced with permission of the John Galsworthy and R. H. Sauter estates.

Library of Congress Cataloging-in-Publication Data

Rose, Carol, 1943–
    Spirits, fairies, gnomes, goblins : an encyclopedia of the little
people / Carol Rose.
        p.   cm.
    Includes bibliographical references and index.
    ISBN 0-87436-811-1 (alk. paper)
    1. Fairies—Encyclopedias.   2. Spirits—Encyclopedias.
3. Supernatural—Encyclopedias.   I. Title.
GR549.R65   1996
398.21'03—dc20   96-8460
                                                        CIP

02 01 00 99 98 97 96 95   10 9 8 7 6 5 4 3 2 1

ABC-CLIO, Inc.
130 Cremona Drive, P.O. Box 1911
Santa Barbara, California 93116-1911

This book is printed on acid-free paper ∞.
Manufactured in the United States of America

For David, Jean-Karim, Rhya-Jeanette, Gina Foong-Lin,
Michelle Mun-Wai, and my grandchildren

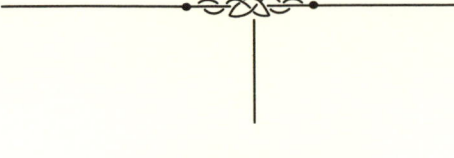

CONTENTS

INTRODUCTION, ix

SPIRITS, FAIRIES, GNOMES, AND GOBLINS

AN ENCYCLOPEDIA OF THE LITTLE PEOPLE

1

APPENDIXES, 349

BIBLIOGRAPHY, 367

INTRODUCTION

Between the gods and heroes and mere mortals, there is another group of beings that holds a very special place in the cultural development and expression of human society. These are the "Little People." This group of supernatural beings and individual spirits is an important part of the religions, cultures, and folk beliefs of human societies throughout the world. The lesser spirits included in this encyclopedia are not powerful like supreme deities or extremely evil in the satanic sense; the spirits presented here occupy a different place in the supernatural spectrum. Some of these spirits, such as *Fairies* and *Angels,* have volumes devoted to them and are referred to frequently; but there are hundreds of other fascinating groups of supernatural beings throughout the world that are not well known except to the social group that reveres them and the specialists who have recorded their legends.

There is no exact, all-encompassing concept of this range of spirits, but they are described by C. S. Burne in *The Handbook of Folklore* (1914) as "various races of beings, not human and yet not divine, who are supposed to share this lower earth, more or less invisibly with mankind." These beings may have an association with a "supreme" power, such as that of messenger, or they may be quite independent of any superior influence. These spirits may be either entirely good or entirely evil or both good and evil at different times. Although possessing some supernatural powers, they are mostly restricted to their own sphere of operation and their powers are quite limited and subordinate. In fact, that is why they are called "Little People"—they are "little" in the sense of limitation rather than size. While some of these spirits are described as being small, such as the *dwarfs* and *Orang Bunyi,* or even invisible, such as the *encantados,* others such as the *djinns* may assume any proportion and shape at will.

These spirits come from a range of origins: Some are the transformed souls of humans or transformed human ghosts that have become *demons, keremets,* or *afrits.* Others are the debased deities of a conquered people, such as the *Tuatha dé Danann, Coventina,* and *Legua.* Yet other spirits are the personification of a fear such as the *Exotica* and *Fad Felen,* or of a natural phenomenon such as *Kornwolf* and *Virra Birron.* Some supernaturals are the descended memory of ancestor worship such as the *Banshee* or the *Domovoi,* or the debased memory of an ancient supreme being such as *Auld Hornie, Herne the Hunter,* and the *Wild Huntsman.*

In general these spirits tend to interfere with the lives of humans, sometimes promoting the person's interests as a *familiar* or *Guardian Angel,* sometimes being mischievous such as *Puck* or *Blue Jay,* and at other times being entirely malevolent such as *Lucifer* and *Melalo.* These supernaturals may be categorized to some extent by their activities. There are messenger spirits, including *angels;* and spirits associated with animals, the arts, celestial bodies, corn, and vegetation. Some spirits like demons and devils are associated with death, disease, and fate; others are associated with fortune, luck, and treasures. Some are familiar spirits, guardian spirits, and tutelary spirits; others protect the family and children. Some spirits inhabit the graveyards, the home, mills, and mines, while others dwell in the elements of the earth, water, wind, and fire. Still others serve to warn humans in the guise of nursery bogies, cautionary spirits, and weather spirits. There are others who fit none of these categories because their activities are diverse and ambivalent towards both the deities and humans. These include the *fairies, djinns, tricksters,* and *trolls* who may work good deeds, feed the poor, spin thread, steal human babies, blight crops, or bring disasters, all for the same human group.

The appearance of these beings also varies. Some invariably manifest in the shape of humans like the *elves*. Others may manifest as part-human like the *mermaids*, or as modified humans with heads and feet pointing backwards like the *Obda*, or as half a human vertically divided like the *Nashas*, or with some odd feature such as grossly extended ears like the *Dogai*. Others may manifest most often in animal form. *Familiars* tend to be domestic creatures, while *bogies*, *barguests*, and *Wisht hounds* often manifest as *Black Dogs*. The *Phooka, Kelpie,* and *Cheval Bayard* can transform from human to horse shapes at will. Some spirits such as *Boneless*, as the name implies, have little by way of shape at all, while others such as the *devils*, *djinns, guardian spirits,* and *tricksters* can shape shift to assume whatever guise their purpose requires.

Most of these lesser spirit beings are immortal, but they may sometimes be mortal after hundreds of years like the *Peri*. They may live in societies similar to those of humans, having royalty, armies, and activities reflecting that of human society. They may even intermarry with humans. Others may be solitary, shunning people or their own kind; while others such as the *nymphs* may consort with deities and produce offspring by the gods. Their places of abode are sometimes restricted to woods, hills, deserts, roads, buildings, or water, while others move about freely.

Whatever and whoever they are, these "Little People" have been with every society since the beginning of time. That they are revered and propitiated is evidenced by the numerous euphemisms by which these spirits are known. In Britain, the most common of these euphemisms is the *Little People*, a name that has an equivalent in many other languages. The stories of these spirits may represent the expression of social needs or the personification of natural phenomena. However, there are deeper anthropological meanings that folklorists say indicate the very real invasions and battles for survival of our distant ancestors. These legends may depict their human hopes and fears, their defeats and triumphs, and the transformation of once superior adversaries to those of a less superior group, like the *Tuatha dé Danann* who were conquered by the Milesians and demoted from a superior race to the status of underground fairies. The "Little People" form the subjects of fascinating and engrossing legends, which may be appreciated through the accumulation of imaginative embellishments over the centuries. Some of these spirits also belong to modern folk tales, e.g., the *Hobbit, Gumnut babies,* and *Gremlins*, indicating that the process of identifying these supernaturals is as much a part of our present as it is of our past. Whether they are the expression of our collective conscience or our guilty conscience, these "Little People" are a common cultural heritage around the world,

and as such they deserve to retain a prominent place in the expression of our traditions.

Research and Organization

Being from Yorkshire, England, my own background is deeply rooted in local culture and traditional tales. While studying for a fine arts degree, I came across many references to visual perceptions of the supernaturals in paintings, weavings, sculptures, and masks from different nations. However, researching their meanings was difficult because there were no comprehensive sources. Later, as a student in psychology studying beliefs, superstitions, and fears in cultural traditions, I encountered the same research difficulties. This lack of reference sources demonstrated that these spirits are not restricted to any particular subject, and that the realm of the "Little People" transcends linguistic, geographical, historical, chronological, and cultural boundaries. My fascination with them and their legends resulted in the accumulation of my own library of specialist folklore and antiquarian books; and the concept of this work evolved to fill what was clearly a gap in reference publishing.

To be included in this book, a spirit must exert some active, willful, supernatural influence on humans and/or their domestic creatures, without being divine. In this respect, the spirit could neither be a hero, nor a ghost since these beings retain the human condition (only the *demonized* soul of a human, such as the *hantu* or *keremet*, was the exception).

The material for this work has been drawn from several different reference areas. Encyclopedias and dictionaries of classical and nonclassical mythology for the major groups of religions from antiquity to present-day; books of folk tales and folklore of different periods from different cultures; sources of traditional superstitions and local legend; literature from different cultures; chronicles and annals of historical events; travel and regional descriptions of social groups in geographical and anthropological surveys; and nursery rhymes and fables for children were used.

The entry head represents the most common name of the spirit. Any alternative spelling with a simple doubling of letters, or the addition of the letter 'e' is shown, e.g., *Afrit/e, djin/n;* closely related spellings also appear in the entry head. Other names or euphemisms for the being are located in the text. Very dissimilar names are mentioned and may appear as a separate entry. The reader is directed to this by way of a cross-reference.

The spirit names from other cultures and languages, including ancient ones, are transcribed as far as possible into a modern English equivalent. However, this presents some difficulties. The nature of legend and folklore means that the majority of such spirits, except literary ones like the *Hobbit*, have survived through oral reports and stories. When these stories were finally written down, the spirits were an interpretation of the pronunciation of the spirit's name and its activities. Many accounts survive from ancient times, as hand-written documents such as scriptures, and from about the fifteenth century as hand-cut wood-block prints. However, the standardization of spelling did not really occur until the twentieth century. (Even so differences still occur in the types of English used around the world.) Add to the problems of spelling, the number of regional names and differences in dialect for each country, and the number of possible interpretations can be enormous.

Indeed some spirits have the same name but have a different description of character and activities, e.g., *Nereid*. Others have the same description of character and activities but have a completely different name, e.g., *Rumpelstiltskin* and *Tom Tit Tot*.

The names of general groups of spirits are given in the lower case, e.g., *angel*; capitals are used for specific types within the group, e.g., *Guardian Angel*, and also for individual spirit names, e.g., *Michael*. The name of a spirit within its own entry is capitalized to highlight its importance over other beings discussed within the same text.

Each entry gives information about the physical description, character, powers, and activities of the spirit. Where possible, a traditional tale or anecdote is incorporated. Full information is not always available, but every endeavour has been made to give details that identify the spirit.

The entry description of each spirit is in the present tense because these spirits, being supernatural, are deemed to exist to eternity, unless specifically stated as having been destroyed. Activities that are habitual and that form part of the description of the being's character are also given in the present tense. Actions and anecdotes that were unique occurrences are in the past tense. However, if a tale is repeated habitually as a tradition, it is often folkloric convention to tell the story as though it is actually happening, i.e., told in the present tense. This convention is used for dramatic impact. When such tales are included, the original tense is maintained.

Names of religions, countries, and regions are given in the forms used during the period of belief in the particular spirit. Names of beliefs such as Manicheism and Zoroastrianism and places such as Bohemia and Prussia are included. Although boundaries and names may since have changed and the religion may have been superseded by another faith, giving these original names will indicate the historical context of belief in the spirit being described.

Belief in these lesser spirits is not confined to particular areas. Absorption of these spirits into the legends and folklore of different groups of people often happens with demographic migrations and trade. Similarities in the character or activities of these spirits is indicated in cross-referencing throughout this work as well as in the appendixes.

The traditions that have been passed down to us are essentially human interpretations of someone's record of human experiences. This presents the difficulty not only of spellings and names earlier discussed, but also of different versions of the same stories. While the source may be sincere, there must always be a certain caution in accepting such interpretations, since embellishments may have been added with the passage of time and the emphasis may have been distorted in the retelling.

Inevitably selections have been made with regard to the salience of information for each entry. Cross-referencing and guides to source material are given for the reader to pursue further inquiry into this fascinating aspect of human culture.

I have come to realize through my research into these supernaturals that those beliefs that I once thought were exclusive to my own culture are common to so many others, and the spirits are much the same in all but name. Pervading many of the accounts of the spirits' characters and their activities is a stoic sense of humor by which it is possible to discern how societies have coped with their difficulties. Through the legends of the "Little People," I have discovered that in this shared heritage it is possible to relate to people the world over in a way that transcends historical, cultural, and linguistic barriers. This is an experience I hope other readers will also be able to enjoy.

*   *   *

I wish to acknowledge the following for their invaluable professional assistance: D. G. Rose, for photographic preparation of the illustrations from my collection; C. Oates, Chief Librarian of the Folklore Society; and the library staff of the University of Kent, England.

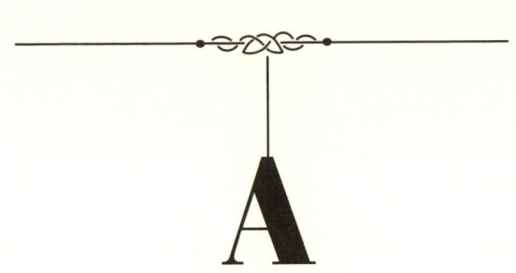

A

AATXE

This is the name of an evil spirit or devil in the folklore of the Basque people of southwestern France and northwestern Spain. Aatxe, which means Young Bull, is also known as Etsai. This spirit is a shape-shifter who most frequently appears in the shape of a bull, but he may also assume human form. Aatxe inhabits mountain caves, from which he emerges only on stormy nights to wreak havoc and cause destruction.
References 93
See also Devil, Spirit

ABA

See Čembulat

ABAC

See Addanc

ABADDAN, ABBADON

This is the demon or devil known in Christian scriptures and writings as the Angel of the Bottomless Pit. He is also called the Angel of Hell and the Lord of the Plague of Locusts in the Apocalypse, and is known in Greek as Apollyon, which means the Destroyer. Abaddan, whose name means Downfall or Ruin in Hebrew, is one of the most destructive of the Fallen Angels. His character is used in scriptures and literature, as in Milton's *Paradise Regained,* to epitomize evil just short of the extreme of Satan.
References 23, 40, 92, 93, 107, 114
See also Angel, Apollyon, Demon, Devil, Fallen Angel

ABARBAREA

This is the name of a nymph in the classical mythology of Greece and Rome. She is mentioned in Homer's *Iliad* as being the consort of Bucolion and mother of Æsepus and Padasus.
References 130
See also Nymph

ABBEY LUBBER

These are minor devils also known as Buttery Spirits in the folklore of England. They inhabited the abbeys and religious houses that had become wanton and overluxurious after the fifteenth century. The Abbey Lubber's aim was to tempt the monks and brothers from their life of piety into drunkenness, gluttony, and other excesses so that their souls would be damned.
References 17
See also Buttery Spirit, Devil, Friar Rush, Appendix 22

ABDIEL

This is the name of a Seraph or angel in Milton's *Paradise Lost.* His name is Hebrew and means Servant of God. Abdiel opposed the revolt of Satan against the Lord, who cast out Satan and his accompanying Fallen Angels from Heaven. He is portrayed as an evil spirit in Milton's *Paradise Lost,* Book VI.
References 40, 114
See also Angel, Fallen Angel, Seraphim, Spirit

ABDULLAH AL-KAZWINI

This is the name of a merman in the Arabic legends called the *Thousand and One Tales of the Arabian Nights.* He befriends and assists a poor fisherman also named Abdullah.
References 88
See also Havmand, Merman

ABERE

This is the name of an evil spirit in the folk beliefs and legends of Melanesia. She is a female demon portrayed as a "wild" woman, with young female attendants. Abere seduces men to come willingly to her in the waters of a lake. Then she commands rushes and reeds to grow around and conceal her. Hidden by the reeds, she entraps the gullible men searching for her and murders them.
References 29
See also Demon, Spirit, Appendix 25

ABGAL

This is the name of a group of spirits in the mythology of the ancient Sumerians. There were seven spirits in the group, also known as Apkallu. The Abgal are portrayed as part man and part fish like mermen,

and are protective guardian spirits. They derive from the earlier Apsu or Abzu in the entourage of Enki, the god of wisdom.
References 93
See also Guardian, Merman, Spirit, Appendix 25

ABHAC
See Addanc

ABIGOR
This is the name of a fiend or devil featured in the mysticism and demonology of medieval Europe. This evil spirit was considered to be a powerful, high-ranking demon of Hell.
References 53
See also Demon, Devil, Fiend

ABIKU
These are evil forest spirits of the Dahomey and Yoruba people of West Africa. The Abiku possess babies and young children, drawing away their life essence until the child dies. The spirits may enter a child in infancy or be permitted by the Creator, Mawu, to be born to a family. Once in possession of the infant, the Abiku are unceasingly hungry and thirsty. They devour all the food intended for the child, often providing for other Abiku without a host. The host child, in pain and deprivation despite the efforts of the parents, ultimately sickens and dies, whereupon the Abiku seeks another host.

Parents may protect their children in different ways: They may adorn the child with bells, which the Abiku hates; they may dedicate the child to a Vodu (a god); they may rub pepper into tiny cuts, as this may drive out the evil spirit; or they may disfigure the child's appearance to be unrecognizable and un-wanted by the spirit, which will go back to the forest. Sometimes the infant is detained by iron anklets and bracelets with bells to prevent the Abiku from taking possession in the first place.
References 87, 100
See also Alp Luachra, Joint Eater, Spirit, Appendix 19, Appendix 22

ABONSAM
The name of a house devil or evil spirit of dwellings and settlements in the folklore of Ghana. The Abonsam will take up residence in the home, causing problems and misfortune. Once a year the neighbors of the village hold a special ceremony to rid them-selves of the unwelcome spirits, who hate noise. Inhabitants remain silent for four weeks prior to the very noisy ceremony; then everyone beats drums and gongs to rid every corner of the houses of each evil spirit.
References 48
See also Devil, Spirit, Appendix 22

ABUNDIA
See Habonde

ABZU
See Abgal

ACACILA
See Achachilas

ACAVISER
This is the name of a spirit in the beliefs and mythol-ogy of the ancient Etruscans. Acaviser is a female supernatural also known by the name Achvistr.
References 93
See also Lasas, Spirit

ACEPHALI
See Acephalos

ACEPHALOS
This is a supernatural being in the mythology of ancient Greece. It was also known as Acephali, Akephale, or Aképhalos. The Acephalos is described in Egyptian, Greek, and medieval European religion and folklore as a frightening spirit. It is a demon that manifests in the shape of a human being but without a head, causing terror and panic in those to whom it appears. In the later folklore of modern Greece, the spirit known as Phonos (the Greek word for Death) has the same physical description and ability to incite terror.
References 39, 40
See also Coluinn Gun Cheann, Demon, Spirit

ACHACHILAS
This is the name of a group of nature spirits or demons in the folk beliefs of the Aymara people of Bolivia. These spirits, also known as Acacila, are described as looking like old people and are said to dwell underground in the mountains. The Achachilas control the prevailing weather and send frost, hail, or rain to the region according to how benevolently dis-posed to humans they may be at the time.
References 87, 88, 119
See also Demon, Mekala, Spirit

ACHERI

This is a female disease spirit in Indian folklore. She lives on the mountaintops, but attends nightly revels in the valleys beneath. She respects all who wear the color red, and children are given necklets of this color to protect them. If a child falls ill, it is said that the spirit has passed by, and the sickness is called Acheri's Shadow.
References 87
See also Spirit, Appendix 22

ACHVISTR

See Acaviser

ADAMASTOR

This is the name of a unique spirit that seems to have appeared only once in history. Adamastor is named as the Spirit of the Cape of Good Hope or the Spirit of the Cape of Storms. According to records detailed by the famous Portuguese poet Luis de Camões (1524–1580), Adamastor was described as a hideous spirit that appeared to Vasco da Gama prior to rounding the Cape, foretelling disaster for all those attempting the voyage to India.
References 40, 114
See also Spirit

ADARO

This is the name of a sea spirit of Melanesian and Polynesian mythology.
References 102
See also Spirit

ADDANC

The name of a dwarf or water spirit that inhabited Lake Llyon Llion in Wales. According to the region of the narrator and the spirit's activities, he was known by different names: Abac, Afanc, and Avanc. This dwarf or demon was considered to be responsible for terrible flooding by making the waters of the lake overflow into the surrounding country. He was eventually dragged from his abode by the oxen of Hu Gadarn and, some say, killed by Peredur.
References 41
See also Afanc, Demon, Dwarf, Appendix 25

AD-HENE

This euphemistic name, meaning Themselves in Manx Gaelic, is used when referring to the fairies in the Isle of Man (United Kingdom). It was always considered prudent not to offend the Little People. The fairies could be offended by invoking them directly or even by calling them by the wrong name, and they could be malicious to humans when slighted.
References 81
See also Little People, Appendix 6

ADRAMELECH

This is the name of an ancient Babylonian spirit to whom child sacrifices were made. In later European scriptures, he is portrayed as one of the Fallen Angels and one of the highest in the infernal order in European medieval demonology. In English literature of the seventeenth century, Adramelech was overthrown by Uriel and Raphael in Milton's *Paradise Lost*.
References 40, 53, 114
See also Fallen Angel, Raphael, Spirit, Uriel, Appendix 22

ADRASTEA

A nymph of ancient Crete, whose abode was a Dictæan grotto. In Roman mythology, she is credited with suckling the infant king of the gods, Jupiter.
Reference 41
See also Amáltheia, Nymph, Appendix 22

AELFRIC

See Alberich

AËLLO

See Harpy

AELLOPUS

See Harpy

AENGUS

The name of one of the fairies in the folklore of Ireland. Aengus is one of the Tuatha dé Danann in Irish mythology and a member of the Sidhe.
References 18
See also Sídhe, Tuatha dé Danann, Appendix 6

AEOLUS

This is the name of the spirit of the winds, also known as Æolus in ancient Greek mythology. He was guardian of the winds on his island of Lipari, from which he released the winds by request from the gods or in answer to the prayers of humans. In the classical myths, Aeolus befriended and tried to help Odysseus on his epic voyage.
References 119
See also Guardian, Spirit, Appendix 26

AËRICO

In Albanian folklore, this is the name of a devil that inhabits particular trees, especially an old cherry tree. It will attack anyone who comes near it or interferes with its trees. The very shadow of Aërico's tree is deemed responsible for painful swellings of the hands and feet.
References 110
See also Aerika, Kirnis, Appendix 17, Appendix 19

AERIKA

These are demons or spirits in the folklore of modern Greece. Aerika, also known as Ayerico, inhabit the air and are considered to be responsible for bringing disease to humans.
References 12
See also Aërico, Spirit, Appendix 17

AES SÍDHE

See Sídhe

AESHMA, AESMA

(1) Aeshma, also known as Aesma in Iranian and Zoroastrian mythology, is a particularly evil fiend, deva, or demon, third in the hierarchy of demons and high in the retinue of Angra Mainyu. Aeshma, whose name means Madness, is particularly charged with inducing rage, vengeance, and lust, and prolonging outrage. He will do this even to the point of inciting strife among demons themselves when unsuccessful with humans. He harries the vulnerable souls of the dead before they can approach salvation, and Ahura Mazda (the Supreme Being) has assigned Sraosha to control and ultimately defeat this demon. In the earlier Hebrew scriptures, Aeshma is the Asmodeus of the Book of Tobit.

(2) In the Parsee mythology, Aesma Deva is the demon whose rage and destructive vengeance is particularly directed toward the cow, a sacred animal, and only the hero Saosyant can ultimately defeat him.
References 41, 53, 87, 88, 93, 102
See also Asmodeus, Demon, Deva, Fiend, Sraosha

AFANC

This is a name for an evil spirit in the folklore of Wales. It may be known in other localities as Abac, Abhac, Addanc, or Avanc. The Afanc is described variously as a dwarf, a water demon, a supernatural crocodile, or a beaver. Afanc was said to inhabit deep river pools near Brynberian Bridge, Llyn yr Afanc above Bettws-y-Coed, Llyn Barfog (the Bearded Lake), or in Llyn Llion. This water demon not only dragged down and devoured any creature that fell into the water, he caused disastrous flooding when he allowed the waters of the pool to burst out onto the surrounding area. Legend has it that through this flooding all the inhabitants of Britain were drowned except one man and one woman, who became the ancestors of the present British people. The Afanc was such a menace that it was decided to destroy or remove him.

Two versions of this feat exist:

(1) The Afanc was dragged from the pool by chains attached to Hugh Gadarn's great oxen and dragged to dry land, where his powers were useless.

(2) The Afanc was enchanted out of the pool by the caresses of a damsel who let him sleep on her knee.

In his trusting slumbers, men from the village bound Afanc with chains attached to oxen. The demon woke immediately, furiously wrenching the damsel's breast in his attempt to break free and regain the safety of his pool. Afanc was dragged to Llyn Cwm Ffynnon, where he is said still to exist.
References 15, 133
See also Addanc, Spirit, Appendix 4, Appendix 25

AFFRIC

This is the name of a water nymph, possibly derived from the older name Aithbrecc of ancient Britain, in the locality of Glen Affric in Scotland. With the coming of Christianity to the islands, she may have been debased from the ancient goddess whose name was that of the Scottish river she protected.
References 123
See also Nymph, Appendix 25

AFREET

See Afrit

AFRIT/E

In Arabic and Muslim mythology, the Afrit are the second most powerful of the five classes of demons known as djinns. In different regions they are also known as Afreet, Efreet, Efrit, Ifreet, and Ifrit. Not only were they of enormous size, they were extremely malicious, inspiring great fear. They were particularly adept at shape-shifting to achieve the downfall of humans. In Kenya and along the east coast of Africa, these spirits inhabit the murky depths of pools and rivers, waiting, like Jenny Greenteeth, to drag down unwary bathing children by the legs. Legend has it that King Solomon made an Afrit submit to being his servant. Lord Byron featured such a demon in his work *The Giaour*.
References 29, 40, 41, 53, 92, 107, 114
See also Djinn, Jenny Greenteeth, Spirit, Appendix 22

AGA KURMAN

This is the name, meaning Plowing Man, of a demon or keremet in the folk beliefs of the Cheremis/Mari people of the former Soviet Republic. This spirit is propitiated at the time when the earth is prepared for sowing a new crop.
References 118
See also Demon, Keremet

AGANIPPE

A spring water nymph in the classical mythology of Greece and Rome. Her abode was on Mount Helicon, where the waters of her spring were said to give inspiration to those who drank there.
References 102, 130
See also Nymph

AGANIPPIDES
See Muses

AGAS
This is the name of a demon of Iranian mythology. His name is taken from the Avestan word meaning Evil-Eye, and this devil caused his evil work to be effected through the sense of sight. This demon's domain is the temptation to sin through visual experiences such as voyeurism, lust, and covetousness. Agas is delighted when he sees men falling into his traps, bringing the opportunity to inflict diseases of the eyes on tempted humans.
References 93
See also Demon, Devil, Appendix 17

AGATHODEMON, AGATHODÆMON
See Agathos Daimon

AGATHOS DAIMON, AGATHODEMON
In ancient Greek mythology, this term was used for a benevolent guardian spirit of the individual or abode, sometimes conceived of as a hovering, winged supernatural serpent. The name is derived from the Greek term Good Demon, used for an otherwise nameless Genius. In households an offering of wine would frequently be reserved for this protective spirit. During the Greek occupation of Egypt, a cult of the Agathos Daimon became important and linked with the spirit of Good Fortune, Agathe Tyche.
References 39, 53, 93, 107
See also Aitvaras, Guardian Angel, Spirit, Appendix 22

ÆGERIA
See Egeria

AGIAOPHEME
See Siren

ÆGINA
The name of a nymph in the classical mythology of Greece and Rome. She was the daughter of the river god Asopus and the lover of Zeus.
References 102, 130
See also Nymph

AGLAIA
See Graces

ÆGLE
In ancient Greek mythology there are three nymphs by this name:
(1) One of the Hesperides, transformed into part of the constellation of that name.

(2) A Naiad, considered to be the most beautiful of this group of nymphs.
(3) The name of the nymph who stole the love of Theseus away from Ariadne.
References 130
See also Hesperides, Naiad, Nymph

AGLOOLIK
A tutelary guardian spirit in the Inuit mythology of North America, Agloolik lives beneath the ice floes. The particular guardian of the seals and their pups, Agloolik provides sufficient game for the hunters to feed their families, while protecting the survival of the seals.
References 29, 38, 119
See also Fylgja, Nagual, Spirit, Tutelary Spirit, Zoa, Appendix 18, Appendix 21

AGNEN
An evil genius or demon in the mythology of the Amazonian Tupinamba people, Agnen is a particularly frightening spirit who is mentioned in the myth of the Twins as devouring one before being beaten by the other.
References 102
See also Demon, Spirit

AGUN KUGUZA
This is a spirit in the folk beliefs of the Cheremis/Mari people of the former Soviet Republic. The name Agun Kuguza means Drying House Old Man. He is usually invisible, but inhabits the buildings used for drying and storing the grain after the harvest. If he is not propitiated properly, the harvest will be ruined. To make sure that the Agun Kuguza is well disposed to the humans of the farm, a small animal is sacrificed to him each autumn.
References 118
See also Kuguza, Spirit, Appendix 22

AGUNA, AGUNUA
See Figona

AHASPENDS
See Amesha Spentas

AHI AT-TRAB
In Muslim Tureg folklore, these are mischievous spirits that live just beneath the surface of the Sahara sands. They are rarely visible, but during a sandstorm may manifest as a whirling pillar of sand. The Ahi At-trab cause all manner of problems for these nomadic people, such as drinking dry the water of the oases and springs just as the Tureg arrive, or

causing the camels to trip and miss their footing in the shifting dunes.
References 87
See also Djinn, Spirit

AHIFATUMOANA
See Pahuanuiapitaaiterai

AHREN KONIGEN
This is the name of the corn spirit embodied in the last sheaf ceremonially cut at the end of the harvest in Salzburg, Austria. Its effigy was celebrated as the Ahren Konigen, which means the Corn King, at the feast given for the completion of the harvest. It is unusual in that the spirit is envisaged in a male form rather than the more customary female.
References 48
See also Cailleac, Corn Spirit, Appendix 15

ÄI
This is the name of a disease spirit in the folklore of southern Estonia. It may also be known as Äijo or Äijätär in different areas. It is said to inhabit the forests, and will attack any humans that venture there. This spirit is comparable with the Aiatar, Ajatar, and Ajattara in Finland.
References 87
See also Spirit, Appendix 17

AIATAR
This spirit is known as the Devil of the Woods in Finnish folklore. It is a demon that inhabits the forest and may also be known as Ajatar or Ajattara in different regions of Finland. Aiatar is described as an evil female spirit that sometimes manifests as a serpent or a dragon. Aiatar is said to suckle snakes and to bring disease to mankind. It is comparable with the Äi, Äijo, or Äijätär of southern Estonia.
References 87
See also Demon, Spirit, Appendix 17, Appendix 19

AICHA KANDIDA
A water djinn in the folklore of Morocco who is to be found by the banks of the River Sebu, around the Aquedal at Marrakech, and sometimes in the sultan's palace grounds. Her husband is the Afrit Hamou Ukaiou. Aicha Kandida takes the form of a very beautiful woman who will approach a man traveling alone at night in the area, calling him by name and pursuing him if he tries to escape. She hates humans, and if her quarry cannot reach another human or inhabited dwelling in time, she will drag him into the river and consume him under the water. Sometimes, if men gratify her willingly, she may be magnani-

mous and release them back to their world, and even laden them with rich gifts.
References 90
See also Afrit, Djinn, Hamou Ukaiou, Appendix 25

ÄIJÄTÄR
See Äi

ÄIJO
See Äi

AIKEN DRUM
This is the name of an individual brownie in the folklore of Scotland. He was said to have inhabited Blednoch in Galloway. Aiken Drum was described as wearing only a kilt made of green rushes. During the night he would complete all the tasks left unfinished by the humans at dusk. But when given new clothes as payment for his work, like all such brownies he disappeared from that location forever.
References 17
See also Brownie

AIKREN, A'IKREN
This is a spirit in the folk beliefs and mythology of the Karok people of South America. He is the guardian spirit of the village of Kitimin, located beneath Sugar Loaf Mountain. A'ikren, whose name means He Who Dwells Above, appears as the Duck Hawk, which lives on the summit of the mountain. He is benevolent, and in one story shows compassion to two young maidens grieving for the loss of their warrior suitors.
References 87, 88
See also Guardian, Spirit

AILLEN MAC MIDHNA
This is the name of the fairy musician of the Tuatha dé Danann in the legends and folklore of Ireland. Aillen Mac Midhna is described as particularly dark with fiery breath, and is the owner of an evil, poisonous spear. He possessed a magic *tuinpan* (an Irish tambourine), or harp, on which he played so enchantingly that all who heard him were lulled to sleep. On the Celtic festival of Samhain (Halloween), when the Tuatha dé Danann came each year to the royal palace of Tara from the sidh of Finnachaid, Aillen would play for the assembled company. Annoyed because they would be lulled to sleep, he would take his magic spear and blast three fiery bellows from his nostrils, which destroyed the palace of Tara. Finn of the Fianna, at last tiring of Aillen's destruction of 23 years, destroyed him by turning Aillen's own spear on him and forcing the weapon's owner to inhale its poisonous fumes.
References 17
See also Fairy, Tuatha dé Danann

AINE, AINÉ

This is the name of an Irish fairy of the Tuatha dé Danann, a woman of the Sidhe and queen of the fairies of South Munster owing allegiance to Finvarra, Onagh, and Cliodna. There are two main versions of Aine's identity: (1) She and her sister Fenne were the daughters of King Egogabal of the Tuatha dé Danann, and (2) she is the daughter of Owel of Munster, the foster son of Mannan; as a woman of the Sidhe of Munster, Aine used her magic to slay the king of Munster, who had raped her. Whichever derivation, a further legend survives that she was seen combing her hair on the banks of Lough Gur by Gerald, the earl of Desmond. In love at first sight, he stole Aine's magic cloak and persuaded her to marry him. As with all such supernatural unions, the bargain was subject to a promise—that he should never express surprise. The child of the union was Gerald Fitzgerald, fourth earl of Desmond (from whom the present family claims descent). The childhood antics of Gerald surprised his father, thus making him break the promise, and caused Aine and their child to be reclaimed by the waters of the Lough and returned to their fairy family. Knockainy/Knock Aine is a hill near Lough Gur named after Aine. Her son is said to have a fairy castle in the depths of the Lough, from which he emerges on a white steed every seven years.
References 17, 87
See also Cliodna, Fairy, Finvarra, Onagh, Sídhe, Tuatha dé Danann

AINSEL

This is the name of a playful little spirit or a fairy child in the folklore of Northumberland (England). She is the subject of a local fairy tale, the theme of which is to be found in many other cultures. The story tells how the willful son of a widow would not go to bed when requested and preferred to remain beside the fire. His mother warned him that the fairies would come for him if he stayed too long by the embers, and she went to bed expecting him to follow soon after. Just then, to his amazement, a dainty little fairy child popped down the chimney and frolicked about the room. The boy asked her name, to which she replied "Ainsel," which in dialect means Ownself. Therefore, upon the fairy inquiring his name, the boy playfully answered "My Ainsel," meaning My Ownself. The embers glowed dimmer, so the boy poked the fire into lively sparks that flew at Ainsel, who screamed. Then an enormous booming voice called down the chimney, "Who's hurt you?" In terror, remembering his mother's words, the child leapt into bed just as the fairy mother appeared. The wailing fairy child cried,

"My Ainsel did it," whereupon the fairy mother kicked her silly child back up the chimney for being the cause of her own harm.
References 17
See also Cheval Bayard, Fairy, Kallikantzari, Spirit, Appendix 22

AIPALOOKVIK, AIPALOOVIK

This is the name of an evil sea spirit in the folk beliefs of the Inuit of North America. Aipalookvik is a particularly terrifying spirit bent on destruction, especially attacking and biting those fishing the sea.
References 29, 102, 119
See also Spirit, Appendix 25

AIRI

This is the name of an evil spirit in the folklore of India. It is a bhut, or demon, that dwells in the hills and will do anything to cause harm to the humans who travel there.
References 87
See also Bhut, Demon, Spirit

AITVARAS

This is a house spirit of Lithuanian folklore that assumes various shapes according to its environment. In the house it is described as looking like a black cat or black cockerel, but when traveling outside it may be like a flying dragon or serpent with a fiery tail. This "luck-bringer" may be "purchased" from the Devil for one's soul, hatched from the egg of a seven-year-old cockerel, or brought home unrecognized until too late. Once in the home, it is very difficult to dislodge it. The Aitvaras's responsibility is to make its owner rich by any means. This is usually by the theft of milk, corn, and gold, frequently at the expense of the neighbors. It demands sustenance only of omelets in return for the goods it brings. The first mention of this spirit was in a 1547 document. Since then, numerous stories of suspicious wealth may mention an Aitvaras.

One traditional account describes how a bride is given the task of grinding the corn for her new mother-in-law. She cannot understand why she can never finish grinding the grain from the corn bin. Taking a consecrated candle from the church she peeps into the bin and sees an Aitvaras disgorging constant streams of corn. The sacred candle is its demise much to the grief of the mistress of the house. Not only has the mother-in-law lost the source of her wealth but also her soul, which will now be claimed by the Devil for the lost Aitvaras.
References 87, 88, 93
See also Kaukas, Para, Pukis, Smiera-Gatto, Appendix 22

AIWEL

He is a nature spirit in the folklore of the Dinka people of Sudan. The son of a river spirit, Aiwel is charged with helping the people and their herds with his magical powers.
References 119
See also Spirit

AJATAR, AJATTARA
See Aiatar

AKAANGA

This is the name of a demon in the folk beliefs and mythology of Mangaia Islanders (Cook Islands) of the South Pacific. It is one of the devils said to come from hell.
References 110
See also Amaite-Rangi, Demon, Devil, Miru

AKAKASOH

These are tree spirits or nats in Burmese folklore. These spirits are much like the Hamadryads of Greek mythology in that they inhabit the trees. The Akakasoh dwell in the highest branches of their tree.
References 110
See also Boomasoh, Hamadryad, Hmin, Nats, Shekkasoh, Spirit, Appendix 19

AKEPHALE, AKÉPHALOS
See Acephalos

AKHKHAZZU

The name of a disease spirit in the mythology of ancient Babylon. He is particularly responsible for inflicting yellow jaundice on humans.
References 31
See also Appendix 17

AKHTYA
See Drug

AKO-MANO

This is the name of a demon or devil in the mythology of ancient Persia. He was subject to the supremely evil Ahriman, and the adversary of the beneficent spirit Vohu Mano.
References 102
See also Demon, Devil, Spirit, Vohu Mano

AKOSA-SAPATA

This is the name of a spirit or encantado in the Afro-Brazilian cult Batuque. This spirit belongs to the "family" of Dā or Danbiera spirits.
References 89
See also Akossi-Sapata, Encantado, Spirit

AKOSSI-SAPATA

He is a dangerous disease spirit and encantado of the Afro-Brazilian cult Batuque. Possibly a borrowing from the spirit of the same name in the Casas das Minas cult in São Luís, he derives from a deity of Dahomey, West Africa. Akossi-Sapata is associated with Saint Lazarus, whose feast day is 11 February. This is the only day in the year when this spirit is invited to be received by a medium; otherwise, if Akossi-Sapata is not treated correctly, he may take offense easily and inflict the most terrible skin disease on his medium. [He is *not* the same as Akosa-Sapata.]
References 89
See also Akosa-Sapata, Encantado, Spirit, Appendix 17

AKSELLOAK

This is the name of a beneficent spirit in the Inuit folklore of North America. Akselloak is said to inhabit swaying or rocking stones in the harsh landscape.
References 102
See also Spirit

AKUAKU

These are supernatural beings in the folklore of the Easter Islanders. These spirits were believed to exist on the aroma of food. One of them is called Rapahango, a supernatural who had arrived from beyond the seas.
References 22
See also Peri, Spirit, Tatane

AKVAN

Akvan is the name of a demon in the ancient legends and mythology of Iran. He was defeated in a famous fight by the mythical hero Rostom.
References 30
See also Demon

AL

A disease spirit or demon in the folk beliefs of North Africa, Al is considered responsible for giving infections to women in childbirth.
References 6
See also Demon, Appendix 17, Appendix 22

ALAKAI
See Pey

ALAN

This is a group of spirits in the folklore of the Tinguian people of the Philippine Islands. The Alan are said to inhabit the forests. They manifest as part bird and part human, with fingers and toes reversed. Their abode is the jungle, where they rest by suspending themselves from the trees like bats, but when not there, they live in homes constructed of

pure gold. Although they can be malignant or simply mischievous, the Alan are usually benevolent and considered to be the guardians of many of the mythical heroes.
References 87
See also Guardian, Spirit

ALARDI
A disease spirit in the folklore of the Osset people of the central Caucasus, Alardi is often described as taking a human form but having wings. Although he is a demon responsible for inflicting smallpox, Alardi is regarded as the guardian of women.
References 93
See also Con-Ma-Dāu, Demon, Guardian, Minceskro, Šedra Kuba, Tou Shen, Appendix 17

ALASTOR, ALASTORES (pl.)
An avenging spirit or evil genius in the mythology of the ancient Greeks, Alastor is also described as a cacodemon. As a spirit usually associated with either the family or its home, the Alastor is responsible for exacting revenge for wrongdoing. It will do this by pursuing the offender indefinitely in order to exact retribution. If the offender is not punished sufficiently before death, even the descendants of the first offender may receive the punishment. These spirits are also associated with inflicting and spreading pestilence. Alastor was the subject of a work by the English poet Shelley, titled *Alastor, or the Spirit of Solitude.*
References 40, 53, 107, 130
See also Cacodæmon, Emizimu, Furies, Genius, Spirit, Appendix 17, Appendix 22

ALB
See Alp

ALBASTOR
The Albastor is a house spirit of the Cheremis/Mari peoples of one of the former Soviet Republics. This spirit, also known as Labasta, inhabits the bathhouses in the guise of a man or woman, but it may appear as a giant with long, flowing hair. Although said to originate as the soul of an unbaptized, illegitimate infant, it is capable of shape-shifting to the form of any animal while on the ground. When this spirit travels through the air, it takes the appearance of a shooting star with a trail of sparks. It has also been described as synonymous with Šükšəndal, or as a spirit of marshland and ravines in forests. Like the succubus, the Albastor's activities include sexual intercourse with humans, and it punishes those who overindulge by providing such sexual excess as to cause their death from exhaustion. The attentions of the Albastor may be discerned from a sore left on the

victim's lips by its kiss. The human lover or husband of any woman visited by an Albastor will also become ill. The Albastor may be defeated in two ways, either by catching it and breaking the little finger of its left hand, thereby breaking its power, or by placing a cross over each door, thus preventing its entry.
References 118
See also Aitvaras, Bannik, Household Spirit, Incubus, Spirit, Succubus, Šükšəndal, Appendix 22

ALBEN
See Alfar

ALBERICH
In Teutonic and Scandinavian mythology, Alberich is the King of the Dwarfs, or the Dark Elves, and brother to King Goldmar. He is also known as Aelfric, Alferich, Alpris, Andvari, and Elberich in Wagner's adaptation of the *Nibelungenlied*. Alberich is reduced to the description of a hideous gnome. He lives in a magnificent underground castle decorated with gemstones in which he guards a great treasure. He is also the keeper of a magic ring, an invincible sword Balmung, a belt of strength, and a cloak of invisibility. He is responsible for forging many of the fabulous gifts for the gods, such as Freya's necklace. Alberich is featured in many of the legends of the *Volsunga Saga* and the *Nibelungenlied,* which detail the theft of the treasures and the retribution that follows.
References 41, 87, 95, 114, 119
See also Andvari, Dwarf, Elf, Gnome, Goldmar, Nibelung

ALCYONE
This is the name of one of the nymphs known as Pleiades in the classical mythology of Greece and Rome. She was one of the daughters of Atlas and Pleione.
References 130
See also Nymph, Pleiades

ALDER KING
See Erl King

ALECTO
In the mythology of ancient Greece and Rome, Alecto, whose name means the Unceasing, is the spirit or genius of war, pestilence, and ultimate revenge. She is one of the Furies who exact retribution from those whose hideous crimes, especially matricide or patricide, remain unpunished by human law.
References 53, 93, 130
See also Alastor, Erinys, Eumenides, Furies, Genius, Spirit

ALF
See Alfar

ALFAR
In Scandinavian and Teutonic mythology, these are the elves of northern Europe; the spelling may vary as Alf, Elben, Ellen, Elven, and Elfvor. From this Nordic name comes the Old English word Ælf. There are two races of elves described in the *Prose Edda*.

(1) The first of these are the Döckalfar, also spelled Döcálfar, which means Dark Alfar. They are also known as the Swartalfar, Svartalfar, or Black Alfs, whose character and appearance are described as darker than pitch. They were supposed to have developed from maggots that ate the flesh of the dead giant Ymir. The Dark Alfs live underground and are sinister and powerful, especially in the fashioning of magic metal weapons and other gifts for the gods whom they assist. They were considered to be the bringers of fertility, and as such were the subject of a widespread cult. Later development transformed the Dark Alfs into demonic beings, responsible for disease and misfortune.

(2) The Liosalfar, or the Light Alfs, are the second group; their character and appearance are whiter than the sun. In Denmark these elves are called Elven or Ellen, while in Sweden they are named Elfvor. The Light Alfs live between earth and heaven in a luminous place called Alfheim, and unlike their counterparts are benevolent toward mankind.
See also Elf, Elven, Elves of Light

ALFERICH
See Alberich

ALICANTO
This is a spirit in the folk beliefs of the mining communities of South America. It is a night spirit that assumes the shape of a bird, the wings of which give out a golden or silvery light. It inhabits the mountains and forests of Chile. The Alicanto has a taste for gold and silver, and when it locates a vein, it feasts until it is unable to fly. Any human prospector who thinks that he can follow the Alicanto's light in the darkness to find a source of gold will be deceived and misled by it. The wily Alicanto will flicker its wing-light enticingly until it lures the greedy human to his doom, usually over the edge of a cliff.
References 56
See also Spirit, Will o' the Wisp

ALIORUNA
See Alraune

ALOCER
This is the name of a powerful demon in the mysticism and demonology of medieval Europe.
References 53
See also Demon

ALP
A supernatural being of Teutonic mythology and later Swiss folklore, the Alp, also known as Alb, is described as part dwarf or elf and part god. In the original concept of the Alps, they are magical workers of metals that inhabited the underworld deep in the mountains. This status was later diminished in folklore to that of a demon responsible for diseases and the disturbance of sleeping humans.
References 93
See also Demon, Dwarf, Elf, Incubus, Appendix 17

ALP LUACHRA
An evil fairy or spirit in the folklore of Ireland. Being entirely invisible, it is difficult to know when they are about until it is too late. The Alp Luachra is acquired when a person sleeping by a stream accidentally swallows a newt. This spirit invisibly devours the food of its victim, who, though apparently greedy, continues to be emaciated and undernourished, to the astonishment of family and friends. Douglas Hyde describes a version of this story in his book *Beside the Fire*, in which the victim managed to get rid of the spirit by eating a huge quantity of salt beef without a drink, then lying with his mouth open over a stream, into which the thirsty Alp Luachra jumped in desperation.
References 17
See also Abiku, Fairy, Joint Eater, Spirit

ALPAN
See Lasas

ALPRIS
See Alberich

ALRAUN/E
(1) A female demon in Teutonic mythology. The supernatural powers of this spirit were invoked with the aid of an effigy cut from the root of a tree, usually an ash. This was given the name Alraun, which in Germany was also the ancient name of the wild Bryony plant that develops by strangling its host.

(2) Alrauns is an alternate collective name in earlier Germanic mythology for the Norns or Valkyries, whose other names are variously Alioruna, Alrunes, Dises, or Idises.
References 53, 95
See also Dis, Norns, Spirit, Valkyries

ALRICHE
See Eldrich

ALRUNES
See Alraune

ALVIS, ALVÍSS, ALWIS
This is one of the kings of the dwarfs in Nordic mythology. His name means All-wise, and his story is told in the *Alvis-Mal-Edda*. Alvis fell in love with Thrud, a Valkyrie and the daughter of the god Thor, and asked for her hand in marriage. Thor agreed, if Alvis could answer 13 questions about the naming of the sun, moon, night, world, sky, wind, clouds, stillness, fire, sea, forests, wheat, and beer in the languages of the Gods, the Giants, the Æsir, the Vanir, and the Elves. Knowing how easy the questions were that Thor had posed for him, Alvis, who had just traveled throughout the nine worlds, confidently went to claim his bride. But crafty Thor knew how long it would take to answer the questions. As Alvis triumphantly gave the last answer, he was horrified to realize that the first rays of the morning sun had reached him. He turned to stone upon the spot, unable to take the bride he had won.
References 41, 87, 95
See also Dwarf, Elf, Valkyrie

AMADÁN
The name of a fairy spirit in the folklore and mythology of Ireland, Amadán is the "fool" of the Irish Sidhe, also known as the Stroke Lad. He is also called Amadán Mór and Amadán na bruidne because he is said to live in a castle called Bruidean. Amadán chooses humans indiscriminately to punish or curse with his incurable crippling touch. His victims and their disfigurements of face, limbs, or body may be forever subjected to ridicule or accusations from their fellow humans. A more severe affliction from Amadán could result in the victim's early demise. According to Lady Gregory, his touch may be counteracted by repetition of the prayer "The Lord between us and harm," should one be unfortunate enough to meet Amadán, which is more likely in June than any other time of the year. Amadán punished, with a stroke, a miserly man whom he caught mending shoes on a Sunday. (The Christian sabbath was formerly decreed a day of religious observance only; work was forbidden.)
References 87
See also Fairy, Sídhe, Spirit

AMADÁN MÓR
See Amadán

AMADÁN NA BRUIDNE
See Amadán

AMAHRASPANDS
See Amesha Spentas

AMAIMON
In European medieval demonology, Amaimon is a devil ruling the eastern territories of Hell, or of the universe, and accountable to Asmodeus. Shakespeare includes the naming of this evil power in *The Merry Wives of Windsor* (Act II, scene ii), and describes Amaimon as a fiend. It was considered possible to restrain the activities of Amaimon at certain hours of the morning and evening when his power was at its weakest.
References 40, 53
See also Asmodeus, Devil, Fiend

AMAITE-RANGI
This is the name of a sky demon in the mythology of the Mangaia people of the Cook Islands. He waged war on and was defeated by Ngaru.
References 41
See also Akaanga, Demon

AMÁLTHEIA, AMALTHÉA
This is the name of a nymph in the mythology of ancient Greece. Amáltheia suckled the infant god who became Zeus, king of the gods of Olympus.
References 93
See also Adrastea, Nymph, Appendix 11, Appendix 22

AMBROSIA
See Hyades

AMERETAT
In the Zoroastrian religion of Iran, this spirit is one of the six Amesha Spentas, and one of the attendants of Ahura-Mazda. Ameretat is the spirit of immortality and the guardian of all plants and trees.
References 41, 53, 119
See also Amesha Spentas, Attendant Spirit, Guardian, Spirit, Appendix 18

AMESA SPENTAS
See Amesha Spentas

AMESHA SPENTAS
This is the name for a group of spirits in the Zoroastrian religion of Iran said to equate with the archangels of Christianity. Amesha Spentas may also be referred to as the Ahaspends, Amahraspands, Amesa, Amesa Spentas, or Amshaspands. Translated as the Bounteous Immortals, Amesha Spentas is the collective name of the spirits that are the six attendants of Ahura-Mazda. Each of the spirits is the genius presiding over a particular earthly quality, and the means by which divine will is conveyed. Their individual names are Ameretat, Aramaiti, Asha,

Haurvatat, Kshathra, and Vohumanah. They are the symbols of intellect and bringers of glad tidings. Their individual roles have been ascribed as: (1) Achievement, (2) Inspiration, (3) Wisdom, (4) Intellect, (5) Sensitivity, and (6) Love.
References 41, 53, 119
See also Ameretat, Angel, Aramaiti, Asha, Attendant Spirit, Genius, Haurvatat, Izeds, Kshathra, Spirit, Vohu Mano

AMMIT, AMMUT

This female demon, also known as Ammut, is the spirit of the underworld in ancient Egyptian mythology. She is described as having the head of a crocodile, the body of a cat or lion, and the rear end of a hippopotamus! Ammit lurked in the proximity of the hall of judgment, where the souls of the dead were sent to heaven or hell. In this position she was able to pick off and devour those condemned as sinners.
References 29, 93
See also Demon, Spirit

AMON

In European medieval demonology, Amon is one of the most powerful demons.
References 53
See also Demon

AMORETTI, AMORETTO

See Erotes, Putti

AMPHITHOE

See Nereids, Nymphs

AMPHITRITE, AMPHYTRITE

In ancient Greek mythology, Amphitrite was a Nereid nymph who was married, reluctantly, to the sea god Poseidon. Tiring of Poseidon's affairs and jealous of Scylla, Amphitrite changed Scylla into a sea monster.
References 40, 56, 92, 93, 114, 130
See also Nereid, Nymph, Scylla

AMSHASPANDS

See Amesha Spentas

AMY

In European medieval demonology, Amy is a particularly powerful demon.
References 53
See also Demon

ANA

In Romany Gypsy folklore, she is the Queen of the Fairies, known in Romany as the Keshalyi. Ana is described as the embodiment of the fairy-tale princess, being pure and beautiful, and her abode is a wonderful mountain castle—that is, until the fateful liaison with the king of the demons, which condemns her offspring to be demons also. Her name may be the derivation of the Celtic goddess Dana, from whom the Tuatha dé Danann of Irish legend take their origins. The Celtic word *Ana* translates as abundance, while in the Sanskrit from which the Romany language derives, *Anna* translates as sustenance or nourishment, which also shows a remarkable similarity.
References 31
See also Fairy, Keshalyi, Loçolico, Melalo, Tuatha dé Danann

ANAMELECH

An evil demon in the medieval demonology of Europe, his task is to deliver unhappy messages and cause distress to humans.
References 53
See also Demon

ANANSI, ANASI

This is the name of a trickster of West African, West Indian, South American, and southern U.S. folklore. As a typical shape-shifting, cunning, sly, supernatural spirit of folktales, Anansi features extensively in moralizing tales, with other animal spirits and sometimes humans as his dupes. His origin, according to West African folklore, was human, but he was transformed by the gods and used as a spirit messenger.

In West Africa, the names of this supernatural spider vary from Gizō and Kwaku Ananse among the Hausa and Akan peoples, respectively, while in the New World his names vary from Mr. Spider, 'Ti Malice in Haiti, and Nansi in Curaçao, to the feminine forms of Aunt Nancy and Miss Nancy in parts of South Carolina in the United States. The original name for this trickster survives in stories from Jamaica and Surinam.

The most common tales involve Anansi in some attempt to fool another creature by supernatural manipulation, but Anansi does not always succeed and sometimes falls prey instead of his intended victim. Some tales are unique to one area, but others like the Tar Baby feature under one name or another wherever the Spider stories have survived. The spider may be adapted to a different animal form and his demise effected by some other sticky substance. In the Ashanti and Yoruba form, this tale is known as The Pot Always Full of Food, in Surinam as Anansi and the Gum Doll, in Angola as The Hare and the Gum Doll, and in South African Hottentot folklore as The Jackal and Gumdoll. Some tales remain essentially the same, while the characters have been changed. Thus, in West Africa, Anansi may be the

Hare and the Tortoise in Bantu tales, B'Rabby in the Bahamas, and Brer Rabbit in the southern United States. In this way an original tale becomes in Sierre Leone Turtle Rides a Leopard, in Surinam Anansi Rides a Tiger, and in the southern United States Brer Rabbit Rides Brer Fox/Brer Wolf.

One of the most delightful of the original tales describes how, when caught in a bush fire, Anansi changes into his spider shape and jumps into the ear of a frightened antelope. He tells her which way to run clear of the fire, and they both escape. The grateful spider promises that he will repay her. Some time later, the antelope and her fawn are in the path of some hunters and she runs desperately to lure them away from her baby but to no avail. When she returns, exhausted, she cannot find the baby and believes it to be slaughtered, until Anansi reveals where he has hidden it safely—inside an enormous web.

References 33, 56, 87, 119
See also Bamapama, Basajaun, Blue Jay, Coyote, Eshu, Manabozo, Mink, Spider, Trickster

ANANTA-SHESHA
See Nagas

ANASI
See Anansi

ANATIVA
This is the name of an evil supernatural spirit who, in the folklore of the Koraya people of eastern Brazil, is the cause of the flood that precedes the creation of their ancestors.
References 41
See also Spirit

ANCHANCHO, ANCHANCHU
In the folklore of the Aymara people of Bolivia, Anchancho is an evil spirit and demon living in isolated places, especially rivers in the Peruvian Andes. The Anchancho is essentially a disease spirit, but is also associated with terrible whirlwinds, which signal his presence. The Anchancho befriends and accompanies unwary travelers whom he either afflicts with sickness or feeds from by sucking their blood while they sleep.
References 87, 119
See also Ccoa, Demon, Incubus, Larilari, Mekala, Spirit, Appendix 17

ANCHUNGA
In the folklore of the Tapirape people of central Brazil, this term is applied to (1) spirits of the dead and (2) particularly evil demons. They are described as having such long hair that it drags along the ground behind them. Ware, a famous Tapinare

shaman hero, is said to have destroyed all the Anchunga that plagued the Tapinare people in the south of the country by setting fire to their hair, but the evil spirits of the north escaped this fate and still plague the Tapirape people there.
References 87
See also Demon, Spirit

ANDRAS
A particularly powerful demon in the medieval demonology of Europe, he is considered responsible for sowing discord and provoking quarrels among humans.
References 113
See also Demon

ANDVARI
King of the Dwarfs in Nordic mythology, he is also known by the names Aelfric, Alberich, Alferich, Alpris, and Elberich. Andvari is the guardian of the treasure and the magic ring, upon which he placed a curse. A series of legends tells how these were stolen and subsequently brought disaster to whoever possessed them, including Sigurd and the family of Hreidmar.
References 29, 40, 41, 87, 95, 114, 119
See also Alberich, Dwarf, Guardian

ANGATCH
This is the name of an evil spirit in the folklore of Madagascar.
References 56
See also Spirit

ANGEL
The term Angel is an ancient one, and various spellings of it are to be found in manuscripts, including: Ængel, Ængle, Engel, Enngell, Enngle, Angil, Eangel, Angle, Aungel, Aungele, Aungelle, Aungil, Angell, Angelle, and Angele. Originally the word may have derived from the Greek word *anglos*; the Hebrew translation *mal'akh* meant Messenger. These concepts and namings were adopted throughout Europe in various forms. Until the end of the thirteenth century, the English pronunciation used a hard "G" from Old English and Teutonic traditions, but it was later softened through the influence of Old French. Angels are included as a concept in many different religions and have various descriptions according to the particular theological tradition. In ancient Mesopotamia, huge winged spirits were depicted, the Amesha Spentas of Zoroastrianism are invisible, and the Shên of China have human form. Early Hebrew concepts were humanoid but sexless; later identification of individual Angels gave them masculine names. The Angels of Islamic tradition, created from

pure bright gems, were sometimes named and described as having two, three, or four pairs of wings.

The Christian concept of Angels, which was derived from the Hebrew Testaments, became a highly developed element of the church doctrine. A complete hierarchical system was described. Divided into seven divisions, each headed by an Archangel, Angels were estimated to number 496,000. Each level of this hierarchy had a separate physical description: (1) Seraphim, Cherubim, and Thrones in the first circle; (2) Dominions, Virtues, and Powers in the second circle; and (3) Principalities, Archangels, and Angels in the third circle. The following are the descriptions of each as they were portrayed in religious art through the ages:

Seraphim—a child's head and wings depicted, usually in red, and may have a candle; or in human form with three pairs of wings.
Cherubim—a child's head and several pairs of wings, usually blue or gold, with a book.

The following are usually of human shape, dressed in flowing white and gold garments from which large gold wings protrude, either outstretched or folded, and they are mostly barefoot:

Thrones—may hold a throne.
Dominions—may be crowned and hold an orb and scepter.
Virtues—hold a rose or a lily.
Powers—may be in armor.
Principalities, Archangels, and Angels—unless named, have a youthful, feminine appearance.

Angels are, by tradition, the divine messengers and ministering attendant spirits of the Supreme Deity in the above religions. They bring guidance, healing, comfort, and hope, but are also likely to be the medium of bringing punishment to sinners or forgiveness to penitents. It is their duty to guide the souls of the righteous to Heaven.

With the Christian theological hierarchy and the naming of ranks and individual Angels, specific responsibilities or actions were ascribed to them. The angels in the first circle were the immediate circle of adoration, those in the second circle were responsible for the heavens and the elements, and those in the third circle were responsible for the earthly kingdoms, and humans in particular. It was from this last rank that Guardian Angels were drawn.

The seven named, most revered Archangels are: Michael, Gabriel, Raphael, Uriel, Chamuel, Jophiel, and Zadkiel. These Angels were associated in medieval theology with the seven planets then known to astronomers, and their names are recorded

in the Apocrypha. Only Michael and Gabriel are mentioned in the Bible; they are also in the Koran, which mentions other Angels called Malik, Harut, and Marut. Izra'il, the Angel of Death, and Israfil are angels mentioned in Islamic literature. In the Hebrew Talmudic tradition, the three Angels Sanvi, Sansavi, and Semangelaf were charged with encouraging the errant Lilith to return to Adam, and they provide a charm to protect children from her evil.

The presence of evil in the human world was accounted for in Christian theology of the Middle Ages by a "revolt" of the Angel Lucifer and his followers, who would not acknowledge "man." They were cast out from Heaven to become the adversarial Devil/Satan and his demon followers or the Fallen Angels, some of whom repented and try to return to Heaven.
References 39, 40, 56, 59, 62, 75, 91, 92, 107, 113, 114
See also Amesha Spentas, Angiris, Archangel, Attendant Spirit, Azrael, Demon, Devil, Fallen Angel, Gabriel, Guardian Angel, Haruts, Israfel, Lar, Lilith, Lucifer, Malik, Manes, Michael, Pitris, Raphael, Shên, Spirit, Uriel, Zadkiel, Appendix 1, Appendix 3, Appendix 7

ANGEL OLIVER
Until Satan's revolt in Heaven against the Lord, Angel Oliver had been a Prince of Archangels, but he was disgraced and cast out with the other Fallen Angels. From that time, in the Christian tradition, he has been responsible for cruelty to the poor, and his assigned adversary is Saint Lawrence. However, he is said to be remorseful and ever hopeful of regaining his place in Heaven.
References 87
See also Fallen Angel, Appendix 7

ANGIRIS
In Hindu mythology these spirits are named after Angiris, the King of the Pitris. They are Rishis, the "sons of the gods," who have immortality and the friendship of Indra. Like angels, they act as divine messengers and intermediaries for mankind, and to some extent they are protectors in much the same way as the Guardian Angels. They were also the givers of fire to mankind, and therefore preside over sacrificial fires and associated ceremonies.
References 29, 102
See also Angel, Guardian Angel, Lars, Manes, Pitris, Spirit

ÆNGUS MAC OG, ANGUS MAC OG (YOUNG SON)
See Angus Og

ANGUS ÓC
See Angus Og

Angels bring forgiveness.

ANGUS OG

One of the Tuatha dé Danann of Irish legend and fairy tradition, he is variously known as Angus Óc, Ængus/Œngus Mac Og (Young Son). He was the son of Dagda and the queen of the Sidhe, and his abode was the Bruigh na Bóinne (New Grange mound in County Meath). He had a magic cloak of invisibility, and with his magic he could control time and transform his shape to that of a swan. The supernatural Swan Maiden Ibormeith visited him in a dream, and having fallen in love with her, he pined until he discovered her with 149 of her Swan Maidens on Lough Bel Dracon. As she had human form only every alternate year, Angus Og transformed himself to the swan's shape to be with her on the Lough, singing sweetly as they glided over its waters. All who heard them were soothed into a magic sleep until Angus and his love returned to Bruigh na Bóinne.
References 56, 87
See also Fairy, Sídhe, Swan Maiden, Tuatha dé Danann, Urvasi

ANHANGA

(1) This is an ancient forest spirit or vegetation spirit in the folk beliefs of the Tupi people of Brazil. He is the guardian spirit of the forest and its animals.

(2) This is also a forest demon in the folklore of the modern Caboclos, derived from the shamanistic beliefs of native South Americans of the Amazon Basin. Like the Leshii of the Russian forests, this spirit tricks, misguides, and leads astray hunters and travelers in his domain, causing them misery and discomfort.
References 87
See also Demon, Guardian, Leshii, Spirit, Appendix 18, Appendix 19

ANIRAN

A lesser spirit in the Zoroastrian religion of Iran, Aniran is an attendant of Kshathra, who is one of the Amesha Spentas.
References 41
See also Amesha Spentas, Attendant Spirit, Kshathra, Spirit

ANITO

This is a general term for supernatural spirits in the Philippine Islands that includes those of all activities, whether good or evil in nature.
References 87
See also Spirit

ANITSUTSA

This is the name by which the Pleiades maidens are known in the mythology of the Cherokee Native American people.

References 25
See also Nymph, Pleiades

ANPIEL

Anpiel is an angel in the Hebrew literature whose responsibility is guardian of the birds.
References 53
See also Angel, Guardian Angel, Appendix 12

ANTARIKSHA

This is the name of a spirit in the Hindu mythology of India. Antariksha, whose name means Sky, is one of the eight attendant Vasus of Indra.
References 41
See also Angel, Spirit, Vasus

ANTIOPE

This is the name of a nymph in the classical mythology of Greece and Rome. She was the daughter of the river god Asopus.
References 102, 130
See also Nymph

ANTONIO LUIZ CORRE-BEIRADO

See Caboclo

ANUNNAKI

In ancient Babylonian mythology, these were the spirits that represented the stars below the horizon and were therefore invisible to humans.
References 87
See also Igigi, Spirit

AŒDE

See Muses

AOIBHINN

This is the name of one of the fairies in Irish folklore and one of the members of the Sidhe. Aoibhinn is the Queen of the Fairies of North Munster. She owes allegiance to Finvarra and Onagh of the Sidhe and their subordinate, Cliodna.
References 125
See also Cliodna, Fairy, Finvarra, Onagh, Sídhe

ÆOLUS

See Aeolus

AONIDES

See Muses

APARĀJITA

This is the name of the chief of the demons in the ancient folklore of India. Aparājita, whose name means the Unvanquished, was destroyed by Bhūtadāmara, who put an end to the demon by tram-

pling on him. (Aparājita has since been elevated to the status of one of the Krodhadevatās, one of the Buddhist fierce deities.)
References 93
See also Demon

APCI'LNIC
In the folklore of the Montagnais of Labrador, Canada, these Little People are described as about the height of the human knee; they inhabit remote mountain wilderness areas. The Apci'lnic are well known for stealing human children, and can materialize anywhere at will. Naturally, they are viewed with caution, and their presence is associated with imminent danger.
References 87
See also Changeling, Dwarf, Little People, Appendix 22

APEP
A demon also known as Apophis in ancient Egyptian mythology, he materialized in the shape of a serpent, living deep in the Nile and symbolizing all the dark features of existence such as storms, night, and death. He was a co-conspirator of the god of evil, Set. Apep fought to devour Ra each day but, protected by Mehen, Ra always escaped to bring light to the world again. Sometimes Apep was almost successful and an eclipse would occur, but Apep was always forced to regurgitate the celestial boat with Ra, its occupant.
References 29
See also Buber, Demon, Mehen, Nagas, Rahu

APKALLU
See Abgal

APO
(1) Apo is one of the celestial spirits, known as the Yazatas, in the Zoroastrian religion of Iran. Apo is especially the guardian spirit of fresh, sweet waters.
   (2) This is a general term for the spirits in the beliefs of the Quechua people of Peru.
References 41
See also Angel, Arariel, Spirit, Yazatas

APOIAUEUE
Apoiaueue was a benevolent nature spirit of the Tupi Guarani peoples of Amazonian Brazil. Apoiaueue was responsible not only for ensuring that the earth received a bountiful supply of rain when necessary, but also reported back to the Supreme Deity about events on earth, similar to angels in European theology.
References 56, 102
See also Spirit, Yazatas

APOLLYON
This is the name of one of the fiends in ancient Greek mythology. Apollyon, whose name means the

Destroyer, was a ruler of the underworld. He features in John Bunyan's work *Pilgrim's Progress*.
References 99, 107
See also Abaddan, Fiend, Appendix 16

APOPA
This is a spirit resembling a dwarf in the folklore of the Inuit and Ihalmiut people of North America. Although described as of human shape, Apopa is deformed and ugly. Apopa behaves rather like the kobolds and Puck of Europe, but unlike them, his activities never extend to benevolent acts. The Apopa are always mischievous, though relatively harmless.
References 101
See also Dwarf, Kobold, Puck, Spirit

APOPHIS
See Apep

APPLETREE MAN

In the West of England folklore of Cornwall, Devon, and Somerset, the spirit of the apple orchard is said to reside in the oldest tree, which is given the title of Appletree Man. To ensure a good crop for the year, it is the custom each year, traditionally Eve of Epiphany (5 January), for the farmer and his workers to take a pail filled with good cider and roasted apples to the Appletree Man. Each takes a drink and toasts the spirit with the words:

> "Health to thee old Apple tree
> Well to bear pocketsful, hatsful,
> Pecksful, bushelsful."

The remaining cider is for the Appletree Man, and is poured on the roots of the tree while the crowd cheers. Sometimes, just to make sure that no witches have entered the orchard, guns are fired to scare them from the trees.
References 69
See also Colt Pixy, Lazy Laurence, Old Roger, Spirit, Appendix 19

APSARAS

These are nymphs, also known as Asparas, who were originally water spirits of Hindu mythology. These beautiful and voluptuous nymphs made their appearance at the Churning of the Waters, and now dance in Indira's heaven. Their abode is the fig and banana trees, where the music of their lutes may be heard. They are the companions of the Gandharvas, spirits of air and music. The Apsaras's reputation for promiscuity stemmed from the legend that no one group of beings would take them as wives; consequently, they are reserved for the heroic dead on their arrival in paradise. This lively reputation extends to their concerns with bestowing good fortune in games of chance, and also causing irrationality or possibly madness.
References 29, 52, 87, 93, 102
See also Deev, Gandharvas, Guardian, Nymph, Spirit, Urvasi, Vrikshakas

APSU

See Abgal

APU

This is the name of a spirit in the religious texts of Peru. Apu is a spirit of the mountains in the religion of the Quechua people.
References 94
See also Spirit

APUKU

The Apuku are spirits in the Afro-South American folklore of Surinam. These Little People inhabit the natural clearings in the bush and jungle, which humans are too terrified to use. They resemble the dwarfs of European myths, with a powerful physique and frightening appearance.
References 87
See also Aziza, Bakru, Dwarf, Ijimere, Little People, Mmoatia, Pukkumeria

ÀRÀK

In the folklore of Cambodia, this is a tutelary or beneficent family guardian spirit who lives in the family home or a tree nearby. Considered to be a transformed ancestor, this spirit is called upon especially in times of sickness. A special festival is held at the beginning of the year to honor the Àràks of each family.
See also Agloolik, Fylgja, Guardian, Lar, Manes, Nagual, Spirit, Tutelary Spirit, Zoa, Appendix 21, Appendix 22

ARALEZ

In ancient Armenian belief, these spirits assumed a shape similar to that of a dog. Through their supernatural powers they were able, by licking the wounds of the dead and the injured, to restore warrior heroes to life on the battlefield.
References 93
See also Badb, Spirit, Valkyries

ARAMAITI

This is the name of one of the Amesha Spentas, also known as Armaiti, who is an attendant of Ahura-Mazda in the Zoroastrian religion of Iran. The name Aramaiti means Holy Harmony and is closely associated with guardianship of the earth's fruitfulness.
References 41
See also Amesha Spentas, Attendant Spirit, Appendix 21

ARAPTEŠ

This is a female forest spirit in the folklore of the Cheremis/Mari peoples of the former Soviet Republic. It may materialize as a pretty girl in an abandoned bathhouse, but only after nightfall.
References 118
See also Bannaia, Jekšuk, Spirit, Appendix 19

ARARIEL

This is the name of an angel in Hebrew tradition and literature. Arariel is the guardian of the waters of the earth.
References 53
See also Angel, Apo, Guardian, Appendix 25

ARATHRON

An Olympian spirit in the medieval European literature of Mysticism, Arathron was considered to

be the personification of Saturn, celebrated as Saturday, ruling over 49 provinces of the Olympian Universe.
References 53
See also Olympian Spirit, Spirit

ARAWOTYA
This is the name of a sky spirit in the mythology of the Australian Wonkamala peoples, whose homeland is around Lake Eyre. Arawotya was originally said to have been an earth spirit, providing unexpected water supplies and springs in the most arid regions of southern Australia and western Queensland.
References 119
See also Spirit, Appendix 18

ARCHANGEL
A chief angel ranking above others in the celestial hierarchy in the theology of several religions. The Christian concept of angels derived from the Hebrew Testaments and became a highly developed element of the church doctrine. Angels in seven divisions, each headed by an Archangel, were estimated to number 496,000. Unless named, Archangels and angels were depicted as having a youthful, feminine appearance.

Hebrew theological and literary works mention Raphael, Gabriel, Ariel, Michael, Kafziel (Cassiel), Zadkiel, and Samael. Some of these are included in the Christian list of the seven named, most revered Archangels: Michael, Gabriel, Raphael, Uriel, Chamuel, Jophiel, and Zadkiel. These Archangels were associated in medieval theology with the seven planets then known to astronomers, and their seven names are recorded in the Apocrypha. Only Michael and Gabriel are mentioned in the Bible; they are also named in the Koran. An alternate list is given in the Book of Enoch with the four primary names of Raphael, Gabriel, Ariel, and Michael, and also includes Raguel, Sariel, and Jerahmeel as the other three. A total of four Archangels is recorded in the Koran: the previously mentioned Michael and Gabriel, and Azrael and Israfil.

In Europe during the Middle Ages, the Archangels were associated with the 12 signs of the zodiac and were often called upon by herbalists and others trying to effect unorthodox cures.
References 40, 87, 107, 114
See also Amesha Spentas, Angel, Ariel, Azrael, Gabriel, Israfel, Kafziel, Michael, Raphael, Samael, Uriel, Zadkiel, Appendix 1

ARCHONS
In Mysticism, Occultism, and Gnosticism these are spirits of primordial existence. In Manichaeism, they were deemed to have swallowed the light to deprive the first humans of its radiance.
References 53
See also Spirit

ARDAT LILI
This is a demon of the night, also known as Lilitu or Lilu, in ancient Sumerian, Babylonian, Assyrian, and Hebrew traditions. The name Ardat Lili means Maid of Desolation. She is described as a wild-haired, winged spirit of the wind by the Assyrians, but as the screech owl in Hebrew writings. She is the demon that does everything possible to harm all mortals with whom she comes into contact. Ardat Lili will entice humans to lonely and desolate places especially to attack them.
References 31, 87, 93
See also Demon, Lilith, Spirit

AREMATAPOPOTO
See Pahuanuiapitaaiterai

AREMATAROROA
See Pahuanuiapitaaiterai

AREMHA
This is the general term used for all supernatural spirits in modern reference to the ancient traditions of the Tanna people of the New Hebrides. Even the status of once powerful deities has now been reduced to that of minor spirits.
References 102
See also Spirit

ARETHUSA
Arethusa is a Nereid in the classical mythology of Greece and Rome.
References 56
See also Hesperides, Nereid, Appendix 11

ARGYRA
She was a nymph in the classical mythology of Greece and Rome; she was loved by the shepherd Solemnos.
References 102, 130
See also Nymph, Appendix 11

ARIĀ
In the folk beliefs of the Maori people of New Zealand, the Ariā is the physical manifestation of the Atua spirit. It may take the shape of an insect, a dog, a star, or others. Ariās were mostly deemed responsible for inflicting disease or misfortune, and the sight of one was a severe warning that had to be heeded to avoid more terrible consequences. Conversely, if protection were required from a particular spirit, then its Atua would be welcome; their representations were

frequently carved on important buildings. The most fearsome of the Ariās is that of the green gecko. An anecdote recorded in 1823 tells of a ship's officer carrying a green gecko to a young Maori woman to ask its Maori name. "She shrunk from him in a state of terror that exceeds description, and conjured him not to approach her as it was in the shape of the animal he had in his hand that the Atua was wont to take possession of the dying and to devour their bowels."
References 63
See also Atua, Spirit

ARIAEL
See Ariel

ARIEL, ARIAEL
(1) An Archangel or a chief angel in Judeo-Christian scriptures, in the astrological calendar Ariel was associated with the planet Venus in early Jewish writings, as well as in medieval Christian astrology. Described by Heywood (1635) as one of the seven angelic princes, he is later named by Milton as one of the rebel angels in *Paradise Lost* (1667).

(2) Ariel is a spirit of the air in English literature and folklore, whose most famous description is to be found in Shakespeare's *The Tempest,* in which he is a spirit imprisoned by the witch Sycorax and rescued by his later master, Prospero, who eventually sets Ariel free. In Pope's *Rape of the Lock* (1712), Ariel is described as a sylph and as Belinda's guardian. Alchemists and other practitioners invoked this spirit to do their bidding. Ariel communicates through music in the air, by which humans come under Ariel's enchantment and sometimes are driven to distraction. He is a mischievous spirit and, though willing to work magic, he will work trickery whenever he can. Able to materialize at will, Ariel controls both fire and air, but like a fairy, he is said to ride on the back of a bat and sleep in the bell of a cowslip flower.
References (1) 40, 107; (2) 40, 44, 107, 114
See also (1) Angel, Archangel, Fallen Angel; (2) Fairy, Guardian, Puck, Spirit, Sylph

ARIFA
This is a benevolent female djinn in the folk beliefs of Morocco. She will not only protect the family and household, but she is also a guardian spirit for any infant. Arifa will watch over and protect the sleeping child against other evil djinns that may wish to do harm.
References 90
See also Djinn, Guardian, Khadem Quemquoma, Appendix 21, Appendix 22

ARIOCH
Meaning Fierce Lion, this is the name of a demon of vengeance in the mysticism of medieval Europe.

Milton used this name for one of the Fallen Angels in *Paradise Lost.*
References 40, 53
See also Demon, Fallen Angel

ARMÉE FURIEUSE, L'
This is the name given in the folklore of Switzerland to the Wild Hunt. L'Armée Furieuse, which means the Furious Host or the Raging Host, is blamed in particular for the abduction of unbaptized babies.
References 99
See also Wild Hunt, Appendix 22

ARMAITI
See Aramaiti

ARNAKNAGSAK
See Sedna

ARZSHENK
In the Zoroastrian religion of Iran, he is a king of the Devs who are demons and servants of the supreme evil, Ahriman, and constantly combating the good works of the Amshaspands or Izeds. Arzshenk is described as taking human form but having the head of a bull, which is eventually struck off in the final battle with the hero Rootsam.
See also Amesha Spentas, Demon, Deev, Izeds

AS
See Čembulat

ASA
See Asa Vahista

ASA VAHISTA
(1) In the Zoroastrian religion of Iran, this is one of the Amesha Spentas and the attendant genius of Ahura-Mazda. This spirit is also known as Asa, Asha, or Asha Vahishta, and the name means Righteousness. He is associated with guardianship of fire and the sun.

(2) In the Hindu religion, this spirit is described as an archangel whose overzealous, moralizing tone is criticized by Indra.
References 41
See also Amesha Spentas, Archangel, Attendant Spirit, Genius, Spirit

ASAG
This is the name of a disease demon of ancient mythology and beliefs of Sumer and Mesopotamia. He was also known as Asakku. Asag is considered responsible for spreading disease, and also for poisoning the earth and causing the wells to dry up.
References 93, 119
See also Demon, Appendix 17

L'Armée Furieuse, the French Wild Hunt, chases the souls of the damned.

ASAKKU
See Asag

ASASEL
This demon is also known by the names Azazel, Azazil, and Azael. He is a spirit in the Hebrew, Christian, and Muslim religious texts. In the Book of Enoch, he is described as the chief of the rebellious angels and a Fallen Angel cast out from heaven. In the Hebrew tradition, he is the demon of the wilderness, the recipient of the scapegoat on the Day of Atonement (Yom Kippur).

In the Muslim tradition, Asasel or Azazil was a devil, sometimes identified as Iblis, the offspring of a djinn, who was similarly cast out from heaven for refusing to acknowledge Adam, the first human. Asasel, along with Shemyaza, is credited with teaching humans how to forge weapons and make war on each other, and how to deceive one another by using the mask of cosmetics.
References 93
See also Demon, Devil, Djinn, Fallen Angel, Iblis, Shemyaza, Spirit

ASƏRA
This is the name given to a demon in the folklore of the Cheremis/Mari people of the former Soviet Republic. Asəra is thought to be responsible for causing colic in horses. Asəra is derived from the Tartar word for an evil spirit.
References 118
See also Demon, Spirit, Appendix 17

ASH BOYS
These are spirits in the folk beliefs and legends of the Zuñi Native American people. They are the spirits associated with fire in mythology.
References 88
See also Ashes Man, Grandmother Fire, Spirit

ASHA, ASHA VAHISHTA
See Asa Vahista

ASHAKKU
This is the name of a disease demon of ancient Babylonian mythology considered responsible for spreading tuberculosis.
See also Demon, Appendix 17

ASHES MAN
This is a spirit in the folk beliefs and legends of the Zuñi Native American people. He is one of the spirits associated with fire in mythology.
References 88
See also Ash Boys, Grandmother Fire, Spirit

ASHMEDAI, ASHMADAI
He is the king of the demons in Hebrew mythology. He returns to Heaven daily only to find out how many souls have been rejected as unworthy of Heaven so that he can claim them and take them to Hell. This demon is the subject of numerous legends and folktales. Ashmedai was credited in the times of Solomon with knowing the whereabouts of a *shamir* (supernatural worm) that could split rocks by its touch. Solomon sent Benaiah ben Jehoiadah to capture them for his service in the construction of the temple. Curious to learn how a powerful demon could be subjugated, Solomon was persuaded to return a ring to Ashmedai to demonstrate his power. The king was thus usurped by the demon for some time until Solomon, with the aid of another magic ring, regained his kingdom.
References 87
See also Demon

ASHRAPA
See Dakini

ASIA
This is the name of a nymph of the Oceanids, variously described in the classical mythology of Greece and Rome as the mother of Prometheus, and in English literature as his wife.
References 114
See also Nymph, Oceanids, Appendix 11

AS-IGA
This is a benevolent water spirit in the folklore of the Ostyaks, a Finno-Ugric people living in the region of the River Ob in Siberia. As-iga, whose name means Old Man of the Ob, was the guardian of the river creatures and protector of those who depended on the river.
References 102
See also Guardian, Kul, Spirit, Tchatse-olmai, Tonx, Vu-kutis, Vu-nuna, Appendix 21, Appendix 25

ASKAFROA
In Nordic and Teutonic folklore, this spirit is the Wife of the Ash Tree, also known as the Eschenfrau, and was the guardian spirit of the ash tree. She was regarded as particularly malicious. (It is reported that a propitiation was rendered to the Askafroa on Ash Wednesday, but as this Christian feast day has nothing to do with ash trees, but rather fire ashes, the two seem to have become rather confused.)
References 110
See also Guardian, Spirit, Appendix 19

ASMAN
This is the name of a spirit in the Zoroastrian religion of Iran, an attendant of the Amesha Spenta known as Kshathra.

References 41
See also Amesha Spentas, Attendant Spirit, Kshathra, Spirit

ASMODAIOS
See Asmodee

ASMODEE
This is the name of a devil with a mischievous sense of humor in a French literary work. He is also known as Asmodeus. Asmodee is described as lame by Alain-René Lesage in his book *Le Diable boiteux* (The Devil upon Two Sticks, 1707). In the story, Asmodee accompanies Don Cléofas on a tour of Madrid by night. While accompanying the devil, the Don discourses with him on philosophical matters. From the vantage point of Saint Salvador's steeple, Asmodee makes his argument by displaying the wickedness and duplicity of his fellow humans to the Don. The devil does this supernaturally by lifting the roof of each house and exposing the private events of the family.
References 114
See also Asmodeus, Astarotte, Devil

ASMODEUS
A particularly evil demon and an archfiend, his name possibly derives from Aeshma or Aeshma Daeva, the Zoroastrian fury demon. He is also sometimes identified with the Assyrian Pazuzu or the Christian Fallen Angel Samael. In Hebrew Rabbinic literature, Asmodeus is the chief of the Sheddim, and in the Book of Tobit he is described as the son of Naamah, the sister of Tubal-Cain. Asmodeus is considered to be the demon who incites marital jealousy and discord. He is also known by the names Asmodaios and Asmodee.

The story of Asmodeus is told in the Book of Tobit, now more frequently encountered in literature and art under the title of Tobias and the Angel. Sarah, daughter of Raguel, suffered the unwanted attention of Asmodeus, who destroyed each bridegroom on her wedding night on the seven occasions that she was to be married. Asmodeus was rendered powerless by the intervention of the Archangel Raphael, who showed Tobias the means (burning the heart and liver of a fish) by which this could be achieved. Tobias married Sara, and Asmodeus fled to Egypt, where he was enchained by Raphael.
References 39, 40, 41, 53, 87, 93, 114
See also Aeshma, Asmodee, Demon, Fallen Angel, Fiend, Pazuzu, Samael

ASPARAS
See Apsaras

ASRAI
A water spirit or water fairy in the English counties of Cheshire and Shropshire. It may appear in human form, but is very small. In one local tradition, a fisherman caught an Asrai, and despite its distraught cries he was determined to take it to shore. He tied it up and put it in the bottom of the boat under some water weeds. When he reached the shore, the fairy had faded away as its cries had grown weaker. All that was left was a pool of water under the weeds and a weal on the fisherman's hand where he had touched its cold, wet skin to tie it up. This weal remained with him for the rest of his life.
References 17
See also Fairy, Spirit, Appendix 25

ASTAROTH
In European medieval demonology, Astaroth is one of the most powerful and high-ranking demons of Hell.
References 53
See also Demon, Devil

ASTAROTTE
This is the name of a demon or fiend in the literary work *Morgante Maggiore* (1481) by Luigi Pulci, in which Astarotte transports the hero Rinaldo to the battle of Roncesvalles by supernatural means. While traveling with the hero, Astarotte engages him in grotesque theological discourse.
References 114
See also Asmodee, Demon, Fiend

ASTEROPEA
See Pleiades

ASTŌ VIDĀTU
Originally, he was a demon in Persian mythology and chief agent of the supreme evil. An approximate translation of his name means Disintegrator of Bodies. Astō Vidātu was given the task of consuming those destined for hell. He was later venerated as the god of death.
References 93
See also Demon

ASUMAN
A general term for nature spirits in the Ashanti folklore of East Africa.
References 57
See also Spirit, Appendix 18

ASURA
In ancient Persian mythology, the Asuras were beneficent spirits, and their opponents were the evil Daevas. In India this was also the original tradition (in the Rigveda the word signifies a god), until

The title page illustration from Alain-René Lesage's book Le Diable boiteux (The Devil upon Two Sticks), *published in 1707.*

superseded by the Hindu tradition in which a reversal took place and the Asuras were debased to the status of demons and the Devas elevated to the status of gods. The Asuras included the Rakshasas, Vritra, the Piśācas, and the Daityas, as well as others not regarded as supernatural. The Asuras are credited with luxurious tastes, supernatural skills, greed, and the ability to restore the dead to life. Although constantly warring with the Devas, they are not always defeated, and indeed some stories tell of them assisting the Devas. At the Beginning and the Great Churning, the Asuras stole the Draft of Immortality. Vishnu assumed the shape of a beautiful, voluptuous maiden and his disguise so enchanted the lecherous

Asuras that he was able to snatch back the precious liquid and return it to the Devas.
References 29, 39, 53, 56, 92, 93, 111, 119
See also Daitya, Deev, Piśācas, Rakshasas, Spirit, Vritra

ASURAKUMARA
These are powerful demons of the underworld in the Jain religion. They are in the upper group in the hierarchy of devils and portrayed as being black with red garments. The Asurakumara are considered to be responsible for causing rainstorms and thunder.
References 93
See also Demon, Devil, Appendix 26

ATAKSAK

He is a benevolent spirit of Inuit mythology invoked by *Angakoks* (shamans). Ataksak is described as being like a sphere, wearing garments decorated with shining cords. He is the personification of happiness.
References 102
See also Aulanerk, Spirit

ATAMAN

This is the name of a nature spirit in Russian folklore. Ataman is the chief of the forest spirits.
References 75
See also Spirit, Appendix 19

ATHLASHI

See Koyemshi

ATLANTIDES

In ancient Greek mythology, this is the name of a group of nymphs who were the sisters of the Hyades. They were also known as the Hesperides, with a different tradition of their derivation. The Atlantides were the seven daughters of Atlas and Plieone, changed into the constellation in Taurus known as the Pleiades.
References 129
See also Hesperides, Hyades, Nymph

ATROPOS

In the classical mythology of Greece and Rome, Atropos is one of the Fates. She is depicted with a pair of shears cutting the thread of mortal life.
References 41
See also Fates

ATTENDANT SPIRIT

A supernatural companion, an attendant spirit is one that renders service or guidance, whether for good or evil purposes, such as a Guardian Angel or a familiar spirit. They may be in attendance and at the service of the Supreme Deity or of the supreme of evil, other deities, other spirits, or humans. Their attendance is usually inferred as being by some obligation, pact, or command.
References 41, 107
See also Familiar, Guardian Angel, Spirit

ATUA

This is the term used for the invisible aspect of a supernatural in the beliefs and legends of the Maori of New Zealand. Each of these Atua had a particular domain of influence, and were most frequently malevolent toward humans. Their Ariā, or physical manifestation, was therefore to be avoided at all costs by humans in order to remain unmolested by the Atua and avert the resultant misery. The following are the names of some of the Atuas with their activities: Korokioewe attacked pregnant women to cause problems with the birth, Mokotiti inflicted problems of the lungs and chest, Tatariki inflicted swelling of the ankles and toes, Te Makawe caused people to be scalded in hot pools and geysers, Titihai brought pains to the feet, and Tonga inflicted headaches and nausea.
References 63
See also Ariča, Appendix 17

AUFHOCKER

This is the name in German folklore for the demon with the same characteristics as the Belgian Kludde. Aufhocker, which means Leap Upon, is a malignant shape-shifting demon that might appear as a domestic animal, or be completely invisible, to terrorize travelers at night on lonely roads. This spirit might jump on the back of the victim and cling with its talons, becoming heavier the more the terrified human tried to dislodge it, until the victim might die of exhaustion. Only dawn breaking or the sound of the church bell could save the traveler. As a Black Dog, it would suddenly appear and prance along the road, stretching on its hind legs until it reached the throat of its victim. Its most usual manifestation is as a horse that, like the Hedley Kow, encouraged the unwary to ride it. The person would be unable to dismount until, after a horrific ride, the victim was ejected into a river.
References 66, 104
See also Demon, Hedley Kow, Kludde, Old Man of the Sea, Oschaert, Spirit, Appendix 12, Appendix 24

AUKI

These are mountain spirits in the beliefs of the Quechua people of Peru. These spirits inhabit the high Andes, where their abodes are the equivalent of the *haciendas* below. The vicuñas are their spirit servants, the condors are their spirit poultry, and the fearsome Ccoa is their spirit cat. The Auki are called upon by the *brujos* (shaman curers) to heal the sick. The curing ceremony commences when the *brujo* places a paper on the floor of the sick person's house as the Auki's seat, and whistles three times as a signal to the Auki to descend. Then the *brujo* holds a dialogue with the spirit in which he enquires (by ventriloquism) the nature of the illness and its cure. When the spirit has given its answers, the Auki departs through the roof.
References 87
See also Anchancho, Ccoa, Larilari, Spirit, Appendix 17

AULANERK

This is the name of a sea spirit in the folk beliefs and legends of the Inuit people of North America.

Aulanerk is a spirit of joyfulness, described as resembling a naked human, but he dwells in the sea like a merman. It is Aulanerk's movement in the sea that creates the waves.
References 102
See also Ataksak, Merman, Spirit, Appendix 25

AULD ANE
See Auld Hornie

AULD CLOOTIE
The Scottish familiar name denigrating the Devil to the status of a lesser demon. The name Auld Clootie derives from the word *cloot,* meaning the cleft of the goat's hoof. It is a term often used to express the spiritual perpetrator of minor mischief and annoyance.
References 28, 40, 114
See also Auld Hornie, Demon

AULD HANGIE
See Auld Hornie

AULD HORNIE
A Scottish and North of England euphemism and derisory name for the Devil in denigrated and depleted form, equating with the status of an imp. The derisory or humorous terms used in England are: Grime, Grim, Lord Harry, Old Boot, the Old Gentleman, Old Harry, Old Horny, the Old Lad, Old Nick, the Old One, Old Simmie, and Old Teaser. In Scotland the following terms are used: Auld Ane, Auld Clootie, Auld Hangie, Auld Nick, Graham, Grahame, Auld Scratch, and Scratch. These terms were particularly used after the eighteenth century, when people had lost belief in the Devil's supremely evil power and the spirit had been relegated to literary and common familiarity. His description coincides with that of the Christian denigration of the ancient nature god Pan with his goat horns, beard, and feet, and his hooked nose and pointed ears. "Auld" or "old" applied to a spirit in northern Britain tends to imply a draining of power and a mellowing of character with the passage of time. Auld Hornie may be familiar and mischievous rather than outright evil, but his last "sparks" may still catch out the unwary.
References 28, 40, 114
See also Asmodee, Astarotte, Imp, Spirit

AULD NICK
See Auld Hornie

AULD SCRATCH
See Auld Hornie

AULD SCRATTY
This is the name of a frightening spirit or devil used mostly as a nursery bogie by parents in Britain to threaten their young children into good behavior. It may be a minor devil whose name is derived from Auld Scratch.
References 17
See also Auld Hornie, Devil, Nursery Bogies, Spirit, Appendix 22

AUMANIL
A benevolent spirit in Inuit belief and folklore in North America, he is said to dwell on land, but nevertheless he is the guardian spirit of the whales. Aumanil ensures the presence and abundance of the whales where the Inuit people hunt.
References 29, 102
See also Guardian, Spirit

AUNT NANCY
See Anansi

AVANC
See Addanc

AVEREKETE
Also called Verekete, he is an encantado or guiding spirit of the Afro-Brazilian cult Batuque. He is described as the Owner of the Night or the Saint of the Night, and is identified with the black Saint Benedict, one of the most popular saints in the Amazon region. Averekete is derived from the Dahomean god of the same name; however, in Bélem, unlike his African predecessor, he is portrayed as old and dignified. He is a member of the Kevioso/ Badé encantado "family." Averekete's "family" includes Averekitano and his "foster daughter," Princesa d'Alva. It is believed in Maranhão that Santa Barbara created the *terrieros,* where the Batuque ceremonies take place, and appointed Averekete as the introductory guiding spirit. Consequently, Averekete is always the first spirit to be called on by mediums taking part in the ceremony, followed by Rainha Barba.
References 89
See also Badé, Encantado, Princesa d'Alva, Rainha Barba, Senhor, Seu Turquia

AWAR
See Iblis

AWD GOGGIE
This is the name of a malicious spirit in the folklore of East Riding of Yorkshire, England. Awd Goggie is a nursery bogie or demon, the invention of children's nannies, parents, and protective farmers. Awd Goggie was the malicious guardian spirit of ripening fruit in

orchards and woods. He may be invisible, but he lurks behind trees, waiting to "get" any venturesome, greedy children who help themselves to fruit without permission.
References 17
See also Demon, Nursery Bogies, Guardian, Spirit, Appendix 21, Appendix 22

AWKI

A type of nature or earth spirit in the folklore of the Quechua peoples of southern Peru. It is said that an Awki inhabits each *moqo* (knoll or rounded hill) in the region.
References 94
See also Spirit

AWL-MAN

The tutelary spirit of the awl in the folk beliefs of the Pueblo Native Americans. He is the spirit personification of one of the most useful implements given to humans. Awl-man is portrayed in many legends in which the spirit often saves humans with his guidance.
References 87
See also Agloolik, Àràk, Clay Mother, Corn Mother, Fylgja, Nagual, Salt Woman, Spirit, Tutelary Spirit, Zoa

AXEKI

This is the name of a spirit in the folk beliefs and legends of the Shasta Native American people of California. He is a protective or guardian spirit.
References 99
See also Guardian, Appendix 21

AYERICO

This is the name of a demon in the folklore of Macedonia in Europe. It is a spirit that may take human form, but more usually dwells invisibly in the air. Ayerico is a disease spirit, responsible for spreading plague and malaria.
See also Aërico, Aerika, Demon, Appendix 17

AYNIA

This is the name of a fairy in the folklore of Ireland. Aynia is a woman of the Sidhe and is a fairy queen of Ulster in northern Ireland.
References 125
See also Fairy, Sídhe

AYS

This is the name of an evil nature spirit or demon in the folklore of Armenia. Ays is the spirit of the wind. He is so powerful that he is feared as being able to penetrate humans through their skin and drive them mad.
References 93
See also Demon, Spirit, Appendix 26

AZ

(1) This is the name of a female demon in the beliefs of eastern Europe. She is the spirit of excessive sexual desire, instilling lassitude and corrupting intellectual strength.

(2) Az is also the name of a very powerful female demon in the ancient Persian religious cult of Manichaeism.
References 33
See also Demon, Spirit

AZAEL, AZAZEL

See Asasel

AZAZIEL

This is the name of a Seraph whose story is told in Byron's work *Heaven and Earth.* Azaziel fell in love with the granddaughter of Cain, a devout young woman called Anah. When the deluge was sent to destroy the evil on the earth, Azaziel rescued Anah from the earth's floods by holding her under his wings and transporting her to another planet.
References 40
See also Angel, Seraphim

AZIDAHAKA, AZI DAHAKA, AZHI DAHAKA

This is the name of a powerful demon in the Persian Zoroastrian creation myth. Azidahaka is portrayed in the shape of a serpent with three heads, six eyes, and three pairs of fangs. He conspired to overthrow and destroy the first human being, Yima. When the demon succeeded, he was in turn made powerless by the hero Thraetona and bound in chains under Mount Demavand.
References 41, 102
See also Demon, Drug

AZIZA, AZIZAN

The Aziza are nature spirits and the Little People in the folklore of Dahomey in West Africa. These spirits inhabit the deep forests. Through the relationship of these Little People with the human hunters who go into the forests, the knowledge of some supernatural powers has been brought to the Dahomey people. Humans propitiate these spirits for their benevolence.
References 48, 87
See also Bakru, Ijimere, Little People, Mmoatia, Pukkumeria, Spirit, Appendix 19

AZRAEL

This is the name of an Archangel in Judeo-Christian texts and a chief angel in the Koran. He is the angel of death and is also known as Azra'il or Izra'il. Azrael is mentioned in very early Jewish mythology and is described as having a terrifying appearance, his feet being on the edge of the world while his head towers

above in heaven. His numerous eyes see all, but one is said to close as a mortal dies. Ultimately only four eyes, representing the Thrones of God will remain open and Azrael will be the last to expire on Judgment Day. Azrael is charged with collecting the soul from each dying mortal; in a white silk cloth for the faithful, and in a rag for those destined for Hell. He knows where the souls are that are about to depart, as he receives the names of the dying for each day. A Tunisian tradition tells how humans were originally almost immortal, living for centuries. One who became weary of continuous life after 500 years requested that her life should cease; Allah instructed Azrael to gather the soul henceforth after the allotted three score years and ten (seventy).
References 33, 40, 41, 56, 87, 114
See also Angel, Archangel, Azren

AZRAFIL
See Israfel

AZRA'IL
See Azrael

AZREN, AZREN KUBA, AZREN KUGUZA
This spirit of the Cheremis/Mari peoples of the former Soviet Republic, is variously described as the angel of death, as the spirit helper of a Keremet or devil, or a Keremet in its own right. Azren may manifest in a female or male human form known as Azren Kuba and Azren Kuguza, which mean Azren Old Woman and Azren Old Man. However, Azren is usually described as having the appearance of a Tartar who is very thin and so tall that his head touches the roof. He appears in dreams foretelling the death of a human. Only the dying ever see him other than in dreams. He is always seen carrying some weapon, a knife, a chisel, a scythe etc. with which to despatch the victim. The more sharp the implement in the dream, the quicker the death predicted; the more blunt or further from the head the first blow is made, then the person will endure a lingering painful death. It is said that he crushes children to death between two wooden boards. This spirit is propitiated by the sacrifice of a chicken.
References 118
See also Angel, Azrael, Čembulat, Devil, Keremet, Kugə Jeŋ, Spirit

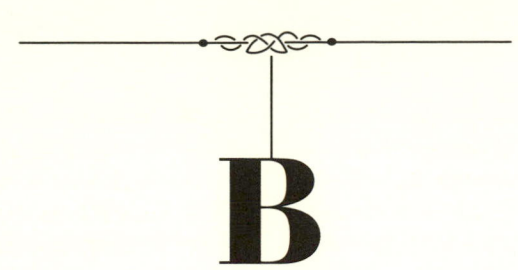

B

BAALBERITH

In medieval European demonology this spirit was regarded as one of the most powerful demons of Hell.
References 53
See also Demon, Spirit

BAALZAPHON

In medieval European demonology Baalzaphon was regarded as a powerful demon of Hell.
References 53
See also Demon

BABA

This was the name of a fairy in the earlier folk beliefs of Hungary. The status of Baba gradually evolved to that of an evil spirit resembling a hag or a witch.
References 93
See also Baba Yaga, Fairy, Spirit

BABA, BOBA

See Cailleac

BABA YAGA

In Russian and East European folklore Baba Yaga, also known as Jezi-Baba, is a female supernatural forest spirit of entirely malicious intent. She either entices human victims, usually children, to their horrific death and cannibal end or travels with Death eating the soul of his victims. She is described as a hideous hag with teeth of stone. She is so large that when she lies down, her head is at one end of her little hut and her feet at the other, with her blue hooked nose touching the ceiling. She lives in a clearing in the forest, behind a fence decorated with skulls, in a little hut that constantly whirls around on hen's legs. When she travels, she flies through the air either in a mortar propelled by its pestle or in an iron kettle, sweeping the air with a fiery broom. She is sometimes given other sisters of the same name, all equally demonic.
References 18, 93
See also Black Annis, Cailleach Bheur, Hag, Spirit, Appendix 19, Appendix 22

BABBAN NY MHEILLEA

In the folklore of the Isle of Man (United Kingdom) the Babban ny Mheillea, which means the Harvest Baby in the Manx language, is a fertility spirit of the crop at the time of reaping. The spirit of the corn at the harvest is trapped in the last sheaf and kept by cutting the sheaf and making it into an effigy of the Corn Spirit. Then it is decorated and ceremoniously paraded and feasted. The Babban ny Mheillea is then kept until the next sowing season when the spirit is released to continue the fertility of the next corn crop. In his nineteenth-century Manx poem, William Kennish describes the tradition:

> Then Kitty Eldest of the Youthful Band
> Of females, challenged all within the field
> To be the first to cut with friendly hand
> The last oat sheaf the farm that year did yield
> To form the "Maiden" in its usual style
> With ribbon-bows and plaited straw-made arms....
> She bore it forth in triumph in her hand....

In this episode the "corn" grain is oats. "Corn" is a general term in Northern Europe for grain cereal crops such as rye, oats, barley, and maize, but mostly for wheat. The tradition of the Corn Doll is not always as gentle as the Manx one—some involved enactments of simulated or even real murder.
References 81
See also Cailleac, Kornmutter, Kornwolf, Sara-Mama, Spirit, Appendix 15

BABI

The name of a demon in ancient Greek and Egyptian mythology. Babi is also known by the names Bapho and Bebon. Babi inhabits the regions of darkness and death. He is named in the Books of the Dead and in Greek incantations for the afterlife of the dead.
References 93
See also Demon

BÄCKAHÄST

This is the name of an evil spirit and an alternative form of the Näcken in Scandinavian folklore. The Bäckahäst dwells in fresh water lakes and rivers, where it may be seen in the guise of a water-horse, but it could also resemble an upturned boat or a drifting log. Those who are tempted into the water by it are doomed.
References 99
See also Cabyll-Ushtey, Each Uisge, Kelpie, Näcken, Spirit, Appendix 12, Appendix 25

BAD

The name of an evil spirit or djnn in ancient Persian mythology. Bad is considered to be responsible for storms and winds that cause structural damage, disaster, and death.
References 53
See also Djinn, Appendix 26

BAD HOUR, THE

In modern Greek folklore a demon or type of evil spirit that may also be known as the Dangerous Hour, the Ugly Hour, or the Shameful Hour. This kind of demon is usually invisible, but it may take the shape of a little black dog, a beautiful woman, a whirlwind, a shadow under a fig tree, or some animal. It may be invoked by human bad temper, which allows the demon to invade the individual, causing the person to do wicked things. It may also be attracted to possess humans when they pass by a crossroads or through a narrow pass between high mountains, where it also lurks. When possessing or attacking a human, the Bad Hour may "take" the voice of the individual and render the person unable to talk. The Bad Hour is also considered to be a Nightmare or disease demon. When the Bad Hour enters children or others in their houses at night, it may cause sudden fevers, painful eyes or limbs, and possibly death. One may exorcise it by saying special prayers known as *xemetrima* and calling in the aid of a priest or a type of local exorcist known as a *praktika*.
References 12
See also Demon, Nightmare, Shameful Hour, Spirit, Ugly Hour

BADB, BADHBH

A female evil spirit, the daughter of Ernmas of the Tuatha dé Danann in the mythology of Ireland. Badb was a shape-shifter, but she usually took the form of a crow. She had two sisters, Macha and Neman. Badb not only incited conflict but also appeared on the battlefield, like the Valkyries, to those who were to be defeated or killed.
References 87
See also Aralez, Banshee, Bodua, Macha, Morrigan, Neman, Spirit, Tuatha dé Danann, Valkyries

BADÉ

A family of spirits, or encantados, in the Afro-Brazilian cult Batuque. They are associated with the Christian Catholic Saint Jerome and his feast day, 30 September. The name is derived from a Dahomean deity of West Africa.
References 89
See also Encantado, Senhor, Xangô

BADHB/H, BADHBH CHAOINTE

See Banshee

BADI

This is a type of spirit in the beliefs and folklore of the Malay people of West Malaysia. Badi are considered to inhabit invisibly everything on Earth, where they create mischief and incite discord. The first Badi were supposed to have originated from three drops of blood spilled by Adam, the first man. Now there are supposed to be more than 190 of them creating mischief wherever they can.
References 120
See also Bes, Imp, Spirit, Sprite

BADJANG, BAJANG

This is the name of a malicious demon and disease spirit in the folk beliefs of the Malay people of West Malaysia. Bajang is the term used for a familiar spirit that takes the form of a *Musang* (civet-cat). It is invoked by a human family who uses it for its supernatural powers, and the family to which it owes allegiance feeds it eggs and milk in an abode made of bamboo. The Bajang is particularly malicious towards children, and disaster or disease soon afflicts the victim whom its master family has sent it to attack. It is sent to disturb the sleep of people at night and especially to cause harm to women in childbirth.
References 87, 120
See also Aitvaras, Al, Demon, Familiar, Hantu, Kalu Kumāra Yaka, Mara, Pontianak, Tçaridyi, Appendix 22

BÀ-DÚC-CHÚA

See Dúc-Bà

BADUH

A benevolent spirit also known as B'duh or Beduh in Arabic mythology. This spirit is thought to be responsible for ensuring the swift transmission of messages. His assistance is invoked by inscribing the numerals 8 6 4 2, which signify the (reversed) Arabic script B D U H, representing the spirit's name. This inscription was still apparently used in Iran and Egypt well into the twentieth century on documents and communications that needed the assurance of swift delivery.
References 41, 53
See also Spirit

BAEL
In medieval European demonology one of the most powerful demons of Hell.
References 53
See also Demon

BAETATA
This is the name of a spirit in the folklore of the Tupi Guarani peoples of the Amazon Basin. Baetata is a mischievous spirit similar to a Will o' the Wisp. It will encourage humans to follow the being wherever it leads, until they are hopelessly lost or in some difficult terrain.
References 102
See also Spirit, Will o' the Wisp

BAGHLET EL QEBOUR
This is an evil female spirit in the folklore of Morocco. Baghlet el Qebour, whose name means the Mule of the Graves, was said to be transformed by Allah from the spirit of a woman thought to have taken a husband before the end of the prescribed widow's mourning. In the shape of a mule, she roams the Houz of Marrakech and such deserted places at night. She seeks out lazy and thoughtless men who are away from their homes at night, and she buries them alive.
References 90
See also Spirit

BAGUL
The name of a demon or malevolent spirit in the legends of India. The Bagul is featured in the Mahratta in Hindu mythology.
References 92
See also Bogle, Demon, Spirit

BAINIKHA
See Bannaia

BAJANG
See Badjang

BAKA
This is the term for a group of malevolent spirits in the folk beliefs of Haiti. These cannibal demons may be spirits taking human form or humans who have become demons.
References 67
See also Demon, Spirit

BAKEMONO
This is the general term for a malevolent little spirit in the folklore of Japan. The Bakemono manifests as a type of goblin.
References 87
See also Goblin, Spirit

BAKRU
This is a name for the little spirits in the folklore of Surinam, particularly the region of Paramaribo and the coast. These Little People are derived from the West African evil Apuku of the forests. The Bakru are described as being half flesh and half wood with very large heads on bodies like those of small children. A male and female Bakru always appear together. The Bakru are obtained as the servants of a human only after an evil pact has been made to forfeit the soul for the riches the Bakru servants will bring, in much the same way as the Aitvaras of Europe.
References 87
See also Aitvaras, Apuku, Aziza, Ijimere, Little People, Mmoatia, Pukis, Pukkumeria, Spirit

BAKŠ IA
This is the spirit of the grain mill in the folk beliefs of the Cheremis/Mari people of the former Soviet Republic. The Bakš Ia, whose name means Mill Devil, is also known as the Bakš Kuba and the Bakš Oza (Mill Master). This supernatural is the guardian of the mill and its working, similar to the Killmoulis. The Bakš Ia may inhabit the space beneath the floorboards or behind the water wheel, and it comes out at night to keep the mill working for the miller with whom the spirit has a pact. In return for his work each day, the Bakš Ia will receive a bowl of porridge with some butter, left in a suitable place for the spirit to find it. If this is forgotten the angry spirit will take revenge and cause problems with the machinery and the condition of the grain.
References 118
See also Bakš Kuba, Brollachan, Kaboutermannekin, Kuba, Spirit

BAKŠ KUBA AND BAKŠ KUGUZA
This is the spirit of the grain mill in the folk beliefs of the Cheremis/Mari people of the former Soviet Republic. This supernatural is more often called Bakš Ia or Bakš Oza. It may manifest in the form of a woman called Bakš Kuba, whose name means Mill Old Woman. She is described as wearing a traditional peasant dress decorated with silver coins. It may also manifest in the form of a peasant man called Bakš Kuguza, whose name means Mill Old Man. They are addressed by the euphemisms Kuba and Kuguza so that they will not be offended and seek revenge.
References 118
See also Bakš Ia, Kuba, Kuguza, Spirit

BAKŠ OZA
See Bakš Kuba

BALAM
The general term for a guardian spirit or ancestral supernatural spirit in the beliefs of the Quiché

peoples of Mexico. The Balam, whose name means Tiger or Jaguar, were originally assigned as guardians of the Four Directions. Their names were Iqi-Balam (Moon Jaguar), Balam-Agab (Nocturnal Jaguar), Balam-Quitzé (Smiling Jaguar), and Mahu-Catah (Famous Name), possibly a euphemism for a terrifying spirit. These spirits have now been relegated to the role of nature spirits in the modern Mayan folklore. The Balam now protect the inhabitants, the villages, and their agricultural land.
References 87
See also Guardian, Spirit

BALAN

A supremely powerful demon in European medieval demonology.
References 53
See also Demon

BALI

In Hindu mythology Bali is a demon. The grandson of an incarnation of Ravana called Hiranyakasipu, whom he succeeded as the ruler of the heavens and earth. The gods had lost their power and domain to Bali, and Vishnu was requested to take another incarnation, as a dwarf Brahmin, to overthrow Bali. Vishnu paid a visit to Bali as a guest and was granted his right of a guest's desire, in this case the territory he could cover in three paces. Vishnu immediately assumed his own incarnation, and the powerful god took two paces that covered the entire universe. Bali acknowledged defeat, and with the third pace Vishnu banished Bali to the underworld to reign there. In another version, Bali is forced to live in the form of an ass in a mud hut.

A different version of the defeat of Bali is accomplished by Indra in a battle led by Jalandhara and his demons. When Bali eventually fell, instead of blood issuing from the body, jewels poured from his mouth. Out of curiosity Indra cut up the body, and Bali's corpse became pearls from the teeth, rubies from his blood, sapphires from his eyes, crystals from his flesh, diamonds from his bones, and emeralds from the marrow.
References 29, 41, 93, 102
See also Demon, Ravana

BALUBAALE

A general term for spirits in the beliefs of the Ganda people of East Africa. Although the group includes ancestral heroes who have been deified, the majority are nature spirits and personifications of natural phenomena through whom Katonda (the Creator) exercises his will on earth. At least 50 Balubaale are named, the best known being Kibuka (war) and Walumbe (death). The latter must receive a visit from a deceased person's soul before Walumbe allows relatives to bury the corpse.
References 33
See also Spirit

BAMAPAMA

A spirit, also known as Crazyman, who is a trickster in the folk beliefs and legends of the Murgin peoples of the Arnhem Land region in Australia. This spirit is credited in folklore with stirring up conflict, hostility, and bitterness between humans. He caused these reactions by deliberately violating tribal taboos, including incest, to the open horror and secret mirth of the tribes people.
References 87
See also Anansi, Basajaun, Blue Jay, Coyote, Eshu, Manabozo, Mink, Spirit, Trickster

BAN NIGHECHAIN

In Celtic Scottish folklore Ban Nighechain, whose name means Little Washer Woman, is a female spirit of foreboding and doom. She is also known as Nigheag na H-ath, which means Little Washer of the Ford. She is described as a little old woman with only one nostril, protruding teeth, and red webbed feet. The Ban Nighechain is seen standing in the ford of a river, washing the blood-soaked clothes of the dying taken from battle. Death or disaster are imminent for anyone she sees, but if the traveller sees her first and can grab her, she must tell the name of the doomed person and grant three wishes.
References 87, 88
See also Banshee, Bean Nighe, Caointeach

BANKSIA MEN

This is a group of evil nature spirits in the shape of *Banksia serrata* (a shrub native to Australia). These demons are also referred to as the Big Bad Banksia Men. They were the creation of the author May Gibbs in the first decade of the twentieth century in Australia and appear in her fairy tales of Snugglepot and Cuddlepie. Banksia Men have huge eyes, warts on their noses, thick-lipped mouths with whiskers, and protruding navels. They are aggressive pursuers and persecutors of the Gumnut Babies and are to be found in groups sitting on the shrub branches, awaiting the opportunity to do harm.
References 55
See also Demon, Fairy, Gumnut Babies, Spirit, Appendix 18

BANNAIA

This is the name of a spirit in the folklore of Russia. She is also known as Bainikha, and is the spirit wife of the Bannik, the evil demon of the bathhouse.
References 75
See also Bannik, Demon, Spirit, Appendix 22

A Banksia man abducts a Gumnut Baby.

BANNIK

This is the spirit of the bathhouse, or *banya* (a type of outdoor sauna), in the folklore of Russia. He is described as resembling a little old man with long white hair and beard. He was, however, rarely seen, but when he materialized he was also able to shape-shift to resemble a familiar person, (and in a steamy room) a true description would be difficult. The Bannik could be as generous as he could be evil, and anyone who had the misfortune to enter the bathhouse when it was the Bannik's turn (one in every four sessions was allotted to him) might be peeled or scalded to death. To propitiate this fearful spirit, not only was a bathing time given to him and his fellow demon household spirits, but people left offerings of soap, fir branches, and water as they finished, and the Bannik was thanked for his presence.

When a new bathhouse was to be built, the villagers would sacrifice a black hen and bury it unplucked under the threshold to please the Bannik. An offended Bannik was quite capable of burning down a bathhouse. To avert his vengeful mood a similar ceremony would be performed, and again the villagers would depart backwards, bowing and reciting incantations as they left the newly constructed bathhouse.

Not surprisingly few humans would venture into the bathhouse alone, especially after dark; not only was it considered an unclean place, but also the haunt of other demons. The Bannik protected the villagers from other forces. Although not a pleasant place, the bathhouse was the place of birth for many of the children, and some believed that the Bannik was particularly protective of these children; others, however, believed that he attempted to steal unbaptized infants, so new mothers and their babies were never left there alone.

At Yuletide the Bannik was asked to perform a sort of divination ceremony by the young girls of the village. They would stand at the entrance to the bathhouse one by one with their skirts brought over their heads and their exposed buttocks towards the interior of the bathhouse. If the Bannik gave a rough scratch, then the coming year would be bad, if he patted or caressed the girl, then the new year would be good. In some districts it was even the custom for the Bannik to give a ring to signify good fortune. One story of a particularly malicious Bannik says that when one unfortunate girl looked at her hand thinking that she had a ring, she found that all her fingers had been trapped in hideous iron links. Other tales of Banniks describe how elderly women who were asked to attend a bathing visitor were found later either strangled or peeled to death. Another woman who tried to get the Bannik to dispose of her husband was found with her skin peeled and a bucket over her head. Not all tales of Banniks reflect his gruesome aspects: in one tale from Belozersk, some girls who were terrified by demons chasing them were given protective refuge in a *banya* by its guardian Bannik.
References 29, 75, 87
See also Demon, Domovik, Spirit, Appendix 22

BANSHEE, BAN SHEE

The name of this Celtic Irish spirit, which means Woman of the Hill or Woman of the Mound, is derived from the Irish *bean*, a woman, and *si* or *Sidhe* an ancient "mound" and later "fairy." The Banshee is known by different names in various regions: in Waterford as Badbh; in Wexford, Kildare, and Wicklow as Badhbh; and in Kilkenny and Laois as Badhbh Chaointe. The Banshee is said to look like an old woman with glowing red eyes in hollow sockets and long flowing white hair; she wears a gray cloak over a green dress (the fairy color). Another description is of a woman dressed in white (the color of death) with a ghastly face surrounded by long red hair; but Lady Wilde described her as beautiful but veiled in mourning. She is the attendant spirit of old Celtic families having O' or Mac in the surname. The Banshee's wailing or *keening* under the window of a family member portends their demise. Sometimes the name of the spirit is known to the family; Cliodna attends the McCarthy family of South Munster, and Aoibhill attends the Dalcassian family of North Munster.

References 15, 17, 41, 53, 56, 66, 87, 92, 105, 107, 114, 136
See also Attendant Spirit, Badb, Ban Nighechain, Bažaloshtsh, Bodua, Cliodna, Cyhiraeth, Morrigan, Spirit, Valkyries, Appendix 22

BAOBAN SITH

Although this Scottish Gaelic name has exactly the same meaning as the Irish Banshee "woman of the fairies," in the Highlands the name refers to beautiful but evil female spirits. They are usually dressed in green and can be recognized by their deer's hooves if they appear in human form, but they may also take the shape of hooded crows or ravens. The Baoban Sith live on the blood of humans, especially young huntsmen on the moorlands. In his *Scottish Folklore and Folk Life*, D. A. McKenzie tells of four young huntsmen resting overnight in a *shieling* (a shepherd's shelter), who wished for company and were delighted when four beautiful young women entered. While making music for the others, one hunter noticed that the "women" had hooves and drops of blood on them, and he fled to hide with the horses, whose iron shoes were protection. He realized that these were the fearful Baoban Sith and his friends had succumbed to the enchantment of these demon women. Try as she could, his supernatural partner the Baoban Sith could not reach him, and she disappeared at sunrise. Later, to his horror, he discovered the drained and bloodless bodies of his companions.
References 15, 17, 37
See also Banshee, Demon, Fairy, Succubus

BAPHO

See Babi

BAR

This is the name of a beautiful female sea spirit in the mythology of Scandinavia. She became the wife of Ögir the Dane, who, because of her love, became a spirit also and the King of the Seas. In the legends Bar not only held the souls of the drowned, but actively sought humans to pull into the depths, where she buried them in the sands of the the ocean bed.
References 95
See also Spirit, Appendix 25

BARÃO DE GORÉ

This is the name of a high-ranking spirit or encantado in the Afro-Brazilian cult Batuque. Barão de Goré, whose name means the Shark, belongs to the same "family" group of spirits as Gorézinho, which are derived from the shamanistic reverence of nature spirits.
References 89
See also Encantado

Bar claims the soul of a drowned sailor.

BARAVASHKA
This is the term for a poltergeist-type household spirit in the folklore of Russia.
References 46
See also Poltergeist, Spirit, Appendix 22

BARBA SUEIRA
See Rainha Barba

BARBASON
A demon or fiend in the documents and literature of sixteenth- and seventeenth-century England. Barbason was named in Scott's *Discoverie of Witchcraft* (1584) and later mentioned in Shakespeare's *Merry Wives of Windsor* and *Henry V*.
References 40
See also Demon, Fiend

BARDHA
These are nature spirits or earth spirits in the folklore of Albania. The Bardha, whose name means the White Ones, are said to materialize as formless white beings. To make sure of their benevolence, Albanian housewives scatter sugar and sweet cakes on the ground for them.
References 93
See also Maahiset, Spirit, Appendix 22

BARGHEST
See Barguest

BARGUEST
A bogie or fiend known also as Barghest and Boguest in the northern English counties of Northumberland, Durham, and Yorkshire. It is possibly derived from the German *Bahrgeis*, meaning Spirit of the Bier. The Barguest is variously described as having the shape of a black dog the size of a mastiff, with horns, fangs, and fiery eyes, or of a large shaggy-haired dog or even a bear, with huge claws and eyes like glowing coals. Sometimes it drags a chain, sometimes it is wrapped in chains. At other times it has been described as a headless man, a headless woman, a white rabbit, cat, or dog that disappears in flames. The Barguest is a fiend attached to a particular locality and is known as a portent of disaster or death for those who see it, or one of their family. If anyone tries to approach it or pass in front of it, then it is said to inflict a terrible wound on the person that never heals. Around the area of Leeds in Yorkshire, a Barguest would appear and set all other dogs of the city howling when anyone of importance was about to die.
References 15, 17, 28, 66, 87, 123
See also Black Dog, Black Shuck, Boggart, Bogie, Bullbeggar, Capelthwaite, Church Grim, Fiend, Freybug, Gytrash, Headless Woman, Mauthe Dhoog, Padfoot, Rongeur d'Os, Skriker

BARIAUA
The name of a group of nature spirits in the folklore of the Tubetube and Wagawaga peoples of Melanesia. These shy, benign spirits hide from mortals and make their abode in the trunks of ancient trees. They are occasionally said to borrow the canoes of humans, but if seen, they will disappear immediately.
References 87
See also Dryad, Karawatoniga, Spirit, Appendix 19

BARQU
In medieval European demonology this was the name of a demon reputed to be the guardian of the mysteries of the Philosopher's Stone.
References 53
See also Demon, Guardian

BARTEL
See Knecht Ruprecht

BASA-ANDRE
See Basajaun

BASAJAUN, BASA-JAUN
A nature spirit and culture trickster in the Basque folklore of northwestern Spain who takes the shape of a faun or wood sprite. The French name for this spirit is Homme de Bouc. Basajaun is credited with teaching humans about agriculture and iron-working. He is also mischievous and plays tricks on others. Basajaun lives high in the Pyrenean Mountains in the woods and caves, where he protects the flocks of sheep and goats. He has a wife called Basa-Andre who is depicted as a sort of siren who sits combing her long hair and luring mortals to their demise.
References 87, 93
See also Anansi, Bamapama, Blue Jay, Coyote, Eshu, Manabozo, Mink, Siren, Sprite

BASHKIR
See Paškəče

BASILIO BOM
An encantado spirit also known by the name Guillerme in the Afro-Brazilian cult Batuque. Described as the son of Seu Turquia, he was fostered into the encantado family of Dom João Sueira. Basilio uses the name Guillerme in curing ceremonies.
References 89
See also Dom João Sueira, Seu Turquia

BATHYM
In medieval European demonology one of the most powerful and high-ranking demons of Hell. He is also known as Marthim.

References 53
See also Demon

BAUBO

A female spirit or demon in the beliefs of ancient Greece and Asia Minor who personified the concept of female fertility. She is depicted as having her head placed between her open legs, or having no head at all. She is supposed, by the obscene display of her genitalia, to provide a charm against death and to have made the Greek gods laugh with this grotesque show.
References 93
See also Demon, Karina, Sheela-na-gig

BAUCHAN

This is a type of hobgoblin in the folklore of England. It may also be known as a bogan. The Bauchan is sometimes benevolent and often mischievous.
References 17, 40
See also Hobgoblin

BAUMESEL

A type of demon or goblin in the folklore of Germany. Baumesel, whose name means Ass of the Trees, is said to inhabit the trees in the forests.
References 110
See also Demon, Goblin, Appendix 19

BAŽALOSHTSH

A type of fairy or Banshee in the folklore of the Wend district of the eastern region of Germany. Bažaloshtsh, whose name means God's Plaint, is described as a tiny long-haired woman. This spirit will only make an appearance in order to sit and weep beneath the window of a human about to die.
References 87
See also Banshee, Cyhiraeth, Spirit

BDUD

Although originally a divine spirit in the Bon religion of Tibet, with the advent of Lamaism, the bDud was degraded to the status of a demon. He is portrayed as a black demon living in a black castle with a well of milk and nectar. He is supposed to be appeased by the sacrifice of a pig.
References 87, 93
See also Demon, Spirit

B'DUH

See Baduh

BEAN NIGHE

This is a spirit of foreboding in the Highlands of Scotland, particularly the Hebrides. Also known as "the Little Washer by the Ford," she is the equivalent of the Ban Nighechain but of more malevolent character like the Caointeach. The Bean Nighe, which means Washing Woman, is described as being small, wearing green clothes, and having red webbed feet and is a portent of war or other mortal disaster. The Bean Nighe may be chanced upon, washing the bloodstained linen of those about to die, this may be the observer, or one of their family. If the Bean Nighe sees the observer, she will lash out with the linen, the touch of which will break both legs. If anyone happens on her without being seen and can grab and suckle a dangling breast, then the "foster child" can demand such favours as "second sight." A less dangerous ploy is to arrive at the water's edge before she can, in which case three wishes will be granted, but only if the mortal first answers three questions faithfully. In general, humans traveling through wild, isolated moorlands, who hear the violent noise of slapping water on stones will wisely make a detour, for the Bean Nighe is surely at her washing there. During such times as the Forty-five Rebellion (1745), the Bean Nighe could be seen before each battle, washing the bloodstained clothes of Highlanders about to be slain.
References 17, 123
See also Ban Nighechain, Banshee, Cannered Noz, Caointeach, Spirit

BEAN-SIDHE

See Banshee

BEBON

See Babi

BEDIADARI, BIDADARI

This is a euphemism that means the Good People, used to refer to the Little People or fairies in the folk beliefs of the Malay people of West Malaysia.
References 120
See also Fairy, Little People

BEDONEBYASYOUDID, MRS.

A fairy of nineteenth-century English moral values in Charles Kingsley's classic story The Water Babies (1863). Like Mrs. Doasyouwouldbedoneby, she is portrayed as an elderly, strict schoolmarm who tutors the Water Babies in their underwater realm.
References 37
See also Fairy

BEDUH

See Baduh

BEELZEBUB

One of the spellings of the name of an infernal devil also known as the "Lord of the Flies" in Hebrew and

Christian scriptures. The other variants of the name are Baalzebub, Baalzebul, Beelzebul, Belsabub, Belsabubbe and Belsebub. He is described as the "prince of demons" in the New Testament and as a Fallen Angel next in rank to Satan in Milton's *Paradise Lost*. His particular temptation is to lead humans into the vice of gluttony.
References 40, 53, 107, 119
See also Demon, Devil, Fallen Angel

BEFANA
This is the name of a good house fairy in the folklore of Italy. Befana is usually described as an ugly old hag, but sometimes, especially on Twelfth Night, the Feast of the Epiphany (January 6), she is portrayed as a kindly grandmother figure. A Christian Christmas legend tells how she was so busy with her housework when the traveling Magi called on their way to Bethlehem to see the Christ Child that she postponed offering any hospitality until their return trip. One tradition says that she was invited to accompany them but was busy and later got lost trying to follow them. Since then, the legend says, she sets out a welcome every Twelfth Night in the hope that they will come. So Befana, who missed sending gifts to the Child Jesus, fills the shoes of Italian children at Epiphany in the guise of a parent. Those children who are awake and hear her, cry out *"Ecco la Befana."* Her name is a mispronunciation of Epiphania (Epiphany). A traditional celebration of singing, music, and merrymaking with effigies of Befana in house windows has been practiced in Italian towns and cities every Twelfth Night.
References 40, 87, 93
See also Berchta, Butzenbercht, Fairy, Santa Claus, Appendix 22

BÉFIND
A Celtic fairy and in Ireland a woman of the Sidhe. She is one of the three guardian fairies who attended the birth of each child in order to endow it with gifts of abilities or character and make predictions for its future life. A custom in northern Brittany, France, of preparing a festive table in the room of the birth and inviting these fairies to attend survived until the last century. The most famous traditional tale involving these fairies is that of the Sleeping Beauty.
References 35
See also Chang Hsien, Eshu, Fairy, Fati, Guardian, Moiræ, Oosood, Parcae, Pi-Hsia Yüan-Chün, Sídhe, Ursitory, Appendix 22

BEHEMOTH
In medieval European demonology Behemoth is a most powerful demon who appears in the shape of a grotesque elephant. His domain is the "delights of the belly," and he is charged with tempting humans into the vice of over-indulgence.

References 53, 113
See also Demon

BEHIR, BEITHIR
The name of one of a group of fearsome spirits known as fuaths in the Highland folklore of Scotland. Their name is associated with lightning and snakes, and when these are seen during the long-light summer nights, one may be sure that the Beithir are close by. Although they are rarely seen, it is known that these spirits, like the snakes, inhabit the corries and caves of the Highlands, which humans avoid as much as possible.
References 17
See also Fuath, Spirit

BELIAL, BELIAR
This is the name of a powerful devil, demon, or fiend in Hebrew and Christian writing, and in medieval European literature. Belial means worthless or base, and Beliar means the Unholy One. Milton later uses Belial as one of the Fallen Angels in his work *Paradise Lost*.
References 40, 53, 67, 87, 93, 107
See also Demon, Devil, Fallen Angel, Fiend

BELIAS
See Devil

BELPHEGOR
In ancient Assyrian mythology Belphegor was a god noted for orgiastic celebrations, but he was demoted in medieval Roman Catholic writing to the status of a demon. In this latter capacity Belphegor tests the felicity of human marriage and tempts partners to commit acts of indiscretion and adultery.
References 40, 53
See also Demon, Devil

BEN BAYNAC
A goblin in Scottish folklore who resided with his goblin wife Clashnichd Aulniac in the region of Craig Aulniac. They were, as all sprites, virtually immortal, except for a conspicuously vulnerable mole on Ben Baynac's chest. The two goblins were particularly quarrelsome; Ben Baynac beat and tormented his wife such that her shrieks would disturb the neighborhood every night. A highlander called James Gray, on hearing the cause of Clashnichd Aulniac's distress, put an end to the problem by shooting an arrow into Ben Baynac's mole, killing the vindictive goblin. But that only served to leave Clashnichd Aulniac so grateful that she attached herself to the local families, where her greed knew no bounds. The goblin's thieving appetite at last so angered a housewife that she hurled boiling water over Clashnichd as she was

attempting to steal. The scalded, shrieking goblin fled, never to be seen there again.
References 47
See also Goblin, Sprite

BEN SOCIA, BENSOCIA
A name used in French folklore as a euphemism for a fairy. Ben Socia, which means Good Neighbor, was derived originally from an epithet of the Norse goddess Frigg whose status was similarly reduced with the coming of Christianity. In Holland the goddess and her epithet were transformed to either Pharaildis or Vrouelden, which are now the local names for Frau Hilde.
References 95
See also Fairy, Holle

BEN VARREY
The Manx word for the mermaid in the folklore of the Isle of Man (United Kingdom). She is described as a beautiful being with golden hair who enchants fishermen and lures them to their doom. Sometimes the Manx mermaid can be benevolent, as in the tale in Dora Broome's *Fairy Tales from the Isle of Man* in which a grateful mermaid tells her mortal rescuer where to find a hoard of treasure. However, the simple fisherman does not recognize the value of Spanish Armada gold and he disposes of his treasure by throwing it back into the sea!
References 17
See also Fairy, Mermaid, Appendix 25

BENDITH Y MAMAU
See Tylwyth Teg

BENG
This is the Romany Gypsy name for a devil that inhabits dark woods and forests. This demon will attack humans but also leaves the forest in order to work evil at night. The term *O'Bengh* is used to signify Satan, the Devil.
References 31, 93
See also Demon, Devil

BENSHI
See Banshee

BERCHTA
This winter spirit of south German, Austrian, Swiss, and Alsatian folklore has many descriptions according to the role that she fulfills at the time. She is therefore known by a number of different regional names, which are: Berkta, Bertha, Brechta, Butzenbercht, Eisenberta, Frau Berchta, Frau Berta, Precht, Percht, Perchta, Spinnstubenfrau, and Stomach-slasher.
　She can be a hag with a hooked nose, bright beady eyes, long straggly grey hair, wearing dishevelled clothes, and carrying a distaff. She is easily identified by one of her feet, which is flattened and longer than the other from continuous pounding of the spinning wheel treadle. This spirit is supposed to reside deep in hollow mountains. As the hag, Berchta presents a nursery bogie image with which untidy or unruly children are threatened into good behavior and tidiness—especially just before the Christmas season, when, as Butzenbercht, she is expected at Epiphany Eve (*Perchtentag*) to deliver gifts to those children who have been good. As the "Stomach-slasher" she will inflict dire consequences if not included in the celebration to feast on herrings and dumplings or pancakes.
　In another guise, Berchta is a tall, elegant, and youthful beauty. She has long flaxen hair braided with pearls; her pallid face is obscured by a fine white veil that extends to her long, flowing white silken robes. She carries in one hand the keys of happiness and in the other a spray of mayflowers.
　She is also Perchta, which means Shining, the fearsome guardian of cornfields, barns, and the activity of spinning. Any of these areas left untended will incur her plagues on livestock or humans. In order to ensure fertility of her domain, dancers known as *Berchten/Perchten,* representing both the ugly and beautiful Berchta, dance in the fields of those farmers providing the harvest feast, to drive out any lurking evil spirits. In this guise she is also associated with the Raging Host, whom she leads through the winter storms gathering up *Heimchen,* the souls of the infant dead, especially on *Perchtennacht* (Twelfth Night). It is believed that the Devil sometimes joins them in order to grab a victim as they howl through the night skies.
　In the guise of the White Lady, Berchta is a predictive spirit of death and disaster appearing to those who will be involved in the coming events. She was reported as appearing in 1806 before Napoleon's Prussian conquest and occupation of Berlin, and before such battles as Waterloo. It is said that anyone who receives a cowslip flower from her or can release her from her enchanted world will be blessed with good fortune.
References 87, 88, 93, 95
See also Banshee, Butzenbercht, Corn Spirit, Father Christmas, Guardian, Hag, Holle, Nursery Bogie, Pelznickel, Santa Claus, Sprite, Stomach-slasher, White Lady, Wild Hunt, Appendix 15, Appendix 22, Appendix 23

BEREGINI
These are water spirits in the folklore of Russia. They are benevolent spirits associated with the rivers and streams and are said to inhabit the banks over the water where the Rusalka may be found.
References 75
See also Rusalka, Spirit, Appendix 25

BERG PEOPLE
This is the Danish name of the Little People resembling dwarfs, also known as Bergfolk, Bjerg-Trolde, or Skovtrolde (the wood troll). They are a species of troll often appearing in the shape of toads. There is a well-known tale of a midwife who, on her way home from a successful human delivery, notices in the road a fat toad with white stripes and remarks to it that she will gladly deliver it too. A fortnight later, on hearing a cart draw up outside her door, she sees a little man with a long white beard. He entreats her to attend his wife just as she had promised. This the midwife does, but she cannot help remarking on their poor abode. The little new mother tells the midwife to anoint her eyes with liquid from a pot nearby, whereupon a vision of great beauty and wealth is revealed to her, and she receives much gold for her service. The little mother then tells her to jump from the cart when she reaches boggy ground, otherwise the little man will not take the midwife home and may dispose of her. In fear she does as she is told and arrives home safely with her reward. Some time later in the market place she recognizes and greets the little old man who immediately pokes her eyes out.
References 18, 38, 133
See also Dwarf, Little People, Troll

BERG FOLK
See Berg People

BERITH
A powerful demon in medieval European demonology.
References 53
See also Demon

BERKTA, BERTHA
See Berchta

B'ES
This is a term for an evil spirit or devil in the folk beliefs of the Cheremis/Mari people of the former Soviet Republic.
References 118
See also Bes (1)

BES
(1) The word for a devil in Russian folklore who could be either benevolent or malignant depending on which of your shoulders he was sitting on. Good Bes, the equivalent of a Guardian Angel, sat on the right shoulder, and Bad Bes, the tempter, sat on the left shoulder.

(2) Originally this was the name of a grotesque, dwarf-like demi-god of Egyptian mythology clothed in a lion pelt. As a deformed protector against demons with a love of music, pleasure, and buffoonery, he was transposed into Greek mythology as Silenus the satyr.

References (1) 46, 75; (2) 29, 39, 41, 87, 93, 114, 119
See also (1) Chert, Devil, Guardian Angel; (2) Demon, Dwarf, Satyr, Silenus

BĒTĀLA
See Vetāla

BETHOR
This spirit appears in the medieval mysticism of Europe. Bethor is described as an Olympian spirit and guardian of 42 provinces of the universe.
References 53
See also Guardian, Olympian Spirit, Spirit

BETIKHÂN
This is a nature spirit in the folklore of India. Betikhân is a forest spirit or type of faun who hunts the animals of the Neilgherry Hills.
References 110
See also Faun, Spirit, Appendix 19

BEUGIBUS, BUGIBUS
See Bug-a-Boo

BHAIRON
In Indian mythology Bhairon is a field spirit elevated by association with the god Bhairava to act as guardian of temples dedicated to Siva in Benares. In this guise, in Bombay, Bhairon is depicted carrying a sword and a bowl of blood.
References 87
See also Guardian, Spirit, Appendix 18

BHUT/A
In Indian folklore these malignant spirits or demons, also known as Bûtûs, can materialize in many shapes, usually that of an animal such as a pig or horse. When the Bhuts manifest in human form they are said to resemble a goblin who talks with a nasal twang. They can be identified by the fact that they throw no shadow and cannot lie down on the earth. They may be encountered in cemeteries and dark forests. In order to avoid the Bhuts one may lie on the ground where they cannot follow or ignite a stick of turmeric, of which they are apparently afraid. They may be appeased by throwing grain to the cardinal compass points and the center point.
References 29, 87, 93, 110
See also Chûtâs, Demon, Goblin, Pey, Piśācas

BIA
A river spirit in the mythology of the Akan peoples of Ghana.
References 119
See also Spirit, Appendix 25

BIASD BHEULACH

A demon spirit of regional Scottish folklore that haunted the locality of Ordail Pass in the Hebridean Isle of Skye (United Kingdom). This demon could assume many shapes, but mostly manifested as a greyhound or as a man with only one leg. At night it could be heard howling and shrieking, causing terror to all who heard it or needed to travel through the pass. According to the local tradition, one morning a workman was found dead with horrifying wounds to both his leg and side, but after this, the Biasd Bheulach never reappeared.
References 17
See also Cacy Taperere, Demon, Dodore, Fachan, Nashas, Spirit

BIB AND BUB
See Gumnut Babies

BIBUNG
A dwarf who appears in the ancient German *Book of Heroes* as the protector of Virginal the ice fairy.
References 58
See also Dwarf, Fairy, Virginal

BIČA KUBA AND BIČA KUGUZA, BIČA IA, BIČA OZA
Biča Kuba and Biča Kuguza are the Old Woman of the Animal Pen and Old Man of the Animal Pen spirits in the folklore of the Cheremis/Mari peoples of the former Soviet Republic. As their name implies, they are guardians of the livestock in the pens. These spirits share their responsibilities with two other categories of pen spirit known as: Biča Ia, Pen Devil, and Biča Oza, Pen Master. Biča Kuba is described as a little old woman dressed in white who may be seen inspecting the livestock in the evenings. These spirits have favorite animals, and if they take a dislike to one, they may torment it and allow it to suffer. Sometimes, like the pixies of England, they may ride a horse all night so that it is covered with sweat and exhausted in the morning.
References 118
See also Guardian, Ia, Kuba, Kuguza, Pixie, Spirit, Appendix 12

BIERSAL
This is the name of a kobold or goblin in the folklore of the German region of Saxony. This household spirit has as his abode the *bierkeller* of inns. In these establishments the Biersal will gladly clean the bottles and steins that have been used in return for his own stein of beer each day.
References 87
See also Cellar Demon, Goblin, Kobold, Spirit, Appendix 22

BIG PURRA
The storm spirit in the Dreamtime legends and mythology of the Native Australian people.
References 14
See also Spirit, Virra Birron, Appendix 26

BIG WATER MAN
This is a powerful river spirit of the Native American Taos Pueblo people's beliefs. He is described as having a spiny body, yellow eyes, and a huge mouth. Big Water Man is a guardian spirit of good health and protection against disease. He controls all the areas around the rivers and can cause floods, alter the depth and flow of the rivers, and even cause landslides when he decides to move swiftly. Big Water Man is constantly rebuffed by the Corn Maidens and seeks to punish them for rejecting him.
References 88
See also Deohako, Guardian, Spirit, Appendix 25

BILBERRY MAN
This is a demon in the folklore of the Franconia region of Germany who inhabits the forests and brush. He is essentially a guardian spirit of the bilberry fruit bushes and will attack anyone traveling through his territory. Anyone who wishes to gather the ripe fruit must appease the Bilberry Man. This is done by placing an offering of bread or fruit conspicuously on a stone.
References 110
See also Appletree Man, Demon, Guardian, Appendix 21

BILLY BLIN
(1) A household spirit of the Borders country between England and Scotland. He was a benevolent spirit also known as Billy Blind or Blind Barlow, who was described as wearing a blindfold. This spirit was particularly concerned with maintaining family and matrimonial happiness and was credited with giving copious good advice and removing spells of evil enchantment.

(2) A Malevolent seven-headed fiend in Cornwall who hid in a barrel to spy on King Arthur and his court. Billy Blin was beaten in combat by Sir Bredbedal, the Green Knight, and delivered to King Arthur to serve the knights of the Round Table.
References 15, 37, 87, 135
See also (2) Fiend, Green Knight, Spirit, Appendix 22

BILLY BLIND
See Billy Blin

BILLY WINKER
This is a sleep spirit in the folklore of Lancashire, and known elswhere in England as Wee Willie Winkie.

He is a nursery spirit invoked at bedtime for young children to be gently coaxed to sleep.
References 17
See also Dormette, Dustman, Ole Luk Øj, Sandman, Spirit, Appendix 22

BILOKO
A malignant dwarf in the folklore of Zaire. He is described as having an enormous mouth and hair that looks like grass. Biloko has huge vicious claws and wears a covering of leaves. He inhabits hollow trees, where he awaits his victims.
References 56
See also Dwarf

BILWIS
A nature spirit in the folklore of Germany and Austria during the Middle Ages. This spirit was also known by the names Pilwiz and Bimesschneider. He lived in trees and was invoked for curing illness. This relatively gentle character was later changed to a sort of demon in human form and recognized by the sickles protruding from his big toes. At night the Bilwis was supposed to torment humans by entangling their hair and playing tricks. The pranks he played in the fields involved cutting strips through the farmer's ripening crops and spoiling the harvest with the sickles on his feet. Although sometimes given small offerings for protecting children against sickness, he is now regarded mostly as a type of bogie.
References 87, 93
See also Demon, Spirit

BIMESSCHNEIDER
See Bilwis

BINAYE ALBANI
These are demon spirits in the beliefs and mythology of the Navajo Native American people. These demons, until they were destroyed, were able to kill just by a look from their eyes.
References 87
See also Demon, Spirit

BISAN
A female nature spirit in the folklore of the Malay people of West Malaysia. The Bisan is specifically the guardian of the camphor-bearing tree and appears in the shape of a cicada. Bisan must be approached correctly for camphor to be found, and therefore only *bahasa kapor* (camphor language) is spoken while people search for it in the jungle. A white cockerel may be sacrificed and some food presented for Bisan, otherwise she may not reveal the whereabouts of any camphor for the people to take back.

References 87
See also Guardian, Spirit, Appendix 19

BITÂBOHS
These are evil and malignant spirits in the folklore of the Bongo and Niam-Niam peoples of Gabon, West Africa. These spirits are also known by the name Hitâbohs. They are believed to inhabit the trees of the forest, where they are intent on the destruction of any humans who travel through their territory. Old women are frequently accused of being their accomplices.
References 110
See also Spirit

BITNƏZƏ
See Kugə Jeŋ

BITOSO
A disease demon in the folklore of the Romany Gypsies of Europe. This evil spirit was the result of the union between Ana and the king of the demons after he had eaten cloves of garlic covered in his urine. Bitoso, whose name means One Who Fasts, takes the shape of a tiny many-headed worm. He is responsible for causing humans loss of appetite, headaches, and stomach aches. Bitoso has several "children," each buzzing around human bodies causing problems such as earache, toothache, cramps, and colic.
References 31
See also Keshalyi, Loçolico, Melalo, Schilalyi, Appendix 17

BJERG-TROLDE
See Berg People

BLACK AGNES
See Black Annis

BLACK ANNIS
This is the local demon or hag also known as Black Agnes of the Dane Hills near Leicester in England. The original character may have derived from the Celtic goddess Danu, the same derivation as the Tuatha dé Danann. She was a powerful and terrifying supernatural hag with long claws and yellow fangs who lived in a cave called Black Annis's Bower, which she is said to have clawed from the rock. Black Annis fed on the local children whom she caught at dusk when they strayed into the Dane Hills. She was said to have skinned and devoured her victims, scattering their bones and hanging the skins on a tree to dry. Later her influence became no more than that of a nursery bogie.
References 47, 123
See also Baba Yaga, Demon, Hag, Nursery Bogie, Tuatha dé Danann, Appendix 22

BLACK BEAR

A guardian spirit also known as Wacabe in the beliefs of the Osage Native American people. He inspires humans with courage and strength, and he is also the spirit of longevity.
References 87
See also Guardian, Spirit, Appendix 12

BLACK DOG

This is the name of a type of fiend or terrifying spirit found in folklore throughout most of the southern and eastern English counties, and sometimes in Scotland. They appear under many different names in other regions. These spirits take the shape of a huge shaggy-haired black dog, said to be about the size of a calf, with enormous glowing, fiery red eyes. Some are reported to be malicious, and some can be quite benevolent at times. Black Dogs, or Black Hounds, are usually encountered on lonely tracks, ancient roads and crossroads, bridges, and entrances—the places of transition in human lives. They are normally benign if left alone and are often said to be the guardian spirit of some ancient treasure (e.g., at Lyme Regis, Somerset) or sacred place (e.g., at Wambarrows, Somerset).

If anyone attempts to strike out or engage them in any way, then the Black Dogs can show most frightful powers, inflicting savage wounds, paralysis, and death, then they vanish before the eyes of any survivor. To see one is supposed to portend death within the year, however, in some parts of England (e.g., at Weacombe, Somerset), there are well known instances of Black Dogs appearing to lost travelers or frightened girls traveling alone and guiding them safely home.

The most famous anecdote is of the Black Dog of Bungay which Abraham Fleming (d. 1607) reported as having terrified, killed, and devastated people in the Church of Bungay, near Norwich, on Sunday, 4 August 1577. (A report of the same incident in Stow's Annales, published in 1600, makes no mention of a dog!) There are numerous local tales on Dartmoor, including that of a white "Black" dog, which were the inspiration for Sir Arthur Conan Doyle's famous The Hound of the Baskervilles. Other famous Black Dog traditions may be found at Oakhampton Castle, Devon, Newgate in London, Cromer in Norfolk, Torrington in north Devon, and Tring in Hertfordshire. Hundreds of Black Dog sightings have been recorded in Britain over the last 400 years, and some instances have been recorded in Brittany (France), Denmark, and other areas of Scandinavia. More recently the author has been given anecdotes of otherwise inexplicable crashes of police cars on a dark empty road in Hampshire, which were ascribed to the appearance of the local supernatural

Black Dog. The Black Dog is still a potent feature of local folklore!
References 15, 16, 17, 19, 99, 126, 133
See also Barguest, Black Shuck, Boggart, Bullbeggar, Capelthwaite, Church Grim, Freybug, Guardian, Gytrash, Mauthe Dhoog, Padfoot, Rongeur d'Os, Skriker, Spirit, Appendix 12, Appendix 24

BLACK HOUND

See Black Dog

BLACK SHUCK

A fiend also known as Shuck, Shuck Dog, or Old Shuck, of the Black Dog type in the folklore of East Anglia, England. The name is possibly derived from the Anglo-Saxon *Scucca* meaning a demon. It is described as about the size of a shaggy black donkey with huge glowing red eyes, or a single eye that showers sparks of green or red fire. At Clopton Hall near Stowmarket, however, this fiend is described as resembling a monk with a hound's head. Its abode is variously the salt marshes or the sea itself, from which Black Shuck emerges only at dusk to patrol the lanes, marshes, river banks, and graveyards. This demon may be encountered on the roads, where its icy breath and shaggy pelt may be felt as it draws alongside a traveler. In Suffolk it will offer no harm if left alone, but death soon follows for any who challenge it. In Norfolk merely seeing the Black Shuck was enough to invoke sickness or death. There is a variant of this demon reported as having the face of a monkey. This spirit haunts the area between Balsham and Wratting in Cambridgeshire, where it is known locally as the Shuck-Monkey. The Essex Shuck, however, is a benevolent spirit that has been known to guide lost travelers and protect those under attack. The fact that it haunts the place of a gallows, gibbet, or cemetery links it with the demon Shuck.
References 19, 47, 69, 133
See also Barguest, Black Dog, Boggart, Bullbeggar, Capelthwaite, Church Grim, Demon, Fiend, Freybug, Gytrash, Lubin, Mauthe Dhoog, Padfoot, Rongeur d'Os, Skriker, Spirit, Appendix 12, Appendix 24

BLACK SOW

A winter demon of the border Welsh Hills on the Borders between England and Wales. It may also be known as the Cropped Black Sow or the Cutty Black Sow. This spirit is associated with the local traditional bonfires lit on Halloween (31 October, Beltane in the Celtic calendar). In local superstition the last to leave the scene of this bonfire invoked the possibility of being chased and caught, supposedly in ancient times as a sacrificial victim. This demon was also used as a children's bogeyman.
References 123
See also Bogyman, Demon, Spirit, Appendix 12

BLACK SPIDER OLD WOMAN
See Spider

BLACK TAMANOUS
A cannibal spirit in the Native American folklore of the coastal Pacific Northwest.
References 87, 88
See also Spirit

BLACK VAUGHAN
An evil spirit sometimes described as a goblin and sometimes as a Black Dog in the folklore of Herefordshire, England. It is said to have been invoked by or to represent Vaughan, the owner of Hergest Court many centuries ago. The demon materialized at any time in different shapes causing fright and destruction, raging as a bull in church, or tipping farmers' loaded wagons. Eventually the folk of the neighborhood called for Black Vaughan to be confined by "reading him down" from the Bible. Although this was done, and his prison is supposed to be a silver snuff box, no one dares to enter the room in which it remains and from which Black Vaughan's footsteps and clanking chains are said still to be heard.
References 123
See also Black Dog, Demon, Goblin, Spirit

BLIND BARLOW
See Billy Blin

BLOODY CAP
An evil sprite or goblin that is also known as Red Cap or Red Comb in the folklore of the Borders between England and Scotland. Bloody Cap inhabited the ruins of castles and peel towers (fortified Border towers), the sites of previous skirmishes and bloodshed. This evil spirit looks like a very small old man with long grisly hair, fiery red eyes, protruding teeth, and hideous talons on his skinny fingers. He wears iron boots, a red blood-soaked cap, and carries a pikestaff. If any travelers who have lost their way are foolish enough to shelter in one of these old ruins, Bloody Cap is waiting to butcher them and catch their blood in his cap. The only way to protect oneself from his intentions is to recite the scriptures, whereupon Bloody Cap will shriek and disappear, leaving one of his fangs behind. There is said to be a Red Cap that inhabits Grandtully Castle. He is supposed to be benevolent towards humans and may bring good fortune. However, the more usual legends of the Red Cap are similar to the gruesome tale of Lord Soulis and his familiar, whose horrific activities and demise in a boiling cauldron are the subject of Border legend.
References 15, 17, 66, 133
See also Goblin

BLOODY-BONES
See Raw Head and Bloody Bones

BLOSSOM BABIES
See Gumnut Babies

BLUE BONNET
See Blue Cap

BLUE BURCHES
A house spirit or hobgoblin of the Blackdown Hills in Somerset, England. He was able to assume many different shapes, such as a cloud of blue smoke, a white horse, or a little black piglet. Blue Burches' usual shape was that of a little old man wearing blue breeches (burches). Blue Burches played tricks in the house that were alarming but harmless, such as making the house glow from within, causing those outside to scurry in fear, believing that it was on fire.
References 17
See also Hobgoblin, Spirit, Appendix 22

BLUE CAP
This is a spirit of the coal mines in English folklore. Blue Cap, or Blue Bonnet as he was sometimes known, appeared as a light blue flame but was otherwise invisible, like the knockers of the tin mines. Blue Cap was extremely industrious and put in the day's work, moving the loaded tubs in the same way as a human miner. Like the human miners, Blue Cap expected his due wages, which were calculated and left in an appropriate corner. An account of this practice was written in some mine documents of 1863.
References 17
See also Knockers, Mine Spirits, Spirit

BLUE FAIRY, THE
The guardian fairy in the Italian fairy tale of Pinocchio the puppet, whom she helps to become human. Her image, now established in the depiction from the Walt Disney production, is of a tall, blond, beautiful female dressed in a long blue gown with gossamer wings shimmering from her shoulders and carrying a magic wand.
References 37
See also Fairy, Guardian

BLUE JAY
A semi-supernatural, shape-changing being of the Chinook, the Jacarilla Apache, and other Native American creation legends. He is a mischievous trickster spirit. Among the many tales of magic and deception is one involving Blue Jay's sister Ioi. Ioi needs help with her work and persuades Blue Jay to take a wife. Blue Jay agrees to marry the chief's daughter Stikua. But she has just died, so he takes her

corpse to the Great Ones, who restore her life. When the outraged chief demands Blue Jay's hair in exchange for his "dead" daughter, the trickster changes into a bird and makes his escape. The chief's daughter returns to the "dead ones," who take Ioi, Blue Jay's sister, to marry one of the ghosts as punishment for Blue Jay's tampering. Blue Jay searches for and finds his sister with the heap of bones that is now her family. They assume their threatening human shape, but Blue Jay knows the words to reduce them to bones again. He takes delight in redistributing them so that the next time the bones take shape they have a mixture of each other's legs, arms, hands, and heads.

References 41, 87
See also Anansi, Bamapama, Basajaun, Coyote, Eshu, Manabozo, Mink, Trickster

BLUE MEN OF THE MINCH
These malignant sea spirits are a type of merman unique to the Minch Passage of the Outer Hebrides off Scotland. They are believed by the islanders to be Fallen Angels. The Blue Men are only found in the folklore of the Outer Hebrides, where they may be seen floating in the Minch, known in Gaelic as *Sruth nam Fear Gorma,* which means the Channel of the Blue Men, between the Isle of Lewis and the Shiant Isles off the Scottish mainland. They have the appearance of humans but are entirely blue with grey beards.

The seas around these islands are particularly treacherous, and the weather is said to be calm when the Blue Men and their chieftain are in their underwater caves. When they appear, they summon up fearsome storms and swim out to any foolhardy vessel attempting to make a run through the Minch, with the intention of wrecking the ship and sending the sailors to their doom. The local skippers know that the Blue Men may be thwarted since they love rhyming contests and will challenge the captain before condemning the ship. If the captain has an agile tongue and can always get the last word, then the Blue Men will spare the vessel and its crew.

There is strong evidence that these beliefs were derived from the Moorish slaves who were pressed into sailing the Viking longships and were marooned by the Norsemen in the Minch in the ninth century. Like their descendants today, the Tuaregs, these unfortunates wore long blue robes and grey-blue veils.

References 15, 17, 47, 123
See also Fallen Angel, Merman, Spirit, Appendix 25

BÓANN
In ancient Irish mythology Bóann was a queen of the Tuatha dé Danann, the wife of Dagda, and mother of Angus Og. Bóann boasted that the curse of the well of Nectan (that the eyes of anyone looking down the well would burst from their sockets) would not affect her. After looking down the well and running round it thrice in defiance, a wave of water surrounded her, taking from her an eye, a hand, and a thigh. In desperation she tried to escape to the sea but the waters totally engulfed her and she became the Boyne, the river that retains her name.

References 87
See also Angus Og, Dagda, Sídhe, Tuatha dé Danann

BOCAN
This is a local form of the spirit name Bogan in English folklore. This variant is found in the Isle of Man (United Kingdom), Cheshire, and Shropshire. Other variant names are Bauchan, Bogan, and Bugan. Under the name Bocan the sprite is a type of nuisance spirit in the folklore of Ireland.

References 17
See also Hobgoblin, Spirit, Sprite

BOCKMANN
A type of forest demon in German folklore, whose appearance, like the satyr, is part man and part goat. His existence is used by parents as a nursery bogie to frighten children into staying away from the forests.

References 110
See also Demon, Nursery Bogie, Satyr, Appendix 19, Appendix 22

BODACH, BODACH GLAS
This is the name of a frightening spirit and a form of the Celtic bugbear. The Bodach, which means Old Man in Scottish Gaelic, was thought to enter human houses at night by way of the chimney in order to carry off naughty children. In this respect it was used by Scottish parents as a nursery bogie. In the more seriously terrifying aspect of the spirit he is known as the Bodach Glas, the Dark Grey Man. In this guise he is a portent of imminent death in the family.

References 15, 17, 56
See also Ainsel, Banshee, Bugbear, Nursery Bogie, Spirit, Appendix 22

BODACHAN SABHAILL
A type of brownie or barn spirit in the folklore of the Irish, Manx, and Hebridean people of northwestern Britain. The Bodachan Sabhaill, whose name means Little Old Man of the Barn, lived in the farm buildings. Although he does not seem to have done general work of the brownie kind, he did the threshing in the barn for farmworkers who were too old to keep up with the younger ones.

References 17
See also Brownie, Capelthwaite, Dobie, Massariol, Ovinnik, Spirit, Appendix 22

BODB

In old Irish mythology, Bodb is one of the Tuatha dé Danann. He is the son of Dagda and also a king of the Sidhe in County Tipperary, Munster. When Aoife betrayed the children of Lir, Bodb changed her into a demon.
References 87
See also Dagda, Demon, Sídhe, Tuatha dé Danann

BODƏŽ

This is chiefly a term for nature spirits in the folk beliefs of the Cheremis/Mari peoples of the former Soviet Republic. Bodez is usually a suffix or appended to another name to denote the class of spirit to which the spirits belong. When used alone, this name may also refer to a water spirit or to a lesser demon.
References 118
See also Demon, Spirit

BODUA

An evil spirit in the mythology of ancient Gaul (France), whose presence signified imminent death or disaster.
References 87
See also Badb, Ban Nighechain, Banshee, Cyhiraeth, Morrigan, Spirit, Valkyries

BOE BULBAGGER

See Bullbeggar

BOG, BOGGE

See Bogie

BOGAN

See Hobgoblin

BOGEY, BOGY, BOGUEY

See Bogie

BOGGART

A spirit or hobgoblin in North Country English folk-lore who may also be known as a Bag, Boggard, or Buggard. The Boggart can take numerous forms and behave both as a demon and a poltergeist or even as a benevolent brownie. Whichever form they take, it is only rarely that they materialize, and therefore only specific Boggarts will have a description. The Boggarts that take human shape are frequently more vicious than those that materialize as animals. The Boggart is well known for playing tricks either in the household—where it delights in frightening people by pulling at bedclothes, tripping cooks in the kitchen, rapping on and slamming doors—or lurking in dark lonely roads or moorland, where it terrorizes travelers. The friendly household Boggart, however, acts much like a brownie and will work hard wash-ing, cleaning, and doing heavy farmwork if treated well. If upset, this spirit will destroy or displace everything in the house and farm buildings.

There are many stories about Boggarts. One from Lincolnshire is almost identical to that of the farmer and the bogie. It relates how a tormented farmer decided to leave his home, and hopefully the Boggart with it. However, as he was on his way out of the farm gate with his family and all his possessions, a neighbor expressed surprise and asked where he was going. Before anyone could answer, a voice from deep in the possessions replied, "Aye we're flittin'" (leaving). The farmer returned sadly, realizing that there was no escape.

Another tells of the Boggart of the Brook, at Garstang in Yorkshire, which appears as a woman in a hooded cloak at the roadside requesting a lift from travelers, usually those on horseback. When the "hitchhiker" has become a passenger, she reveals her-self to be a skeleton, and her demonic cackle and clawing grip spur the traveler into a frenzied ride, causing injury or death. A similar example of this Boggart terrorized children who walked through a gloomy pass between two hills, known as Bunting Nook, in Norton (the author's childhood home) near Sheffield, Yorkshire. Very few people braved this route after dark.

The Boggart of Hackensall Hall took the shape of a horse, the work of which was so much appreciated that it was allowed to lie by its own fire in winter.
References 15, 17, 47, 69, 87, 92, 107, 123, 133, 135
See also Barguest, Black Dog, Black Shuck, Bogie, Brownie, Bullbeggar, Capelthwaite, Church Grim, Demon, Freybug, Gytrash, Hobgoblin, Mauthe Dhoog, Padfoot, Poltergeist, Rongeur d'Os, Skriker, Spirit, Appendix 22, Appendix 24

BOGGELMANN

This is a type of nuisance spirit in German folklore. It is also known by the name Bumann and behaves much like the English boggle or bogie.
References 41
See also Bogie, Poltergeist, Spirit

BOGIE

A class of frightening goblin or bugbear in English folk-lore. These spirits may be called by the following varia-tions of the name: Bog, Bogge, Bogey, Bogy, Boguey, Bogie Beast, Bogyman, Bogeyman, Booger Man, Booman, and Budge Fur. The Bogie is generally described as little, black, and hairy. They can be dan-gerous but are more frequently mischievous or sly, and as they are not renowned for their intelligence, a quick-witted human may easily foil the Bogie's evil inten-tions. The Bogie is also used frequently as a nursery Bogie to frighten children into good behavior. In other

The Boggart of the Brook rides behind her victim.

countries the following spirits equate with the activities of the Bogie: The German Bumann or Boggelmann, the Irish Bocan or Púcá, and the Bubák of Bohemia.

A Northamptonshire story told by Sternberg in *Dialect and Folklore of Northamptonshire*, tells how a lazy Bogie decided to torment a farmer by demanding half the crop despite doing no work himself. The farmer, knowing what evil could be inflicted if he refused, quickly agreed and asked the Bogie whether he wanted the top half or the bottom half. The Bogie demanded the bottom half, so the farmer planted wheat. Having only the roots from that year, the next year the Bogie demanded the tops, and this time the farmer planted turnips. The exasperated Bogie then demanded that the field be divided into two and whoever reaped the fastest would win the lot. This time, the day before harvest commenced, the farmer planted thin metal rods between the wheat stalks in that half of the field that the Bogie would cut. The Bogie used the scythe with magical vigour, but it only became blunt. When told that the "wiffle-waffle," or communal sharpening, would take place only at noon, the exhausted Bogie admitted defeat and tormented the farmer no more.
References 15, 17, 18, 40, 92, 107
See also Bugbear, Nursery Bogie, Spirit

BOGIE BEAST
See Bogie

BOGIL/L
See Bogie

BOGLE, BOGGLE, BOGGLE BOO
A frightening bugbear, goblin, or hobgoblin in the folklore of the northern English counties. These spirits are also known locally as Bogill, Bugell, and Bugil in England and Bo-lol, Bwgwl, and Bygel Nos in Wales. Scotland has Bogil, the regional name of this malicious spirit. Descriptions are difficult since these supernaturals had the power to shape shift to almost anything from a gloomy, dark miasma hovering over a deserted road to a distinct shape such as a Black Dog, a strangely animated sack of corn, or even a human shape, which would quickly vanish. Bogles were renowned for the frightening tricks they played on lone travelers, but it was rare that they actually did any harm except to "the guilty, the murderer an' the mansworn an' the cheaters o' the widow an' the fatherless."

Some famous Bogles were recognized by a name, such as the one called Jesse recorded in the 1870s as belonging to Westlands End Farm in Northumberland. Others were specific types of Bogle with individual characteristics and behavior such as the Hedley Kow and the Shellycoat.

The Bogle actually had a celebration day (much like Halloween) in Scotland, which was held on 29 March. This has long been discontinued.
References 15, 17, 53, 87, 92, 104, 107, 123, 133
See also Aufhocker, Barguest, Black Dog, Bogie, Bug, Bugbear, Goblin, Hedley Kow, Hobgoblin, Shellycoat, Spirit, Appendix 22, Appendix 24

BOGUEST
See Barguest

BOGYMAN, BOGEYMAN
This is a type of bogie also known as a Booger Man in the folklore of the mainland areas of Britain. It appeared in a fearsome and grotesque human shape in lonely places, terrifying people traveling alone on the roads at night. This spirit is known as the Booman in the Orkney and Shetland Islands off the north coast of Scotland. More recently its use has been more in keeping with that of a nursery bogie.
References 15, 17, 53, 87, 92, 104, 107, 133
See also Bogie, Nursery Bogie, Spirit

BOIADEIRO DA VISAURA
This is a spirit or encantado of the Afro-Brazilian cult Batuque. This encantado belongs to the Caboclos low-status group of spirits. Boiadeiro da Visaura, whose name means Cowboy of Visaura, is said to be skilled in healing ailments and is invoked for the curing sessions.
References 89
See also Caboclo, Encantado, Spirit

BOLƏK PIAMBAR
See Piambar

BOLL, BOLLY, BOLLEROY
These are the Lancashire dialect words for a bogle in the folklore of England. A Boll is a supernatural spirit that inspires dread. "Bolly" is the lesser or diminutive form, while "Bolleroy" is a local alternative name for the same bogie.
References 107
See also Bogie, Bogle, Spirit

BO-LOL
See Bogle

BOLOTNYI
This is a water spirit in the folklore of Russia. The Bolotnyi is a spirit of the swamps.
References 75
See also Spirit, Appendix 25

BOMBIERO
See Legua Bogi da Trinidade

BONELESS

This is a terrifying supernatural spirit mostly in the folklore of Oxfordshire, England. It is described as a clammy, white, stinking, shapeless mass. Boneless inhabits the lonely lanes of the countryside, especially on dark or foggy nights. The spirit is said to move along the ground, then it overtakes and engulfs travelers on dark, lonely roads.
References 17
See also Brollachan, Caointeach, Spirit, Appendix 24

BONGA

The name of an evil spirit in the folklore of the Santal people of India. These are the transformed spirits of certain dead humans that become malicious female supernaturals inhabiting the rivers, woods, and hills. Bongas can take up physical relationships with humans but may also play sinister tricks on them. At other times they can be quite benevolent, as with the cowherd who was given special powers of "second sight" for helping a Bonga, but the gift was removed because he confided in his wife.
References 87
See also Spirit

BONITO MAIDENS

These are spirit maidens of the sea in the beliefs of the Sa'a people of the Solomon Islands. These spirits are not unlike the European mermaid, but the Bonito Maidens are the exclusive guardians of the bonito fish, with which they live in the deep pools of the ocean bed. These beautiful spirits wear jewelry of cowrie shells and porpoise teeth. They are also the guardians of all ancient ivory bonito fishing hooks lost at sea, and it is from the spirits that these must be retrieved. When the time is right for a shoal of bonito fish to be released for the Sa'a fishermen, the Bonito Maidens leave a bunch of areca nuts by the head of the sleeping shaman. On seeing this he will build a special shrine for the Bonito Maidens, upon which the first bonito fish to be caught will be cleaned and laid as a sacrifice. From there the first fish will be paraded to the canoe house, where it will be baked and eaten by the shaman to ensure a good season's catch.
References 87
See also Guardian, Mermaid, Sedna, Spirit, Appendix 25

BONNES DAMES

This name as well as Nos Bonnes Mères, which means Our Good Mothers, is a name given as an epithet in the folklore of Brittany, France, to refer to the fairies. It is well known that to invoke the fairies by naming them without due cause is to invite their anger and incite their malevolence.
References 87
See also Fairy, Appendix 6

BOOGER, BOOGER MAN, BOOMAN

See Bogie

BOOMASOH

These are tree spirits or nats in Burmese folklore. These spirits are much like the Hamadryads of Greek mythology in that they inhabit the roots of the trees.
References 110
See also Akakasoh, Hamadryad, Hmin, Nats, Shekkasoh, Spirit, Appendix 19

BORARO

These are malignant demons of the Amazon forests in the folklore of the Tukano people. The Boraro, whose name means the White Ones, when they take human shape, are tall, pallid, hairy-chested beings with protruding ears and enormous phalluses. They materialize without knee joints and with their feet pointing backwards, so if they happen to fall over they have difficulty righting themselves. The Boraro carry a stone hoe when hunting in the forest, where they ensnare and devour unwary humans.
References 33
See also Demon, Appendix 19

BORI

These are disease spirits in the beliefs of the Hausa peoples of northern Nigeria. They were invoked to take possession of human mediums in the Bori cult dances. There are more than 178 different Bori spirits, each of which is responsible for causing a particular sickness. When a human becomes ill, the medium for that spirit is asked to invoke the supernatural to remove the disease; if this takes place, then the cured human is forever bound to dance in the cult as the subject of that particular spirit. This cult has been banned for some time.
References 56, 87
See also Encantado, Spirit, Appendix 17

BORONIA BABIES

See Gumnut Babies

BORUTA

In the folklore of Poland, this is the name of a female forest spirit that inhabited the fir trees.
References 110
See also Spirit, Appendix 19

BOSSU

This is the name of a clan of spirits and also of one evil and criminal spirit subject to *Mait' Carrefour* in the Voodoo cults of the West Indies. Bossu, also known as Kadja Bossu, is a three-horned man representation in art or ceremony. He is possibly derived from a being of Dahomey.

References 29
See also Spirit

BÔTO BRANCO
See Falange de Bôtos

BOTO TUCUXÍ, THE
See Falange de Bôtos

BOTTLE IMP
This is a folkloric form of classifying a spirit usually in a folktale, in which some lesser demon or spirit becomes imprisoned through human magic arts, in a container (e.g., a lamp, a bottle, or a jar). The spirit is then obliged to remain imprisoned and must use its supernatural power for its new human master. This method of encapsulating the power of the Little People is common in the folklore of Arabia, the Philippine Islands, Scandinavia, Switzerland, and the Baltic Coast. Typical of these traditional tales is Aladdin and the Magic Lamp from the Arabian *Tales of a Thousand and One Nights*.
References 87
See also Demon, Djinn, Little People, Spirit

BOUDA
An evil and malicious demon in the folklore of Ethiopia that took possession of young and beautiful people, torturing them with foul and unseemly practices. An account from 1865 states that a normal, healthy servant began one day to exhibit the symptoms of a Bouda possession. First, this hard-working person became exhausted and faint; by the evening she had become unconscious. Her frightened fellow servants called in an exorcist, at whose appearance the possessed woman immediately behaved like a raving maniac, laughing, biting, kicking, and screaming. The exorcist commanded the Bouda to leave the woman, which, in an horrific voice from the possessed, it refused, until threatened with burning coals. Before it would comply, the Bouda demanded sustenance of its choosing. Excrement mixed with other dung and water were to be placed in a dish. When this was done the possessed woman leapt at the dish on all fours and lapped up the filth with sickening relish. She then took hold of the most enormous rock (which several men could not have shifted), straightened up and whirled it around her head and catapulted it away. She then fell senseless to the ground. On her recovery shortly after, she was totally unaware of what had happened to her.
References 57
See also Demon

BRAG
This is a term for a class of shape-shifting, malicious spirits in the folklore of the Northern Counties of England. Like the phooka of Irish folklore, it often materialized as a horse, as well as other shapes. The Brags would be seen in fields, on moorland, and on lonely roads. But instead of being the expected friendly farm animal, Brags are deceptive bogies that frequently mislead travelers in to dangerous situations. A well-known instance of their trickery is told of the Picktree Brag.
References 17
See also Bogie, Picktree Brag, Pooka, Spirit, Appendix 12, Appendix 24

BRASH
See Skriker

BREAS
This is the name of a king of the Tuatha dé Danann, also known as Bres or Eochu Bres in Irish mythology. Breas, whose name means beautiful, betrayed his own people to the Formorians.
References 105
See also Formor, Tuatha dé Danann

BRECHTA
See Berchta

BRITOMARTIS
A nymph of ancient Crete who, being pursued by King Minos, threw herself into the Mediterranean, where she was caught in the nets of some fishermen.
References 130
See also Nymph

BROCK
A dwarf in Nordic mythology, he is the brother of Sindri, the acknowledged supreme magic metalsmith. Brock boasted to Loki of his brother's superiority and wagered his own head in a contest. Brock then had to assist his brother by keeping the magic bellows filled with air, despite the blood-sucking flies sent by Loki, while Sindri forged the most incredible magic gifts. These were the boar named Gullinbursti, the magic ring called Draupnir, and Thor's great battle hammer. Thus Brock won his bet and kept his head.
References 95
See also Dwarf

BROLLACHAN
This is a diminutive spirit in the folklore of Scotland. The Brollachan, whose name means Shapeless Thing in Scottish Gaelic, was deemed to be the offspring of a fuath and was supposed to inhabit mill streams. The Brollachan, although essentially a miasma without formal shape, did possess both eyes and a mouth. While having the power of speech, the spirit could only pronounce two phrases: *Mi phrein* (myself) and *Tu phrein* (thyself). One anecdote of the Brollachan

An exorcist is called to help a woman possessed by a Bouda.

told by J. F. Campbell in his *Popular Tales of the West Highlands* follows almost exactly the same theme as that of Ainsel.
References 15, 17
See also Ainsel, Boneless, Fuath, Spirit

BROONIE
A family spirit of the Balfour family of western Scotland. It was a spirit of the brownie type that was renowned for pulling the moored boats to shore for safety during storms and for making roads in difficult terrain.
References 47
See also Brownie, Spirit, Appendix 22

BROTHER MIKE
The name of a local fairy in the folklore of Suffolk, England.
References 17
See also Fairy

BROUNGER
A malignant sea spirit that inhabited the eastern coast of Scotland and particularly the Firth of Forth. The Brounger is described as a male spirit, "a flint the son of a flint," which would indicate a connection with thunder storms, or possibly the phenomenon known as Saint Elmo's Fire. Brounger is said to have extorted a teind, or tythe, of fish and oysters from every fishing vessel in his region and to have terrorized the fishermen by appearing suddenly in the ship's rigging. If this happened (or if some prankster had suggested this as a curse), then the only way to remove the evil of Brounger was for the captain to order the boat to be steered three times the full 360 degrees, before resuming the proper course.
References 123
See also Spirit, Appendix 25

BROUNY, BROWNY
See Brownie

BROWN MAN OF THE MUIRS
This is a guardian spirit of the wildlife of the moors in the folklore of the Elsdon district (Scotland). He is described as a dwarf with red grizzled hair, fierce glowing eyes, a squat stout body with gnarled hands and bare feet, and wearing russet-colored garments. The Brown Man is regarded as particularly malignant towards human beings, especially those who hunt for sport and not for food, as the Brown Man eats no meat and lives only on whortleberries, apples, and nuts. A story of 1744, retold by Sir Walter Scott, tells how two young men hunting game for sport stopped by a burn to rest and eat. One went to the burn for a drink, where he saw, on the opposite bank, the Brown Man,

who rebuked the man for shooting so many animals. Then the dwarf invited the young men to accompany him to a place where he would show them many secrets of the moors. While one young man started to make for the opposite bank, the other grabbed him back, whispering that the dwarf had no good intentions towards them and would tear them to pieces. The Brown Man stamped in rage and instantly vanished. On their way back the imprudent young man defied the warning and shot another hare, invoking the Brown Man's curse, and within the year he died.
References 15, 17, 18, 44, 66
See also Duergar, Dwarf, Guardian, Spirit, Appendix 12

BROWNEY
In the folklore of Cornwall, England, this invisible brownie type of spirit is the guardian of the honeybees. When the bees swarm in early summer, the farmer's wife will summon up Browney to help collect them back safely into the hives.
References 99
See also Brownie, Cyrene, Guardian, Spirit, Appendix 12

BROWNIE
This is a household spirit of northern English and Scottish folklore, where the name may also be spelled Broonie, Browney, Brouny, or Browny; in southern England he goes by the name of Robin Goodfellow. The Brownie is described as being like a very small, brown, shaggy human, sometimes naked and sometimes wearing ragged brown clothes. In some instances Brownie is said not to have a nose, but just two nostrils; in some regions Brownies had all the fingers attached with a web, or joined completely together apart from the thumb. There are numerous recorded instances of particular Brownies such as Aiken Drum, Mieg Moulach, Maggy Moloch, and Puddlefoot. Families were proud of their Brownies as they brought good fortune; to lose one was disastrous. Outside of the family a Brownie was viewed with caution, as they were prone to mischief when annoyed.

In general the Brownie was the most industrious of the household spirits, ploughing, reaping, grinding grain, cleaning the house and barns, churning butter—in fact, most of the tedious jobs he would gladly do. In return the Brownie was entitled to a bowl of the best cream and new baked cake or bread, to be put within his reach. To offer the Brownie any form of payment other than this, especially to take pity and to give him new clothes, was an insult, and he would vanish immediately. Furthermore, if the Brownie were criticized, then not only would he undo everything that he had done but also destroy a good deal more as well. Lazy servants and bad workmen were often exposed by a watchful Brownie, who would punish them with trickery and devilment. In the lawless Borders region of past centuries, reivers and rustlers would bury their money and invoke a treasure-guardian Brownie with the sacrifice and burial of some animal as payment for his watchfulness.

One anecdote in Henderson's *Popular Rhymes of Berwickshire* tells how the Brownie of Cranshaws Farm, who had served the family well for years, over-heard a farmworker criticizing the harvest mow that year. That night an incredible noise was heard from the barn along with the voice of the Brownie muttering, "It's no weel mowed! It's no weel mowed! Then it's ne'er to be mowed by me again; I'll scatter it o'er the Raven Stane and they'll hae some work e'er it's mowed again." In the morning it could be seen that the furious Brownie had taken the corn all night from the barn and thrown it over the Raven's Rock into the river below. Having wreaked his revenge, he was never seen again at Cranshaws Farm.
References 15, 17, 18, 28, 39, 40, 56, 66, 87, 92, 107, 114, 133
See also Aiken Drum, Gobelin, Kobold, Maggy Molock, Mieg Moulach, Nis, Piskey, Puddlefoot, Robin Goodfellow, Spirit, Tomtar, Appendix 22

BROWNIE CLOD
A household spirit of the brownie type in the folklore of Scotland. But unlike most brownies, this one, the son of Mieg Moulach, was a dobie and so stupid that even the servants played tricks on him! He was said to inhabit the old farmhouse of Achnarrow at Glenlivet in Banff, Scotland.
References 17
See also Brownie, Dobie, Mieg Moulach, Spirit, Appendix 22

BRUDER RAUSCH
This is the German monastic folklore equivalent of the English ecclesiastical spirit called Friar Rush. Bruder Rausch means Brother Intoxication. This spirit was a demon that was sent by the Devil to haunt the monasteries in the guise of a fellow monk of the order. The demon's task was to tempt the monks from their life of piety, devotion, and abstinence and lead them into debauchery, drunkenness, and damnation. Instead of the Lord God, whom the monks were supposed to serve in their order, they became, through the work of Bruder Rausch, the servants of the Evil One they were meant to oppose!
References 114
See also Abbey Lubber, Buttery Spirit, Demon, Friar Rush, Spirit, Appendix 22

BRUNHILDE
This is the name of a Valkyrie also known as Brynhilde, in Scandinavian and Teutonic mythology.

She is a Swan Maiden and one of the attendants of Odin. The legend in which she is featured tells how the Swan Maiden cloak of Brynhilde had been stolen by Agnar to be returned when she favoured him in war. Against the will of Odin, she allowed Agnar victory in battle over Hialmgunnar. For this Odin imprisoned her in a wall of fire, from which she was rescued by Sigurd, who had fallen in love with her. After being given a magic potion, Sigurd married Gudrun instead and matched Brynhilde with Gudrun's brother, Gunnar. Heartbroken, Brynhilde invoked conflict between Sigurd and Gunnar. When Sigurd was destroyed, she leapt into the fire and destroyed herself too.
References 87, 95, 119
See also Attendant Spirit, Sigrun, Swan Maiden, Valkyries

BTSAN
This is the name of a group of fierce demons in the folk beliefs and legends of Tibet. They are the demons of the air, inhabiting the mountains. These spirits are portrayed as red huntsmen on red horses.
References 129
See also Demon, Spirit

BUB
See Gumnut Babies

BUBÁK
See Bogie

BUBER
A demon or evil spirit also known as an Uber in the folklore of the Cheremis/Mari people of the former Soviet Republic. This spirit is capable of shape-shifting into many different guises. Sometimes it is seen as a type of Will o' the Wisp traveling over the ground with a trail of sparks. It may take the form of an old woman with long gray hair, or an old man with a long gray beard, both of whom may float above the ground. A Buber is capable of drawing the life from a living being. It also pecks at trees until all the sap is gone and they remain only as hollow stumps. It takes possession of humans and makes them do evil things while they are supposedly sleeping. They think this is a nightmare, and if they can recall exactly what happened and can tell someone else, then they can reject the spirit possession. Bubers can take possession of a human or animal fetus by disguising itself in the food eaten by the mother-to-be.

These demons putrify both food and drink, causing diseases, especially sores on the skin. Bubers suck milk from cows in the night, and at milking time this may be recognized because the milk contains blood or dirt. Bubers will kiss humans while they are asleep and drain blood from them and within a short while they will die. These spirits will also eat out the eyes of cattle and humans, turning the eyes completely white. It is believed that this can be cured with the pulped bark of the mountain ash tree. The voracious Bubers even bite mouthfuls of the moon, causing an eclipse!

Charms can be used as protection against these spirits, such as a horseshoe pinned over the threshold, or removing the shirt's waist band or bast shoe bands, or splitting a wooden pitchfork if the spirit is sensed to be near. Anyone brave enough may chant a spell to bring a Buber close enough to beat it to ashes; unfortunately, the spirits usually reactivate shortly after, and their evil deeds begin once more.

References 118
See also Apep, Demon, Nightmare, Rahu, Spirit, Will o' the Wisp

BUCCA

This is a sprite in the folklore of Cornwall, England, that has the alternative Cornish dialect names of Bucca Boo, Bucca Dhu, and Bucca Gwidden, according to the circumstances in which the spirit may be encountered. The Buccas, also known as Bwca or Bwciod in Wales, were not visible, but their actions could be observed. They used to be propitiated by fishermen with offerings of fish and by farmers at harvest time with offerings of bread and beer to ensure their benevolence. The Bucca was held by the fishermen, especially around the harbour of Newlyn, to be responsible for the stormy winds, and therefore the spirit was considered able to predict the numerous wrecked ships on this dangerous coastline. These fishermen would propitiate Bucca with an offering of fish left on the shore, to ensure favourable weather and catches. Buccas were also encountered as the spirits of the tin mines, much the same as the kobolds in Germany, and in this guise, Bucca takes the name of Knocker. By the end of the nineteenth century, these practices had declined and the Bucca's role diminished to that of a nursery bogie.

References 10, 17, 18, 40, 59, 87, 107
See also Bucca Dhu, Knockers, Kobold, Nursery Bogie, Puck, Spirit, Appendix 26

BUCCA BOO

See Bucca, Bug, Bug-a-boo

BUCCA DHU AND BUCCA GWIDDEN/GUIDDER

Bucca Dhu, which means Black or Evil Bucca, is the name given to the Bucca in Cornish folklore, whose intentions and actions are mostly malevolent. This spirit was frequently invoked as a nursery bogie with which to threaten children who misbehaved. However, the name Bucca Gwidden or Bucca Guidder, which means White or Good Bucca, referred to the Bucca whose intentions and actions are entirely benevolent.

References 17, 18, 40, 87, 107
See also Bucca, Nursery Bogie, Spirit, Appendix 22

BUČə ÜMBAL ŠUČə

See Šuča

BUCKIE

This is the name of an imp or demon in the folklore of Lowland Scotland. It inhabited deserted moorlands, valleys, woods, and roads. The few descriptions of it indicate that it somewhat resembles a goat. Travelers on horseback would be sure to ride with company at night through lonely country known to be haunted by this supernatural, for the Buckie would jump up behind solitary riders and attempt to garrote them.

References 17, 133
See also Demon, Imp, Appendix 24

BUCKLAND SHAG, THE

A demon that manifests in the shape of a water horse in the folklore of Buckland in Devon, England. In this location indelible red stains on a large rock were said to be the result of the Buckland Shag taking its victims there to be slain. Few people dared to venture in this vicinity alone for fear of encountering the Buckland Shag, until the vicar of Buckland exorcised the spirit with bell, book, and candle.

References 47
See also Cabyll-Ushtey, Demon, Kelpie, Neugle, Shag Foal, Spirit, Appendix 24

BUDGE FUR

See Bogie

BUG BOY

See Bug-a-Boo

BUG-A-BOO, BUGABO

This is a variant form of the Old English Bug, meaning a demon or bugbear. It may also be known as Buggy Bow, Bucca Boo, Bogle Bo, or Bug Boy. This spirit is no longer considered seriously by adults and is mostly used as a nursery bogie to threaten mischievous children into good behavior.

References 92, 119
See also Bogle, Bug, Bugbear, Demon, Nursery Bogie, Appendix 22

BUGAN

See Hobgoblin

BUGBEAR/E

This is a class of spirits that are an object of terror in English folklore. The Bugbear is a demon or malevolent

spirit thought to take the shape of a bear or large beast. It was later said to be fond of devouring naughty children and used mostly as a nursery bogie to threaten children into good behavior.
References 17, 40, 107
See also Bogie, Bogle, Demon, Nursery Bogie, Spirit, Appendix 22

BUGELL, BUGIL
See Bogle

BUG/G, BUGGE
An archaic name from the early Celtic form *Bwg* and the Middle English *Bugge* for a malevolent sprite, demon, or hobgoblin. The name mostly survives in the use of Bug-a-boo, Bugbear, Bogle, and Bogie. From a terrifying spirit in early centuries, debased in later times to a form of nursery bogie, a Bug now has no impact in any of the folklore from which it was derived and may simply be used as a word denoting annoyance.
References 7, 17, 28, 40, 92, 107
See also Aufhocker, Bagul, Barguest, Bogie, Bogle, Bug-a-boo, Bugbear, Demon, Hobgoblin, Nursery Bogie, Spirit, Sprite

BUGGANE
This is a particularly malevolent shape-shifting spirit in the Manx folklore of the Isle of Man (United Kingdom). It may take the shape of an enormous man, with or without a head, a black calf or a heifer lying in the road with or without head and tail, and at other times a large shaggy dog with a white collar and huge glowing eyes.

There are several stories of the evil deeds of the Buggane, but the most widely known is that of the tailor and the Church of Saint Trinian. This church was called by the locals *Keeill Brisht*—"the Broken Church." This was because when the church was being built, each time the stone masons went home at night a Buggane emerged from under the ground in the aisle and destroyed all their hard work. No one knew what to do until a brave tailor named Timothy sat in the chancel after the masons had left, determined to make a pair of breeches before the Buggane appeared. He had almost finished when the floor was rent and the Buggane started to emerge, ranting at the intrusion of this foolhardy mortal. Whatever the Buggane threatened, the terrified tailor gave the appearance of calm as he replied, "I see, I see." Finishing his work, Timothy leapt through the window just in time, for the Buggane pulled down the entire roof as he emerged completely. The tailor ran as fast as he could for the consecrated ground of the Marown churchyard. The enraged Buggane, unable to pursue him, tore off its own head and threw it over the wall at the tailor,

where it shattered into little pieces. From that time the Buggane was never seen again, either with or without his head. The brave tailor's scissors and thimble were displayed at an inn on the Douglas to Peel road, where all could hear the story.
References 17, 76, 81, 134
See also Spirit

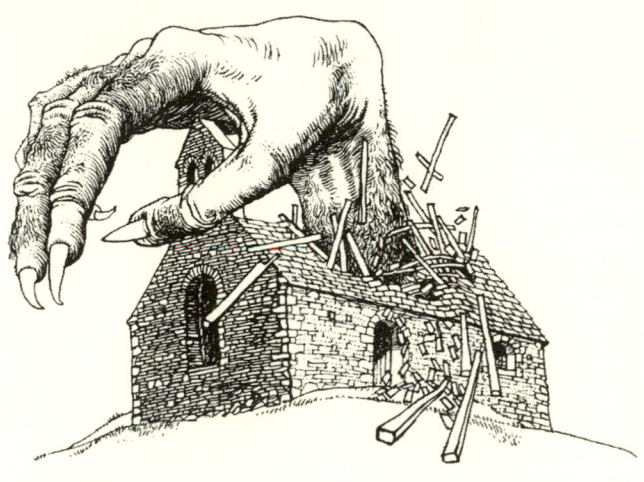

BUGGY BOW
See Bug

BUGIBUS
See Bug-a-Boo

BUJ ŠUČƏ
See Šučə

BUKURA E DHEUT
A very powerful fairy in the folklore of Albania, Bukura e dheut, whose name means the Beauty of the Earth, lives in a fairytale castle guarded by wonderful creatures. She can be benevolent like a Guardian Angel, but there are other times when she can be destructive and in league with the demonic forces.
References 93
See also Demon, Fairy, Guardian Angel

BULLBEGGAR
A demon or bogie also known as Boe Bulbagger in English folklore. It is a tricksy spirit that assumes the shape of an injured person lying in the road. When any well-meaning person attempts to render assistance, the Bullbeggar leaps to its enormous, shadowy height and chases the terrified traveler until he or she reaches safety, and the spirit vanishes, howling with laughter. Alternatively it may manifest as a black uncanny shape, or as the sound of following footsteps that stop and start as the night-bound traveler attempts to see who is so close behind. One instance of the following footsteps reported frequently at Creech Hill in Somerset was supposed to

be explained in the late eighteenth century when the bodies of two men, thought to be those of a Saxon and Norman, were uncovered lying across each other.

References 17, 133
See also Barguest, Black Dog, Bogie, Demon, Spirit, Appendix 24

BULLEKLAS
See Knecht Ruprecht

BULLERMAN
This is the name of a spirit in the folklore of Germany. The name is from the German *bullen*, to knock. It is the German form of the Bullbeggar, a demon or nuisance spirit that knocks on walls and doors in the manner of a poltergeist.

References 123
See also Bullbeggar, Demon, Poltergeist, Spirit

BULLKATER
A corn spirit or field spirit in the folklore of the German region of Silesia. When the last swathe of corn has been reached, the Bullkater, which means Tomcat, will be trapped with no more corn in which to hide, and the reaper whose section it is in is then deemed to be possessed by the Bullkater. This last reaper is decked in a rye-straw costume with a plaited green tail which represents the spirit. He then chases all around the field with a stick, beating anyone who does not escape. This ritual pursuit takes place in order to eliminate the old Bullkater and ensure the fertility of the next corn crop.

References 87
See also Cailleac, Corn Spirit, Kornwolf, Spirit, Appendix 15

BUMANN
See Boggelmann

BURRYMAN
A vegetation spirit from the South Queensferry district of the Scottish Firth of Forth. At harvest time this spirit is represented by a youth dressed in a garment entirely covered with burs and other seed cases, which appear to be moving on their own. The "spirit" is taken from house to house where those wishing for future good harvests and its linked prosperity propitiate the spirit with gifts.

References 123
See also Corn Spirit, Green Knight, Green Man, Jack-in-the-Green, Spirit, Appendix 15, Appendix 18

BUSHYASTA
This is the name of a demon in the mythology of the Zoroastrian religion of Iran. He is portrayed as a

human shape entirely in yellow. He is responsible for making men slothful and lethargic, thus given to oversleeping and neglecting their religious duties.

References 87
See also Demon, Mazikeen

BUSO
These are evil and dangerous demons in the folklore of the Bagobo Malay peoples of the Philippine Islands. They are described as tall and thin with curly hair, flat noses, only one huge yellow or red eye and two protruding teeth. Although considered fearsome, they are also stupid. The Buso live in lonely forests, rocks, and trees that grow in cemeteries. Here they consume the rotting flesh of the dead and are constantly provoking the deaths of more humans. There are two particular types of Buso called Tigbanua and Tagamaling. Although they are especially dangerous, there are many folk tales concerning their being outwitted. One amusing story tells how a cat agreed that the Buso could take her human owner so long as the Buso had counted every hair on the cat's tail before morning. Every time the Buso got anywhere near completing its task, the cat flicked its tail, until the dawn broke and the Buso was compelled to disappear.

References 87
See also Demon, Kappa, Tagamaling, Tigbanua

BÜT BODƏŽ
This is the guardian spirit of fresh water in the folklore of the Cheremis/Mari people of the former Soviet Republic. Büt Bodəž inhabits springs and rivers that are often used by humans. If someone violates the waters by drinking directly from them, or, worse still, urinating into the water, then Büt Bodəž will inflict an appropriate punishment, in these cases a sore on the lips and sores on the penis, respectively. Anyone crossing rivers or brooks must be sure to do so respectfully, as any transgression will be evidenced by the appearance of ulcers or sores on the parts of the body that touched the water. These will then be attributed to the spirit under the name of that water course—e.g., Amše Bodəž Čer is the infection caused by the spirit in the Amše Brook. Propitiation with either porridge or a sacrificed hen may prevent such an occurrence or cause it to be cured.

References 118
See also Büt Ia, Spirit, Appendix 25

BÜT IA
A fresh water spirit in the folklore of the Cheremis/Mari people of the former Soviet Republic, Büt Ia inhabits the bottom of lakes and rivers. Büt Ia, which means Water Devil, may be called Büt Oza, which means Water Master. It sometimes appears in the guise of a horse (Büt Imnə), an ox (Büt Uskəz), or

as a huge fish with its head pointing upstream. Büt Ia is more usually described as Büt Kuguza, which means Water Old Man. In this guise he appears as an old man with horns and long gray hair. Less frequently he assumes the form of Büt Kuba, which means Water Old Woman. Sometimes Büt Ia is without clothes, but when wearing garments, they reflect the size and status of its domain. Consequently, the Büt Ia of a large lake or vast river will be richly dressed, while the spirit of a brook or pool wears rags. These spirits are thought to live in underwater communities with families and possessions.

Büt Ia may be either malignant or benevolent. When appeased with suitable offerings, such as *bliny*, money, or vodka, the spirit will ensure good catches of fish from its waters and allow humans who enter the water to return to land safely; otherwise it will drown all who venture near. To see a Büt Ia sitting in the sun combing its hair, although the spirit will vanish instantly, is an omen of disaster or death. When the spirits are addressed directly, the polite forms Büt Kuba and Büt Kuguza, are used.

References 118
See also Büt Bodəž, Büt Ian Üdəržə, Kuguza, Spirit, Appendix 12, Appendix 25

BÜT IAN ÜDƏRŽƏ

This is the name of a water spirit in the folklore of the Cheremis/Mari people of the former Soviet Republic. The Büt Ian Üdəržə, which means Water Devil's Daughter, is a female fresh-water spirit of human shape. This spirit is subordinate to the main spirit venerated for a stretch of water and is therefore called the "daughter" of that spirit, in this case Büt Ian. Büt Ian Üdəržə may sometimes be seen on a river bank combing her long golden hair with a gold or silver comb. Mortal men may be able to marry her if they can catch her, by touching her with iron, which renders her unable to escape. However, if the true identity of the spirit is ever revealed, she will die like a mortal immediately.

References 118
See also Büt Ia, Fin Folk, Mermaid, Melusina, Selkies, Appendix 25

BÜT IMNƏ

This is the name of a demon or devil in the folklore of the Cheremis/Mari people of the former Soviet Republic. It is also known as a Büt Ia that appears in the guise of a horse.
See also Büt Ia, Demon, Devil, Each Uisge, Kelpie, Appendix 12

BÜT USKƏZ

See Büt Ia

BUTTERY SPIRIT

This is the secular form, in English folklore, of the demon from the monasteries known as the Abbey Lubber. The Buttery Spirit could only exist in the store-cellars (buttery) of establishments such as coaching inns, taverns, and country houses where gifts were ungraciously received, or where the hospitality was grudgingly given. This involved miserly portions, or dishonestly prepared food from unhealthy stock. In these regimes the Buttery Spirit grew fat and bloated on the greed of the landlord or head of the household. In establishments where visitors or travelers were welcomed with honest portions of well-prepared fine food, and where gifts were graciously received, the poor Buttery Spirit starved and declined. The demon lost its power over the inhabitants to instil dishonesty and greed, and in a starveling state faded away to find a more promising abode.
References 17
See also Abbey Lubber, Demon, Friar Rush, Appendix 22

BÛTÛS

See Bhut

BUTZENBERCHT

This is an alternative name for the spirit called Berchta in the folklore of Germany. Under the name Butzenbercht, which means Bringer of Gifts, she is responsible for delivering gifts to German children on the night before Epiphany (6 January). This feast was known originally in Old High German as *Perahtun naht*.
See also Befana, Berchta, Santa Claus, Spirit, Appendix 22

BWBACH, BWBACHOD (pl.)

This spirit in the folklore of Wales is similar to the northern English brownie, and is similarly described as brown and hairy. The Bwbach will take up residence with a household where it will perform many of the household tasks at night. If the Bwbach is affronted or annoyed it can become a malicious spirit given to the behavior of a poltergeist. An account by Giraldo Cambrensis (circa 1147–circa 1223) gives descriptions of Bwbachod tearing clothes and throwing dirt at the people in the Pembrokeshire homes of Steven Wiriet and William Not. Bwbachod have a particular dislike of teetotallers, dissenters, and their ministers. In his book *British Goblins* (pp. 30–31) Sikes tells how a Bwbach plagued a dissenting minister by pulling away his seat during services and appearing at other times as his double.
References 15, 17, 18, 59, 123, 125
See also Brownie, Bucca, Bwca, Poltergeist, Spirit, Appendix 22

Bwca flees the farm where his work was not appreciated.

BWCA, BWCI (pl.)

The Welsh variant name of the Cornish Bucca. He is a household spirit very similar to the northern English brownie and Puck. Like the English brownie, Bwca performed all manner of menial household tasks for the family at night, expecting only a bowl of sweet milk or flummery with some wheaten bread in return. Although almost entirely loyal and benevolent, Bwca could be most vindictive and malicious if affronted. There was a Bwca resident at Trwyn Farm who was called Bwca'r Trwyn. He was particularly friendly with a serving maid who was said to have the Twylwth Teg in her. One night, however, out of sheer devilment, instead of leaving poor Bwca his posset of flummery, she filled his bowl with the stale urine used as a mordant in the dyeing of wool. When she woke the following morning, Bwca was waiting for her. He leapt upon her, grabbed her by the throat, and dragged her kicking and screaming all over the house. Soon the whole household was wondering what was happening; since Bwca was invisible, it was hard to understand what was taking place. When the men came running from the lofts Bwca let go his hold and would neither stay nor work there anymore.
References 17, 18, 123
See also Brownie, Bucca, Puck, Tylwyth Teg, Appendix 22

BWCÏOD

The Welsh variant name for the Cornish Bucca, as well as a comprehensive term for all sorts of other spirits such as demons and poltergeists.
References 17, 18, 123
See also Bucca, Demon, Poltergeist, Spirit

BWGAN

In the folklore of Wales this spirit is a type of goblin or poltergeist.
References 59
See also Bwbach, Goblin, Poltergeist, Spirit

BWGWL

A spirit regarded as an object of terror in Welsh folklore.
References 104
See also Bogle, Spirit

BYGEL NOS

A bogle or demon in the folklore of Wales that appears only at night.
References 104
See also Bogle, Demon

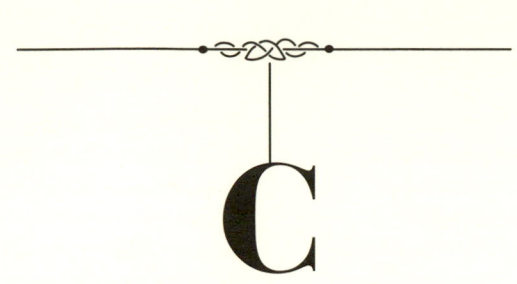

C

CABOCLO
Originally applied as the name of uneducated back-woodsmen or the original inhabitants of Brazil, this name has been used by association for the nature spirits revered by those people and has come to include that group of spirits in the pantheon of the Afro-Brazilian Batuque cult. These spirits are regarded as the lower-status encantados and are characterized by unrefined behavior in possession of devotees; however, they are renowned for their helping the sick in curing sessions. The most prominent of the Caboclos are Boiadeiro da Vasura, Constantino, Antonio Luiz Corre-Beirado, Herondina, and Mestre Marajó.
References 89
See also Boiadeiro da Visaura, Constantino, Encantado, Spirit

CABOCLO VELHO
See Japetequara

CABYLL-UISGE
See Cabyll-Ushtey

CABYLL-USHTEY
A fierce water spirit in the folklore of the Isle of Man (United Kingdom) also known by the Gaelic name of Cabyll-Uisge, which means Water-Horse. This demon takes the form of a water-horse but can transform himself into the shape of a handsome young man. The Cabyll-Ushtey will attract humans or their live-stock to accompany it into the water, where the victim will be torn to pieces.
References 17, 99
See also Ceffyl-dwr, Demon, Kelpie, Neugle, Spirit, Appendix 25

ČACCE-HALDDE
In the folklore of the Lapps in the extreme north of Scandinavia and the Baltic states, this is the name for the spirit of the waters.
References 88
See also Čacce-olmai, Haldde, Spirit, Appendix 25

ČACCE-OLMAI
In the folklore of the Lapps of the extreme north of Scandinavia and the Baltic States, this water spirit is known as the Man of the Water.
References 88
See also Čacce-haldde, Haldde, Spirit, Appendix 25

CACODÆMON
In the classical mythology of Greece, those dæmons with evil intent were called Cacodæmon. Also spelled Kakodaimon, the name Cacodæmon was derived from Greek *Kakos daimon*, meaning an evil spirit. In English folklore and literature, the Cacodæmon is an evil spirit or demon sometimes described as one of the Fallen Angels.
References 40, 53, 107
See also Dæmon, Demon, Fallen Angel, Spirit

CACY TAPERERE
A spirit in the shape of a dwarf in the folklore of the native people and people of mixed ancestry in southern Brazil. He is also called Saci and Sasy Perere. This supernatural is described as having fiery eyes and only one leg, wearing a red cap, and smoking a pipe. Cacy taperere, like many other household spirits, plays jokes on the family by moving or hiding their belongings and disturbing household objects.
References 87, 88
See also Dwarf, Nashas, Spirit, Thrummy Cap, Appendix 22

CAILLAGH NY GROAMAGH
This supernatural being, whose name means Old Woman of Gloom in Manx Gaelic, is a weather spirit in the folklore of the Isle of Man (United Kingdom). As the *Caillagh ny Gueshag,* or Old Woman of Spells, she was thrown into the Irish Sea for practicing her evil magic. On Saint Briget's Day (1 February) she was cast up on the Manx shores, where she gathered sticks for a fire to dry herself. The ensuing spring was wet, and every year after this Caillagh ny Groamagh goes to gather sticks on Saint Briget's Day. If the day is fine, then she will have plenty of fuel for a wet spring; if

the day is wet and she cannot go out, then she is obliged to ensure a dry spring for her own comfort.
References 17, 81
See also Cailleach Bera, Cailleach Bheur, Spirit, Appendix 26

CAILLAGH NY GUESHAG
See Caillagh ny Groamagh

CAILLEAC, CAILLEACH
The Cailleac, whose name means Old Hag in Scottish Gaelic, is a corn spirit, particularly in the Hebridean Island of Islay. The very last cut of corn is deemed to contain the spirit, which could not escape. It is cut with ceremony and fashioned into the sheaf known as the Old Wife and taken to a safe place in the farmhouse ready for the plowing season. When the new year's sowing is to commence, the mistress of the farm takes down the Old Wife and divides the sheaf among the plow-hands who, on reaching the field, give a portion to the plow horses to eat as they work the field. This ensures that the Cailleach's spirit enters the field for the fertility of the new crop. The Cailleach may be given its own garments and suitable offerings of bread, grain and a harvest sickle in the Isle of Lewis (Hebrides) and is held with suitable honor in safekeeping until the spring. In some areas, however, since the first reaper to finish makes the Cailleach and passes it to the next to finish, the final holder of the Cailleach is thus shown to be the laziest in the district, and its possession is no longer an honor. In other countries similar reverence and ceremonies are associated with the corn spirit under the following names: Ahren Konigen in Salzburg, Austria; Baba in Poland; Boba in Lithuania; Carlin in some Scottish regions; the Granny in Belfast, Ireland; and the Wrach in Pembrokeshire, Wales.
References 87, 107
See also Ahren Konigen, Baba, Babban ny Mheillea, Bullkater, Carlin, Corn Spirit, Granny, Kornmutter, Kornwolf, Sara-Mama, Spirit, Wrach, Appendix 15, Appendix 18

CAILLEACH BERA, CAILLEACH BEARA, CAILLEAC BHÉARRA
The Cailleach bera, whose name means Hag of Beare, is not only the Celtic corn spirit of Irish folklore, but also in Irish mythology a supernatural being of strength and cunning. She is associated with the Beare Peninsula near Cork, which she carried in her apron as stones that were dropped to form the rocky promontory when the strings broke. In this way she is also credited with the formation of some of the other offshore islands. This spirit was considered to be a prolific harvester of crops and would challenge reapers to a contest knowing that only she could win.

She was said to manifest in the shape of a hare, which raced through the crop ahead of the reapers. The process of catching the spirit in the last sheaf was therefore known as driving out the hare. The effigy of the spirit made from this sheaf was called the Cailleac. In other countries similar reverence and ceremonies are associated with the corn spirit. The Cailleach bera is also credited with showing the people how to plant winter sowings which could be harvested as green corn before the arrival of the autumn gales. This sowing was called *Coirce na bhFaoilli*, the oats of February, which was recognized as more productive than the chaff of an April sowing.
References 17, 88, 105
See also Cailleac, Cailleach Bheur, Hag, Appendix 12, Appendix 15

CAILLEACH BHEUR
The Cailleach Bheur, whose name means the Blue Hag, is a weather spirit who inhabits the Highlands of Scotland. Also known by the phonetic spelling Cally Berry, she is usually described as a hideous blue-faced hag wearing a plaid and carrying a mallet or a strong staff. She is the guardian spirit of wild deer, boar, goats, cattle, and wolves; her plants are the gorse and holly. She also guards the Highland streams and wells. From Halloween (31 October, Samhain) to Beltane Eve (the eve of May Day in the old Celtic calendar), she is the personification of winter, turning the ground hard by beating it with her staff to prevent new growth and bring on the snow. In this role she is represented as an ugly, sometimes giant, blue-faced hag, the daughter of Grianan, the lesser Celtic winter sun. She lives in a cave beneath Ben Nevis where the Summer Maiden, who is her captive, endures torments until she is rescued by one of the Cailleach Bheur's compassionate sons on Saint Bride's Day (1 February). This prompts the Cailleach to unleash the *Faoiltach* (the Wolf Storms) in an effort to prevent Summer from existing. When Beltane (May Day) and spring return, the Cailleach Bheur casts away her staff under a holly or gorse, where no other plants may thrive. She is then transformed, some say, into a beautiful maid, or into a sea serpent, or into a stone, until next Halloween.

The Cailleach Bheur and her two sons are considered to be responsible for changing the landscape. The Cailleach Bheur, like the Cailleach bera, created land features, in this case the Hebridean Islands, when the rocks she was carrying fell through holes in the container. In her role as guardian of the springs, she accidentally created Loch Awe when she forgot to cover the spring of Ben Cruachan. Her two sons are constantly arguing and cast rocks at each other across Invernessshire. The Cailleach Bheur, like the Cailleach bera, also challenges young reapers to harvesting con-

tests that only she could win, and in the West Highlands she is held responsible for blighting the crops. At Kilberry (cf., Cally Berry) in Argyllshire, the Cailleach's seat is located on the summit of the hill. To have a wish granted by her, the request must be made when a stone is thrown as an offering onto the seat, but she must never be addressed by her real name.
References 15, 17, 18, 44, 69, 123
See also Ahren Konigen, Baba, Baba Yaga, Cailleac, Cailleach Bera, Caillagh ny Groamagh, Guardian, Appendix 12, Appendix 25, Appendix 26

CAIRPRÉ

This is the name of the son of Ogma and the poet of the Tuatha dé Danann in the mythology of Ireland. As a poet he expected to be welcomed at the court of other kings and treated with respect. Similarly, if treated disrespectfully by a host, it was unheard of to be rude in return. So when Cairpré was treated badly at the court of King Bress, the poet responded with verse of double meanings for anyone with the wit to interpret his veiled criticism. He was therefore credited with the first satirical verse and the return of Nuada to the throne, which had been usurped by the Formorian King Bress.
References 123
See also Formor, Tuatha dé Danann

CALLICANTZARI
See Kallikantzari

CALLIOPE
See Muses

CALLISTO

A nymph, also known by the spelling Kallistó, in ancient Greek mythology. She was the attendant of Artemis. Callisto was seduced by Zeus, king of the gods, in disguise. In a fit of jealousy, Hera, the queen of the gods, changed Callisto into a she-bear. In this form, the nymph would have been killed by her own son Arcas while he was out hunting if Zeus had not transformed the two of them into the constellations of Ursa Major and Ursa Minor.
References 87, 93, 114, 119, 130
See also Nymph, Appendix 13

CALLY BERRY
See Cailleach Bheur

CALYPSO

This is the name of a sea nymph, also spelled Kalypso, in the classical mythology of Greece and Rome. In Homer's *Odyssey* she rescued and detained the shipwrecked Ulysses for seven years. Declaring her love for him, she promised him immortality if he would stay. However, on Ulysses' refusal and declaration of loyalty to his wife, Zeus commanded Calypso to help Ulysses return safely.
References 20, 93, 114, 130
See also Nymph, Appendix 25

CAMENÆ
See Egeria

CAMPANKITĀCI

The name of a queen of the demons in the Tamil mythology of southern India. In the story of Kāttavarāyan, this hero defeated Campankitāci in a game of dice.
References 68
See also Demon

CANKOBOBUS

A bogie in the folklore of Cornwall, England, which seems mainly to have been used as a nursery bogie. It is a variant of Tantrabobus, or Tankerabogus as it is sometimes called, in the area of north Devon.
References 17, 19
See also Bogie, Nursery Bogie

CANNERED NOZ

Cannered Noz, which means Washer Woman of the Night, is the name of a group of fairy spirits in the folklore of Brittany in northwestern France. They are said to resemble diminutive elderly peasant women when they materialize, but they are more often invisible, and only the sound of their activities may be heard. They inhabit the lonely fords of rivers and stony banks of streams. In these places the spirits can be heard at night washing the linen of those humans dying without absolution. Local people will not venture near if they can hear the Cannered Noz at work.
References 87, 123
See also Bean Nighe, Caointeach, Fairy, Spirit

CAOINEAG

One of a group of spirits in Scottish folklore of mainland Scotland, known as fuaths. The Caoineag is never seen, unlike the Caointeach or the Banshee of Ireland, but has a role much like theirs. The Caoineag is a female family spirit and each notable family, or clan, has its own. She is to be heard *keening* (lamenting or weeping) at night in anticipation of a forthcoming disaster to the clan with which she is associated. The Caoineag of the Macdonald clan was said to be heard some nights before the Massacre at Glen Coe.
References 17, 87
See also Ban Nighechain, Banshee, Boneless, Caointeach, Cyhiraeth, Fuath, Spirit, Appendix 16, Appendix 22, Appendix 23

CAOINTEACH

This is a death spirit in the folklore of the Hebrides Islands and southwest Scotland, whose name means the *Keener* (one who wails or cries for the dead). She was envisaged as a nebulous, formless white presence, or as a very small woman dressed in green, washing bloodstained linen in a stream. She was associated with the clans of the Curries, Kellys, MacFarlanes, Mackays, MacMillans, Mathisons, and Shaws, for whom she set up a lament if any disaster were imminent. In this respect she is identical with the Caoineag. The Caointeach is more normally heard than seen, but if one happens upon her by the water and approaches too closely and is seen by her, she may lash out with the wet linen, which will invoke complete paralysis of the limbs for life.
See also Ban Nighechain, Banshee, Boneless, Caoineag, Cyhyraeth, Spirit, Appendix 16, Appendix 23

CAPELTHWAITE

In the folklore of Westmoreland in England, this is a bogie that most frequently assumes the shape similar to a Black Dog type of spirit. Capelthwaite could shape shift at will. As an inhabitant of Capelthwaite Barn at Milnthorpe, he was benevolent in his dealings with the farm folk, often assisting in rounding up the livestock. He was not so well-disposed to strangers, who might be chased on the road at night by Capelthwaite and thrown into a hedge or ditch.
References 17
See also Barguest, Black Dog, Black Shuck, Boggart, Bogie, Bullbeggar, Church Grim, Freybug, Gytrash, Mauthe Dhoog, Padfoot, Rongeur d'Os, Skriker, Spirit, Appendix 12, Appendix 22

CARLIN

The corn spirit when caught in the last sheaf is called Carlin, which means Old Woman in some Scottish regions. Special harvest cakes are made, formerly for the reapers, known as Gyre-Carlins.
References 123
See also Cailleac, Corn Spirit, Gyre-Carling, Spirit, Appendix 15

CARMENÆ, CARMENTA, CARMENTIS

The Carmenæ were a group of nymphs in the classical mythology of Rome. They took their name from Carmenta or Carmentis, their leader. These nymphs were renowned for their prophetic abilities. At one time they were so frequently consulted and revered that Carmenta had an altar dedicated to her and a location named for her at the Porta Carmentalis in Rome.
References 130
See also Egeria, Nymph, Appendix 23

CARREAN

See Devil

CARRIVEAN

See Devil

CASSIEL

See Archangel

CASSOTIS

See Castalia

CASTALIA

Castalia and Cassotis are two prophetic nymphs in the classical mythology of Greece and Rome. They dwelt close to inspirational springs on Mount Parnassus, where they were consulted for their divination abilities.
References 102, 130
See also Nymph, Appendix 23

CASTALIDES

See Muses

CATACLOTHES

See Fates

CAUCHEMAR

This is the French name for the European medieval fiend of the night known in Latin as the Incubus. It goes by different names in the folklore of each country. In England it is the Nightmare, from the Anglo-Saxon *Mara*, meaning Crusher. Mara is also the name used in Lithuania. In Germany it is known as Mahr but in Greece it is known as Ephialtes, which means the Leaper. This night demon leaps upon the chests of sleeping humans with the intent of inflicting evil and crushing the life out of them. When people have been the subject of a Cauchemar's attention, it is evident from their exhaustion and agitation but their unwillingness to sleep at night. People tried many different ways of keeping this terrifying spirit from entering the sleeping chamber. Iron nails were placed under the mattress; some placed their shoes at the bedside toes outwards, while others slept with their heads in any direction but the north—the direction of death and darkness. (A famous painting titled *The Nightmare* (1781) by the artist Henry Fuseli depicts these spirits.)
References 40, 104
See also Alp, Demon, Ephialtes, Fiend, Incubus, Mahr, Mara, Nightmare, Spirit

ČAUGA

This is the name for a group of evil spirits in the folklore of the people of the Andaman Islands.

References 88
See also Lau, Spirit

CAULD LAD OF GILSLAND

A supernatural being in the folklore of the district of Gilsland in Cumberland, England. This spirit is said to be transformed from the ghost of a boy who died of cold and neglect. The spirit now appears in much the style of the banshee shivering and moaning beside the beds of members of the family who are soon to perish. If their demise is to be brought about by disease this is indicated when the spirit puts his icy hand on that part of the body to be affected and intones, "Cauld, cauld aye, cauld; An' ye 'se be cauld for evermair."

References 66
See also Banshee, Spirit, Appendix 16, Appendix 22

CAULD LAD OF HILTON

A spirit of the brownie type that inhabited the Castle of Hilton in the county of Northumberland in England. Like the Cauld Lad of Gilsland, this spirit is said to be transformed from the ghost of a stable boy killed by the Baron Hilton for failing to saddle-up a horse on time. The legend tells how the baron hid the body and then disposed of it in the estate pond. Many years later the pond was drained and the skeleton of a boy was discovered.

The Cauld Lad of Hilton was not seen but could be heard by the servants at night as he tidied up for them everything that was left in disorder. But he did as much damage as he did well, for he created chaos when all had been left tidy. Although the Cauld Lad of Hilton was quite benign, the servants decided to rid themselves of his tampering in the traditional way. Since household spirits are offended by the offer of reward or the gift of clothes, by giving him a gift of a green cloak and hood, the servants were rid of him forever.

References 15, 18, 66, 133
See also Brownie, Cauld Lad of Gilsland, Spirit, Appendix 22

CAYPÓR

A type of forest demon in the folklore of Brazil. He is described as ugly, with red skin and hair that is very long and shaggy. Caypór is primarily a nursery bogie used by parents to control young children and prevent them from wandering into the forest alone.

References 110
See also Demon, Nursery Bogie, Appendix 19, Appendix 22

CCOA

An evil spirit in the shape of a cat in the mythology of the Quechua people of Peru. The Ccoa is described as having a grey body with darker horizontal stripes and a very large head from which glow huge fiery eyes that spit out hail. This weather demon does the bidding of the Aukis, bringing devastating hail storms to destroy the crops and cause the demise of the human planters. In order to prevent his anger and the blight he might inflict, Ccoa is placated with frequent offerings during the growing season.

References 87
See also Anchancho, Auki, Demon, Larilari, Spirit, Appendix 12, Appendix 26

CE SITH

The Highland Scottish variant of the English Black Dog spirit. In Scottish folklore the Ce Sith, which means Fairy Dog, is green and, some say, as large as a bullock.

References 15
See also Black Dog, Fairy, Appendix 12

CEARB

This is an evil spirit in the Highland folklore of Scotland that was recorded by MacKenzie. The Cearb, whose name means the Killing One, was considered responsible for many of the afflictions suffered by both the humans and their cattle.

References 17
See also Spirit, Appendix 17

CEASG

This is the mermaid of the Scottish Highlands. She is a beautiful woman above the waist, but the lower part of her body resembles a large salmon tail. She is also known as the *Maighdean na tuinne,* the Maiden of the Wave. Like most fairy people she is tricksy and although seemingly benevolent, she can also be malevolent. The Ceasg may grant three wishes to anyone who can catch her, but if she catches them first she will swallow them completely.

References 17
See also Fairy, Liban, Mermaid, Appendix 25

CEFFYL-DŴR, CEFFYLL-DŴR

The Ceffyll-dŵr, whose name means Water-Horse, is a fearsome water spirit of Welsh folklore. This demon is to be found in mountain pools and waterfalls and usually takes the shape of a gray horse, which has a glow of light that illuminates its surroundings. It has also been known to appear as a goat or a handsome young man. Although appearing to be solid—and indeed, humans have been known to mount and ride to their cost—the Ceffyll-dŵr will evaporate into insubstantial mist. The beauty of the Ceffyll-dŵr belies its true nature, for it will leap out of the water at any lone traveler and, by gripping the back and the shoulders, squeeze its victim to death, or kill them by kicking and trampling on them.

References 48, 87
See also Cabyll-Ushtey, Demon, Kelpie, Neugle, Spirit, Appendix 12, Appendix 25

CELÆNO, CELENO
See Harpy

CELLAR DEMON
In medieval English monastic folklore, this spirit was reputed to inhabit the cellars of wealthy religious houses and monastic orders. There the Cellar Demon protected the provisions and wines from those who would take the cellars' contents for themselves.
References 17
See also Biersal, Buttery Spirit, Cluricaun, Friar Rush, Spirit, Appendix 21, Appendix 22

CELŒNO
See Pleiades

ČEMBULAT
This spirit is a keremet in the folk beliefs of the Cheremis/Mari people of the former Soviet Republic. He is also known by the names of Kurək Kuga Jeŋ, Kurək Kuguza, Nemdə Kurək Kugə, Nemdə Kurək Kuguza, and Lemdə Kurək Kuguza. This spirit was revered from ancient times, when he was said to have been a transformed hero prince of long ago. Sacrifices, especially of a black horse, were made to Čembulat, and a sacred stone that was dedicated to him at Chembulatova was demolished by Christian missionaries in 1830. Čembulat has now come to be a term for a devil, and the alternatives of Kurək Kuga Jeŋ and Kurək Kuguza now signify his guardian activities in the mountains and waters of the Nemda River. If this spirit is offended he will cause drought, sickness, or bad harvests, so he is propitiated when any of these are threatened. Among the other spirits associated with Čembulat are Aba (means Mother), As, Azren, Bitnəzə, Bodəž, Er Orolək, Kapka Orol (means Gate Guard), Kübar Kuguza, Osər Pamaš (means Oser Spring), Piambar, Šüč Pundəš (means Burnt Stump), Sərt, Telmač (means Interpreter), Tiak (means Scribe), Üstel Orol, Ümbač Koštšə (means One Who Walks Over), Ümbal Keremet (means Over Keremet), Üstel Orol (means Table Guard), and Užedəš (means Disease).
References 118
See also Devil, Guardian, Keremet, Kugə Jeŋ, Kuguza, Spirit, Appendix 9

CERUBIN
See Cherub

CHAARMAROUCH
This is the name of one of the kings of the djinns in the folk beliefs and traditions of Morocco.

Chaarmarouch is said to inhabit a cave on the sides of the range of the Goundafi Mountains. He is never seen and is considered to be of a malicious nature. His presence, which is to be avoided, may be recognized by the shower of stones that will be cast to blind any human intruder.
References 90
See also Djinn

CHAHURU
This is the name of a water spirit in the folklore and legends of the Pawnee Native American people.
References 25
See also Spirit, Appendix 25

CHAMUEL
See Archangel

CHANEKOS, CHANES
See Chanques

CHANG HSIEN
This is a spirit in Chinese folk belief described as an old man with a long gray beard who is often portrayed with a small boy who walks at his side, or depicted shooting his bow and arrow at T'ien Kou Hsing, the Heavenly Dog or Dog Star. Chang Hsien is the guardian of women in childbirth and particularly invoked for a male heir; he protects the women from the evil influence of T'ien Kou Hsing. However, if the family astrology is ruled by the Dog Star, the life of any male child will be short, or there may be no sons at all.
References 87, 131
See also Béfind, Eshu, Guardian, Oosood, Pi-Hsia Yüan-Chün, Spirit, Appendix 21, Appendix 22

CHANGELING
In European folklore the fairies coveted the beautiful, robust, well-fed children of humans instead of their own sickly, ugly offspring. As a result fairies were said to steal human babies left unattended before baptism and leave in their place the Changelings of their own. The Changeling could be recognized because it was not only wizened and ugly, but also lacking in normal development and was frequently precocious for its supposed age. Alternatively, if the fairy had no "child" to leave, then an enchanted log of wood might be left that shriveled and "died" almost immediately; or an aged member of their group who was willing to be cosseted by feigning the likeness of the human child might be substituted. Although the Changeling phenomenon is substantially European folklore, there are other societies in North America and the Far East with similar beliefs.

There were many tests practiced to establish the identity of the Changeling and be rid of it. Most of these were performed in the mistaken belief that if it were made very unwelcome, the Changeling would be resubstituted for the real child. These practices ranged from the simplistic placing of salt on a shovel with the sign of a cross and baking the shovel and salt over the fire, rubbing the Changeling with digitalis, or benign neglect, through to a whole range of vicious, cruel, and bizarre activities. In the belief that fairies were exorcised by fire, many suspected Changelings were "tested" in the hearth of a blazing fire or put on the shovel with the salt over the fire in the expectation that the spirit would fly up the chimney. Others were pelted with iron nails or exposed on hillsides or dung heaps all day.

One test of which one might approve arose from the belief that exorcism would occur if the Changeling could be made to laugh. There is a story of a prudent mother who took an egg, broke it in half, threw away the contents, filled the shells with water, and set them in front of the fire to boil. This made the Changeling howl with laughter and exclaim, "In my thousand years I've never seen the like." Then in an instant he was gone, and her true child returned. On a more encouraging note, there have been instances when the mother has been advised that kindness to the Changeling would result in the return of her own child, and happily in each case it did.
References 17, 28, 40, 44, 53, 56, 59, 76, 80, 87, 92, 107, 136
See also Corpán síde, Elf, Fairy, Mannikin, Nix, Sibhreach, Spirit, Appendix 22

CHANQUES
These are Little People or dwarfs in the folklore of Mexico and Central America, where they are also known by the names Chanekos and Chanes. The Chanques are the guardian spirits of the forest animals. These spirits may be benevolent, but more frequently they cause illness or death in humans by stealing their souls. They are said to be afraid of tobacco smoke, which may be used to keep them away. When the Popoluca people of Veracruz wish to have success in hunting, they invoke the assistance and approval of the Chanques with offerings and incense.
References 87
See also Dwarf, Guardian, Appendix 12, Appendix 19, Appendix 21

CHAPEAU DE COURO
See Constantino

CHARITIES
See Graces

CHARLOT
An evil spirit said to inhabit the forests around Lake Mékinac north of Quebec in Canada. Charlot was supposed to have made a demonic pact with certain loggers isolated in the forest long ago.
References 99
See also Spirit

CHARON
In classical Greek mythology Charon was originally a dog-shaped demon of death who was transformed to be the ferryman who transported the dead across the River Styx to the entrance of Hades.

In modern Greek folklore Charon is an evil spirit usually taking the form of a little black dog. It is said to follow humans or pad along silently at their side on lonely roads. It may also come into the house with a member of the family and sit in a corner of the room until it disappears. The Charon is regarded as a portent of misery and a coming death in the family.
References 93
See also Black Dog, Charos, Demon, Spirit, Appendix 12, Appendix 16

CHARONTAS
See Charos

CHARONTES, CHARUN
These are both male and female demons of death in ancient Etruscan mythology and are usually depicted wielding hammers. The male demon was called Charun. He is depicted as having a beak-like nose, pointed ears, and snakes for hair like that of Medusa.

Sometimes he is shown with wings, but he always carries a hammer. Charun was responsible for ensuring that the dead reached their final abode, and in this respect he was the guardian of the entrance to graves.
References 93
See also Charon, Charos, Demon, Guardian, Appendix 16

CHAROS
The demon or terrifying angel of death in modern Greek folklore. Charos, also known as Charontas, rides through the skies mounted in an enormous saddle on a huge black horse. Charos gathers up the dead by way of this huge wooden saddle on the black horse.
References 87, 93
See also Angel, Charon, Charontes, Demon, Appendix 16

CHARUN
See Charontes

CHASSE D'HÉRODE
This is one of the French names for the Wild Hunt. Chasse d'Hérode means Herod's Hunt or the Hunt of Herodias. There are two possibilities for the derivation of this name: (1) King Herod/Herodias, who was responsible for the death of John the Baptist and the Massacre of the Innocents, is given as the Christian derivation; (2) Hrodso, which means Glory Bearer, was a pagan epithet for Odin of Norse mythology, the leader of the Norse Wild Hunt. As the Normans settled Normandy in northern France, the latter may be the more likely of the two. It is also known as Chasse de Caïn, la Chasse d' Artu, L'Armée Furieuse, or Mesnie Herlequin in other parts of France.
References 95
See also Armée Furieuse, Mesnie Hellequin, Wild Hunt, Appendix 16, Appendix 23

CHASSE DE CAÏN
See Chasse d'Hérode

CHELONE
She is a nymph in the classical mythology of Greece and Rome. Chelone was condemned to exist in the form of a tortoise by Mercury for making fun of the wedding ceremony between Jupiter and Juno, the king and queen of the gods.
References 130
See also Nymph, Appendix 12

CHERRUVE
The name of a group of spirits in the folk beliefs of the Araucanian people of Chile. These spirits were the servants of the thunder god Pillan. They were depicted as snakes with human heads and were considered to be the portents of evil. The Cherruve were responsible for sending shooting stars and comets across the skies, bringing disasters to the communities. The location of the misfortunes was indicated by the direction in which their shooting stars and comets landed.
References 102
See also Spirit

CHERT
See Devil

CHERTOVKA
This is the name for a female devil or water demon in Russian folklore. Chertovka, which means Jokestress, is an alternative name for the Rusalka. This is a malignant spirit that mostly inhabits deep still or stagnant pools of water.
References 75
See also Bes (1), Demon, Devil, Jenny Greenteeth, Rusalka, Spirit, Appendix 25

CHERUB, CHERUBIM, CHERUBIN, CHERUBYM, CHERUBYN, CHERUBIS
Cherub is the singular and Cherubim is the collective name for these heavenly spirits in Christian and Hebrew tradition. The Cherubim, also known as Cerubin, Cherube, Cherubin, Cherubym, Cherubyn, Cherubis, and Kerubim, are the attendants of God and the Guardian Angels of Heaven in the first (or second) circle of the hierarchy of angels. They may be described as having the form of a lion, a man, or an eagle, or a combination of these with wings. However, in art they are usually depicted as having a child's head and several pairs of wings, usually blue or gold, and holding a book. Hebrew religious writings state that images of Cherubim guarded the Ark of the Covenant and Solomon's Temple. They were later adopted into the Christian religious doctrine and art. Not only are the Cherubim divine messengers and ministering attendant spirits, but they are also concerned with the dissemination of universal knowledge. It is possible that the Cherubim are derived from the Assyrian Lamassu or Šedu.
References 39, 93, 107, 119
See also Angel, Attendant Spirit, Guardian Angel, Lamassu, Šedu, Spirit

CHEVAL BAYARD, LE
In the folklore of Normandy, France, this is a type of water spirit that may appear as a human or as a horse. The Cheval Bayard inhabits the banks of rivers, pools, and marshland. The spirit entices foolhardy humans to attempt to ride it, but as soon as they get on its back, the spirit will toss them into the water or the bushes. A story is told of the Cheval

Heavenly Cherubim attend the throne of the Almighty.

Bayard that is similar to that of Ainsel. The sprite, in the form of a handsome young man, had taken to calling on a peasant woman whose husband found out. The jealous husband placed a bar of iron to heat in the kitchen fire and, concealing himself in his wife's clothes, sat at her spinning wheel to await the sprite. Soon enough the spirit entered the room and with loving words enquired "her" name. "Myself" replied the husband, hurling the red-hot iron bar at the sprite, who yelled for his spirit comrades to come. The other spirits enquired who was attacking him, and when the Cheval Bayard told them "Myself did it," they chided him for causing his own harm and departed.
References 11
See also Ainsel, Cabyll-Ushtey, Each Uisge, Kallikantzari, Kelpie, Näcken, Neugle, Spirit, Sprite, Appendix 25

CHI LUNG WANG

This is a spirit in the legends and popular folklore of China. He was deemed to be in charge of the provision of domestic water. Chi Lung Wang, whose name means Fire Engine Dragon King, was propitiated for assistance in providing sufficient water and efficient working of the pumps in times of house fire. This lesser spirit is derived from the religious cult of the Dragon King, Lung Wang, provider of the earth's water.
References 87
See also Diuturna, Spirit, Appendix 22, Appendix 25

CHIH NÜ

In Chinese folklore and legend Chih Nü is a celestial nymph. She was the Celestial Weaving Maid responsible for weaving the beautiful cloth that made the robes of the gods. There are several versions of her story. In one she was banished to the earth, where she spent her time with an oxherd, and they were ultimately transformed into the stars Vega and Altair. In another version, she and her sister saw the things on the earth from their place in heaven and decided to go there to bathe. A mortal cowherd was informed by a cow of how he could win the love of the most beautiful maiden by stealing her celestial garments. Without them she could not return to heaven. While she and the cowherd dwelt in bliss, the gods received no more fine clothes, so she was recalled to heaven. The distraught cowherd pursued her wrapped in the skin of the magic cow. But the celestial guards stopped him. The Jade Emperor took pity and allowed them to meet once a year across a bridge made by the wings of the magpies. They are the subjects of several traditional tales not only in China but also in Korea and Japan.
References 87
See also Nymph

CHILD MEDICINE WOMAN
See Sand Altar Woman

CHIMMEKEN
See Kobold

CHIN CHIA

This is the name of a spirit in the legends and popular folk beliefs of China. He is a tutelary spirit particularly concerned with literature and scholastic attainment. Chin Chia, whose name means the Gentleman in Golden Armor, is to be seen waving a flag in front of the houses of those whose descendants will be academically successful. It is known that he will also punish those who are lazy scholars or who abandon their studies.
References 87
See also Spirit, Tutelary Spirit

CHINOI
See Mat Chinoi

CHINÜN WAY SHUN

In the beliefs of the Kachin people of Burma, Chinün Way Shun, also known as Ka, is the first and most important nat. He is the spirit of fertile soil. In the legends he was responsible for the formation of the other nats: Chitōn, Jān, Mbōn, Mu, Ponphyoi, Shitta, Sinlap, and Wāwn. Each of these donated some magic element to a pumpkin from which the first human was formed.

References 87
See also Mbōn, Mu, Nats, Ponphyoi, Shitta, Sinlap, Spirit, Appendix 10

CHISIN TONGBŎP

These supernaturals are the Earth Imps of Korean folk belief. They are particularly malevolent and will enter houses hidden in new items crossing the threshold for the first time, or may be invoked by accident when the earth is moved on an inauspicious day to build the foundations of a new home. Unless they are detected and banished by a *Mansin* (a female shaman), the Chisin Tongbŏp will cause family discord and illness.
References 79
See also Imp, Moksin Tongbŏp, Nanggu Moksin, Tongbŏp

CHITAR ALI

The name of an angel in the Islamic beliefs of the people of West Malaysia. Chitar Ali means Lord of the Whirlpool.
References 120
See also Angel, Sabur Ali

CHITŌN

See Nats

CHITRAGUPTA

This is a spirit in the Hindu mythology of India. Chitragupta is a supernatural concerned with the afterlife. He records the virtuous and evil deeds of each human, which are then judged to determine the person's entry to heaven or hell.
References 87
See also Angel, Spirit, Appendix 16

CHLEVNIK

The spirit of the cow byre and guardian of the cows in Russian folklore. The Chlevnik must be propitiated correctly when a new byre is being built or a new cow is being introduced, as the wrong site or the wrong color may incite the spirit to a malevolence that destroys all around. As a result of the Chlevnik's destructive tendencies he was often encouraged to depart with the beating of the walls and loud noise or was simply asked to leave.
References 87
See also Domovik, Guardian, Spirit, Appendix 12

CHONCHONYI, CHONCHÓN

A group of evil spirits in the folk belief of the Araucanian people of Chile. The Chonchón is described as being like a human head with such enormous ears that they are used as wings. The Chonchonyi seek and prey upon those humans who are sick. They wait until the person is left alone, then they will leap onto the person and drain their life from them.
References 29, 56, 102
See also Mara, Spirit

CHU PA-CHIAI

This spirit is the Pig Fairy in the folklore of China and companion of the Monkey King in the story of the Journey to the West. Originally a celestial official, he was banished to earth for drunkenness and reincarnated as a piglet. In disgust at his predicament, he gobbled up his pig mother and siblings, then made off to the Fu-Ling Mountains, where he attacked all humans who ventured there. Then the goddess of mercy, Kwan Yin, converted Chu Pa-Chiai to Buddhism, and he was readmitted to the Western Paradise as the Chief Altar Washer.
References 131
See also Fairy, Spirit, Appendix 12

CHUCKLEBUD

See Gumnut Babies

CHUDANG

This is the name of an evil spirit in the folklore of Korea.
References 79
See also Spirit

CHURCH GRIM

This is a guardian spirit and portent of impending death in the family in the folklore of Yorkshire, England. It usually takes the form of a Black Dog that patrols the churchyards and burial grounds at night or in stormy weather, where it is said to protect the dead from the Devil and other malignant spirits. Only a minister of the church may see the Church Grim without being affected by its usual portent of death, as it may be seen at the funerals and cause the bell to toll for the departing soul. Both William Henderson and Ruth Tongue give details of this Northern spirit as derived from the belief that the first human to be interred in a graveyard would become its spiritual guardian. To absolve them from this duty, a black dog was sacrificed and buried in the north corner of the plot.
References 17
See also Barguest, Black Dog, Black Shuck, Boggart, Bullbeggar, Capelthwaite, Freybug, Guardian, Gytrash, Kirkegrim, Mauthe Dhoog, Padfoot, Rongeur d'Os, Skriker, Spirit, Appendix 12, Appendix 21

CHURNMILK PEG

This is the name of an individual nature spirit in the folklore of Yorkshire, England. Churnmilk Peg protected the growing hazelnuts from humans who might be tempted to take them before they were ripe. She took the form of a female goblin whose presence could be detected by the smoke that drifted from her tiny pipe. If anyone ate the hazelnuts before they were ready, Churnmilk Peg would inflict severe bloat or stomach cramps on them.
References 17, 44
See also Goblin, Melsh Dick, Spirit, Appendix 21

CHÛTÂS

These are forest demons in the folklore of India.
References 110
See also Bhut, Demon, Appendix 19

CHUTSAIN

An evil spirit in the beliefs of the Tinneh Native Americans, Chutsain is a personification of death.
References 122
See also Spirit, Appendix 16

CHU-UHÀ

In the folk beliefs of the Annamese people of Vietnam, this is the guardian spirit of the household. Chu-Uhà inhabits the lime-jug possessed by each family for preparing betel nuts. If the jug is accidentally broken, it is a portent of disaster for the family. The only way to avert this is to carry the broken jug to the nearest shrine with the new jug so that the placated spirit will accept its new abode.
References 87
See also Guardian, Appendix 21, Appendix 22

CIHUATETEO, CIUATETEO

These are evil demons in the Aztec beliefs of Mexico. Cihuateteo, also called Ciuapipiltin, were the servants of Cihuacoatl, the serpent woman, who carried the sun for her to the lords of the underworld. The Cihuateteo appeared in their female form at crossroads to terrify travelers. They also brought sickness and epilepsy to children and inspired lustfulness in men. These demons were supposed to have been the transformed spirits of women who had died in childbirth. Under the later Spanish culture, the Cihuateteo were gradually metamorphosed to the form of La Llorona.
References 41, 53, 87
See also Demon, Llorona, Appendix 22

CIN-AN-EV

The trickster wolf, supernatural hero of the Ute Native American beliefs.
References 87
See also Trickster

CITIPATI

The Citipati are demons in the mythology of Tibetan Buddhism. These evil spirits, whose name means Lord of the Graveyard, inhabit the cemeteries and are depicted as dancing skeletons.
References 93
See also Demon, Spirit, Appendix 16

CIUAPIPILTIN

See Cihuateteo

CLAP-CANS

This is an invisible spirit of the bogie type in the folklore of Lancashire, England. Although not harmful, it does cause some fear from the crashing noises it makes in the buildings that it inhabits.
References 17
See also Bogie, Spirit

CLASHNICHD AULNIAC

See Ben Baynac

CLAY MOTHER

This is the name of a guardian spirit in the folk beliefs of the Pueblo Native American people. She is the tutelary spirit of clay and pottery crafts and is the spirit responsible for one of the most useful skills given to humans. Clay Mother is the subject of many legends and folk tales.
References 87
See also Agloolik, Àràk, Awl-man, Corn Mother, Grandmother Fire, Guardian, Salt Woman, Spirit, Tutelary Spirit, Appendix 14

CLIM

An imp or nursery bogie in the folklore of Sussex, England. Clim was said to inhabit the chimneys of the nursery room where children would be taught and would sometimes play. This sprite was said to be watching the youngsters while he was in the bottom of the chimney, from which he would shout at naughty children.
References 123
See also Imp, Nursery Bogie, Sprite, Appendix 22

CLIO

See Muses

CLIODNA

An Irish fairy of the Tuatha dé Danann, a woman of the Sídhe, and queen of the fairies of Munster owing allegiance to Finvarra and Onagh. Cliodna's abode in County Cork is a *sidh*, or long barrow, near Mallow. Aoibhinn of North Munster and Aine of South Munster owe allegiance to Cliodna.
References 125

See also Aine, Aoibhinn, Banshee, Fairy, Finvarra, Onagh, Sídhe, Tuatha dé Danann

CLOTHO
See Fates

CLOUD CHIEFS
See Cloud People

CLOUD PEOPLE
These are supernatural beings, known as the Shiwanna in the beliefs of the Pueblo Native Americans. They may be equated with the Cloud Chiefs of the Hopi or the Rain People of the Jemez Pueblo Native Americans. These are all spirits that bring rainfall and their blessings to mankind. The Cloud People may inhabit the cardinal regions of the universe, taking on the associated colors, or they may be found, like nature spirits, in natural phenomena such as lakes and mountains. The Cloud People are associated with the souls of the dead, and they are represented by Kachina masks in Kachina ceremonies.
References 87, 88
See also Kachina, Spirit

CLUPRICAUNE
See Cluricaun

CLURACAN, CLURICAINE, CLURICANE
See Cluricaun

CLURICAUN/E
In Irish folklore this malicious spirit is also known as Clupricaune, Cluracan, Cluricaine, Loghery Man, and Luricadaune. He is said to be like an elf, resembling a little old man who wears a long red pointed cap, red coat with a silver buckle, blue stockings, and buckled shoes. He inhabits the wine cellars of houses, where he makes sure that the bungs are tight and the casks' taps not left running. Although nearly always appearing to be drunk, he would frighten the household servants to prevent them from helping themselves to the wine cellars' contents. Like the leprechaun, the Cluricaun is associated with the guardianship of hidden treasure. One anecdote tells a similar story to that of the Boggart "flitting," but the Cluricaun hid inside one of the casks of wine before he was discovered to be accompanying the family who were leaving their home to be rid of him.
References 15, 17, 18, 38, 40, 41, 53, 87
See also Biersal, Boggart, Cellar Demon, Elf, Leprechaun, Spirit, Appendix 21, Appendix 22

CLYM OF THE CLOUGH
An imp in the folklore of Suffolk, England.
References 123
See also Clim, Imp

CLYTIE
In classical Greek mythology Clytie, or Klytie, was an ocean nymph or mermaid who, when cast up on the seashore, saw Apollo take his sun's course across the sky. She fell in love with him and could not take her eyes off him day after day. Eventually, as she pined unnoticed, her tail took root to the earth, her arms and hands grew into leaves, and her hair turned into petals around her face. Clytie, as the golden sunflower, would forevermore follow her sun's progress across the sky.
References 20, 40, 114, 121
See also Mermaid, Nymph, Appendix 25

COB
See Gnome

COBALT, COBOLT
A gnome or demon of the mines in German folklore. It is considered to be responsible for the evil effects of the cobalt ore named after the spirit. The Cobalt could be both helpful, in locating the ore, and malevolent if not propitiated.
References 17, 87
See also Coblyn, Gnome, Kobold, Mine Spirits, Spirit

COBLYN, COBLYNAU (pl.)
These are mine goblins in Welsh folklore similar to the kobolds of Germany and the knockers of Cornwall, England. They are described as having either black- or copper-colored faces, which are extremely ugly. Though very small, they are dressed like the miners. The Coblynau are entirely benevolent and can be heard tapping in the tunnels and shafts, indicating where rich veins may be found. To see one is said to be very lucky, but if anyone jeers at them, they will be pelted with stones from invisible hands.
References 17, 87, 125
See also Goblin, Knockers, Kobold, Mine Spirits

COBRA GRANDE DA LAGOA
See Dona Rosalina

ČODRA KUBA AND ČODRA KUGUZA
These are spirits of the forests in the folklore of the Cheremis/Mari people of the former Soviet Republic. Čodra Kuba and Čodra Kuguza mean Forest Old Woman and Forest Old Man, respectively. Although these spirits are invisible, there are always signs of their presence in the forests that they inhabit. Čodra

Kuguza rustles the leaves of the trees as he passes. If he is angry with hunters who have not propitiated him with porridge, then Čodra Kuguza will shake the trees wildly, scaring away the game, and lure the hunters deep into unknown areas of the forest where they may be lost for days. Čodra Kuba is guardian of the wildlife of the forests. She likes to play cards with the other female spirits, using the forest game as her stake. If she loses, then the animals will migrate to the area guarded by the winner until she can win them back again. Hunters are not allowed to hunt while the stake is being paid (i.e., while the animals are migrating), as this would cause serious discord in the forest.

References 118
See also Guardian, Laskowice, Leshii, Spirit, Appendix 19, Appendix 21

CO-HON

These are evil spirits in the folk beliefs of the Annamese people of Vietnam. They are said to be the transformed souls of those who have died a violent death and received no burial rites. As supernaturals, the Co-Hon inhabit the undergrowth of trees, waiting to attack and deliver misfortune to passersby. Some humans consider their powers to be necessary to success, and businessmen in particular will propitiate these demons with offerings.

References 87
See also Demon, Spirit

COLANN GAN CEANN

See Coluinn Gun Cheann

COLEMAN GRAY

This is the name of an individual pisky in the folklore and traditional tales of Cornwall in England. This pisky was found as a diminutive boy and captured by a farmer, or fisherman according to the variation. The pisky was then taken home and adopted by human parents who gave him the name of Coleman Gray.

References 17
See also Green Children, Piskey, Skilly Widden, Undine, Appendix 22

COLO-COLO

This is a disease spirit in the folklore of the Araucanian people of Chile. The Colo-Colo is said to be hatched from a cock's egg. It is a malicious demon that attacks humans and drinks their saliva. In this way it is able to inflict fever on its victims and ultimately causes their deaths.

References 29, 102
See also Aitvaras, Demon, Spirit, Appendix 17

COLT PIXY, COLT PIXIE

A mischievous sprite in the folklore of the English counties of Hampshire, Somerset, Devon, and Cornwall, where it may also be known as Colle Pixy or Colt Piskie. It generally takes the form of a young horse that leads astray travelers and their horses, who often end up in bogs or thickets. The sprite then vanishes. In Somerset, however, the Colt Pixy is the guardian of the apple orchard who will frighten humans intent on damage or theft.

References 17, 28, 40, 107
See also Appletree Man, Brag, Churnmilk Peg, Dunnie, Guardian, Old Roger, Sprite, Appendix 12, Appendix 21

COLUINN GUN CHEANN

Known also as the Colann Gan Ceann, the Colann Gun Cheann, and the Headless Trunk, this malevolent spirit or Bauchan was the guardian spirit of the Macdonalds of Morar in the Isle of Skye (Inner Hebrides, Scotland). Toward women and children or men traveling in groups by day it offered no harm, but any male traveling alone at night on the Smooth Mile to Morar House was sure to be found dead and mutilated in the morning. There are two versions of its defeat: one by banishment effected by MacLeod of Raasay, and the other by a clever coolheaded clansman who caught Coluinn Gun Cheann's head on his sword and would only return it if the spirit departed forever.

References 17, 47
See also Acephalos, Bauchan, Guardian, Spirit, Appendix 21, Appendix 22

CON-ION

In the folk beliefs of the Annamese people of Vietnam, these evil spirits are supernaturals that enter a human life by birth but cause the child to be stillborn or miscarried. A woman who has lost more than one child in this way is a host to these evil spirits and may not be touched or mentioned. In order to get rid of the Con-Ion, a dog is sacrificed and interred beneath the bed of such a woman when she is about to give birth.

References 87
See also Spirit, Appendix 22

CON-MA-DĀU

This is the name of a group of demons in the folk beliefs of the Annamese people of Vietnam. The Con-Ma-Dāu are disease spirits associated with bringing smallpox.

References 87
See also Alardi, Demon, Minceskro, Šedra Kuba and Šedra Kuguza, Spirit, Tou Shen, Appendix 17

CONSTANTINO

This is the name of an encantado in the Afro-Brazilian cult Batuque. Constantino is also known as Chapeau de Couro, which means Leather Hat. He is one of the spirits in the group called Caboclos.
References 89
See also Caboclo, Encantado

CON-TINH

Said to be the transformed souls of girls who died prematurely, these malevolent nature spirits of the Annamese folk beliefs of Vietnam reside in trees. The Con-Tinh will attack any human near their tree, cackling and driving them mad and attempting to steal their souls. Anyone foolish enough to try to cut down their tree will be made to suffer. The prudent Annamese get someone of another faith or nationality to fell the tree of a Con-Tinh.
References 87
See also Hamadryad, Sankchinnis, Spirit, Appendix 19

CONTROL

A familiar spirit that takes over the normal consciousness of a medium or other human, forming a spirit link between humans and other supernaturals.
References 98
See also Familiar

ČOPAKIN

This is the name of a keremet or evil spirit in the folk belief of the Cheremis/Mari people of the former Soviet Republic.
References 118
See also Keremet, Spirit

COQUENA

The guardian spirit of the vicuñas in the folklore of the Quechua of the Puna de Atacama. Coquena is described as being like a little man dressed in white clothes. He moves large herds of vicuñas in the mountains at night and will punish anyone who tries to harm them.
References 87
See also Guardian, Appendix 12

CORANIANS

A mythical tribe of supernatural dwarfs of ancient Britain from the time of King Ludd. The Coranians were greatly feared because they could hear everything in the land and no weapon could cause them injury. They used fairy money, which appeared to be real on payment but quickly turned to toadstools when they had gone.
References 125
See also Dwarf, Fairy

CORN MOTHER

This is the name of a spirit in the beliefs and legends of the Arikara Native American people of the Great Plains. She is a tutelary spirit who emerged through the earth and taught the people how to grow maize. She also taught the people about astronomy and the mysteries of the sacred medicine bundles. Before she left, Corn Mother charged the humans to make regular offerings to the gods in all the cardinal directions.
References 25, 45, 87
See also Agloolik, Àràk, Awl-man, Clay Mother, Corn Spirit, Flint Boys, Fylgja, Grandmother Fire, Salt Woman, Spirit, Tutelary Spirit

CORN SPIRIT

The fertility spirit of the grain harvest was trapped in the last sheaf of the harvest in the folk beliefs of many societies. In Europe, "Corn" refers most frequently to cereal crops such as oats, barley, rye, and more usually to wheat. In other parts of the world, especially the Americas, it most usually denotes maize. As the embodiment of the corn spirit, the sheaf was given various names. In Wales it was called the Wrach or the Hag; in Ireland the Kirn or the Granny. In Northumberland it was the Kern Baby, while further south in England it was the Kirn Dolly (today simply the corn dolly), the Harvest Lady, or Harvest Queen. In Scotland its various names were the Maiden or the Auld Wife (if taken before or after Halloween, respectively), the Carlin, or the Cailleach. In the Isle of Man it is known as Babban ny Mheillea. In most accounts the trapped spirit was shaped into its image and often given diminutive clothes. It was usually kept safely after being feasted and then was fed to the plow horses at the next season's sowing of the grain-seed, or was fed to a cow in calf or a mare in foal, so that the spirit would be reborn in the new seed. Similar beliefs exist throughout the world, some of which are the Baba in Poland and Boba in Lithuania, the Bullkater in Germany, and the Ahren Konigen in Austria.
References 123
See also Ahren Konigen, Babban ny Mheillea, Bullkater, Cailleac, Carlin, Corn Mother, Hag, Kornmutter, Kornwolf, Kuršis, Sara-Mama, Spirit, Wrach, Appendix 15, Appendix 18

CORNWOLF

See Kornwolf

CORONIS

This is the name of a nymph who was one of the Hyades in ancient Greek mythology. Coronis was, for a time, the consort of the god Apollo. This union produced Æsculapius, one of Jason's Argonauts.
References 13
See also Hyades, Nymph

CORPÁN SÍDE
The Irish Gaelic words for a changeling, also known as Síod Brad.
References 80
See also Changeling

CORRE-BEIRADO, ANTONIO LUIZ
See Caboclo

CORRIGAN
See Korrigan

ČORT
A devil or evil water spirit in the folk beliefs of the Cheremis/Mari people of the former Soviet Republic. This spirit, also sometimes known as Šərt, often takes the form of a human but can easily be spotted as he has no eyebrows. Čort is often seen with the evil Keltəmaš. Čort will appear by the water at midnight, noon, or six o'clock in the morning or evening in the hope of attracting some unwary bather or fisherman to their doom. Čort will also help a keremet in its evil purposes.
References 118
See also Devil, Keltəmaš, Keremet, Spirit, Appendix 25

CORYCIA
A nymph in the classical mythology of Greece and Rome. Corycia was one of the lovers of the god Apollo and, by him, the mother of Lycorus.
References 130
See also Nymph

CORYCIDES
See Muses

COSME
An encantado in the Afro-Brazilian cult Batuque associated with the feast day of Saint Cosmos, 2 September. With Damião, Cosme was supposed to have been thrown into the sea at Baia by their human mother and saved by the encantado Queen Rainha Oyá, who brought them to her encantaria under the sea. Like the saints with whom they are associated, Cosme and Damião are invoked as healers, but they attend ceremonies in their childlike characters with an unchildlike thirst for rum!
References 89
See also Damião, Encantado

COURIL
A dwarf or fairy in the Celtic folklore of Brittany in northwest France and Cornwall in southwest England. The Couril inhabited the stone circles that abound in these areas and could be seen sometimes flitting between the ancient stones. These Little

People appeared in the form of diminutive people but were distinguishable by their webbed feet.
References 53
See also Dwarf, Fairy, Little People

COVENTINA
A water spirit of pre-Roman Britain that was the guardian spirit of the well at Carrawburgh. Coventina was possibly a river goddess who was debased to the status of a nymph after the Roman invasion of Britain and the superimposition of their pantheon on the local religion.
References 133
See also Guardian, Nymph, Spirit, Appendix 25

COWLUG SPRITES
In the local folklore of Bowden and Gateside in the north of England, these sprites or imps were distinguished by their huge ears resembling those of cows. Although supposedly working their mischief on Cowlug E'en, in his account Mr. Wilkie could find no record of when or how this took place.
References 17, 66
See also Imp, Sprite

COYOTE
This supernatural being is variously a trickster, a culture hero, a nature spirit, or a demon clown that plays a prominent part in the mythology of the Achomawi, Chinook, Crow, Jicarilla Apache, Kato, Kutenai, Maidu, Navajo, Rschochimi, Shushwap, Sia, Tuleyone, Yana, Yoku, and Zuñi Native American peoples. Coyote is also known as Isakawuate, Italapas, Italapate, Koyote, Mahih-Nah-Tieyhey, Old Man, Old Man Coyote, and Our Mother's Brother.

Coyote can shape shift at will but most frequently takes the form of the prairie wolf or human and can be compared with Blue Jay in this respect. Similarly, his character may be benevolent or mischievous to the point of malevolence. He is described as amoral, cunning, greedy, sly, resourceful, antagonistic, and sometimes destructive in the abundant tales of his activities. Coyote is considered responsible, in his positive aspect, for giving knowledge of creative artwork, the game for hunting, the gift of fire, and the planting of seeds, while his negative aspect is responsible for all manner of troubles, including sickness and misery to mankind and irritation to the supreme powers.

One tale of Coyote's deceitfulness tells how he encounters Owl, who is on his way to hunt men with his bow, arrows, and club. Coyote tells Owl that only those who vomit human flesh are capable of killing men. On Coyote's instructions, Owl closes his eyes and spews human flesh and grasshoppers. The trickster quickly picks up the human flesh and leaves the grasshoppers for Owl to see, then Coyote shows

the flesh as his own vomit. The puzzled Owl is told his legs are not fast enough, but if he closes his eyes again, Coyote will fix them. So the demon swipes Owl's legs, breaks them, and then flees with the bow and arrows. Owl repeatedly flings his club at Coyote, calling it back until at last the trickster has been hit and injured. Coyote curses all missiles from that time to remain exactly where they fall.
References 29, 33, 41, 53, 56, 87, 88, 93
See also Anansi, Bamapama, Basajaun, Blue Jay, Demon, Eshu, Kachina, Kokopelli, Manabozo, Mink, Spirit, Trickster

CRAOSA

This is the name of a benevolent spirit in the mythology and beliefs of the Zoroastrian religion of Iran. Craosa is the good spirit whose duties are to oppose and prevent the evil of Aesma.
References 41
See also Aeshma, Spirit

CRAZYMAN

See Bamapama

CREDNÉ

In Irish mythology Credné is the fairy bronze-worker of the Tuatha dé Danann.
References 125
See also Fairy, Tuatha dé Danann

CROPPED BLACK SOW

See Black Sow

CROQUEMITAINE

This is the name of an individual hobgoblin or bogie in the folklore of France. The Croquemitaine is essentially a nursery bogie whose activities are used to frighten children into good behavior.
References 40
See also Bogie, Hobgoblin, Nursery Bogie, Appendix 22

CU SITH

This is the fairy dog in the Highland folklore of Scotland. It is described as being the size of a bullock with a green shaggy coat, a long plaited tail, and enormous feet. Like the Black Dogs of English folklore, it was a portent of disaster and a fearsome spirit for a human to encounter on the road at night.
References 18, 119
See also Black Dog, Fairy, Padfoot, Spirit, Appendix 12, Appendix 24

CUACHAG

An evil water spirit or fuath in the folklore of Inverness, Scotland, where it is supposed to inhabit the river of Glen Cuaich.

References 17
See also Fuath, Spirit

CUDDLEPIE

See Gumnut Babies

CUÉLEBRE, EL

A spirit in the folklore of northwest Spain. It inhabits the high mountains, where it is said to dwell in the forests and caves. El Cuélebre is the guardian of secret treasures, and humans who venture into its domain to search for the treasure will be deceived and misled by el Cuélebre's enchantment.
References 88
See also Aitvaras, Guardian, Spirit, Appendix 21

CUGHTAGH

This is the name of a type of spirit in the folklore of Scotland. The Cughtagh is a class of buggane that inhabits the caves in Scottish Highlands and mountains.
References 17
See also Buggane, Spirit

CULSU

This is a female demon in the ancient Etruscan mythology. Culsu awaits the arrival of each human at the gates of the underworld. She is armed with scissors with which she will cut the thread of life, and she holds a flaming torch to guide them onward to heaven or hell.
References 93
See also Demon, Fates, Norns, Appendix 16

CÜNAWABI

This is the name of a trickster supernatural, also known as Sünawavi, in the mythology of the Ute Native Americans of Colorado.
References 88
See also Trickster

ČURPAN ŠƏRT

This is a keremet or evil spirit in the folklore of the Cheremis/Mari people of the former Soviet Republic. The name Čurpan Šərt means Stump Devil, and this demon may be encountered where trees have been felled. It is thought to be necessary to placate the demon with the sacrifice of a hare.
References 118
See also Čort, Keremet, Spirit

CURUPIRA

(1) This is a male forest demon, which may also be called Kurupira or Curupiri, in the folklore of the Tupi-Guarani people and the caboclos (mestizos) of Brazil. He is described as looking like a gnome with a bright red face and cloven hooves on his feet, or as

being entirely covered in shaggy hair and having feet turned backwards. He is credited with having a wife and children living with him in the trees and undergrowth. The Curupira may be heard in the forest making a resounding hollow or piercing noise. He is the guardian of the game and will reward hunters who have made offerings, but will punish those who abuse the forest. Curupira and his family have been blamed for the theft or destruction of crops where the forest has been cleared.

(2) These spirits are encantados of the Afro-Brazilian cult Batuque. The Curupira are tree spirits whose usual abode is the dense thorn trees in the rain forest. When a medium is possessed by a Curupira, it may be known by the wild manner in which the human will dance and make yelping noises and is able to climb the thorn trees without feeling the thorns. The Curupiras belong to the Japetequara "family" of spirits, and when they materialize are said to look like black children. The Curupiras are mischievous spirits and if anyone ventures into the rain forest alone, the spirits will delight in luring the person off the track until the traveler has entirely lost the way. It is considered wise to propitiate the Curupiras with their favorite rum, tobacco, and honey to avert such a trick.
References (1) 29, 56, 87, 102, 110; (2) 89
See also (1) Gnome, Guardian, Appendix 19, Appendix 21; (2) Encantado, Japetequara, Leshii

CURUPURI
See Curupira (1)

CUT-CUT
An evil spirit in the Dreamtime beliefs of the Native Australians. Cut-Cut preys on the vulnerability of others to work his evil deeds. One story tells of how he was supposed to help Kara-Kara find her lost husband in the bush. As payment he took, one by one, each of her children until none was left and Kara-Kara was changed into a cuckoo.
References 14
See also Spirit

CUTTY BLACK SOW
See Black Sow

CUTTY DYER
An evil, bloodthirsty spirit in the local folklore of Ashburton, Somerset, England. He is said to inhabit the bridge or culvert of the River Yeo. Cutty Dyer was described as having the shape of a huge man with eyes as big as saucers. He would wait at night for unwary travelers to cross the river, from which he would emerge behind them. Then the demon would either pull them down to drown under the river or

slit their throats to drink their blood. It is reported that an aged blind man resident in Taunton, but who was born in Ashburton, before he died in 1972, recited the following remembered rhyme of his youth:

"Dawn't'ee go down the riverzide
Cutty Dyer do abide
Cutty Dyer ain't no gude
Cutty Dyer'll drink yer blood."

Young children were told of this spirit's activities, and in this respect Cutty Dyer was a nursery bogie.
References 29
See also Demon, Nursery Bogie, Spirit, Appendix 22, Appendix 24

CUTTY SOAMS
A spirit or bogle of the mines that mischievously cut the traces, or soams, that yoked the mine workers to the wooden tubs used for transporting the coal to the surface. Although Cutty Soams mostly played this trick on the workers, from time to time he would take their grievances in hand and thrash an unpopular deputy or overman.
References 17
See also Bogle, Knockers, Kobold

CWN ANNWN
These are fearsome spirits in the folklore of Wales. The Cwn Annwn, which means Hounds of Fairyland/Hell, are also known as Cwn Mamau, which means Hounds of the Mothers. They may be invisible, but when they appear they take the form of white hounds with red ears. They are to be heard or seen in certain locations howling and gathering the souls of the dead for delivery to Hell. The Cwn Annwn are said to search for unbaptized babies, or those without penitence, to kidnap if there are no dead to take. They may be led by the Devil or a master huntsman clothed in grey.
References 69, 87, 125
See also Gabriel Hounds, Herne the Hunter, Spirit, Wild Hunt, Appendix 12, Appendix 22, Appendix 23

CWN MAMAU
See Cwn Annwn

CYANE
The name of a nymph in the classical mythology of Greece and Rome. She dwelled in the countryside of Sicily. When Persephone was kidnapped by the god of the underworld, Cyane tried to help her to escape. But for trying to help Persephone away from Hades, Cyane was changed into a fountain.
References 130
See also Nymph, Appendix 25

CYHIRAETH, Y CYHYRAETH
This is the name of an invisible spirit in the folklore
of Wales. Y Cyhyraeth, like the banshee and
Caoineag, is to be heard wailing and groaning as the
portent of some disaster to the inhabitants of the district. If the community is to suffer an epidemic, the
Cyhyraeth may pass along the street at night, moaning and howling as she progresses. Even if the person
to be afflicted has emigrated abroad, y Cyhyraeth will
still rattle the shutters of their former home.
References 17
See also Banshee, Caoineag, Gwrach y Rhibyn, Spirit,
Appendix 22, Appendix 23

CYMODOCE
In the classical mythology of Greece and Rome, this is
the name of a nymph or Nereid mentioned by Virgil
and by Spenser in his work *The Faerie Queen*.
References 130
See also Nereid, Nymph, Appendix 25

CYMOTHOE
In the classical mythology of Greece and Rome,
Cymothoe was a sea nymph or Nereid, the daughter

of Nereus and Doris. She assisted in refloating the
sinking ships of Æneas.
References 130
See also Nereid, Nymph, Appendix 25

CYRENE
In the classical mythology of Greece and Rome,
Cyrene is a nymph and the daughter of the river god
Peneus. Abducted by Apollo, Cyrene bore a son by
him—Aristaeus, who became the first keeper and
guardian of honeybees.
References 40, 110, 130
See also Browney, Guardian, Nymph, Appendix 12

CYTHRAUL
This is an evil spirit in the folklore of Wales. Cythraul
means a type of devil or a demon in the Welsh
language.
References 59
See also Demon, Spirit, Ysbryd Drwg

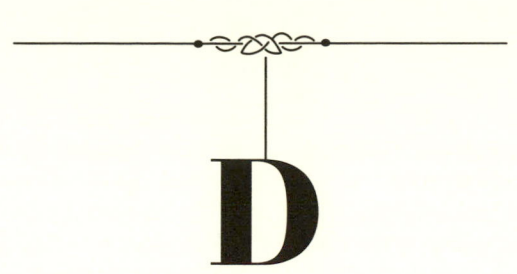

D

DAEVA
See Deev

DAGDA
He is the king and the most powerful of all the fairy race of the Tuatha dé Danann in Irish mythology. He was celebrated not only for his prowess with battle club, magic harp, and cauldron, but also known for his greed and cruelty.
References 44, 76
See also Fairy, Tuatha dé Danann

DAIMON, DÆMON
These are spirits in the classical mythology of ancient Greece. The Daimons were benign supernatural beings equated with Dæmones, but they were alternatively described as an individual's personal guardian spirit.
References 93, 130
See also Agathos Daimon, Dæmon, Guardian, Spirit

DAIN
He is a dwarf in Teutonic and Scandinavian mythology. Dain is always associated with the dwarf Thrain. The two dwarfs, whose names Dain and Thrain mean Dead and Stiff, respectively, are associated with the underworld and prophecy. They are believed to have knowledge of the coming Nordic Armageddon known as Ragnarök.
References 95
See also Dwarf

DAITYA, DAITEYA
In the Hindu mythology of India, the Daityas are a race of demons. These evil spirits constantly opposed the good works of the gods and tried to prevent the proper sacrifices and sacraments from taking place. They were later destroyed.
References 93, 111
See also Demon, Spirit

DAJOJI
In the mythology of the Iroquois Native American people, Dajoji is the spirit personification of the west wind, taking the form of a panther. He was called by Ga-oh to combat the storms and control the tempests. He is also powerful enough to make high waves in the sea and flatten forest trees.
References 87
See also Ga-oh, Spirit, Appendix 18, Appendix 26

DAKINI
They are female demons, also known as Ashrapa, which means Drinkers of Blood, in Indian Buddhist mythology. They can appear as beautiful but wrathful naked maidens, or as maidens with the head of a lion or bird, from which protrudes the face of a horse or dog. They are the servants of Kali and enjoy the flesh of humans. The Dakini fly through the air and have supernatural powers. Sometimes they may be invoked by a Yogin for the initiation of novices into the secrets of learning the *Tantra* and gaining spiritual insight. They may also sometimes perform the function of personal guardian spirit.
References 56, 93, 111
See also Demon, Guardian, Appendix 12

DAKTYLOI, DACTYLI
In ancient Greek mythology, these are three supernatural beings who were individually called Celmis the Smelter, Damnameneus the Hammer, and Acmon the Anvil. As a consequence of their skills, they were termed dextrous (i.e., with the fingers) and named Daktyloi, which means Finger. They were credited with the invention of working with metals, understanding botany, and the arts of music, medicines, and sorcery. They inhabited Mount Ida in Phrygia and Crete; the pointed pinnacles of these mountains may also have contributed to their name. In some legends these beings are referred to as the original inhabitants in much the same manner as the formorians of Irish folklore and the dwarfs of Teutonic myths.
References 93, 130
See also Dwarf, Formor

DALA KADAVARA
This is the name of a former Singhalese elephant goddess in the mythology of Sri Lanka. However, with the introduction of Buddhism to Sri Lanka, Dala Kadavara, also known as Gara Yaka, was reduced to the status of a male disease demon.
References 93
See also Demon, Appendix 17

DALHAM
This is the name of a djinn in the Islamic mythology of the North African coasts and the Arabian peninsula. Dalham is said to materialize as a man riding on a camel. This ferocious djinn inhabits desert islands, where he causes passing ships to be wrecked. He devours the bodies of the shipwrecked sailors who have been brought ashore by his powers.
See also Djinn, Siren

DAME ABONDE
See Habonde

DAME ELLERHORN
See Elder Mother

DAME HIRIP
See Tündér

DAME JENÖ
See Tündér

DAME RAMPSON
See Tündér

DAME VÉNÉTUR
See Tündér

DAMIÃO
This is an encantado in the Afro-Brazilian cult Batuque. In the Batuque ceremonies, this spirit usually appears in association with the encantado known as Cosme. Damião is associated with Saint Damian and the feast day of 27 September.
References 89
See also Cosme, Encantado, Spirit

DÆMON, DÆMONES
These are spirits in the classical mythology and beliefs of ancient Greece. These spirits or genii do not equate with our modern concept of demons. The Dæmones of ancient times were essentially shape-shifting supernatural beings presiding over the daily lives of humans. Their relationship to humans varied, with beneficent or malignant intent at different times. Those with good intent were called Agathodæmon, and those with evil intent were called Cacodæmon.

References 130
See also Agathos Daimon, Cacodæmon, Demon, Genius, Spirit, Appendix 2

DANAVAS
These are demons in the classical Hindu mythology of India. These evil beings were of divine descent, like the Asuras. Indra ultimately banished them to the oceans.
References 7, 39, 93, 119
See also Asura, Demon

DANCING VARGALUSKA
See Rumpelstiltskin

DANDO AND HIS DOGS
This is the Cornish variant of the Wild Hunt of English folklore. These supernatural spirits manifest as baying hounds with their demonic master flying through the midnight sky. They are said to hunt the souls of the unbaptized and the dead and carry them off to Hell. They are portents of death and disaster to those who see them. Upon hearing their approach, any belated traveler would throw themselves face-down until Dando and His Dogs had passed.
References 18, 133
See also Cwn Annwn, Gabriel Hounds, Spirit, Wild Hunt

DANGEROUS HOUR, THE
See Bad Hour

DAOINE BEAGA
See Daoine Sidhe

DAOINE MAITE
This is a euphemism for the fairies of Irish folklore. It means the Good People, and is used in Ireland to refer indirectly to the spirits and ward off any of their trickery.
References 88
See also Fairy, Sídhe, Spirit, Tuatha dé Danann

DAOINE SIDHE, DAOINE O'SIDHE
These are the fairies of Irish folklore, also known as Daoine Beaga, which means the Little Folk. They are the descended race of the heroic spirits, the Tuatha dé Danann of Celtic mythology. The Daoine Sidhe may resemble humans, but they can shape shift and even become invisible. They inhabit the *sidh* (the Long Barrows from which they are named), the loughs, the forests, wild places, and solitary thorn trees. They are akin to the Sleeth Ma of Highland Gaelic folklore. Like human realms, the Daoine Sidhe have their own kings and queens, who are often renowned for healing the sick and warding off disease. These spirits are the

sociable Trooping Fairies, who enjoy feasting, dancing, and parading, especially on the Celtic festivals of Beltane and Samhain. They can be quite boisterously malicious, and they enjoy battles, stirring up dust storms, stealing human brides and babies, and inflicting blight and other problems on human beings. The Daoine Sidhe may be propitiated with offerings of milk, but to avert their less favorable intentions they are referred to by euphemisms such as the Gentry, the Good People, the Little People, or the Wee Folk.
References 15, 17, 18, 53, 76, 87
See also Aine, Aoibhinn, Cliodna, Fairy, Finvarra, Onagh, Sleagh Maith, Tuatha dé Danann, Appendix 22

DAPHNE

In the classical mythology of Greece and Rome, she was a nymph, the daughter of Peneios, the river god. She spurned the love of the god Apollo, and was pursued by him. As she reached the riverbank, Daphne implored her father to rescue her. She became rooted to the spot, with bark covering her body, and her hands, arms, and head growing feathery leaves—safely changed into the laurel tree.
References 110
See also Nymph

DARAGO

See Mandarangan

DARRANT

He is a river demon specific to the River Derwent in Derbyshire, England. Like Jenny Greenteeth, he lurks in the pools to drown unwary strangers who venture too close to the water's edge. (Since this river was made famous for its fishing by Izaak Walton, numbers of such drownings were reported during the eighteenth and nineteenth centuries.)
References 123
See also Demon, Jenny Greenteeth

DASIM

See Iblis

DASYUS

These are the dwarfs in the mythology and folklore of India. The Dasyus, which means Dark Folk, are described as the dark, primeval dwarfs that later became the demons of folklore.
References 56
See also Demon, Dwarf

DATAN

A nature spirit or field spirit of Polish folklore, Datan was derived from an ancient god now debased.
References 102
See also Spirit, Appendix 18

DAVALIN

In Nordic mythology, Davalin is one of the four dwarfs (the others are Dain, Durathror, and Duneyr) whose names were those of the Harts that ate the buds of Yggdrasil, and were possibly originally guardian spirits of the World Tree. Davalin was father to at least one of the Norns, who sustained the World Tree from their wellspring.
References 95
See also Dwarf, Guardian, Norns, Spirit

DÆVAS

(1) In Hindu mythology, the Dævas are divine beings resembling, in some respects, the angels of Christian doctrine. They derive from the Devs of ancient Persia, who were divine beings. A later change was brought about by the Zoroastrian doctrines that replaced the ancient concepts. The celestial status of the Dævas was reversed, and they were relegated to the role of demons. In India the Dævas still maintain the status of benevolent heavenly spirits.

(2) In Iran, after the acceptance of Zoroastrianism, the Dævas were regarded as demons and devils. They became the assistants of the supremely evil Ahriman, and their task was to oppose the good works of the Amesha Spentas.
References 23, 93, 119
See also (1) Angel, Demon, Spirit; (2) Amesha Spentas, Deev, Demon, Devil

DAVY JONES

This fiend or evil spirit of the sea in the folklore of sailors warns of impending drowning and traps the souls of the drowned in his "locker" in the deep. The derivation of the name has several probable sources. It is possible that the name Davy is derived from the Celtic name for a watercourse: *Tau* or *Taff*, which is the derivation of many river names in the United Kingdom such as the Tavy and Tywi. The Jones part of the name may be from the Celtic diminutive *Shon*, from which come the first names Sean and John, and which are used in the same way as in Jack Frost, and reminiscent of the Highland Shoney. There is also evidence of numerous mythological underworld and underwater bone-constructed prisons for lost souls, the Celtic example being called Ochren. A further possibility is that the name Davy is from the West Indian term for a ghost or devil known as the Duppy, and Jones may be derived from Jonah, the biblical symbol of death and misfortune at sea, all of which would be familiar to the seventeenth-century mariner.
References 40, 107, 116
See also Devil, Fiend, Jack Frost, Shoney, Spirit

DE HI NO HINO
See Heng

DECUMA
See Parcae

DEEV, DEV, DEVA, DEVI
This is the name of a group of spirits in many different cultures, but they probably originated in the ancient religion of Persia. With the various migrations of peoples by way of conquering invasions, removal from ecological catastrophes, and missionary zeal, the original concepts of these spirits have spread and evolved. They are therefore referred to under many variants of the name: Daeva, Deev, Dev, Deva, Devi, Div, and Díve. The four main concepts of these supernaturals are given below.

(1) Deevs: Malignant spirits or demons of Persian mythology and folklore. They are constantly doing battle with the peris, whom they imprison in iron cages hung from the very tops of trees. All things of any beauty are reviled by the evil Deevs.

(2) Devs: In the Zoroastrian religion of Iran, the Devs are evil genii or demons who are servants of the supreme evil, Ahriman, and are constantly combating the good works of the Asuras, Amshaspands, or Izeds. There are said to be 28, of whom six are arch-Devs, among them Arzshenk, Demrush, Hondkonz, and Munheras, led by Hares or Iblis. They are depicted as having a deformed human shape with shaggy hair, horns, protruding eyes, great fangs, animal paws, and tail. They loathe and are repelled by sweet fragrances. The Devs are supposed to devour corpses and torture the souls of the damned.

(3) Devs: In Armenia the Devs are powerful malignant spirits of male or female human form who can shape shift to a snake or other wild animal that, although possessing only one eye, may have as many as seven heads. They inhabit caves and forests, and a sure sign of their presence is when a human faints, itches, or sneezes. Protection from them may be gained by cutting the air with a blade.

(4) Devas: In the Hindu and Buddhist traditions, the Devas are the Shining Ones, and are usually identified as divine or semidivine, but occasionally they are referred to as benevolent spirits, heroes, or goblins.
References 78, 88, 92, 93, 100, 107, 110
See also Aeshma, Amesha Spentas, Arzshenk, Asura, Demon, Demrush, Genius, Goblin, Iblis, Izeds, Munheras, Peri, Spirit

DEIVE
In Lithuanian folklore this is the name for a fairy. The Deive was previously a goddess, but was debased with the arrival of Christianity. The Deives are described as being beautiful with blue eyes, long blond hair, and large breasts. They are adept at home-making skills, and when they are caught by and marry a human, they are excellent wives and mothers. However, like the Swan Maidens, if a taboo is broken, they will return to their true identity. The Deives take particular care of women and their work (no washing may be done after sunset, or spinning on a Thursday), and men must show respect for this or be subject to punishment. Similarly, they resent insincerity or selfish greed. In later regional folklore, the Deives have become associated with hags. One folktale relates how a woman, who was exhausted after many tedious hours in the fields, returned without her baby. In the morning, the infant was found slumbering, surrounded by gifts from the Deives. The mother went home joyfully with her child and told the neighbors. Hearing this, a rich woman of the same village left her child in the field overnight and returned in the morning to find it strangled by the Deives.
References 93
See also Fairy, Hag, Laumé, Selkies, Swan Maiden, Appendix 22

DEMOGORGON
This is the name of a terrible demon in the beliefs of Europe. The very name of the Demogorgon brought such dread in ancient times that he was rarely mentioned. He is named first by Lactantius in the fourth century A.D., and later by Spenser, Milton, Dryden, and Shelley. Aristo describes Demogorgon as the king of elves and fays of the Himalayas, but for the most part his abode is the "terrible abyss." He may be invoked just by the mention or thought of his name, and with it bring death and disaster to mankind.
References 40, 107, 114
See also Demon, Elf, Fairy

DEMON, DAEMON
In ancient times these spirits were called Daimon, and were of both good and evil dispositions. However, the term was later applied only to those devils of malignant intent. The Demons, or devils, have been described as the followers of Satan, and Fallen Angels who refused to acknowledge Adam. They are frequently depicted in the image of Satan, having horns, a tail, and cloven hooves. Demons are deemed to oppose the work of the angels, and to be the messengers of the Prince of Darkness. They do his evil work by bringing misery, sickness, disease, and death on Earth and luring mortals into sin so that their souls will be sent to Hell. They are also able to enter and take possession of humans and other creatures in order to perform more evil deeds.

Demons in Different Cultures

Buddhism: Although there is no particular place for Demons in the Buddhist doctrine, the existing evil spirits (e.g., the Yakkhas and Piśācas) of a culture overtaken by Buddhism were usually absorbed into the belief system. Demons in general are confined to temptation and annoyance of monks and sacred activities on the Indian subcontinent, while farther east the Demons of previous regimes assume a greater predominance. In *Tibetan* Buddhism, Demons are the agents of Khön-ma; they constantly try to enter and do evil in human homes, but the Demons are deceived by effigies in containers located above the house door and do not enter to wreak their usual havoc.

Celebese Islands: Demons are said to inhabit those dwellings not yet occupied by living beings (e.g., new houses), and must be propitiated by a priest.

Chinese Taoism: Demons or Kuei have been the object of superstition and dread for centuries and form a large body of tales in Chinese folklore. They are considered to be able to take possession of both the animate and the inanimate and inhabit all aspects of nature, either visibly or invisibly. Intricate ceremonies and methods have been devised and are practiced by the people and the Taoist priests to ward off the evil dispositions of Demons and their activities. In Amoy, Demons riding spectral horses are said to inflict disease on children with the purpose of drawing the soul from the weakened child. To combat this attack, the mother would swirl the child's garments above the roof of the house while a relative banged a gong.

Christianity: As with the angelic order, there is a Christian hierarchy of Demons, among them Asmodeus, Astaroth, Beelzebub, and Beherit, derived from the Hebrew debasement of pagan deities from the surrounding countries of the Middle East. Converted Christians often continued to believe in their pagan Demons, which were then absorbed into the folklore along with former pagan deities. Belief in Demons, fiends, and familiars in fact supported the doctrine of salvation and the purges of witchcraft and heresy in Europe well into the eighteenth century. Exorcism rites are still available in the Roman Catholic and Anglican churches, as well as in Orthodox and Nonconformist churches. Belief in Demons still forms a prominent part in the literature of European folklore. A Demon in eastern Russia took the form of a grieving widow who at noonday wandered into the fields during harvest time. Any reaper not able to avert his eyes would suffer broken legs and arms. The bark of certain sacred trees was said to remedy this evil affliction. In the folklore of Denmark, a type of Forest Demon hid especially in cherry trees with malicious intent toward any human that approached and tried to eat the fruit.

In ancient cultures, although not usually named, Demons appear to have been a part of the underworld regime of punishment, where they are referred to by such functions as the "breaker of bones." Others of importance are mentioned, such as Bes, Bebon, or Babi, the Demon of Darkness, but numerous activities such as misfortune and disease are attributed to unnamed Demons for which protective rituals have been recorded.

Greece: The modern "Demon" is derived from the ancient Greek word *Daimon,* which signified both benevolent and malevolent dispositions. From the more evil ones of that time (e.g., the Harpies and Alastor) later beliefs developed in Demons such as the Stringlos and Exotika of modern Greek folklore.

Hebrew: Belief in Demons is recorded very early in Hebrew writings, with references to Lilith and Azazel. The horde of Demons as servants of the Devil was later established as the Fallen Angels, and demonic hierarchies after this described the regimes of such as Asmodeus, Beelzebub, and Belial. The modern demon Shedeem can be traced back to Canaanite deities known as Shēdîm, mentioned in the Book of Deuteronomy, demonstrating a continuing tradition in both religious beliefs and accepted folklore.

Iran/Persia: Prior to the introduction of Zoroastrianism, Persian belief in Demons was of the Aesma, while the Dævas were considered to be beneficent (as in the Hindu beliefs). With the introduction of Zoroastrianism, the system was reversed and the Dævas became the Demons, created by Ahriman to make continuous conflict with Ahura Mazda and the Aesma. Demons such as Az are the result of evil thoughts and deeds of mankind; they haunt the most foul and noxious places, bringing constant misery.

Islam: Prior to the coming of Islam, Demons existed in the cultures of each society that were later either absorbed or dismissed as insignificant. A wide knowledge still exists of such Demons as the famous djinns of numerous tales, and evil spirits such as the Afrit and Dalham of the deserts, which have inspired protective ceremonies and provided a rich source of literature.

Japan: Demons existed in the early folklore of Japan mostly as nature spirits and evil spirits, such as the Kappa manifest in animal form. In the Shinto beliefs, the Demons are the Oni, who are mostly considered to be responsible for misery and disease. These rarely have a specific name but often, like Yuki Onna, take human form. There is a rich tradition of tales from regional folklore concerning such Demons as the Fox spirits, which are common to both China and Japan.

Middle East/Ancient Mesopotamia: Demons played a prominent role in the beliefs of ancient Mesopotamia.

The spirits were subdivided into those that were vengeful ghosts and the supernaturals. The latter category comprised dangerous spirits of deserts, wild places, and diseases, such as the Labartu and Lilitu, while others, such as the Lamassu, could also take the role of guardian spirit. Cuneiform evidence of exorcism and protective amulets form a large part of the archaeological finds.

Demons manifest in many guises throughout the cultures of the world and form the subject of numerous religious and folkloric traditions.

References 7, 23, 27, 39, 40, 48, 53, 62, 91, 92, 107, 110, 114, 126, 136

See also Aeshma, Afrit, Alastor, Angel, Ardat Lili, Asmodeus, Astaroth, Az, Babi, Beelzebub, Bes (1), Daimon, Dævas, Devil, Djinn, Exotika, Fallen Angel, Familiar, Fiend, Guardian, Harpy, Kappa, Kuei, Labartu, Lamassu, Lilith, Mazikeen, Oni, Piśācas, Spirit, Stringlos, Yakkhas, Yuki-Onna, Appendix 2

DEMON LOVER, THE

This spirit is the subject of many ballads in Scottish folklore. In the legend this "elfin knight" wins the love of a mortal maiden and they become betrothed. He swears that although he has to leave her for a while, he will return and they will be wed if she will be faithful to him. Seven years passed, and in that time the grieving maiden found another, married him, and bore a child. The fairy knight returned in a galleon with silken sails and golden masts, and immediately sought his betrothed, who was once more under his spell. This time he carried her off on his galleon, which, only three leagues from shore, sank forever to the bottom of the sea.

References 44

See also Demon, Elf, Fairy, Spirit

DEMRUSH

In the Zoroastrian religion of Iran, this is one of the fiercest Devs. These spirits, who are evil genii or

A devil receives gifts from witches as demons lurk overhead.

In the folklore of the Highlands of Scotland the Green Woman is a particularly malicious demon.

demons, are attendants of the supreme evil Ahriman, and are constantly combating the good works of the Amshaspands or Izeds. Demrush is said to inhabit a gloomy cave in which all the plundered wealth of India and Persia is piled.
References 114, 136
See also Amesha Spentas, Attendant Spirit, Deev, Demon, Genius, Izeds

DEOHAKO
In the beliefs of the Iroquois and Seneca Native American people, this is a collective name for the guardian spirits of corn, beans, and squash. They are usually depicted as three maidens dressed in the leaves of the plants they protect.
References 25, 87
See also Guardian, Onatah, Spirit

DERRICKS
The name of a type of fairy or dwarf in the folklore local to Devon, England. The Derricks' appearance is much like that of little wizened humans, and their disposition is tricksy. The people of the region are wary of these Little People as they are not particularly benevolent, and they are inclined to pranks such as leading travelers astray.
References 17
See also Dwarf, Fairy, Little People, Piskey, Pixie

DEVA
See Deev

DEVIL
Originally a Devil was an entirely malignant evil spirit, demon, or fiend, the Servant of the Devil; and in the Hebrew and Christian tradition, as the Fallen Angels were condemned to the infernal regions. Their particular mission is to lead mankind into temptation and sinfulness, so that human souls will be damned and claimed by the Devils' master for Hell. They may take any shape necessary to accomplish their task, but are generally described as having diminutive human shapes with horns, hairy body, tails, and cloven hooves.

In Europe, demonologists classified the various Devils by name into hierarchies in much the same way as the angels:

Binsfield (1589) classified Devils and their regions of temptation as:
Lucifer (Pride), Mammon (Avarice), Asmodeus (Lechery), Satan (Anger), Beelzebub (Gluttony), Leviathan (Envy), Belphegor (Sloth).
Father Sebastien Michaelis (1612) classified the Devils under their previous angelic status, region of temptation, and adversary saint:

First angelic hierarchy:
> Seraphim, Lucifer, pride; Seraphim, Beelzebub, (adversary Saint Francis)
> Seraphim, Leviathan, heresy (adversary Saint Peter the apostle)
> Seraphim, Asmodeus, wantonness (adversary Saint John the Baptist)
> Cherubim, Balberith, quarrelsomeness (adversary Saint Barnabas)
> Prince of Thrones, Astaroth, sloth (adversary Saint Bartholomew)
> Throne, Verrine, impatience (adversary Saint Dominic)
> Throne, Gressil, impurity (adversary Saint Bernard)
> Throne, Sonneillon, hatred of enemies (adversary Saint Stephen)

Second angelic hierarchy:
> Prince of Powers, Carrean, hardness of heart (adversary Saint Vincent)
> Prince of Powers, Carrivean, obscenity (adversary Saint John the Evangelist)
> Prince of Dominions, Oeillet, breaking vows of poverty (adversary Saint Martin)
> Dominion, Rosier, love (adversary Saint Basil)
> Prince of Principalities, Verrier, breaking vows of obedience (adversary Saint Bernard)

Third angelic hierarchy:
> Prince of Virtues, Belias, arrogance and fashion display (adversary Saint Francis de Paul)
> Prince of Archangels, Olivier, cruelty to the poor (adversary Saint Lawrence)
> Prince of Angels, Iuvart (no temptation or adversary recorded)

Francis Barrett (1801) classified Devils and their regions of temptation as:

> Mammon (Prince of Tempters), Asmodeus (Revenger of Evil), Satan (Prince of Deluders, i.e., witches), Beelzebub (Prince of False Gods), Pytho (Prince of the Spirit of Lies), Belial (Prince Over Vessels of Iniquity), Merihim (Prince of Pestilence Spirits), Abaddan (Prince of Evil War), Astaroth (Prince of Accusers and Inquisitors)

Lists such as the above were frequently the work of theologians, as were estimates of the number of the infernal host, which ranged from 133,306,668 (de Spina 1459) to 7,405,926 (Weyer). Devils have played an important part not only in the religious sphere but also in the arts and literary and social development of culture as entities of terror, veneration, or fun. In their diminished state, especially in Europe after the fourteenth century, Devils were considered not only capable of extreme evil and demonic possession of humans, but also as familiars, and even the subject of humor. A fourteenth-century Miracle Play describes them as: "Smooth devils, Horned devils, Sullen devils, Playful devils, Shorn devils, Hairy devils and Foolish devils."

Devils in Other Cultures

Cheremis/Mari: In the folk beliefs of these people of the former Soviet Republic, a whole system of belief involves elaborate ceremonies to acknowledge the everyday control exerted by Devils known as Chert, Ia, and Keremet, with appellations signifying their area of influence. The more venerated Devils were given the appellation *Kuba* (Old Woman) or *Kuguza* (Old Man). While some were definitely fearsome, others were regarded almost as family friends and benefactors.

Russia: In Russian peasant folklore (before 1917), Devils such as Bes and Zloi Dukh were envisaged as having a social order much like that of human beings with families, and engaging in the pleasures of smoking, drinking, and gambling. Their weddings were celebrated at crossroads, where the riotous festivities caused whirlwinds and dust storms. Snow and windstorms were the playthings of the Devil children. Devils lived in dark lakes, swamps, thickets, abandoned human abodes, and bathhouses, emerging from Hell through holes in the earth. Normally the peasants had amulets to ward off any evil intent, and only in the bathhouse were they at risk. Devils and evil spirits were most at work during the long winter darkness, and would put in an appearance at winter parties in the guise of a neighbor to cause havoc.

Korea: Devils play a particularly important part in the folk beliefs of Korea. A calendar system of "safe" and inauspicious days is learned by heart, and female shamans or *Mansins* become adept at propitiating the benevolent Devils and ridding the family of those that are undesirable, such as the Tongbŏp.

Morocco: In the folklore of Morocco, Devils take the guise of extremely beautiful women who will approach a man in the street between the hours of twilight and early morning. If any man is tempted to follow, he may be sure of a horrible end if, when plainly visible, she is seen to have vertical eyes and the feet of a goat.

As with other such evil spirits, Devils of some form feature in the beliefs of most religious and social groups, with an associated literature and cultural tradition describing their activities in relation to that of humans.
References 53, 56, 59, 75, 88, 91, 92, 107, 113, 114, 133
See also Angel, Bes, Demon, Deive, Djinn, Fallen Angel, Familiar, Fiend, Ia, Keremet, Spirit, Tongbŏp, Zloi Dukh, Appendix 3

DEVIL-FISH PEOPLE

In the mythology of the Haida Native American people, these fish spirits exist under water in the same kind of society as human beings, but have magical gifts such as

Bat-like wings, horns, and a tail are common characteristics of a devil, as pictured here.

shape-shifting and changing the states of other beings. A traditional tale relates how a shaman went fishing with his family and saw a Devil-fish, which he tried to capture. Instead, the female Devil-fish dragged him down to her underwater world, where she introduced him to her father, the chief. After a while, the shaman married the chief's daughter who had captured him. His human family, believing him dead, paddled away sadly. Years elapsed, and he became nostalgic and wished to see his mortal family, so he persuaded the Devil-fish People to let him go home once more. He and the Devil-fish Wife took many gifts and trade goods, and he was welcomed with honor. During one of the many feasts, his Devil-fish Wife pined for the ocean and slowly started to assume her liquid form, eventually slithering between the planks of the flooring into the water. To his surprise, the shaman changed as well, and he followed her silently back to their watery home.
References 122
See also Selkies, Spirit

DEVILET

This is a diminutive devil of inferior rank that equates with the cherub in angelic hierarchies. Like the cherub, it is portrayed as a childlike image, usually with a tail and miniature horns.
References 82, 107

DEVIL'S DANDY DOGS

They are a version of the Wild Hunt in the folklore of Cornwall, England; the demonic huntsman and his demon dogs are described as black, with fiery eyes, and breathing fire. They seek the souls of the damned and the unbaptized, chasing them through tempestuous nights to carry them off. The victims are doomed unless saved by the dawn breaking, a cock crowing, or saying their prayers.
References 15, 17, 18, 66, 87
See also Cwn Annwn, Dando and His Dogs, Demon, Gabriel Hounds, Wild Hunt

DEWAS

This is the genie or spirit of trees in the Buddhist folk beliefs of India.
References 110
See also Djinn, Hamadryad, Spirit

DGEN
See Djinn

DHARMAPALA
This is the collective name in the Buddhist beliefs of Tibet for a particular group of guardian spirits. The Dharmapala, whose name means Protector of the Teaching, are spirits who protect the faithful from evil demons. In Chinese Buddhism, they are known as the Hu Fa.
References 93
See also Demon, Guardian, Spirit

DHUNDH
See Dund

DIABLOTIN
This is the French word for a little devil or imp.
References 107
See also Devil, Imp

DIAKKA
This is a term invented by A. J. Davis to depict, in Spiritualist teaching, the imps who are thought to harass the disembodied spirits of mortals in "Summerland."
References 53
See also Imp

DIANCÉCHT
This is the name of one of the Tuatha dé Danann in Irish mythology and folklore. Diancécht is their magic healer, who could restore those slain in battle (so long as their heads were intact) and create magic limbs from silver.
References 88
See also Tuatha dé Danann

DIAVOL
This is the Russian word for a devil, also used to denote the Devil.
References 75
See also Devil

DIAWL, DIAWLIAID (pl.)
This is an evil spirit in the folklore of Wales. Diawl (the plural is Diawliaid) is a type of devil in the Welsh language.
References 59
See also Cythraul, Devil, Spirit

DICK O' TUESDAY
See Will O' the Wisp

DIEFEL, DIFLE, DIEVEL/E, DIJEVEL, DIOBUL, DIOFUL, DIOUL, DIOWL, DIOWUL, DIWL
See Devil

DIEVINI
The name of a household spirit in the folklore of Latvia. The Dievini are protective or guardian spirits of the house and family.
References 93
See also Guardian, Spirit, Appendix 22

DIFF ERREBI
This name is used as a euphemism in the folk beliefs and folklore of Morocco. Diff Errebi, which means the Noble One, is the polite form used for referring to a king of the djinns in order to invoke his goodwill and blessings. As with the fairies of Europe, referring directly to a tricksy spirit was considered likely to cause offense, thus invoking the spirit and resulting in vengeful actions.
References 90
See also Djinn, Fairy, Spirit

DIMME
This is the name of a female demon in ancient Sumerian mythology. She is a disease demon who brings puerperal fever to mothers who have just given birth, and sickness to their babies.
References 93
See also Demon, Lamaštu, Appendix 17, Appendix 22

DINGBELLE
This is a female gremlin found in association with the Women's Division of the Canadian Armed Services during World War II. These demons were particularly adept at triggering the public address system for disclosure of personal conversations, jamming the key mechanisms on typewriters when urgency was essential, and flipping photographs of a handsome officer from a girl's personal bag while on a date with her Private/LAC boyfriend, or vice versa.
References 87
See also Demon, Fifinella, Gremlins

DINGIR
In ancient Sumerian mythology, this word denotes any supernatural.
References 88, 93

DINNY MARA
The Dinny Mara is a type of merman in the folklore of the Isle of Man (United Kingdom). This spirit is also known by the variants Doinney Marrey and Dooinney Marrey, which mean Man of the Sea in the Manx language. He was regarded as more benevolent than the mermen of the mainland. However, no one was ever allowed to whistle onboard the ship for fear of attracting his attention, and with him, more wind than was required.

Some time ago there was a fishing vessel called *Baatey ny Guillyn* (the Boys' Boat), crewed by only seven single young men. Every time they set sail they made an offering of herring to the Dinny Mara, who rewarded them each time with a full net. The other crews were curious, and the admiral (fleet controller) requested that they show the others where the herring congregated in such quantity. Willingly, the young men told them that they had fished off the Calf of Man, and accordingly the fleet set sail. During the night, the Dinny Mara was heard by the crew of the *Baatey ny Guillyn* to say: *"Te kiuneas aalin nish agh bee sterrym Çheet dy gerrid."* (It is calm and fine now but a storm is coming shortly.) The crew drew in their nets and regained the harbor just as a fierce storm arose; the rest of the fleet was lost. Since that time the fleet controller has decreed crews should have both single and married men.
References 17
See also Dooinney-Oie, Howlaa, Mermaid, Merman, Spirit, Appendix 25

DIRAE
See Erinys

DIRNE-WEIBL
In the folklore of Germany, this little forest spirit is a type of Wood Wife who would emerge from the forests and ask travelers to accompany her, but would vanish, weeping, if this were refused. She is usually dressed in white, but in Bavaria she is dressed in red and carries a basket of apples that turn into money for the lucky recipient.
References 110
See also Skogs Fn, Spirit, Wood Wives, Appendix 19

DIS
In Teutonic mythology, the Dises are spirit maidens of fate and war, also known as the Idises, who usually appeared in human shape wrapped in dark veils. They could materialize to warn of impending doom, and one is believed to have assumed an imposing image to warn the Roman commander Drusus of his own demise.
References 53, 95
See also Alraune, Norns, Spirit, Valkyries, Appendix 23

DIUTURNA
In classical Roman mythology, this is the name of a nymph, also known as Juturna, who was changed by Jupiter into a fountain. She became the guardian of healing springs and wells, and by association, the protector against destruction by fire. Juternalia, 11 January, was a festival for workers building aqueducts and wells. She was also celebrated with other protective nymphs at the feast of Volcanalia, 23 August, for preventing fires.

References 87, 130
See also Chi Lung Wang, Guardian, Nymph, Appendix 21, Appendix 25

DIV
See Deev

DÍVE
See Asura

DI-ZANG
This is the name of the appointed ruler of Hell in Chinese mythology and folk belief. Di-Zang is also a Bodhisattva, and in this capacity he is the guardian of those human souls who will entrust him to guide them back to salvation.
References 93
See also Guardian

DJALL
This is a name for a devil or the Devil in the folklore of Albania. Another word used is Dreqi.
References 93
See also Devil

DJIN/N
(1) These spirits feature prominently in the beliefs and folklore of the peoples who follow the faith of Islam, especially of the Saharan regions of North Africa and some countries of the north and eastern Mediterranean. The name is variously spelled as Dgen, Dschin, Genie, Ginn, Jann, Jinn/i, Jinnee, or Jnun. It is said of the beings created by Allah that the angels were formed from light, the Shaitans from the fire of His anger, the humans from earth, and the Djinns from the Saharan wind (the Simoon). Taranushi was the first Djinn charged with controlling the rest, but like the Fallen Angels the Djinns rebelled, and Azazel and Iblis became their most terrifying leaders, opposed by an army of angels.

Djinns may be invisible or take any shape, including that of a gigantic human. They may be beautiful or hideously deformed. When a Djinn appears as a beautiful woman, the deception may be detected by noting the vertical eyes and the feet of a goat or camel. However, by the time a human is close enough to observe this, it is usually too late for them to be saved. Djinns may be beneficent or thoroughly evil, but even those using their supernatural powers for human benefit cannot be trusted. Djinns inhabit the desert; isolated, ruined places; or remote islands where they may be solitary or congregate to work mischief on the community. Their most famous descriptions are to be found in the *Thousand and One Tales of the Arabian Nights*.

When benevolent, they may fall in love with and have children by human partners. Their offspring can walk through walls and fly, and they age very slowly. Djinns can bring great wealth, beauty, and fabulous possessions to those they like or to magicians who can control them. To those they dislike or have been directed to harm, their powers bring disasters, nightmarish tortures, and horrifying death.

Morocco: It is believed that each human has their personal Djinn or Grine throughout their life, as well as independent Djinns who inhabit dark and isolated places. Earth Djinns dwell in drains, wash places, lavatories, cemeteries, and ruins. They are easily offended, and if the correct procedures are not taken before excavating for drainage or building foundations, they will exact terrible retribution. Water Djinns dwell by rivers, fountains, and wells, and are particularly malevolent toward humans, whom they will entice into the water for the pleasure of killing them. Tree Djinns such as Hamadryads inhabit trees and are usually well disposed toward humans, allowing them to rest in the shade they provide—all except the fig tree. The Djinn of the fig tree incites people to quarrel, and so the shade of this tree is to be avoided.

Egypt: The whirlwinds of sand and dust devils in the desert are said to show where an evil Djinn is traveling. One must take precautions against them because they shower people with stones from the rooftops, and steal any good food or beautiful woman that attracts their attention. Calling the name of Allah will dispel them, and the shooting stars over the desert are said to be Allah's arrows directed against the Djinns.

Serbia and Albania: Djins are evil nature spirits inhabiting mountains, lakes, and forests. They will terrify and lead astray any unwary traveler who does not respect the area of the Djin's control. A Djin inhabiting the woods near the Lake of Skutar would envelope in a miasma of nightmare visions any person who so much as touched a leaf of his forest abode.

(2) "Djin" is the name given by Elephas Levi as the "emperor" of the Elementals known as Salamanders.
References 36, 39, 40, 53, 78, 90, 92, 93, 107, 114
See also Afrit, Aicha Kandida, Angel, Azaziel, Chaarmarouch, Diff Errebi, Elemental, Fallen Angel, Grine, Had al' Khorine, Hadduok Ennass, Hamadryad, Iblis, Lalla Mira, Lalla Mkouna Bent Mkoun, Lalla Rekya Bint el Khamar, Lalla Zouina, Maezt-Dar l'Oudou, Malik el Abiad, Moulay Abdelkader Djilani, Nass l'Akhorine, Redjal el Marja, Salamander, Shaitan, Sidi Hamou, Sidi Mimoum el Djinnaoui, Sidi Mousa el Bahari, Spirit, Taranushi, Appendix 2

DJOK

This is a name for lesser spirits in the folk beliefs of the Alur peoples of Uganda and Zaire.

References 33
See also Spirit

DMU AND RMU

These are spirits in the ancient Bon religion of Tibet. They are described as bloated purple fiends that live in the skies and are subservient to the sky god dMu-bdud- kam-po sa-Zan.
References 88, 93
See also Fiend, Sa-bDag, Spirit

DOASYOUWOULDBEDONEBY, MRS.

See Bedonebyasyoudid

DOBBS

This is the name of a household spirit in the folklore of Sussex, England, who was also known as Master Dobbs. He was a type of brownie, and was said to be particularly caring toward humans in old age.
References 17
See also Bodachan Sabhaill, Brownie, Dobby, Spirit, Appendix 22

DOBIE, DOBBIE, DOBBY

This is a brownie, elf, hobgoblin, or household sprite of the counties and Borders area of northern England. The name is a diminutive and derivative of the name Robert, denoting a certain familiarity or patronizing attitude to these spirits. Although usually attached to a household, the Dobies were not as helpful as the Brownies and were considered to be rather lazy, gullible, and stupid. They might have a place in the house, but usually their abode was the barn or stable, where they could keep watch over the animals. The family Dobby would be invoked in times of trouble to be the guardian of the family treasures.

Unattached Dobies had a different character, and were considered particularly malevolent. They dwelt by rivers, isolated peel towers, and derelict ruins, where they awaited the lone traveler on horseback. Like the Buckie of Lowland Scotland, they would leap behind the traveler to garrote them.
References 15, 17, 40, 66, 123, 133
See also Brownie, Brownie Clod, Elf, Guardian, Hobgoblin, Sprite, Appendix 22

DÖCKALFAR, DÖCÁLFAR

See Alfar

DODORE

These are the Little People in the folk belief of the Malaita people of the Solomon Islands. The Dodore are described as having only one leg, arm, and eye each, and very long, red hair resembling a horse's tail. They could be malevolent, and were even known to kill men with their long fingernails, but they could

usually be outwitted. One tale tells of a man who made a sleeping mat from the bark of a banyan tree inhabited by a Dodore. The offended spirit appeared to him every night while he slept. One night the Dodore rolled up the mat with the sleeper in it and started to take it away. The man suddenly awoke and realized that this time it was no dream. He managed to grab a protruding branch of a tree as they passed, pulling himself out of the rolled mat to safety, while the Dodore went on heedless without his victim.
References 109
See also Biasd Bheulach, Cacy Taperere, Fachan, Hinky-Punk, Little People, Nashas, Paija, Shiqq, Spirit

DOGAI
This is an evil spirit in the folk beliefs of the people of the Torres Straits Islands. A Dogai can shape shift to any form, but it is mostly feared when seen as a beautiful young woman. The deception can be detected when its limbs bend backward or its head swivels around on its neck. It also has very long earlobes and very thin legs. The Dogai will terrorize and kill humans, particularly children, and bring disease. They will also destroy crops and keep the shoals of fish from the fishermen's nets.
References 88, 102, 109
See also Spirit, Appendix 22

DOINNEY MARREY
See Dinny Mara

DOM CARLOS
This is the name of an encantado in the Afro-Brazilian cult Batuque. Dom Carlos is supposed to have been a human who fell into a drunken stupor under a Jurema tree. He emerged from his demise three days later as an encantado of the Jurema "family" of spirits.
References 89
See also Encantado, João da Mata, Jurema

DOM JOÃO SUEIRA
This is the name of a principal encantado of the Afro-Brazilian cult Batuque and of the Sueira "family" in particular. *Sueira* is a colloquial word for *Suliera,* meaning a Southerner. He is said to have tamed the evil Exus, and his character is said to have been derived from Ogun, the Yoruban god of war. His "wife" is the spirit Fina Joia, whose name means Fine Jewel. It has been suggested that these characters have a historical development from the legendary exploits of João Fernandez de Oliviera and his mistress, Chica da Silva of Minas Gerais, during the eighteenth century. Dom João Sueira is associated with Saint John the Baptist, and his feast day is 24 June.

Other spirits invoked within the Sueira "family" are: Menino Agudui, Conceição Sueira, João de Ouro, Joãozinho Sueira, Leovergio Sueira, and Basilio Bom.
References 89
See also Basilio Bom, Encantado, Exus, Spirit

DOM JOSÉ
An encantado in the Afro-Brazilian cult Batuque, he is also known as Rei Florioano and associated with Saint Joseph and the feast day of 19 March. His "family" includes Zezinho.
References 89
See also Encantado, Zezinho

DOM LUIZ
An encantado in the Afro-Brazilian cult Batuque, he is said to be the transformed spirit of King Louis XVI of France (executed in 1793). This spirit was first received by Dona Maria de Aguiar, the *mai de santo* (medium leader of ceremonies) over 35 years ago in the city of São Luís.
References 89
See also Encantado, Spirit

DOM PEDRO ANGAÇO
A principal encantado in the Afro-Brazilian cult Batuque and a member of the Seu Turquia "family," he is equally important in the districts of Maranhão and Pará. Dom Pedro Angaço is associated with Saint Peter and the feast day of 29 June. Through his "wife," Rainha Rosa, the following are identified as "offspring" spirits: Esmerelda Edite, Moça da Guia, Angacino, Caboclo Nobre, Bombiero, Floriano, Pedro Estrelo, and Legua Bogi da Trinidade, whose own "offspring" belong to the same spirit "family." Dom Pedro Angaço and his "family" were supposed to have been "defeated" by Seu Turquia and banished to Maranhão to rule the spirits of the Codo Forest. Coboclo Nobre, his "son," was surrendered to the Turquia clan.
References 89
See also Encantado, Floriano, Legua Bogi da Trinidade, Rainha Rosa, Seu Turquia, Spirit

DOMAVICHKA, DOMAVIKHA
See Domikha

DOMIKHA
In Russian folklore, she is the wife of the Domovoi. The Domikha may also be known as Domavikha, Domavichka, Kikimora, or Shishimora. She is supposed to live under the floorboards of the house and emerge only at night to do her spinning. In Smolensk Province it is said that if the child of the Domikha is heard crying, one should throw a piece of cloth over the place where it is heard. The Domikha will not be

able to locate her child, and will answer any questions for its safe return.
References 75
See also Domovik, Kikimora, Appendix 22

DOMINATIONS, DOMINIONS
See Angel

DOMOVIK, DOMOVOI, DOMOVOJ
In Russian folklore, this household spirit, also known as Domovik in the Ukraine, is similar to the English brownie. The name derives from the Russian *dom*, which means a house or home. He is attached as guardian spirit to a particular family, and may be derived from ancient ancestor spirits. The Domovoi can shape shift, but is usually described as a little old gray-bearded, hairy man who usually abides by the house stove (a large chimney incorporating the fire and oven is central to Russian houses). Sometimes he was said to have a wife called Domikha, who lived under the floorboards.

The Domovoi loves fire and warmth, and if offended will quite happily punish the family by burning the house down. Naturally, the family always wishes to please him, so a portion of the supper is habitually left for him. When the family moves to a new home, the Domovoi escorts them with a brand from the old fire to kindle the new one. The Domovoi is never referred to directly, but always by some euphemism such as *chelovek* (fellow), or *Dedushka, Dedko* (grandfather).

He is particularly busy at night, and the groans and creaks of the house signal his activity, clearing unfinished work. Primarily, though, he warns the family of impending problems or defends the household against evil spirits or human intruders, even to the point of strangling them or boiling them to death. The Domovoi is also the means of foretelling the future: If a person is brushed by him in the dark and the feeling is warm and furry, they will have good luck, but if the feeling is clammy and cold, bad luck will follow. The Domovoi has favorites in the household on whom he always bestows good fortune, but those without his favor are likely to have tricks played on them.

It is said that the Domovoi and related spirits once resided in heaven, and that they rebelled and were cast out and fell to the earth. Those that fell into human homes were the Domovoi, who became benevolent toward their hosts. Those that fell outside the home but around it—the Dvorovoi, Bannik, Ovinnik, and Chlevnik—became quite well disposed to guarding their new residences, but wary of humans. Those that fell into wild places such as the Polevik, Leshii, Vodyanoi, and the Rusalka remained malevolent toward human beings.

References 29, 56, 75, 87, 119
See also Bannik, Brownie, Chlevnik, Dvorovoi, Ekkekko, Gobelin, Guardian, Household Spirit, Kobold, Leshii, Nis, Ovinnik, Polevik, Robin Goodfellow, Rusalka, Spirit, Tomtar, Vodyanoi, Appendix 22

DONA ROSALINA
This is the name of an encantado, also known by the name Cobra Grande da Lagoa, in the Afro-Brazilian cult Batuque, second to Japetequara in importance. Although associated with the cult of the giant snakes of the Amazon, Dona Rosalina as a spirit is noble and dignified, accepting tea and a pipe but spurning alcohol.
References 89
See also Curupira, Encantado, Japetequara, Spirit, Seu Turquia

DONGO
This is the name of a weather spirit in the folklore of the Songhay people of West Africa. The Dongo is said to be responsible for causing thunder-flashes.
References 119
See also Appendix 26

DOOINNEY MARREY
See Dinny Mara

DOOINNEY-OIE
He is a benevolent weather spirit in the folklore of the Isle of Man (United Kingdom). Dooinney-Oie, whose name means the Night Man, may manifest as the misty outline of a human shape, or as a gentle voice on the wind, and sometimes as a booming horn. Like the Howlaa, Dooinney-Oie warns the farmers and fishermen of imminent storms.
References 17, 18, 69
See also Dinny Mara, Howlaa, Appendix 26

DOONIE
This is the name of a road spirit in the folklore of Scotland. It manifests as an old woman or man, or sometimes as a pony. Unlike the other spirits that assume this guise, the Doonie is entirely benevolent. It will find and guide lost travelers back to the road.
References 17
See also Dunnie, Spirit, Appendix 24

DORCH
See Dwarf

DORIS
This is the name of a sea nymph or Oceanid in the classical mythology of Greece. She was the daughter of Tethys and Oceanus, also the mother of the Nereids by Nereus.

References 130
See also Nereid, Nymph, Oceanids, Appendix 25

DORMETTE, LA
This is the name of a sleep spirit or nursery spirit in the folklore of France. Also called La Dormette de Poitou, this fairy, like the Sandman of England and Ole Luk Øj of Denmark, ensures sleep and pleasant dreams for infants in their beds at night.
References 17
See also Billy Winker, Dustman, Ole Luk Øj, Sandman, Spirit, Wee Willie Winkie, Appendix 21, Appendix 22

DOTO
See Nereid

DOUL
See Devil

DRAC, DRACAE (pl.), DRACS (pl.)
These water spirits are a type of malignant fairy described by Gervaise of Tilbury, the medieval English historian. They were said to exist in the rivers and appear to humans in the form of golden rings or wooden dishes floating on the surface. In this guise they would entice the unwary, and when grasped would assume their normal form, dragging their victim under the water. The Dracs were said to entice suckling mothers and abduct them to nurse the fairy offspring in the depths of the rivers.
References 15, 18
See also Fairy, Nix, Spirit, Appendix 22, Appendix 25

DREQI
See Djall

DROICH
See Dwarf

DROWS
See Troll

DRUDE, DRUDEN (pl.)
In the folklore of southern Germany and Austria, this evil spirit is a demon that harries humans in their sleep in much the same manner as a nightmare. The Pentagram, which is said to be a charm against evil spirits, is called a *Drudenfusz*.
References 93
See also Alp, Demon, Incubus, Mare, Nightmare, Spirit

DRUG, DRUJ
In ancient Persian mythology, this class of demons was known by the name Druh (from the Persian *Drauga*). In the Zoroastrian form, the Drugs or Drujs are usually female demons in the hordes of Ahriman, said to dwell in caves. They were supposed to have been created by Angra Mainyu as the opponents of the Amesha Spentas, called Asha Vahishta. The Drujs are considered to be responsible for deceit, treachery, and vice. Three particularly evil Drujs are Azidahaka, Jahi, and Nasu. Later reference to the Drujs includes other evil supernaturals such as the Daevas, the Kavi, and the Yatus, whose chief was Akhtya.
References 87, 93
See also Amesha Spentas, Asa Vahista, Azidahaka, Daevas, Deev, Demon, Nasu

DRUGGEN HILL BOGGLE
In the folklore of this district of Cumberland in England, a story of the disappearance of a peddler in the nineteenth century coincided with the appearance of a Black Dog type of bogle that terrorized and attacked travelers in the district at night. This spirit was named for the district in which it lurked and was known as the Druggen Hill Boggle. The local people connected the incidents, and when the peddler's body was found and interred in the churchyard, the Black Dog was no longer reported. Furthermore, the injuries the bogle had inflicted on its victims at last started to heal.
References 47
See also Black Dog, Bogle, Appendix 24

DRYAD
(1) This was the name of a group of nymphs in the classical mythology of Greece and Rome. The Dryad's name is derived from the Greek *Drys*, which means oak. These nymphs were the guardian spirits of trees, groves, and woods, and would punish any mortals offering harm. They were the attendants of the goddess of hunting, Artemis (Diana), and to see them was considered unlucky. They could be propitiated with milk, honey, and oil. Sometimes they would perish at the same time as the tree they were associated with like the Hamadryads, but unlike them the Dryads were free to move from tree to tree. A famous Dryad was Eurydice, the wife Orpheus tried to rescue from Hades.

(2) This was also one of a group of nature spirits or Elementals defined by the mystical philosopher Paracelsus (1493–1541) in terms of the natural elements from which they were supposed to be derived. The Dryads were spirits of vegetation inhabiting the trees and fields.
References 29, 40, 53, 88, 93, 98, 107, 110, 114, 129, 136
See also Attendent Spirit, Elemental, Guardian, Nymph, Spirit, Appendix 19

DRYOPE
In the classical mythology of Greece and Rome, she was a nymph who bore a son, Amphissos, for the god

Apollo. When Amphissos built a temple to his father, Dryope went there and was carried off by the Hamadryads who had tutored her as a child, replacing her with a poplar tree in the temple grounds.
References 110
See also Hamadryad, Nymph

DSCHIN
See Djin/n

DÚC-BÀ
In the Annamese belief of Vietnam, these nature spirits are the Three Mothers, who are called Dúc-Bà, Bà-Dúc-Chúa, and Dúc-Thánh Bà. They are the Spirit of the Forest, Spirit of the Air, and Spirit of the Waters, and were supposed to have been created by the Jade Emperor. They are often venerated in small rooms in pagodas dedicated to the Buddha, and offerings are made to them locally as the feminine spirits of the trees.
References 87
See also Spirit, Appendix 19

DÚC-THÁNH BÀ
See Dúc-Bà

DUENDE
In the folklore of Spain, the Duende are household sprites or dwarfs that inhabit the fabric of the white-washed walls of the village houses. As nightmare spirits, they may disturb the sleeping humans of the house.
References 38
See also Dwarf, Nightmare, Spirit, Appendix 22

DUERCH/E, DUERGH, DUERI, DUERY, DUERZ
See Dwarf

DUERGAR, DVERGAR
These are the dwarfs of Scandinavian and Teutonic mythology who lived under the hills, in dark woods, and in the rocks of isolated places. In northern England they are described as the Black Dwarfs, which is exactly the meaning of their other Germanic name of Svart Alfar. They were said to have been created from the maggots that infested the body of the defeated giant Ymir, and like them, were intent on bringing about corruption and misery to mankind. The first of their kind was called Modsognir; others were Durin and Dvalin.

They are described as resembling very small humans, with dark skin, green eyes, long grey beards, stocky and powerful bodies, and legs with the feet of crows. The English description credits them with lambskin coats, moleskin breeches and shoes, and a green moss hat decorated with a pheasant's feather. Their magic cloaks rendered them invisible, but if they were ever caught in the sunlight they would perish and, in some legends, turn to stone. The Duergars were experts in working all metals, especially gold and silver. They made many wonderful weapons for the gods, but any that were exacted by force would bring calamity to the owner.
References 78, 88
See also Alfar, Berg People, Brown Man of the Muirs, Durin, Dwarf, Modsognir

DUGNAI
This is the name of a female household spirit in the folklore of the Slav people of Europe. Dugnai looked after the housewives' bread dough and prevented it from going sour.
References 102
See also Kikimora, Matergabia, Spirit, Appendix 22

DULACHAN
In Celtic mythology and folklore, the Dulachan is a malicious goblin resembling a Cluricaune. It is said to manifest as a rider without a head, and terrifies humans traveling at night on lonely roads.
References 41
See also Cluricaune, Dund, Goblin

DULE
See Devil

DUND
This is a horrifying spirit, also known as the Dhundh, in the folklore of India. The Dund can be recognized as it manifests in the form of a rider without hands, feet, or head. The head may appear to be tied to its saddle. It calls at night to the occupants of the houses it passes, but humans must not answer, because they will go mad or die.
References 87
See also Dulachan

DUNNIE
This is a mischievous, prank-playing spirit much like the Hedley Kow or the Picktree Brag. The Dunnie inhabits the area around Haselrigg in Northumberland, England. It will most frequently materialize in the form of a donkey, plowhorse, or pony to be harnessed by an unsuspecting human at the start of some errand. The human will usually be left holding the empty harness after being dumped in the mud, with the shape-shifting spirit laughing as it disappears.
References 17, 66, 123
See also Colt Pixy, Hedley Kow, Picktree Brag, Spirit, Appendix 12

DUNTERS
These are spirits, also known as Powries, that in the local folklore are said to inhabit the ancient, ruined

peel towers and forts of the northern Border counties of England. If the ruins are approached, the spirits may be heard in the depths making a noise like grain being milled through a quern or the beating of flax. When their noise gets louder and prolonged, it is an omen of imminent disaster.
References 17, 29, 66
See also Red Cap, Spirit, Appendix 23

DUOROW
See Dwarf

DURGĀ
This is a malicious demon in the Hindu religion, portrayed as a yellow woman riding a tiger.
References 87
See also Demon, Deev

DURIN
Durin, also known as Dyrin, is associated with Dvalin and Modsognir in Scandinavian and Teutonic mythology. These three powerful dwarf leaders are responsible for forging, by magic, many of the fantastic weapons used by the Norse gods. Like the sword Tyrfing forged for Svafrlami, any weapon demanded from them by force would ultimately kill its owner.
References 95, 102
See also Duergar, Dwarf, Modsognir

DURWE
See Dwarf

DUSII
This is the name given by the ancient Gauls of France to the Celtic hobgoblin. These spirits were also called the Pilosi, which means the Hairy Ones. It was probably a hairy type of household spirit much like the brownie of English folklore.
References 37
See also Brownie, Hobgoblin, Spirit, Appendix 22

DUSTMAN, THE
This is the name of a nursery spirit in the folklore of England. The Dustman is a sleep spirit who comes at night to small children, and by sprinkling magic dust over their eyes, like the Ole Luk Øj of Denmark, the children fall asleep. By his enchantment he ensures that they have pleasant dreams.
References 17
See also Billy Winker, Dormette, Ole Luk Øj, Sandman, Spirit, Wee Willie Winkie, Appendix 22

DVALIN
See Durin

DVERGAR
See Duergar

DVOROVOI
In Russian folklore this is the spirit of the farmyard. He hated beasts with white fur and would tease them, but he would tolerate white hens. Young calves and foals were not safe from his malevolence, and had to be reared in the farmhouse until they were strong enough to withstand the Dvorovoi's teasing. He could be appeased with bread and gentle conversation, but if he had been particularly vindictive, he could be punished by piercing the yard fence with a pitchfork or by whipping the air in the yard with a thread from a shroud. Although not normally visible, the Dvorovoi is said to resemble the Domovik. However, in one tale he materialized as a handsome young man with the capacity for human jealousy. When the young woman he had helped through difficulties on the farm planned to marry, the Dvorovoi strangled her with her own hair.
References 29, 56, 75, 88, 119
See also Domovik, Spirit, Appendix 22

DWAERUH, DWARGH/E, DWARW
See Dwarf

DWALIN
See Durin

DWARF, DWARFE, DWARFF/E
Dwarfs are a type of elf or goblin found in the mythology and folklore of most of the world's societies. In general their description is of a humanoid shape but very small, looking old and wizened, with odd-shaped legs and feet. They usually inhabit caverns and underground palaces or dark forests, and are often associated with watercourses. Their most outstanding accomplishment in most folklore is their magical gift of transforming metals into beautiful and dangerous artifacts that frequently carry some curse. They can shape shift at will, and usually have either a magic cap, cloak, belt, or ring that renders them invisible. They are the guardians of underground treasures such as jewels or precious metals, which they may reveal to the fortunate, or use as a lure for their victims. Although usually immortal, they may be tricked and immobilized, or even turned to stone, when the light of the morning sun falls on them.

Teutonic Dwarfs
On the Baltic island of Rügen, dwarfs are considered to be of three types, according to the color of their garments: (1) White Dwarfs, (2) Brown Dwarfs, and (3) Black Dwarfs. The White Dwarfs are gentle and pleasant of manner and appearance. They work fine

pieces in gold and silver in their underground forges all through the winter months. They spend the summer dancing in the assumed shapes of butterflies and other creatures until winter, when their work resumes. The Brown Dwarfs dress and behave in much the same way as the English brownie, except that they are prone to stealing human babies as well as playing tricks on their chosen household. They dance by the light of the moon and also create wonderful gifts in precious metals. When they favor a member of the family, they will leave fine presents and protect them. But if people are lazy or careless, the Dwarfs will bring them trouble and bad dreams. The Black Dwarfs are ugly, malicious, and of evil intent toward humans. They will lure ships onto rocks with false lights to plunder them, and lead travelers astray. They are particularly skilled in working iron and steel and fashioning the most dangerous weapons. When not thus engaged, the Black Dwarfs may take the form of a screech owl to fly through the night or sit under an elder tree in the long summer twilight. It is extremely dangerous for a human to see them. In other parts of Germany, the kobolds are the Dwarfs of the mines, whose expertise with metals and ore also extends to revealing to the miners where the richest veins are, and giving warning of disasters such as roof falls. Legend tells of the Dwarfs' King Goldmar and his brothers Alberich and Elbgast.

Scandinavian Dwarfs

In Scandinavia the Dwarfs form the subject of a large part of the myths and folklore as the craftsmen forging artifacts for the Æsir and Vanir. They are supposed to have developed from maggots that crawled from the body of the giant Ymir. There were three groups of dwarfs: Modsognir's folk, Durin's group, and Dwalin's alliance with Lovar. Their skill with metals extended to making replacement hair for the goddess Sif, Gungnir the magic spear, and the magic ship Skidbladnir which could be reduced to the size of a handkerchief. The Dwarfs were responsible for deceit, murder, transformations, and revenge. But of all the supernatural beings, the two Dwarfs called Dain and Thrain are the ones who will herald the coming of Ragnarok.

Other Cultures

In the folklore of the *Slav* peoples of central Europe, the Karliki, the Ljeschi, and Lychie are Dwarf mischief-makers of the dark forests. In *French* folklore, the Korrigans of Brittany are mound-dwelling Dwarfs, while *Spanish* folklore describes the wall-dwelling Duende as a Dwarf. These had the same habits and tricksy nature as their more conventionally-dwelling eastern European counterparts. *Welsh* Dwarfs are supposed to derive from human souls that were spat upon

by the Devil. *English* Dwarfs take many guises and names, from the Spriggans of Cornwall, Tom Thumb of folktale, the mine-working Knockers, the Northern Counties Duergar, and the Brown Man of the Muirs of *Scotland*. All of these beings dress and look like the conventional description, usually having long gray beards. They are sometimes helpful and sometimes malicious, often taking punitive revenge on those humans who offend them.

The most famous *Irish* Dwarf is the Leprechaun, dressed in dapper green; others are the Goibniu, the Luchorpain, and the Luchtaine. These have a prominent place in the folklore of Ireland; they are mostly solitary, and may work with wood rather than metal. There is a tradition of Dwarfs in the legends of the ancient culture of *Yucatán*, and in *Mexico* the Dwarfs are called Chanques. In *Native American* mythology, a rich tradition of Dwarfs exists among the Paiute, the Cherokee, the Cayuga Iroquois, the Seneca, the Shawnee, and others who describe these Little People variously as malicious and sometimes benevolent. Like their European counterparts, they are at all times tricksy and unreliable in their approach to humans, and to see them is often regarded as a portent of disaster. A tale in the folklore of the *Kodiak* people tells of good fortune bestowed on two hunters who found Dwarfs in a kayak on a fogbound lake and took them home to look after them. *Baffin Islanders* believed that a race of Dwarfs lived under the sea.

In *India* the dark, evil, underground-dwelling Dasyus resemble the Black Dwarfs of German legend, while Vamana was a Dwarf incarnation of Vishnu, who had taken that form to deceive the demon Bali. The *South African* Dwarf is the evil Uhlakanyana, part supernatural and part human. In *Zaire*, the Biloko is an evil tree-dwelling Dwarf. In East Africa it is thought that if a human speaks to a Dwarf, the supernatural will fade away to invisibility to escape.

Tales of Dwarfs continue to form a rich part of folkloric heritage, from the retelling (and Disney animation) of traditional stories by the Grimm Brothers such as Snow White and the Seven Dwarfs to the development of new traditions such as J. R. Tolkien's cycle of stories featuring the Hobbit.

References 26, 40, 41, 59, 69, 78, 87, 95, 107, 114, 119
See also Addanc, Alberich, Apopa, Bali, Biloko, Brown Man of the Muirs, Brownie, Chanques, Couril, Dain, Dasyus, Duende, Duergar, Durin, Dwarf, Elbgast, Elf, Goblin, Goibniu, Goldmar, Guardian, Karliki, Knockers, Kobold, Korrigan, Leprechaun, Little People, Ljeschi, Lovar, Luchtaine, Lychie, Modsognir, Spriggans, Tom Thumb, Uhlakanyana, Appendix 4, Appendix 22

DWEARF
See Dwarf

Dwarfs at work.

DWELLER ON THE THRESHOLD
This is a term invented by Bulwer-Lytton to describe a demon or elemental capable of possessing a human and subordinating the personality to its control.
References 53
See also Demon, Elemental

DWEORH, DWEORZ
See Dwarf

DWERF/E, DWERFF/E, DWERGH, DWERK, DWERUF, DWERUZ
See Dwarf

DWEROWE, DWERWE, DWERWH/E, DWERY, DWERZ/E
See Dwarf

DWRF/E
See Dwarf

DWYLLE
See Devil

DYAVO
This is a term for demons in the folklore of Serbia.
References 41
See also Demon

DYBBUKIM
This is the name of a demon in the Hebrew traditions and folk beliefs.
References 91
See also Demon

DYEVEL, DYEVLE, DYVELL
See Devil

DYINYINGA
In the folklore of the Mende people of Sierra Leone, these nature spirits are the genies that inhabit the rivers, forests, and rocky places of the land. Different types of Dyinyinga include the Tingoi and the Ndogbojusui, and if humans do not wish to have misfortune, it is said that these spirits must be dealt with boldly.
References 33
See also Genie, Djinn, Ndogbojusui, Spirit, Tingoi

DYN
See Vasus

DYNON BACH TEG
See Tylwyth Teg

DYOMBIE
In the folklore of Surinam in South America, this spirit of the silk-cotton tree is derived from a Dahomean forest spirit. Possibly the name of this spirit has the same derivation as the Jumby of the West Indies.
References 88
See also Huntin, Jumby, Sasabonsam, Shamantin, Spirit

DYRIN
See Durin

DZIWITZA
In the folklore of Poland, this forest spirit appears as a beautiful young woman hunting with a pack of hounds and a *zylba* (javelin). She may materialize suddenly and terrify anyone alone in the forest at midday or on a moonlit night, although no actual harm has been recorded.
References 110
See also Spirit, Appendix 19

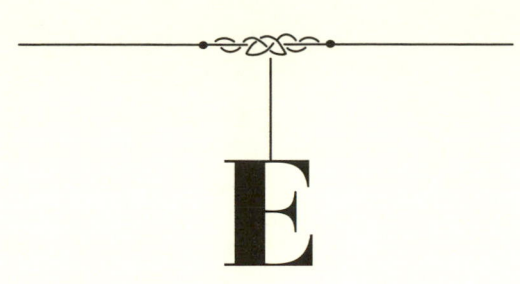

EACH UISGE, EAČ UISGE

This supernatural, whose name means Water-Horse in Scottish Gaelic, is a fearsome water spirit in the Highland folklore of Scotland. It is distinguished from the kelpie in that it only haunts salt water and the inland lochs, while the kelpie haunts fresh running watercourses. The Each Uisge is a shape-shifting spirit that sometimes appears as a handsome young man with seaweed in his hair, or as a bird known as the Boobrie. However, its usual form is that of a beautiful horse prancing on the shores of the loch. If anyone is foolish enough to mount and ride the Each Uisge, it will head for the water immediately with the rider fixed to its back and unable to dismount. The Each Uisge submerges to its underwater lair, where it will devour its victim, leaving only the liver floating on the surface of the loch.
References 17, 18, 87, 99
See also Bäckahäst, Büt Imnə, Cabyll-Ushtey, Kelpie, Näcken, Neugle, Spirit, Appendix 12, Appendix 25

EAGER

This is the personification of the Trent River Tidal Bore as a malicious water spirit responsible for floods in the region of Nottingham (United Kingdom). This spirit was particularly local to the bargemen working the river in the eighteenth and early nineteenth centuries, when warnings of this imminent danger were very necessary and took the form of calling to each other, "Look out! Eager is coming." It is conjectured that this spirit name may be derived from the Scandinavian god of the sea Ægir, who would have been familiar to the Danish invaders who settled the area after the Romans left Britain.
References 123
See also Spirit, Appendix 25

EARTH PEOPLE
See Honga

EBLIS
See Iblis

ECHENAIS

This is the name of a nymph in the classical mythology of Greece and Rome. She was also known as Xenæa or Lyca. Echenais was loved by the shepherd Daphnis.
References 102, 130
See also Nymph

ECHO

She was an Oread nymph in the classical mythology of Greece and Rome, whose body disappeared while her voice remained. There are several stories as to why Echo became a disembodied voice: (1) She pined for the unrequited love of Narcissus until her body disappeared; (2) She refused the advances of Pan, who bewitched some shepherds into tearing her to pieces until only her voice was left; (3) Her continuous prattling to distract the queen of the gods, Hera, from her husband's indiscretions, so annoyed Hera that she condemned Echo to speak only by repeating the last syllables that others had just spoken.
References 40, 78, 87, 114, 119
See also Nymph, Oread

EEYEEKALDUK

In the folklore of the Inuit people this benevolent spirit takes the shape of a little man with a black face who inhabits a stone. He is invoked as a healer of the sick, but it is considered dangerous to look into his eyes.
References 102
See also Spirit

EFREET, EFRIT
See Afrit

EGERIA

This is the Roman form of the name of this water nymph known as Ægeria in ancient Greek mythology. She belonged to the group of prophetic nymphs known as Camenæ and received offerings from pregnant women for a safe and easy childbirth. Legend

has it that Egeria favored the second king of Rome, Numa Pompilius (753–673 B.C.), with prudent counsel, thus giving her name to female counselors of state office, and was so full of grief at his death that the goddess Diana changed her into a fountain.
References 29, 93, 114, 129
See also Nymph, Appendix 22, Appendix 23

EINGSAUNG

In the folk beliefs of the Burman and Talaing people of Burma, these nats are benevolent house guardians that dwell in the south corner of the home in a post decorated with leaves. They are propitiated with offerings of coconuts.
References 87
See also Guardian, Nats, Appendix 10, Appendix 21, Appendix 22

EISENBERTA
See Berchta

EKAKO, EKEKO
See Ekkekko

EKKEKKO

A spirit of the Aymara people of Peru and the Mestizos of Bolivia. Ekkekko, also spelled Ekako, Ekeko or Eq'eq'o, is usually portrayed as a small corpulent man decorated with and carrying tiny household utensils. He is revered as a benevolent house spirit who can bestow not only good luck but also fertility. His feast day, formerly celebrated in midsummer, is now 24 January.
References 87, 119
See also Brownie, Domovik, Gobelin, Kobold, Nisse, Spirit, Robin Goodfellow, Appendix 22

ELABY GATHAN

This is the name of a fairy familiar invoked in magic spells in seventeenth-century England.
References 113
See also Fairy, Familiar

ELBEN
See Alfar

ELBERICH
See Alberich

ELBGAST

The name of a dwarf in Teutonic mythology. He was the brother of the dwarfs' King Goldmar and also the brother of Alberich.
References 95
See also Alberich, Dwarf, Goldmar

ELDER MOTHER, ELDER QUEEN

This is the name of the guardian spirit of the elder tree. She was revered as belonging to the Little People in the folklore of northern Britain and known as Elder Mother, Elder Queen, and Old Lady of the Elder Tree. In Scandinavia she was known as Hylde-Moer, and in Germany as Dame Ellerhorn, Hyldemoder, and Hylde-Vinde. In Germany she is said to belong to the group of tree spirits known as Waldgeister. In all these areas permission was sought of the spirit for any necessary cutting of her tree. In a field where any of her trees were growing, the surrounding earth would be left untilled, otherwise the Elder Mother would inflict terrible penalties on the humans and their livestock.
References 15, 17, 18, 44, 123
See also Guardian, Hylde-Moer, Hylde-Vinde, Little People, Spirit, Waldgeister, Appendix 25

ELDRICH/E, ELDRITCH/E

In old Scottish folklore these and the local names of Alriche, Elphrish, Elrage, Elraige, Elrisch, Elrish, or Eltrich describe a hideous elf-like spirit. It was said to inspire fear in any human who saw one.
References 92, 107
See also Elf, Spirit

ELECTRA

(1) In the classical Roman mythology of Homer she is a daughter of Atlantis and one of the nymphs who became the Pleiades. She is (by Jupiter) the mother of Dardanus, the mythical ancestor of the Trojans. Electra is said to have disappeared from the celestial constellation in order not to witness the destruction of Troy, and only resumes visibility occasionally in the guise of a comet.

(2) The name of a nymph in the classical mythology of Greece and Rome, one of the Oceanides, the wife of Thaumus and mother of Iris, goddess of the rainbow.
References 40, 130
See also: Nymph, Oceanids, Pleiades

ELEGBA
See Eshu

ELEL

This is the name of a malevolent disease demon in the folklore of the Puelche people of Argentina. Elel is also responsible for storms, disaster, and death.
References 87
See also Demon, Appendix 17

ELEMENTAL

A group of nature spirits defined by the mystical philosopher Paracelsus (1493–1541) in terms of the natural elements from which they were supposed to be derived. The defined groups are: spirits of the air, Sylphs; spirits of the earth, Gnomes; spirits of animal life, Fauns; spirits of vegetation, Dryads; spirits of fire, Salamanders; spirits of water, Undines.

Other malevolent spirits such as poltergeists and goblins are often popularly included in the list. These groups of spirits have been described in accordance with the "element" that they inhabit. The occultist Elphas Levi gave names of their "emperors." Their occult descriptions do not correspond with their mythological or folkloric characters and are for the most part much more inclined to malevolence or mischief. Elementals are supposed only to be visible to those humans having the "second sight," and are held responsible for trickery, cheating, and discord between humans, as well as inflicting irritations associated with the natural element involved.
References 40, 53, 69, 91, 98, 107, 136
See also Djinn, Domovik, Dryad, Dwarf, Elf, Faun, Gnome, Goblin, Nymph, Poltergeist, Salamander, Spirit, Sylph, Undine

ELF/E, ELVES (pl.)
This is a type of sprite or mannikin in British, Icelandic, Scandinavian, and Teutonic legend. The name may be spelled Ælf, Alfe, Alve, Elve, or Ylf. Originally the word in the Anglo-Saxon meant all types of fairies, but it later denoted a special class. This change of meaning was then adopted into the other cultures. Elves are tiny human-shaped supernaturals who can shape shift at will.

In England the Elf men are described as being like little old men, but the Elf maidens are young and beautiful, and they are believed to live in communities with kingdoms and kings in the same way as humans. They exert their supernatural powers over humans whenever they can, sometimes benevolently but more often with mischievous intent. The Elves live in the forests and woods, often in the hollows of tree trunks; they also live in old long-barrows and ancient burial mounds from which they emerge at night to dance in the grass by moonlight.

In Teutonic mythology the Alfar are subdivided into Dark and Light Elves who are malicious and benevolent, respectively. In German folklore the Forest Elf is called Schrat.

In Danish folklore the Ellen or Elle Folk are particularly malicious toward humans if seen in the woods. They reward a housewife whose home is particularly clean, but are prone to stealing her bread and other things from her kitchen.

In Sweden the Elves are known as Elvor, Grove Folk, or Grove Damsels.

In Iceland they are known as Spae-wives. Sometimes they will be friendly towards humans,

and stories are told of them asking for help, but the Elf community is usually quite independent and very powerful, taking terrible revenge on any human who offends them. They may steal babies, cattle, milk, and bread or enchant and hold young men in their spell for years at a time. An example of this is the well-known story of Rip Van Winkle.

So well known is the harm that Elves offer to humans that many conditions and phenomena have been attributed to them, as follows:

Elf Arrows—Neolithic arrowheads, supposed to have been shot at humans by elves
Elf Bolt—a disease of farm animals caused by Elf Arrows
Elf Bore—a piece of wood from which the knot has dropped out
Elf Cake—an enlargement of the spleen
Elf Child—a changeling
Elf Cup—a stone with a hollow from dripping water
Elf Fire—Will o' the Wisp
Elf Locks—tangles and knots in the hair caused by elves tangling the hair at night
Elf Marked—natural defects at birth or birth marks caused by mischievous elves
Elf Taken—bewitched or enchanted humans
Elf Twisted—said of a person who suffered a stroke; or of fasciated, deformed vegetation
References 7, 15, 17, 18, 20, 28, 40, 41, 59, 78, 92, 93, 95, 97, 107, 110
See also Alfar, Elle Folk, Fairy, Grove Folk, Mannikin, Spae-wives, Sprite, Appendix 22

ELFVOR
See Elf

ELLE FOLK, ELLE KING, ELLEN
These are the Danish forms of the English elf. An elf man looks like a little old man wearing a dark low-crowned hat, and sometimes he may be seen sitting near the Ellemoors. However, it is dangerous to go near him as he will blow his breath as a fog of sickness over any human who comes too close. The Ellewoman appears as a tiny, beautiful young woman who may be identified by her entirely hollow back, "like a dough trough." She is equally unlucky to meet and dangerous to approach. She will enchant young men, especially hunters in the forest, by playing the lyre and singing so sweetly that they are lost to her. The Ellen live in the Ellemounds in a human-like society with kings, celebrations, and weddings. They congregate for these festivities under the linden or lime trees, and no human is safe under these after sunset. According to the local Danish folklore of Store Hedding in Sjæland, the remains of an ancient oak

Elves make their homes in the darkness of the forest, old long-barrows, or ancient burial mounds and emerge nightly to dance in the moonlight.

forest are the transformed Elle King's soldiers, who resume their supernatural form at night.
References 110
See also Alfar, Elf, Grove Folk

ELLYLLDAN
This is the name of a spirit in the folklore and beliefs of Wales. Ellylldan is the Welsh name for the Will o' the Wisp who mischievously leads night-bound travelers into bogs.
References 17
See also Spirit, Will o' the Wisp

ELLYLLON
This is the name for the fairy or elf of Welsh folklore. The Ellyllon are described as diminutive mannikins that are very fair of skin and hair and dressed in beautiful silken garments which are usually white. These Little People are said to exist on "fairy butter" and toadstools. They live in communities in the hills, and on islands in lakes, where they may keep their fairy cattle. They are very keen on cleanliness and will reward the household that has a tidy home with gifts and good fortune, but will punish those that are dirty or lazy. They like human children, and if not guarded carefully, babies may be switched with changelings. There is a particular group of fairies that live on an invisible island off the Dyfyd coast called the Plant Rhys Ddwfn, which means the Children of the Deep Rhys. They are normally very tiny on their island, but they transform to the size and appearance of humans to do their shopping one day each week at the local market.
References 15, 17, 59, 87

See also Changeling, Fairy, Little People, Nix, Appendix 22

ELPHRISH, ELRAGE, ELRAIGE, ELRISCH, ELRISH, ELTRICH
See Eldrich/e

ELVEN
(1) The female form of elf used in England before the thirteenth century.
   (2) One of the three Danish names for elf, the others being Ellen and the Elle folk.
References 40, 41, 87, 114
See also Alfar, Elf, Elle Folk

ELVES OF LIGHT
There are two cultures using this descriptive name (translated from the original language) for spirits:
   (1) The English translation of *Liosalfar* from Teutonic mythology in Europe.
   (2) The supernaturals of Algonquin in Native American beliefs.
References 122
See also Alfar, Summer

ELVOR
See Elf

EMANDWA
This is the name of spirits in the folk beliefs and traditions of the Ankore people of Uganda. These spirits are protective guardian spirits of the tribe who are benevolent to the people.
References 33
See also Emizimu, Guardian, Spirit

Mannikins play amongst the mushrooms.

EMIZIMU

This is the name of the family guardian spirit in the beliefs of the Ankore people of Uganda. These spirits act in judgement of the behavior of members of their society and punish any transgressors.
References 33
See also Alastor, Emandwa, Guardian, Appendix 21, Appendix 22

EMPUSA, EMPUSAE (pl.)

In the classical mythology of ancient Greece, the Empusa is a terrible female demon described as having one leg of brass and the other that of an ass. Sent by Hecate, these demons could shape shift from the form of a beautiful seductive woman to that of a chosen animal which would patrol the roads and terrify travelers. In the folklore of modern Greece the Empusa is a shape-shifting evil spirit. She may manifest in the form of an ox, a dog, a mule, or a beautiful woman. She is a frightening spirit to humans who is considered responsible for causing injury to the sheep on the mountains in the noonday heat.
References 6, 12, 130
See also Black Dog, Demon, Spirit, Appendix 12, Appendix 24

EN

Originally an Illyrian god, he has, with the advent of Christianity, been demoted to the position of a demon in Albanian folklore. However, in keeping with his original status, his name is still the Albanian word for Thursday.
References 93
See also Demon

ENCANTADO

In the beliefs of the Afro-Brazilian cults of Batuque, Candomblé, Catimbó, Mina-Nagô, and Umbanda, the Encantados are spirits that inhabit the same supernatural universe as God and the angels in the Roman Catholic faith. They occupy a status between their human devotees and the angelic order. Each Encantado has a special association with one of the order of saints including their feast day, and the saint's image may come to be representative of the physical description of the Encantado. Some Encantados can be described in terms of their original form—they may be transformed "old" gods, historical personalities, folk heroes, or forest or animal spirits from another culture of West Africa, Native South America, or Portugal. However, they are mostly described in terms of their character when possessing a devotee, whose behavior will signify which spirit is in control.

The Encantados are allied in terms of either "families," such as those of Averekete and Rei Turquia or "lines" of status and affiliation such as the Falange de Bôtos. The most important Encantados are titled Rei (king), Raihna (queen), Senhor, or Dom to signify their status. They may also be referred to as Brancos, Orixás, or Gente Fina, while the Encantados of lowly status are referred to as Cabaclos or Pretos Velhos.

The Encantados are believed to have particular powers. As guardian spirits they will offer supernatural protection and, most importantly, cures for all types of malady. As demons the Encantados known as the Exus behave like poltergeists and can inflict mischief, disease, madness, or even death.

These spirits are invoked by mediums during a special ceremony called a *batuque* to take possession of the participant devotees. Within the different cults, the same spirit may have different names, but the main objective of the cults is to gain the Encantados' supernatural protection.
References 89
See also Angel, Averekete, Demon, Exu, Falange de Bôtos, Guardian, Poltergeist, Princesa d'Alva, Senhor, Seu Turquia, Appendix 5, Appendix 21

EŊER BODƏŽ

A river spirit in the folklore of the Cheremis/Mari people of the former Soviet Republic. If offended this spirit will inflict swelling of the hands or feet or even cause a human to lose his sight. Propitiation of salt and porridge must be offered for a cure.
References 118
See also Spirit, Appendix 25

EPHIALTES

This is the medieval European fiend of the night, known in Latin as the Incubus. It goes by different names in the folklore of each country. In modern Greece it is called Ephialtes, which means the Leaper. It comes to humans at night in their homes while they are asleep and leaps upon their bodies, transfixing them supernaturally. In this state the human can neither sleep nor arise and instead suffers until day break, when the demon vanishes.
References 88
See also Cauchemar, Fiend, Incubus

EPREM KUGUZA

A keremet or devil in the folklore of the Cheremis/Mari people. His name, which means Ephraim Old Man, is a derivative of the biblical Elias.
References 118
See also Keremet, Kuguza

EQ'EQ'O

See Ekkekko

ER OROLƏK

See Čembulat

ER TÜTRA

This spirit, whose name means Morning Mist, is a weather spirit in the folklore of the Cheremis/Mari people of the former Soviet Republic. Said to be present in the morning mist, the Er Tütra is responsible for the growth of the grain crops.
References 118
See also Corn Spirit, Spirit, Appendix 26

ERATO

See Muses

ERDLEUTE

This is the name of an individual dwarf in the folklore of Germany.
References 38
See also Dwarf

EREM ČAUGA

See Lau

ERGE

A demon in the folklore of the Basque people of southwest France and northern Spain that attempts to kill every human it meets.
References 93
See also Demon

ERINYS, ERINYES

The name in classical Greek mythology for the three avenging female spirits. Their names are Alecto, Magæra, and Tisiphone. These terrifying spirits are described as black, their hair and hands are entwined

with snakes, their faces are deformed with suppurating eyes, and they wear soiled robes. They pursued and exacted retribution from those guilty of blood crimes against the human family or people who had oppressed others.
References 20, 33, 39, 40, 48, 92, 93, 95, 114, 129
See also Alecto, Dirae, Eumenides, Furies, Magæra, Semnai, Spirit, Tisiphone, Appendix 22

ERL KING
A particularly malevolent goblin who is also known as Erlkönig, Alder King, and Oak King. He haunts the forests and woodlands, especially in the Black Forest of Germany, where he lures children and travelers to their destruction. This spirit was the subject of one of the works by Goethe and further popularized by Schubert's musical setting of the poem.
References 40, 92, 107, 114
See also Goblin, Oakmen, Spirit, Appendix 18, Appendix 22

ƏRLƏGAN KUBA AND ƏRLƏGAN KUGUZA
These are disease demons in the folk beliefs of the Cheremis/Mari people of the former Soviet Republic. The names Ərləgan Kuba and Ərləgan Kuguza mean Measles Old Woman and Measles Old Man, respectively. Their description and activities are identical with those of Šedra Kuba and Šedra Kuguza, who also spread disease by way of hemp seeds.
References 118
See also Demon, Kuba, Kuguza, Šedra Kuba, Appendix 17

ERLIK
A demon in the folk beliefs of the Altaic peoples of Siberia. Erlik is deemed responsible for human misery and for tempting the first woman, Edji, to share the forbidden fruit with her husband, Törongoi.
References 33, 93, 110
See also Demon

ERLKÖNIG
See Erl King

EROTES
Diminutive spirits in the classical mythology of Greece and Rome (and in Renaissance art) who were the messengers of Eros, the god of love. The Erotes, also known in art forms as Amoretti or Putti accompanied humans throughout life and guided the soul afterwards; in this guise they are genii. They were associated with Erato and Venus in their role of messengers of the arts and profane love. Their depiction in art, resembling corpulent cherubs, both in religious and secular works, reached its greatest expression during the Renaissance and Counter-Reformation periods.

References 62, 93
See also Cherub, Erotes, Genius, Muses, Putti, Spirit

ERYTHEIA
A nymph in the classical mythology of Greece and Rome. She is one of the Hesperides transformed into part of the constellation of that name.
References 130
See also Hesperides, Nymph

ERYTHESIS
See Hesperides

ESCHENFRAU
See Askafroa

ESHU
The trickster spirit of the Yoruba people of Nigeria, Eshu is known as Elegba and Legba to other people of West Africa. He caused discord and misery through his pranks and mischief-making but was also a protector of mankind against evil spirits and other dangers. As such he is the patron of mothers in childbirth and the miners of the Nigerian coalfields. Eshu is depicted as having an enormous lock of plaited and sculpted hair resembling a penis, adorned with the fruit of the oil palm, extending from the back of his head. Initiates into his cult both in West African countries and the Americas wear a mask or their hair resembling this feature.
References 24, 119
See also Anansi, Bamapama, Basajaun, Béfind, Blue Jay, Chang Hsien, Coyote, Encantados, Eshu, Manabozo, Mink, Oosood, Orisha, Pi-Hsia Yüan-Chün, Spirit, Trickster, Appendix 21

ESTANTIGUA
This is the night demon in the folklore of northern Spain. She wears white robes and appears with lighted candles, ringing a bell and intoning prayers for the dead. Estantigua, despite her apparently benevolent description, is a malicious spirit who attacks all mortals who meet her. The name la Güestia, by which she is also known, is derived from *Hueste antigua* (the Ancient host) of the Middle Ages, which referred to the host of demons.
References 88
See also Demon

ETSAI
See Aatxe

EUDORA
See Hyades

The Erlkönig entices children and travelers to his lair in the forest.

EUMENIDES

This is a euphemistic term for a group of spirits in classical Greek mythology. The name Eumenides, which means the Good-Tempered Ones or the Kindly Ones, was used to placate the avenging spirits the Erinyes. They were also known in Roman mythology by the name Furies.
References 40, 119, 130, 132
See also Furies, Spirit

EUNICE

The name of a nymph in the classical mythology of Greece and Rome. Eunice was a member of the group known as the Nereids.

References 130
See also Nereid, Nymph

EUPHROSYNE

In the classical mythology of Greece and Rome, she is one of the three Graces. Her name means Cheerfulness.
References 130
See also Graces

EURYNOME

The name of a nymph in classical Greek mythology. Eurynome is an Oceanid and, by Zeus, the mother of the Charities.

Sheltering from the rain, the Erotes with a broken bow will send no arrows of love this day.

References 130
See also Graces, Oceanids

EVAN
See Lasas

EXOTICA, EXOTIKA
A general term in modern Greek folklore for spirits, which may include the Dangerous Hour, the Nereids, and Stringlos. The Exotica, whose name means From out There, shape shift from the appearance of a Black Dog to that of a horse or a man and his bride on horseback or other human shapes, or they may resemble inanimate objects or be invisible. The Exotica are malevolent to humans and may abduct or torture and eventually kill their victims.
References 12
See also Bad Hour, Black Dog, Nereid, Spirit, Stringlos

EXU
A dangerous and powerful trickster spirit in the beliefs of the Yoruba people of West Africa, also assumed into the Afro-Brazilian cult Batuque.
References 89
See also Encantado, Exus, Spirit, Trickster

EXUS
This is a powerful and dangerous group of encantados in the Afro-Brazilian cult Batuque. They are derived from the Yoruban trickster spirit Exu and are also known as the Exun or *Homem da Rua* which means Men of the Street. They are considered to be demons and propitiation is made with offerings of rum, gunpowder, and candles before a *batuque* ceremony. This is done in the hope that these demons will *not* take possession of the devotees who do not want them. Possession by one of these spirits is characterized by wild antics and staring, unfocussed eyes displayed by the human, who will be "brought round" as fast as possible by the other devotees before any harm can be accomplished by the spirit. Principal spirit members of this group are Biranan, Cibiru, Exu-Mirim, Inambé, Pomba Gira, Sete Encruzillados, Tiriri, and Tranca Rua. Some devotees consider the Exus to be associated with Saint Anthony, and his feast day of 13 June is celebrated by them.
References 89
See also Demon, Exu, Spirit, Tranca Rua, Trickster

EZÚ
An evil spirit or demon in the Afro-Brazilian cult called Macumba. Ezús are similar in characteristics and activities to the Exus of the Batuque cult of the same region.
References 67
See also Demon, Encantado, Exu, Spirit

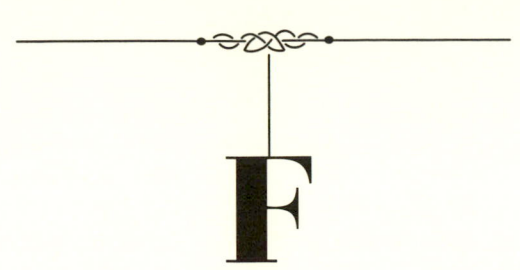

FA

This is the name of a spirit in the beliefs of the Benin people of West Africa. Fa, also known as Ifa, inhabits a celestial palm tree. He is a prophetic spirit, and certain initiated people may consult the spirit for knowledge concerning future events. This divination of the future may be obtained by devotees who throw palm nuts in a specified ritual and deliver their interpretation.
References 119
See also Spirit, Appendix 23

FACHAN

The Fachan is a hideous goblin in the folklore of Ireland and the Scottish Highlands. He is described as having one hand that protruded from his chest, one leg from his hip, one eye, and one tuft of hair on his head, all of which were usually concealed by a cloak of rough matted feathers. This is an evil spirit that belongs to the group known as the fuaths. The Fachan inhabited deserted places and would attack any mortal who strayed there.
References 17, 123
See also Biasd Bheulach, Cacy Taperere, Dodore, Fuath, Goblin, Hinky-Punk, Nashas, Shiqq, Spirit

FAD FELEN

A disease spirit of ancient Britain that is described as having a repulsive human form with golden eyes, hair, and teeth. The Fad Felen, whose name means Yellow Death, inhabited marshland from which it would emerge and fix upon its victim with its eyes. From that point the person was inflicted with the deadly sickness from which they rarely recovered. Maelgwn, a prince of the ancient Britons, is reported to have died as a victim of this spirit.
References 123
See also Hongaek, Y Wrach, Appendix 17

FAINGAA

An evil spirit in the folklore of Tongatabu people of Samoa. Together with the spirit Sisi, he pursued a man called Pasikole who had unusual yellow hair.

This human knew how gullible this pair of supernaturals could be, so one day he told them that if they each climbed into a basket on either end of a pole he would take them on a journey. As all that the spirits could see from the top of the baskets was the sky, they did not notice that they had been suspended from the top of a tree until the baskets rotted and they fell out. The two spirits went once more in search of Pasikole, who this time told the silly pair that he was going to a feast under the sea. Naturally they wished to go, too. Pasikole took them in his boat, and when they had reached the open sea he allowed them to go first in the weighted net. Now when human children see the phosphorescence glowing in the sea, they are told that it is Faingaa and Sisi trying to find Pasikole again.
References 109
See also Spirit

FAIRY

There is a long tradition in myth and legend of these diminutive enchanting spirits throughout Europe and the Middle East, although they figure less in other countries of the world. The Fairies may vary in their apparel and abodes, but in general they resemble tiny humans and are usually described as beautiful. They may be divided into two groups: Trooping Fairies, who have communities, kingdoms, and monarchies in the same fashion as humans (e.g., the Irish Sidhe); and the Solitary Fairies, who exist as individuals, although they may be associated with a particular place, activity, or family (e.g., Robin Goodfellow and Fairy Godmothers).

While most Fairies have a benign approach to human beings, they have a tricksy and unreliable character and are more likely to bring about magical mischief than to benefit any mortal. Indeed, they may kidnap a thriving human child and replace it with their own weakling, known as a changeling. However, where the poor, deprived, or unfortunate are concerned, Fairies seem to offer genuine, though often partially successful, supernatural intervention. This may take the form of money made from toadstools and coaches made from pumpkins, which unfortunately for the beneficiary usually resume their original state.

There is a further subdivision of the Fairies according to their character. The Seelie Court are those who are generally engaged in their own society, existing relatively peacefully within the human world and enjoying feasting, hunting, and dancing in the earth's rural idyll. The Unseelie Court, however, comprises those malignant spirits whose purpose is the destruction of humans at every opportunity. These are generally of ugly appearance, existing in the wilderness areas and places associated with bloodshed.

Fairies of Different Countries

England: Fairies play a prominent part in the English literature, culture, arts, and folklore from a very early time, such that their descriptions and activities are well established. Indeed, Spenser's work *The Faerie Queene* (1590) was dedicated to Queen Elizabeth I, and Malory's *Morte D'arthur* (1470) details not only the supernatural court of King Arthur but also the Fairy realm of Avalon.

The benign Trooping Fairies may be human size but are usually described as being very tiny. They resemble the human shape, but are always comely and dressed exquisitely in green, gold, or blue, their gossamer wings protruding from their backs. The Fairies can, however, shape shift to any form or render themselves invisible at will. An excellent account of them is to be found in Shakespeare's *A Midsummer Night's Dream* (1596), which also names their king Oberon and queen Titania, with Puck and Flower Fairy members of their court. This is changed in Poole's work *Parnassus* (1657) to Oberon as emperor and Mab as his empress, with Puck, hobgoblin, and Tom Thumb listed among the courtiers. The most notable of the Solitary English Fairies are Puck and Robin Goodfellow.

The Fairies inhabited kingdoms and palaces either underground, often associated with the ancient stone circles and barrows, or in Fairyland, where time did not correspond to human reckoning. Here the Fairies pursued activities and pleasures similar to those of humans but with supernatural speed and quality. They loved music and dancing and would often "invite" human musicians or dancers to join them, especially on the Celtic festivals of Beltaine (May Eve), Midsummer Eve, or Samhain (Halloween). Human "guests" who spent the night often returned to their village to be confronted angrily by their unrecognized great-grandchildren. Similarly, wealth and possessions "donated" to helpful humans had a horrible habit of either returning to the donor or turning into leaves.

Perhaps it is this unpredictability and humorous mischief that gives Fairies their enduring charm.

Wales: The Welsh Fairies are mostly known as the Tylwyth Teg, but other epithets such as Dynon Bach Teg, Bendith y Mamau, and Plant Rhys Ddwfn are regional names. They are described as resembling beautiful fair humans with golden hair. One group is tiny in size and the other group is up to the height of a man's knee. But as the Fairies can shape shift at will, they can assume an even taller form when necessary. They live on a mixture of milk and saffron, and their females may marry mortal men so long as their *tabu* is not broken.

Their king is Gwyn ap Knudd, and although the Fairies usually wear green, the king's courtiers are described as being dressed in red and blue silk. Lesser Fairies in local areas may be dressed in white, red, blue, or green, or even the homespun of the local Welsh countryfolk.

The Welsh Fairies inhabit lonely islands off the coast or in lakes, as well as the hills and woodland areas of the mountains, where they may be seen making music and dancing in their fairy rings by moonlight or in the mist. Any human caught in these rings will be obliged to dance for a year and a day, although he would swear that it was only minutes. A stick from a rowan tree laid across a ring may liberate any enchanted human, but any who plow through them is cursed forever.

The group of smaller Fairies is more beautiful and virtuous than the others, often rewarding humans for their cleanliness and hospitality, but they are inclined to punish just as severely any slight against them. The group of taller Fairies is more inclined to dishonesty and will steal butter, milk, cows, and goats, as well as babies, and leave behind their ugly changelings. Among the more common tales are those of the midwife and the magic eye ointment, and the unknown name, told of Sili Ffrit, Sili-go-dwt, and Trwtyn-Tratyn, which are common themes elsewhere in Europe.

Ireland: The Irish Fairies are called the Daoine Sidhe, who are said to be derived variously from the Fallen Angels, the ancient gods of the earth. But mostly they are the transformed legendary supernatural race the Tuatha dé Danann, whose deeds are recorded in the medieval Irish Books of the *Dun Cow,* of *Lecan, Lismore,* and others.

They inhabit the ancient *sidh* (mounds and barrows), lakes, and stone circles to be found in rural Ireland, in organized communities and kingdoms. Their kings are called Finvarra and Dagda, and their queens are called Onagh, Aine, Aoibhinn Aynia, and Cliodna. They too have their Solitary Fairies, of whom the most famous are the Leprechaun and the Banshee, which have a particular activity or are associated with a particular region or family.

These Fairies, like those elsewhere in the British Isles, can be benevolent to those who are kind to them, but they do not hesitate to wreak supernatural revenge on those of evil intentions toward them or other humans. It is commonly told that they will generously lay *bannocks* in the road for hungry mortal travelers, who are sure to receive a severe (invisible) beating if the cakes are spurned. Ever mindful of this capricious nature, prudent humans only ever refer to the Fairies as "the Gentry," the "Little People," or some other respectful euphemism.

In stature the Gentry are usually very tiny, when visible, and may be very beautiful, but they can assume any size or form. Their garments may be of the richest silks or the poorest rags but nearly always are emerald green. They love feasting, hunting, and above all, making music and dancing on the Celtic festivals. Although they may steal human brides and children for themselves, they are secretive, and woe betide any mortal who happens upon them uninvited.

The Isle of Man: The Manx Fairies were called Adhene and known as *Cloan ny moyrn*, which means the Children of Pride/Ambition, because they were regarded as having been Fallen Angels cast from Heaven but too good for Hell. They could be benevolent but were mostly mischievous in association with humans, taking babies or wives when they wished, although it was believed that their powers were not effective over any human on an errand of mercy. About the size of a small child when visible, they fished at sea and herded their cattle on the hills. The Manx people knew there would be good fishing or harvests when they heard the Fairies making storage barrels in the caves.

Scotland and the Islands: The Fairies of Scotland are also capable of appearing in any shape and size, but are usually recognized as being quite small human shapes. Often the females are extremely beautiful but malevolent. Their unpredictable nature is wisely placated by referring to them as the People of Peace or the Good Neighbors, while contact with the solitary Caointeach is to be avoided at all costs. In a work of the thirteenth century by Thomas the Rhymer (Thomas of Erceldoune, a legendary Scots historian), the Fairy Queen is described as wearing green and riding a horse with silver bells plaited into its mane. Thomas claimed to have lived in Fairyland for seven years, thus giving a rich description of these supernaturals and their powers.

Although divided between the Seelie Court and Unseelie Court, benevolent and malevolent groups respectively, the Scottish Fairies tend to be more aloof from human contact, preferring the more remote moorland and mountainous regions. They inhabit the hillforts, peel towers, brochs, and dolmens, emerging to dance, hunt, and make merry on the Celtic feast days and during the long warm twilight of summer nights. The long winter nights are the domain of the Unseelie Court, when wise mortals remain indoors.

France: The French Fairies, or Fées, seem predominantly to be female, as their epithets imply: Nos Bonnes Mères, Bonnes Dames, and Ben Socia. As all these names testify to their goodness, this also implies their fearfully unpredictable association with humans. There is a very strong historical and rich tradition from the earliest records in French medieval times, most notably the romance of Melusine, from whom the French kings were proud to claim descent. The Fairies could change shape, from looking like beautiful humans to hideous shapes or complete invisibility. They could be dressed in the finest garments or resemble the local folk. In Brittany, where the tradition of the Celts is strong, even their names and characters are shared with those of England, Wales, and Ireland in Béfind and Couril, who inhabit the dolmens and hillforts of those areas.

Spain: The Fairies are called Fada, acknowledging the derivation from the Latin *fatum*, meaning fate, which they could control by enchantment. Their description is much more of the Solitary Fairy resembling the local country folk, with a malicious ability for deception and vindictive spite even for their own kind. Some inhabit human buildings, while others, like the Basque Basa Jaun, inhabit the mountainous areas.

Italy: Like the Fada of Spain, the name Fata is derived from the Latin *fatum*, but as there is a vast classical repertoire of nymphs, the folklore of the Fairies does not have the same strength as in northern Europe. The Italian Fairies vary from the vicious Fata Morgana, equally at home in England as Italy, to the gentle Befana and Blue Fairy, who are entirely industrious and benevolent toward humans.

Germany: The Teutonic culture is rich in heroic literature in which the place of Fairies overlaps those of the Alfar and the Valkyries. However, the role of the latter as Swan Maidens recalls that of the Tuatha dé Danann. A further resemblance to the Celtic tradition is the Bazaloshtsh, meaning God's Plaint, who behaves in the same way as the Banshee. Other Fairies in the Teutonic legends reflect the regional winter traditions of the Ice Fairies and their queen Virginal's adventures.

Scandinavia: As with the Germanic traditions, those of the *Prose Edda* and other heroic literature of this region deal mainly with the deities and dwarfs. There is, however, some overlap with the Elle folk and the Trolls. However, some Fairies, such as the punitive Hyldemoer (Elder Mother) and other guardian Fairies, play a minor part in their rich folklore.

Lithuania: The Deives and Laumé are beautiful, blond, blue-eyed female Fairies transformed from

A fairy King and Queen receive fairy courtiers from their flower throne.

former deities and now assigned to give supernatural protection to human females.

Hungary: In Hungarian folklore the fairies are predominantly female, and individuals are venerated with the title Dame even though they may be a Fairy queen, as in the case of Dame Rampson. They are for the most part benevolent, taking a shape and size similar to that of humans but much more magical in appearance. There are others who have no love of humans, such as the Baba, who works any evil she may.

Romany Gypsies: There are numerous legends concerning the Keshalyi, who are the gentle Fairies of the Romany people. These Fairies have a queen called Ana who was forced to marry the king of the demons. It is through the story of her tragic liaison that the arrival of human sickness and diseases are explained.

Albania: Here Fairies form a rich part in the local folklore. Most are like the magnificently beautiful Bukura e dheut, meaning Beauty of the Earth, who lives in a fairy castle on the top of a mountain. They are entirely capricious in their relationships with humans and other spirits.

Persia/Iran: The Fairies of Persian mythology were called Peries. They were light, tiny gossamer creatures who were entirely benevolent. They existed on the choicest of perfumes from woods and flowers. The evil Deevs constantly tried to imprison the Peries in iron cages hung from the tops of the highest trees. If any Peries were caught, the other Peries sustained the captives by feeding them with perfumes, which repulse the Deevs.

Nigeria: The Dahomean Azizan and Yoruban Ijimere are the tiny gentle Fairy people of the bush and forests.

Malaysia: There are two types of Fairies, known as Bediadari and Orang Bunyian. The Bediadari are much like the Trooping Fairies of Europe, whose fickle benevolence requires respect; whereas the Orang Bunyian are a somewhat unsophisticated group whose mischief may easily be outwitted by a shrewd human.

China: Within the rich legends and folklore of the Chinese traditions, the lesser celestial spirits such as Chih Nü (the Celestial Weaving Maid) and Chu Pa-Chiai (the Pig Fairy) have the role that Fairies occupy

The Snow Queen, a Fairy Queen.

in Western cultures, with fewer powers than the gods but controlling the destinies of humans through their benevolence or interference.

Canada: With the European occupation of the New World, old traditions were transferred and modified such that in the mountainous regions of Labrador, Fairy beings called Apci'lnic were just as adept at stealing children as their European counterparts.

United States of America: The Native American people have their own rich traditions and mythology, including such beings as the gentle, beautiful Cloud People and Shiwanna, who shape shift into rainbow colors or remain invisible to work their magical powers.

References 17, 18, 28, 40, 44, 48, 52, 56, 59, 81, 87, 91, 92, 93, 98, 107, 108, 110, 133, 134, 136

See also Ad-hene, Aine, Alfar, Ana, Aoibhinn, Apci'lnic, Aynia, Aziza, Baba, Banshee, Bažaloshtsh, Bediadari, Befana, Béfind, Ben Socia, Blue Fairy, Bonnes Dames, Bukura e dheut, Caointeach, Changeling, Chih Nü, Chu Pa-Chiai, Cliodna, Cloud People, Couril, Dagda, Daoine Sidhe, Deev, Deive, Demon, Dwarf, Elle Folk, Fata, Fallen Angel, Fée, Finvarra, Flower Fairy, Gentry, Good Neighbors, Guardian, Gwyn ap Knudd, Hobgoblin, Hylde-Moer, Ijimere, Keshalyi, Laumé, Leprechaun, Little People, Mab, Melusina, Nos Bonnes Mères, Nymph, Oberon, Onagh, Orang Bunyian, Peri, Plant Rhys Ddwfn, Puck, Robin Goodfellow, Seelie Court, Sídhe, Sili Ffrit, Spirit, Swan Maiden, Tom Thumb, Trwtyn-Tratyn, Troll, Tuatha dé Danann, Türdér, Tylwyth Teg, Valkyrie, Virginal, Appendix 6, Appendix 22

FAIRY HELEN
See Tündér

FALANGE DE BÔTOS
A prominent group of encantados whose name means the Phalanx of Dolphins in the Afro-Brazilian cult Batuque. They are derived from the local shamanism of Pará, but are only ever described in human form. They inhabit the lakes, rivers, and coastal creeks of the Amazon Basin. They are regarded as gentle protective spirits. This group includes Belo Encanto, Bôto Araçu, Bôto Branco, Bôto Castanho, Bôto Preto, Bôto Tucuxí, Bôto Vermelho, Dona Dada, Dona Ina, Dur Encanto, João da Lima, and Parajito.
References 89
See also Mermaid, Appendix 25

FALLEN ANGEL
In the religious traditions of Christianity, Islam, and Judaism, certain of the angels of the heavenly host rebelled against the Lord, for which they fell from grace and were cast out from Heaven.

In the Hebrew tradition the Fallen Angels were identified as demons and devils in Satan's entourage of Hell and were responsible for inflicting misery and suffering on humans in the form of disease, conflict, and disasters. Their character and activities can be traced to the ancient pantheism of surrounding nations, especially to such as Lilith and Canaanite deities known as Shēdîm.

In the Christian concept of Fallen Angels, the disgraced spirits, when they fell from Heaven, scattered into the provinces of the Earth—the air, the land, the waters, and the mountains—as well as into Hell. Those that fell into the realms of earth became the Little People, the elves, the fairies, and other spirits who were too malicious for Heaven but too good for Hell. The most malevolent of them fell as demons and devils directly into Hell. While the folklore of the Little People constantly attests to remorse at their demise and the desire for a soul in order to regain their place in Heaven, the demon traditions detail only the Fallen Angels' allegiance to Satan and their place in Hell, even when being moderately benevolent towards humans, e.g., Asmodee or Angel Oliver.

In the Islamic tradition some of the angels also became resistant to the position of mankind, so Allah sent Hārūt and Mārūt as tutelary spirits to Earth in human form, where they used their powers to indulge themselves. As a result of this they were cast out forever from Heaven to join other Fallen Angels, such as Iblis, and undertook to initiate humans into the black arts.
References 87
See also Angel, Angel Oliver, Asmodee, Demon, Devil, Elf, Fairy, Hārūt and Mārūt, Iblis, Lilith, Little People, Spirit, Tutelary Spirit, Appendix 3, Appendix 7

FALM
A demon of the Scottish Highlands described by the "Ettrick Shepherd" James Hogg as particularly haunting the highest crags around Glen Avon. This spirit could sometimes be glimpsed at dawn, but his presence was so evil as to contaminate wherever he had passed until the morning sun dispelled his powers. Any mortal unfortunate enough to venture across his path before sunrise was doomed to an early demise.
References 6
See also Demon, Spirit

FAMILIAR, FAMILIAR SPIRIT
In general a spirit that attends a human either invisibly or in some recognizable shape. The term Familiar is derived from the Latin *famulus,* meaning a servant. There are two main categories:

(1) An attendant spirit whose role is to give supernatural protection, warnings, and advice in much the

same way as a Guardian Angel. The poet W. B. Yeats was said to converse with such a spirit, which took the form of a musk-scented miasma.

(2) A demon, devil, or imp that could appear in any shape. It was invoked through the black arts in order to do the bidding of the human, usually for divination, healing, or malevolent purposes, for which the demon received "nourishment" from its master. The term Familiar was first used in this sense by Reginald Scot in his work *Discovery of Witchcraft* (1584). Many of the witch-hunting episodes in Europe and North America from the sixteenth to the eighteenth centuries were considered "proven" by the presence of a Familiar (such as a cat, dog, bird, or hedgehog) in the household, or a mark on the body of the accused from which the Familiar suckled. Cotton Mather introduced this element into the detection of witches in America between 1563 and 1604.

In most of Europe, and for the Europeans of North America, Familiars could take the shape of any domestic animal or bird, as well as many of those to be found in the fields and hedgerows such as hedgehogs, frogs, toads, beetles, lizards, mice, etc.

In Wales, Familiars are mostly demons who are usually invisible.

In the folklore of Lapland, Norway, and Finland, Familiars take the shape of flies.

In Siberia the Familiar is known as a Yakeela, which may be required to combat the Familiar of an adversary shaman.

The familiar of Arab folklore is an attendant spirit known as a Tabi.

The Zulu of South Africa have the services of Umkovu or Zombies as their Familiars, while the Bantu Familiars, called Obe, take the shape of large animals, and Familiars of the Yoruba of Nigeria take the form of an owl.

In India and Malaysia the Familiar will take the shape of an owl, badger, or civet-cat.

In the New Hebrides and New Guinea a Familiar will take the form of a snake.

Native Australian Familiars are usually lizards.

Some Native American shamans' Familiars give voice but remain invisible.

The familiars of both the Inuit and Jewish folk belief take possession of a prepared inanimate object known as a Takela and Ob, respectively.
References 7, 40, 53, 59, 87, 98, 107, 113, 114, 128
See also Attendant Spirit, Badjang, Control, Demon, Devil, Guardian Angel, Imp, Obe, Tabi, Yakeela, Appendix 8, Appendix 22

FANTINE
This is the name for a group of Little People in the regional folklore of the Vand Province of Switzerland. They are nature spirits who are particularly con-

cerned with the safety of the herds in the Alpine pastures. The Fantine will ensure the safety of the herds by providing each cow with a bell to signal its location in the Alps. If propitiated properly these spirits will also provide the most favorable conditions for excellent harvests.
References 87
See also Little People, Spirit, Appendix 12

FAR DARRIG
See Fear Dearc

FARAONY, FARAONYI, FARAONKI
In Russian folklore these are alternative names for the Rusalki and Vodianyi. These terms signify, in popular Christian belief, the descent of these water spirits from the Pharoah's forces lost under the Red Sea while in pursuit of Moses and the tribes of Israel.
References 75
See also Rusalka, Spirit, Vodianoi, Appendix 25

FARRISTA
This is a term for an encantado group in the Afro-Brazilian cult Batuque. These spirits are boisterous and are given to carousing and vulgar behavior when in possession of a devotee.
References 89
See also Encantado, Spirit

FAT LIPS
The name of a spirit of the goblin type in the early folklore of the Borders Country of northern England. Fat Lips was claimed to be the companion of a woman hermit in Dryburgh Abbey in Berwickshire. The woman had lost her lover in the 1745 Jacobite rebellion, and as a result of her distress it was said that she had lost her mind. The woman became a kind of vagrant, settling in a cell of the deserted abbey from which she would emerge to beg for food. She talked to a supernatural companion that she identified as Fat Lips, who she said kept the cell dry for her by trampling the damp from the clay floor of the cell with his iron boots. (Iron boots are usually the footwear of the Borders spirits known as Redcaps.)
References 47
See also Goblin, Red Cap, Spirit

FATA
This term means fairy in Italian. These spirits figure rather less in the folklore of Italy than elsewhere in Europe. The Fata are almost always female. Notable tales are those of Fata Silvanella and Fata Morgana, who is reputed to cause the mirages in the Straits of Messina.
References 40, 87, 114
See also Fairy, Fata, Spirit

FATES, THE

In the classical mythology of Greece and Rome, these are the three spirits also known as Cataclothes, which means the Spinners, Parcae, and Moiræ. Their individual names are Clotho (or Kloto), Lachesis, and Atropos. Clotho is depicted with a distaff or spinning wheel spinning the thread of mortal life. They are usually depicted as old women who spin, measure, and cut the thread of life for every mortal. They are still propitiated in modern Greece at the birth of a child for good fortune and long life to be allotted to the infant.

See also Atropos, Lachesis, Moiræ, Norns, Oosood, Parcae, Spirit, Appendix 22, Appendix 23

FATHER CHRISTMAS

In English folklore this winter spirit of rejuvenation can possibly be traced to the druidic ceremonies of pre-Roman Britain and was certainly a part of the winter Feast of Fools, originating in the Roman Saturnalia. Father Christmas became the embodiment of joy and hope for the renewal of the sun and promises of spring. He inherited, like Sinter Klaas, the white hair and long white beard of Odin and, traveling either on a donkey or a goat, presented gifts to the midwinter revelers. From the fourteenth century Father Christmas was the presiding figure over the Mummers' plays during the twelve days of Christmas, and this tradition lives on in rural England. To English children he is the benevolent spirit who distributes gifts to each good child on Christmas Eve (24 December) in recognition of the first Christmas gifts to the Christ Child.

References 34

See also Befana, Father Frost, Julenisse, Knecht Ruprecht, Nicolai Chudovorits, Pelznickel, Santa Claus, Sinter Klaas, Spirit, Appendix 22

FATHER FROST

In Russian folklore this is the spirit of winter and is said to be a descendant of Nicolai Chudovorits. He inhabits the forests and the wilds of the Arctic Circle with his daughter, the Snow Maiden. Father Frost has a long white beard and hair and is dressed in furs. He roams through his forests, where unwary travelers may be doomed by his freezing embrace. But Father Frost is not an evil spirit, for on New Year's Day he and his daughter travel throughout Russia in their reindeer sleigh, rewarding all the good children by placing presents for them under the decorated tree in their homes.

One of the many stories of this spirit tells of how an uneducated girl living with her stepmother and two stepsisters was persuaded that Father Frost would make a suitable husband. The father of the girl, under the influence of his new wife, made no protest but took his innocent daughter to the forest to await her bridegroom. Chilled to the bone in the blizzard, when the spirit arrived she bravely affirmed that she was well, even though his embrace was cold enough to freeze her to death. Touched by her gentleness, Father Frost wrapped her in furs and gave her rich gifts that amazed and delighted her father when he returned the following day. The jealous stepmother encouraged her own daughters to take Father Frost as their husband in order to receive such gifts. However, when the spirit arrived they had nothing but complaints about the cold and discomfort, and when the father returned in the morning he found the quarrelsome pair frozen to death in the snow.

References 34, 44

See also Achachilas, Father Christmas, Jack Frost, Jüstə Kuba, Morozko, Pokšem Kuba, Spirit, Appendix 22

FATHER TIME, OLD FATHER TIME

This is the name of the European spirit of time. He is possibly transformed from the classical god Cronos (Saturn), whose own description is usually that of an old man with long white hair and beard carrying a sickle. Like Cronos, Old Father Time may carry a sickle or scythe but also has an hourglass. Wings sometimes protrude from his monk-like habit. At the stroke of midnight on 31 December in the Christian calendar, Father Time is eclipsed by the Baby New Year, which develops into Father Time as the year progresses, only to be superseded in his turn by the next Baby New Year.

References 87

See also Fates, Spirit

FATI, FATIT (pl.)

This is the name for the spirits of destiny in the folklore of Albania. The Fatit are sometimes also called the Miren. This Albanian term is the group name for the three Fates who, like the Fates of classical Greek and Roman mythology, are all women. They are portrayed very much like the fairies and are seen riding through the air behind the wings of butterflies. The Fatit come to the cradle of the newborn shortly after the baby's birth and determine the future of the child.
References 93
See also Béfind, Fairy, Fates, Moiræ, Spirit, Appendix 22, Appendix 23

FAUN

(1) One of a group of nature spirits or Elementals defined by the mystical philosopher Paracelsus (1493–1541) in terms of the natural elements from which they were supposed to be derived. The Fauns are spirits of animal life and dwell in woods and forests as the guardian spirits of the animals.

(2) Nature spirits, the offspring of the classical Greek demigod Faunus, which resembled him in their semihuman form with the legs, hooves, and horns of a goat. They are likened to the Satyrs and are guardians of the wildlife of the woods and fields they inhabit.
References 40, 98, 107, 136
See also Betikhân, Elemental, Guardian, Satyr, Appendix 12, Appendix 18

FAUNI FICARI

This is the name of evil spirits in the folklore of Sicily. These are evil bloodthirsty spirits or demons whose name means Fig Fauns. They are said to inhabit the fig trees, each one residing on a separate leaf. At Avola it is said that they will present themselves in the form of a nun carrying a knife to anyone resting in the fig's summer shade. If asked which end of the knife to take, it is prudent to ask for the handle, as the point will bring immediate death.
References 110
See also Demon, Faun, Spirit

FAY

See Fairy

FEAR DEARC

An elf or fairy, whose name means the Red Man, in the folklore of Ireland. He is also known by the names Far Darrig, Fir Darrig, and Fir Dhearga. This spirit may assume different guises in the various parts of Ireland. In Munster he resembles a wizened long-gray-haired gnome about 2½ feet high and wears a scarlet coat and sugarloaf hat. In this form he would arrive at a human's home and beg to warm himself by the fire. It was deemed prudent to let him in, for good luck would follow. In another guise the Fear Dearc has red hair and is a practical joker. But the Fear Dearc of Donegal can appear huge and dressed in red. In this form he is described as a prankster and enjoys invoking evil hallucinations for unwary humans.
References 17, 18
See also Elf, Fairy, Gnome, Spirit

FÉE

See Fairy

FEEORIN

The name of a type of diminutive fairy in the folklore of England. It is described as wearing a red cap and green coat. The Feeorin loves dancing in the fairy rings.
References 17
See also Fairy

FENE

The name of a demon in the folklore of Hungary. It was once greatly feared but is now diminished to a status of no importance. The folk memory of it is perpetuated, however, and its evil practices live on in such expressions as *"Egye meg a fene"* ("Fene eat you").
References 77
See also Demon

FENODYREE, FENODEREE

In the Manx folklore of the Isle of Man (United Kingdom), this is a type of brownie or hobgoblin. The Fenodyree is also known as Finnoderee, Fynnoderee, Phynnodderee, and *Yn Foldyr Gastey*, which mean the Nimble Mower. It is described as a huge hairy being that is amazingly strong and very ugly. He was said to have been one of the Ferrishyn transformed as a punishment for falling in love with a human girl in the Glen of Rushen and missing the appointed revels of his own kind. The Fenodyree, like all brownies, works extremely hard at farm tasks such as herding, mowing, reaping, and threshing, all accomplished between dusk and dawn. His only reward was the comfort of his food and drink from the farm. A grateful farmer innocently lost the services of Fenodyree by offering as a reward the insult that all brownies fear, a suit of new clothes.

References 17, 18, 41, 81, 110
See also Brownie, Hobgoblin, Appendix 22

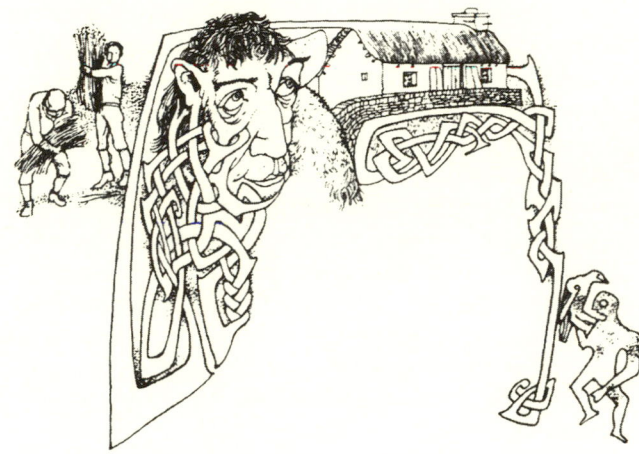

FERIERS, FERISHERS

A local name for a type of fairy in the county of Suffolk, England. They are described as tiny, sandy-colored Little People with sandy, long hair and are sometimes dressed in green coats with golden belts and yellow satin shoes. The Feriers enter human homes through the cracks in the floorboards and will bring in firewood and gifts of money for those humans who are tidy and clean. If the recipient discloses the secret of their good fortune, then the Feriers will depart, leaving misfortune instead. Like all fairies, they have a liking for human infants, and given the chance will steal a baby, leaving a changeling in its place. An account from about 1840, related by a lady 80 years old, tells how as a baby she was nearly abducted in this way. Her mother saw the Feriers in the moonlight with her child, and being discovered, they fled through the floorboards. After that her mother kept her child pinned to the bed sheets while sleeping between herself and her husband.

References 133
See also Changeling, Fairy, Little People, Appendix 22

FEROHERS

This is the collective name for the Guardian Angels and attendant spirits of Ormuzd in the Zoroastrian religion of Iran.

References 78
See also Attendant Spirit, Guardian Angel

FER-SIDHE

This is another euphemistic name in the Irish folklore for the male members of the Sidhe and the Tuatha dé Danann. Fer-Sidhe means Man of the Hill or Mound.
References 125
See also Sidhe, Tuatha dé Danann

FIDEAL

The name of a malignant demon in the folklore of Scotland. It was said to inhabit the waters of the Gairloch. This female water spirit preyed upon any mortal foolish enough to venture by the loch alone. But Fideal was destroyed by Ewen when she tried to devour him under the loch, as she had done with all her other victims.
References 17
See also Demon, Spirit, Appendix 25

FIELD SPIRIT

The Field Spirit is most frequently the guardian spirit or fertility spirit of agricultural fields and especially of grain crops. In this respect they are closely associated with the Corn Spirits; occasionally they are one and the same. Field Spirits are to be found in every society with an agricultural tradition. This spirit may be envisaged in a human form, but it is more usually considered to manifest in the shape of an animal such as a wolf, a goat, a dog, or a deer. The presence of the spirit is signified by the rippling movement of the crop as the wind blows through it in the field, or by a sound made in the fields, or by conditions of the crop or herds that it protects. The character of the spirits ranges from the gentle benevolent fairy that cares devotedly for the field to malignant evil devils that intimidate the humans, who must then propitiate the spirits to prevent any damage they threaten to inflict.
References 87
See also Corn Spirit, Devil, Fairy, Guardian, Spirit, Appendix 18

FIEND

This is a designation for a demon, a devil, or some totally evil spirit from Hell having only ever-malicious intent. It is an ancient term for an evil being and has many variants of which the following—Feigne, Feint, Fend/e, Feond/e, Feont, Feynd, Find/e, Fint, Fiond, Fond, Fynd/e, Fynt, Veond, and Vyend—may be seen in manuscripts from different periods. Fiends may appear in any guise, but they are usually in the form of a human or a dog, or they may be invisible.

Some Fiends of different cultures described in this book are: Aesma, Aeshma, Amaimon, Asmodeus,

Astarotte, Barbason, Barguest, Belial, Billy Blin, Black Dogs, Black Shuck, Cauchemar, Davy Jones, Ephialtes, Flibbertigibbet, Freybug, Ghul-I-Beaban, Hantu Ribut, Harry-ca-nab, Incubus, Karina, Kelpy, Mara, Mahr, Mauthe Dhoog, Nightmare, Old Man of the Sea, Rongeur d'Os, Smolenkos, Succubus, Tom Dockin, and Vatak.
References 40, 52, 107
See also Demon, Devil, Imp, Spirit

FIFINELLA

A female spirit of the Gremlin type in the folklore of the British, American, and Canadian armed forces. This spirit is closely related to the Dingbelle. Although invisible, this sprite was able to tickle Air Force bombers and pilots just as their target coordinates were correct, thus causing an overshoot or an abort.
References 87
See also Dingbelle, Gremlins, Spirit, Sprite

FIGONA

These are nature spirits, in the beliefs of the San Cristoval Islanders of Melanesia. The Figona are also known as Higona or Hi'ona by the Arosi people and as Vigona by the people of Florida Island in Melanesia. They may be invisible or take the shape of snakes or stones. Their chief is called Aguna or Agunua.
References 87, 88
See also Spirit

FIN FOLK

In the folklore of the Shetland and Orkney Islands (United Kingdom), these are a race of supernaturals that inhabit the seabed and sunken offshore islands, such as Eynhallow. Selkies and mermaids are members of the Fin Folk. Unlike the mermaids, however, Fin Wives grew old and ugly, so Fin Men were in the habit of stealing human wives. One famous tale tells of Evie, a fisherman whose wife was stolen. He went secretly and performed the sacred rites at the Odin Stone at the Stones of Stenness, to be able to see the island home of the Fin Folk called Eynhallow. The story continues with the fight on his way to rescue his wife and tells how he finally outwitted the Fin Folk.
References 47, 132
See also Mermaid, Merrow, Selkies, Appendix 25

FINA JOIA
See Dom João Sueira

FINIS

This is the name of a spirit in the folklore of the Orkney and Shetland Islands off the north coast of Scotland. Finis is said to be the offspring of a Kunal

A fiend huddles near a fire of burning bones and skulls.

Crashing over the waves, a Fin Man catches a ride a top a dolphin.

Trow and a sorceress. It is thought only to appear in the likeness of a person about to die. Its name is interesting in that *finis* is the Latin word denoting the limit or end.
References 17
See also Spirit, Troll, Trow

FINN BHEARA, FINBEARA
See Finvarra

FINNODEREE
See Fenodyree

FINVARRA, FINVARA
Finvarra is the king of the Connaught Fairies in the mythology and folklore of Ireland. His name may also be spelled Finn Bheara, Finbeara, or Fionnbharr. Onagh is his consort, and together they are the supreme King and Queen of the Sídhe in Irish folklore. Other noble supernaturals, such as the tributary provincial queens Cliodna, Aoibhinn, and Aine, owe them allegiance. Finvarra is famed for his benevolence toward humans in his domain at Cnoc Meadha in Galway. He will ensure good harvests, fine bred horses, and riches for those who are not afraid to assist him. He was prone to carrying off any young wife he desired. In one story he kidnapped Etain, the wife of the Lord Kirwan. This led to his becoming the patron and guardian spirit of the family and all their possessions after returning her unharmed.
References 17, 88, 105
See also Aoibhinn, Cliodna, Fairy, Guardian, Onagh, Sídhe, Spirit

FINZ-WEIBL
See Moss Folk

FIONNBHARR
See Finvarra

FIR BHOLG, FIR BOLGS
In the folklore and traditions of Ireland, these were the first inhabitants before being defeated by the Tuatha dé Danann. The Fir Bolgs were really three tribes called the Fir Domnann (the Men of Domnu) of North Munster, Fir Gaillion (the Men of Gaillion) of South Munster, and the Fir Bolgs (the Men of Bolg) of Connaught. They were thickset and dark, giving rise to the names Corca-Oidce (People of Darkness) and Corca-Duibhne (People of the Night). After their defeat they retreated to the mountains, caves, and forests, where they practiced their magic arts and became the first grotesque Little People of Ireland.
References 17, 18, 125
See also Little People, Tuatha dé Danann

FIR CHLIS
In the folklore of the Highlands of Scotland, the aurora borealis was considered to be the manifestation of Fallen Angels, whose fall from grace had been suspended between heaven and the earth. They were also known as the Merry Dancers and the Nimble Men.
References 17
See also Fallen Angel, Perry Dancers

FIR DARRIG, FIR DHEARGA
See Fear Dearc

FIRE DRAKE
In the folklore of the Fens of England, this fiery spirit may manifest as a snake or flying fiery dragon over marshes, where it is said to be guarding treasure. It is a manifestation of the Ignis Fatuus or Will o' the Wisp.
References 107
See also Aitvaras, Spirit, Will o' the Wisp, Appendix 21

FIRTOS
See Tündér

FITTLETROT
See Whoopity Stoorie

FJALAR
An evil dwarf in Nordic mythology who, with Galar, murdered the wise and gentle man called Kvasir, collecting his blood and making it into a magic mead. All who drank this potion gained the gifts of eloquence, and soon the dwarfs' fame spread. They invited to feast, and again murdered, the giant Gilling and his wife. Suttung, the giant's nephew, became suspicious and took revenge upon the dwarfs

by taking away the magic potion, which became known as Suttung's mead.
References 41, 95
See also Dwarf, Galar

FLAGAE
Prophetic familiar spirits in the folk beliefs of medieval Europe. It is said that they are only visible through a mirror, by which means they may reveal future events.
References 53
See also Familiar, Spirit, Appendix 23

FLANNEL FLOWER BABIES
See Gumnut Babies

FLAY-BOGGART
In English folklore a frightening bogie or boggart.
References 17, 107
See also Boggart, Bogie

FLIBBERTIGIBBET
A spirit in English folklore, which may be found in texts with the variant spellings Flebergebet, Flibbergib/be, Flibber de jibb, Flibirgibbit, and Flybbergybe. The name may be applied in two different ways:
   (1) An alternative name for Puck;
   (2) The name of a fiend identified by Harsnet (1603) as one of the demons cast out by Jesuits at an exorcism, and named in Shakespeare's *King Lear* (1608) as possessing "poor Tom."
References 40, 107
See also Demon, Fiend, Puck, Spirit

FLINT BOYS
See Grandmother Fire

FLOWER FAIRY
In the folklore and literature of England, especially of the sixteenth and seventeenth centuries, Flower Fairies were in constant attendance of the Fairy King and Queen in the rural idyll as nature spirits. Their role was further defined in the later Victorian and Edwardian (nineteenth and early twentieth centuries) concepts as painting the most brilliant blossoms, guarding the roses, giving perfume to the night air, and promoting the fertility of the countryside. They were tiny delicate spirits, dressed in the colors of their guardian flower, with shimmering translucent wings. They danced in the summer dew and were the patrons of all young lovers. When these fairies quarreled or were slighted by man, then the crops and flowers would be blighted or covered in mildew. Shakespeare gave these spirits a prominent part in his *A Midsummer Night's Dream* (1596). They later became a feature of the books of May Gibbs with the tales of

Bib and Bub and other Australian bush Flower Fairies in the stories of Snugglepot and Cuddlepie.
References 1, 41
See also Fairy, Gumnut Babies, Spirit, Appendix 18

FODDEN SKEMAEND
See Troll

FOLIOTS
This is a type of spirit in Italian folklore described by Robert Burton (1577–1640) in his *The Anatomy of Melancholy*. Although able to shape shift to the form of a crow, hare, or black dog, the Foliots appear to have behaved like poltergeists in the ruins they inhabited, without offering real harm.
References 17
See also Black Dog, Poltergeist, Spirit, Appendix 12

FOLLET
See Incubus

FOLLETTO
See Incubus

FOMAGATA
This is the name of a demon in the ancient mythology of the Chibcha people of central Colombia. Fomagata was a weather spirit who was responsible for violent storms. He was defeated by the sun god Bochica.
References 56
See also Demon, Spirit, Appendix 26

FOMHÓIRE
See Formor/Formorian

FORCAS, FORAS
This is the name of a powerful demon in European medieval demonology. He was also known as Furcas.
References 53
See also Demon

FOREST FOLK
See Moss Folk

FORMOR, FORMORIAN
In the folklore and legend of Ireland, this race, also known as the Fomhóire, was deemed to be the original people of the land. They were defeated and transformed into grotesque demons by the invading Firbolgs, who were themselves defeated by the Tuatha dé Danann. The Formorians are often identified as weather spirits associated with storms, fog, and blighted crops.
References 17, 88, 93, 105
See also Demon, Fir Bholg, Spirit, Tuatha dé Danann, Appendix 26

Thumbelina is the female counterpart of Tom Thumb.

FORNEUS

This is the name of a demon in the traditions and literature of Germany. Forneus, also known as Fornjotr, was also described as an evil spirit that inhabited the seas. This demon was invoked, according to medieval German literature, for the purpose of sorcery.
References 93
See also Demon, Spirit

FORNJOTR
See Forneus

FOSSEGRIM

The name for a type of water spirit in the folklore of Norway. The Fossegrim was described as a little golden-haired, handsome male spirit that inhabited waterfalls. He was said to be particularly fond of music and enjoyed human company. He could be seen in the water pools beneath the falls, where everyone came to hear him singing, on sunny days.
References 88
See also Grim, Nix, Spirit, Appendix 25

FRAU BERCHTA, FRAU BERTA
See Berchta

FRAU HILDE
See Holle

FRAU WACHHOLDER

This is the name of a tree spirit in the folklore of Germany. Frau Wachholder is described as a female goblin who was the guardian spirit of the juniper tree. More curiously, she was invoked in a particular ritual for the return of stolen property. The procedure involved bending one of the lower branches to the earth and, while securing it with a heavy stone, calling for the thief to be present. The thief and property

would be brought to the accuser by the intervention of Frau Wachholder, whereupon the stone and branch would be released.
References 110
See also Goblin, Guardian, Spirit, Appendix 19

FRAU WELT

This is the name of a spirit in the secular and ecclesiastical folklore of Germany. Frau Welt was a female supernatural lover or fairy mistress who came to monks, brothers, and other clerics in monastic houses during the medieval period. Frau Welt was purported by some to be a succubus, a demon, or the Devil in other guise.
References 88
See also Demon, Fairy, Friar Rush, Gan Ceanach, Incubus, Spirit, Succubus

FRAVASHI, FRAVAŠI

This is a group of spirits in the Zoroastrian religion of Iran. The Fravashis, whose name means She Who Confesses or She Who Is Chosen, are the Guardian Angels assigned to each human at birth to accompany them throughout their lives. The Fravashis were venerated as the bringers of good things, but remained invisible to the human. They are the assistants of Ormuzd/Ahura Mazda in the promoting of growth and combating evil. In the later folk beliefs of Armenia, they were still regarded as human Guardian Angels that dwelled near the burial places of the ancestors.
References 29, 41, 53, 88, 93, 102, 114
See also Grine, Guardian Angel, Manes, Pitris

FREYBUG

This is the name of a demon of the roads in English folk beliefs of the Middle Ages. It was described as a Black Dog fiend and referred to in an English document of 1555.
See also Barguest, Black Dog, Boggart, Demon, Fiend, Appendix 24

FRIAR RUSH

This is the name of a demon or spirit that took the form of a friar in a monastic order. Friar Rush is also variously described in the English chapbooks of the sixteenth century as having a "cow's tail, cloven feet, and hooked nails." He was sent (by the Devil, presumably) to lead the monks by trickery into wanton and debauched behavior, and thus into damnation. His favorite haunts were the kitchens and cellars of wealthy monasteries. There he made mischief and tricked the monks into gluttony and stupor. In one account the demon is eventually exposed by a holy Prior, who transforms the spirit into the shape of a horse and expels it to haunt a ruined castle. Then

Rush escapes and starts his pranks again, until the Prior again tracks him down and deals with him. The stories, from about the fourteenth to the sixteenth centuries, have similar versions in Denmark and Germany, where Friar Rush is called Bruder Rausch. Although the spirit starts off as a demon, in later stories his pranks and escapades are more in keeping with those of Robin Goodfellow or a hobgoblin.
References 17, 18, 41, 87, 114
See also Abbey Lubber, Bruder Rausch, Buttery Spirit, Demon, Hobgoblin, Robin Goodfellow, Spirit, Appendix 22

FRID, FRIDEAN (pl.)

The name of a type of spirit to be found in the folklore of the Scottish Highlands. The Fridean are mentioned by MacKenzie in his *Scottish Folklore and Folk Life,* where he suggests that they might have been the original inhabitants of the areas of Gairloch and Ross and Cromarty. The Fridean are said to inhabit the interiors of the rocks or to dwell under them in caverns. The Frid of each place was propitiated with offerings of milk and bread strewn on the ground.
References 17, 18
See also Spirit

FUATH, FUATHAN (pl.), OR FUATHS (pl.)

This is a general term for a group of malignant spirits that often take human shape and are usually associated with water in the folklore of Scotland. They are described as having a hideously deformed human shape often covered in shaggy hair. They are full of malice and evil intent toward human beings but are rarely seen because of the remote terrain that they normally inhabit. The following spirits are known to be Fuaths described in this book: Beithir, Brollachan, Caoineag, Cuachag, Fachan, Fideal, Glaistig, Peallaidh, Shellycoat, Urisk, and Vough.
References 15, 17, 99
See also Spirit

FURCAS

See Forcas

FURIES

This is the collective name given to the avenging spirits in the classical mythology of Rome. The Furies, whose name means the Angry Ones, were also known as the Dirae, but in Greek mythology they were known as the Erinyes, Eumenides, or Semnai. These spirits have been given various origins: as the daughters of the gods of the Earth, or the Night, or the blood drops from the castration of Uranus. They are sisters whose names are Alecto, Tisiphone, and Magæra and are described variously as being snake-haired, human-shaped hags that may have bat's

wings or the head of a dog. They avenge the unpunished wrongs committed by humans with horrible zeal, to exact revenge even after death. In this respect they were so dreaded that they were only referred to by the euphemisms of Eumenides and Semnai.
References 40, 53, 56, 107, 129, 130
See also Alecto, Erinyes, Eumenides, Hag, Magæra, Meliæ, Semnai, Spirit, Tisiphone

FURIOUS HOST, THE
See Armée Furieuse

FUTRUS
The name of an angel in the Islamic faith who was said to have offered his services to Hussain, the Prophet's grandson.
References 30
See also Angel

FYLGJA, FYLGIR (pl.), FYLGJUR (pl.)
These spirits of Teutonic and Norse mythology are hereditary protective guardians of individual humans from birth, passing from ancestor to descendant. The Fylgja, whose name means the Follower, may manifest as a woman bearing arms and riding through the skies, or may appear in the form of an animal. But whatever form they take, they appear as tutelary spirits only in dreams, giving warnings or advice about future events. To see one's Fylgja when awake was the portent of imminent death. With the advent of Christianity, the Fylgja was considered to be a demon.
References 88, 93, 102
See also Agloolik, Àràk, Awl-man, Chin Chia, Clay Mother, Corn Mother, Demon, Guardian, Harut and Marut, Leib-Olmai, Nagual, Spirit, Tutelary Spirit, Zoa, Appendix 22

FYNNODEREE
See Fenodyree

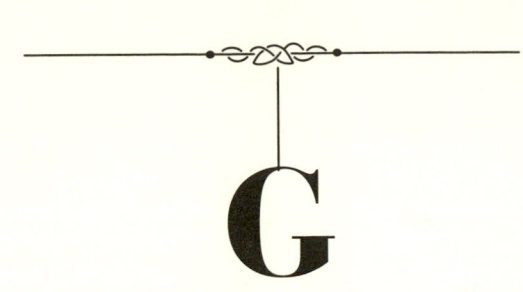

G

GABBLE RETCHETS
See Wild Hunt

GABIETA, GABETA
See Gabija

GABIJA
The name of a female spirit in the folklore of Lithuania. Gabija, also known as Gabieta or Gabeta, is the guardian spirit of the household fire. This spirit could be both benevolent and malevolent according to the fastidiousness of the housewife. If the fire ever went out, then the household would experience misfortune unless the housewife took a brand from a neighbor's fire and placated Gabija with an offering of salt. The male counterpart of Gabija is Gabijaujis, who is the household guardian spirit of the kiln fire.
References 88, 93
See also Guardian, Spirit, Appendix 22

GABIJAUJA
This is the name of a demon in the folklore of Lithuania. Originally Gabijauja had been a deity of the corn and grain crops. The spirit was then demoted to the status of a demon with the advent of Christianity.
References 93
See also Demon

GABIJAUJIS
See Gabija

GABRIEL, GABRA'IL
An Archangel and a chief angel in Judeo-Christian scriptures, who is known as the Herald, and the angel of death who will blow the final trumpet blast before the Day of Judgment. He is also an Archangel mentioned in the Koran as Gabra'il who took Mohammed to heaven and revealed the holy laws to the Prophet. He is known by the name *Sidna Djebril*, the Lord Gabriel, in Morocco, where this angel was said to have delivered all the tools that Adam needed to survive outside Paradise. He is also known as the

angel that presides over the deathbed to ease the human's transition to the next world. In the astrological calendar, Gabriel was associated with the moon in early Jewish writings as well as in medieval Christian astrology.
References 39, 40, 88, 93, 107, 114, 119
See also Angel, Archangel, Appendix 1

GABRIEL HOUNDS, GABRIEL RACHETS
This is the name of the supernatural host of death spirits known in Durham, Lancashire, and Yorkshire in northern England. The name may vary as the Gabble Rachets, Gabbleracket, or Gabble Retchets. The Gabriel Hounds rode high in the skies on stormy nights, appearing with human heads and the bodies of dogs. They are said to be a group of demons, or the souls of the unbaptized, or the souls of human sinners sent by the Devil to hunt and bring misfortune to the living. Anyone who saw or heard them hover over a dwelling knew that someone within was doomed. As a form of the Wild Hunt there are numerous tales of this portent of disaster being recorded throughout the centuries.
References 15, 17, 123, 133
See also Demon, Spirit, Wild Hunt, Appendix 23

GAHE
These are powerful healing spirits in the beliefs of the Chiricahua and Mescalero Apache Native Americans. The Gahe are also known as the Mountain People, as they inhabit the interior of the mountains. These supernaturals are known to the White Mountain Apache as G'an, to the Lipan Apache as Hactci, and to the Jicarilla Apache as Hactcin. They are represented in ceremonies by dancers wearing the special Kachina masks. Kachina is the name by which the Gahe are known to the Pueblo Native American people. Stories are told of how these spirits have protected the oppressed and guided humans. One account tells of how the spirits provided an escape for a persecuted community. They caused the entombment of an entire army that had pursued the people into the mountains. The Gahe lured the army

into a mountain cave and sealed the entrance with a rock fall.
References 88
See also G'an, Hactci, Kachina, Spirit, Appendix 21

GAHONGAS

This is the name of one of the three groups of dwarfs in the folk beliefs of the Iroquois Native American people. They are said to resemble little grotesque humans when they materialize. The Gahongas inhabited the rocks and stretches of water in lonely places.
References 102
See also Dwarf, Gandayaks, Ohdowas

GAKI

See Oni

GALAR

See Fjalar

GALATEA

This is the name of a nymph in the classical mythology of Greece and Rome. Galatea was a spirit of the sea, or Nereid, who was in love with a mortal called Acis. However, the legend tells that Cyclops was infatuated with Galatea, and in a jealous rage he destroyed Acis. When Galatea discovered this she threw herself into the sea, out of reach, to grieve the loss of her lover.
References 40
See also Nereid, Nymph, Appendix 25

GALLA, GALLU

This is the name of a demon in the ancient mythology of Sumer. Galla was known by the name Gallu in Babylon.
References 93
See also Demon

GALLEY-BEGGAR

A Galley-beggar is said to be a frightening bogie, demon, or Bullbeggar in the folklore of England. This bogie was reported to haunt the more desolate areas of Suffolk and Somerset. When it materializes, it manifests in skeletal form with a human head under its arm, the air around it glowing strangely. A rather comical tale concerning this spirit relates how it was seen to slide on a hurdle (a type of fencing used for sheep folds) down the hill at Nether Stowey, cackling and shrieking with laughter.
References 17
See also Bogie, Bullbeggar, Demon, Spirit

GALLEY-TROT

This is the name of a type of bogie or demon in the folklore of Suffolk, England. The Galley-trot, also

known as the Gilitrutt, takes the form of a large white shaggy dog about the size of a bullock, or a nebulous, white miasma. Like the Shuck and the Black Dog type of demon, it would silently appear beside humans on lonely roads, engulfing or harassing them. It particularly haunted the area of Woodbridge and Dunwich, as well as a bog called Bathslough, from which it would emerge to chase passing travelers.
References 17, 69, 123
See also Black Dog, Black Shuck, Bogie, Demon, Galley-beggar, Appendix 24

GAMAINHAS

In the folklore of Native South American people of Venezuela, this is the collective name of the spirits of the waters and the forest.
References 110
See also Mauari, Saraua, Spirit, Appendix 19, Appendix 25

G'AN

In the folk beliefs of the White Mountain Apache Native Americans, these powerful supernaturals have associations as vegetation spirits celebrated in the masked sacred dances of the Kachinas. It is said that these spirits once inhabited the earth but went into the center of the mountains to retreat from mankind and his misery.
References 88
See also Gahe, Kachina, Spirit, Appendix 18

GAN CEANACH, GANCANAGH, GANCONER

This is an elf or fairy, whose name *Gan Ceanach* means the Love Talker, in the language and folklore of Ireland. This debonair little man would appear in lonely glens smoking his *dudeen* (clay pipe). The Gan Ceanach, also known as the Gancanagh or Ganconer, could be recognized by the fact that he had no shadow, the birds stopped singing and a mist unfurled about him. It was considered to be very unlucky to meet him, and those young men who dissipated their fortune on trinkets for the ladies were said to have met with the Gan Ceanach. The Love Talker would seduce young mortal maidens with his twinkling black eyes and enchanting gentle voice. Once they kissed him they were doomed, for he would disappear as quickly as he had come, leaving them to pine to death.
References 15, 17, 18, 44
See also Elf, Fairy

GANAS

These are dwarfs or demons in the mythology of India. They are ruled by the elephant-headed god of wisdom, Ganesha.
References 98, 102
See also Demon, Dwarf

GANDAREWA

In the Zoroastrian religion of Iran, Gandarewa is a water demon disposed of by Keresapa.
References 93
See also Demon

GANDAYAKS

This is the name of one of the groups of dwarfs in the folk beliefs of the Iroquois Native Americans. The Gandayaks were vegetation spirits whose particular responsibility was as the guardians of freshwater fish.
References 102
See also Dwarf, Gahongas, Guardian, Ohdowas, Appendix 12, Appendix 18

GANDHABBAS

See Gandharvas

GANDHARVAS

In the classical mythology of India, these are vegetation spirits, also known by the Pali name of Gandhabbas, that inhabit the air, forests, and mountains. They are described variously as being shaggy half-animal beings or fragrant, richly clothed warriors. The Gandharvas are the companions of the Apsaras and are renowned for their beautiful music in the heavens. Their leaders are Visvavasu and Tumburu.
References 29, 39, 40, 56, 93, 102, 114,
See also Apsaras, Deev, Fauns, Guardian, Nymph, Spirit, Urvasi, Vrikshakas, Appendix 18

GANFER

See Trow

GA-OH

In the mythology of the Seneca and Iroquois Native American people, this is a powerful and benevolent wind spirit. Ga-oh controls the activities of the associated wind spirits known as Dajoji, O-yan-do-ne (the south wind, who appears in the form of a mouse), Ne-a-go (the east wind, who appears in the shape of a fawn), and Ya-o-gah (the north wind, who appears in the shape of a bear).
References 88
See also Dajoji, Spirit, Appendix 26

GARA YAKA

See Dala Kadavara

GARDSVOR

This is the name of a household spirit in the mythology and folklore of Scandinavia. Gardsvor, whose name means House Guardian, manifests in the form of a dwarf. He inhabits the home, where he protects the family and its possessions.

References 88
See also Domovik, Dwarf, Household Spirit, Nis, Appendix 21, Appendix 22

GARTHORNES

A local name in the folklore of Cornwall, England, for the mine spirits, who are also known as knockers.
References 18
See also Knockers, Mine Spirits

GAUEKO

In the folklore of the Basque people of southwestern France and northern Spain, this spirit is a type of demon. It only manifests in the darkness, as a gust of wind or a farm animal, to work mischief in the night. However, the Gaueko can also be benevolent.
References 93
See also Demon, Spirit

GAUNAB

This is an evil spirit in the beliefs of the Hottentot people of South Africa. Gaunab is considered to be responsible for the creation of the rainbow, which is not thought to be benign as it is in other folklore. The demon was vanquished by the almighty deity Tsui-Goab, to reside in a pile of stones.
References 102
See also Demon, Spirit

GAURI

In Indian classical mythology this is an alternative name for Devi in her benign form.
References 88
See also Deev

GAYA

In classical Indian mythology this is the name of a particularly devout Asura. His worship of Vishnu accumulated so much purity that all who touched him became purified and went to Brahma's heaven, until the entire universe was empty of sinners. Since the gods were no longer receiving devotion from sinners, they made a pact with Gaya that one region only would be reserved for the blessings of his purity to pilgrims who journeyed there. This is how, according to legend, the place called Gaya in Bihar Province came into being.
References 88
See also Asura

GÉDE, GÉDE L'ORAGE

In the Voodoo of Haiti, Géde is an outrageous trickster spirit of sexual activity, deceitfulness, and death. When in possession of devotees, he drinks rum and eats the hottest chilies. An epithet used as a euphemism to deflect the malice of Géde is the

flattering name Géde l'Orage, which means Spirit of the Storm.
References 67
See also Anansi, Bamapama, Basajaun, Blue Jay, Coyote, Eshu, Exus, Manabozo, Mink, Spirit

GENIE
See Djinn

GENIUS, GENII (pl.)
The name of a group of spirits in the classical Roman, Etruscan, and Assyrian mythologies. They are essentially guardian spirits of the individual beings and phenomena that have been created. There is a Genius for crops, trees, water, mountains, each kind of animal, and of course, humans. A Genius was assigned to each individual at birth. The Genius of each man (women were protected by Juno) controlled his character and destiny, eventually conducting his soul out of the mortal world. They were variously depicted as naked winged youths or bird-headed beings, while the Genius of a family in Pompeii was portrayed as a snake. There were good Genii, called Shedu or Lamassu, and bad Genii, called Utukku.
References 28, 29, 40, 56, 88, 92, 93, 102, 107, 114, 129
See also Guardian, Lamassu, Lar, Penates, Spirit, Utukku, Appendix 22

GENTLE ANNIS, GENTLE ANNIE
In the folklore of the Scottish Lowland area of the Cromarty Firth, this blue-black–faced hag is a treacherous weather spirit that brings unexpected squalls. The name is a euphemism to ward off her vengeance against local fishermen, but it may be derived from the Celtic Danu, whose people are the Irish Tuatha dé Danann.
References 17, 47, 123
See also Cailleac Bera, Hag, Spirit, Tuatha dé Danann, Appendix 26

GENTRY, THE
See Fairy

GHADDAR
In the traditions of the Yemen and Upper Egypt, the Ghaddar are the djinn offspring of Iblis. They are responsible for ensnaring gullible humans, whom they terrify and torture, eventually abandoning their victims in some remote place.
References 41
See also Djinn, Iblis

GHILLIE DHU, GILLE DUBH
Ghillie Dhu, also known as Gille Dubh in the folklore of Scotland, is a black-haired elf or sprite whose name means Black Gillie. This sprite was described as

being dressed much like the nature spirit the Green Man, in leaves and green moss. He inhabited the birch woods and thickets around Loch a Druing and Gairloch, where he was regarded as a benevolent being.
References 17
See also Elf, Green Man, Spirit, Sprite, Appendix 18

GHOL, GHOLE, GHOOL
See Ghoul

GHOUL/E, GHOWL, GHUL/I
This is the name of a species of djinn in Islamic traditions and beliefs. In pre-Islamic times they were identified as the male Qutrub and the female Gulah. Other spellings of the name are Ghol, Ghool, Ghowl, and Goul, while Ghulah is the female form. The Ghouls are fiends known and feared from the north of Africa, across the Middle East, to the Indian continent and beyond. They are said to inhabit the wilderness, or lonely forests, islands, and caves, as well as their more usual place of abode where humans have died or are buried. The Ghouls have been described as dark, hairy, quick-witted, and lustfully attracted to humans. Another manifestation is as a grotesquely ugly being, resembling an ostrich with only one eye. However, these evil spirits are shape-shifters that can transform themselves to any guise in order to seduce humans. Ghouls prey on the unwary traveler and may kidnap them or terrorize them. They may haunt the sites of human tragedy, such as battlefields, murder sites, or cemeteries, devouring the bodies of the recent dead in deserted graves.
References 41, 53, 56, 67, 88, 107
See also Baba Yaga, Demon, Djinn, Fiend, Ghul-i-Beaban, Lamia, Qutrub, Yogini

GHRTAMĀRI
See Mahāmāri

GHULAH
See Ghoul

GHUL-I-BEABAN
A ghoul in the folklore of the wilderness regions of Iran and Afghanistan, where this fiend attacks and devours strangers traveling alone.
References 6
See also Fiend, Ghoul

GID-MURT
This is the spirit of the cow byre and the cattle sheds in the folk beliefs of the Finno-Ugric Votyak people of the Vyatka region of Russia. Gid-murt, which means the Man of the Cattle House, is the guardian spirit of the cattle in much the same way as the

Chlevnik of Russia. He must be propitiated to ensure his benevolence.
References 88
See also Chlevnik, Guardian, Gunna, Kudə Ört Kuba, Lauko Sargas, Murt, Nur Kuba, Spirit

GILITRUTT
See Galley-trot

GILPIN HORNER
This was a goblin or bogle in the folklore of Eskdale, England. It made its appearance in the eighteenth century but spoke of incidents in the seventeenth century. It was described as very short and strong in the legs and above the waist resembled a little old woman. It was known locally as the Bogle of Todshawhill; the name Gilpin Horner was given to the goblin after it had left Eskdale.

Gilpin Horner appeared out of the mists to some youths who were tethering some horses one evening in a paddock. Terrified, they ran back to the milking sheds, but it got there before them. The women doing the evening milking were equally frightened until the sprite spoke quite gently. It followed them home and installed itself in the home of James Moffat, taking some of their barley and milk for supper. Gilpin Horner disappeared each day but returned by evening; the sound of hooves was heard in the courtyard, but the sprite was invisible. They shut the goblin into the barn for the night but were surprised to see him immediately on its roof and then on a hayrick. After about a week the sprite vanished, and although he was reported sitting on a rock in the Barmpool, he never went back to Eskdale.
References 73
See also Bogie, Goblin, Sprite, Appendix 22

GINN
See Djinn

GIRÁITIS
This is the name of a nature spirit in the folklore of Lithuania. The Giráitis inhabits the woods and forests. It is described as appearing in the form of a young man. He is the guardian of everything in the woods, and his female counterpart is known as Medeine.
References 88
See also Medeine, Spirit, Appendix 18, Appendix 19, Appendix 21

GIRLE GUAIRLE
The name of a fairy in Irish folklore whose story follows the same motif as that of Habetrot and Rumpelstiltskin. A very busy Irish wife working late into the night was so anxious about the completion of the spinning and weaving of her flax, that a fairy overheard her distress and offered to complete the work by the following day. The only payment was that the wife should remember the name of her helper, which was Girle Guairle. As with all fairy things, no sooner had the spinster gone than the name was lost to the wife. She had neither the name nor her flax now. Terrified of what her family might say, and even more terrified of the vengefulness of the fairy, she wandered into the fields by a fairy-ring. By chance she heard the fairy singing "If yon woman knew my name to be Girle Guairle, I would have neither frieze nor canvas." The happy wife ran home and waited for the fairy spinner to arrive and greeted her by name. Girle Guairle was obliged to hand over the completed work according to the bargain and disappeared in a rage.
References 88
See also Fairy, Habetrot, Rumpelstiltskin, Sili Ffrit, Appendix 14

GIWOITIS
This is the name of a household spirit in the folklore of the Slav people. The Giwoitis usually manifest in the form of a lizard. It was regarded as a protective spirit that was propitiated in the home with the offering of a bowl of milk.
References 102
See also Smiera-Gatto, Spirit, Appendix 22

GIZŌ
See Anansi

GLAISTIG
The Glaistig is a complex fairy spirit and a member of the group known as fuaths in the folklore of the Highlands of Scotland. She is able to shape shift from the form of a woman to half-woman and half-goat, or completely to the form of a goat. As a water spirit the Glaistig might beg to be carried across a stream by an unsuspecting mortal, whom she may very well devour or, at the least lead astray. As a benign household spirit she might willingly do domestic tasks while the family sleeps, or herd the cattle for the farm. In this capacity the Glaistig appears to protect the infants, the infirm, and the elderly, and as the Green Glaistig she will wail for the imminent departure of one of her charge much like a banshee. The Glaistig, although of questionable motives, does not seem to have been totally at fault. One anecdote of a smith who entrapped a Glaistig tells how the smith, when the Glaistig produced the magic cattle and inviolable house he demanded, seared off her extended hand of farewell. The vegetation in the place where she met this horrible reward, Lochaber, Inverness, is said to be stained red to this day.

References 15, 17, 47
See also Banshee, Fairy, Fuath, Spirit, Appendix 22, Appendix 25

GLASHAN

In the folklore of the Isle of Man (United Kingdom), this Manx spirit is of the same group as the more well-known Fynnoderee. The Glashan inhabits the south of the island, where he is the hard-working friend of the farming community. This shy supernatural will reap, thresh, and mill the wheat in the twilight and return in secrecy to the hills before dawn.
References 60
See also Dobie, Fenodyree, Spirit

GLASHTIN

This is a water spirit in the Manx folklore of the Isle of Man (United Kingdom). The Glashtin, also spelled Glastyn, is a form of the Scottish Each Uisge, or the water-horse. In his human shape, the Glashtin appears as a handsome dark-haired young man. The only clue to his real nature is the presence of horse's ears within his curly hair. The Glashtin usually inhabits the banks of rivers and lochs where, in his equine form, he encourages humans to mount his flanks. With his quarry firmly in place, the spirit takes the unfortunate person to be devoured beneath the waters. A common theme of tales concerning the Glashtin describes how a young woman left at home alone unbolts the door to the cottage to admit someone she thinks is her father caught in the rainstorm. It is only when the stranger uncovers his head to dry by the fire that she notices the horse's ears. The spirit makes a grab for her, but the cockerel in the yard is wakened by her piercing screams, and she is saved by the cockcrow.
References 17, 81, 87
See also Each Uisge, Kelpie, Neugle, Spirit, Appendix 12, Appendix 25

GLYKON

This is the name of a demon in the texts and mythology of the early European Gnostic-Mithraic cult. This spirit was portrayed as a human-headed snake demon.
References 93
See also Demon, Spirit

GNOME

There are two different groups of lesser spirit that go by this name:

(1) One of a group of nature spirits or elementals defined by the mystical philosopher Paracelsus (1493–1541) in terms of the natural elements from which they were supposed to be derived. The Gnomes are described as being like little old men

able to shape shift to the size of giants. They are malicious, greedy, and miserable. Their emperor, according to the occultist Elephas Levi, is called Cob.

(2) In Teutonic mythology, these earth spirits closely resembled dwarfs in that they were small, stocky, grotesque beings. They invariably appear like little old men in monks' habits. They dwell in the earth and are able to disappear at will into the substance of the earth or the trees. These gnomes are industriously occupied within the quarries and mines deep in the earth, where they are supposed to be guardians of treasures.
References 7, 17, 18, 40, 67, 88, 93, 98, 107, 114, 136
See also Dwarf, Elemental, Gnome, Guardian, Spirit, Appendix 21

GNYAN

These are disease spirits in the beliefs of the Tibetan people. These demons dwell in the trees and stones and may inflict humans with the plague and other pestilence, causing them misfortune and death.
References 87, 93
See also bDud, Demon, Lha-mo, Ma-Mo, Spirit, Appendix 17

GOBELIN

This is the household spirit of Normandy in northern France. He is said to resemble the appearance of a little old man, like the goblin of England, but the Gobelin behaves more like the English brownie.
References 107
See also Brownie, Goblin, Kobold, Nis, Piskey, Tomtar, Appendix 22

GOBHAN SAER

See Goibniu

GOBLIN

In European folklore this is a grotesque, diminutive, and generally malicious earth spirit or sprite. Goblins may be known by the alternative spellings of the

name: Gobblin, Gobelin, Gobeline, Gobling, and Goblyn. Goblins are said to be about the height of a man's knee and have gray hair and beards. Like the more friendly brownie, Goblins inhabit the homes of humans, where they indulge in tricks and make noises much as the poltergeist does. The Goblin does have the endearing trait of liking children and bringing them little gifts when they are well-behaved. For the adults, however, a resident Goblin can become a nuisance with upset kitchens and furniture and horses ridden to a lather in the stables at night. There is only one recommended method of getting rid of a household Goblin, and that is to cast flax seed all over the floors. When the sprite comes to do mischief at night he will be obliged to pick up all the seed, but there will be so much that he cannot finish before dawn. After a few repeats of this tedium, he will give it up and leave.
References 7, 17, 18, 40, 53, 67, 69, 88, 92, 107, 114
See also Bakemono, Baumesel, Ben Baynac, Brownie, Hobgoblin, Pixie, Poltergeist, Spirit, Sprite, Appendix 22

GODDA
The name of a fairy who became the wife of Wild Edric in the folklore of Shropshire, England.
References 18
See also Fairy

GOFANNON
This is the name of a fairy in the folklore of Wales. He is the supernatural smith of the Tylwyth Teg.
References 105
See also Fairy, Goibniu, Tylwyth Teg, Wayland Smith

GOGOL
In Russian folklore this is the name for a devil or the Devil.
References 75
See also Devil

GOIABEIRA
This is the name of a group of encantados in the Afro-Brazilian cult Batuque. They are thought to be derived from the tree spirits of the local Amazonian shamanistic beliefs.
References 89
See also Encantados, Spirit, Appendix 19

GOIBHLEANN
This is the alternative name in folklore for the smith of the Tuatha dé Danann called Goibniu in Irish mythology. In Irish folklore and legend, under the name of Goibhleann, he is the owner of the magical cow Glas Ghoibhneann. The milk yield of the cow was unending for those in need, but dried up imme-diately for any who sought to profit from the supernatural gift.
References 105
See also Goibniu, Tuatha dé Danann

GOIBNIU, GOIBHNIU
In the folklore and legend of Ireland, Goibniu, also known as Goibhleann or *Gobhan Saer*, meaning Goibniu the Architect, is the supernatural smith of the Tuatha dé Danann who fashioned weapons that never missed their mark. His smithies were located all over Ireland, but he was especially active in Beare, County Cork. As Goibhleann he is the owner of the magic cow, but under the name of Gobhan Saer he is famed for creating the round towers and the strongest bridges.
References 105
See also Gofannon, Goibhleann, Tuatha dé Danann, Wayland Smith

GOLDMAR, GOLDEMAR, KING
This dwarf in Teutonic mythology is the king of the malicious Black Dwarfs. According to Keightley, King Goldmar was the name of a kobold that in the fifteenth century haunted the house of Neveling von Hardenberg. Although invisible, the touch of his hands was said to feel like the paws of a frog. Goldmar demanded, like Hinzelmann, a place at the table, a room in the castle, and stabling for his invisible horse, although he seems to have done no more for his host than to sing and play the harp. He was particularly adept at exposing the knavery of servants and the hypocrisy of the resident clergy to his own advantage. Goldmar is said to have hacked to death, broiled, and eaten one of the servants who had tried to trick him into becoming visible and therefore vulnerable.
References 18, 95
See also Alberich, Dwarf, Hinzelmann, Kobold, Appendix 22

GÖLL
See Valkyries

GONDUL
See Valkyries

GONG GONG
This is the name of an evil spirit or devil in the folk beliefs and legends of China. This demon manifests in the form of a black dragon that causes deluges. Gong Gong is responsible for disaster and misery brought to humans as a result of these great floods. His attendant is Xiang Yao.
References 93
See also Attendant Spirit, Demon, Devil, Spirit, Xiang Yao

GOOD NEIGHBORS

In English and Scottish Lowland folklore, this name is used instead of referring directly to the fairies who may be listening and be offended by a direct naming. The naming of a member of the Little People was a direct affront to them and showed disrespect. It was sufficient to cause such offense that they would either vanish or exact some retribution. Most humans who acknowledged the part that these supernaturals played in their lives would rarely risk such an event.
References 18
See also Ben Socia, Fairy, Little People

GOOSEBERRY WIFE

This is the name of a spirit in the local folklore of the Isle of Wight (United Kingdom). The Gooseberry Wife is the guardian spirit of the gooseberry bushes. She manifests in the form of a very large hairy caterpillar in order to guard the ripening gooseberry fruit from inquisitive and greedy children. In this respect the Gooseberry Wife is a nursery bogie.
References 17
See also Guardian, Nursery Bogie, Spirit, Appendix 22

GORSKA MAKUA

A hideous hag of Bulgarian folklore who inhabits the woods like the Nočnitsa.
References 88
See also Hag, Nočnitsa

GOU MANG

In Chinese mythology this supernatural is always associated with Rou Shou. Together they are the spirit messengers of the sky-god and share the form of the double dragon. Gou Mang presages good fortune and the return of springtime. He is associated with the benefit of longevity, and he comes from the eastern directions.
References 93
See also Rou Shou, Spirit

GOUL

See Ghoul

GRACES, GRATIÆ

In classical Roman mythology these three maidens (although there were sometimes more) were probably early vegetation spirits elevated to represent the benefits of gifts. Their names are Aglaia, which means Brilliance; Euphrosyne, which means Cheerfulness; and Thalia, which means the Flowering. The Graces are depicted usually as naked graceful maidens with flower garlands. They are the guardians of developing blossoms and fruitfulness, bestowing beauty and idyllic charm. They are also known as Charities, the classical Greek name by which the Roman Graces

were known. In Greek mythology these maidens were the daughters of the king of the gods, Zeus, and the Oceanid Eurynome. They were the personification of the arts and were frequently portrayed in sculpture and painting, especially of the Renaissance period.
References 40, 56, 93, 100, 114, 130
See also Euphrosyne, Eurynome, Guardian, Oceanid, Spirit, Appendix 18

GRAHAM/E

See Auld Hornie

GRAND VANEUR, LE

See Wild Huntsman

GRANDMOTHER FIRE

This is the name of the benevolent spirit of the fire in Zuñi Native American folk belief and legends. She is a tutelary spirit who is associated with the spirits called the Ash Boys, Ashes Man, Flint Boys, and Poker Boys.
References 88
See also Spirit, Tutelary Spirits

GRANNY, THE

The corn spirit when revered in the last harvest sheaf is called the Granny in Belfast, Ireland.
References 87
See also Cailleac, Corn Spirit, Spirit

GRANT

A spirit described by Gervaise of Tilbury, the English thirteenth-century chronicler, as being a type of demon. It took the form of a yearling colt with glowing eyes, much like the Picktree Brag, but traveled only on its hind legs and presented a terrifying aspect for those who saw it. Although frightening, the Grant seems to have been a warning spirit. It usually appeared in the town during the heat of the day or at sunset, setting the dogs barking and chasing it in vain, while the alerted residents would be warned of an imminent town fire.
References 15, 17, 123
See also Demon, Picktree Brag, Spirit, Appendix 12, Appendix 23

GREEN CHILDREN

In medieval English texts this is the name given to fairy children who were described as having green skins and were often dressed in green (the fairy color). In an account by the thirteenth-century English Cistercian chronicler Ralph of Coggeshall, two Green Children were found naked at the edge of a wolf pit, looking disoriented and distressed. They were given clothes by the local people and taken into the household of the local lord of the manor, Sir Richard de

Calne. In one version of the story, their fairy parents found them and took them away; in another version, related by William de Newburgh, the boy died and the girl eventually married a local man from Lynn.
References 15, 17, 133
See also Coleman Gray, Fairy, Skilly Widden, Undine, Appendix 22

GREEN GLAISTIG
See Glaistig

GREEN GEORGE
See Jack-in-the-Green

GREEN KNIGHT, THE
In the legendary tales of King Arthur and the Knights of the Round Table, the Green Knight is a supernatural fairy knight whose skin, clothes, armor, and weapons are green. As an immortal soldier, the Green Knight may lose his head, but he always retrieves it and carries on fighting. He is the symbol of vegetation rebirth, like Jack-in-the-Green. In one tale, Sir Gawain, one of Arthur's favorite knights, is entrapped by the wiles of the Green Knight's wife. During the Christmas jousts, the Green Knight (in disguise, calling himself the Knight of the Green Chapel) challenges Sir Gawain, who severs the fairy knight's head. Picking up his head, the Green Knight demands satisfaction one year hence at his own castle. Sir Gawain keeps the appointment, meeting the knight and his lady. In his return joust with the fairy knight, Sir Gawain retains his life only because he has refused further advances from his hostess, who is none other than Morgan le Fay.
References 37
See also Billy Blin, Fairy, Jack-in-the-Green, Morgan le Fay

GREEN LADY, THE
This is the name of a spirit in the folklore of the Scottish Highlands. The Green Lady is a supernatural of the Gruagach type that inhabited Skipness Castle by Loch Fyne. She is described as manifesting in the form of a woman with long hair. She was a guardian spirit, and in times of danger the Green Lady would protect the human residents of the castle by causing supernatural confusion among their enemies.
References 47, 76
See also Gruagach, Guardian, Spirit, Appendix 21

GREEN MAN, THE
A woodland or vegetation spirit of ancient European origins, whose pagan image of a grotesque severed head with emergent foliage from mouth, beard, and hairline decorate Christian churches from as early as the sixth century. As the Wild Man of the Woods he is the guardian and spirit of the ancient woodlands, and

the mysterious Green Man may be malevolent, tricksy, and unpredictable. In the folk legends and literature of England and Scotland he becomes Robin Hood and the Green Knight. The Green Man is a potent symbol of renewed fertility. He plays a prominent role in the festivities of May Day in the guise of the Garland, or King of the May (each of these is a person dressed in floral cages representing the spirit), or as Jack-in-the-Green.
References 47, 107, 123
See also Green Knight, Guardian, Jack-in-the-Green, Spirit, Appendix 18, Appendix 19

The Green Man.

GREEN WOMEN, THE
In the folklore of the Highlands of Scotland these are particularly malicious demons that appear at night in the guise of beautiful women dressed in green. In one anecdote, two young men who had been out hunting late into the night were obliged to take refuge in a *bothy* (hunting shelter). Feeling the isolation of the wilderness, they began to make merry with music, but still wished for company to dance with. No sooner had

their words been uttered than two beautiful women dressed in green danced in through the door. Enraptured by her charms, one of the young men accompanied his lady outside, leaving his suspicious partner playing a sacred melody. When daybreak came the Green Women vanished and the other young man had not returned, so his partner left the bothy to search for him. The bones of his unfortunate friend lay where the beautiful Green Woman had turned back into her demon form and devoured him. As a warning this area is now known as the Glen of the Green Women.

References 16
See also Baoban Sith, Demon

GREMLINS

These spirits of the ether owe their existence to the fertile imaginations of a British Royal Airforce crew of Bomber Command stationed on the Northwest Frontier of India, who required an entity to blame for inexplicable problems with their aircraft. The name Gremlin is reported to have been coined from an amalgam of the title of the only book in the Officers' Mess—*Grimm's Fairy Tales*—and the only beer available—Fremlin's.

Group Captain Geoffrey Leonard Cheshire V.C. used the name of Gremlin in the context of aircraft problems at a Yorkshire (north England) airfield, where the author Charles Graves heard it and incorporated it into his work *The Thin Blue Line* (1941). Gremlins were the subject of articles in *Punch* (11 November 1942), *The Spectator* (1 January 1943), and the *New York Times* magazine (11 April 1943).

Gremlins have variously been described as a type of elf, spirit, demon, or imp, which may be about 20 inches high, weigh about 17 pounds, and look like jackrabbits with sparse hair and sour expressions; or about 12 inches in height, wearing red jackets and green trousers; or as only 6 inches tall with horns protruding from their heads, wearing leather flying jackets and boots. Furthermore, a species with fins on the heels of their webbed feet has been reported by the Fleet Air Arm. A species operating at above 10,000 feet is sometimes referred to as a Spandule. Whatever the description, all agree that the Gremlins, having no wings of their own, are obliged to be passengers in whichever aircraft they plague.

Immense technical and meteorological ability is attributed to Gremlins, such that they have been credited with removing entire navigational points from their expected vicinity; raising or lowering runways as much as 10 feet just at the point of touchdown; consuming all the available fuel before the end of the flight; nibbling holes in the fuselage; distracting gunners and navigators at crucial moments so that the target is missed; or chewing through essential cables

A Green Woman.

in midair. Although generally mischievous, the Gremlins' intentions do not appear to be malicious, as they have been known to congregate in order to help a pilot fly the remnants of his aircraft back to base.
References 40, 87
See also Demon, Dingbelle, Elf, Fifinella, Imp, Nobody, Spirit

GRESSIL
See Devil

GRIG
A dwarf, elf, or sprite in the folklore of Somerset, England. They are described as little merry folk wearing green clothes and red stocking caps. It was common to leave the smallest apples of the harvest hanging on the tree for the Little People, and in Somerset these were referred to as the Griggling apples.
References 17
See also Dwarf, Elf, Little People, Sprite

GRIM
This is an ancient European spirit of the night. Originally an alternative name for one of the aspects of Odin, it was later applied to the goblin or demon assuming a terrifying form, usually that of a large black dog or an owl, whose wails beneath the windows of the sick predicted their demise. This aspect of the fairy Grim is described in *The Life of Robin Goodfellow* (1628). Different aspects of the spirit's role are denoted by a prefix, as in the Fossegrim of Norway and the Kyrkogrim, Kirkegrim, and Church Grim of Sweden, Denmark, and England, respectively. Essentially the Grim is a warning rather than terrifying spirit.
References 17, 133
See also Banshee, Black Dog, Church Grim, Demon, Fossegrim, Goblin, Kirkegrim, Kyrkogrim, Robin Goodfellow, Spirit, Appendix 23

GRIME
See Auld Hornie

GRINDYLOW
In the folklore of Yorkshire, England, this water demon is a nursery bogie. Like its Lancashire counterpart, Jenny Greenteeth, Grindylow inhabits deep stagnant pools of water, waiting to drag down any curious unwary child to its doom.
References 17
See also Demon, Jenny Greenteeth, Kappa, Nellie Longarms, Nursery Bogie, Peg Powler, Appendix 22, Appendix 25

GRINE
In the folklore of Morocco this is a type of djinn that inhabits a parallel world with that of the human

beings. When a child is born, its Grine will be created at the same time, and their existences are inextricably locked by fate. The Grine's function may be compared with that of the Guardian Angel or the Russian form of Bes.
References 90
See also Bes, Djinn, Guardian Angel, Appendix 22

GROAC'H
In the folklore of the Brittany peninsula of France, this is a female water spirit or nix that takes the form of a beautiful young woman on the banks of a river or on the seashore. The Groac'h enchants men with her charming manner, then enmeshes them in her silver nets, enslaving them in the form of frogs to do as she wills. Like most malignant sprites she may be defeated by iron.
References 132
See also Nix, Spirit, Sprite, Appendix 25

GROAGACH, GROGACH, GROGAN
See Gruagach

GRØNJETTE
In the folklore of Denmark this green wood spirit hunts the Wood Wives on the islands of Møn and Falster.
References 110
See also Spirit, Wild Hunt, Wood Wives

GROVE FOLK, GROVE DAMSELS
This is the name for the elves in the folklore of Sweden, where they are also known as the Elvor. The Grove Folk, or Grove Damsels, are the guardian spirits of the woods, and like the Dryads of ancient Greek mythology, the Grove Folk inhabit the trees.
References 110
See also Dryad, Elf, Elvor, Guardian, Hamadryad, Appendix 19

GRUAGACH
In the folklore of the Scottish Highlands and of Ireland, these are spirits of the brownie type. The Gruagach, also known as the Groagach, Grogach, or Grogan, are variously described as being golden-haired, hairy Little People dressed in fine clothes. However, in Ulster they are described as about the height of a man's knee and without clothes, or as a large-headed, soft-shaped, almost formless hairy being. Whatever the description, the Gruagach helps the homestead or the farms in which it abides. Its protective qualities and cattle-herding abilities make up for the other mischief it may wreak on the household.
References 17, 47, 76
See also Brownie, Green Lady, Little People, Spirit, Appendix 22

GUAPINDAIA

An encantado, also known as Tango do Pará and Mestre Belamino, in the Afro-Brazilian cult Batuque. He is an important member of the Turquia family of spirits and is regarded as a sibling of Mariana and Tapinaré. Guapindaia is regarded as a powerful supernatural healer and in curing sessions will be addressed under the names of Tango do Pará and Mestre Belamino during the process of these ceremonies.
References 89
See also Encantado, Mariana, Seu Turquia, Spirit, Tapinaré

GUARDIAN, GUARDIAN SPIRIT

A tutelary or protective spirit that advises, warns or defends the subject of its protection. This aspect of guardianship is often associated with a personal spirit assigned to a human at birth. This may be a Guardian Angel or a Grine or, in the ancient Greek and Roman cultures, a Daimon or Lar. For the Native Americans and Native Australians, acquiring their Guardian Spirit was an important step to achieving maturity and status within the community. Their Guardian Spirit was often manifest in the form of an animal. Other Guardians in European folk beliefs appear only at the time of most urgent need and fulfill that role in many different forms, often in the shape of a familiar animal, especially that of a dog. While most instances of Guardian Spirits tend to involve the care of a human, such spirits may also be assigned to protect places or objects of veneration that require supernatural care. Ancient mounds, standing stones, treasures, and luck-bringing artifacts figure in legends from around the world of supernatural guardianship.

Many stories tell of humans who have been saved by the unexpected appearance of a guardian dog. One such story relates how an old farmer had been caught in a freezing fog on the top of the Quantock Hills in Somerset, England. Feeling his way with difficulty in the cold, he suddenly felt what he took to be the familiar coat of his sheepdog and urged him, "Home, Boy!" When he emerged out of the fog in front of his house, the farmer heard his own dog barking from within. Turning swiftly, the man observed his guardian "dog" assume unnatural proportions before it evaporated into the fog.
References 17, 92, 107
See also Daimon, Deev, Gandharvas, Genius, Grine, Guardian Angel, Lar, Nymph, Tutelary Spirit, Urvasi, Vrikshakas, Appendix 21, Appendix 22

GUARDIAN ANGEL

In the beliefs of the peoples who belong to the Latin, Greek and Russian Orthodox and Anglican churches (though not official doctrine), a Guardian Angel is

A Guardian Angel protects a sleeping child.

assigned by the Almighty to each individual from the hour of birth until their final judgment. The ancient Egyptians considered that each individual had three Guardian Angels; both the ancient Greeks and Romans considered that there were two. The latter believed that one was good and the other evil. In Russian folklore this prevails as good and bad Bes. Two Guardian Angels, Michael and Raphael, are named in the scriptures, and the Roman Catholic Church celebrates a feast day for Guardian Angels on 2 October. In the Islamic faith, four Guardian Angels are assigned to each human, two to ward off danger during the day and two for the night. In general the Guardian Angels accompany their charges, usually invisibly, taking note of their good and bad deeds and bringing supernatural intervention when they have piously prayed for divine help. Their responsibility to the individual is guidance and support in adversity, particularly in warding off temptation. They also record the activities of the individual for the coming of the Day of Judgment.
References 52, 92, 107
See also Angel, Bes, Michael, Raphael

GÜBICH

This is the name of an evil spirit in the folklore of Germany. Gübich is a demon of the forests in the Harz region of the country.
References 110
See also Demon, Katzenveit, Rübezahl, Spirit, Appendix 19

GÜESTIA, LA

See Estantigua

GUI XIAN

These are evil spirits in the beliefs and legends of China. They were the transformed and demonized souls of those humans who had drowned or committed suicide.
References 93, 131
See also Demon, Spirit

GUIA

The designation of an unnamed spirit or encantado that guides other spirits to enter the Afro-Brazilian cult Batuque ceremonies. *Guia* means Guide.
References 89
See also Encantado, Legba

GUILLERME

See Basilio Bom

GUILLYN BEGGEY, NY

In the folklore of the Isle of Man (United Kingdom), this term, which means the Little Boys, is a Manx

euphemism for the fairies. They have been described as being about 6 inches tall with pale faces and small eyes and ears. The males have no beard, and they are usually dressed in blue coats, which they spread out in order to fly from the ground.
References 81
See also Fairy

GULAH

See Ghoul

GULL

In the English folklore and chapbook tale *The Life of Robin Goodfellow,* Gull is a malevolent sprite that behaves much like an incubus. This spirit steals infants, deceives mortals into betraying each other, brings horrors and pain to sleeping humans, and steals their milk and cream to share with sibling sprites.
References 17
See also Incubus, Spirit, Sprite, Appendix 22

GUMNUT BABIES

In the folk literature of European Australia, these fairy beings were the creation of Cecelia May Gibbs. (Gibbs was born in Kent, United Kingdom, in 1877 and moved to Perth, Australia in 1881, where she died 1969). The Gumnut Babies first made their appearance in January 1914 and, like the Flower Fairies of England, swiftly became an enduring part of the lore of children and their parents.

The Gumnut Babies may be described as tiny, chubby elves or a type of Flower Fairy, each dressed according to the flower it personifies. In the case of the eucalyptus flower, the females wear flower-stamen skirts, while the males wear the operculum. They may have blond or red hair formed from the stamens or seed capsules of the flowers. The most famous are Bib and Bub, Snugglepot, Cuddlepie, Ragged Blossom, Narnywo, Nittersing, and Chuckle-bud. The Gumnut Babies inhabit Gumnut Town in the Australian Bush, where their attendants are the insects to be found there. Like most Trooping Fairies they are communal in their activities and especially love music and dancing. They can exist in any environment and may often visit their friends in the air or under the water. Their adventures with the Blossom Babies, Flannel Flower Babies, Boronia Babies, and Wattle Babies all seek to avoid the evil Banksia Men.
References 1, 55
See also Banksia Men, Elf, Fairy, Flower Fairy

GUNNA

In the folklore of the Isle of Tyree, Ireland, this spirit is rather like a brownie. Although he is rarely seen, he has been described as being extremely thin with long yellow hair and clad only in a fox skin. Gunna is

Gumnut Babies take a walk through Ann Chovy's sea garden.

like the Glaistig, who inhabits farms and herds the cattle for the farmer, keeping the animals away from the ripening crops.
References 17
See also Brownie, Gid-murt, Glaistig, Gunna, Kudǝ Ört Kuba, Lauko Sargas, Nur Kuba, Spirit

GUTA
In the folklore of Hungary this is a particularly evil demon that encourages immoral behavior in humans and rewards them with destruction.
References 93
See also Demon

GUYTRASH
See Gytrash

GWARWYN-A-THROT, GWARYN-A-THROT
In the folklore of Dyfed, Wales, this is the name of a bwca who remained invisible while inhabiting and working for a homestead. Gwarwyn-a-Throt, whose name means the White-naped One with the Trot, would spin and weave for the family. All would be well with the relationship so long as the family was not curious about their supernatural worker, and like the story of Rumpelstiltskin or Tom Tit Tot, did not enquire about his name. Like most household spirits the provision of clothes or pronouncing of the name would be sufficient to drive him away. There are two anecdotes of Gwarwyn-a-Throt working and existing in harmony with a family. The first one ends when a servant girl learns his name, and the second when his human host leaves to fight for Henry of Lancaster against Richard III of England. This dates the story to the fifteenth century. Thereafter Gwarwyn-a-Throt degenerates to the status of a boggart who is finally exorcised to the Red Sea, a common place of exile for troublesome British spirits.
References 17, 18, 59
See also Boggart, Bwca, Rumpelstiltskin, Spirit, Tom Tit Tot, Appendix 14, Appendix 22

GWENHIDWY, GWENHUDWY
This is the name of a mermaid in the folklore of Wales. Her flocks of sheep were the waves, and every ninth one was a ram. The bard Rhys Llwyd ap Rhys ap Rhuert wrote in the sixteenth century:

Haid ddefaid Gwenhudwy
A naw hwrdd yn un a hwy.
(A troop of the sheep of Gwenhuwy
And nine rams along with them.)

References 59
See also Mermaid, Appendix 25

GWILLION, GWYLLION
These are the evil mountain fairies in the folklore of Wales. The Gwillion are described as hideous hags seen walking on the roads in foul weather. They could also materialize in the shape of goats. It is said that they combed the goats' beards on Wednesdays, the fairy sabbath. The most feared of them is the Old Woman of the Mountain. The Gwillion, when not leading night-bound travelers astray in the mountains and forests, may call at the homes of the community about Aberystwyth, where the terrified inhabitants allow the Gwillion to shelter on stormy nights. These supernatural hags, like many others of their kind, are vanquished and disappear at the sight of an iron knife.
References 17, 44, 123, 125
See also Fairy, Hag, Old Woman of the Mountain

GWRACH Y RHIBYN
In the folklore of the Powys, Wales, this is a spirit whose name means the Hag with the Dribble. This hideous hag is described as having long, dishevelled red hair, sunken eyes above a hooked nose, fang-like black teeth, and disproportionately long wrinkled arms. She might appear to humans at a crossroads or a ford, where she would shriek or dash the water in a frenzy. Usually invisible to all but those who receive her attention, Gwrach y Rhibyn, also known as y Cyhiraeth, behaves in much the same way as the Irish banshee, as a supernatural warning of a death or misfortune in the family. However, the Gwrach y Rhibyn accompanies the spouse or the parent of the one who will be lost, and wailing audibly on reaching any crossroad, "My wife!" or "My husband!" or "My little child!", alerts the spouse or parent to their fate. If the wailing is heard but is unintelligible, then the one who hears it is the subject of the warning.
References 17, 87, 108, 123
See also Banshee, Baba Yaga, Hag, Spirit, Appendix 22

GWRAGEDD ANNWN
These are the Lake Fairies or Ladies of the Lake in the folklore of Wales. They are described as beautiful maidens with long golden hair, but unlike the mermaids the Gwragedd Annwn are gentle and have no fish's tail. The Gwragedd Annwn live harmoniously in families under the lakes and are known sometimes to marry mortals. Typical of such tales is one where a widow's son falls in love with one of the Gwragedd Annwn whom he sees combing her hair on the surface of the lake. He entices her to come to him, but after several days of testing his tenacity, at last he is requested to identify his lady from among others. Successfully choosing her he is only allowed to take her as his bride, with her dowry of cattle, so long as he never strikes her, and treats her kindly; otherwise,

Taking the form of a dog, Gytrash prepares to attack a kneeling victim.

all will be lost. As with all such tales, the promise is broken unintentionally, and the distraught husband loses his wife, his children, and his cattle.
References 15, 17, 18, 44, 123, 125
See also Fairy, Lady of the Lake, Selkie, Undine, Urvashi, Appendix 25

GWRAGEN ANNWN
See Plant Annwn

GWR-DRWGIAID
This is the name for an imp or little devil in Welsh folklore.
References 108
See also Bwca, Devil, Imp

GWŶLL
This is the name of a spirit or sprite in the folklore of Wales. This invisible spirit behaves like a goblin or pixy as it delights in riding the horses in the stables at night. These sprites perform such frantic riding of the horses, that the animals are in a lather when found in the stable the next morning.
References 59
See also Goblin, Pixie, Spirit, Sprite

GWYN AP KNUDD
In early Welsh legends Gwyn ap Knudd is the Celtic deity of battles and the dead. With the coming of Christianity, his status was relegated to that of the supernatural controller of demons in the Arthurian underworld. In this capacity from his court on Glastonbury Tor in Somerset, England, Gwyn ap Knudd is the leader of the Wild Hunt, gathering the unbaptized for his underworld. The further degeneration of the status of Gwyn ap Knudd reveals him as the king of the Plant Annwn or the Tylwyth Teg, the Welsh fairies.
References 17, 119, 125
See also Demon, Fairy, Tylwyth Teg, Wild Hunt

GYHLDEPTIS
A gentle vegetation spirit inhabiting the area of the northwest Pacific coast in the folk beliefs of the Native Americans. Gyhldeptis, whose name means Hanging Hair, like the Greek Dryads, dwelt in and protected the trees as well as the mortal inhabitants of the forests. There is a story of how she was instrumental in getting other spirits to remove the great whirlpool spirit Keagyihl Depguesk from the river.
References 25

See also Dryad, Keagyihl Depguesk, Spirit, Appendix 18

GYL-BURNT-TAYL
This is a local name in Warwickshire English folklore for the female Will o' the Wisp. Gyl or Jill was a name often used over a century ago to refer the flirtatious tendencies of a young woman, and in this case it is used as the name for the spirit, whose flirting and enticing light also lead the follower into trouble.
References 17
See also Spirit, Will o' the Wisp

GYRE-CARLIN, GY-CARLIN
In the area of Fyfe in Scotland, this is the name given to the queen of the fairies. She was particularly the patron of the spinsters, and it was considered disrespectful to leave flax unfinished on New Year's Eve. The Gyre-Carlin's anger would be invoked, and she would take it from the lazy spinner. This may be the basis of the present haste to complete knitting before New Year's Day.

Gyre-Carlin was also the name given to certain special cakes made in celebration of the completion of the harvest and the taking of the Carlin.

References 17
See also Carlin, Fairy, Appendix 14

GYTRASH
In the folklore of the north of England this evil road spirit, also known as Guytrash, is a portent of death and disaster. It is a shape-shifting spirit and can take any form, usually taking that of an animal such as a horse, cow, mule, or dog. It is most frequently seen as a large shaggy-haired dog with glowing eyes. The Gytrash, like the Padfoot, follows night-bound travelers on lonely moorland roads and brings misfortune and terror to those who are too slow to get away. Charlotte Brontë describes the Gytrash in *Jane Eyre* (1847).
References 17, 28, 40, 107
See also Barguest, Black Dog, Black Shuck, Boggart, Bullbeggar, Capelthwaite, Church Grim, Freybug, Lubin, Mauthe Doog, Padfoot, Rongeur d'Os, Skriker, Spirit, Appendix 12, Appendix 24

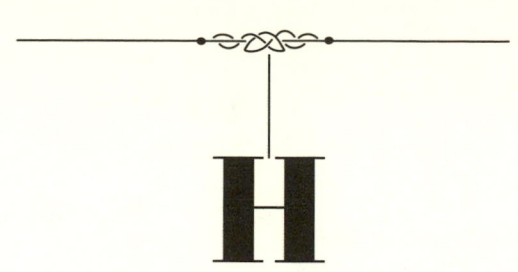

H

HABETROT, HABITROT, HABTROT

In the folklore of the northern counties of England, she is a fairy who, though appearing old and ugly with a deformed lip, is the kind-hearted patron of spinsters and their spinning. She inhabits the underside of a huge stone in a grassy knoll with sisters who resemble her, one of whom is Scantilie Mab, who is more ugly, with bulging eyes and a hooked nose. A garment woven by Habetrot was said to ward off any ailment for the wearer.

A tale from the English Border Country tells how a young girl could not spin no matter how hard she tried, at a time when spinning was the way to a successful marriage settlement. In despair she wandered by a grassy knoll where Habetrot observed her distress. The fairy promised the girl to do her spinning so long as she never disclosed the fairy's name. The yarn was duly delivered and the happy girl ran home, arriving after her mother had gone to bed. In the morning the mother discovered the yarn so finely spun that she immediately ran bragging to the neighbors. A *laird* passing on his horse was so impressed that he demanded to see this girl, and it was love at first sight. After a short period, the wedding took place, but the bridegroom demanded her fine spinning for his clothes. Habetrot again came to her aid and invited the bride and groom to visit her and her sisters while they did their spinning. The groom accepted and when he entered by the stone on the grassy knoll he did not show any disdain for his wife's supernatural friends. However, he inquired if he might know how they came by their strangely deformed lips. Habetrot cleverly told him that the deformity was the result of spinning, and from that moment the *laird* swore that his wife would never spin again.

References 17, 66
See also Fairy, Appendix 14

HABONDE

The name of a fairy of English folklore who was said to be the consort of Hobany. She is described as a beautiful young woman with dark plaited hair, wearing on her head a golden circlet on which there is a star. This is to signify that she is a queen of the fairies, and possibly of the French fairies. Habonde is also known as Abundia or Wandering Dame Abonde.

References 10
See also Fairy, Hobany, White Lady

HABORYM

In medieval European demonology, the demon that causes destructive fires.

References 53
See also Demon

HACTCI, HACTCIN

These spirits are known in the beliefs of the Apache Native American people as the children of the Black Sky and Earth.

References 88
See also Gahe, Spirit

HAD AL' KHORINE

A euphemism for the djinns in the folklore of Morocco. The name Had al' Khorine means Those Others and is used as a safe manner of referring to the spirits without invoking their presence or their malevolence.

References 90
See also Djinn, Spirit

HADARNIEL

A powerful angel who is described in the Jewish scriptures (Exodus 24:18) as challenging Moses on Mount Sinai before Moses received the Ten Commandments.

References 30
See also Angel

HADDUOK ENNASS

A euphemism in the folklore of Morocco for the djinns. The name Hadduok Ennass means These People and is used as a safe manner of referring to the spirits without invoking their presence or their malevolent activities.

References 90
See also Djinn, Spirit

HAFERBOCKS

In German folklore this is a field spirit whose name means the Oats Goat. The Haferbocks is invoked at harvest time when the spirit is trapped in the final swathe of the crop and the final sheaf is taken. An effigy of the spirit may be made with the final sheaf in the likeness of the Oats Goat, which is celebrated at a festival.
References 87, 88
See also Bullkater, Cailleach Bera, Corn Spirit, Kornwolf, Oats Goat, Spirit, Appendix 18

HAG, HAGGE

A supernatural being taking the form of a crone. The spirit may be benevolent but is more often of malicious intent. Hags abound in Celtic and Teutonic folklore, and the term is often applied to the queens of the Sidhe and corn spirits such as the Scottish Cailleac. They are said to build islands, cromlechs, and other topographical features. The activities of these spirits are often associated with the weather, harvests, and spinning. A hag may also be a succubus plaguing a sleeper, especially during the Celtic feasts of Beltane and Samhain. In this respect the term Hagge is the sixteenth-century English name for the Nightmare.
References 17, 88
See also Cailleac, Cailleach Bera, Corn Spirit, Nightmare, Sídhe, Spirit, Succubus, Appendix 14, Appendix 26

HAGITH

An Olympian spirit of the universe whose name was used in the mysticism of medieval Europe.
References 53
See also Spirit

HAGNO

In classical Roman mythology she was one of the three nymphs who provided the infant Jupiter with his education. Her sisters, Neda and Thisoa were the other two.
References 130
See also Nymph, Appendix 22

HAIKUR

See Nicker

HAIRY JACK

In the folklore of Lincolnshire, England, this is the name of a type of barguest or evil spirit.
References 17
See also Barguest, Spirit

HAIRY MEG

See Mieg Moulach

HAIRY ONES, THE

See Dusii

HAKEL-BÄREND

In the region of Westphalia in Germany this is a term for the Wild Huntsman. The name Hakel-Bärend means Mantle-Bearing. There are two possible reasons for this name. The first reason is the great black cloak that the demon wears that flies around him on his stormy rides. The second reason is related to a human by the name of Hans von Hackelberg. Von Hackelberg was the Duke of Brunswick's chief huntsman who was said to have been condemned to hunt until eternity with the hounds of Hell for hunting instead of attending church on Sundays.
References 95
See also Demon, Devil's Dandy Dogs, Holle, Wild Hunt, Wild Huntsman

HAKENMANN

This is a malevolent water spirit in Teutonic mythology and folklore.
References 88
See also Havmand, Merman, Nix, Spirit, Appendix 25

HALAK GIHMAL

See Mat Chinoi

HALDDE

In the folk beliefs of the Lapp people of northern Scandinavia and Russia, this is the name for a nature spirit. This name is also used in combination with other subsidiary names to indicate a close relationship of activities.
References 88
See also Čacce-Haldde, Haltia, Mära-Halddo, Appendix 18

HALDJAS

This is the name for nature spirits in the folk beliefs of the Estonian people, and this term is used as a suffix in combination with other terms to show the relationship of their activities.
References 87
See also Haldde, Haltia, Koduhaldjas, Majahaldjas, Metsänhaltia, Appendix 18

HALTIA

This is a general term for the protective spirits in the folk beliefs of the Finnish people. This name is also used in combination with other names to show the relationship of their activities.
References 88

See also Domovoi, Haldde, Haldjas, Kodinhaltia, Metsänhaltia, Talonhaltija, Tonttu, Vedenhaltia, Appendix 21

HAMADRYAD
In the classical mythology of Greece and Rome, this is the name of nymphs of the trees who inhabited and were part of the trees they protected. They are described as being beautiful females to the waist, and the lower parts of their bodies are the trunk of the tree and its roots. Hamadryads die with their tree but if it is cut down by a mortal, the nymph will cry out as the first cut is made.
References 7, 53, 92, 107, 110
See also Akakasoh, Boomasoh, Dryad, Nymph, Shekkasoh, Appendix 19

HAMINGJA
This is the name of a female household guardian spirit in the folklore of Cumbria and the Isle of Man (United Kingdom). She is the protector of the family and the bringer of good fortune or luck to its family. In this way the spirit is passed from generation to generation. It is believed that the name Hamingja and the spirit's description derive from the Norse traditions when the Vikings invaded these lands a thousand years ago.
References 133
See also Domovoi, Spirit, Appendix 21, Appendix 22

HAMOU UKAIOU
This is the name of an evil and malicious Afrit in the folklore of Morocco. He is said to be the husband of the djinn Aicha Kandida. Hamou Ukaiou pursues women traveling alone at night, as his wife does with men, in order to attack and devour them. It is said that sharpening a knife on the ground may put them to flight.
References 90
See also Afrit, Aicha Kandida, Djinn

HAMPELMANN
This is a name for a goblin or mannikin in the folk-lore of Germany.
References 133
See also Goblin, Mannikin

HANGING HAIR
See Gyhldeptis

HANTU
In the folk beliefs of the Malay people of West Malaysia, this is a general term for spirits of all descriptions, including demons, ghosts, goblins, fairies, and all types of evil spirits. The Hantu may also be referred to as Sheitan, a word from which the Christian "Satan" is derived.

References 88
See also Demon, Fairy, Goblin, Shaitan, Spirit

HANTU AYER
This is a general term for water spirits in the folk beliefs of the Malay people of West Malaysia. The name Hantu Ayer means Water Spirit, but these supernaturals are confined to the fresh water such as rivers, streams and lakes.
References 120
See also Hantu, Appendix 25

HANTU BAKAL
In the folk beliefs of the Malay people of West Malaysia, this is an evil nature spirit that inhabits the jungle.
References 120
See also Hantu, Spirit

HANTU BAN DAN
The name of a water spirit in the folk beliefs of the Malay people of West Malaysia. The Hantu Ban Dan is the demon of the waterfall. This spirit manifests in the shape of a copper cooking pot lying prone on the water surface where the torrent meets the rocks.
References 120
See also Ceffyll-dŵr, Demon, Fossegrim, Hantu, Nix, Spirit, Appendix 25

HANTU BELIAN
In the folklore of the Malay people of Selangor, West Malaysia, this is the spirit of the tiger. It takes the form of a bird sitting on the back of a tiger, where it is always safe. This demon is invoked by humans as a familiar to enrich the person who controls it, as its speciality is stealing diamonds.
References 120
See also Aitvaras, Demon, Familiar, Hantu, Spirit, Appendix 12, Appendix 20

HANTU B'ROK
This is a spirit or demon in the folk beliefs of the Malay people of West Malaysia. It takes the shape of the baboon when it materializes in the forests. He may take possession of entranced dancers, inducing them to perform fantastic feats of climbing.
References 120
See also Curupira (2), Demon, Hantu, Spirit, Appendix 12

HANTU DENAI
This is a demon in the folk beliefs of the Malay people of West Malaysia. The name Hantu Denai means Spirit of the Tracks. This demon is said to be present in the tracks of wild beasts, awaiting the opportunity to attack human hunters following their quarry.

References 120
See also Demon, Hantu, Appendix 12

HANTU GAHARU

The demon or guardian spirit of the Gaharu or aloe
wood tree (the source of a perfume) in the folklore of
the Malay people of West Malaysia. The Hantu
Gaharu, whose name means Spirit of the Aloe Wood,
will not allow his trees to be cut down by humans
unless a human life is given in exchange. When a
human needs to cut down such a tree, the Hantu
Gaharu will visit him in a dream and demand the
sacrifice. The victim is selected from among those
who are still asleep and the person's forehead is
smeared with lime. When the spirit sees this, Hantu
Gaharu takes the soul of the victim and the tree may
be cut down and taken in return.
References 110, 120
See also Dryad, Guardian, Hantu, Hantu Gharu,
Hantu Hutan, Hantu Kayu, Spirit, Appendix 19

HANTU GHARU

A powerful and dangerous demon in the folk beliefs
of the Malay people of West Malaysia. The name
Hantu Gharu means the Spirit of the Eagle Wood
Tree, and, as this implies, he is the guardian spirit of
that tree. When an eagle wood tree has to be felled
care must be taken in the preparations for its fall to
the earth, as the spirit will take every opportunity to
harm those who chop it down. Even when the tree is
on the ground, no one should pass between the severed trunk and its root stump, or the Hantu Gharu
will take their life.
References 110, 120
See also Demon, Dryad, Guardian, Hantu, Hantu
Gaharu, Hantu Hutan, Hantu Kayu, Spirit,
Appendix 19

HANTU HANTUAN

This is the collective name for the group of spirits in
the folk beliefs of the Malay people of West Malaysia.
These demons inhabit the jungle and take delight in
confusing people who venture there by echoing their
human voices.
References 120
See also Demon, Hantu, Spirit

HANTU HUTAN

In the folk beliefs of the Malay people of West
Malaysia, this is a general term for the evil spirits or
demons of the forest. The name Hantu Hutan means
Forest Spirit.
References 110, 120
See also Demon, Dryad, Hantu, Hantu Gaharu, Hantu
Gharu, Hantu Kayu, Spirit, Appendix 19

HANTU KAYU

In the folk beliefs of the Malay people of West
Malaysia, this is a general term for the spirits or
demons that inhabit the trees. The Hantu Kayu,
whose name means Wood Spirit, are greatly feared as
they are frequently malicious and are considered
responsible for bringing sickness to humans who
venture into the forests.
References 110
See also Demon, Hantu Bakal, Hantu Gaharu, Hantu
Gharu, Hantu Hutan, Spirit, Appendix 17,
Appendix 19

HANTU KOPEK

This is an evil spirit in the folklore of the Malay peo-
ple of West Malaysia. Hantu Kopek means the Flaccid
Spirit and is the term in Bahasa Melayu (Malay
Language) for the spirit known in Europe as the
Nightmare. This spirit will come in the night to
oppress those who are trying to sleep and disturb
those who are already sleeping.
References 120
See also Hantu, Nightmare, Spirit

HANTU KUBOR

This is a fearsome spirit in the folk belief of the Malay
people of West Malaysia. The Hantu Kubor, which
means Grave Spirit is the name of grave demons
that—like the ghoul—hover where humans have
been interred, awaiting the opportunity to attack the
living as well as the dead.
References 120
See also Demon, Ghoul, Hantu, Spirit

HANTU LAUT

A general term for sea spirits in the folk beliefs of the
Malay people of West Malaysia. The name Hantu
Laut means Sea Spirit.
References 120
See also Hantu, Si Raya, Spirit, Appendix 25

HANTU LONGGOK

The Hantu Longgok, which means the Spirit of the
Rubbish Heaps, is a demon in the folk beliefs of the
Malay people of West Malaysia. It is a male disease
spirit. When humans have been attacked by this
spirit it can be recognized from their behavior since
they look upwards at the sky all the time and foam at
the mouth.
References 120
See also Demon, Hantu, Appendix 17

HANTU PEMBURU

This is the name of a fearful spirit in the folk beliefs
of the Malay people of West Malaysia. Hantu
Pemburu, which means the Hunter Spirit in Bahasa

Melayu (the Malay Language), is a version of the Wild Huntsman. The Hantu Pemburu hunts through the stormy skies with his pack of supernatural hounds, as in the European Wild Hunt. Like his European counterpart, this spirit searches for those who are traveling alone, and for the lost souls of sinners to transport them directly to hell.
References 120
See also Hantu Si Buru, Spirit, Wild Hunt, Wild Huntsman, Appendix 24

HANTU RAYA
In the folk beliefs of the Malay people of West Malaysia, this is a powerful demon. Hantu Raya, whose name means Great Spirit, inhabits the center of a crossroads awaiting any late or unwary traveler to prey upon.
References 120
See also Demon, Hantu

HANTU RIBUT
The name of the storm demon or fiend in the folk beliefs of the Malay people of West Malaysia. The name Hantu Ribut means Spirit of the Storm in Bahasa Melayu. He stirs up the whirlwind and screeches through the forests causing destruction.
References 120
See also Demon, Fiend, Hantu, Kompagnin, Virra Birron, Appendix 26

HANTU RIMBA
The name of a forest demon in the folk beliefs of the Malay people of West Malaysia. The name Hantu Rimba means Spirit of the Primeval Forest in Bahasa Melayu. He inhabits the deep jungle, where it is dangerous for humans to penetrate.
References 120
See also Demon, Hantu, Appendix 19

HANTU SAWAN
This is a demon in the folk beliefs of the Malay people of West Malaysia. Hantu Sawan, whose name means Spirit of Convulsions, is the evil spirit that causes children to have fits and convulsive attacks.
References 120
See also Demon, Hantu, Appendix 17, Appendix 22

HANTU SI BURU
This is the name of a spirit in the folk beliefs of the Malay people of West Malaysia. Hantu Si Buru, whose name means the Spirit that Hunts, is a demon hunter who roams the jungle with his pack of hounds at the time of the full moon. It is said that the call of the brik-brik bird warns that the Hantu Si Buru is coming. It is fatal for any human to see him, for the Hantu Si Buru is the portent of sickness and

death. Offerings and propitiation are made to the spirit for cures which sometimes occur. The Hantu Si Buru was once a man whose pregnant wife craved the meat of a mouse deer in calf to guarantee the birth of a son. Her husband was eager to hunt for the meat and vowed that he would not return without it, but, having misheard his wife, he set out to kill a buck big with calf. His child was born, but still the father pursued his impossible chase, sending his dogs into the sky and swiveling his neck to search in all directions, thus gradually becoming the demon hunter for all eternity.
References 88
See also Demon, Hakel-Bärend, Hantu Pemburu, Spirit, Wild Hunt, Wild Huntsman

HANTU SONGKEI
In the folk beliefs of the Malay people this spirit is known as the Loosening Demon. He is described as having an enormous nose and eyes stretching around his head so that he can see all around; he is invisible below the waist. This demon releases the animal traps set by humans for food, so that the animals are not caught.
References 120
See also Demon, Hantu, Spirit, Appendix 12

HAPIÑUÑU
In the folk beliefs of the Quechua and Aymara people of Bolivia, these are female demons that fly through the night skies, entrapping humans in their dangling breasts and carrying off their victims.
References 88
See also Demon, Harpy

HARES, AL HARIS
See Iblis

HĀRITI
This is the name of a female demon in the mythology of India; of China, where she is known as He-Li-Di or Kishimojin; and of Japan, where she is known as Karitei-mo. In the mythology of India and China this demon trapped and devoured children until converted by the Buddha. Hāriti is now a guardian of children and elevated to the status of a goddess able to bless couples with children and cure sick children. As Kariteimo, her original Japanese name, she is especially venerated by the Shingon and Nichiren sects in Japan, where she is represented holding a child or the flower of happiness.
References 93, 102
See also Demon, Guardian, Appendix 22

HAROOT AND MAROOT
See Harut

HARPY

In classical Greek and Roman mythology the Harpies were originally wind spirits personifying the storm winds, hurricanes, and whirlwinds, and later transformed to the role of vengeful hideous demons or fiends. There are various accounts of their origins: They are the daughters of Thaumas and Electra, or the daughters of Neptune and Terra, or the daughters of Typhon and Echidna. Their number also varies from one to five according to the author. Homer mentions Podarge, meaning Swift-Foot; Hesiod mentions Aëllo, meaning Swift as the Storm, and Ocypete, meaning Swift-Flying; and others mention Celeno, Keliano, meaning Black, and Aellopus, meaning Storm-Footed. They are described as having bird bodies with the heads and torsos of ugly women, bears' ears, and human arms with talons for fingers. They were not only ugly but foul-smelling, and they contaminated whatever they touched. The Harpies feature in the tales of Jason and the Argonauts, who eventually help to bring about the demise of these demonic sisters.
References 20, 29, 40, 56, 88, 92, 93, 107, 129, 130
See also Demon, Electra, Fiend, Podarge, Spirit, Appendix 26

HARR

The name Harr, which means the Old One or the High One is one of the rock dwarfs mentioned in the Eddas of Nordic mythology.
References 41
See also Dwarf

HARRY-CA-NAB

This is the name of an individual spirit in the local folklore of the Lickey Hills near Bromsgrove in Worcestershire, England. He is one of the chief demons or huntsman fiends who rides in the Wild Hunt across the skies of Worcestershire. Harry-ca-nab rides on a white bull escorting the Devil and his hounds on stormy nights in search of lost souls.
References 47
See also Demon, Fiend, Spirit, Wild Hunt, Wild Huntsman

HARUN, HARUNA

In the folk beliefs of Morocco, these are dangerous water spirits that may manifest as snakes in the rivers. Offerings of couscous and bread are made to placate them.
References 93
See also Spirit, Appendix 25

HARUT AND MARUT

In the Islamic tradition, these are two angels, also known as Haroot and Maroot, who were sent to Earth by Allah as tutelary spirits in human form, for the benefit of mankind. However, they used their powers to indulge themselves in all manner of human sins, and as a result of this they were cast out from Heaven forever. They joined other Fallen Angels such as Iblis and undertook to initiate humans into the black arts, bringing conflict and misery.
References 41, 88, 114
See also Agloolik, Angel, Fylgja, Haruts, Iblis, Nagual, Shemyaza, Tutelary Spirit, Zoa

HARUTS

In the classical Hindu mythology of India, this is the name for the sons of Rudra, the god of storms, and the reason that these storm-cloud spirits are also called the Rudras. Their number varies according to the version of the legend, between two and 180. The Haruts are the military attendants of the god Indra. They are described as warriors in golden armor riding chariots drawn by spotted deer, traveling across the thunderclouds armed with spears of lightning. They chase and defeat Vritra the demon of drought, releasing the sacred cows bearing rain. In their more violent activities as winds uprooting trees and howling through the forests, they resemble the activities of the Wild Hunt of European folklore.
References 29, 56, 88, 93, 102, 110, 119
See also Demon, Vritra, Wild Hunt, Appendix 26

HATIF

This invisible spirit in Arabic pre-Islamic traditions is a type of djinn or nature spirit. Far from being dangerous, unlike later djinns, Hatif gave advice and warnings to humans who possessed the ability to hear him.
References 41, 53
See also Djinn, Spirit, Appendix 18

HAUGBONDE

This is the name of a spirit in old Norse folklore. Haugbonde was regarded as the guardian of the farms and those who lived there.
References 47
See also Guardian, Hogboon, Spirit

HAURA

See Houri

HAURVATAT

This is the name of a spirit in the Zoroastrian religion of Iran. Haurvatat means Well-Being, Saving Health, or Wholeness. He is one of the Amesha Spentas and Yazatas and is an attendant genius of Ahura Mazda. Haurvatat is also the benevolent spirit associated with the water of the earth and the afterlife. He may have been derived from an earlier river deity.

References 41, 88
See also Amesha Spentas, Attendant Spirit, Genius, Yazatas

HAUS-SCHMIEDLEIN

In the folklore of Bohemia these are the dwarfs or knockers of the silver mines. Although rarely seen, they are described as being like squat, little old men with over-large heads and dressed in the same kind of clothes as the miners. The Haus-Schmiedlein, like the knockers of Cornwall, would rap from within the walls of the tunnels to indicate to the miners where they could find a rich vein of silver ore. The closer the miners got to it, the louder the noise would be. When the miners heard the Haus-Schmiedlein hammering from all directions in the tunnels, it was then that they knew that the Little People were warning them of an imminent roof fall and to flee the mine shaft. In return for their help the miners would leave food or infants' clothing for the Haus-Schmiedlein.
References 38
See also Dwarf, Knockers, Kobold, Little People, Mine Spirits

HAVFRUE

In Danish folklore the Havfrue is a very beautiful mermaid with long golden hair, which she may be seen combing while floating on the surface of the sea. The Havfrue can be both benevolent and malevolent. She is regarded as being able to foretell events of importance, and the birth of the Danish king Christian IV of Denmark was supposedly foretold by a Havfrue. She may be seen driving her milk-white cattle over the dunes to feed on the shore, or glimpsed through the early summer sea mists hovering on the surface of the water. But these sightings are usually portents of wild and stormy weather. She has been reported as visiting the fishermen's night fires on the shore in the guise of a beautiful maiden who is wet and suffering from the cold. Any who are unwary and enticed to her side may be taken by her to her watery underworld with all the other bodies of the drowned who never resurface.
References 18, 78, 88
See also Bar, Havmand, Mermaid, Appendix 25

HAVMAND

In Scandinavian folklore the Havmand is a beneficent merman also known as the Havstrambe in the folklore of Greenland. He is described as being very handsome in human shape, having either a green or black beard and hair. When not in his water home under the sea, he may be in the cliff and rock caves along the shore.
References 18, 78, 89, 99
See also Havfrue, Mermaid, Appendix 25

HAVSTRAMBE
See Havmand

HAYAGRIVA

There are two spirits sharing this name although one is a deity. This is the name of a demon in the classical mythology of India. Hayagriva, whose name means Horses Neck, is described as having a little pot-bellied human torso with a horse's head. In the mythology of the Vedas, this evil member of the Daityas stole the scriptures but was ultimately defeated by Vishnu in the *avatar* of a fish.

(In Tibetan Buddhism Hayagriva is a protective deity who guards humans from demon attacks.)
References 15, 33, 41
See also Daityas, Demon, Spirit

HEA-BANI

In the epic legends of ancient Chaldea, Hea-Bani seems to have been a nature spirit or satyr. He lived in the forests and communicated with living and supernatural beings including the trees and their spirits. Hea-Bani interpreted the dreams of Izdubar and accompanied the future king of Erech in his battles and journeys to his future kingdom. When Izdubar rejected the advances of the goddess Ishtar, she destroyed Hea-Bani in revenge.
References 110
See also Satyr, Spirit, Appendix 18

HEADLESS WOMAN, THE

In the folklore of Lancashire, England, this is a boggart in the shape of a Headless Woman said to haunt the lanes in the district of Longridge. This malicious spirit would appear in the guise of an old woman wearing the old-fashioned shawl and "coal-skuttle" bonnet, hobbling along the roads and carrying a basket on her arm. She would walk along with any traveler, head bent, seemingly listening to their conversation. When she turned to look at her companion the human would be startled to see that the bonnet contained nothing. Then her animated head would leap cackling with laughter from the basket and chase the terrified traveler for miles. One tale relates how a husband, after a night's drinking, was accosted by the Headless Woman and, in his terror, miraculously vaulted hedges and gates to achieve the safety of his home. His pragmatic wife commented, "If it meks tha fain o' thi own hearthstoan, I'se be some glad on it, for it's moor nor a woman wi' a heead on her showters hae bin able to do." (If it makes you appreciate your own home, I'll be glad, because its more than a woman with a head on her shoulders has ever been able to do.)
References 47
See also Boggart, Spirit, Appendix 24

HEDAMMU

In the mythology of the Horites, invaders of ancient Mesopotamia, Hedammu was a sea demon who manifested in the shape of a snake.
References 93
See also Demon, Appendix 25

HEDLEY KOW

In the folklore of Hedley near Ebchester in Northumberland, northern England, this is a type of mischievous sprite or bogey beast. Although called the Hedley Kow, this spirit could transform itself into almost any shape to work its pranks. In the shape of a cow, the Hedley Kow would resemble the farmer's milch cow up to the point of being milked, when it would kick over the pail, slip its noose, and run away laughing; or it would wander into the farmwife's kitchen, scattering the cheeses, giving the cream to the cats, and unraveling the spinning and knitting. The exasperated farmer once took a cane to it, but to his surprise the stick was grabbed and laid to his own back. In the shape of a horse, the sprite would allow itself to be harnessed and ridden as far as a brook or bog, when it would slip from the tack and toss its riders into the mire, laughing at their plight. The Hedley Kow would tease old women out to gather fire sticks by assuming the shape of a bundle of kindling in the road. As soon as the poor dame tried to pick it up, the sprite would roll just out of reach, leading the unfortunate woman on a merry dance, then running off giggling.

Henderson, in *Folk-Lore of the Northern Counties* (1866), gives an unusual story of how the Hedley Kow assumed two shapes simultaneously. Two young men had arranged to meet their young ladies near Newlands in the same district. They saw their sweethearts walking ahead, but no matter how they tried to catch up with them, it was almost impossible. At last, when just within reach, the men found they were up to their knees in a bog. The image of their young ladies dissolved into a horrible cackling bogey beast that harried them as they scrambled terrified out of the bog, running as fast as their legs could carry them. As they approached the river Derwent, in their confusion, the young men blundered into each other and fell headlong into the water, each thinking the other was the Hedley Kow and thrashing at him to get away. They eventually reached the safety of their homes separately.
References 15, 17, 18, 66, 69, 133
See also Bogie, Bogle, Shellycoat, Spirit, Sprite

HEINZE

See Kobold

HEINZELMANN, HEINZELMÄNCHEN (pl.)

In the folklore of Cologne, Germany, these were friendly household spirits like the brownies of English folklore. They worked at night in the bakeries and trades shops with such excellent skill that the masters needed fewer apprentices. No one knew what they looked like, but people were content to accept the wonderful craftsmanship, until one tailor's wife could not bridle her curiosity. She was determined to have a look at them, so she scattered dried peas all over the floor of the workshop, thinking that if one of the Heinzelmänchen were to fall, he would not be able to retreat. She was wrong, the Heinzelmänchen avoided her trickery and departed forever.
References 8, 18, 88
See also Brownie, Spirit, Appendix 22

HEITSI-EIBIB

In the folk beliefs of the Khoisan people of South Africa, this bush spirit is revered and propitiated as a "grandfather" and guardian of those who go out to hunt.
References 93
See also Guardian, Spirit, Appendix 21

HELD

The name of one of the Norns in the later versions of the Teutonic myths where there are more than the original three. In some versions of the legend, Held was considered to be the bad fairy in the traditional tale of *Sleeping Beauty*.
References 95
See also Fairy, Norns, Appendix 23

HELICONIADES

See Muses

HE-LI-DI

This is the Chinese name for the spirit in Buddhist belief known as Hāriti.
References 93, 102
See also Hāriti, Spirit

HENG

In the beliefs of the Huron Native American people, this is the energetic but blundering spirit of thunder. He is also known as De Hi No, Heno, or Hino. He was so clumsy in his charging through the forests that he frequently smashed down too many trees and uprooted others. The damage was so great that his brothers decided to confine Heng to an island where he could do no more harm. Although now he still sometimes splits the trees with thunderbolts hurled from his chariot clouds, he also delivers the warm rain needed for agricultural success.
References 25, 119
See also Spirit, Appendix 26

HENKIES

In the folklore of the Orkney and Shetland Islands off the north coast of Scotland, the Henkies are a type of troll. Among these trolls or trows, as they are called in these islands, were ones that had a pronounced limp or *henk* when they danced, and this particular group of spirits was therefore identified by this name.
References 17
See also Spirit, Troll, Trow

HENO

See Heng

HERECGUNINA

The name of a powerful evil spirit in the beliefs of the northern forest-dwelling Native Americans.
References 25
See also Spirit

HERENSUGUE

This is a demon in the folk beliefs of the Basque people of northern Spain and southwestern France. The Herensugue is said to manifest in a form with seven heads or as a snake that can fly through the air like the Aitvaras to do its evil deeds.
References 93
See also Aitvaras, Demon

HERLETHINGUS, HERLETHINGI, HERLE'S RADE

This is a name for the Wild Hunt in English folk beliefs recorded as long ago as the twelfth century, and this name was later transformed in France to Mesnie Herlequin. The tradition is derived from a supposed early English King Herle (or Herlewin, or Hurlwain) who was duped into attending the wedding feast of a fairy or dwarf that lasted three fairy days (300 human days). When the king returned to his domain he was given a fairy dog to accompany him and his troops and was told that under no circumstances should they dismount until the dog had leapt to the ground. Several of the king's men were eager to be home and dismounted without waiting for the fairy dog. As their feet touched the earth, they crumbled to dust. The dog is said still to be on the pommel of the king's saddle, and he and his troops have long since transformed to being the hunters of lost souls. "Herlewain" is also possibly a corruption of Hell Wain, the Old English words for the Hell Waggon, which was a part of folklore in the west of England well into the nineteenth century.
References 88, 95, 133
See also Fairy, Wild Hunt

HERNE THE HUNTER

This legendary spirit is entirely local to the Windsor Great Park surrounding Windsor Castle, one of the main residences of the English monarchy. He is described as an imposing human shape with billowing cloak over deerskin garments and his head covered by the skull and antlers of a stag. His whole form is said to emanate a sort of phosphorescent glow. Sometimes he has been observed standing statuesque beneath Herne's Oak, at other times riding a great black steed breathing fire. The origins of this guardian spirit have been speculated to be from the Celtic horned fertility god Cernnunos or the transformed ghost of a forest keeper, as described in Shakespeare's *The Merry Wives of Windsor* (1623). Shakespeare's is the first written account of the spirit and the great tree known as Herne's Oak, which was said to be over 600 years old when it ceased to grow in 1790 (in the reign of George III). There is some confusion as to when it was replaced; some say by Queen Victoria in 1863, while others state that the new Herne's Oak was planted by Edward VII on 29 January 1906.

To see Herne the Hunter is a portent of death or disaster, and there are numerous recordings of such sightings in the twentieth century: 1931, the start of the economic depression; 1936, the abdication crisis; 1939, the declaration of war; 1952, the death of King George VI. Herne the Hunter is also sometimes associated with the Wild Hunt as its supernatural huntsman, gathering the souls of the damned and delivering them to Hell. Although there are numerous legends about the appearance of Herne the Hunter, none seems more disturbing than that told to the folklorist Ruth Tongue in 1964. Three youths dressed in the "Teddy Boy" style of the sixties and bent on a night of wanton vandalism were breaking saplings in the Great Park when one found an old hunting horn in the leaves. Thinking that a recent film crew had left it there by mistake, he picked it up and gave a blast on it. The other two could not remember seeing a film crew, and, having second thoughts about being there, started to run. The blast had invoked the baying of hounds, and the youth, now feeling "rather strange," called to the others as he staggered after them towards the old chapel. By now they could hear the padding of feet in the soft earth and the breathing of the hounds pursuing them. As the staggering youth reached the chapel door, there was a sound like a whistling arrow through the air, and though the others saw nothing behind him, the lad screamed and fell. When they reached him they could see that he was dead with no apparent cause, and the forest was totally silent once more.
References 17, 40, 48, 69, 133
See also Guardian, Spirit, Wild Hunt, Appendix 12, Appendix 19

HEROK'A
These are benevolent earth spirits in the folk beliefs of the Native Americans of the northern forests. Their name means Those Without Horns.
References 25
See also Maahiset, Spirit

HERSCHEKLOS
See Knecht Ruprecht

HESPERESTHUSA
See Hesperides

HESPERIDES
This is the collective name for a group of nymphs in the classical mythology of Greece. They were also known as the Atlantides and under this name accorded a different derivation. As the Hesperides these nymphs are the daughters of Hesperus and Atlas; in other traditions they are the daughters of Nyx and Erebus, or of Phorcys and Ceto. Their number is also variable from seven to the usual three named Ægle, Erytheia, and Hesperesthusa. Others include Erythesis, Hestia, or Arethusa. The Hesperides were the guardians of the queen of the gods' grove of golden apples, which Hercules was to gain as one of his legendary labors.
References 88, 93, 110
See also Ægle, Arethusa, Atlantides, Erytheia, Guardian, Nymph

HESTIA
See Hesperides

HIBIL, HIBIL ZIWA
In the beliefs of the Gnostics, Hibil is an Uthra who defeated the "entity" of Hell by wearing spiked armor in his battle.
References 29
See also Uthra

HICKS
See Undine

HIDDEN FOLK
See Little People

HIGONA
See Figona

HIISI
In the ancient religion of the Finns, Hiisi was a forest god, but with the coming of Christianity he was demoted to the status of a guardian forest spirit. Described as being a ragged, beardless human shape with lidless eyes, Hiisi is now relegated to the role of a minor devil.

References 29, 88, 93
See also Devil, Guardian, Spirit, Appendix 19

HILDE
In Teutonic mythology she was one of the Valkyries whose name means War. In battles she was able to restore the slain and their weapons to the state before the battle began, and thus perpetuate the conflict indefinitely.
References 95
See also Valkyries

HILLE BINGELS
See Hinzelmann

HILL FOLK, HILL PEOPLE
In the folklore of Scandinavia, and particularly in Denmark, where they are known as the Høgfolk, these spirits are rather like elves. They are said to be of a pleasant human shape and they live in little hills or caves. They are entirely benevolent but rather melancholy, and they may be heard sometimes singing wistfully on the long, light summer nights.
References 17, 40, 78
See also Berg People, Elf, Spirit

HILL-MEN
These are a particularly formidable type of fairy in the folklore of the Isle of Man (United Kingdom). The Manx people propitiated these spirits, also known as the Hogmen, with offerings of fruit. However, it was considered prudent to avoid them, especially when they changed their abodes on Hollantide (11 November) each year.
References 17, 78
See also Fairy, Spirit

HIND ETIN
This is the name of a Hillman or dwarf in the folklore of Scotland. Hind Etin, according to the legend, enchanted a king's daughter into living with him secretly, thus producing seven sons. In the end the princess died when the magic spell was broken and the secret was revealed to her royal parents.
References 88
See also Dwarf, Hill-Men

HINKY-PUNK
In the folklore of the West Country of England this is a version of the Will o' the Wisp also known as Hunky Punk. The sprite is described as having only one leg, but this does not stop him from misleading travelers into following his candlelight into bogs.
References 17, 18
See also Biasd Bheulach, Cacy Taperere, Dodore, Fachan, Nashas, Paija, Shiqq, Sprite, Will o' the Wisp

Hilde, one of the Valkyries whose name means War, rides the clouds over human battles.

HINO
See Heng

HINZELMANN
In the local folklore of Hudemühlen Castle near Aller in Germany, this household spirit, although usually invisible, became a companion to the family and familiar with the servants. Sometimes he would appear in the guise of a curly-haired little boy when with the younger children. He told the family that his other name was Lüring, and that of his wife was Hille Bingels. At first the lord of the castle was anxious to be rid of the presence, so the lord packed up his family, his belongings, and retinue and traveled away from his castle in order to live in one of his other residences. However, while on the journey they stopped at an inn and the Hinzelmann was discovered to be still with them. The Hinzelmann proved that there was no escaping him, so the lord reluctantly returned his household to the castle. (This story is also recorded of the Boggart and Hobthrush of England, the Nis of Denmark and the Cluricaune of Ireland). Hinzelmann worked like a brownie and played pranks like Robin Goodfellow. He had a particular affection for the lord's two daughters and frightened away suitors until the girls remained spinsters. It is

recorded that in 1588 Hinzelmann gave three presents to the lord of the castle, a woven silk cross, a straw hat, and a pearl-embroidered glove, stating that these together would always bring good luck. Hinzelmann then took his leave and was never seen again.
References 18
See also Boggart, Brownie, Cluricaune, Hob Thrush, Nis, Robin Goodfellow, Spirit, Appendix 22

HI'ONA
See Figona

HIRANYAKASIPU
In the Vedic mythology of India this demon is one of the Daityas and an incarnation of Ravana. He was destroyed by Vishnu in the *avatar* of Narasinha.
References 41
See also Bali, Daitya, Demon

HIRGUAN
This is the name of a demon in the folk beliefs of the people of Gomera, one of the Canary Islands. When Hirguan becomes visible, the evil spirit is described as having a woolly-haired appearance. He is the enemy of the deity Orahan.
References 93
See also Demon, Spirit

HISA-ME
This is a collective name for a group of demons in the folk beliefs of Japan. The Hisa-Me, whose name means Frowning Women, are also known as Shiko-Me. They are hideous female demons that inhabit the land of the dead.
References 29
See also Demon

HITÂBOHS
See Bitâbohs

HKUM YENG
This is a particularly aggressive nat also known as Tak-Keng in the beliefs of the Wa people of Burma. He is propitiated as the guardian spirit of the village.
References 88
See also Guardian, Nats, Appendix 10

HMIN
In the mythology of Burma this nat is a demon of the forests. His special quarry are travelers, whom he shakes violently if they meet him. In this way Hmin is responsible for inflicting malaria on his victims.
References 41, 88
See also Akakasoh, Boomasoh, Demon, Irra, Namtar, Nats, Phi, Shekkasoh, Appendix 10, Appendix 17

HOB, HOBBE
This is a class of household spirit whose name is a corruption of the English first name Robin. Hob is also called Hobany, Hobredy, or Lob in the folklore of the Northern Counties of England. The Hob resembles a brownie, for the only people who have seen this nocturnal spirit have described him as naked, brown, and very hairy. The Hobs were almost entirely benevolent spirits who would come unseen to work at night when the family was in need of urgent help. Unlike brownies, who did all types of domestic work, the Hobs specialized in particular activities. They threshed or ground corn, churned milk into butter, and the Hobhole Hob was renowned for curing the whooping cough. Like all brownie types of spirit, the Hob could be "laid" by a gift of clothes. The earliest account we have of a Hob is made in the fourteenth century by John of Bromyard, a Dominican friar. He describes such an incident and the Hob's reaction thus: *"Dicens Anglice, 'Modo habeo capam et capuciam amplius bonum non faciam.'"* ("Saying in English, 'Now I hold a cape and hood, I'll cease doing further good.'") Hobs attached themselves to families or localities, and each was known by a particular name. Thus such names as Hob of Close House, Hob of Hart Hall, Hob of Sturfit House, and Hobhole Hob of Runswick Bay designate places inhabited by such a spirit.

There is one instance, in North Yorkshire, of a malevolent Hob called Hob Headless whose many activities included springing on unsuspecting travelers, changing the directions of the signposts, and causing vehicles to skid on the road between Neasham and Hurworth. The spirit was said to have been "laid" and banished to a hole under a huge stone at the roadside for 99 years and a day. The stone itself is so cursed that any human unfortunate enough to choose it for his rest will be unable to rise from it ever again.
References 15, 17, 18, 28, 66, 69, 92, 123
See also Hob Thrush, Hobany, Hob-Lantern, Household Spirits, Lob, Lob-Lie-by-the-Fire, Spirit, Appendix 22, Appendix 24

HOB THRUSH, HOBTHRUST, HOBTRUSH
The Hob Thrush is an English North Country goblin similar to the hob, but unlike the hob, the Hob Thrush is not a domestic spirit but is said to inhabit tumuli, caves, crags, and woods in lonely places, the name of which would usually contain the spirit's name. Thus we have Hobthrush Rock, 'Obtrush Tumulus, and Hob Thrush's Mill Nick (a deep rock cleft). The name has certainly been used since the sixteenth century, and in 1787 Francis Grose described these spirits as inhabiting the woods. The origins of the name are variously given as Hob o' t' Hurst, meaning Hob of the Woods; or Hob *Thurse*, an Old

English word for a giant; or the more ancient Hob *Thrys*, the Anglo-Saxon word for a spirit. This spirit was mostly mischievous, although he could also be malevolent, behaving much like a poltergeist. The same story of "Ay we're flittin'" told of the boggart and the nis is told of the Farndale Hobthrush (1853).
References 15, 17, 18, 28, 66, 69, 92, 123
See also Boggart, Goblin, Hob, Nis, Poltergeist

HOBANY
This is the full name of the hob of English folklore as the spirit is called in the county of Worcestershire, where the alternative Hobredy is also used. Hobany was said to have a consort known as Habonde.
References 10
See also Habonde, Hob, Spirit

HOBBEDY'S LANTERN
See Hob-Lantern

HOBBIT
This dwarf-like being is the creation of J. R. R. Tolkien. The Hobbit resembles a gnome, is about as high as a man's knee, and loves bright colors. The exploits of the Hobbit are related in the works *The Hobbit* (1937) and *The Lord of the Rings* (1955).
References 40, 114
See also Dwarf, Gnome

HOBBY
A local name for a brownie in the folklore of the East Anglian region of Stowmarket, England.
References 27
See also Brownie

HOBGOBLIN, HOBGOBLINET
This is the term used for a kind of nature spirit in the folklore of England. The Hobgoblin is described as being like a very ugly little elf. The Hobgoblin, also known as Robgoblin, or the diminutive form Hobgoblinet, can be helpful and well-disposed to humans, like a brownie. Though usually good-natured and not malicious like the goblin, he can nevertheless be easily offended and is capable of playing spiteful pranks.
References 7, 17, 18, 28, 40, 53, 92, 107, 114
See also Bauchan, Brownie, Elf, Goblin, Spirit

HOB-LANTERN
In the folklore of the English Midlands, this is a name for the Will o' the Wisp, also known as Hobbedy's Lantern. The name indicates that a hob was considered to be responsible for misleading travelers.
References 18
See also Hob, Will o' the Wisp, Appendix 24

The Hobgoblin laughed till his sides ached

HOBREDY
See Hobany

HOBYAH
In English folktales these nursery bogies were said to be terrifying cannibal spirits that trapped unwary children. The only thing of which these spirits were afraid was black dogs, one of which eventually destroyed them all.
References 17
See also Nursery Bogie, Spirit, Appendix 22

HOCEREU WAHIRA
This is a disease spirit in the beliefs of the Native Americans of the northern forest regions.

HODEKIN
A forest sprite in pre-Christian England whose name may have been assumed by the outlaw Robin Hood as a pseudonym. This in turn may be related to the German Hödekin, a type of kobold.
References 69
See also Kobold, Sprite, Appendix 19

HÖDEKIN
See Kobold

HODGE, HODGE-POCHER, HODGE-POKER
These names were used in England well before the twentieth century to denote a devil or bugbear. Even then the names were used to indicate a nuisance spirit rather than one of which one might be afraid. Hodge is the diminutive form of the first name Roger.
References 107
See also Bugbear, Devil, Spirit

HOGBOON, HOGBOY
In the folklore of the Orkney Islands (United Kingdom), this spirit inhabited the ancient earth mounds and old farmyards. He is described as looking like a tiny gray man. Although he never entered human buildings, he would mend household implements left for him and guard the farm's animals from the trows. In return for his benevolence he expected libations of milk and ale to be presented at his abode. If anyone offended him by attempting to plough up his abode or forgetting to propitiate him, then he could inflict all manner of misfortunes on them. The same "Aye we're flittin'" story told of the boggart is told of the Hogboon.
References 47
See also Boggart, Haugbonde, Trow, Appendix 12

HØGFOLK
See Hill Folk

HOGMEN
See Hill-Men

HOITA
In the beliefs of the Mandan Native American people this is the spirit that manifests as the spotted eagle.
References 25
See also Spirit

HOLLE, FRAU HOLLE
This important Teutonic spirit may have been derived from an earlier deity of the sky or fertility or the underworld. She is described in many guises and may be known by the variant names Hoide, Holda, Hulda, Huldra, Huldu, Hulla, and Mistress Venus. As the guardian spirit of the home, she cares for the activities of spinning and weaving. However, in her guise of a beautiful fairy she inhabits the Thuringian Mountains of Venus with her entourage, enticing men to her domain, which is described in the legend of Tannhäuser. As the beautiful white sky spirit, she rode the wind, and when she shook her duvet the snow fell to the earth. In this guise she also rode with the Wild Hunt, for in her underworld she ensured the emergence of infants to be born, and gathered back to her the souls of those that died before baptism. This underworld could be reached by diving deep into the pool or Fountain of Youth, where Holle could be seen bathing, or reached at the bottom of the well guarded by her kobolds or Hollen. Today this spirit is relegated to the status of a nursery bogie. Looking and behaving like Baba Yaga, she seeks the badly behaved child to take as her meal in the dark forests.
References 41, 88, 95
See also Baba Yaga, Berchta, Deive, Guardian, Kobold, Nursery Bogie, Spirit, Wild Hunt, Appendix 14, Appendix 22

HOLLEN
See Holle

HOLLOW MEN
See Troll

HOLZ-FRAU
See Wood Wives

HOMME DE BOUC
See Basajaun

HONDKONZ
See Deev

HONGA
This is the collective name for a group of spirits in the beliefs of the Osage Native American people. The Honga are guardian earth spirits or Earth People who live below the ground.
References 25
See also Guardian, Hill Folk, Maahiset, Spirit

HONGAEK
These are a group of evil spirits in the folk beliefs of the Korean people. The Hongaek, whose name means Red Disaster, may manifest as a noxious miasma at the scene of a fatal accident, suicide, murder, or other mortal affliction. They feed off and multiply their power over humans with every victim that they can infect. The Hongaek engulfs and infects humans who

pass too closely by the scene of a human misfortune; so taxi and ambulance drivers, as well as people whose horoscope predisposes them to contagion, are particularly vulnerable to these demons.
References 79
See also Demon, Fad Felen, Spirit

HONOCHENOKEH
This is the collective name for a group of beneficent spirits that give help to humans in the beliefs of the Iroquois Native American people. Their name means Invisible Helpers.
References 25
See also Spirit

HOOPER OF SENNEN COVE, THE
This is a spirit that used to inhabit Sennen Cove in Cornwall, in southwest England. It took the form of a rolling misty cloud, from which a strange glow and whooping noise emanated. It would also rest in the vicinity of a rock called Cowloe Rock. If the spirit manifested at night, the mist would emit showers of sparks. The Hooper was always beneficent, as it came to warn the fisher folk of impending violent storms, and they regarded this supernatural as their guardian spirit. However, one fisherman and his son defied the Hooper's warning and put out to sea. Neither they nor the Hooper were ever seen again.
References 17, 69
See also Dooinney-Oie, Guardian, Howlaa, Spirit, Appendix 25, Appendix 26

HOST, THE
See Slaugh

HOTUA PORO
This is the name of an evil spirit in the beliefs of the people of Samoa. Hotua Poro is a demon lover or an incubus that comes in the night to disturb the sleep of its victim with sexual intent. It will copulate with humans in their sleep while also depriving them of their breath. The victim will be totally exhausted and may even die.
References 88
See also Demon, Incubus, Spirit, Succubus

HOURI
In the Muslim tradition, these are beautiful, pure nymphs whose name may also be spelled as Haura, Hur, or Huri in different texts, and the plural form is Huran. These shapely female spirits inhabit Paradise, where they dance and make music awaiting the pleasure of the faithful, to whom they are promised in the afterlife.
References 88
See also Nymph

HOUSEHOLD SPIRITS
These supernatural beings are mostly to be found in the folklore of Europe, but some examples have been recorded in cultures of the Far East and South America. They usually inhabit homes and farms as guardian spirits. Household spirits may be helpful, often doing much of the tedious work left unfinished at night. They are benevolent and protective of the property and the family. However, these spirits may also be mischievous and sometimes malignant, often showing a perverse loyalty to a family that may be anxious to be rid of them. The Hinzelmann of Germany is a particular example of this type of spirit.
References 87
See also Guardian, Hinzelmann, Appendix 22

HOWLAA
This is the name of a weather spirit in the folklore of the Isle of Man (United Kingdom). It was always invisible, but as a guardian spirit of the Manx people it howled a warning of impending violent storms. Its place in folk legend is very similar to that of the Dinny Mara and Dooinney-Oie.
References 17, 18
See also Dinny Mara, Dooinney-Oie, Guardian Spirit, Appendix 26

HRIST
See Valkyries

HSIEN
In Chinese folklore and mythology these spirits are variously compared with demons or fairies. They can remain invisible or assume any shape, including the semblance of a member of the family, to work their confusion on unsuspecting humans.
References 87
See also Demon, Fairy, Kuei, Spirit

HU FA
See Dharmapala

HU HSIEN
These spirits, also known as Fox Spirits in the folklore and beliefs of both China and Japan, may take the form of foxes when visible, but usually they transform into beautiful young women. In China they are often benevolent and regarded as the bringers of good fortune, but can mischievously cause marital problems. They are the patrons of civil-service officials, who would keep their documents in a Fox Box. In Japan the Fox Spirits usually appear as malevolent but beautiful women prone to trickery, causing the misfortune or death of their victims. They induce the love and surrender of their prey, and when the human is completely in their power, they withdraw

An Houri welcomes the faithful to pleasures in Paradise.

the life essence of the human, who sickens and dies.
References 88, 131
See also Green Women, Spirit

HUACAS
In the ancient Inca religion of Peru the term *Huacas* denoted supernatural beings in general, including lesser spirits, and sacred items associated with them. Today this word has been relegated to a description of anything unusual or inexplicable.
References 88, 119
See also Spirit, Vilcanota

HUASA MALLCU
This is the name of a spirit in the folk beliefs of the Aymara people of Bolivia. Huasa Mallcu is the guardian spirit of the vicuña herds in the mountains. He protects them by making them invisible to would-be hunters.
References 88
See also Guardian, Appendix 12

HUECUVU
These are the evil spirits in the folk beliefs of the Araucanian people of Chile. The Huecuvu are shape-shifting disease demons. They are controlled by the evil Pillan, god of thunder and volcanoes.
References 56, 102
See also Cherruve, Rasogonaga, Spirit, Appendix 17

HULDA, HULLA
See Holle

HULDEN, HULDE-MEN
See Holle

HULDRA, HULDRE (pl.)
There are two beings with this name:
  (1) In the folklore of Scandinavia, this spirit is described as a beautiful wood nymph or an ugly old Wood Wife. Whatever image the Huldra presented in front, from behind she was always hollow and had a long tail like that of a cow, which she was anxious to conceal. When not caring for their flocks and singing on the mountainsides, the Huldre would pursue mortal men. The men could be warned that these were no mortal women if they caught a glimpse of the hollow reverse or the tail, but the Huldre were usually too careful and most alluring. Any man who succumbed to their advances was likely to lose his mind or be scarred in some way.
  (2) Huldra is an alternative name for the German spirit Holle.
References 18, 44, 110
See also Holle, Nymph, Spirit, Wood Wife, Appendix 19

HULDU
There are two concepts of beings having this name:
  (1) This is an alternative name for the German spirit Holle.
  (2) In Scandinavian folklore the Huldu Folk are the Hidden Folk, or the Little People, or the Elle Folk.
References 18, 40, 114
See also Elle Folk, Holle, Little People

HULDU FOLK
See Elle Folk

HUMBABA
In the mythology of ancient Mesopotamia this is the name of the guardian spirit of the cedar forests, and he may originally have been a deity of nature. He was later demoted to the status of a giant demon, the adversary of Gilgamesh.
References 119
See also Demon, Guardian, Appendix 19

HUNESSAI
This is the collective name for a group of spirits in the folk beliefs of the Witoto people of South America. The Hunessai are the guardian spirits of freshwater and its plant life.
References 88
See also Guardian, Spirit, Appendix 25

HUNKY PUNK
See Hinky-Punk

HUNTIN
This is the name of a vegetation spirit in the folk beliefs of the Nigerian people. Huntin is the spirit of the silk-cotton tree and can be particularly malevolent. This powerful spirit must be propitiated with offerings of palm oil and fowl if one of his "residence" trees must be felled.
References 41, 110
See also Dyombie, Sasabonsam, Shamantin, Spirit, Appendix 18, Appendix 19

HUR, HURAN, HURI
See Houri

H'URARU
This is the name of the spirit of the earth in the beliefs of the Pawnee Native Americans.
References 25
See also Maahiset, Spirit

HURGEON
See Urchin

HUTKIN

The name of a household spirit in German folklore said to have been resident in the home of the Bishop of Hildersheim. Although described as hardworking and benevolent, Hutkin gave ill treatment to a kitchen boy in return for the torments the boy had inflicted on the sprite.

References 18
See also Household Spirit, Sprite, Appendix 22

HYADES

This is the name of a group of seven nymphs, whose name means the Rainy, in the classical mythology of Greece and Rome. They are the daughters of Atlas. Because they were so disconsolate at the death of their brother Hyas, they were transformed into the constellation that bears their name. Three of the main individual names are Ambrosia, Coronis, and Eudora.

References 40, 102, 129, 130
See also Atlantides, Nymph, Appendix 13

HYLDEMODER

See Hylde-Moer

HYLDE-MOER

This is the name of a wood spirit in both the German and Danish folk beliefs. The name Hylde-Moer means Elder Mother, and she is the guardian spirit of the elder tree. No one may take any fruit or wood from the tree without first giving respect to the Hylde-Moer and requesting her permission.

References 18, 88
See also Elder Mother, Guardian, Appendix 19

HYLDE-VINDE

This is the German name for the guardian spirit of the elder tree. She is also known as the Elder Mother and Hyldemoder. The name Hylde-Vinde means Elder Queen.

References 18, 88
See also Elder Mother, Appendix 19

HYTER SPRITES

In the folklore of Lincolnshire and East Anglia, England, these fairies can assume many shapes. They are usually described in their human form as having sandy-colored skin and hair like the Feriers, with beautiful green eyes. But they can also appear as sand martins, birds that nest in sand banks. In return for gentle behavior towards them, these spirits have been known to help humans and even to search for and find their lost children.

References 17
See also Fairy, Feriers, Spirit, Appendix 22

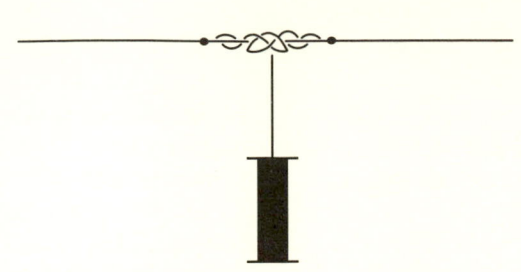

IA

This is the word for an evil spirit or devil in the folk beliefs of the Cheremis/Mari people of the former Soviet Republic. The Ia may be generated from the spittle of evil men or careless people who spit on the ground, or from the evil soul of a debauched priest after his death. An Ia is described as having long hair that blazes like the trail of a comet as it travels in its whirlwinds. Otherwise it can shape shift to any form, especially those that seem to be familiar and trustworthy, to work its evil temptations. Sometimes, like the Aitvaras, this devil will bring wealth to the householder who leaves offerings of food, but it cannot touch food that has been blessed. If an Ia inhabits a particular place, it may be addressed as Oza, but as with all dangerous spirits, other epithets are used, such as Kuba and Kuguza, to avert any evil attention. In some other regions, the name Ia may refer only to a water spirit.

Each person has an Ia on the left shoulder noting the wicked things, just as they have a Guardian Angel on the right shoulder noting all the good deeds of the person's life. Whichever has the longer list takes the soul when the human dies. Those who drown or die of alcohol will be taken by an Ia and transformed into the shape of a horse. Numerous stories tell of a farrier shoeing a hoof that turns into a human foot in his hands. The Ia may even inhabit the stable with the horses, taking good care of the ones it favors and starving (or like the pixies, night-riding to a lather) the ones it hates. Farmers may daub tar on their horses' backs to prevent this.

These devils take every opportunity to work their evil; they will get into empty objects such as a storage box, a baby's cot, or holes in wooden things, causing the next mortal to use it to sicken and die. They may be seen through knots in the boles of hollow trees and, like the Leshii, cause those who travel through the forests to lose their way. Lightning is the heavenly weapon sent to destroy the Ia, but humans may be struck if there is a devil close to them. To protect themselves from the Ia, humans may draw a protective Iron Fence, or circle, around themselves with an iron object to divert both the lightning and the devils.
References 118
See also Aitvaras, Bes, Devil, Guardian, Kuba, Kuguza, Leshii, Oza, Pixie, Spirit

IA KUBA AND IA KUGUZA

In the folk beliefs of the Cheremis/Mari people of the former Soviet Republic, these devils or Ia take the form of long-haired humans inhabiting meadows and banks of rivers. Their names mean Devil Old Woman and Devil Old Man. If a human does not recite a prayer or magic formula before the Ia Kuba and Ia Kuguza see him, the person may be made to wander about all night, or pulled beneath the water.
References 118
See also Ia, Kuguza

IA SALTAK

This is an evil spirit in the folk beliefs of the Cheremis/Mari people of the former Soviet Republic. This devil, whose name means Devil Soldier, is also known as Oksa Saltak, which means Money Soldier, or Oksa Orola, which means Money Guard. It takes the form of a glowing green flame, usually seen between Easter and Pentecost (March to June). This spirit, armed with sword and gun, is supposed to be the infernal guardian of hoards of money. When humans see the flames, the spirit is supposed to be airing the money to dry, and the humans may attempt to take it and make themselves rich, if the Ia Saltak doesn't destroy them in the process.
References 118
See also Devil, Guardian, Ia, Spirit, Will o' the Wisp, Appendix 21

IACHOS

In classical Greek mythology, this spirit is described as the son of Demeter or Persephone, and personifies exuberance.
References 93
See also Spirit

IBAŚKA

This is the name of a keremet in the folk beliefs of the Cheremis/Mari people of the former Soviet Republic.
References 118
See also Keremet

IBLIS

This is the name of a djinn, also known as Eblis or Hares, in the beliefs of Islam and the folklore of the Arab peoples. He is considered to be one of the Fallen Angels who refused to acknowledge the place of Adam, the first man in Allah's creation. As a result, Iblis, who had hitherto borne the name of Azazel, was turned into a Shaitan and condemned to rule over only the evil djinns. Iblis had five evil progeny: Awar, Dasim, Sut, Tir, and Zalambur. In the Zoroastrian tradition, Jan-ben-Jan, a suliman of the Devs, offended heaven and Iblis was sent to chastise him. Instead, Iblis overthrew the suliman and usurped the throne, thus rebelling against heaven. For this evil defiance, Iblis and his Dev followers were condemned to the infernal regions. He inhabits the unclean places such as wastelands, cemeteries, and ruins, and hovers at markets, crossroads, and other meeting places to trap the unwary and sinful humans.
References 40, 41, 53, 78, 88, 92, 93, 114
See also Asasel, Azazel, Deev, Djinn, Fallen Angel, Shaitan, Sut, Tir, Zalambur

IBORMEITH

See Angus Og

ICTCINIKE, ICTINIKE

In the beliefs of the Ponca and Omaha Native American people, he is the evil, deceitful trickster spirit that taught the humans how to mistrust one another and make war. In traditional legends he is outwitted by the hospitality and magic of the Beaver, the Muskrat, the Kingfisher, and the Flying Squirrel, grandfathers of his wife. He is known by the names Ikto or Iktomi in the legends of the Teton Sioux, Ictcinike in the legends of the Missouri Sioux, and Unctome in the legends of the Santee Sioux. Unctome is also identified as the Spider Trickster.
References 88, 122
See also Spider, Spirit, Trickster

IDƏM KUBA AND IDƏM KUGUZA

In the folk beliefs of the Cheremis/Mari people of the former Soviet Republic, these represent the harvest spirit of corn threshing. Their names mean Threshing-Floor Old Woman and Threshing-Floor Old Man. Like most helpful supernaturals, they are reluctant to be observed at their work, and if seen in the early morning mists they will disappear.

Libations are offered for successful threshing before bad weather.
References 118
See also Bodachan Sabhaill, Corn Spirit, Fenodyree, Kuguza, Mannikin, Ovinnik, Robin Round-Cap, Spirit, Urisk, Appendix 15

IDIS

See Norn

IDUN

In the Scandinavian mythology of the *Prose Edda*, Idun is the daughter of the dwarf Svald. She is the guardian of the gods' golden apples of eternal youth. Legend tells how the evil god Loki deceives her into leaving the apples unguarded, and thus they were removed by the giants.
References 40, 119
See also Dwarf, Guardian, Iwaldi

IFA

This is the Yoruban name of the Benin spirit Fa in the folk beliefs and legends of Nigeria.
References 119
See also Fa, Spirit

IFREET, IFRIT

See Afrit

IGIGI

This is the name for the spirits of the heavens to be seen above the earth's horizon in the mythology of ancient Babylon. Like the angels, these spirits assisted the deities. The Igigi were invoked for blessings before any trial or battle so that justice might prevail.
References 93
See also Angel, Anunnaki, Spirit

IGUMA

This is an evil spirit in the folklore of the Basque people of northern Spain and southwestern France. It invisibly seeps into the homes of humans after nightfall and chokes them to death in their sleep.
References 93
See also Spirit

IGUPIARA

In the beliefs of the Tupi-Guarani people of the Amazon region of South America, these are evil water spirits or demons. Although usually invisible, the Igupiara lurked beneath the surface of the rivers to pull down any humans into the depths.
References 56, 102
See also Afrit, Darrant, Demon, Jenny Greenteeth, Spirit, Appendix 25

IGWIKALLA

This is a malicious demon in the beliefs of the people of Nigeria. It was said to inflict sickness on humans who ventured into the woods. In an account from 1865, Igwikalla was described as being particularly powerful and requiring an offering in propitiation to be left in the bushes it inhabited.
References 57
See also Demon, Appendix 17

IJIMERE

This is the collective name for a group of spirits in the West African folklore of the Yoruba people. These are the Little People of Nigeria who inhabit the deep forests and wild places of the country.
See also Apuku, Aziza, Bakru, Little People, Mmoatia, Pukkumeria, Spirit, Appendix 19

IJRAFIL

This is the name of the angel Israfel in the Islamic beliefs of the people of West Malaysia. Sometimes he is called Serafil, and is deemed to control human breath.
References 120
See also Angel, Israfel, Mala'ikat

IJRAIL

This is the name of the angel Azrael in the Islamic beliefs of the people of West Malaysia.
References 120
See also Angel, Azrael, Mala'ikat

IKŚA KEREMET

In the folk beliefs of the Cheremis/Mari people of the former Soviet Republic, this is a keremet or demon. As the translation of its name (Spring Keremet) indicates, this evil spirit inhabited the spring water sources. Any humans or cattle that drink from a spring inhabited by Ikśa Keremet will die very shortly after.
References 118
See also Demon, Keremet, Spirit, Appendix 25

IKTO, IKTOMI

See Ictinike

ILLIKE

This is the name of a group of spirits in the folk beliefs of the Samoyed people of the Asian Arctic. The Illike are evil spirits or demons.
References 88
See also Demon, Spirit

ILMARINEN

Once the earth god in the mythology of the Fino-Ugric peoples of Siberia, Ilmarinen is now relegated to a status similar to the dwarfs or Wayland Smith of European myth. He is a supernatural metalworker in his underworld.
References 24
See also Dwarf, Wayland Smith

ILOGO

A benevolent spirit in the former beliefs of Nigerian people, Ilogo was said to reside in the moon. He was regarded as a prophetic spirit, and invoked for healing the sick. He could be consulted for curing sickness or prophecy only at the period just before the full moon.
References 81
See also Spirit, Appendix 17

IMANJA

This is an encantado in the Afro-Brazilian cult Batuque. This spirit is a mermaid member of the Cabaclos group of encantados. The name is derived from the Yoruban deity of the same name, although as a mermaid, she derives from the shamanistic beliefs local to that region of Brazil. She is associated with the feast of Our Lady of Conception on 8 December.
References 89
See also Caboclo, Encantado, Jamaína, Mermaid, Oxun, Spirit, Appendix 25

IMDUGUD

This is a spirit in the mythology of ancient Mesopotamia. Imdugud is a dual spirit of benevolence and evil, and was portrayed as having an eagle's head on the body of a winged lion. He brought misfortune and disease to domestic animals.
References 119
See also Spirit, Appendix 12, Appendix 17

IMP/E, IMPA

In the folk beliefs of Europe, this is a mischievous little devil, devilet, or minor fiend that is often described as being the childlike offspring of the Devil. It is a very old term, and may be seen in ancient documents in various spellings such as Emp, Himpe, Hympe, or Ymp/e. Imps may manifest in any form, but are often portrayed as evil-looking infants with tiny horns protruding from their heads and tiny wings from their shoulders. The Imp may also feature in witch trials as the familiar spirit of the accused. The legend of the Lincoln Imp tells how the Devil, in a frivolous mood, set loose some of his more playful Imps to create mischief. One of them descended from the air into the English town of Lindum, as Lincoln was then known, entered the new cathedral being built, and started to wreak havoc. An angel observing the little fiend put a stop to his pranks by turning the

Imps make mischief.

Imp into stone on the column where he had alighted, and that is where he remains to this day.
References 7, 17, 47, 53, 92, 98, 107
See also Angel, Devil, Devilet, Familiar, Fiend

INA PIC WINNA
This is said to be a sprite or local supernatural of the coast of Somerset, southwest England. Ina Pic Winna is possibly the name of a spirit invoked for a good catch of fish in the folklore of the fisher folk of Weston-super-Mare.
References 17
See also Spirit, Sprite

INCUBUS, INCUBI (pl.)
This is the European medieval male fiend of the night known in Latin as the Incubus, which means That Which Lies Upon. As indicated by its name, this is an evil spirit that mounts a sleeping woman for the purpose of sexual relations. It may take on any shape, male or female, but is usually a semblance of the woman's husband or lover, or it may be entirely invisible. An Incubus was said to be recognized by his cloven hooves and stinking breath.

The European names for this demon are Follet (French), Folletto (Italian), Alp (German), and Duende (Spanish). The activities of this kind of fiend are to be found in most cultures from the earliest times and make their appearance as the pre-Islamic Lilith, the Celtic Dusii, the Teutonic Mara, the Greek Ephialtes, the Hindu Bhutas, and the Samoan Hotua Poro. In Europe, the Incubus was recognized in both civil and ecclesiastical law during the Middle Ages, and many deformed births, unwanted pregnancies, and unholy night visits were pronounced the work of this convenient demon. By the time that the witch-hunting fervor of the sixteenth and seventeenth centuries had run its course, the change in accusation from demonic "possession" to demonic "cooperation" had sealed a horrific fate for thousands of terrified victims.
References 7, 17, 40, 56, 88, 91, 92, 93, 98, 107, 113
See also Alp, Bhut/a, Cauchemar, Demon, Duende, Dusii, Ephialtes, Fiend, Hotua Poro, Lilith, Mara, Spirit, Succubus

INDRA
In the mythology of the Zoroastrian religion of Iran, this evil spirit is the deceiver and tempter of all humans, drawing them into sin and evil deeds. Indra (*not* the Indian deity of the same name), is the enemy of the Amesha Spentas named Asha-Vahishta.
References 102
See also Amesha Spentas, Asa-Vahishta, Spirit

INHAÇAN
See Rainha Barba

INLƏKAN KUBA AND INLƏKAN KUGUZA
See Ərləgan Kuba

INO, INUA (pl.)

In the beliefs of the Inuit and Ihalmiut people of Canada, this is a term for spirits of both animate and inanimate origin. The Inua Mikikuni, or Little Spirits, are the less powerful, and the Inua Angkuni, or Great Spirits, are more powerful. Both may be benevolent or malevolent toward humans.
References 101
See also Spirit

INVISIVEL

This is an alternate designation for the encantados of the Afro-Brazilian cult Batuque. *Invisivel* means Invisible, which is what they are, since the encantados do not materialize physically. These spirits' descriptions exist through the devotees' experience of their "possession" and the spirits' communication.
References 89
See also Encantado, Spirit

IRĀ-KEWA

This is the name of a spirit in the beliefs of the Maori of New Zealand. Irā-Kewa is capable of causing disorientation and death. One story says that this spirit was invoked against the tribe of Maruiwi in order to gain revenge for tribal war. The Maruiwi, under the influence of the spirit, were so confused on a journey one night that they blundered about in what should have been familiar territory. As a result of their disorientation, few members of the tribe survived stumbling over a precipice near Tohue.
References 63
See also Spirit

IRDLIRVIRISSONG

In the beliefs of the Inuit people of Canada, this is the name of a female demon. Irdlirvirissong obtains victims in a very unusual manner. She cavorts and plays pranks on unwary humans in order to induce laughter. At this sign of human weakness, the evil spirit will desiccate their bodies and devour their intestines.
References 26, 119
See also Demon, Spirit

IRRA

This is a disease demon in Babylonian mythology who is particularly responsible for spreading the plague. When Ishtar, the goddess of fertility, visited the underworld in search of Tammey, the god of spring, the two were tormented by Irra on the orders of Allatu, queen of the underworld.
References 29, 41
See also Demon, Namtar, Appendix 17

IRUCI

See Pey

ISAKAWUATE

See Coyote

ISRAFEL, ISRAFIL

Israfel is an Archangel and a chief angel in the Hebrew, Christian, and Islamic scriptures. He is known by the variant names Azrafil and Israfel, and he is considered the patron of music. In the scriptures, Israfil accompanied Gabriel and Michael to warn Abraham of the impending destruction of Sodom. In Islamic tradition, he is the angel who will blow the last trumpet to signal the Day of Judgment and the resurrection of the faithful.
References 40, 93, 114
See also Angel, Archangel, Gabriel, Michael

IT

In the folklore of the Shetland Islands (United Kingdom), this supernatural spirit frequently makes an appearance at the Christmas season, and can take on any shape or form. Those who see It are unlikely to agree on the form it took or how it traveled, yet they will agree to a curious telepathic manner in which It communicated or, more frighteningly, repeated their thoughts.
References 17
See also Kallikantzari, Spirit

ITALAPAS, ITALAPATE

See Coyote

ITHURIEL

In Milton's *Paradise Lost,* this is the name of an angel whose spear is capable of exposing deceit. Ithuriel is the angel sent by the Archangel Gabriel to search out Satan in Paradise.
References 114
See also Angel, Archangel, Gabriel, Zephon

IUBDAN

This is the name of the king of the Lupracan in the folklore and legend of Ireland. His story appears in a fifteenth-century manuscript, where he is described as a noble and truthful being.
References 88
See also Leprechaun

IUVART

See Devil

IWA

Iwa is a trickster spirit in the folk beliefs of Hawaii. This demon could shape shift at will to any form

when visible, and was renowned for his thieving from humans. Iwa was challenged by other spirits to see who could steal the most in a single night. The trickster remained calmly inactive until all the other spirits had finished, then he removed everything they had stolen to his own abode. Thus, the thieves were the victims of theft, and the trickster Iwa won.
References 29
See also Demon, Kapua, Spirit, Trickster

IWALDI, IWALDUR

This is the name in Scandinavian mythology of the most skilled of the dwarf metalworkers. Iwaldi is also known as Svald, and he is said to be the father of Idun. He and his dwarf brethren made Odin's spear Sindri, forged Sif's golden wig, and constructed the folding ship Skidbladnir.
References 93, 95
See also Dwarf, Idun

IWANČI

In the beliefs of the Jívaro people of the Amazon region of Equador, the Iwanči are shape-shifting demons. The Iwanči may manifest as the Macanči (water snake) or the Paŋi (anaconda), or enter a tree in the forest in order to kill their victims.
References 64
See also Demon

IYA

This is the name of a disease demon in the folk beliefs of the Sioux Native American people. This spirit may

manifest in the form of a hurricane and swallow up animals and humans in his path.
References 93
See also Demon, Spirit, Appendix 17

IZƏ NUR KEREMET

In the folk beliefs of the Cheremis/Mari people of the former Soviet Republic, this is a keremet or demon. As the translation of the name, Little Field Devil, suggests, this demon is intent on inhabiting and controlling the fertility of the smaller fields, and may destroy them if slighted.
References 118
See also Demon, Keremet, Appendix 18

IZEDS

This is the collective term for a group of spirits in the Zoroastrian religion of Iran. The Izeds are beneficent spirits who were created to be guardians and attendants of the Amshaspands (Amesha Spentas) surrounding Ormuzd.
References 78, 100
See also Amesa Spentas, Attendant, Guardian, Spirit

IZRA'IL

See Azrael

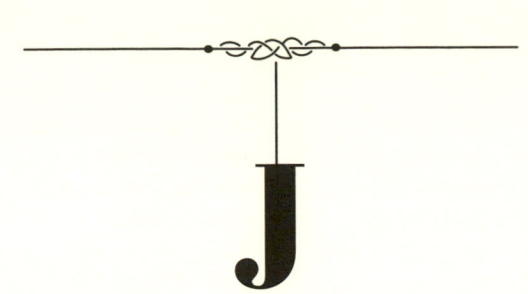

JABOL
This is one of the terms for a devil in the beliefs of the Cheremis/Mari people of the former Soviet Republic.
References 118
See also Devil, Ia

JABRA'IL, JIBRA'IL
This is the name of the angel Gabriel in Bahasa Melayu (Malay Language), in the Islamic beliefs of the people of West Malaysia. He is sometimes called Raja Brahil, and is regarded as the angelic messenger of Allah.
References 120
See also Angel, Gabriel, Mala'ikat

JACK FROST
In English popular folklore, this is the mischievous spirit personification of freezing weather. He is usually portrayed as a type of elf dressed entirely in white, with icicles dangling from his clothes. Jack Frost nips the fingers and toes of those who venture outside on such cold days, and will playfully turn human noses the color of ripe cherries. He frolics along the countryside, leaving twinkling frost crystals decorating everything he has touched.
References 41
See also Achachilas, Elf, Father Frost, Jüstə Kuba, Morozko, Pokšem Kuba, Spirit, Appendix 26

JACK THE WHITE HAT
In the folklore of Devon, England, this mysterious water spirit, also known as Old White Hat, is recognized by the large white hat with a glowing lantern that he wears. Jack the White Hat was said to signal to the ferries at Appledore from Braunton Burrows. Possibly he was another form of Will o' the Wisp.
References 19
See also Spirit, Will o' the Wisp, Appendix 25

JACK UP THE ORCHUT
This is the name of a frightening spirit or devil used mostly as a nursery bogie by parents in Britain to threaten their young children into good behavior. He is possibly derived from a guardian spirit of ripening fruit and fruit trees such as Churnmilk Peg.
References 17
See also Churnmilk Peg, Devil, Guardian, Nursery Bogie, Spirit, Appendix 22

JACK-IN-IRONS
This is the name of a road bogie in the folklore of Yorkshire, England. This spirit was likely to leap upon unwary travelers at night and terrify its victims before it disappeared. It may be derived from the habit of placing executed felons on gibbets at the side of roads or at crossroads, as a gruesome warning to passersby.
References 17
See also Bogie, Spirit, Appendix 24

JACK-IN-THE-GREEN
Jack-in-the-Green is an alternate name for the vegetation spirit called the Green Man in English folk belief. His counterpart in the German regions is Latzman in Württemburg, Leaf King in Hanover, and the Little Leaf Man in Thuringia. In the regions of European Russia, Slovakia, Rumania, and Transylvania, a similar spirit known as Green George is celebrated by the local people and especially revered by the Romany Gypsies. Celebration of the Jack-in-the-Green, like many of the European counterparts, involves the creation of a cage of vegetation, which is worn and paraded by a human "stand-in" for the spirit. The emptied effigy is then ritually disposed of and returned to the earth. In more ancient periods, as described by Frazer in *The Bough* (1922), a similar ritual took place with the Wicker Man, in which the human representative was also sacrificed.
References 47, 48, 88, 107
See also Babban ny Mheillea, Corn Spirit, Green Man, Spirit, Appendix 18

JACKY LANTERN
See Will o' the Wisp

JADE MAIDENS
See Yü Nü

JA'FAR

This is the name of a powerful djinn and the "son" of Za'far, a king of the djinns. An Islamic legend tells how Ja'far offered his services to Hussain, the Prophet's grandson.
References 30
See also Djinn, Za'far

JAHI

In the Zoroastrian religion of Iran, this is a female druj. She is also known by the Pahlavi names of Jah or Jeh. Jahi is the personification of female human vices, sins, and afflictions. She is considered to be responsible for introducing these sinful practices to the unwary and gullible.
References 87, 102
See also Drug

JAL ÜMBAČ KOŠTŠƏ KEREMET

This is the name of a demon in the folk beliefs of the Cheremis/Mari people of the former Soviet Republic. As implied by this demon's name, which means Keremet Passing Through the Village, the Jal Ümbač Koštšə Keremet passes its evil influence from home to home and then departs, leaving misery in its wake.
References 118
See also Demon, Keremet

JALANDHARA

See Bali

JALJOGINI

This is a water spirit in the folklore of the Punjab area of India. Jaljogini is an evil female demon who is considered to be responsible for causing waterborne diseases and misfortune to women and children.
References 6
See also Demon, Spirit, Appendix 17, Appendix 22, Appendix 25

JALPARI

This is the name of a spirit in the folk beliefs of the Punjab region of India. This evil female water spirit entices men to her embrace in order to kill them. She may be placated with gifts of lamb's meat or flowers.
References 87
See also Spirit, Appendix 25

JALXTER BODƏZ

See Keremet

JAMAÍNA

This is the name of an encantado in the Afro-Brazilian cult Batuque. She is a mermaid, and inhabits saltwater of the estuaries. Like the spirit Imanja of the same group, Jamaína is derived from the shamanistic beliefs of the local region.
References 89
See also Encantado, Imanja, Mermaid, Spirit, Appendix 25

JAMŠENER

This is a keremet or demon in the folk beliefs of the Cheremis/Mari people of the former Soviet Republic. This evil spirit is also known by the names Emsener and Jomšeŋer. Jamšener particularly inhabits freshwater springs, and will inflict horrible diseases on any human who lets his clothing or hair contaminate this water. An offering of a fish or a woodpecker may induce the spirit to remove the sickness.
References 118
See also Demon, Keremet, Spirit, Appendix 17, Appendix 25

JĀN

See Nats

JANN

This is the name used for the less powerful, lower order of djinn in pre-Islamic tradition.
References 56
See also Djinn

JAPETEQUARA

This is the name of an important encantado in the Afro-Brazilian cult Batuque. Japetequara, whose name means the Alligator, is identified and described as a dignified chief of the Native South American people and as a powerful alligator spirit. As a term of respect he may also be addressed as Velho, the Old One, or Caboclo Velho, which means Old Man Indian, also indicating a derivation from the local shamanistic traditions. His abode is said to be in the forest of Ararí on the island of Marajó. From his name is derived the title of the Japetequara "family" of encantados comprising the following spirits: Cabocla Tartaruga de Amazonas, Caboclo Pemba, Curupira, Curupira-airara, Curupira Chica Baiana, Curupira Piriri, Dona Rosalina, Guerriero, Itapaquara, Itaquara, Itaquari, and Jacitaria.
References 89
See also Curupira, Dona Rosalina, Encantado, Spirit

JARČIK

See Moča Kuba

JARINA

An encantado spirit in the Afro-Brazilian cult Batuque. The name Jarina means Ivory Palm Tree, and indicates that this supernatural is possibly derived from a tree spirit in the local shamanistic traditions. She is said to be the "daughter" of Rei Sebastião. During Batuque ceremonies she manifests as a wanton, playful, and

heavy-drinking spirit. Batuque tradition tells of how Jarina was imprisoned for her wantonness by her "father" and rescued by Mariana.
References 89
See also Encantado, Mariana, Rei Sebastião, Spirit

JAUŠ KEREMET
See Keremet

JAVERZAHARSES
These are female spirits in the folklore of Armenia whose name, Javerzaharses, means the Perpetual Brides. They are the personification of bridal innocence, and are invisible to mortals. They represent the involvement with, and the preparations for, the marriage ceremony in their concern for the grooming, dress, and festivity of the occasion.
References 87
See also Spirit

JEKŠUK
See Arapteš

JEMALANG, JEMBALANG
This is the name of an earth spirit or jin in the folk beliefs of the Malay people of West Malaysia.
References 120
See also Djinn, Jin, Maahiset, Spirit

JENNIE OF BIGGERSDALE
This is the name of an evil spirit in the folklore of the North Riding of Yorkshire, England. She was said to inhabit the Mulgrave Woods of the area, and was probably a nursery bogie.
References 17
See also Nursery Bogie, Spirit

JENNY GREENTEETH
This is a spirit of Lancashire, northeast England. She is an evil and malignant water spirit of stagnant pools. She particularly awaits the unwary child who may go too close to the water; then she grabs the child in her long green fangs and drags the child down under the water to drown. Jenny Greenteeth may be found in any pool or pond that is covered with green slime or scum. She is a spirit that belongs to a class of nursery bogies described with vigor by watchful nursemaids and anxious parents in order to prevent the untimely death of children in such fearful places.
References 15, 17, 123, 133
See also Kappa, Nellie Longarms, Nursery Bogie, Peg Powler, Spirit, Appendix 22, Appendix 25

JER BODƏŽ
This is an invisible lake spirit in the folk beliefs of the Cheremis/Mari people of the former Soviet Republic.

The fisher folk make offerings of bread and vodka to this water spirit in return for a good catch.
References 118
See also Spirit, Appendix 25

JER KUBA AND JER KUGUZA
In the folk beliefs of the Cheremis/Mari people of the former Soviet Republic, this is the male and female form of the powerful lake spirit called Jer Bodəž. The names Jer Kuba and Jer Kuguza mean Lake Old Woman and Lake Old Man. They may manifest as a cow or an ox bellowing at the lakeside. This spirit may benevolently deliver good hauls of fish when propitiated correctly, but if anyone washes soiled clothing or hair in its waters, the spirit will exact revenge. Any human that offends this spirit may be struck down with an illness, or the fish stocks may dwindle. In more serious offenses, the house or town may be flooded; worse still, the spirit may remove the entire lake.
References 118
See also Kuba, Kuguza, Spirit, Appendix 25

JER OZA
This is the name of an Obda in the Cheremis/Mari folk beliefs of the former Soviet Republic. This spirit, as the translation of the name (Lake Master) implies, inhabits lakes. His abode is stretches of water in isolated places such as in the forests. Jer Oza is a malevolent spirit who will call the name of unwary men and entice them into the water, where they will be drowned. However, Jer Oza never harms women.
References 118
See also Obda, Spirit, Appendix 25

JERAHMEEL
See Archangel

JERSEY DEVIL, THE
In the popular folklore of New Jersey (United States), this devil was reported to inhabit Leeds Point, and is therefore also known as the Leeds Devil in the folklore of Pleasantville, Estelleville, and other locations nearby. The devil was said to be the result of an invocation by a woman so weary of childbearing that she declared she would sooner have a devil. The Jersey Devil was reported to be seen at night, frolicking with mermaids in the surf, sitting and prattling on chimney stacks, or terrifying the residents by peering in through their unshuttered windows. There is some speculation that this being was of human origin, yet others avow that it was supernatural.
References 87
See also Devil

JERŠUK
In the folk beliefs of the Cheremis/Mari people of the former Soviet Republic, this is a wind demon. He tries to make mischief by blowing into the campfires of travelers and hunters resting for the night in the forests, scattering sparks and flaming embers. A rowan branch placed at entry points to the track will avert his dangerous pranks.
References 118
See also Demon, Appendix 26

JETAITA
This was a terrifying earth spirit in the beliefs of the Yamana people of Tierra del Fuego.
References 93
See also Spirit

JEWA-JEWA
This is an intercessional spirit in the beliefs of the Malay people of West Malaysia. Like the angels, his duty in heaven is to mediate with the Creator on behalf of humans.
References 87
See also Angel, Spirit

JEZI-BABA
See Baba Yaga

JILI FFRWTAN
In the folklore of Wales, this is the name of a fairy servant of the Rumpelstiltskin or Habetrot type. Jili Ffrwtan performed some work that a woman had found impossible to do without assistance, and the supernatural demanded that the woman must be able to state the fairy's name in three days' time or forfeit everything. Before the time was up, the desperate woman came upon Jili Ffrwtan unnoticed. While at her work, the fairy was overheard to sing: *"Bychan ŵyr fy meistres i, Mai Jili Ffrwtan ydw i"* (Little does my mistress know that I am Jili Ffrwtan). With this, the woman was able to relate the supernatural's name in time and retain the completed work.
References 59
See also Fairy, Habetrot, Rumpelstiltskin, Sili Ffrit, Appendix 14

JIN, JINN/I
Jin is the spelling used in Bahasa Melayu in West Malaysia for the djinn of Islamic folk belief.
References 110
See also Bottle Imp, Djinn

JIN ASLAM
See Sang Gala Raja

JIN KAFIR
See Sang Gala Raja

JIN TANAH
This is the name for evil spirits in the folk beliefs of the Malay people of West Malaysia. As the name Jin Tanah (meaning Demon of the Earth) implies, they are demons that come from the earth. They inhabit the forests and have power over anything that walks there.
References 110
See also Demon, Djinn, Hantu, Spirit

JINN, JINNEE
See Djin

JNUN
This is the name of a type of djinn in the folklore of Morocco. This demon usually manifests in the form of a toad. It is not the usually destructive djinn, but most people will be respectful; therefore, if it enters the home, no one will molest it. Instead, they will ask it politely to depart.
References 87
See also Demon, Djinn

JOAN THE WAD
This is the Cornish variant of the spirit known elsewhere in England as Will o' the Wisp. It is possible that this spirit is derived from a Cornish piskey, and if approached correctly, would probably guide travelers to safety. Images of Joan the Wad are frequently offered as good-luck charms to tourists in the area because this is supposed to ensure that the traveler will never be lost.
References 17, 18
See also Piskey, Spirit, Will o' the Wisp, Appendix 24

JOÃO DE MATA
This spirit is a powerful and important encantado in the Afro-Brazilian cult Batuque. He was originally a human, transformed mysteriously to his present state. João de Mata, also known as Rei da Bandeira, is a spirit with a reputation for curing certain illnesses. This encantado's "family" includes Dorina and Tanbacê. He is a carefree spirit associated with Saint John of Matha and the feast day of 8 February.
References 89
See also Encantado, Spirit, Appendix 17

JOÃOZINHO
This is an encantado in the Afro-Brazilian cult Batuque associated with the feast day of Saint John and the encantado "family" of Legua Bogi da Trinidade.
References 89
See also Encantado, Legua Bogi da Trinidade

JOCOO
This is the name of a devil in the beliefs of the Mbousha people of Nigeria.

The Jin Tanah are earth demons with power over anything that walks in the forests that they inhabit.

References 81
See also Devil

JOHN BARLEYCORN

This spirit of English and Scottish folklore is the personification of the cultivation of barley and the resultant beer (and often, by extension, intoxication from beer). Robert Burns's poem "John Barleycorn" (1786) catalogs the "life and demise" of the spirit, which in some respects compares with that of the Kornwolf or the Cailleach. Apparently at the instigation of Prohibition in the United States, many breweries enacted the "death" of John Barleycorn.
References 24, 87
See also Cailleach, Kornwolf, Spirit

JOINT EATER

In English folklore this spirit was described as a type of malignant fairy or elf. The Joint Eater, also known as the Just Halver, is always invisible but in constant attendance of its victim. Its sole purpose, like the Alp Luachra of Irish folklore, is to cause the demise of humans. It accomplishes this by invisibly devouring their food, leaving the victim starving and constantly hungry despite apparently consuming enormous meals.
References 17
See also Abiku, Alp Luachra, Elf, Fairy, Spirit

JOLA SVEINAR

This is the name given in the folklore of Iceland to the Scandinavian Julenisse.
References 34
See also Julenisse

JOMBOL

In the beliefs of the Native Australians, he is the sea wind spirit.
References 14
See also Kompagnin, Spirit, Appendix 25, Appendix 26

JOPHIEL

See Angel, Archangel

JOSÉ TUPINAMBÁ

This is the name of an encantado in the Afro-Brazilian cult Batuque. He is derived from the character of the local Tupinamba people, who were thus named by the early Portuguese explorers. José Tupinambá is believed to reside in his ancestral home, and is described by devotees as a dignified old gentleman inclined to delivering moralistic speeches.
References 89
See also Encantado

JOŠKAR SER

This is the name of a keremet or devil in the folk beliefs of the Cheremis/Mari people of the former Soviet Republic. The name Joškar Ser means Red Bank.
References 118
See also Devil, Keremet

JUAN CABRITO

See Nubero

JUČUZO

This is a keremet in the folk beliefs of the Cheremis/Mari people of the former Soviet Republic.
References 118
See also Keremet

JUJU

At one time in southern Nigeria, this term applied to the evil spirits or demons that inhabited a fetish or representation. It is now a general term for sorcery or tabu.
References 88
See also Demon, Spirit

JUL SER KUGƏRAK

This is a term for a local keremet of the River Volga in the folk beliefs of the Cheremis/Mari people of the former Soviet Republic. This name, used as a euphemism to avert the demon's annoyance and resultant revenge, means Volga Bank Prince.
References 118
See also Demon, Keremet

JULE TOMTE
This is the name given in Sweden to the Christmas spirit, called the Julenisse in Norway and Denmark.
References 34
See also Julenisse, Spirit

JULENISSE
An important member of the Scandinavian Little People is the Julenisse. In Danish and Norwegian folklore he is described as looking like a little bearded goblin wearing red garments and a pointed red night-cap. He is the nisse charged with delivering gifts at Christmas to all the good children in Denmark and Norway. A dish of his favorite porridge is left on the table to welcome him. Nisse is the old form of *Nils,* the Scandinavian version of the first name Nicholas. This would seem to indicate that the derivation of this spirit is closely linked with that of Saint Nicholas's metamorphosis into the spirit called Santa Claus.
References 34
See also Goblin, Jola Sveinar, Jule Tomte, Little People, Nis, Santa Claus, Appendix 22

JUMBY
This is the general term for a spirit used by Caribbean Islanders of African descent.
References 88
See also Dyombie, Spirit

JUODS
Juods is the term for a devil or the Devil in Latvian folklore. In Estonian and Finnish folklore, the term is Juudas and Juutas, respectively. Although the name means Black, it is possibly derived from the biblical Judas.
References 88
See also Devil

JŪRASMĀTE
This is a female nature spirit in the folk beliefs of the Latvian people. Jūrasmāte means Mother of the Sea. She is the guardian spirit of the creatures in the seas.
References 88
See also Guardian, Māte, Spirit, Vējasmāte, Appendix 12, Appendix 25

JUREMA, JUREMA VELHA, SEU JUREMA
The name Jurema is that of an important "family" of encantados, derived from tree spirits, in the Afro-Brazilian cults of Batuque, Umbanda, and Catimbó. At the head of this clan are Jurema Velha, which means Old Lady Jurema, and Seu Jurema, which means Sir Jurema. Other spirits of the Jurema group are: Jureminha, Mirací, Dom Carlos, Cabocla Roxa, Capingueiro, Capingueiro de Jurema, Flechiero, Juçara, Junquiera, Juremeia, Juruwa, Paranguaçu,

Pena Verde, Rompe Mato, and Sete Flechas.
References 89
See also Dom Carlos, Encantado, Oxossi, Pena Verde, Rompe Mato, Spirit

JURONG
This is the name of a spirit in the mythology and folk beliefs of China. Jurong is an avenging spirit of fire that punishes those who offend the gods. It may manifest as a bird.
References 119
See also Spirit, Appendix 12

JURUA, JURUWIN
In the beliefs of the people of the Andaman Islands, these are evil sea spirits that belong to a group of invisible supernaturals having their abode under the sea. Jurua is the name used in the northern islands, and Juruwin is the name used in the southern islands. The Jurua will devour anything that falls into the water. In order to encourage this, they will fling their spears at the legs of fishermen and swimmers, causing them to have cramps, so they can be dragged down to the underwater world to be consumed.
References 88
See also Lau, Spirit, Appendix 25

JUST HALVER
See Joint Eater

JÜŠTƏ ERGE AND JÜŠTƏ ƏRBEZƏ
This is the frolicsome winter-child spirit in the folklore of the Cheremis/Mari people of the former Soviet Republic. The names mean Cold Boy and Cold Child. Although invisible, this supernatural child can be heard on freezing nights playing with a ball that bounces all over the doors and roofs of the houses. He calls in the wind for the children of the house to come and play. During the day, they know when he is there because he will nip at their fingers, toes, noses, and cheeks, trying to get them to chase him.
References 118
See also, Jack Frost, Jüšta Kuba, Spirit, Appendix 22

JÜŠTƏ KUBA AND JÜŠTƏ KUGUZA
These are the female and male forms of the spirit of freezing-cold weather in the folk beliefs of the Cheremis/Mari people of the former Soviet Republic. Their names mean Cold Old Woman and Cold Old Man. Although invisible, the spirits can be heard as they pound on wooden fences, house walls, and trees on freezing nights. They try to call people out, but if they catch anyone (especially drunken men, whose singing makes them angry), they trip them and push them about in the snow. If no one comes out, people inside can sometimes hear Jüšta Kuba as she

spitefully sews the door with her ice needle. During the day the two spirits tease humans who have to go outside by pinching their noses, knocking their heads, and even killing them.
References 118
See also Father Frost, Jüšta Ərbezə, Jüšta Erga, Kuba, Kuguza, Pokšem Kuba, Spirit, Appendix 26

JÜŠTƏ MUŽƏ

This is a disease demon in the folklore of the Cheremis/Mari people in the former Soviet Republic. This spirit is responsible for inflicting chills and colds on humans, as the translation of its name (Cold Illness) implies. This demon is said to manifest in many other guises, which are named Jüštə Mužə Üdər, Jüštə Erge and Jüštə Ərbezə, and Jüštə Kuba and Jüštə Kuguza.
References 118
See also Demon, Jüštə Erge, Jüštə Kuba, Kuba, Kuguza, Spirit, Appendix 17

JÜŠTƏ MUŽƏ ÜDƏR

This is a female disease spirit in the folk beliefs of the Cheremis/Mari people of the former Soviet Republic.

Jüštə Mužə Üdər means Cold Illness Daughter, and this is her domain. She is responsible for climbing into the beds of humans and bringing freezing chills and hot fevers associated with the ague.
References 118
See also Jüštə Mužə, Spirit, Appendix 17

JUT BODƏŽ

This spirit is regarded very much like a Guardian Angel in the folk beliefs of the Cheremis/Mari people of the former Soviet Republic. Jut Bodəž means the Night Spirit, and he protects humans during the hours of darkness. He may be requested to keep away demons while the family sleeps.
References 118
See also Demon, Guardian Angel, Spirit, Appendix 21, Appendix 22

JUTURNA
See Diuturna

JUUDAS, JUUTAS
See Juods

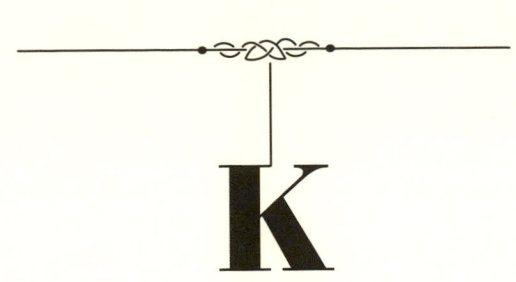

K

KA

This is a name used in two different cultures to denote a spirit being.

(1) In the beliefs of ancient Egyptians the Ka was a protective or guardian spirit. It was assigned to an individual at birth and, like the Grine, lived a parallel supernatural life. It was given its own container and effigy when the human died, and the container became known as a "Ka."

(2) In the beliefs of the Kachin people of Burma, it is the alternative name for Chinün Way Shun, the nat or spirit of fertile soil.

See also (1) Daimon, Grine, Guardian; (2) Chinün Way Shun, Nat, Appendix 10, Appendix 18

KABA PIAMBAR

See Piambar

KABANDHA

This is the name of the metamorphosed and deformed state of the demon Gandharva in the epic Indian legend the Ramayana. Gandharva quarreled with Indra, who dealt the demon such a blow that his head and legs were swallowed up into his body, swelling it like a barrel, his eye and mouth emerging though his huge hairy torso. As Kabandha, whose name means Barrel, he quarreled with Rama, who destroyed the demon by fire, from which he re-emerged in his original form as Gandharva. In gratitude for being restored to his original form, Gandharva helped in Rama's wars against Ravana.

References 119
See also Demon, Gandharva, Ravana

KABOUTERMANNEKIN

A type of goblin or brownie in the folklore of Holland. This spirit could be naked and hairy or wear rather old and dusty red clothes and cap, which is why he would sometimes be called Red Cap. This sprite would work at night in the mills grinding corn, storing the sacks of flour, or resetting the heavy mill stones if they had become worn. All that he would receive for his services would be a slice of bread and

butter and a glass of beer. As with all such spirits, a gift of clothes, once accepted, would ensure that he never worked there again. A miller of Kempnerland who did not understand this had given his Kaboutermannekin such a gift then tried to get the spirit to return by lying in wait at a bridge where he was sure to pass. Just as the goblin saw him, the miller heard what he thought was his wife falling into the water screaming. Running to rescue his wife, the miller realized that he had been duped and all the sprites had vanished.

References 17, 66
See also Brollachan, Brownie, Goblin, Killmoulis, Spirit, Sprite, Appendix 15

KACHES

This name, which is a euphemism meaning the Brave Ones, is used for a group of malicious spirits in the folk beliefs of Armenia. They were invisible and inhabited wilderness places in communities. The Kaches were entirely malevolent towards humans, stealing from them and, when they could, torturing those they could entrap. In modern folklore their place has been overtaken by the Devs.

References 88
See also Deev, Spirit

KACHINA, KATCINA

In the beliefs of the Pueblo, Zuñi, Hopi, and other Native American people of the American Southwest, this is a term for benevolent agricultural nature spirits that revisit the earth every year during the winter months. These spirits are represented in the Kachina masks worn by dancers during important ceremonies. The Kachinas originally visited the people in person, showing them how to grow melons and corn and providing rainfall for good harvests.

References 25, 45, 119
See also Gahe, Appendix 15, Appendix 18, Appendix 26

K'DAAI

This is a demon in the folk beliefs of the Yakut people of Siberia. K'daai is the spirit of fire, and is believed

to have introduced the skills of smelting and working iron to the Yakut people.
References 93
See also Demon, Spirit, Appendix 14

KAFZIEL
This is the name of an Archangel or a chief angel in Judeo-Christian scriptures. In the astrological calendar, he was associated with the planet Saturn in early Jewish writings. He was similarly associated with the same planet in medieval Christian astrology under his alternative name of Cassiel.
References 40, 87, 107, 114
See also Angel, Archangel

KAHAUSIBWARE
An evil female spirit or demon in the beliefs of the Solomon Islanders. She usually manifests in the form of a snake. Kahausibware was responsible for creating certain animals, such as pigs, and trees. She can be extremely malicious and destructive and is blamed for strangling the first baby born to the first woman.
References 33
See also Demon, Kaia, Spirit, Appendix 12, Appendix 22

KAIA
In the beliefs of the people of the Gazelle Peninsula in New Britain (Melanesia), these demons were originally creator spirits. They can manifest in human shape but more frequently appear as snakes, eels, or pigs. The Kaia inhabit the depths of the earth or volcanoes from which they emerge to bring misfortune to humans.
References 93
See also Demon, Kahausibware, Spirit, Appendix 12

KAIAMUNU, KAIEMUNU
This is an important demon in the beliefs of the people of the Purari Delta, Papua New Guinea. Although invisible, his form is believed to be represented in the shape of a wicker effigy. During the initiation ceremonies of boys, Kaiamunu is believed to engulf each boy and regurgitate him as a new initiate.
References 93
See also Demon, Green Man, Kaia

KAITORAK
This is the name of a forest spirit in the beliefs of the Inuit and Ihalmiut people of Canada.
References 101
See also Spirit, Appendix 19

KAJƏK KEREMET
This is a demon in the folk beliefs of the Cheremis/Mari people of the former Soviet Republic. As the translation of its name, Game Bird Keremet, implies,

it is the guardian of those birds and animals that are hunted in the forests. Kajək Keremet is propitiated by those who go into his forests for success in the hunt.
References 118
See also Demon, Guardian, Keremet, Appendix 12

KAJIS
This is the collective name of a group of demons in the folklore of the Georgian people of the Caucasus Mountains. A story is told of how a hero, known as Mindia the Snake Eater, was captured and enslaved by these demons in their terrible underworld. Left alone one day he investigated the foul-smelling cauldron of snakes from which they ate. Ignoring the stench, Mindia ate from the cauldron and was immediately filled with some of the supernatural power of the Kajis. The returning demons were horrified to find their slave had found the source of their powers, which had allowed Mindia to outwit them and make his escape.
References 30
See also Demon

KAKAMORA, KAKANGORA
These are the Little People in the folk beliefs of the Melanesian people of San Cristoval. On other islands of the same group these spirits may be known as Kakangora or Pwaronga. Although their size may change from very tiny to almost knee-high to a human, the Kakamora are always described as having long hair and sharp, long nails and teeth. As supernaturals they are afraid of anything white and have a vulnerable place on the body, which is their buttocks. They inhabit the caves and banyan trees in forest communities with a king and queen, and they are fond of hoarding money. The Kakamora were known to hunt humans as meat long ago, and they would peer into the human homes to await their opportunity to kill the inhabitants. Humans learned how to grab the hair of the Kakamora through the cracks in the walls and prod their buttocks to drive them away. After this the Kakamora confined themselves to playing pranks on the humans, especially children.
References 119
See also Little People, Spirit, Appendix 22

KAKODAIMON
See Cacodæmon

KAKUA KAMBUZI
A spirit in the folk beliefs of the Basoga people of Uganda. It is a protective tree spirit much like the Dryads of ancient Greek and Roman mythology.
References 110
See also Spirit, Appendix 19

KALA, KALAU (pl.)

A general name given for the evil disease spirits in the beliefs of the Koryak people who inhabit the Kamchatka Peninsula of the former Soviet Republic. The spirits are also known by the names Kalak, Kamak, Ñe'nveticñin, and Ñi'nvit. These spirits may appear in human shape with pointed heads or take the shape of animals. They may inhabit an underworld or the wilderness of the earth. The Kalau are particularly malevolent towards humans. While invisible they may cause headaches by beating people over the head, or inflict diseases by breathing in a person's face. They may bite or nip the flesh of humans, causing sores or painful swelling of the limbs. These demons have also been accused of devouring human flesh.

References 88
See also Demon, Kalak, Ñe'nveticñin, Ñi'nvit, Appendix 17

KALAK

This is the collective name of a type of evil spirit in the beliefs of the Paren people of Siberia. This group of Koryak people who inhabit the Kamchatka Peninsula also call these spirits by the name Kamak. But these demons are more generally known elsewhere and also in Siberia by the name Kalau.

References 88
See also Demon, Kala, Spirit

KĀLANEMI

This is the name of a demon in the epic Indian mythology of the Ramayana. Kalanemi is a Rakshasa and the uncle of the demon Ravana. In the classical legends Kalanemi is defeated by Hanuman and propelled on to the island of Lanka to join Ravana in exile.

References 88
See also Demon, Rakshasa, Ravana

KALEVANPOJAT

In the folklore of Finland this name, meaning Sons of Kalavala, is used for a group of destructive spirits. These demons despoil agricultural land, scattering it with rocks and stones. They also flood the forests to make them uninhabitable.

References 93
See also Demon, Spirit, Appendix 18

KALFU

This is the name of the guardian spirit of doors and entrances in the Voodoo beliefs of Haiti. It is Kalfu who guides other spirits to the ceremonies. He is derived from a deity of West Africa.

References 138
See also Guardian, Guia, Legba, Spirit

KALKES

See Kallikantzari

KALLIKANTZARI

These are evil and malignant spirits in the folk beliefs of modern Greece. The Kallikantzari are also called Kalkes in the district of Panorio. They are described as being little hairy beings with long tails. They are particularly attracted to open fires at night in the winter months, and if the fire is left unattended, they will urinate on it and put it out. For this reason the household Christmas fires are well guarded, as these spirits may enter and wreak havoc, stealing all the good food and extinguishing the fires. The Kallikantzari often visit the campfires of shepherds at night and may attempt to get solitary people to divulge their names. This is a ploy the spirits use to attack humans. A story resembling those of the English Ainsel and the French Cheval Bayard is told of a shepherd who saw the Kallikantzari come to his fire demanding food from his pot. When they asked his name he answered, "I myself." When he got the chance the shepherd threw hot coals at the spirits, who fled, screaming for their companions to destroy their persecutor. Asked who this was, they replied, "I myself," to which the reply was, "You deserve what you got." Not surprisingly, the shepherd was left unharmed.

References 12
See also Ainsel, Cheval Bayard, It, Satyr, Spirit

KALLISTÓ

See Callisto

KALU KUMĀRA YAKA

In the Buddhist beliefs of the Sinhalese people of Sri Lanka, Kalu Kumāra Yaka was originally a holy man who succumbed to the temptation of earthly love. He was destroyed and became a demon. As the demon he preys upon the vulnerability of women in pregnancy and childbirth, causing complications and puerperal fever.

References 88
See also Demon, Labartu, Lilith, Putana, Tçulo, Appendix 17, Appendix 22

KALUKS

This is a name used for the spirits that inhabit trees in the folk beliefs of Burma and Thailand. Although they are invisible, a sure sign of their presence is when the leaves flutter without any wind. Care must be taken to consult these spirits respectfully before a tree is to be felled. Otherwise, according to the En people, the human who cuts the tree will die.

References 110, 119
See also Hamadryads, Spirit, Appendix 19

KALYPSO
See Calypso

KAMAK
See Kalak

KAMALLO
This is an evil spirit of the Isuama region of Nigeria propitiated for malicious events to be brought upon others.
References 57
See also Spirit

KAMANG
In the folk beliefs of Korea, this is a spirit guardian of the underworld.
References 79
See also Guardian, Spirit, Appendix 16

KAMI
These are two groups of spirits that are named Kami.
(1) In the folk beliefs of Korea this is a general term for a spirit or supernatural being.
(2) A general term for spirits in the Shinto religion of Japan.
References 79, 119
See also Spirit

KAMSA
This is the name of an evil demon, or Asura, in the mythology of India who was eventually destroyed by Krishna.
References 88, 119
See also Asura, Demon

KANAIMA
This is a collective name for malignant forces and evil spirits in the folk beliefs of Guiana. These are mostly demons that shadow their victims until they find the opportunity to inflict a mortal disease or death blow.
References 88
See also Demon, Spirit

KANNUK
The name of a powerful spirit in the beliefs of the Native Americans of the Pacific Northwest coast. Kannuk manifests in the shape of a wolf.
References 25
See also Spirit, Appendix 12

KAPKA OROL
See Čembulat

KAPPA
These are demons in the mythology of Japan. They are described as being small and in the shape of mon-

keys, with scaly skin and webbed fingers. The Kappa, also known as Kawako, which means Child of the River, inhabit ponds and rivers. The Kappa are particularly malicious and entice humans and animals into the water, where the spirits devour their victims and drink their blood. If a human is clever enough to negotiate with the Kappa, he may keep his life. The Kappas' potency may be drawn from them by making a low bow, which convention decrees must be returned even by a demon. As they do so, the water, which is the source of the Kappas' power, will drain from their heads.
References 29, 88, 93, 119, 132
See also Buso, Demon, Jenny Greenteeth, Llamhigyn y Dwr, Peg Powler, Spirit, Appendix 12, Appendix 25

KAPUA
This is the term for a group of supernatural tricksters in the folk beliefs of Hawaii. They could assume any shape or size when visible, and no object was a barrier to their deceitful and chaotic exploits.
References 29
See also Iwa, Kawelo, Ono, Pekoi, Trickster

KARAWATONIGA
In the folk beliefs of the Tube-Tube people of Melanesia, these are benign spirits that inhabit the littoral rocks and vegetation. They look vaguely like humans, with ill-defined features and long hair.
References 88
See also Bariaua, Kakamora, Spirit

KARINA
In the beliefs of Islamic people in North Africa, Karina is a powerful demon. She may manifest as a beautiful young woman, as a dog, as an owl, or as a snake. She is said to have been a human mother who ate her own children and turned into a fiend. Like Sheela-na-gig she would disgust and curse humans by displaying her genitalia, condemning those who saw her to a future of stillborn offspring and sickness. She also brings barrenness to the land and its animals. A tradition tells of her appearing as a beautiful young woman to Solomon while he was hunting in the desert. She considered herself too powerful for any man to defeat her, but revealed that the Archangel Gabriel was superior. Solomon immediately invoked the Archangel who subdued her and transformed Karina into the shape of an old hag.
References 56
See also Archangel, Baubo, Demon, Fiend, Gabriel, Sheela-na-gig, Appendix 22

KARITEI-MO
See Hāriti

KĀRKOTAKA
See Nagas

KARLIKI
This is the name for dwarfs in the folklore of the Slav people. These spirits were believed to have originated as Fallen Angels who arrived on earth and remained there as Little People.
References 41
See also Dwarf, Fallen Angel, Little People, Spirit

KARMAN KURƏK KUGUZA
This is the name of a keremet in the folk beliefs of the Cheremis/Mari people of the former Soviet Republic. Karman Kurək Kuguza is a powerful demon whose name means Castle Mountain Old Man.
References 118
See also Demon, Keremet, Kuguza

KAS PEREŠTA
See Perešta

KASAGONAGA
A spirit in the folk beliefs of the Chaco people of the South American Pampas. She is a female weather spirit who hovers in the skies and delivers the rain to the grasslands.
References 33, 56
See also Spirit, Appendix 26

KATAVI
This is a demon in the folk beliefs of the Nyamwezi people of Tanzania. Katavi inhabits the wilderness and also leads the evil water spirits.
References 93
See also Demon, Spirit, Appendix 25

KATCINA MANA
The name for the Sprouting Maize Spirit in the beliefs of the Hopi Native American people.
References 25, 45
See also Corn Spirit, Kachina, Kerwan, Appendix 15

KATCINAS, KATSINAS
See Kachinas

KATZENVEIT
This is a demon in the folklore of the Fichtelgebirge region of Germany. Katzenveit inhabits the forest, where he is said to entrap unwary humans who venture there. The threat of this demon is used by parents as a nursery bogie to prevent small children from wandering into the forest alone.
References 110
See also Demon, Gübich, Nursery Bogie, Rübezahl

KAUKAS
This is a household spirit in the folklore of Lithuania. The Kaukas may manifest as a sort of goblin or, like the Aitvaras, as a kind of flying dragon with a fiery tail. This demon brings good fortune and stolen goods for the family to which it is attached. It may also be the guardian of treasure hoards.
References 87, 88, 93
See also Aitvaras, Demon, Goblin, Guardian, Household Spirit, Para, Pukis, Smiera-Gatto, Appendix 20, Appendix 22

KAWAKO
See Kappa

KAWELO
In the folk beliefs of Hawaii this is the name of a trickster spirit. This demon could shape shift at will to any form when visible and was renowned for the pranks and jokes he played on humans.
See also Iwa, Kapua, Pekoi, Spirit, Trickster

KAZNA PERI
This is the name of a demon that means Treasure Devil, in the folk beliefs of the Cheremis/Mari people of the former Soviet Republic. Kazna Peri is supposed to be the guardian of a treasure that it lifts from the ground to cook over a blue flame between the Feast of the Pentecost (Whitsuntide, seven weeks after Easter) and Midsummer's Day (usually 24 June). If a human is able to see this take place he may be able to locate and remove the treasure before the fire goes out.
References 118
See also Demon, Guardian, Kladovik, Kudeiar, Peri, Will o' the Wisp, Appendix 20

KAZNA PIAMBAR
See Piambar

KEAGYIHL DEPGUESK
This is the great whirlpool spirit in the beliefs of the Native American people of the Pacific Northwest. There is a legend that tells how Gyhldeptis was instrumental in getting other spirits to remove Keagyihl Depguesk from the river.
References 25
See also Gyhldeptis, Spirit, Appendix 25

KEELUT
This is a malevolent spirit in the folk beliefs of the Inuit people of Canada. The Keelut appears in the shape of a dog without fur.
References 102
See also Ke'lets, Spirit, Appendix 12

KE'LETS

This is the name of a fearsome demon in the folk beliefs of the Chukchi people of Siberia. With his dogs he tracks human hunters and travelers to kill them in the wilderness.
References 93
See also Demon, Keelut, Appendix 24

KELIANO

See Celæno

KELPIE, KELPY

This is the fearsome and malevolent water spirit of Scottish folklore. Although it could assume the form of a rough, ragged old man or a handsome young man, the Kelpie mostly took the form of a black or gray horse with flashing eyes and a silken coat. It could be identified as the water spirit by the green rushes that always clung to its hair. It was to be found on the shores of the lochs, at fords, and at ferry points. To see a Kelpie is considered a portent of drowning or other waterborne catastrophe. In human form it could leap onto the horse behind the rider and crush the terrified traveler to death. It would appear to unsuspecting young women as a lover, eventually abducting them and devouring them under the water. The Kelpie would also entice wandering children or unwary young men to mount him in the guise of a sleek horse on the shore of the loch. The fiend would then gallop off into the water, dragging down his victims and devouring all but the entrails, which would float to the surface. If anyone could get a bridle over the Kelpie's head, it was said that the spirit would do the work of several horses. The spirit was also known to keep the waterwheels of the mills turning at night, but he was just as capable of destroying them.
References 15, 17, 18, 28, 40, 41, 44, 56, 88, 92, 99, 107, 114, 123
See also Bäckahäst, Cabyll-Ushtey, Cheval Bayard, Each Uisge, Fiend, Näcken, Neugle, Spirit, Appendix 12, Appendix 22, Appendix 25

KELTƏMAŠ

The Keltəmaš is an evil forest spirit in the folk beliefs of the Cheremis/Mari people of the former Soviet Republic. It can appear in any form. The Cheremis hang mirrors by the doors and windows as a protection against this spirit. The Keltəmaš confuses people late at night and leads them astray in the dark. One evening while a man was in the bathhouse, the Keltəmaš entered in the guise of his wife and told him that it was snowing outside. When the man recovered from his confusion he found that he was shivering naked in the woods miles from his home, a victim of the Keltəmaš's trickery.
References 118

See also Čort, Spirit, Xuda Sila, Appendix 19, Appendix 22

KER, KERES (pl.)

These are two versions of this Greek spirit:

(1) This is the name of a spirit in the classical mythology and beliefs of Greece. The Ker was an angel of death responsible for guiding the souls of the dead to Hades.

(2) In modern Greek folklore the Ker is a malevolent demon bringing sickness and death to the humans upon whom it fixes its attention.
References 12, 93
See also Angel, Demon, Appendix 16, Appendix 17

KEREMET

A Keremet is a powerful nature demon or devil in the folk beliefs of the Cheremis/Mari people of the former Soviet Republic. It is described as being dressed in clothes like those of the Tartars with a blue shirt and a turban-style head covering. Keremets have many origins: they may have been wicked humans, like Black Vaughan in the Wild Hunt of England, who were transformed after death and continued to do evil. They may have been legendary heroes, like Čembulat, assigned to lead a pack of demons. A Keremet may evolve from the spittle of an evil person, but they are usually the spirits of natural phenomena. Whatever the origin, there are Keremets controlling all aspects of natural occurrences in the lives of the people. These spirits are ever present bringing misfortune, disease, and in extreme cases, death. In order to placate these malignant beings and avert their influence, the Cheremis make propitiating sacrifices, which descend into their underworld. Sorcerers try to use the Keremets as familiars in their spells to bring sickness or misfortune to others. In order to avoid the attention of a Keremet, people usually refer to them as: Kuguza, Old Man; Kugə Jeŋ, Great Man; Kugərak, Prince; or Bodəž, Spirit.
References 118
See also Black Vaughan, Bodəž, Čembulat, Demon, Devil, Familiar, Kuguza, Spirit, Wild Hunt, Appendix 12

KEREMET ŠƏRT

This is a keremet or evil spirit, in the folklore of the Cheremis/Mari people of the former Soviet Republic, that is placated by the sacrifice of a hare.
References 118
See also Cort, Keremet, Spirit

KERGRIM

In English folklore and local legend this is a term for a churchyard demon or ghoul.
References 69
See also Church Grim, Demon, Ghoul, Grim

The Kelpie, a frightening water spirit, nears his next victim.

KƏRTNÃ BODƏJ

A keremet in the folk beliefs of the Cheremis/Mari people of the former Soviet Republic. This spirit, whose name means Iron Spirit, is described as being richly dressed and traveling in a *troika* drawn by bay horses with an escort of demons ready for battle.
References 118
See also Demon, Keremet, Spirit

KERUBIM

See Cherub

KERWAN

This is the name for the Sprouting Maize Spirit in the beliefs of the Hopi Native American people.
References 25, 45
See also Corn Spirit, Deohako, Katcina Mana, Appendix 15

KESHALYI

In the folk beliefs of the Romany Gypsies of Transylvania, this is the name of the benevolent fairies. The Keshalyi inhabited the remote and beautiful forests and mountains of the region and were ruled by their queen called Ana. Their shape resembles that of beautiful, diminutive, delicate humans, rather like the nymphs of Greek mythology. The derivation of the name seems to be the word *kachli,* meaning spindle, as indicated in a charm against sterility invoking these fairies thus: *"Keshalyi lisperesn"* (Fairies spin).
References 31
See also Ana, Bitoso, Fairy, Loçolico, Melalo, Nymph, Schilalyi

KHADEM QUEMQUOMA

This is a female djinn in the folk beliefs of Morocco. The name Khadem Quemquoma means Black Woman of the Copper Pot. This spirit is particularly wicked to small children and will wake up a sleeping infant and frighten it, causing it to cry in the night.
References 90
See also Arifa, Djinn, Oum Çebiane, Spirit, Zagaz, Appendix 22

KHASM

This is the modern name for Aesma of the Zoroastrian religion, in the beliefs and folk traditions of Iran.
References 41
See also Aeshma

KHEREBU

This is the name of a group of spirits of ancient Assyria whose name is the origin of the Christian Cherubim.
References 41
See also Cherub, Spirit

KHITKA, KHITKHA

See Rusalka

KHMÓC PRÂY

See Pray

KHO-DUMO-DUMO

In the folk beliefs and legends of Lesotho, this is the name of an evil demon. Kho-dumo-dumo was destroyed by the folk hero Ditaolane.
References 29
See also Demon

KHSATHRA, KHSHATHRA VAIRYA

See Kshathra

KHYAB-PA

This is the name of a powerful demon in the pre-Buddhist Bon-po religion of Tibet.
References 119
See also Demon

KIBUKA

See Balubaale

KIKIADES

A name for demons in the folklore of modern Greece. The name means the Bad Ones.
References 12
See also Demon

KIKIMORA

This is a female household spirit in Russian folklore sometimes said to be the wife of the Domovoi. She is described as looking like an old peasant woman with uncovered long hair and chicken's legs. She resided in the cellars of the home and would do domestic chores when the family had gone to bed. The spirit would also look after the chickens in the yard. If the housewife was neat and clean, then she could be sure of Kikamora's help; however, if the housewife were untidy and lazy, then the spirit would break or hide things, turn food sour, and tickle the children at night in their beds. The only way to appease Kikamora would be for a brew of ferns to be made and all the household utensils scrubbed thoroughly in it. Kikimora was also a portent of disaster. Should anyone see her at her spinning on the porch, then they were doomed to die shortly after.
References 29, 75, 102
See also Domikha, Domovoi, Household Spirit, Krimba, Kurinyi Bog, Appendix 22

KILLMOULIS

This spirit inhabited the flour mills of the Lowlands of Scotland. He is described as a grotesque creature with

no mouth and who seems to have taken food by way of a huge nose. The Killmoulis is a spirit of the hob or brownie type, being a family guardian spirit whose labor could be called upon when the miller or his family were in need. The Killmoulis could be relied upon to help with the milking, and at All Hallows Tide (Halloween, 31 October) would cast the future for the family. The Killmoulis could also be mischievous and would play practical jokes, such as puffing ashes over the grain. His favorite haunt was the *killogie,* the outer section of the drying kiln. If any misfortune were about to befall the family, the Killmoulis would howl a warning.
References 17, 66
See also Banshee, Brollachan, Brownie, Domovoi, Kaboutermannikin, Spirit, Urisk, Appendix 22

KIMPRUSHAS
There are two groups of spirits with this name:
(1) In the Hindu mythology of India, these are demon spirits and attendants of the evil Kubera. They are described as having the torso of a horse and human heads.
(2) A group of spirits in the folklore of the Yaghan people of Tierra del Fuego.
References 88
See also Attendant, Demon, Kubera, Spirit, Appendix 12

KING GOLDMAR OF VOLLMAR
See Goldmar

KINGMINGOARKULLUK
In the folk beliefs of the Inuit people of Canada this tiny benevolent spirit appears in the same shape as the people. He enjoys making music.
References 102
See also Spirit

KINGU
The name of a powerful demon in the ancient Babylonian creation myths.
References 88, 93
See also Demon

KINNARA
There are two groups of spirits with this name:
(1) A group of spirits or Gandharvas in Indian mythology. They are variously described as being like birds with human heads or having the torso of a man and the head of a horse. They are the attendants of Kubera. Under the name Keinnara, they feature in the mythology of Burma.
(2) The name of a group of spirits in the mythology of the Yaghan people of Tierra del Fuego.
References 88, 93
See also Gandharvas, Kubera, Spirit, Appendix 12

KIRKEGRIM
Like the Church Grim of Yorkshire, England, this guardian spirit of Danish folklore patrols the churchyards to protect those interred there from evil spirits. The Kirkegrim usually takes the form of a "grave-sow."
References 17
See also Church Grim, Guardian, Kirkogrim, Appendix 12, Appendix 21

KIRKOGRIM
Like the Church Grim of Yorkshire, England, this guardian spirit of Swedish folklore patrols the churchyards to protect those interred there from evil spirits. The Kirkogrim usually takes the form of a lamb, said to be derived from the sacrificial lamb that used to be buried beneath the altar before the consecration of a church.
References 17
See also Kirkegrim, Kyrkogrim, Appendix 12, Appendix 21

KIRNIS
In the folklore of Lithuania this is the demon or guardian spirit of the cherry trees who ensured a successful harvest.
References 102, 110
See also Aërico, Demon, Guardian, Spirit, Appendix 19

KISHIMOJIN
See Hāriti

KISKIL-LILLA
This is the name of a demon in the ancient Sumerian mythology. Kiskil-lilla was a female night demon who was destroyed by Gilgamesh.
References 93
See also Demon, Lilith

KIVATI
See Kwati

KLABOTERMAN
This is the name of a kobold in the folklore of the fishermen and sailors of the Baltic Sea. Klaboterman is described as dressed in yellow with a nightcap-style sailor's hat and smoking a pipe. This spirit is skilled in the ways of sailing ships and is said to help sailors in their tasks aboard their vessels, but will punish those who are lazy. Klaboterman is never seen on the ships until the vessel is doomed to disaster, and then he will become visible to those who will perish.
References 114
See also Kobold, Paravoj Ia, Spirit, Appendix 25

KLADOVIK, KLADOVOI

This is the name of a demon in the folklore of Russia. The Kladovik is said to be the guardian of treasure
References 75
See also Demon, Guardian, Kazna Peri, Kudeiar, Appendix 20

KLIPPIE

The name of a tiny brown-faced elf or fairy in the folklore of Forfarshire, Scotland.
References 17
See also Elf, Fairy

KLOTO

See Fates

KLUDDE

A malignant shape-shifting bogle or demon in the folklore of Belgium. The Kludde would appear as a dog, cat, frog, bat, or horse, or stay completely invisible to terrorize night-bound travelers on lonely roads. The Kludde could, however, be identified by telltale blue flames flickering ahead of it. This spirit might jump on the back of the victim and cling with its talons, becoming heavier the more the terrified human tried to dislodge it, possibly until the human died of exhaustion. Only dawn breaking or the sound of the church bell could save the traveler. As a Black Dog it suddenly appeared and pranced along the road, stretching on its hind legs until it reached the throat of its victim. Its usual manifestation was as an old horse, which like the Hedley Kow, encouraged the unwary to mount on its back, from which they were unable to dismount until, after a horrific ride, they were ejected into a river.
References 66
See also Aufhocker, Black Dog, Bogle, Demon, Hedley Kow, Old Man of the Sea, Oschaert, Spirit, Appendix 12, Appendix 24

KMNKAMTCH

A demon that tried to destroy the Earth by fire in the mythology of the Klamath Native Americans of Oregon.
References 41
See also Demon

KNECHT RUPRECHT

In the Christian tradition of Germany, the supernatural giver of gifts at Christmas had several spirit helpers. They looked like gnomes and dressed in furs or fur-trimmed garments. Knecht Ruprecht, whose name means Servant Rupert, was one of many such helpers. The names of the others were Bulleklas, Rugeklas, and Sumerklas in Macklenberg and Pomerania; Pelznickel in Brandenburg; Rubbet or Rower in Schleswig-Holstein; and Herscheklos in Thuringia. In Austria, Bohemia, and Switzerland the names are Bartel, Ruprich, and Sammichlaus, respectively. The Austrian Krampus had a malevolent character. These attendants were charged with making sure that all the good children received gifts and that the naughty ones received the "means of correction."
References 34, 88
See also Attendant Spirit, Father Christmas, Gnome, Krampus, Pelznickel, Spirit, Appendix 22

KNOCKERS

In the folklore of the miners of Cornwall, England, these are benevolent goblins or mine spirits. Although they were rarely seen, they were described as little sprites dressed like the human miners. It was believed that these spirits were extracting the tin or gold ore for their own use but were happy to indicate to the humans where the rich deposits lay by tapping on the gallery walls. The Knockers would also hammer furiously in all directions to warn the humans when a rockfall was imminent. In order to keep a favorable relationship with their spirit colleagues, the miners would refrain from swearing, whistling, or making the sign of the cross in the galleries. The Knockers could be offended by any of these things and were known to bring showers of stones or even rockfalls on the work face of any miner who did not respect them.
References 5, 17, 18, 40, 87, 92, 97, 107
See also Blue Cap, Coblyn, Cutty Soams, Garthornes, Goblin, Haus-Schmiedlein, Mine Spirits, Spirit, Spriggans, Sprite

KNOCKY-BOH

In the folklore of North Yorkshire, England, this bogie behaved in much the same way as a poltergeist, knocking from within the fabric of the walls of a house and scaring the occupants.
References 17
See also Bogie, Pokey Hokey, Poltergeist, Appendix 22

KNURRE MURRE

In Danish folklore this is the name of an old and bad-tempered troll whose name means Rumble Grumble. Knurre Murre's quarrel with a young troll and his defeat form the subject of a traditional tale.
References 18, 133
See also Troll

KOBALD, KOBELT, KOBEL

See Kobold

KOBOLD, KOBOLT

This is the name of two types of spirit in Teutonic mythology:
　(1) The goblins who inhabited the underworld of

the mines, like the knockers of Cornwall, and who were skilled in the art of mining and metalworking. They are also known as Cobolts.

(2) The name of the household spirit of German folklore that behaved much like the English brownie. These Kobolds, also known as Kobald, Kobelt, Kobel, looked like gnomes with their wizened little faces and garments with pointed hoods. They inhabited the hearth area of the home or the barns and stables, where at night they would complete all the tasks that the humans had left unfinished. As long as they were treated with respect and given their portion of the family supper, all would be well. However, if this were forgotten, then the Kobold could be most malicious in exacting revenge before leaving. Some Kobolds are known by the local names of Chimmeken, Heinze, Hinzelmann, Hödekin, King Goldmar and Walther.
References 18, 28, 38, 40, 41, 59, 93, 114
See also (1) Cobalt, Goblin, Knockers, Mine Spirits; (2) Biersal, Brownie, Gnome, Goldmar, Hinzelmann, Household Spirits, Appendix 22

KODINHALTIA

In the folklore of the Estonian and Finnish people, this is the name given to a household fairy who behaves in much the same way as the English brownie.
References 88
See also Brownie, Domovoi, Fairy, Haldde, Haldjas, Metsänhaltia, Talonhaltija, Tonttu, Vedenhaltia, Appendix 22

KODUHALDJAS

In the folk beliefs of the Estonian people, this is the guardian spirit of the house and courtyard. The Koduhaldjas must be propitiated to protect and care for the property.
References 87
See also Guardian, Haldde, Haldjas, Haltia, Majahaldjas, Appendix 22

KOKOPELLI, KOKOPÖLÖ

A kachina spirit in the beliefs of the Hopi Native American people. This spirit appears as an insect resembling the dragonfly, but with a hump on his back which is said to be a sack containing precious gifts. Like the Coyote and Nepokwa'i kachinas, Kokopelli is a hunter, but he has a reputation for seducing young girls and giving them bridal gifts.
References 88
See also Coyote, Kachina, Nepokwa'i, Spirit, Appendix 12

KOLLIMALAIKANNIYARKA

In Tamil mythology of India, these are nymphs who educated the infant Kāttavarāyan (son of Siva and Parvati). The name Kollimalaikanniyarka means the Seven Maidens from the Kolli Mountain. A legend tells how they were later turned into the Kolli Mountain Peaks.
References 68
See also Hagno, Meliæ, Nymph, Appendix 22

KOLTƏŠƏ

This is a spirit in the folk beliefs of the Cheremis/Mari people of the former Soviet Republic. This spirit's name means the Sender. This supernatural is propitiated with an offering of a piece of bread.
References 118
See also Spirit

KOMANG

In the beliefs of the Dayak people of Borneo, this is a group of spirits created by Tapa, the chief deity.
References 57
See also Spirit, Triee

KOMOKYATSIKY

In the beliefs and legends of the Pueblo Native American people, this spirit, also known as Old Woman Kachina, produced the Koyemshi from an incestuous union with her brother.
References 88
See also Koyemshi, Spirit

KOMPAGNIN

In the beliefs of the Native Australians, this is the spirit of the whirlwind also known as Willy Wily Man. He had three sons: Jombol the sea wind spirit, Kunubriar the east wind spirit, and Muruwook the inland wind spirit. Although his sons were independent supernaturals, Kompagnin kept them in a shell-nut on a rope around his neck. During the night Kompagnin and his sons assumed human shape. They relaxed around a campfire and, while he played the *didgeridoo*, they would dance. Before he slept Kompagnin changed his sons back into spirits and returned them to the shell-nut. Legend tells how all the sons admired and argued over the same girl. They howled and fought each other all over the territory, creating havoc in their search for her. But she had already escaped them over a rainbow that the rain spirit had created as a bridge to the sky, and there she settled with the night stars.
References 14
See also Hantu Ribut, Spirit, Virra Birron, Appendix 26

KORKA-MURT

This is the "house man" in the folk beliefs of the Finno-Ugric Votyak people of the Vyatka region of Russia. His name Korka-murt means Man of the

House. He is the guardian spirit of the home in much the same way as the Domovoi of Russia. He must be propitiated to ensure his benevolence.
References 88
See also Domovoi, Guardian, Household Spirits, Murt, Appendix 22

KORNƏ BODƏŽ
A demon in the folk beliefs of the Cheremis/Mari people of the former Soviet Republic. The translation of the name Kornə Bodəž is Road Spirit, which implies a demon that may have similar practices to the road spirits elsewhere in Europe.
References 118
See also Demon, Spirit, Appendix 24

KORNEBÖCKE
These are field spirits in the folklore of Germany. Like the Kornwolf they manifest in the form of a male deer prancing through the wheat as the wind causes it to ripple. They might also take the form of the blue cornflower to be found in between the stalks of growing corn. The Korneböcke, whose name means Corn Buck, was the guardian of the wheat in the fields, ensuring that it ripened and provided a good harvest.
References 44
See also Corn Spirit, Field Spirit, Guardian, Kornwolf, Polevik, Appendix 12, Appendix 18

KORNMUTTER
In the folklore of Germany this is the spirit of the developing corn whose name means Corn Mother. She is the guardian spirit of the crop, ensuring its maturation and a good harvest. The spirit is "captured" in the last sheaf to be cut, like the Cailleach, and propitiated for the future planting.
References 44
See also Babban ny Mheillea, Calleach, Corn Spirit, Guardian, Kornwolf, Spirit, Appendix 15

KORNOVKHII
This is an alternative name for the Leshii in the folklore of Russia. Kornovkhii means One Whose Ear Has Been Cut Off. The removal of the left ear was a punishment in medieval Russia for convicted thieves. The peasants, by using this name for the forest spirit indicated the Leshii to be as threatening as these humans when traveling through the forests.
References 75
See also Leshii, Appendix 24

KORNWOLF
The corn spirit of the grain harvest in the folklore of Germany was said to be like a wolf which could be detected by the ripples it made in the corn as it ran through the field. These spirits, also taking the form

of hounds, may be called Cornwolf, Rye Dog, or Roggerhunds. As the harvest progressed the field spirit would retreat before the reapers until it was "trapped" in the last sheaf. In some areas of Germany it would be ritually slain, while in other regions the spirit would be bound up in the last sheaf and kept until the spring plowing, when it would be put back into the earth.
References 44
See also Babban ny Mheillea, Cailleach, Corn Spirit, Korneböcke, Kornmutter, Appendix 12, Appendix 15, Appendix 18

KOROKIOEWE
See Atua

KORRIGAN
These spirits were the elves or dwarfs of Brittany in northwestern France. Also known by the spelling Corrigan, they are described as being usually female, having long hair and wearing white flowing garments. They were often to be seen in woods or by streams at night, where they would enchant any unwary human traveler with their beauty and their singing. With the dawn or the sound of a bell they returned to the form of old hags. They danced at night in the stone circles which abound in the area, often deliberately leading travelers astray with their torchlight. Like the brownies of England, they would attach themselves to a household where they would work at night. The male Korrigans, however, could materialize as a horse or goat and would cause havoc. Female Korrigans were mischievous, especially to Christian priests; they were also known to take human babies and leave a Little Korrigan in its place.
References 18, 87, 110, 114
See also Brownie, Changeling, Dwarf, Elf, Hag, Household Spirits, Appendix 12, Appendix 22, Appendix 24

KORYBANTES
In the mythology of Asia Minor and ancient Greece these were demons renowned for their licentious activities as the companions of the deity Rheia.
References 93
See also Demon, Kurétes

KOTI
A benevolent spirit in the beliefs of the Creek Native American people. He manifests as a water frog.
References 25
See also Spirit, Appendix 12, Appendix 25

KOTRE
This is the name of a nature spirit in the folklore of Lithuania.

References 88
See also More, Spirit, Appendix 18

KOTYANGWUTI
See Spider

KOUKOUDI
The name of a disease demon in the folklore of modern Greece. He appears in the form of a human or as a flaccid shape hanging from a fig tree. Koukoudi wanders about choosing those to whom he gives the plague. A "ring of iron" ploughed around the village by twin calves, which were later buried alive, was said to have kept the plague demon from infecting Panorio village.
References 12
See also Demon, Piśācas, Šajtan, Appendix 17

KOYEMSHI, KOYIMSHI
These are kachina spirits, also known by the names Atlashi and Tachuki, in the beliefs of the Zuñi and Pueblo Native American people. They are considered to be simultaneously sexually immature and behaviorally provocative. In the Kachina dances they are represented as the dancing clowns, each with their own special mask. They were said to have been the progeny of Komokyatsiky and are led by Molanhakto.
References 88
See also Kachina, Komokyatsiky, Molanhakto, Spirit

KOYOTE
See Coyote

KOŽ JEŋ
A keremet in the folk beliefs of the Cheremis/Mari people of the former Soviet Republic. The name Kož Jeŋ means the Pine Man and possibly refers to his habitation. This demon may be propitiated by the sacrifice of a hare.
References 118
See also Demon, Keremet, Toštə Kož Jeŋ, Appendix 19

KOŽ NEDƏK
This is the name of an evil spirit in the folklore of the Cheremis/Mari people of the former Soviet Republic. It is a demon that enters the ears of humans and causes them to have earaches.
References 118
See also Demon, Nedək, Spirit, Appendix 17

KOŽLA IA, KOŽLA OZA, KOŽLA PERI
See Kožla Kuba, Obda

KOŽLA KUBA AND KOŽLA KUGUZA
These are spirits in the folk beliefs of the Cheremis/Mari people of the former Soviet Republic. As their names Forest Old Woman and Forest Old Man imply, they inhabit the forests. These spirits are usually invisible but cause those who travel through the forest to become lost if not propitiated with an offering of bread. It is believed that those who die in the forest and are not found are taken by the Kožla Kuba and Kožla Kuguza to be their servants.
References 118
See also Kuguza, Obda, Spirit, Appendix 19, Appendix 24

KRAMPUS
This is the name of a spirit in the folklore of Austria. Krampus had a malevolent character and was described as looking like a demon with a long red tongue and wild eyes. Although reputedly a Christmas "helper," he spent the winter nights searching for naughty children so that he could punish them. In this respect he is more like a nursery bogie.
References 34
See also Demon, Knecht Ruprecht, Nursery Bogie, Père Fouettard, Spirit, Appendix 22

KRATT, KRATTI
These are the fortune demons in the folklore of Estonia. They usually appear in the shape of a domestic animal such as a cockerel or a cat when on the ground, but as a fiery flying spirit at night in the air. The fortune demon may be obtained as a gift from the Devil in return for the soul of the householder.

These demons are known by the name of Kratti in Finland, Puuk or Pisuhänd in Southern Estonia, Tont in the east of Estonia, and Tulihänd in the west. Like the Aitvaras, the Kratt will deliver goods such as grain, milk, butter, and gold to enrich its master, usually at the expense of the neighbors, who will be unable to see how this is happening. Tales of these demons usually end with the householder being able to outwit the Devil and retain his soul.
References 87, 88
See also Aitvaras, Demon, Para, Pukis, Spirit, Appendix 12, Appendix 20, Appendix 22

KREMARA
This is the name of a nature spirit in the folklore of Poland. Kremara was considered to be the guardian spirit of the domestic pigs, making sure that they were healthy and unharmed. This spirit worked in collaboration with another spirit called Priparchis who was also concerned with the pigs' welfare. A libation of beer was offered to the Kremara to ensure his continued protection.
References 102
See also Guardian, Priparchis, Spirit, Appendix 12

KRICCO
This is the name of a field spirit or nature spirit in the folklore of the Slav people.
References 87
See also Spirit, Appendix 18

KRIKSY
This is an alternative name for the Nočnitsa of Russian folklore.
References 88
See also Nočnitsa

KRIMBA
This supernatural is a female household spirit in the folklore of the Slav people and especially of Bohemia.
References 102
See also Dugnai, Household Spirits, Kikimora, Matergabia, Appendix 22

KRISKY
See Nočnitsa

KRUKIS
A nature spirit in the folklore of the Slav people, Krukis was the guardian of domestic animals.
References 102
See also Domikha, Guardian, Kremara, Spirit, Appendix 12

KRUZIMÜGELI
See Rumpelstiltskin

KSHATHRA
This spirit is one of the Amesha Spentas and an attendant genius of Ahura Mazda in the Zoroastrian religion of Persia. Kshathra, whose name means Rulership or Dominion, may also be referred to by the names Khshathra Vairya, Khsathra, Xšatravēr, or Šahrēvar. He is the guardian spirit of metals and the symbol of the Creator's triumph and power over evil. Kshathra leads Mithra, Asman, and Aniran against the evil Sauru.
References 41, 53, 119
See also Amesa Spentas, Aniran, Asman, Attendant Spirit, Genius, Guardian, Mithra, Sauru, Spirit, Yazatas

KUBA
This is a euphemism used for the female supernatural personification of a natural phenomenon in the folk beliefs of the Cheremis/Mari people of the former Soviet Republic. The name Kuba means Old Woman and is the polite form of address for any spirit in the female form who may offer harm to humans. She is the counterpart of the male form, who is given the title Kuguza.

References 118
See also Kuguza, Spirit

KÜBAR KUGUZA ALSO KÜBAR JUMAL KUGUZA
These are the names used as euphemisms for an evil spirit in the folk beliefs of the Cheremis/Mari people of the former Soviet Republic. The names Kübar Kuguza and Kübar Jumal Kuguza mean Bridge Old Man and Old Man Under the Bridge, respectively. This spirit, for whom these names are a polite form of address, is a demon who lurks under bridges, like Cutty Dyer of English folklore, and he will attack humans who wish to cross the water by way of the bridge. Therefore reference to this spirit is always made using a euphemism to avert his evil intentions.
References 118
See also Čembulat, Cutty Dyer, Demon, Spirit

KUBERA
In the Hindu mythology of India, Kubera, also known as Kuvera, was originally a dwarf born into the Sudra caste, and his half brother is the demon Ravana. He is described as having a squat deformed body with three legs and only eight teeth. In this dwarf form Kubera is the guardian of treasures and metals from his underworld. He is the king of the Yakshas who inhabited Sri Lanka, but when he was driven away by Ravana, they and the Gandharvas, the Kimprushas, and the Rakshasas followed Kubera to the Himalayas. He was later elevated to the status of a deity after honoring Siva and undergoing an austere transformation.
References 88, 93, 111, 114, 119
See also Demon, Dwarf, Gandharvas, Guardian, Kimprushas, Rakshasas, Ravana, Yakkshas, Appendix 20

KUÇEDRË
See Kulshedra

KUDƏ ÖRT KUBA AND KUDƏ ÖRT KUGUZA
These are the male and female personification of the spirit of the cattle sheds and pens in the folk beliefs of the Cheremis/Mari people of the former Soviet Republic. Their names mean Hut Soul Old Woman and Hut Soul Old Man. These invisible spirits would take care of the cattle in the sheds and pens of the farm. Those animals that they favored would become healthy and fat, often being given food from the animals that the supernaturals disliked. The animals they disliked would be tormented and prevented from getting enough to eat.
References 118
See also Gid-murt, Gunna, Kuguza, Lauko Sargas, Nur Kuba, Spirit, Appendix 12

KUDEIAR
This is the name of an evil spirit in the folklore of Russia. The belief in Kudeiar is local to the Sveskii district of the Orel Province, where he is supposed to be the guardian of hidden treasure.
References 75
See also Guardian, Kazna Peri, Kladovik, Spirit, Appendix 20

KUEI
In Chinese folk belief and legend this is the name applied to the spirits, ghosts, and demons that may have developed from the souls of humans who were not honored properly at their death or who died in suspicious circumstances. These Kuei assume a terrifying aspect, seeking and exacting revenge on humans, and are called the Hungry Ghosts.
References 39, 87, 88
See also Demon, Hsien, Spirit

KUGA JEŊ
See Čembulat

KUGƏ AGA KEREMET
This is a demon in the folk beliefs of the Cheremis/Mari people of the former Soviet Republic. The name Kugə Aga Keremet means Great Plowing Devil, and the spirit is propitiated at the time of preparing the land for the new crop so that he will not spoil the seed.
References 118
See also Demon, Devil, Keremet, Appendix 15

KUGƏ JEŊ
This is a fearsome supernatural culture hero or keremet, whose name means Great Man, in the folk beliefs of the Cheremis/Mari people of the former Soviet Republic. He is described as a strong brave leader who rides a white charger and with his battle prowess established the territories of the Cheremis people. The spirits who assisted Kugə Jeŋ are Aš, Azren, Bitnəzə (which means Reporter), Bodəž, Marče, Paškače, and Uжedəš. After his exploits, Kugə Jeŋ retired to his mountain stronghold with his armies, where they await the call to arms in the country's time of war. A man tried to put this to the test and called Kugə Jeŋ, and he and the Cheremis people were punished when the angry spirit found that there was no war to fight. He is credited with being a supernatural healer, and sacrifices are made to him for cures, despite his also being considered an evil spirit.
References 118
See also Azren, Bodəž, Čembulat, Keremet, Spirit

KUGƏ JOMŠƏ
This is a keremet or demon in the folk beliefs of the Cheremis/Mari people of the former Soviet Republic. The name Kugə Jomšə means Great Jomšə. The latter part of the name is thought to be derived from the Churash name *Jomža*, which means a sorcerer.
References 118
See also Demon, Keremet

KUGE KÜBAR
This spirit is a keremet in the folk beliefs of the Cheremis/Mari people. This demon's name means Great Bridge.
References 118
See also Demon, Keremet, Spirit

KUGƏ KURƏK
This is a keremet or devil in the folk beliefs of the Cheremis/Mari people. This demon's name means Great Mountain.
References 118
See also Demon, Devil, Keremet

KUGUZA
The term is a euphemism used for the male supernatural personification of a natural phenomenon in the folk beliefs of the Cheremis/Mari people of the former Soviet Republic. Kuguza means Old Man and is a title of respect used when referring to a spirit that has the power to harm humans, in order to avert his revenge. He is the counterpart of the female form Kuba and is usually identified by the name of the place inhabited. Sometimes the use of the title Kuguza may denote that the spirit is a keremet.
References 118
See also Keremet, Kuba, Spirit

KUKUDHI
This name is applied to two different spirits in the folklore of Albania:
(1) This is the name of a disease demon also known as Kukuth in the folklore of Albania. This female evil spirit is responsible for bringing sickness and plague as an epidemic.
(2) This name is also applied in Albania to the malevolent spirit transformed from the lost soul of a miser seeking to do harm in the world.
References 93
See also Demon, Spirit, Appendix 17

KUKUTH
See Kukudhi

KUL, KUL'
This is an evil water spirit in the folk beliefs of the Ostyak and Ziryen Finno-Ugric peoples of western

Siberia and the Vyatka region, respectively. The Ziryen also call this spirit Vasa or Va-kul'. This demon appears in human shape with long flowing hair and is also thought to have a family. It inhabits deep lakes and still waters, where it lurks, awaiting the opportunity to catch any unwary human. To see one is the portent of misfortune.
References 88, 102
See also As-iga, Demon, Kul-jungk, Spirit, Viz-anya, Viz-ember, Viz-leany, Vu-murt, Vu-vozo, Yanki-murt, Appendix 25

KUL-JUNGK

This is a water spirit in the folklore of the Ziryen, a Finno-Ugric people of Russia. Kul-jungk is a benevolent spirit and the guardian of freshwater fish. In this role he is venerated by the Ziryen fishermen, who rely on the spirit to provide food for them throughout the year. To ensure the start of a good fishing season when the ice is first broken on the river in spring, an effigy of a fish made of birch bark or carved in wood is dedicated with the first catch to Kul-jungk.
References 33, 102
See also As-iga, Bonito Maidens, Guardian, Kul, Spirit, Appendix 12, Appendix 25

KULSHEDËR

This is the male counterpart of the female water demon Kulshedra in the folklore of Albania. Unlike his counterpart, Kulshedër appears mostly to be a terrestrial devil.
References 93
See also Demon, Devil, Kulshedra

KULSHEDRA

This is a malevolent female water demon, also known as Kuçedrë, in the folklore of Albania. It may manifest in two different forms, as a hideous hag with ugly pendulous breasts, or as a flying spirit like the Aitvaras, spitting fiery sparks as it travels through the air. The Kulshedra is entirely evil. It may despoil natural water with its urine, or it may cause a drought. It is thought that a human sacrifice is the only method of placating or averting the evil intentions of the Kulshedra.
References 93
See also Aitvaras, Hag, Kulshedër, Obda, Spirit, Appendix 25

KUNUBRIAR

In the beliefs of the Native Australians, he is the east wind spirit and one of the offspring of Kompagnin.
References 14
See also Kompagnin, Spirit, Appendix 26

KUPLAŊGAŠ

This is the name of a keremet or demon in the folk beliefs of the Cheremis/Mari people of the former Soviet Republic.
References 118
See also Demon, Keremet

KURƏK IA

This is the name of a group of spirits in the folk beliefs of the Cheremis/Mari people of the former Soviet Republic. These spirits, whose name means Mountain Devil, are described as looking like flat-nosed, long-haired dwarfs about knee-high to a human, and their wide mouths seem to have a permanent grin. The Kurək Ia are spirits that inhabit the mountains, and if a human is unwise enough to try to sleep in their territory, they will make his feet so painful that the human will be unable to walk. The Kurək Ia is the most evil of a number of mountain devils whose names are Kurək Kuga Jeŋ, Kurək Kuguza (which means Mountain Old Man), and Kurək Šərt, which means Mountain Devil.
References 118
See also Čembulat, Čort, Devil, Dwarf, Ia, Spirit

KURƏK PIAMBAR

See Piambar

KURÉTES

In the classical mythology of Greece, these were the nature demons that were charged with protecting the infant god Zeus. The Kurétes inhabited the island of Crete. Some authorities state that they were priests of the temple who concealed the crying of the infant Zeus with the crashing of the temple drums and cymbals. They are sometimes associated with, or equated with, the licentious demons known as the Korybantes.
References 93, 130
See also Demon, Korybantes, Appendix 22

KURINYI BOG

In the folklore of Russia, this supernatural was not in effect a deity, although its name means the Chicken God, but a spirit that inhabited a special stone (usually one with a natural hole in it). This spirit was the guardian of the family hens. It was placed in the yard or the pen with the hens in order to counteract the possible evil attentions of Kikimora, who was quite likely to pluck the feathers of any birds she disliked, or simply to spite the family.
References 75
See also Guardian, Kikimora, Spirit, Appendix 12

KURŠIS

This is the corn spirit in the folklore of Lithuania. It is generally considered to manifest in the form of a

man. After the harvest has taken place and the threshing is about to begin, the farmworkers capture Kuršis as an effigy in the last of the straw from the field. The spirit is then kept safely in this guise until the spring sowing.
References 88, 123
See also Cailleac, Corn Spirit, Kornmutter, Kornwolf, Spirit, Appendix 15, Appendix 18

KURUPIRA
See Curupira

KURWAICHIN
The name of a nature spirit in the ancient folklore of Poland. Kurwaichin is revered as the guardian spirit and protector of the lambs during the lambing season and the time of their development to maturity.
References 102
See also Guardian, Spirit, Appendix 12

KUTCHIS
In the Dreamtime mythology of the Native Australians, these spirits are supernatural beings similar to the Mura Mura. They are especially invoked by the medicine men of the Dieri Tribe.
References 41
See also Mura Mura, Spirit

KUTKINNÁKU
In the folk beliefs of the Koryak people of the Kamchatka Peninsula, this is a benevolent culture spirit. Kutkinnáku is described in human form but may appear in the shape of a raven. In the ancient legends he is responsible for helping the Koryak to survive by showing them how to hunt, fish, and make fire. He also gave them the sacred drum, which only the shaman may use.

References 93
See also Coyote, Kwati, Spirit, Tutelary Spirit, Appendix 12

KUVERA
See Kubera

KWAKU ANANSE
See Anansi

KWATI
This is a trickster spirit also called Kivati in the beliefs of the Macah Native American people in the Puget Sound region of Washington. Kwati has similar characteristics to the trickster culture hero called Mink.
References 88
See also Blue Jay, Coyote, Kutkinnáku, Mink, Napi, Trickster

KYRKOGRIM
This is the name in Swedish folklore for the animal spirit guardian of the churchyard, which defends the churchyard and the graves against demons and sorcerers intent on desecrating the human dead. The traditional guardian spirit is derived from the ancient practice of interring a live dog or boar under the foundation stone of the church or the wall of the graveyard, as the vigilant guard of the territory. This absolved the first human soul interred there from this duty.
References 66
See also Church Grim, Demon, Fossegrim, Guardian, Kirkegrim, Kirkogrim, Spirit

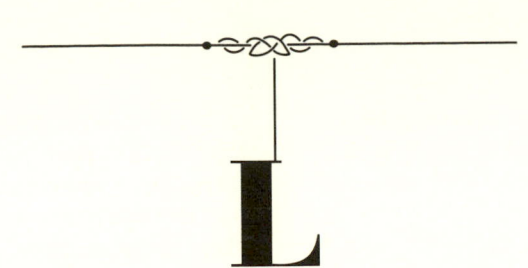

L

LA

In the folk beliefs of the Karen people of Burma, these spirits may represent the human soul, but more frequently the name La is used synonymously for the demons known as nats.
References 88
See also Nat, Spirit, Appendix 10

LABARTU

A female demon in the mythology of ancient Mesopotamia and Babylon. She inhabited marshland or the wilderness of mountains. Labartu attacked children in particular, and she is the spirit blamed for inducing miscarriage in pregnancy.
References 31, 39
See also Demon, Kalu Kumāra Yaka, Lilith, Putana, Spirit, Tçulo, Appendix 22

LACHESIS

In the classical mythology of Greece and Rome, Lachesis is one of the Fates. She is depicted in human female form with a spindle measuring the thread of mortal life.
References 119
See also Fates

LADY OF THE LAKE

In the British and northern French legends of King Arthur, she is a mysterious fairy lady or queen who inhabits the lake surrounding the fabled Isle of Avalon. Apart from an elegant hand and arm rising from the still water, there is only a nebulous description of this veiled spirit. She is the recipient of the sword Excalibur when it is thrown into the lake after Arthur's mortal wounding by his half brother Mordred in the final conflict. With three other fairy queens, the Lady of the Lake then takes Arthur in a boat to Avalon and immortality. There are other Ladies of the Lake that are fairies or evil wraith-like spirits. One fairy creature inhabits Orchardleigh in Somerset, England; another, known as the Lady of Little Van Lake, is a Welsh fairy famed for her magic herbal cures. A malevolent Lady of the Lake is re-

ported as inhabiting Traunsee in Austria. This latter Lady is described as beautiful, with long flowing hair. She may be seen in the lake at noon or by the waterfall on moonlit nights, riding a water-horse that has the appearance of having been flayed. To see her is sure to bring misfortune; she will pursue any mortal, and fishermen are said to have disappeared from the shores of the lake without a trace.
References 17,18, 69, 88
See also Fairy, Spirit, Appendix 25

LAHAMA

In ancient Sumerian mythology the Lahama were water demons, the progeny of the Apsu in the entourage of Enki, the god of wisdom.
References 93
See also Apsu, Demon, Appendix 25

LALLA MIRA, LALLA MIRRA

This is the name of one of the kings of the djinns in the folklore of Morocco.
References 90
See also Djinn

LALLA MKOUNA BENT MKOUN

This is the title of a powerful female djinn in the folklore of Morocco. Her name means Daughter of the Sultan of Demons. Although Lalla Mkouna Bent Mkoun has a formidable title, she is considered to be one of the benevolent djinns. She is invoked with offerings of incense as a guardian spirit to protect a new house when the family is about to move in, and to ensure that no evil djinns are present before the humans enter.
References 90
See also Djinn, Guardian, Appendix 21, Appendix 22

LALLA REKYA BINT EL KHAMAR

A powerful queen of the djinns in the folklore of Morocco. Her name means Lady Rekya Daughter of the Red One, and she is regarded as one of the benevolent djinns. Lalla Rekya Bint el Khamar was the

guardian spirit of the bathhouses. She was invoked by women for protection against the evil djinns that usually lurked there to do harm to the bathers.
References 90
See also Djinn, Guardian, Appendix 21

LALLA ZOUINA
This is the name of one of the powerful djinns controlling other spirits in the folklore of Morocco.
References 90
See also Djinn, Spirit

LAMA
A female benevolent and protective demon in Sumerian mythology. Lama was later associated with the Lamassu of Assyria. Like the Šedu, they were depicted as the winged bull beings that were the guardian spirits of the gateways to palaces.
References 93, 102
See also Agathos Daimon, Demon, Guardian, Lamassu, Appendix 12, Appendix 21

LAMASSU
In the mythology of ancient Assyria and Babylon, these benevolent demons were portrayed as winged bulls or lions with human heads. The Lamassu were regarded as female; their male counterparts were called Šedu or Shedu. In their most important role, they formed the protection of the palaces and temples, where their effigies often remain to this day. They were normally invisible, but just like the Guardian Angels, the Lamassu were assigned to and remained with an individual throughout life to give protection against the evil forces of the Utuku.
References 41, 102, 114
See also Agathos Daimon, Demon, Guardian, Guardian Angel, Šedu, Utukku, Appendix 12, Appendix 21

LAMAŠTU
In Babylonian mythology, this malignant female disease demon is portrayed as naked to the waist and suckling a pig and a dog. She holds a comb and a spinning whorl, the symbols of the wife and mother whom Lamaštu attacks at any opportunity. This evil spirit pursues the pregnant or newly delivered woman, bringing puerperal fever, and sickness or death to infants.
References 93, 117
See also Demon, Dimme, Kalu Kumāra Yaka, Labartu, Lilith, Putana, Spirit, Tçulo, Appendix 17, Appendix 22

LAMIA
There are two spirits known by this name.
 (1) In the classical mythology of Greece and Rome, this was a female demon, of a group of demons called Lamiæ, Lamya, Lamie, or Lamye, said to exist in the North African deserts. They were described as being like a woman to the waist but below the waist had the body of a serpent, though they were able to assume the shape of a completely beautiful woman. There are a number of traditions concerning Lamia's origin. The most usual is that she was a Lybian queen loved by the king of the gods, Zeus (Jupiter), whose queen, Hera (Juno), transformed Lamia to her hideous appearance and then took her children and destroyed them. Henceforth, Lamia seeks and destroys men and children wherever she can entice them. From this earlier legend, used over a thousand years ago as a nursery bogie for Roman children, the tradition developed into the Lamia described by Burton in *The Anatomie of Melancholy* (1621) and by Keats in *Lamia* (1780) as the amorous sorceress or succubus. In more modern times this demon has survived in the dual form of the demonologists' vampire or nightmare or the malignant melancholy fairy road demon of modern Greek folklore.
 (2) In the folklore of the Basque people of southern France and northwestern Spain, the Lamia is a water spirit or mermaid of an entirely benevolent nature.
References 12, 40, 44, 53, 87, 92, 93, 107, 113, 114, 129
See also Ardat Lili, Baba Yaga, Demon, Fairy, Lilith, Llorona, Mermaid, Nightmare, Nursery Bogie, Spirit, Succubus, Yogini, Appendix 22, Appendix 25

LAMINAK
In the folklore of the Basque people of southwestern France and northwestern Spain, these spirits are a race of Little People. Their abode is underground, where they have magnificent castles. They are possibly derived from the same Celtic tradition as the Little People of Ireland and northern Britain.
References 87
See also Little People, Spirit

LANDVÆTTIR
These are the territorial or land spirits in Scandinavian folk belief. They were particularly potent in bringing good fortune to that area, such that should they become offended enough to move, then disaster would befall the property. The benevolent spirits were so important to the well-being of a territory that the Confederation Treaty of Iceland in A.D. 930 made a declaration in Ulfljot's Law. This prevented the display of gruesome figureheads on approaching ships, since these might offend the Landvættir.
References 18, 88
See also Spirit, Appendix 20

LANGHUI
See Langsuir

LANGSUIR, LANGSUYAR

These are malignant female demons in the folklore of the people of West Malaysia. The Langsuir, also called Langhui or Langsuyar, are the transformed spirits of women who have died in childbirth. They can be identified by their long hair, which hangs down to their feet concealing a hole in the back of their necks, and having long talons on their fingers. They wear long green robes, and can fly through the air and adopt different forms in different elements. They are vindictive, especially when they steal fish from the nets of fishermen. However, their other activities are far more malicious, as they will await the moment that an infant is left unguarded in order to suck its blood. Those who can recognize one of these spirits may extinguish her power by cutting her nails and hair, which must then be used to block up the hole in the back of her head. Elaborate rituals are observed for any woman dying in childbirth to prevent her soul from being transformed into a demon.
References 88
See also Demon, Spirit, Appendix 22

LAR, LARES (pl.)

In the beliefs of ancient Rome, these were guardian spirits, said to be the offspring of Lara the Naiad. There were several categories of these guardians according to their location and activities, the principal categories being the domestic and the public Lares. The Lar *Familiaris* was the protector of the household and was often considered to be the elevated soul of the ancestor of the family. This domestic spirit had its special place at the side of the hearth and would be offered part of the family meal each evening. The acknowledged public spirits were the Lar *Praestites* as the guardian of a city; the Lar *Compitales* as the guardian of the subdivisions and crossroads of the city; the Lar *Rurales* as the guardian of the country-side; the Lar *Viales* as the guardian of the roads and travelers; and the Lar *Marini* that protected the seas and fisher folk. They were portrayed as joyful youths dancing and bringing good fortune. With the coming of Christianity their role evolved to that of a household spirit of the hobgoblin type.
References 20, 29, 39, 40, 53, 88, 92, 93, 107, 114, 129, 130
See also Angel, Angiris, Domovik, Genii, Guardian Angel, Guardian, Hobgoblin, Household Spirit, Lara, Larva, Lemur, Manes, Naiad, Penates, Pitris, Appendix 21, Appendix 22

LARA

In classical Roman mythology she was the Naiad who was, by Mercury, the mother of the guardian spirits known as the Lares. She was a particularly garrulous nymph who revealed the infidelities of Jupiter, king of the gods, such that he decreed she should lose her tongue. Her hideous resultant form was used as a nursery bogie from ancient times in Italy, to threaten children into good behavior.
References 29
See also Croquemitaine, Echo, Guardian, Lar, Naiad, Nursery Bogie, Nymph, Appendix 22

LARILARI

This is the collective name for a group of fearful spirits in the folklore of the Quechua people of Peru. The Larilari live in the high Andes, where they may harm humans who enter their domain.
References 88
See also Anchancho, Ccoa, Spirit

LARVA, LARVAE (pl.)

This is a name used for ghosts or the transformed souls of the wicked into evil spirits, goblins, and demons in the beliefs of ancient Rome. The Larvae are mostly invisible. These malignant spirits terrified those about at night and brought misfortune to humans at any opportunity. They are often identified with the Lemures.
References 40, 88, 107, 130
See also Demon, Goblin, Lar, Lemur, Spirit

LASAS

These are a group of spirits or genii in the mythology of the ancient Etruscans. They were portrayed as bejewelled and gracious females, sometimes with wings, carrying a mirror and wreath or garland. They were the attendants of Turan, the goddess of love. Some of their names that have been identified are: Acaviser, Alpan, and Evan.
References 93
See also Acaviser, Attendant Spirit, Genius, Spirit

LASKOWICE

In the mythology and folklore of the Slav people these are forest spirits that are also known as Leschia. They are described as resembling the satyrs, with their hairy bodies, goat's feet, and the upper-parts like a man. They are nature spirits and guardians of the forests and the creatures that reside there, with a particular affinity with the wolf.
References 93
See also Guardian, Leshii, Metsänhaltia, Satyr, Spirit, Appendix 12, Appendix 19

LATZMAN

See Jack-in-the-Green

LAU, LAO

These are fearsome and terrifying demons in the beliefs of the people of the Andaman Islands. These spirits are also known as Erem Čauga and Ti-miku in

the north and south islands, respectively. They do not have an accepted description except that of hideous, but they are associated with death, the presence of women in a male preserve, and the arrival of strangers. The Lau inhabit the jungle, where they endeavor to steal the souls of any human lost there. They can, however, be defeated by using fire, arrows, beeswax, human bones, or red paint.
References 88
See also Demon, Jurua, Spirit

LAUKO SARGAS
In the folklore of Lithuania these nature spirits are the guardians of the fields and the cattle within them.
References 88
See also Biča Kuguza, Gid-murt, Guardian, Gunna, Kudə Ört Kuba, Laukumāte, Nur Kuba, Spirit, Appendix 18

LAUKUMĀTE
This is the name of a female nature spirit in the folk beliefs of the Latvian people. Laukumāte, whose name means Mother of the Fields, is the guardian spirit of agriculture and herds grazing in the fields.
References 88
See also Guardian, Jūrasmāte, Māte, Appendix 18

LAUMÉ, LAUMA
This is the name of a type of fairy in the folklore of Lithuania. The Laumé is called Laūme in Latvia, and she may also be known as Lauma, Spigena, or Ragana. She was often encountered bathing at night in woodland pools or occupied in her spinning and weaving. Laumé was the guardian of the poor and of orphaned children. As time went on the benevolent character of Laumé was transformed to that of a hag much like Baba Yaga.
References 88
See also Baba Yaga, Deive, Fairy, Hag, Appendix 22

LAURIN
This is the name of the dwarf hero of the thirteenth-century German poem *Der Kleine Rosengarten* attributed to Heinrich von Offerdingen. The legend tells of this dwarf king, who lived with his subjects in feasting and merriment in the bejeweled interior of the beautiful mountain peaks (now called the Cantinaccio), protected by a magic silken thread. Laurin's magnificent palace was illuminated by the brilliant glow of the jewels at night and by the surrounding fields of pink roses during the day. Laurin was lonely for a bride, and since he could not marry with other than royalty, on hearing about the beauty of a human princess, he sent sumptuous gifts to woo her. His envoys returned maltreated and robbed, so Laurin transformed himself into thistledown to meet her and attract her for him-

self. He entered the princess's apartments and was so charmed by her that he transformed her also into thistledown so that they could return to his realm. Her brothers eventually found where she was and by treachery defeated the dwarfs and their king, taking the princess from the husband she had come to love. In misery Laurin declared that his mountain castle would no longer glow with the roses of day or the jewels of night, but he forgot the twilight hours, and to this day the beauty of his palace and gardens glow in the dawn and evening skies.
References 38, 40
See also Alberich, Alvis, Dwarf

LAWKAPATIM
In the folklore of Poland this is a field spirit particularly invoked at the tilling and plowing of the soil for the protection of the crop and its successful growth. Lawkapatim was originally an ancient field deity.
References 102
See also Spirit, Appendix 18

LAZY LAURENCE
This is an orchard spirit in the folklore of Somerset and Hampshire, England. Far from being lazy, Lazy Laurence was, like the Appletree Man, the guardian of the fruit in the orchards. He is described as appearing in the form of a young horse that would chase thieves from the property and inflict them with cramps, vomiting, and disorientation to teach them a lesson.
References 17
See also Appletree Man, Churnmilk Peg, Colt Pixy, Elder Mother, Guardian, Nursery Bogie, Spirit

LEAF KING, LITTLE LEAF MAN
See Jack-in-the-Green

LEANAN-SIDHE
This beautiful fairy of Ireland, also called Lhiannan-shee in the Manx folklore of the Isle of Man (United Kingdom), was equally as benevolent as she was malevolent. The Leanan-sidhe, whose name means the Fairy Mistress, would wander through the towns and villages at night in search of romantic young men, on whose door she would knock. When the door was opened to her, she would inspire the occupant with eloquence of word and music within her embrace and bring about his fame and glory. But with that embrace she would gradually withdraw the life force from her lover until he would die of exhaustion, and then she would seek another.
References 17, 44
See also Fairy, Lhiannan-shee, Sídhe, Appendix 14

LEBA, LIBA
See Legba

LEEDS DEVIL, THE
See Jersey Devil

LEGBA, LEGUA
This is a supernatural trickster in the beliefs of Dahomey and Benin in West Africa. He was perhaps originally a god but is now regarded as a powerful demon. He is the guardian of the head of the household and is represented as a clay effigy and phallus covered by a thatched cape. As the messenger of the gods, Legba is in a powerful position to usurp that information and frequently causes discord and misery as a result of his pranks. He is also known as Legua, Leba, or Liba in other regions of Dahomey, and is known as Eshu in Nigeria. Where his cult has been transferred to the New World countries of Guyana, Brazil, Trinidad, Haiti, and Cuba, as well as the southern states of the United States, he retains this latter name. In the New World he is envisaged as an old man covered in tattered clothes. He is the spiritual guide for the other spirits to enter the cult ceremonies.
References 29, 88, 89, 93, 119
See also Demon, Encantado, Eshu, Guardian, Guia, Legua Bogi da Trinidade, Spirit, Trickster, Appendix 22

LE-GEREM
This is a celestial spirit in the folk beliefs of the Islands of Yap in western Micronesia. She guided the old man Anagumang across the seas to the Island of Kokial, where she taught him how to recognize the aragonite stones of great beauty. These stones were brought back to his island, where they were carved into the shape of a wheel. Le-Gerem then charmed these stones to be so desirable that henceforth they were used as money.
References 30
See also Spirit, Appendix 13

LEGUA BOGI DA TRINIDADE
An important encantado in the Afro-Brazilian cult Batuque. His name is derived from that of a Dahomean trickster of West Africa and also from an encantado from Casa de Minas and the Christian Trinity. He is also known as Seu Legua in the cult at Bélem, where his character is regarded as quite serious, although fond of a drink. He is associated not with the Trinity, however, but with the feast of Saint Expeditus. His spirit offspring are mostly regarded as mischievous and playful, possibly reflecting the origins of the group. These offspring—Codoésa da Trinidade, Folha Seca, Joãozinho Joaquimzinho Boa da Trinidade, José Raimundo Boa da Trinidade, Manoelzinho Boa da Trinidade, and Miguelzinho Boa da Trinidade—also belong to the Seu Turquia family.

References 89
See also Encantado, Joãozinho, Legba, Seu Turquia, Spirit, Trickster

LEI CHEN-TZU
This is a transforming spirit in the legends of ancient China. He is said to have been hatched from an egg that was the result of a thunderclap from his father, Lei, the storm god. Lei Chen-Tzu was adopted by Wen Wang, the god of literature. After many adventures, Lei Chen-Tzu discovered that his adoptive father had been taken prisoner, and he sought a way to rescue him. This Lei Chen-Tzu did by eating two apricots and transforming himself into a winged, green, dragon-like form with shining eyes. Then he effected the supernatural rescue.
References 132
See also Blue Jay, Spirit

LEIB-OLMAI
This is an important forest spirit in the folk beliefs of the Lapp people of the North Baltic region. Leib-Olmai, whose name means the Alder Man, is the guardian of the forest creatures and a tutelary spirit in the initiation ceremonies of the Lapp shaman. Leib-Olmai is especially associated with the veneration and hunting of the bear, for which the juice of the alder tree was an integral part. It is in the shape of the bear that his image is portrayed on sacred drums.
References 88
See also Agloolik, Àràk, Awl-man, Black Bear, Chin Chia, Clay Mother, Corn Mother, Fylgir, Harut and Marut, Nagual, Spirit, Tutelary Spirit, Zoa, Appendix 12, Appendix 19

LEMDƏ KURƏK KUGUZA
See Čembulat

LEMMINKÄINEN
In the folk beliefs of the Finno-Ugric peoples of Siberia, this is a trickster spirit that brings merriment and supernatural help to their ceremonies.
References 24
See also Spirit, Trickster

LEMUR, LEMURES (pl.)
There are two groups of spirits known by these names.

(1) These are the spirits of the wicked dead transformed to the status of demon or bogie in the beliefs of the ancient Romans. The Lemures, as evil spirits, were thought to deliver misfortune and terrify the living who were about at night. In order to avert the Lemures' malignant intentions, black beans were burned. The smell, which the Lemures were supposed to detest, would drive the spirits away. The

beans were also left in edible form as a placatory offering on two feast days, 9 November and 13 May.

(2) In occultism the Lemures are regarded as elementals of the air that are responsible for the movement of physical objects in much the same way as a poltergeist.

References 40, 53, 57, 88, 93, 107
See also (1) Bogie, Demon, Lar, Spirit; (2) Elemental, Poltergeist

LEPRECHAUN, LEPRACAUN

In the legend and folklore of Ireland, this is the fairy shoemaker. He goes by numerous names, the original being Luchorpan, meaning Little Body, the designation of a dwarf. In literature the names Lubrican, Lubberkin, Luchorpan, and Lupracan may be used. Other names are used in different districts, such as Luchramán in Ulster; Luchragán, Lurgadán, and Clúracán in Munster; Lúracán in south Leinster and Connacht; and Loimreachan in east Leinster. The Leprechaun is generally described as having a little wizened, gray-bearded face with twinkling eyes and a pointed nose. He is said to wear a red jacket with silver buttons, brown breeches, black silver-buckled shoes, and a high crowned hat. Sometimes he is said to be clothed all in green; however, he usually has a leather apron and appears to be mending a shoe with his little hammer tapping busily. It is this tapping that signifies his presence, but it is not advisable for humans to approach. This elf is tricksy, and despite his reputation for guarding crocks of gold, he will play pranks on any mortals who take their eyes off him for a second, and will vanish laughing. Typical of this is the tale concerning a man who managed to get a Leprechaun to show him the bush in the field where the treasure was located. Having no spade, the man marked the tree with one of his red garters, then kindly released the sprite and went for a spade. Returning almost instantly he found that every one of the numerous trees in the field sported a red garter!

References 17, 18, 38, 40, 56, 87, 88, 105, 114, 137
See also Cluricaun, Dwarf, Elf, Fairy, Iubdan, Sprite

L'ESAK

This is a hideous forest spirit or demon in the folk beliefs of the Cheremis/Mari people of the former Soviet Republic. It is described as able to make itself huge, like a haystack, with a head the size of a beer barrel and a mouth like an open oven. It can be heard howling in the forest or cawing like a raven in the trees. To hear the L'esak is a portent of disaster or even death for one of the family or their livestock. If the L'esak catches anyone in the forest, the spirit may deceive them by making objects resemble other things; a branch will turn into a gun, and animal dung will become bread. To avert the evil of this demon, a

A Leprechaun busily mends shoes.

cross must be painted on all the entrances to a house, so that when the dogs howl, knowing that the L'esak is nearby, the family will be safe from harm.
References 118
See also Demon, Ia, Spirit, Appendix 19

LESCHIA
See Laskowice

LESHACHIKHA
See Lesovikha

LESHAK
See Leshii

LESHII, LESHIYE, LESHY
In Russian folklore this is the name of a nature spirit. He is the guardian spirit of the animals and forests (*Les* means Forest), very similar to the English Green Man. Other regional names for this spirit are Lesovik, Leshak, Lesnoi, Lisun, Lieschi, Ljeschi, and Lychie. He appeared in the shape of a human, but with strangely pallid flesh, green eyes, green beard, and long straggly hair. He wore his bast boots on the wrong feet and threw no shadow. The Leshy was a shape-shifter that could stand as tall as, and in the likeness of, the forest trees, or could assume the size and likeness of a blade of grass. He knew and could make every noise of the forest, mischievously deceiving humans who strayed there. There was usually one Leshii in each forest unless it was very large. Each Leshii was thought to have a wife called Lesovikha and children called Leshonki. One kind of Leshii called the Zuibotschnik delighted in imitating the appearance and sounds of a baby gurgling in its cradle high in a tree.

In the spring, when he had just emerged from his winter death, he would rage with other Leshii, bringing storms and floods at the thought of their autumn demise, but soon calmed down. He would call to humans traveling through the forests or assume the shape of a fellow traveler full of helpful shortcuts and lead them off the track until the travelers were in a bog or thoroughly lost, then disappear laughing. Knowing these and other pranks of the Leshii, herdsmen and hunters thought it best to propitiate the spirits regularly with the traditional offerings of salt and bread. Another way of outwitting the Leshii was to imitate him by turning all one's clothing and boots back to front until the safety of the edge of the forest had been reached.
References 29, 41, 44, 75, 102, 110, 119
See also Domovik, Green Man, Guardian, Hedley Kow, Kornovkhii, Laskowice, Leshonki, Lesovikha, Spirit, Appendix 12, Appendix 19, Appendix 22, Appendix 24, Appendix 26

LESHONKI
In Russian folklore this is the name for the diminutive spirits that inhabited the forests and were regarded as the children of the Leshii and Lesovikha.
References 102
See also Leshii, Lesovikha, Spirit, Appendix 19

LESNOI, LESOVIK
See Leshii

LESOVIKHA
This is a female forest spirit, also known as Leshachikha and Lisovikha in Russian folklore, who is said to be the wife of the Leshii. She is variously described as a beautiful naked girl, a pendulous-bosomed hag, or a wraithlike woman in a white *sarafan*. It was believed in the area of Smolensk that if the Lesovikha were encountered while giving birth to one of her children, known as the Leshonki, and the human covered the child without prayer or cross and departed, then the spirit would follow the person. The grateful Lesovikha would be obliged to ask the human whether they desired money or a happy life. If they chose money, it would appear immediately but turn to ashes at the edge of the forest. If the person wished for nothing, then they would always have good fortune.
References 75, 102
See also Leshii, Leshonki, Appendix 19, Appendix 22

LEUCOSIA
This is the name of one of the Sirens in the classical mythology of Greece and Rome.
References 130
See also Siren

LEVIATHAN
See Devils

LHA-MO
In the beliefs of Tibet this is a powerful female disease demon. She is represented wearing human skins, eating human brains and blood from a skull, and riding a saddle of flayed skin on a white donkey surrounded by fire. She unleashes each of the other demons to cause sickness. Therefore, offerings are made to Lha-mo at the end of the year to prevent her from unleashing any of her demons in the forthcoming year.
References 88
See also Demon, gNyan, Appendix 17

LHIANNAN-SHEE
In the folklore of the Isle of Man (United Kingdom), this fairy, unlike the one bearing the same name in Ireland, was far from benevolent. She has been described as a beautiful woman wearing yellow silken

robes. She entices a young man as the target of her charm. To him she is beautiful and irresistible, but to his companions she is completely invisible. Once under her spell the young man is doomed to pine away to death. The Lhiannan-shee of Ballafletcher was somewhat different. She was the guardian spirit of the Fletcher family of Kirk Braddan, to whom she gave a miraculous crystal cup known as the Fairy Cup. This cup would ensure the line of the Fletchers as long as it was with them. Each year the head of the house would drink a toast to the Lhiannan-shee and their prosperity. The last that was heard of the Fairy Cup of Ballafletcher, it was in the possession of the Bacon family of Seafield, as the Fletcher family line had died out and Ballafletcher House was now a ruin.
References 17, 81, 135
See also Fairy, Guardian, Leanan-sidhe, Appendix 20, Appendix 22

LI

In the mythology of China this spirit is the guardian of fire who was appointed to instruct and organize the daily lives of humans. He is portrayed in human form on a saddled tiger.
References 119
See also Guardian, Spirit

LIBAN

In Irish mythology Liban was originally the daughter of Eochaid and Etain. She was caught up in the floods of a sacred spring that had been neglected and was carried to an underwater cavern with her pet dog while the rest of her community, except Conang and Curman, was destroyed. Liban was trapped for a year until she prayed that she might be as the fishes. She was transformed into the body and tail of a salmon below the waist but remained like a human above. Her dog was changed to become an otter. As a mermaid Liban had become free but remained below the water until, after 300 years, a cleric called Beoc heard her singing. She asked him to bring her out of the water and take her to Saint Comgall. She was baptized and given the choice of another three hundred years of life or immediate entry to Heaven. She chose the latter, but her image may be seen carved on many of the columns and pews in the churches built on the road she took to Saint Comgall.
References 17
See also Ceasg, Finvarra, Mermaid, Appendix 25

LIBETHRIDES

See Muses

LICKE

This is the name of an English fairy who appears in The Life of Robin Goodfellow. It is very probable that this name refers to her duties as a cook.
References 17
See also Fairy, Robin Goodfellow, Appendix 6

LIDÉRC

In the folklore of Hungary this is a type of demon or incubus that fed upon the grief of the widow. In her excessive distress, a bereaved woman might yearn aloud for just one more glimpse of her beloved. This invitation was all that was needed for the Lidérc to descend to the earth in a shower of sparks and assume the form of the deceased. Any woman who did not discover the deception, by seeing the telltale goose foot of the demon, was doomed to wither and die, believing that her husband was visiting her each night.
References 104
See also Demon, Incubus

LIEKKIÖ, LIEKKO

In the folklore of Finland this is a nature spirit that is also the Will o' the Wisp as its name, which means the Flaming One, implies. Liekkiö is said to be the transformed soul of a child buried in the forest that now searches with a flame at night. It is also revered as the guardian of the plants and animals of the wilderness.
References 88
See also Guardian, Spirit, Will o' the Wisp, Appendix 12, Appendix 22

LIESCHI

See Leshii

LIL FELLAS, LI'L FELLAS

This is a name used euphemistically for the fairies in the Isle of Man (United Kingdom).
References 17, 18
See also Fairy, Appendix 6

LILIM, LILIN

In the Hebrew tradition these are spirits of trees or vegetation that are said to be the offspring of Lilith.
References 88
See also Lilith, Appendix 18

LILITH

In the Talmudic tradition of Jewish literature, Lilith was the first wife of Adam. She was transformed into a demon of the night for refusing to accept a status of subservience and inferiority to Adam. She may in fact be derived from the Babylonian demon Ardat Lili. Like her, Lilith is the persecutor and destroyer of children, infants, and pregnant women. Even after being ejected from Paradise, three angels, Sanvi, Sansavi, and Semangelaf, were sent to induce Lilith to return

The eldest son ceremoniously carries the "Fairy Cup," a gift from the Lhiannan-shee to ensure the Ballafletcher family line.

to Adam. This she did, and the demons Shedim and Lilim were created. A charm invoking these three Angels is used to protect infants from the attention of Lilith and her Shedim offspring. As in the Hebrew traditions. Lilith, in Islamic beliefs, haunts the stormy nights in wild places of the desert, ruins, and lonely streets like the djinns that in the Muslim tradition are also supposed to be her offspring.

See also Angel, Ardat Lili, Asmodeus, Demon, Djinn, Kalu Kumāra Yaka, Labartu, Lamia, Lilim, Llorona, Pskégdemus, Putana, Tçulo, Appendix 22

LILITU, LILU
See Ardat Lili

LILYI
In the folk belief of the Romany Gypsies, this is a vicious female disease demon. This evil spirit was the result of the union between Ana and the king of the demons, when Ana had been smeared by him with a fish cooked in asses' milk. Lilyi is the wife of Melalo and is described as having the body of a fish with a man's head, from each side of which hang nine gluti-nous filaments. She seeks the exposed bodies of humans, and should she manage to touch them with her facial filaments, they immediately penetrate the unfortunate's skin and inflict severe catarrhal infec-tion. It is highly probable that the derivation of this spirit is that of Lilu, Lilitu, or Lilith.

References 31
See also Ana, Demon, Lilith, Loçolico, Melalo, Spirit, Appendix 17

LIMENIA
This is the name of a group of nymphs in the classical mythology of Greece and Rome. The Limenia were the guardian spirits of harbors.

References 130
See also Guardian, Nymph, Appendix 25

LIMNÆ, LIMNEAD
This is the collective name for a group of nymphs in the classical mythology of Greece and Rome. The Limnæ were the guardian spirits of marshes.

References 130
See also Guardian, Nymph, Appendix 25

LIMONEADS
This is the collective name for a group of nymphs in the classical mythology of Greece and Rome. The Limoneads were the guardian spirits of meadows and their flowers.

References 107
See also Guardian, Nymph, Appendix 18

LIOUMERE
In the folklore of the Caroline Islands this was the name of a terrible female demon. Lioumere was described as appearing in a hideous female human form with metal fangs in her enormous jaws. She caused havoc with her iron fangs, entrapping and devouring any being that was unwary in her habitat. She was defeated when a man who wanted the magic fangs hired a clown to make the demon laugh. When this happened he leapt forward, smashing out the teeth with a stone and removing her control over the terrified people.

References 33
See also Demon

LIR
This is the name of a chieftan of the Tuatha dé Danann in Irish mythology.

References 108
See also Bodb, Tuatha dé Danann

LISOVIKHA
See Lesovikha

LISUN
See Leshii

LIT, LITUR
This is the name of an individual dwarf in Scandinavian mythology. After the betrayal of Balder and his death brought about by the demon god Loki, a great funeral pyre and ceremony was organized for Balder. The diminutive dwarf Litur was present at the funeral, but was so tiny that he moved forward to see the ritual. Unobserved, he got in the way of Thor's foot as the god was about to deliver the funeral ora-tion. Being so tiny, the dwarf was propelled forward, straight into the fire, and thus was accidentally burned and destroyed on the funeral pyre of Baldur.

References 41, 95
See also Demon, Dwarf

LITTLE FOLK
See Sleigh Beggey

LITTLE OLD MAN OF THE BARN
See Bodachan Sabhaill

LITTLE PEOPLE, THE
Essentially a euphemism for a range of lesser spirits, the term *Little People* is mostly used in Britain for sprites and fairies; it has equivalents in other lan-guages and cultures. It may be used when referring to any lesser spirits in order to avoid offending them and incurring their supernatural revenge. Direct naming of these spirits is said to be offensive, and a

euphemism not only shows respect, but also avoids direct invocation of a spirit whose presence is undesirable. These lesser spirits may also be referred to in this manner by a person visiting a different region, when ignorant of the local name.
References 40, 107
See also Fairy, Mannikin, Old People, Sprite, Appendix 6

LITTLE WASHER BY THE FORD
See Bean Nighe

LIU-MENG CHIANG-CHÜN
In the beliefs and mythology of ancient China, this is a guardian spirit. Liu-Meng Chiang-Chün is often portrayed as a young man surrounded by children. He is particularly vigilant over the crops and fields, which he protects against the ravages of the grasshoppers and locusts.
References 132
See also Guardian, Appendix 18, Appendix 22

LIWA
The name of evil water spirits in the folk belief of the Miskito and Suma peoples of Nicaragua and Honduras. These spirits may manifest as white amorphous shapes under the water, where they are supposed to have their own canoes. The Liwa lie in wait until they can drag down any unwary human to their doom under the water. The Liwa of Caratasca caused the capsizing of fishing boats in the shallows of the river and the drowning of its occupants. One is known to have inhabited a whirlpool at Namakalmuk until a shaman drove it away by burning the skin of an alligator.
References 88
See also Addanc, Darrant, Keagyihl Depguesk, Jenny Greenteeth, Spirit, Appendix 25

LJESCHI
This is the Slavonic name for the Leshii of Russian folklore. This forest spirit is common to many cultures of eastern Europe under different names.
References 29, 41, 44, 119
See also Leshii, Spirit, Appendix 19

LJUBI
This is the name of a demon in the folk beliefs of Albania. This malignant female spirit is said to inhabit a garden full of luscious produce, and in order to keep her garden in all its beauty, she will take all the available water that the humans have on the earth. Ljubi will see that no water reaches the human inhabitants of the region and that their crops are ruined by drought unless she is suitably propitiated, in the past by human sacrifice.

References 93
See also Demon, Spirit

LLAMHIGYN Y DWR
This is a fearful water demon whose name means the Water Leaper in the folklore of Wales. It would manifest in the shape of a toad with a tail and wings instead of legs. Although it could be said to be the guardian of freshwater fish, for other beings it was a malignant spirit of rivers with plentiful fish and grazing sheep on the banks. This demon's favorite preoccupation was to give a shriek and then snap the lines of any fisherman, causing him to fall into the water and be dragged down to his fate. If no humans were fishing, then the Llamhigyn y Dwr would incite the curiosity of the sheep on the bank and lure them into the water to be devoured.
References 17, 59
See also Addanc, Buso, Demon, Guardian, Jenny Greenteeth, Kappa, Liwa, Peg Powler, Appendix 12, Appendix 25

LLORONA, LA
In the folklore of Mexico, this is a female demon who appears as a beautiful woman with a hole in the back of her head. La Llorona, whose name means the Weeper, seems to be sobbing and turning to look behind her, apparently searching for her lost child. In some traditions she has killed her own child and is condemned to wander. Sometimes she is just a wailing voice in the wind. In contrast to her gentle manner, La Llorona, when encountered at night in the alleyways, woods, or riversides, will entice unwary men to follow her. She may simply ask if they have seen her little boy, but more often she is reported as protracting a gruesome liaison that results in a male pregnancy of feces or a more hideous cannibal death. Those who may recognize the telltale ashes in the empty eyes in time may be able to save themselves by poking a lighted cigarette into the hollow behind La Llorona's head. She will then turn into her true demonic shape and slither away.
References 30, 88
See also Demon, Lamia, Lilith, Pskégdemus, Appendix 22

LOA
This spirit, derived from the deities of Africa, is the spirit messenger in the Voodoo cult of Haiti.
References 137
See also Guia, Spirit

LOANGO WINTI
A nature spirit of the African-descended people of Surinam. He is derived from a deity of the Loango region of the Congo Basin.

References 88
See also Encantado, Spirit, Appendix 18

LOB
An uncouth rustic spirit of the brownie type in the folklore of the North of England. They are also called Hobs.
References 17
See also Brownie, Hob, Household Spirit, Lob-Lie-by-the-Fire, Spirit

LOB-LIE-BY-THE-FIRE
In the folklore of England this is a friendly brownie that, as his name implies, was less likely to do household tasks than his nocturnal counterpart. He was supposed to have been the inhabitant of the farmhouse at Lingborough in the north of England, where he would manifest in the shape of a large human and settle before the kitchen fire. Although he would help with the stable work, he was also well known for his pranks and practical jokes. He is described as a Lubber-fiend in the works of the English writers Milton, Blake, and Ewing. Ewing describes Lob-Lie-by-the-Fire as an elf that is "A great rough, black fellow who gets bigger, rougher and blacker every time the cowherd told the tale." Despite his tricksy nature the sprite was greatly missed when he left the farm.
References 17, 41
See also Brownie, Elf, Lubbar-Fiend, Sprite, Appendix 22

LOÇOLICO
The name of terrifying demons in the folk beliefs of the Romany Gypsies. They had originally been humans, but had been transformed by the Devil into these evil spirits that infested the earth. The tradition tells how their king fell in love with the queen of the Keshalyi, called Ana. When she refused his advances, he and his demons captured and devoured her fairy entourage until she agreed to marry the demon king. In order to make her his wife, the king induced her sleep with the help of a golden toad, and from the union came the demons Bitoso, Lilyi, Lolmischo, Mimir, Melalo, Minceskro, Poreskoro, Schilalyi, Tçulo, and Tçaridyi. Consumed with horror at her fate, and driven to despair, Ana managed to part from the demon king on the promise that when a Keshalyi reached 999 years, she would come to one of his Loçolico. Ana hid in shame and remorse forever in her castle, occasionally venturing out in the shape of a golden toad.
References 31
See also Ana, Bitoso, Demon, Fairy, Keshalyi, Lilyi, Lolmischo, Melalo, Mimir, Minceskro, Poreskoro, Schilalyi, Spirit, Tçaridyi, Tçulo

LODONA
The name of a nymph in ancient British mythology, who was supposed to have given her name to the brook that empties into the Thames at Shiplake. Thus, this may be given as an alternative origin of the name of London. This supernatural was a huntress, but being chased by the god Pan, she prayed for safety and was promptly turned into the crystal waters of the stream that now bears her name.
References 40
See also Nymph, Appendix 25

LÖFJERSKOR
This is the general term for wood spirits in the folklore of Sweden. They are described as forest elves or tree sprites that were usually invisible to humans. An individual spirit was called a Rå.
References 110
See also Elf, Rå, Spirit, Sprite, Appendix 19

LOGHERY MAN
This is the Ulster name for the Cluricaun of Irish folklore.
References 17, 40, 41
See also Cluricaun

LOIREAG
In the folklore of the Hebridean Islands of Scotland, this is a fairy woman similar in description to Habetrot, but without the ugly lip. She is usually dressed in white. Like Habetrot, she is an expert spinner and will punish any of the women who are careless at this task. Loireag, or Lorreag, is actually a water spirit and as such is fond of music. She gets very cross if she hears anyone singing out of tune and is likely to cause them mischief to make them cease.
References 17
See also Fairy, Girle Guairle, Habetrot, Jili Ffrwtan, Appendix 14, Appendix 25

LOLMISCHO
In the folk beliefs of the Romany Gypsies, this is a male disease demon whose name means The Red Mouse. This evil spirit was the result of the skin infection of the fairy queen called Ana and the cure advised by Melalo. This involved mice licking the sores, but one mouse entered her abdomen and was born as Lolmischo. In the shape of a red mouse, this demon will inflict sores and eczema on the skin of any human it has touched in the night.
References 31
See also Ana, Demon, Keshalyi, Loçolico, Melalo, Spirit, Appendix 12, Appendix 17

LORD HARRY
See Auld Hornie

LORELEI, LORELEY
This is the name of a female water spirit or siren, also known as Lurlei or Loreley, in the folklore of the German Rhine. Lorelei was supposed to inhabit the rock of the same name, which gave curious echoes in the River Rhine close to Bingen, where her beautiful singing would lure the sailors to certain death. Her existence, however, is not an ancient one, but the work of Klemens Bretano, who published the story in *Lore Lay* (1800). The story was further publicized in England with the popularity of Heinrich Heine's poem on the subject, and a convinced public created a tourist interest in the now-familiar regional attraction.
References 40, 88, 95, 114
See also Siren, Spirit, Appendix 25

LOSKOTUKHA
See Rusalka

LOTIS, LOTUS
This is the name of a nymph in the classical mythology of Greece and Rome. She was chased by Priapus and prayed for escape, and as a result the gods changed her into the Lotus plant.
References 130
See also Nymph

LOVAR
This is a subgroup of dwarfs in Scandinavian mythology. There is not much information about them except their alliance with Dwalin and 11 of their names, which are Ai, Alfr, Eikinsjalldi, Fith, Fjalar, Frosti, Ginnar, Skandar, Skirflir, Virfir, and Yngvi. Afr is perhaps linked to the Alfar.
References 41
See also Alfar, Dwalin, Dwarf

LOVE TALKER, THE
See Gan Ceanach

LU
The name of two disease demons in the beliefs of the Karen people of Burma. The more ancient of the two is less voracious and inflicts less harm. But the younger nat will stop at nothing to inflict horrific contagious diseases on all humans in his area to produce the corpses upon which he feeds. To prevent the Lu from carrying off one of his sick victims, the family will place a dead chicken or some rice in the cemetery to assuage the hunger of the demons.
References 88
See also Demon, Nat, Appendix 10, Appendix 17

LUBBAR-FIEND, LUBBARD-FIEND, LUBBER-FIEND
This is the English farm spirit that John Milton described in his poem *L' Allegro* thus:

> "When in one night, ere glimps of morn,
> His shadowy Flale hath thresh'd the Corn
> That ten day-labourers could not end,
> Then lies him down the Lubbar Fend,
> And stretch'd out all the Chimney's length
> Basks at the fire his hairy strength;
> And crop-full out of dores he flings,
> Ere the first cock his Matin rings."

From this description it may be seen how this tricksy but hardworking brownie spirit came to be known as Lob-Lie-by-the-Fire.
References 17
See also Brownie, Household Spirit, Lob-Lie-by-the-Fire, Spirit, Appendix 22

LUBBERKIN
This is the diminutive form of Lubber and Lob used during the sixteenth and seventeenth centuries in Britain. It usually infers a familiarity and friendly acceptance of the spirit by humans in the place it haunts.
References 17
See also Abbey Lubber, Household Spirit, Lob, Lob-Lie-by-the-Fire, Lubber, Spirit

LUBIN
In the folklore of France this evil spirit haunted the churchyards. It is described as appearing in the shape of a wolf or large gray dog that terrified those who ventured there at night. It is said that the spirit was in search of the souls of the dead to devour.
References 28
See also Church Grim, Grim, Spirit, Appendix 12

LUBRICAN
See Leprechaun

LUCHORPAIN
See Luchtaine

LUCHORPAN
See Leprechaun

LUCHTAINE
In the Celtic mythology of Ireland, this is the supernatural woodworker of the Tuatha dé Danann. Sometimes referred to as Luchorpain, this dwarf with his fellows Credne and Goibniu made the shields and shafts of the spears used by the Tuatha in their fight against the Formorians.

References 41, 125
See also Credné, Durin, Dwarf, Formor, Goibniu, Tuatha dé Danann

LUCIFER

In the Christian religion and literature, Lucifer is the demon or devil associated with pride, who was originally one of the angels. His name in Latin means Bringer of Light. When the Lord commanded that Lucifer should acknowledge the place of Adam, Lucifer refused and led a rebellion of a group of the celestial spirits. They were cast from Heaven for their pride and joined the ranks of the Devil as Fallen Angels. Lucifer has often been equated with the Devil, although the more usual name for the supremely evil spirit is Satan.
References 40, 53, 88, 93
See also Angel, Demon, Devil, Fallen Angel, Appendix 7, Appendix 13

LUCKY DEVIL

This is the spirit of the Australian shrub known as *Lambertia formosa*, or the Mountain Devil, which it resembles. This benevolent being has a head that looks like the spiked pod of the bush, a scaly body, and spiny tail. It is one of the Little People that are the companions of Snugglepot and Cuddlepie, the creation of May Gibb.
References 55
See also Flower Fairy, Gumnut Babies, Little People, Spirit

LUGOVNIK

In the folklore of Russia this is a nature spirit, which is also called Lugovik. This supernatural is the guardian spirit of the meadows and pastures.
References 75
See also Domovik, Guardian, Ia Kuba, Limoneads, Appendix 18

LUIDEAG

In the Scottish Highland folklore of the Isle of Skye, this is an evil female demon whose name means the Rag. She took the form of a human dressed in ragged and squalid clothes, intent on causing the death of any human in her power.
References 17
See also Biasd Bheulach, Coluinn Gun Cheann, Demon

LULL

This is the name of the female fairy nurse who took care of the fairy babies in *The Life of Robin Goodfellow*.
References 17
See also Fairy, Robin Goodfellow, Appendix 22

LUNANTISHEE

In the folklore of Ireland these are the fairy guardian spirits of the blackthorn shrub. This small tree, like the hawthorn, is sacred to the Little People, and it is important that the blackthorn is left uncut on the Celtic festivals of Samhain and Beltane. As these were originally celebrated on 11 November and 11 May, respectively, no human will risk the fairies' wrath and misfortune, so they still refrain from taking blackthorn wood on those days.
References 17
See also Churnmilk Peg, Elder Mother, Fairy, Guardian, Little People, Appendix 19

LUOT-CHOZJIK

This is a benevolent female spirit in the folk beliefs of the Lapp people of northeast Finland. She is the guardian spirit of the reindeer during their summer grazing in the forests on the edge of the tundra.
References 88
See also Guardian, Spirit, Appendix 12

LUPRACAN

See Leprechaun

LURICADAUNE

This is the name given in County Tipperary for the Cluricaun of Irish folklore.
References 17, 87
See also Cluricaun

LURIDAN

This is the name of a household spirit said to have inhabited the Island of Pomonia (now known as Mainland) in the Orkney Islands off the north coast of Scotland. He behaved in much the same way as a brownie, making fires in the hearth, washing dishes, and sweeping the floors. However, Luridan, like a familiar, apparently also conversed with those who could see him.
References 17
See also Brownie, Familiar, Household Spirit, Appendix 22

LURLEI

See Lorelei

LUTIN

These are the elves or mischievous fairies in the folklore of Normandy in northern France. The name was originally Netun for these and farmstead sprites, who were said to like the company of human children. They mostly remained invisible, but their exploits of tangling the horses tails and manes while they rode them all night to a lather would clearly be seen in the morning. Under the name of Le Cheval Bayard these

spirits would present themselves as mounts for any humans foolish enough to attempt to ride them, for the riders would find themselves in a ditch or a bog.
See also Biča Kuguza, Cheval Bayard, Colt, Pixy, Elf, Fairy, Goblin, Gŵyll, Ia, Nain Rouge, Pixy, Sprite, Appendix 12, Appendix 22

LYCA
See Echenais

LYCHIE
This is the Slavonic name for the Leshii of Russian folklore. This spirit is common to many eastern European cultures under various names.
References 41, 44, 53, 56
See also Leshii, Spirit

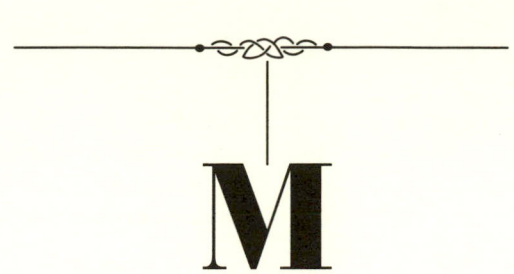

M

MA MIEN
In the mythology of China, this is a demon with the face of a horse. He is the attendant and messenger of Yen-Lo, the ruler of the dead and of those in hell.
References 131
See also Attendant Spirit, Demon, Wu Ch'ang Kuei, Appendix 16

MAAHISET, MAANALAISET
These spirits, whose name means Earth-Dwellers, are the Little People of Finland. They are also known by the name Maanalaiset, which means the Subterranean Ones. They dwell within the earth and are its guardian spirits. Although usually benevolent, any lack of respect for their protected area may bring harsh retribution.
References 93
See also Bardha, Guardian, Herok'a, Honga, H'uraru, Little People, Spirit

MAB
In the folklore and legend of England and Wales, she is a fairy. Mab is mostly described as a Queen of the Fairies, as in Poole' s work *Parnassus* (1657), where she is portrayed as consort to Oberon, emperor of the fairies. She may be portrayed as the fairy midwife, as in Shakespeare's *Romeo and Juliet* (1597). Mab is described as tiny, no bigger than an agate stone, and she travels in a coach drawn by insects.
References 28, 40, 114
See also Fairy, Oberon, Appendix 6

MAC CECHT
With Mac Cuill and Mac Greiné, he was one of the three kings of the Tuatha dé Danann in the legends and folklore of Ireland. When they were defeated by the Milesians, they took their people to the lands beneath the *sidh* (the mounds) to become the Little People of Ireland.
References 125
See also Little People, Tuatha dé Danann

MAC CUILL
See Mac Cecht

MAC GREINÉ
See Mac Cecht

MAC MOINEANTA
He was a king of the Irish fairies of the Tuatha dé Danann who was deposed by Finvarra.
References 125
See also Fairy, Finvarra, Tuatha dé Danann

MACACHERA
This is the name of a spirit in the folk beliefs of the Tupinamba people of the Brazilian Amazon. Macachera is a demon road spirit that brings misfortune, sickness, and even death to those humans that travel on the highways. However, in the beliefs of the Potiguara people, this spirit of the highways is a messenger whose appearance is the portent of good fortune.
References 102
See also Demon, Spirit, Appendix 24

MACARDIT
In the folk beliefs of the Dinka people of Sudan, this is a spirit or demon that is particularly malevolent toward human beings. Macardit brings misfortune, injustice, and disaster to any person he encounters indiscriminately.
References 29
See also Demon, Spirit

MACHA
This is a female evil spirit of conflict and death. Macha is a member of the Tuatha dé Danann in the folklore and legends of Ireland. She is a fairy that takes the shape of a hooded crow in order to gloat over the humans who have fallen in battle.
References 17
See also Badb, Banshee, Bodua, Fairy, Neman, Spirit, Tuatha dé Danann, Valkyrie

MADA
This is a horrific demon in the Hindu mythology and epic legends of India. Mada was created by

Chyavana to coerce Indra into agreeing to the Asvins' inclusion in a ceremony.
References 87
See also Demon

MAEZT-DAR L'OUDOU

This is a powerful and malignant djinn in the folklore of Morocco. Maezt-Dar l'Oudou means the Goat of the Lavatories, a name that indicates its predisposition to take possession of the baths and lavatories at night, and other places where water might be flushed. It takes the form of a bleating goat, which materializes and terrifies anyone imprudent enough to venture to those places after dark.
References 90
See also Djinn, Appendix 12

MAGÆRA

This is the name of a fearsome spirit in the mythology of ancient Greece and Rome. Magæra, whose name means Envious Fury, is the spirit or genius of ultimate revenge. Magæra is one of the Furies who exact retribution from those whose hideous crimes, especially matricide or patricide, remain unpunished by human law.
References 29, 40
See also Erinys, Furies, Genius, Spirit, Appendix 23

MAGGY MOLOCK, MAGGIE MOLOCH

This is the name of a household spirit of the brownie type that inhabited the mill at Fincastle in Perthshire, Scotland. She may be a variant of the spirit known as Mieg Moulach.
References 17
See also Brownie, Household Spirit, Mieg Moulach, Appendix 22

MAHĀMĀRI

This is the name of a female demon of vengeance, also known as Ghrtamāri, who was created by the lord Siva in the classical mythology of India. Mahāmāri was created from a burning lock of Siva's hair anointed with *ghee*. She was sent to do battle with the desecrating fiends called Malla and Mani.
References 68
See also Demon, Fiend, Malla, Mani

MAHIH-NAH-TIEHEY

This name, which means the Changing Coyote, is often used by the Navajo Native American people to refer to the trickster Coyote.
References 41
See also Coyote, Trickster

MAHISĀSURA

This is the name of a demon in the Hindu mythology of India. He was the guardian spirit of the buffalo, and was eventually destroyed by his bride, Mahādevi.
References 68
See also Demon, Guardian

MAHR

This is the European medieval fiend of the night known in Latin as the Incubus. It goes by different names in the folklore of each country; in England it is the Nightmare, from the Anglo-Saxon *Mara*, meaning Crusher. Mara is also the name used in Lithuania. In German and Slavonic folklore, it is known as Mahr. In Poland and Russia it is the Mora. The name variants of Morava and Murawa are used in Bulgarian and Czech folklore, respectively. This demon has the ability to appear in various forms, from being completely invisible to resembling a hair, a wisp of straw, or an ugly little shape that vanishes when observed.
References 93
See also Cauchemar, Fiend, Incubus, Mara, Mare, Nightmare

MAIA

In the classical mythology of Greece and Rome, she is a mountain nymph and one of the Pleiades. Maia, whose name means Mother or Nurse, became the mother of Hermes (Mercury) by the king of the gods, Zeus (Jupiter). She later nursed Arcas after the demise of his mother, Callisto.
References 40, 93, 114
See also Callisto, Nymph, Pleiades, Appendix 13

MAIGHDEAN NA TUINNE

See Ceasg

MAJAHALDJAS

This is the protective household spirit in the folk beliefs of the Estonian people, possibly representing a transformed link with a family ancestor in the same way as the Russian Domovoi. This spirit must not be offended by bad behavior, and must be propitiated with offerings of drinks and food to retain his guardian care of the home.
References 87
See also Demovik, Guardian, Haldde, Haldjas, Haltia, Household Spirit, Koduhaldja, Spirit, Tonttu, Appendix 22

MĀJAKUNGS

In the folklore of Latvia, this household spirit is the equivalent in behavior and description to the Russian Domovoi, and like the Domovoi, is said to be derived

from an ancestor's spirit. In order to protect the family and the home, his abode is either on the threshold of the home or within the hearth.
References 88
See also Domovik, Household Spirit, Appendix 22

MĀJAS GARS
This is a household spirit in the folklore of Latvia whose presence brought good fortune. Like the Domovoi of Russia and the brownie of England, the Mājas gars was placated by small gifts left for him so that he would continue his benevolence.
References 93
See also Brownie, Domovik, Household Spirit, Appendix 22

MAJUJU
This is the name of one of the two demons of Islamic tradition. Together with Yajuju, Majuju is mentioned in the Koran (xxi: 96) as being one of the portents of Doomsday and the Day of Judgment.
References 56
See also Azrael, Dain, Demon, Gabriel

MAKAR
This is a keremet or local field devil in the folk beliefs of the Cheremis/Mari people of the former Soviet Republic.
References 118
See also Devil, Keremet, Appendix 18

MALA'IKAT
This is the name used for angels in the Islamic beliefs of the people of West Malaysia.
References 120
See also Angel, Chitar Ali, Ijrail

MALA'IKAT PUTEH
This is the Guardian Angel of all things in the jungle in the Islamic beliefs of the people of West Malaysia. Mala'ikat Puteh means the White Angel.
References 120
See also Chitar Ali, Guardian Angel, Appendix 19

MALEKIN, MALKIN, MAWKIN
This is the name of a fairy or changeling that inhabited the castle at Dagworth in Suffolk, England. Her story is told by Ralph of Coggeshall, the thirteenth-century Cistercian chronicler. This spirit was precocious by any standards, being able to converse with the lord of the castle in good English, with the servants in dialect, and hold discerning scriptural discourse in Latin with the priest. She was particularly friendly with the servant girl who left a bowl of food for Malekin each night. The spirit would talk happily with the servants

of the castle, but only once made herself visible, and this was to the servant girl, who related the description of her. Malekin appeared to her like a very tiny human child dressed in a white linen tunic.
References 18, 107, 133
See also Changeling, Fairy, Green Children, Spirit, Appendix 22

MALIK
In the Islamic scriptures of the Koran (xliii: 77), this is the name of the angel appointed as the chief guardian of hell. Malik is the angel to whom supplications are made for the release of the damned, but he will bid them to stay.
References 39
See also Angel, Guardian, Appendix 16

MALIK EL ABIAD
This is a benevolent female djinn in the folk beliefs of Morocco. When a human has been possessed by an evil spirit, Malik el Abiad is invoked to assist in removing the malevolent djinn from the human.
References 90
See also Djinn, Spirit

MALLA
In the classical Hindu mythology of India, this is a terrible, destructive demon who, with his brother Mani, worked acts of unspeakable horror and violence on the earth. The lord Siva was so angry that he created a demon of vengeance named Mahāmāri, who was sent to engage in battle with the demons and their horde of fiends. When Mani recanted, Khandoba, who had defeated the demon, allowed him to survive, but Malla fought on. Then Mahāmāri commenced devouring the demon's elephants, warriors, chariots, and weapons. When Khandoba also attacked Malla, the demon appeared to recant just as he was about to lose his head. When the demon asked for three favors to be granted, the wise Khandoba removed the demon's head, replacing it with that of a goat, and buried the original under the temple; then he took the name Malhāri (killer of Malla). All of these actions perversely granted the demon's wishes. In the Maharashtra, the variations of this story give only one demon, whose name is Manimal.
References 68
See also Demon, Fiend, Mahāmāri, Mani

MALLCU
In the mythology of the Aymara people of Bolivia, this is a general term applied to spirits. It is similar in use to the term Apo of the Quechua.
References 88
See also Apo, Spirit

MALLEBRON

In the thirteenth-century ballad "Huon de Bordeaux," this is the fairy servant of Oberon, the king of the fairies. This spirit is sent to assist the chivalrous knights on their journeys to the Holy Land, often rescuing them and transporting them from harm at the instigation of Oberon.
References 21, 58
See also Fairy, Oberon

MALPHAS

In European medieval demonology, this is a powerful demon of Hell.
References 53
See also Demon

MAMAGWASEWUG

In the folklore of the Canadian forests, these Little People are a type of fairy having the same ambivalent relationship with humans as their European counterparts. They can be benevolent, mischievous, and even malevolent when offended.
References 110
See also Fairy, Little People

MAMANDABARI

These are spirits of the Dreamtime in the beliefs of the Walbiri Native Australian people.
References 29
See also Spirit

MAMMON

In the ancient Aramaic language, the name of this spirit meant Property. Agripa of Nittersheim regarded this demon as the personification of ill-derived and undeserved riches. In modern folklore as well, the name of Mammon is mostly used as a devil associated with avarice.
References 93
See also Demon, Devil, Spirit

MA-MO

In the beliefs of Tibet, these are evil female disease demons. They are usually portrayed as being black and dressed entirely in black. The Ma-mo are the "wives" of other fearsome demons.
References 88
See also Demon, gNyan, Appendix 17

MANABOZO

In the beliefs of the Menomeni Native American people, this spirit, whose name means Big Rabbit, is a shape-shifting trickster. He is also known as Nenabushu and Pasikola. Manabozo entered the world from under a bowl, and is said to be the grandson of the Earth Mother. Manabozo will sometimes

fight evil, but is more often concerned with playing pranks, and he is credited with introducing ball games. This great trickster spirit has been immortalized in the more mundane stories of "Brer Rabbit" by J. Chandler Harris.
References 25, 88, 93
See also Anansi, Bamapama, Basajaun, Blue Jay, Coyote, Eshu, Mink, Spirit, Trickster

MANAWYDDAN

In the folklore of Dyfed in Wales, these spirits are a type of fairy. Like the Irish Lepracaun, the Manawyddan occupied themselves with work on cobbling shoes.
References 37
See also Fairy, Leprechaun, Tylwyth Teg

MANDARANGAN

In the folklore of the Philippine Islands, this is a male demon. Mandarangan and his "wife," Darago, are the guardians of Bagobo warriors.
References 88
See also Demon, Guardian

MANDRAGORA

In European occultism and demonology, this is a familiar demon derived from the nature spirit of the mandrake plant. From the earliest times, the legends concerning the fatal results inflicted by the Mandragora on anyone attempting to lift the plant out of the earth brought about the stratagem of harnessing an unfortunate dog to the plant until the root was clear of the ground. The spirit was supposed to scream as it was drawn from the earth, and this is mentioned in Shakespeare's *Romeo and Juliet* (1596). Like the appearance of the roots, the spirit of the mandrake is described as resembling a youthful, naked male or female human, which according to Thomas Newton was produced from the spirit of a buried murderer. The plant was used by alchemists and herbalists from the earliest times for its alleged fertility and curative properties as recorded in the Judeo-Christian scriptures (Genesis 88: 14–16). It was also supposed to inflict vanity and lunacy if the resultant potion were taken to excess.
References 40, 53
See also Demon, Familiar, Appendix 18

MANES

In the beliefs of ancient Rome, this was the term used for the spirits of the dead, who were propitiated and venerated to prevent them from becoming Lemures. Those Manes that were benevolent to humans were called the Lars. However, the term Manes was also used more loosely to denote the supernatural spirits in the underworld and guardians of tombs and burial places.

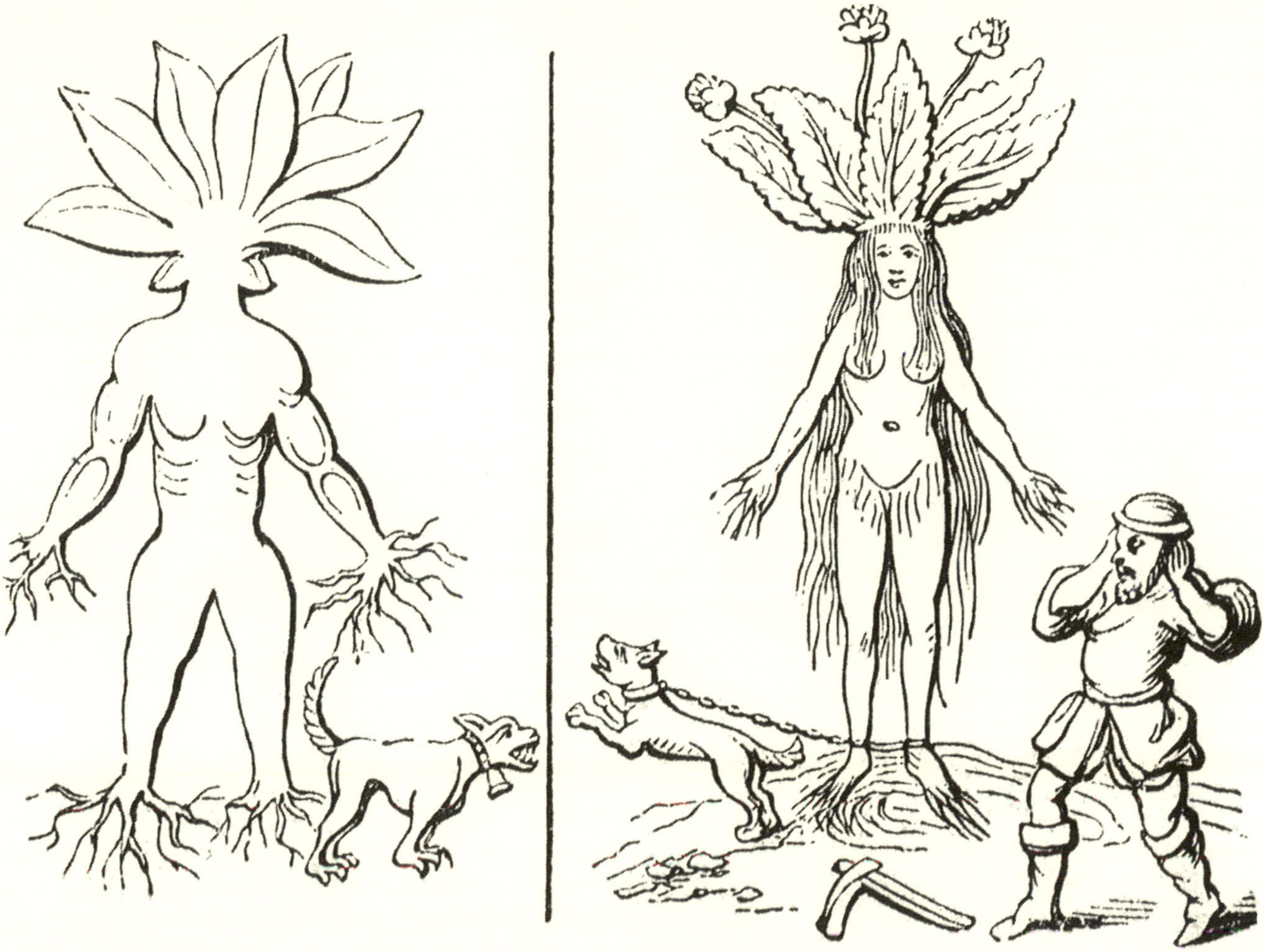

Mandragora is known to scream if uprooted, as depicted by the man (right) covering his ears.

References 29, 39, 40, 88, 93
See also Angel, Angiris, Àràk, Guardian Angel, Guardian, Lar, Lemur, Pitris, Rishis, Spirit, Appendix 16

MANI

This is the name of a terrifying demon in the classical Hindu mythology of India. Mounted on a white horse, he shares in his brother Malla's destruction and war-making before being brought to account by Khandoba.
References 68
See also Demon, Malla

MANIMAL

See Malla

MANINGA

This is the name of a spirit in the folk beliefs and legends of the Mandan Native American people. Maninga is a spirit of floods.
References 25
See also Spirit, Appendix 25

MANNIKIN

In the folklore of Europe, these are the Little People that live in communities much like humans. Their abode is often in the abandoned ruins of human castles, churches, and other fine but decayed and neglected places. They are described as looking much like tiny, youthful humans, given to merriment and a love of music. They will take cream, eggs, bread, and other treats from the farm kitchen, but will be sure to recompense the family by reaping, threshing, making hay, or sweeping the farmhouse.
References 82
See also Elf, Hampelmann, Little People

MANOELZINHO BOA DA TRINIDADE

See Legua Bogi da Trinidade

MANTUS AND MANIA

In the ancient Etruscan religion, these two spirits are the guardians of the underworld.
References 41
See also Guardian, Spirit, Appendix 16

MARA

There are two concepts of spirits, from different cultures, with the name Mara.

(1) In Teutonic mythology he is described as an elf whose specialty is inducing bad dreams for any sleeping human. *Mara* is the Old English word for a demon, from the Anglo-Saxon *Mara*, meaning Crusher. Bad dreams and disturbed sleep are thus ascribed in England even today to the fiend of the night known as the Nightmare. Mara is also the name used in Lithuania, but during European medieval times this fiend was known in Latin as the Incubus.

(2) In Hindu and Buddhist mythology, Mara is the evil demon who attempts at every opportunity to divert Buddha from attaining Enlightenment. This demonic being is the tempter of all those who seek a holy life. The name Mara means Agent of Death, but in the Athara-Veda he is death personified. He also has power over birth and desire, and because Buddha tries to deliver humans from the cycle of birth and desire, Mara constantly attempts to thwart this aim. Mara is a shape-shifter, but he is always recognized as the tempter and consequently defeated. His influence extends only to the three lower planes of existence, and once these have been gained, Mara's influence is no longer relevant to the faithful.
References 15, 17, 33, 39, 41, 56, 87, 93, 104, 119
See also (1) Cauchemar, Demon, Elf, Fiend, Incubus, Mare, Nightmare, Succubus; (2) Demon, Iblis, Mephistophales

MÄRA-HALDDO

This is the name of a sea spirit in the folk beliefs of the Lapp people of northern Norway and Finland. Mära-Halddo means Spirit of the Sea.
References 88
See also Čacce-olmai, Spirit, Appendix 25

MARAWA

See Qat

MARCHOCIAS

In European medieval demonology, this is a demon of Hell often invoked by sorcerers. He is said to have been one of the Fallen Angels, and is described as having the wings of a griffin and the tail of a snake.
References 53, 93
See also Fallen Angel, Appendix 12

MARE

This is the old English word for a demon, which is mostly used today for the frightening dreams said to be caused at night by the Nightmare, or the night demon, known in Latin as the Incubus. The French word for the same spirit, Cauchemar, contains the same word root, which links to the central European

name of Mara for the same fiend. This fiend was said to come during the night to place its weight upon the body of the sleeping human until all the breath had been crushed from it. A further use of the word Mare for a frightening spirit in the English language was that of the Woodmare for the haunting voice that followed the human's own in the forests. This has since been replaced by, and ascribed to, the more gentle Roman nymph Echo.
References 113
See also Cauchemar, Demon, Echo, Fiend, Incubus, Mara, Nightmare, Nymph, Spirit

MARÉT

In the beliefs of the Botocudo people of eastern Brazil, these are guardian spirits. The Marét inhabit the skies, although they can transform their shape to that of a bird or animal to appear on the earth. They can make bad weather overtake those who injure the Botocudo, but are generally well disposed to humans. The Marét taught the Botocudo sacred songs and their special manner of personal adornment.
References 88
See also Guardian, Appendix 12

MARI MORGAN

In the folklore of Brittany in northern France, this is a type of siren or mermaid considered to be both beautiful and extremely dangerous to sailors. They are sometimes known just by the name Morgan or Morgens, which may link with the name of Morgan le Fay. These mermaids inhabit beautiful palaces under the sea in the Isles of Ushant, but they crave the love of mortal men. Therefore, these spirits rise to the surface of the sea whenever a fishing vessel is near, to attract young men to their embrace. Unfortunately, their touch is fatal, and humans try to get away before they are caught in the mermaid's spell. Some say that mortals have survived in their underwater palaces, but the enchanted men can never return to their human world.
References 87, 123
See also Mermaid, Morgan, Morgan le Fay, Siren, Appendix 25

MARIA BARBA

See Rainha Barba

MARIANA

This spirit is a high-ranking and popular encantado in the Afro-Brazilian cult Batuque. She is a member of the Turcos or Turquia "family," and is associated with Nossa Senhora de Batalha (Our Lady of Battle). Mariana is regarded as the guardian spirit of the Brazilian navy as well as a particularly powerful curing spirit for children and pregnant mothers. Her

name is derived from Arara, the name of the macaw, the feathers of which were used by local shamans for centuries in the curing of sickness. She is surprisingly considered adept at arranging for lovers to meet, and for this reason many of the local prostitutes regard Mariana as their protector. Her male counterpart, Mariano, is not so popular in Belém, but more so in Maranhão.
References 89
See also Encantado, Guardian, Seu Turquia, Spirit, Appendix 22

MARIANO
See Mariana

MARICA
This is the name of a nymph in the classical mythology of Greece and Rome. Marica was the guardian spirit of the River Liris and the consort of Faunus.
References 130
See also Guardian, Nymph

MARID
In the Arabic pre-Islamic mythology, Marid is one of the most powerful djinns. It is possible that this name was the derivation of Marut.
References 41
See also Djinn, Haruts

MAROOT
See Haruts

MAROS
See Tündér

MARSABA
This is an evil spirit in the folk beliefs of the people of Ruk Island, Melanesia. This demon was possibly debased from being one of the deities of the underworld.
References 102
See also Demon, Nabaeo, Spirit

MARSAYAS
In the classical mythology of ancient Greece, this spirit was originally a Phrygian demon. Marsayas was adopted and transformed to a status similar to that of Silenus after the occupation of the Phrygian lands by the Greeks. The story of Marsayas tells how he found the discarded *aulos* (flute) invented by the goddess Athena, and learned how to play it so well that he challenged the god Apollo to a musical contest. It was agreed that the winner would do whatever he wanted with the loser. Marsayas lost, and for his presumption was flayed alive, his flowing blood forming the river that now takes his name.

References 88, 93
See also Demon, Silenus, Spirit

MARTHIM
See Bathym

MARTINKO
See Rumpelstiltskin

MARUT
See Haruts

MARZANNA
This is the name of a female field spirit in the folklore of Poland. She promoted the growth and ripening of the fruit before harvest. Marzanna was likely derived from an earlier deity.
References 102
See also Spirit, Appendix 18

MASAN
This is a hideous black disease demon in the folk beliefs of the Hindus in India. It may take the form of a bear or a cloud of ash. This evil spirit is said to emerge from the embers of a funeral pyre and inflict diseases on any child over whom it flings ashes.
References 88
See also Demon, Appendix 17, Appendix 22

MASKIMS
In the religion of the ancient Chaldeans, this was the name given to a group of seven evil spirits against whom the use of pieces of the white cedar tree was said to provide protection.
References 110
See also Spirit

MASSARIOL
This is a dwarf in the folklore of northeastern Italy. He is described as resembling a tiny human with a beard and moustache, wearing red stockings, breeches, jacket, and pointed cloth cap. He was a farm spirit, like the nis of Denmark, equally at home with the tasks of the stable and barn as well as the house. Massariol was a "ladies' man," and when not occupied with work in the stable, could be found in the kitchen flirting with the young maids.
References 38
See also Brownie, Dwarf, Lob-Lie-by-the-Fire, Nis, Robin Goodfellow, Spirit, Tomtar, Appendix 22

MASTÊMÉ
This is one of the Fallen Angels in the Christian literature that tradition said desires a return to Paradise.
References 87
See also Fallen Angel

MASTER DOBBS
See Dobbs

MAT CHINOI
In the folk beliefs of the Semang people of the Malaysian forests, this is the name of the chief of the Little People known as Chinoi. These spirits, like the European fairies, inhabit trees, flowers, and vegetation. Mat Chinoi takes the form of a huge snake, sheltering within his body many of the female Chinoi with their headdresses and fine garments, while on his body he carries a male Chinoi called Halak Gihmal, who is their guardian. An elaborate series of tests must be completed by any male Chinoi before Mat Chinoi will allow them to choose one of the females carried within his body. The Chinoi are called upon by the Semang shamans to help with magic and medicine.
References 88
See also Fairy, Guardian, Little People, Appendix 18

MATABIRI
In the beliefs of the people of Papua New Guinea, the Matabiri are particularly malevolent swamp demons. They are described as appearing in the shape of humans with large bellies and puffed cheeks. They will take every opportunity to bring misfortune to any human who falls into their power.
References 33
See also Demon, Appendix 25

MATAGAIGAI
These are malignant tree spirits in the folk beliefs of the people of Papua New Guinea. Although they appear in the shape of humans, the females are recognizable as being supernaturals from the fact that they have one breast smaller than the other. They can be seen only by people who are sick, and if these spirits manage to poke their fingers into the patient, death is imminent.
References 33
See also Spirit, Appendix 19

MATARISVAN
In the classical Vedic mythology of India, this is the name of the spirit messenger of the gods. Matarisvan was charged with bringing fire to the Rishis.
References 41
See also Angiris, Spirit

MĀTE
The designation of a nature spirit in the folk beliefs of the Latvian people, this term is derived from an earlier deity and means Mother. It now forms a suffix to other names, denoting the status or area of responsibility for the nature spirits.

References 88
See also Jūrasmāte, Laukumāte, Matergabia, Mežasmāte, Spirit

MATERGABIA
This is a female household spirit in the folklore of the Slav people. She directed the work of the kitchen and the organization of domestic activities. To make sure that all would be well, housewives would offer the first piece of bread from the kneading trough to gain Matergabia's protection for the home.
References 102
See also Dugnai, Household Spirit, Kikimora, Krimba, Appendix 22

MATIYA
These are a type of malignant fairy in the folk beliefs of the Romany Gypsies. The Matiya appear as beautiful young maidens. They have an innate need to multiply, but because they have no male counterparts, they entice unwary human males to lie with them. The fate of the human male is his immediate death, while his malicious supernatural partner transforms to a hag that produces three sets of beautiful, identical female twins to perpetuate their kind.
References 31
See also Ana, Fairy, Hag, Keshalyi

MAUARI
These are benevolent water spirits in the folk beliefs of the Maipure and Bamba people of Venezuela. The Mauari belong to a larger group of spirits called the Gamainhas.
References 110
See also Gamainhas, Spirit, Appendix 25

MAUG MOULACH
See Mieg Moulach

MAUG VULUCHD
See Mieg Moulach

MAUI
This is the great trickster spirit in the mythology and beliefs of the Hawaiian, Polynesian, Maori, and other peoples of the Pacific Islands. Although large grotesque representations of Maui are carved on important buildings, he is described as like a diminutive human reared by an ancestor spirit. Maui's supernatural exploits include bringing up earth from the bottom of the Pacific to form the Pacific Islands, trying to lengthen the day by lassoing the sun, and tricking the mud hens into giving him the secret of fire. All of these pranks irritated the deities, and Maui was constantly making reparation. According to one legend, he met his demise when the goddess of the

underworld crushed him after he had transformed himself into a caterpillar.

References 33, 56, 119
See also Anansi, Blue Jay, Coyote, Spirit, Trickster

MÁURARI

This is a malevolent spirit in the folk beliefs of the Maipure and Bamba people of Venezuela.

References 88
See also Spirit

MAUTHE DHOOG, MAUTHE DOOG

This is the evil spirit, also known as the Moddey Dhoo, of Peel Castle on the Isle of Man (United Kingdom). It manifests in the shape of a Black Dog described variously as the size of a calf with eyes like pewter plates, or a spaniel with shaggy hair, that may materialize and inflict harm on all who see it. There are numerous accounts of people who have some experience of the demon, often with variations in the events and outcome. One such tale refers to the time that Peel Castle was occupied by military forces in the seventeenth century. A bored soldier on guard duty, after a few drinks, bragged that he would search for the supernatural fiend. His terrified shrieks brought his fellow officers to the corridor where he lay, and they dragged him back to the guardroom, jabbering about the "Dhoog," before he died. A similar fate befell a Methodist minister brought in to exorcise the evil spirit.

References 69
See also Barguest, Black Dog, Black Shuck, Boggart, Bullbeggar, Capelthwaite, Church Grim, Demon, Fiend, Freybug, Gytrash, Padfoot, Rongeur d'Os, Skriker, Spirit

MAWMETS

A familiar euphemism in England for the fairies, it means Little Mothers.

References 10
See also Fairy, Appendix 6

MAYOCHINA

In the folk beliefs of the Acoma Pueblo Native American people, this is the name of the spirit of summer.

References 25
See also Spirit

MAZIKEEN, MAZZIKIN

These are demons in Jewish mythology that equate with the Arabic djinn. Mazikeen, known also as Shedeem, are said to be the offspring of Adam after his fall from grace and eviction from the Garden of Eden, but before the birth of Cain and Abel. These demons, according to Jewish folklore, still exist to taunt humans. The Mazikeen can take on any shape

Mauthe Dhoog, an evil spirit, can cause harm to anyone who sees it.

to cause havoc, discord, and mischief. One familiar story tells of a lazy servant who neglected his duty of rousing the community for the midnight prayers. Realizing the lateness of the hour, he climbed onto the back of an ass that appeared, and which to his amazement grew and grew. Unable to dismount from the height of its back onto the street, he was obliged to dismount onto the top of the tallest building in the city, where he was found the following morning. This "tall" story gave rise to the expression of disbelief "to swell out like a Mazikeen ass."

References 40, 93
See also Demon, Djinn

MBŌN

In the beliefs of the Kachin people of Burma, this is a powerful nat. He is the guardian or demon of the winds, to whom propitiation is made during the harvest festivities.

References 88
See also Chinün Way Shun, Demon, Guardian, Nats, Appendix 10, Appendix 26

MEBD, MEADHBH

This is the name of a queen of the Tuatha dé Danann and of the Sidhe of Connaught in Irish mythology and folklore. She was said to have had several husbands, as she would not allow a king to rule in Tara unless he took her as his wife. Hers is possibly the derivation of the name of the fairy Queen Mab of later folklore.

References 105
See also Fairy, Mab, Sídhe, Tuatha dé Danann

MEBEDDEL
This is the term for the changeling in the folklore of Morocco. It is left by a djinn in the place of a human child just after its birth. The Mebeddel, unlike a human child, will become wizened, ugly, and thin no matter how much attention it receives. If the mother manages to spot the exchange in time, she may effect the return of her own child. In order to do this she must take the Mebeddel to the graveyard and find a broken tomb, where she must place the Mebeddel with an offering for the djinns. Having done this she will move away, not returning until she hears her own baby's cry, when she will quickly come back to pick up the baby, saying "I have taken my own child and not that of the Other People." Then she must wash her child with holy water and return home.
References 90
See also Changeling, Djinn, Appendix 22

MEDEINE
In the folklore of Lithuania, this is a nature spirit. She is known as the mistress of the forest, and is the guardian of everything in the forests. Her male counterpart is Giráitis.
References 88
See also Guardian, Spirit, Appendix 19

MEDR
In the ancient mythology of Ethiopia, this is an earth spirit.
References 93
See also Spirit

MEG MOLLOCH
See Mieg Moulach

MEGHAMALIN
In the classical mythology and legends of India, this is a demon that attacked Parsva.
References 93
See also Demon

MEHEN
This is the name of a spirit in the beliefs of ancient Egypt. Mehen is described as the guardian attendant of the sun god Ra, and is portrayed as a supernatural serpent.
References 29
See also Apep, Attendant Spirit, Nagas, Spirit

MEKALA
In the folk beliefs of the Aymara people of Bolivia, this is a fearsome evil spirit. This female disease demon caused the fields to decay and the cattle to die.
References 88
See also Achachilas, Demon, Spirit, Appendix 17

MEKUMWASUK
This is the name of a group of the Little People in the folk beliefs of the Passamaquaddy Native American people. These spirits are described as being about three feet high, looking like brightly dressed, ugly humans with their faces entirely covered in hair. They inhabit the woods and wild places, and are said to be the guardian spirits of the Catholic churches in the area. Unlike the Nagumwasuk, these spirits are somewhat malicious and will cause contagious sickness or grave misfortune to any human who stares at them.
References 17
See also Guardian, Little People, Nagumwasuk, Spirit

MELALO
In the folk beliefs of the Romany Gypsies, this is a male disease demon whose name means Dirty or Obscene. This evil spirit was the result of the union between Ana and the king of the demons, when she had eaten the brains of a magpie. He is described as being like a two-headed dirty green bird and having sharp talons. This spirit will render the victim senseless and tear into their hearts and bodies. When the human recovers from the swoon, he is inflicted with unreasonable rage, which may induce him to rape and murder, or to utter the senseless babblings of the madman.
References 31
See also Bitoso, Demon, Keshalyi, Loçolico, Schilalyi, Spirit, Appendix 17

MƏLANDƏ BODƏZ
This is the name of a keremet in the folk beliefs of the Cheremis/Mari people of the former Soviet Republic. Mәlandә Bodәz means Earth Spirit.
References 118
See also Keremet

MƏLANDƏ PEREŠTA
See Perešta

MƏLANDƏ ŠƏRT
This is a keremet or evil spirit in the folklore of the Cheremis/Mari people of the former Soviet Republic. Mәlandә Šәrt means Earth Devil and is a fearsome spirit that is placated by an offering of pancakes and beer.
References 118
See also Čort, Keremet, Spirit

MELETE
See Muses

MELIÆ
The name of nymphs in the classical mythology of Greece and Rome that were created from the drops of

blood from Uranus. This is also the name of nymphs that nursed the infant Jupiter.
References 130
See also Adrastea, Furies, Hagno, Kollimalaikanniyarka, Nymph, Appendix 22

MELIOR
See Melusina

MÉLISANDE
See Melusina

MELISSA
This was an epithet often given to nymphs in the classical mythology of Greece and Rome because they were frequently transformed into bees as the guardian spirits of nature and nurture.
References 130
See also Guardian, Nymph, Appendix 12

MELOBOSIS
This is the name of a nymph in the classical mythology of Greece and Rome who is particularly concerned with feeding sheep.
References 130
See also Nymph, Appendix 12

MELOSINÆ
See Undine

MELPOMENE
See Muses

MELSH DICK, MELCH DICK
In the folklore of West Riding of Yorkshire, England, this is a nature spirit. Melsh Dick is the sprite that protected the hazel trees and their ripening nuts from being damaged by children or taken too soon. Any offenders were severely punished by him with a bout of stomach cramps.
References 17
See also Churnmilk Peg, Nursery Bogie, Spirit, Sprite, Appendix 18, Appendix 22

MELUSINA, MELUSINE
The story of Melusina was already well known in French folk history before it was written down by Jean d'Aras in 1388. Melusine was the daughter of Pressina, the fairy guardian of a fountain, by a mortal king, Elinus of Albany (Scotland). When these two married, it was on the fairy pledge that he should never see her in childbed. Like all such legendary fairy promises, it was broken and he saw her at the last of the births. The broken vow deprived him of his wife and their three daughters—Melusine, Melior, and Platina—who were compelled to return to their fairy court. When these daughters assumed their full supernatural powers, they took revenge on their father, sealing him forever in a cave in Northumbria. Realizing what they had done, Pressina cursed each of her daughters, and Melusine was to become a water serpent from her waist to her feet once a week. It was decreed that she would never experience love until she found someone who agreed not to see her on that day, and if this were broken, she would be condemned to exist only as a hideous winged snake. Melusine met and married Count Raymond of Poitiers, who built the Chateau of Lusignan for her. Most of their children were deformed from the start in some awful manner, but the last two were normal. Eventually the count also broke his vow, and Melusine leaped from the castle ramparts to eternity as the winged serpent mermaid, leaving a noble line of descendants, claimed to be the ancestors of the French monarchy.
References 17, 18, 44, 114, 133
See also Büt Ian Üdəržə, Fairy, Guardian, Mermaid

MEMPHIS
This is the name of a water nymph in the classical mythology of Greece and Rome who was the daughter of the Nile river god. Her name was given to the city of the Egyptians on the River Nile and, later, a city in Tennessee.
References 130
See also Nymph, Appendix 25

MENARA
In the classical Hindu mythology of India, she is a celestial nymph sent to charm and distract Visvamitra from his devotions.
References 114
See also Nymph, Appendix 13

MEPHISTOPHALES
This is the name of the tempter fiend or familiar. His character known also by the variants Mephistopheles, Mephistophiles, Mephistophilis, Mephostophilus, Mefistofele, and Mephisto was well established in the folklore of early Renaissance Europe. He appears in the literature of Marlowe, Shakespeare, and Fletcher in England, and in the story of Faust in the French opera by Gounod as well as in the German poem by Goethe. The story relates how all the riches and knowledge so desired by Faust may be attained at the expense of his soul. This infernal contract is negotiated not by a hideous fiend, but by the urbane and elegantly cynical devil Mephistophales. This pact requires the supernatural to become the servant of Faust until death, and the fulfillment of the contract with the surrender of the mortal's soul to the Devil.

References 40, 93, 114
See also Asmodee, Devil

MERA

This is the name of a nymph in the classical mythology of Greece and Rome. She was the lover of Zeus.
References 102, 130
See also Nymph

MERIHIM

See Devils

MERMAID/E, MEREMAIDEN

This is the name of a female water spirit in the form of a beautiful young woman from the head to the waist; the rest of her body is like the tail of a fish. Mermaids have been part of folklore and mythology of maritime and freshwater cultures since ancient times. The derivation of the name means both sea- and lake-maiden. They are often seen sitting on rocks, holding a mirror and combing their long hair while singing. This singing allies them to the siren, luring sailors to their doom. The ancient accounts, as well as the more modern ones, mention the appearance of these supernaturals in conjunction with misfortune and disaster, although occasionally they can be benevolent. When rescued, they have given the knowledge of herbal cures for fatal sicknesses, rich gifts, and warnings of storms. (These particular tales are told in Scotland, Wales, and Cornwall, England.) They may marry with humans, their offspring having webbed feet and fingers, but usually return to their watery world, where their consorts are called Mermen. A rich tradition of folktales and songs about Mermaids exists in cultures all around the world.
References 15, 17, 18, 40, 47, 56, 59, 88, 87, 92, 114, 123, 132, 134
See also Ben Varrey, Bonito Maidens, Ceasg, Clytie, Gwenhidwy, Havfrue, Imanja, Jamaína, Lamia, Liban, Mari Morgan, Melusine, Merman, Merrow, Roane, Saivo-Neita, Selkie, Siren, Spirit, Appendix 25

MERMAN

This is the male counterpart of the water spirit known as the mermaid. Like her, he appears in the form of a human above the waist with green hair and beard, and like a fish below. The Mermen have a fearsome reputation for bringing violent storms and sinking ships. In British legends they are also thought to be aggressive toward the mermaids and even devour their own offspring, whereas the Scandinavian Havmand is more benevolent. The Merman also has an ancient tradition from the Abgal of ancient Sumer, the Arabic Abdullah al-Kazwini, to the strange tales of the Blue Men of the Minch in the Hebridean Islands off the coast of Scotland.

References 18, 47, 88, 92, 123
See also Abdullah al-Kazwini, Abgal, Blue Men of the Minch, Havmand, Mermaid, Näkki, Spirit

MEROPE

This is the name of a nymph in the classical mythology of Greece and Rome who was one of the Pleiades. She is said to shine less brilliantly in the heavens than her sisters because she had earlier married the mortal Sisyphus.
References 130
See also Nymph, Pleiades, Appendix 13

MERROW

This is the name of the Irish Mer-people, who may also be called the Murdhuacha, Moruadh, Moruach, Muir-Gheilt, Samhghubha, or Suire. The mermaids appear as beautiful young women above the waist with pale skin, dark eyes, and long hair, but as a fish below the waist. Their mermen are ugly, with green skin, teeth, and hair, but a sharp red nose and tiny, narrow eyes. They all have webbed fingers, and are able to shape shift from the appearance of land animals or humans to that of marine dwellers by means of a magic, red feather cap. If this cap is stolen, they are unable to return to their underwater world, and often this is how a mortal man may gain a Merrow bride. The Merrows are usually of a peaceful and

benevolent nature toward humans, often intermarrying; their children may have webbed feet and fingers, and even a scaly skin.
References 15, 17, 18, 123
See also Melusina, Mermaid, Roane, Selkie, Appendix 25

MERRY DANCERS, THE
See Fir Chlis

MESNIE HELLEQUIN, MESNIE HERLEQUIN
This is the name used in France for the Wild Hunt, also known as L'Armée Furieuse and Chasse de Caïn. It is sometimes said to be led by Charlemagne, with the hero Roland carrying the banner at his side. The Mesnie Hellequin is believed to be a portent of disaster, plague, or war, and was reported to have ridden through the skies, twice darkening the sun, before the outbreak of the French Revolution (1789).
References 95
See also Armée, Furieuse, Chasse de Hérode, Wild Hunt, Appendix 23

MESTRE BELAMINO
See Guapindaia

MESTRE MARAJÓ
See Caboclo

METATRON
This is the name of an angel or benevolent demon in Hebrew tradition. Metatron is mentioned in the Kabbalah as the custodian of strength and receiving the prayers of humans to glorify the Lord.
References 53, 93
See also Angel, Demon

METSÄNHALTIA
This is a nature spirit who is the guardian or "ruler" of the forests, in the folk beliefs of the Estonian and Finnish people. He is described as looking like an old man with a gray beard, wearing a garment made of forest lichens. Like the Leshii, he can shape shift to the size of trees or the smallest blade of grass.
References 88
See also Guardian, Haldde, Haldjas, Kodinhaltia, Laskowice, Leshii, Spirit, Talonhaltija, Vedenhaltia, Appendix 19

METSANNEITSYT
This is a female forest spirit of western Finland known as the Forest Maiden. Her appearance is that of a beautiful young woman, and she will entice any unwary human youth to go with her farther into the forest. This spirit's deception may be revealed if her victim can see her from behind, because she is no more than a fine facade concealing a bundle of twigs, a stump of wood, or a hollow log.
References 88
See also Elle Folk, Huldra, La, Llorona, Metsänhaltia, Spirit, Appendix 19

METSHALDJAS
This is a nature spirit in the folklore of the northern Estonians. He is a demon of the forests whose plaintive cry is a portent of misfortune.
References 88, 87
See also Demon, Haldde, Haltia, Koduhaldjas, Leshii, Majahaldjas, Metsänhaltia, Spirit, Appendix 19

METSIK
This is the name of a forest sprite or demon in the folklore of the people of Estonia. It is said that unless he is propitiated correctly, he will work mischief with the cattle and even cause them injury.
References 110
See also Demon, Sprite

MEŽASMÄTE
This is the name of a female nature spirit whose name, also spelled Meža mäte, means Mother of the Forest in the folk beliefs of the Latvian people. She is the guardian spirit of the forests and the creatures that live there. Mežasmäte ensures that the hunters have enough game to feed their families. She has a male consort known as Mežatēus, or Father of the Forest.
References 88, 93
See also Guardian, Spirit, Ūdensmäte, Appendix 12, Appendix 19

MEZATEUS MEŽATĒUS
See Mežasmäte

MHORAG
In the folklore of Scotland, this is the name of the mermaid that inhabited Loch Morar. She behaves in a similar way to the banshee of Ireland, as she only reveals herself when a member of the clan is about to die.
References 99
See also Banshee, Mermaid, Appendix 16

MI FEI
In the mythology of China, this female water spirit is a river spirit and the daughter of Fu Hsi.
References 131
See also Spirit, Appendix 25

MICHAEL
This is the name of an Archangel who is one of the four chief angels in Judeo-Christian scriptures. Michael is known as the "warrior," and he is the main adversary of the supreme evil, Satan, after the

latter's expulsion from heaven. Michael is portrayed as a tall, shining, youthful male spirit clad in either white garments or golden armor, from which huge white wings protrude. He may be depicted with a sword and shield defeating a dragon, or as carrying a set of scales, upon which he will weigh the souls of the risen dead on the Day of Judgment. In the religion of Islam, Michael is also one of the Archangels mentioned in the Koran, and he is regarded as the champion of the Faith. Michael is said to have appeared to a herdsman on Mount Garganus in A.D. 492, and the Christian feast day of 8 May commemorates this. The cult of this Archangel in the Christian faith was at its height during the Middle Ages when many churches and the feast day of Saint Michael and All Angels, 29 September (Michaelmas Day), were dedicated to him. In the astrological calendar, he was associated with the planet Mercury in early Jewish writings, but with the sun in medieval Christian astrology.

References 39, 40, 56, 119

See also Angel, Archangel, Guardian Angel, Israfil, Mika'il, Rashnu, Spirit

MICOL

This is the name of a fairy invoked by European medieval sorcerers. She is said by Magicians of the seventeenth century to be the Fairy Queen of the diminutive Trooping Fairies.

References 17

See also Fairy

MIDAR, MIDHIR

This is the name of one of the kings of the Tuatha dé Danann in the mythology and folklore of Ireland. The abode of Midar was Brí Léith, now known as Slieve Golry, in County Longford. There are two versions of his winning the love of the mortal queen Etain. According to the Ancient Legends of Ireland by Lady Wild, Etain was the wife of Eochaid of Munster, from whom the fairy lord won her in a game of chess. Another legend tells how Midhir chose Etain as his second wife, but his jealous first wife, Fuarnnach, changed Etain into a midge. After a long search, Midhir found her with Eochaid, and won her back in a game of chess. Midhir changed Etain and himself into two swans linked by a golden chain and flew home, only to be confronted by Eochaid and his armies. After many bitter battles Etain eventually returned to Eochaid, her mortal husband.

References 17, 18, 105

See also Finvarra, Liban, Tuatha dé Danann

MIEG MOULACH

This is a household spirit of the brownie type that was attached to the Grant family of Tullochgorm (Strathspey) in Scotland. She was also known as Hairy Meg, Maug Moulach, Maggie or May Moloch, and Meg Molloch. Some accounts say her "son" was Brownie Clod. Mieg Moulach not only performed the usual brownie labors for the household, including assisting the chief of the clan in beating his opponents at chess, she also announced the death of family members by weeping like a banshee. It is unclear whether she is the same spirit as Maug Vuluchd, or the Maggie Molloch that did brownie duties at the farmhouse of Achnarrow in Glenlivet. Each is also a formidable household spirit.

References 15, 17, 18, 40, 47, 114

See also Banshee, Brownie, Brownie Clod, Household Spirit, Appendix 22

MIEHTS-HOZJIN

This is a nature spirit in the traditions and folk beliefs of the Lapp people. Miehts-Hozjin, whose name means Master of the Forest, is described as being dark and having a tail. It was prudent to be quiet in the forests, for if the Miehts-Hozjin heard any human, he would delight in leading them astray.

References 6

See also Leib-Olmai, Spirit, Will o' the Wisp, Appendix 19

MIGAMAMESUS

This is the name of a type of dwarf or elf, also possibly called Mikamwes, in the folklore and legends of the Micmac Native American people. These Little People were said to inhabit the forests of the Gaspé Mountains, where they would dance in the moonlit glades and play tricks on any humans who ventured there.

References 99, 110

See also Dwarf, Elf, Little People

MIGUELZINHO BOA DA TRINIDADE

This is a powerful encantado in the Afro-Brazilian cult Batuque. He is said to be the "son" of Legua Bogi da Trinidade and the "grandson" of Dom Pedro Angaço. He is associated with Saint Michael and his feast day of 29 September.

References 89

See also Dom Pedro Angaço, Encantado, Legua Bogi da Trinidade

MIKA

See Tündér

MIKA'IL

This is the name of the angel Michael in the Islamic beliefs of the people of West Malaysia. He is believed to be the giver of daily bread.

References 120

See also Angel, Mala'ikat, Michael

MIKAK'E
This is the name of the supernatural spirits in the beliefs of the Osage Native American people. They are also known as the Star People.
References 25
See also Spirit

MIKAMWES
See Migamamesus

MIMI
These are spirits, also called Mini, in the folk beliefs of Australia. They inhabit the rocky wastes of Arnhem Land, where they materialize in a human form, but with exceedingly long, thin, brittle bones. (Both humans and yams are the food of the Mimi.) They have a fear of the wind, which will snap their bones and destroy them, so they never appear when the wind is blowing. It is therefore safe for humans to go out in the wind.
References 29, 102
See also Spirit

MIMIR
In the mythology of Scandinavia, this is the name of a giant water demon. He was one of the Jotuns, and the guardian spirit of the Well of Inspiration and Wisdom that lay at the roots of Yggdrasil, the World Tree. When Odin, the king of the gods, wanted to drink from this well, Mimir made him leave an eye in payment for the knowledge that would be thus acquired. Mimir was taken hostage in battle by the Vanir, who beheaded him. Odin retrieved Mimir's head, which continued to advise the lord of the gods.
References 56, 93, 95, 114, 119
See also Demon, Guardian

MIMRING
In the Teutonic and Scandinavian legends, this is the name of a dwarf or wood demon. He was famed for his craftsmanship in metals, especially forging magic swords.
References 95
See also Alberich, Demon, Dwarf, Appendix 4, Appendix 14

MINCESKRO
In the folk beliefs of the Romany Gypsies, this is a female disease demon. This evil spirit was the result of Ana's desire to become sterile after producing so many demon offspring. The cure advised by Melalo was to cover herself up to the neck in a dung heap. But a dung beetle entered her body and was born as Minceskro. She is particularly responsible for diseases of the blood, but her progeny by Lolmischo cause measles, scarlet fever, and smallpox.

References 31
See also Ana, Con-Ma-Dāu, Demon, Loçolico, Lolmischo, Melalo, Šedra Kuba and Šedra Kuguza, Spirit, Tou Shen, Appendix 17

MINE SPIRITS, MINE GOBLINS
These are the spirits that inhabit the mines and tunnels for extracting coal, gold, iron, tin, and other precious commodities. They are usually described as resembling the miners in their dress and habits, but have old, wizened, bearded faces. They can be heard working in parallel seams, drilling, blasting, shoveling, and rolling barrows, but they are rarely seen. The miners who respect and propitiate them are rewarded with the knowledge of rich seams and the advance warning of roof falls and other possible disasters. Those miners who do not respect the supernaturals have pranks played on them and are visited by misfortune and disaster. The Mine Goblins and Spirits detailed in this book have various names: Blue Cap, Bucca, Cobalt, Coblyn, Cutty Soams, Dwarfs, Garthornes, Gnomes, Haus-Schmiedlein, Knockers, Kobold, Nickel, and Wichtlein.
References 17
See also Eshu, Goblin, Spirit

MINGEHE
In the folk beliefs of the Lele people of West Africa, these are forest spirits. They can be both malevolent and benevolent, and are invoked by sorcerers to bring fertility to their people and also to the game that they hunt in the forest.
References 33
See also Spirit, Appendix 12, Appendix 19

MINI
See Mimi

MINK
This is the trickster transformer and culture spirit of numerous legends in the beliefs of the Native American people of the North Pacific Coastal Region. He is both deceitful and clever, being considered responsible for redistributing mountains and providing fresh water and animals for humans. The exploits of this supernatural, such as trying to steal the sun, are as varied and outrageous as those of his southern counterpart, Blue Jay. Like Blue Jay, his amorous adventures often end in his being outwitted by more powerful spirits or in the failure of his own cunning.
See also Blue Jay, Coyote, Kutkinnáku, Kwati, Napi, Spirit, Trickster

MIREN
See Fati

MIRU, MIRU KURA

This is the name of an ugly, deformed female demon of the underworld in the myths of the Mangaia people of the Pacific Islands. There are numerous earthly places where the departing souls of humans set off for the spirit world, known as Avaiki, Haw-aii, or Hawaiki. On the island of Mangaia, the souls depart from a high sea cliff onto a bua tree that emerges for them from the sea, extending the particular branch reserved for their tribe toward the soul. When the soul is on its branch, the tree retracts to the underworld, where all the souls fall off the branches into a net held by a group of demons led by Akaanga. The souls are delivered to Miru Kura, whose name means Ruddy, from the infernal fires she tends. She cooks the souls in the flames of hell and devours them. She was said to be the mother of the fairies known as Tapairu, Kumu-Tonga-I-Te-Po, and Karaia-I-Te-Ata. Miru Kura was eventually defeated by Ngaru, who caused a great flood, putting out the fires on which she roasted her victims.
References 41, 110
See also Demon, Fairy

MISS NANCY
See Anansi

MIST
See Valkyries

MITHRA, MITHRAS, MITRA

This spirit was perhaps originally a human raised to the status of divinity. Mithra was an important deity of ancient Assyria. His cult was adopted into the pantheon of India, where he became known in the Rig Veda as Mitra, one of the Adityas, but he vanished from mention in legend after the development of Hindu Brahmanism. The cult of Mithra, under the name of Mithras, was adopted in the occident as a secret sect spread within the Roman army, but the Christian religion with which it had much in common extinguished its universal acceptance. The name survives in the form of the name of an attendant of the Amesha Spentas, Kshathra, in the Zoroastrian religion of Persia where Mithra was once a deity in his own right.
References 39, 40, 56, 114, 119
See also Amesha Spentas, Attendant Spirit, Kshathra, Spirit

MMOATIA

This is the name of a group of Little People in the folk beliefs of West Africa. The Mmoatia are considered to be the guardian spirits of the forest, the bush, and the wild creatures that inhabit these places, in the folklore of the Ashanti people.
References 88
See also Apuku, Aziza, Bakru, Guardian, Ijimere, Little People, Pukkumeria, Appendix 12

MNEME
See Muses

MOČA KUBA AND MOČA KUGUZA

These are the male and female personifications of the spirit of the bathhouse in the folklore of the Cheremis/Mari people of the former Soviet Republic. The names Moča Kuba and Moča Kuguza mean Bathhouse Old Woman and Bathhouse Old Man, respectively, and they are reported as appearing like elderly humans with long hair. This bathhouse spirit may also be known as Moča Ia, which means Bathhouse Devil; Moča Oza, which means Bathhouse Master; or Jarčik. The spirit is the inhabitant of the bathhouse, and may be heard there at night. Sometimes it may be bathing and using the equipment left there for it; at other times it may moan or cry like a child locked in. When a new bathhouse is built, butter is left on the sweat benches to please the spirits and ensure good saunas. Moča Kuba may be asked by those with a cold to chase away the spirit of mucus, Run Kuguza, or any other bad spirit that has accompanied the human to the bathhouse.
References 118
See also Bannik, Kuba, Kuguza, Run Kuguza, Spirit, Appendix 22

MOČA IA
See Moča Kuba

MOČA OZA
See Moča Kuba

MOČA ŠƏRT

This is a keremet or evil spirit in the folklore of the Cheremis/Mari people of the former Soviet Republic. Moča Šərt means Bathhouse Devil, and is a particularly malevolent supernatural. It is placated by the sacrifice of a bull in order to prevent it from causing deaths in the bathhouse, as the Bannik does in Russian folklore.
References 118
See also Bannik, Čort, Keremet, Spirit, Appendix 22

MODDEY DHOO
See Mauthe Dhoog

MODEINA

This is the name of a nature spirit in the folklore of Poland. It is the guardian spirit of the forests.
References 102
See also Guardian, Spirit, Appendix 19

MODSOGNIR

This is the name of the leader of a group of dwarfs in Scandinavian and Teutonic mythology. Modsognir and his fellow dwarfs are renowned for their ability in forging magic weapons and creating metal objects of supernatural strength and beauty.
References 78, 87
See also Dwarf, Mimring, Appendix 4, Appendix 14

MŒRÆ

See Moiræ

MOIRÆ, MOIRAI

In the mythology of ancient Greece, these are the spirits, also called the Mœræ who were known in Roman mythology as the Fates. These are the birth spirits who, in the changed spelling of Moirai, are still thought in modern Greece to appear in the room of the newborn child three nights after its birth to determine the child's destiny. Not surprisingly, the parents leave propitiatory offerings for the spirits on that evening beside the cradle of their child in order to ensure the blessings of the Moirai.
References 12, 39, 88
See also Béfind, Fates, Oosood, Spirit, Appendix 22, Appendix 23

MOKOTITI

See Atua

MOKSIN TONGBŎP

These are a type of imp, much like the Nanggu Moksin, in the folk beliefs of the people of Korea. These supernaturals are wood imps in that they inhabit objects that are wooden, and are particularly malevolent beings. They may be inadvertently brought into the home with firewood or with timber for shelves. They will also enter houses, hidden in new wooden items crossing the threshold for the first time, on an inauspicious day. If not detected and exorcised by a *Mansin* (female shaman), the Moksin Tongbŏp will be the source of future family illness and discord.
References 79
See also Chisin Tongbŏp, Imp, Nanggu Moksin, Appendix 19

MOLANHAKTO

In the beliefs of the Pueblo Native American people, this spirit, also known as Father Koyemshi, is the leader of the Kachinas.
References 88
See also Kachina, Koyemshi, Spirit

MOLONGA

This is an evil spirit in the beliefs of the Native Australians of Queensland. It is invisible, but would destroy men and violate any women it meets unless propitiated.
References 48
See also Spirit

MONDZO

This is an evil spirit, said in a report of 1865 to inhabit the area of the Bonny River in Nigeria.
References 57
See also Spirit

MONKER AND NAKIR

In the traditions of Islam, these are two black angels. They are described as being of terrifying aspect and thunderous voices. These angels are charged with questioning the newly dead concerning their lives and faith. If the answers are pious, the soul is gently drawn to Paradise. If the person can give no acceptable response, the human's body is beaten with flaming iron cudgels, while the soul is dragged to everlasting torment in hell.
References 114
See also Angel, Appendix 16

MONOCIELLO

This is a type of dwarf or elf in the folklore of Naples in Italy. He is known as the Little Monk because his shape is that of a corpulent friar; he wears sandals on his feet and holds a staff. However, his habit is not brown but bright scarlet, like his ecclesiastical hat. He inhabits houses, where he is far from pious in his behavior, for he will indulge in pinching the bodies of humans or stealing their clothes. He is reputed to be the guardian of a great treasure horde, and anyone who sees him and can steal his cardinal's hat will receive part of his treasure as a ransom for its return.
References 38
See also Dwarf, Elf, Friar Rush, Guardian, Appendix 20

MOOINJER VEGGEY, NY

See Sleigh Beggey

MORA, MORAVA, MURAWA

See Mahr

MORE

This is a female nature spirit in the folklore of Lithuania. She is the personification of fertility, and is venerated with an effigy made in her shape on Shrove Tuesday.
References 88
See also Corn Spirit, Kotre, Kuršis, Spirit, Appendix 18

MORGAN

This is an evil water spirit or merman in the folklore of Wales. The Morgan lived in a lake and would take

any unwary or naughty children into its murky depths. This spirit is clearly used as a nursery bogie, but its origins may have been in the Arthurian Morgan le Fay or the Celtic Breton Morgens. The fact that this spirit is male Rhys attributes to the Welsh use of Morgan only as a man's name.
References 17, 88
See also Merman, Morgan, Morgan le Fay, Nursery Bogie, Spirit, Appendix 22

MORGAN LE FAY
This is a mysterious fairy figure and spirit in the legends of King Arthur. She also goes by the names of Fata Morgana, Morgaine, Morgana, Morgane, Morgan la Fée, Morganetta, and Morgue la Faye. Originally, in the Arthurian legend she is the Lady of the Lake and the healing spirit that takes the wounded Arthur to Avalon. In Malory's *Morte Darthur* (ca. 1469), she is Arthur's fairy half sister, who plots the demise of Guinevere and Launcelot, and thus Arthur's eventual downfall. Morgan le Fay also features in other works such as *Ogier the Dane, Orlando Furioso,* and *Orlando Innamorato.* Her magic is also considered to be responsible for the mirages of the Straits of Messina, which are known as Fata Morgana. It has been suggested that she may be derived from a mermaid or a Celtic water deity, and thus connected with the Morrigan of Ireland and the Mari Morgan of Brittany.
References 17, 18, 40, 41, 44, 56, 78, 91, 114, 119, 121, 123
See also Fairy, Lady of the Lake, Mari Morgan, Mermaid, Morrigan, Spirit

MORITYAMA
This is the name of the spirit in the beliefs of the Acoma Native American people that is the personification of spring.
References 25
See also Spirit

MORKUL KUA LUAN
In the beliefs of the Native Australian people, this is a nature spirit. He is the guardian spirit of sorghum grass, which the people use in their daily food.
References 29
See also Guardian, Spirit, Appendix 18

MORMO
This particular name is used in four cultures to denote a particular spirit:
(1) The name of spirits in the beliefs of the Native Australians. These are evil, frightening spirits that materialize as hairy beings.
(2) The name of a female nuisance spirit in the legends of ancient Greece and Rome.
(3) The name given to terrifying bogies in the folk beliefs of modern Greece.

(4) The name of a nursery bogie in seventeenth-century England.
References 41, 93, 107, 130
See also Bogie, Nursery Bogie, Spirit

MOROS
This is the name of a night demon in the folklore of modern Greece. Although it is usually invisible, it may materialize as a little Black Dog that comes into the house behind people in the dark. More often, it descends onto the bodies of humans while they sleep, and like the Ephialtes, crushes the breath out of them. No matter how much the victims of the Moros may moan and groan, no one can wake them up until the Moros has departed, leaving them drained and exhausted.
References 12
See also Black Dog, Cauchemar, Demon, Ephialtes, Incubus, Mara, Nightmare

MOROZKO
This is the name of the frost demon in the folklore of Russia. He hides in the fir trees in the depths of the forest during the bitter winters, and as he snaps his fingers, he splits and shatters the trees. He jumps from tree to tree, creating mischievous damage wherever he passes.
References 110
See also Achachilas, Demon, Father Frost, Jack Frost, Jüštə Kuba, Pokšem Kuba, Appendix 26

MORRIGAN
This is the name of the evil queen of the Tuatha dé Danann of Irish mythology. Her name, also Mórrígu or Mór-ríoghain, identifies her with Badb, Macha, and Neman. She is later mentioned as a degenerated gray-haired hag. In this guise she takes the form of a scaldcrow that leaps across the weapons of the battlefield, using her supernatural skills to direct the course of the battle. It is in this description that she has also been linked with the banshee.
References 105
See also Badb, Ban Nighechain, Banshee, Bodua, Hag, Macha, Neman, Tuatha dé Danann, Valkyries

MORTA
See Parcae

MOSS FOLK, MOSS MAIDENS, MOSS WOMEN
These are a type of elf or wood nymph in the folklore of Germany that may also go by the names of Forest Folk, Wild Folk, Wood Folk, or Wood Wives. They inhabit the forests, and are the guardian spirits of the trees. They are described as tiny Little People in the shape of wizened humans, usually female, whose bodies and faces are entirely covered by the mosses

Enchanted Moss Maidens watch over three napping travelers.

that they weave to clothe the roots of the trees. Their long hair resembles gray lichens from the branches, and their unclothed limbs, hands, and feet are like the gnarled roots of the maple tree. They are generally benevolent toward humans and may help with herbal remedies for sickness, but will exact revenge for any broken saplings. Their main enemy is the Wild Huntsman, who pursues the Moss Folk as his quarry through the forests on stormy nights. In Voightland, this demon is himself said to be one of the Moss Folk.
References 18, 44, 53, 95, 110
See also Demon, Elf, Guardian, Nymph, Spae-wives, Wild Huntsman, Wood Wives, Appendix 19

MOULAY ABDELKADER DJILANI
This is the name of a powerful leader of the djinns in the folklore of Morocco.
References 90
See also Djinn

MR. SPIDER
See Anansi

MRS. BEDONEBYASYOUDID
See Bedonebyasyoudid

MRS. DOASYOUWOULDBEDONEBY
See Doasyouwouldbedoneby

MU
This is one of the nats in the beliefs of the Kachin people of Burma. He is the demon of the sky.
References 39, 53, 88, 110
See also Chinün Way Shun, Demon, Nat, Appendix 10, Appendix 13

MUCHALINDA
This is the name of the king of the Nagas in the Buddhist beliefs of India. In a famous legend, Muchalinda perceived that Buddha was unaware of an approaching violent storm as he meditated under the great Bo tree. The spirit transformed to his Naga serpent shape and coiled himself around both the Bo tree and the Buddha seven times, then spread his hood to give shelter. When the storm had passed, Muchalinda transformed again to the shape of a young man and paid his respects to Buddha.
References 33
See also Nagas, Spirit

MUILEATACH, MUILEATEACH, MUIR LARTEACH
These are the variant names of an evil sea spirit in the folklore of the Scottish Highlands. Like the Cailleach Bheur, Muileatach is described as a hideous, bald hag with a blue-gray face and one staring eye. She lives in a watery Celtic underworld, and when she rises from

it, she causes great storms. Sometimes she emerges from the shore as a dripping, pathetic old woman hammering at the door of fisher folks' cottages, begging for shelter. But no one should ever let her in, because once inside, she swells to an enormous, terrifying size, wreaking havoc within. She can be benevolent, however, for with the pot of balsam she carries, she can heal the sick or wounded. It is said that she can also restore the dead to life by poking her wizened finger in their mouths.
References 88, 123
See also Cailleach Bheur, Hag, Spirit, Appendix 25, Appendix 26

MUIR-GHEILT
This is an alternate name for the mermaid in Irish folklore.
See also Mermaid, Merrow, Appendix 25

MÜKŠ PEREŠTA
See Perešta

MÜKŠ PIAMBAR
See Piambar

MÜKŠ ŠƏRT
This is a keremet or evil spirit in the folklore of the Cheremis/Mari people of the former Soviet Republic. Mükš Šərt means Bee Devil, and to ensure that this devil will not cause problems, it is placated by the sacrifice of a hare, ram, or ewe.
References 118
See also Čort, Keremet, Spirit, Appendix 12

MUMA PADURA
This is a wood fairy or wood nymph in the folklore of the Slav and Rumanian people. She is entirely benevolent and kindly toward humans. Muma Padura inhabits the forests, but will know when a human child has strayed there and become lost. The spirit will then go in search of the child and restore it to its worried parents.
References 41, 110
See also Fairy, Nymph, Appendix 22

MUMPOKER
This is a frightening spirit in English folklore. He is used particularly in the Isle of Wight as a nursery bogie for encouraging children into good behavior.
References 17
See also Nursery Bogie, Spirit, Appendix 22

MUMY
Mumy means Mother, and is the designation of female nature spirits in the folklore of the Finno-Ugric Votyak people of the Vyatka region of Russia.

They are the guardian spirits of a particular phenomenon, and although not envisaged in human form, they are considered to have a soul that strengthens by propitiation. The term Mumy is used as a suffix to the names of other spirits to indicate the relationship to their area of responsibility. Some of these spirits are Gudyri-mumy (Mother of Thunder), Muzem-mumy (Mother of Earth), Šundy-mumy (Mother of the Sun), and Šur-mumy (Mother of the River).
References 88
See also Elder Mother, Guardian, Kornmutter, Maia, Māte, Murt, Onatah, Spirit, Vizi-anya

MUNHERAS
In the Zoroastrian religion of Persia, Munheras is one of the Devs who are evil genii or demons and servants of the supreme evil, Ahriman. Munheras is described in the first combat with the hero Gershab as having the head of a hog, and in the second combat as having two heads, one that of a boar and the other a bull. Although injured by Gershab, Munheras is finally defeated by Sohab, the son of Rootsam.
References 78
See also Deev, Demon, Genius

MUNYA
See Veeta

MURA MURA
These are spirits that inhabit the trees in the Dreamtime beliefs of the Deiri, Kuynai, and Urabunna Native Australian people. The Mura Mura were supernaturals that helped the humans to emerge from their primeval state, giving them stone knives and other implements. Along with the Kutchis, they are invoked by medicine men, the only humans that can see these spirits.
References 41
See also Kutchis, Spirit

MURAWA
See Mahr

MURDHUACHA, MORUADH, MORUACH
See Merrow

MURT
Murt, which means Man, is the designation for a powerful male nature spirit in the folklore of the Votyak people of the Vyatka region of Russia. It is used in much the same way as the name Kuguza in the folk beliefs of the Cheremis people. This name may have originally signified a deity or worship of the dead. The term is used as a suffix to the names of other spirits to denote their region of responsibility in the same manner as the term Mumy.

References 88
See also Gid-murt, Korka-murt, Kuguza, Mumy, Nules-murt, Obin-murt, Spirit, Vu-murt, Yanki-murt

MURUWOOK
In the beliefs of the Native Australians, he is the inland wind spirit and one of the spirit "offspring" of Kompagnin.
References 14
See also Kompagnin, Spirit, Appendix 26

MURYANS
This is a somewhat euphemistic name given to the fairies or the Small People of Cornwall, England. The Muryans, whose name means Ants, are described as extremely beautiful. The men are dressed in green trousers, blue jackets, and black hats, while the ladies wear lace and silver bells. The Muryans would come into the houses of the poor and the sick to entertain them and bring comfort to those who had little. It was believed that the fairies had once been huge supernatural spirits and that they had offended God, but were too good to be condemned to Hell. Their punishment was to exist on the earth, but their size would diminish each time they shape shifted to another form. They have now dwindled to the size of ants, and will ultimately disappear completely. For this reason it was considered imprudent in Cornwall to kill an ant.
References 14
See also Fairy, Little People, Spirit, Appendix 6

MUSES
These are the nymphs or guardian spirits of the arts in the classical mythology of Greece and Rome. Although usually benevolent, they may exact revenge if offended. According to the places they were supposed to inhabit, they were also named the Aganippides, Aonides, Castalides, Corycides, Heliconiades, Libethrides, Olympiades, Parnassides, and Pierides. They were the daughters of the nymph of memory, Mnemosyne, and Zeus (Jupiter), the king of the gods. Each spirit is the patron of one aspect of the arts who entertained the gods in Olympus by singing, playing, and recitation. Originally there were only three: Acede (singing), Melete (meditation), and Mneme (memory), but Hesiod later names others—Calliope (epic poetry), Clio (history), Erato (love poetry), Melpomene (tragedy), Polyhymnia (eloquence), Terpischore (dance), Thalia (comedy), and Urania (astronomy). These nymphs would often hold contests, which they would nearly always win; the losers—like Thamyris, who was blinded—were often given malicious punishments for their audacity. The riddle of the sphinx, solved by Œdipus, was the creation of the Muses.

References 40, 88, 93, 119, 130
See also Guardian, Nymph, Appendix 11,
Appendix 14

MÜY' INGWA

This is the name of a vegetation spirit in the beliefs of
the Hopi Native American people. Müy' ingwa is the
male spirit of the maize plant. He is portrayed as
wearing a red, yellow, green, white, and black mask,
with his body covered in corn; his feet are heads of
corn. He sits in the underworld surrounded by corn,
squash, and beans of different colors, with colorful
birds and butterflies around him. He is one of the
spirits represented in the Kachina dances.
References 45, 88
See also Deohako, Kachina, Kornmutter, Spirit,
Appendix 15

MUŽƏ

This is an evil spirit in the folk beliefs of the
Cheremis/Mari people of the former Soviet Republic.
Mužə, whose name means Illness, is a disease
demon, a personification of the causes of illness. The
name may also be used as a prefix or suffix to another
spirit's name to show the area of its influence.
References 118
See also Demon, Jüštə Mužə, Mužə Gožo, Spirit,
Appendix 17

MUŽƏ GOŽO

This is a term frequently used for all lesser spirits in
the folklore of the Cheremis/Mari people of the former Soviet Republic.
References 118
See also Mužə, Spirit

MUZEM-MUMY

See Mumy

MYRÉNE, MYRSINE

This is the name of a nymph in the classical mythology of Greece and Rome. There are two accounts as
to how she became transformed into the myrtle tree:
(1) Myrsine beat the goddess Athena in a race, and in
a fit of rage the goddess changed the nymph to the
myrtle tree. This version says that later, as a sign of
her remorse, the goddess took the plant as her
emblem. (2) Myréne was the attendant of Venus, who
transformed the nymph for wishing to be married to
her lover and leave the goddess.
References 110
See also Attendant Spirit, Nymph

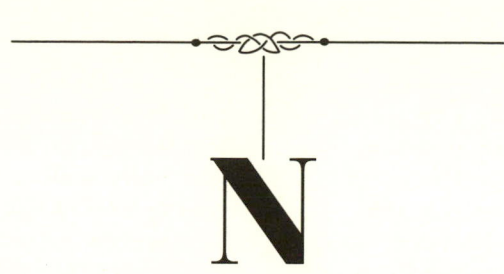

N

NABAEO
An evil spirit in the beliefs of the people of Ruk Island, Melanesia. This spirit may originally have been a benevolent deity, but has since been relegated to the status of a demon.
References 102
See also Demon, Marsaba, Spirit

NÄCKEN
This is a spirit in Scandinavian folklore known as the Water Man. The Näcken was originally a spirit of boundaries, so his appearance on the edge of lakes is in keeping with this first domain. He could shape shift to any form including that of a Bäckahäst, but is most usually seen as a floating log or an upturned boat on the surface of the water.
References 40, 99
See also Bäckahäst, Cabyll-Ushtey, Each Uisge, Kelpie, Spirit, Appendix 25

NAGAS
These are powerful trickster spirits in the myths and legends of India that are described as being human to the waist and a serpent from the waist down. The Nagas live in beautiful underwater palaces with their Nagini wives, who are said to be extremely beautiful. They are ruled by their king, Ananta-Shesha, who protects the god Vishnu, and is equated in the Ramayana with Ravana. The Buddha was protected by a Naga king called Muchalinda, but in general the Nagas' relationship with the deities and humans is ambivalent. In modern Hindu belief, Kārkotaka is the king of the Nagas who control the weather, especially the coming of the rains.
References 33, 56, 88, 102
See also Muchalinda, Nagini Besandi, Ravana, Spirit, Trickster, Appendix 25, Appendix 26

NAGINI BESANDI
This is the name of the Naga wife of Duttabaung, the king of Besandi in the folk beliefs of Burma.
References 30
See also Nagas

NAGINI
See Nagas

NAGLFAR
A dwarf in Scandinavian mythology who was the husband of Noft and one of the builders of the supernatural ship for the Frost Giants.
References 41
See also Dwarf, Appendix 4, Appendix 14

NAGUAL
This is the name of a familiar spirit in the beliefs of the Aztec people of Central America. The Nagual manifested in the form of an animal or other familiar creature and was a tutelary or guardian spirit. It was associated with one individual human from the moment of birth until death and was usually benevolent toward the human, giving guidance and good fortune. As a predatory spirit toward other humans, it was regarded as the being that haunted the night, bringing disease and misfortune.
References 88, 93
See also Agloolik, Àràk, Awl-man, Chin Chia, Familiar, Fylgja, Grine, Guardian, Leib-Olmai, Tutelary Spirit, Zoa, Appendix 12, Appendix 17

NAGUMWASUK
This is the name of the Little People in the folk beliefs of the Passamaquoddy Native American people. These spirits are described as being no more than three feet high and looking like grotesquely ugly humans. They are aware of their ugliness and for this reason rarely make themselves visible. They are the guardian spirits of the Passamaquoddy people and may be heard making merry when there is a human wedding or lamenting when there is a death. To offend them may cause these spirits to exact retribution by inflicting misfortune.
References 17
See also Guardian, Little People, Mekumwasuk, Spirit

NAIAD, NAIADES (pl.)

This is the collective name of a group of water nymphs in the classical mythology of Greece and Rome. The Naiades presided over lakes, rivers, streams, and sometimes fountains. They are portrayed as beautiful maidens with a crown of rushes in their hair, leaning against an urn from which fresh water is flowing. The Naiades are numerous and their individual names are often recorded in legends.
References 20, 40, 62, 92, 114
See also Ægle, Lara, Nymph, Appendix 25

NAIKIYAS

See Naonhaithya

NAIN

There are two different cultures that have this name for spirits in their traditions.
    (1) In Scandinavian mythology this is the name of the dwarf of death.
    (2) In the folklore of France this is the word for dwarf.
References 40
See also Dwarf, Lutin, Nain Rouge, Appendix 16

NAIN ROUGE

This is the dwarf or Lutin in the folklore of Normandy in northern France. Nain Rouge means Red Dwarf, and, as his name implies, this supernatural wears red garments. He is a household spirit who is particularly kind to the families of fishermen. Another of this type of spirit is called Le Petit Homme Rouge, which means the Little Red Man.
References 40
See also Dwarf, Household Spirit, Lutin, Spirit, Appendix 22

NAITAKA

This is a water demon of Lake Okanagan in the folk beliefs of the Shuswap Native American people of British Columbia. This demon was considered responsible for the storms that might suddenly stir the lake into high waves during a crossing. In order to ensure a calm crossing, people would take an effigy or some offering to throw to Naitaka to propitiate the spirit.
References 99
See also Demon

NAKAHET

See Naonhaithya

NÄKINEIU, NÄKINEITSI

This is the name of the female Näkki in the folklore of Estonia. She is described much like the British mermaid as a beautiful, blond-haired maiden to the waist with the tail of a fish below. She is frequently to be seen on the water combing her long golden hair, or looking after her water cattle in the waves.
References 88
See also Mermaid, Merrow, Näkinneito, Näkki, Appendix 25

NÄKINNEITO

This is the name of the female Näkki in the folklore of Finland. She is described much like the British mermaid as a beautiful, blond-haired maiden with a gleaming white body to the waist and the tail of a fish below. This female water spirit is well endowed with such voluptuous breasts that she is able to throw them over her shoulder. Näkinneito is frequently to be seen on the water combing her long curly hair.
References 88
See also Mermaid, Näkineiu, Näkki, Obda, Spirit, Appendix 25

NAKIR

See Monker

NAKISIYYA

See Naonhaithya

NÄKK

This is the name of a fearsome water spirit in the folk beliefs of Estonia, said to be derived from the Näcken of Swedish folklore. The Näkk may manifest in any shape, but usually as a human or a horse or other animal singing at the edge of the water. His voice is so enchanting that any human who hears him falls under his spell and is immediately swallowed up in the Näkk's enormous mouth. Just seeing him is considered to be a portent of a drowning.
References 88
See also Näcken, Näkineiu, Näkki, Neck, Nicker, Nix, Spirit, Appendix 25

NÄKKI

This is the name of a fearsome water spirit in the folk beliefs of Finland. He is said to be an attendant of the water god Ahto in his underwater kingdom, where they have magnificent jeweled palaces. The Näkki may emerge onto land by the lakes in the mornings and evenings. He can assume any form by which to deceive humans who venture into the water. If they have not propitiated him with a coin or a prayer, he will drag people to their doom under the water.
References 87, 99, 102
See also Attendant Spirit, Näkk, Spirit, Appendix 25

NAKSHASTRAS
The name of a spirit in the classical mythology of India. Nakshastras, whose name means Stars, is one of the eight Vasus in the Vedic myths and one of the attendants of Indra.
References 41
See also Attendant Spirit, Spirit, Vasus

NALET
This is the name of a devil or demon in Russian folklore. It is a particularly malignant demon in that it afflicts or even kills those who grieve excessively following the death of a loved one.
References 75
See also Demon, Devil, Appendix 16

NAMPA
The name of a spirit venerated as a fetish of vegetation in the folk beliefs of the people of Senegal. He was the subject of a cult.
References 29
See also Spirit

NAMTAR
There are two cultures that have spirits by this name:

(1) The name of a demon in the mythology of ancient Egypt. He is the guardian of the entrance to the underworld, manifesting in the form of a snake. In legend Namtar also accompanies the sun god in his boat on the journey across the sky before emerging into the morning.

(2) This is a disease demon in the ancient religion of Mesopotamia. Namtar, whose name means That Which Is Cut Off, is the spirit messenger of Ereshkigal, the queen of the underworld. This spirit was regarded as responsible for bringing misfortune, sickness, and death to humans.
References (1) 93; (2) 27, 41, 93, 119
See also (1) Irra, Guardian, Spirit; (2) Demon, Irra, Spirit, Appendix 17

NANGGU MOKSIN
In Korean folk belief, these supernaturals are wood imps much like the Moksin Tongbŏp. They are particularly malevolent and will enter houses while hidden in new wooden items, crossing the threshold for the first time on an inauspicious day. They can also be invoked through certain activities such as building a house, cutting trees, or bringing firewood into the home on any day known to be ill omened for such activities. Once inside the home, the Nanggu Moksin inflict perpetual sickness on the family.
References 79
See also Chisin Tongbŏp

NANIKAHET
See Naonhaithya

NANNY-BUTTON-CAP
This is the name of a fairy or nursery spirit in the folklore of Yorkshire, England. She behaves in much the same way as Wee Willie Winkie, ensuring that all young children are safe and warm in their beds, ready to go to sleep.
References 17
See also Dormette, Fairy, La, Spirit, Wee Willie Winkie, Appendix 22

NANSI
See Anansi

NANTENA
These are the Little People or fairies in the legends of the Tinneh Native American people. These spirits inhabit the elements of earth, water, and air, and may be both benevolent and malevolent.
References 25
See also Fairy, Little People

NAONHAITHYA, NAOSIHAITHYA
In the Zoroastrian religion of Iran, this is one of the fiends of Ahriman. He is opposed to the goodness of Aramaiti and concerned with sowing discord, pride, and rebellion among humans. In the Vedic mythology of India, his name is Nasatya, and his Pahlavi names are Naikiyas, Nakisiyya, and Nakahet; his older Persian names are Naunhas and Nanikahet.
References 88, 102
See also Aramaiti, Fiend

NAPÆÆ
This is the name of a group of nymphs in the classical mythology of ancient Greece and Rome. They were particularly the guardian spirits of forests and groves.
References 129, 130
See also Guardian, Nymph, Appendix 19

NAPFHANS
This is the name of a household spirit or dwarf in the folklore of Switzerland. He behaved in much the same manner as the English brownie, working at night on the household chores. In return he received a daily bowl of cream.
References 38
See also Brownie, Dwarf, Household Spirit, Kobold, Krimba, Mājas Gars, Trasgu, Appendix 22

NAPHÆ
This is the name of a group of nymphs in the classical mythology of ancient Greece and Rome. The Naphæ

were particularly the guardian spirits of glens or small valleys.
References 98, 130
See also Guardian, Nymph, Appendix 18

NAPI

This is a trickster spirit in the legends and beliefs of the Blackfoot Native American people. He is sometimes called Old Man Napi. He is very similar in behavior to Coyote, although Napi is less likely to appear in the shape of an animal and more likely to manifest in the form of a human.
References 88
See also Blue Jay, Coyote, Mink, Trickster

NARAH

This is the name of an evil spirit in the Zoroastrian religion of Persia. This demon is very similar in description and behavior to the Islamic djinn.
References 41
See also Djinn, Naraka

NARAKA

In the Hindu mythology of India, this is an evil spirit. Naraka is one of the most evil of the Asuras and was a shape-shifter. In one legend Naraka took the form of an elephant in order to abduct the daughters of the humans and the gods. The demon held the women in a sumptuous palace in the mountains. Nakara is also the name of one of the Hindu hells.
References 88
See also Asura, Demon, Narah, Spirit, Appendix 12

NARBROOI

The name of a spirit in the beliefs of the people of the Gleevink Bay district of Irian Jaya (New Guinea). This spirit inhabits the tops of the most ancient of the tall trees, where he may be observed as a form in the mists covering the uppermost branches. Narbrooi descends to take the souls of those humans whom he likes, and if one of them is sick Narbrooi may withdraw the soul in advance. Unless the person's friends go to the trees which the spirit inhabits, and negotiate the soul back again, the person may die. Even if Narbrooi has surrendered the soul for a sumptuous offering, he is still so unreliable that he may take the soul back again.
References 41, 110
See also Spirit

NARI

This is the name of a group of spirits in three different cultures.

(1) In the folklore of the Bulgarians, the Nari are demons that manifest in the shape of birds.

(2) In the folklore of the Slavs, the Nari are mischievous demons whose origins may have been the souls of dead children.

(3) In the folklore of the Ukraine, the Nari are mischievous household spirits, much the same as the Domovoi of Russia.
References 93
See also Demon, Domovik, Household Spirit, Appendix 12, Appendix 22

NARNYWO

See Gumnut Babies

NASATYA

See Naonhaithya

NASHAS

The Nashas were a type of djinn in the pre-Islamic folk beliefs of Yemen and the Hadramut. They were said to be the offspring of humans and the Shiqq. When they materialized they could only assume the shape of half a human with one arm, one leg, and half a head. Another group that inhabited an island in the China Sea appeared with bat wings.
References 41
See also Biasd Bheulach, Cacy Taperere, Djinn, Dodore, Fachan, Hinky-Punk, Paija, Shiqq

NASS L'AKHORINE

This is a term used as a euphemism for the djinns in the folklore of Morocco. Nass l'Akhorine means the Other People and is used as an oblique reference to the djinns in direct speech, in much the same manner as "Kuba" is used in the Cheremis folklore or "Ad Hene" in the Manx folklore to avert their offense and possible vengeful actions.
References 90
See also Ad Hene, Djinn, Kuba

NASTE ESTSAN

See Spider

NASU

In the mythology of Zoroastrianism in Iran, this evil spirit is the Druj of corpse contamination. Nasu assumes the form of a fly and takes possession of the dead in order to fulfill his purpose to infect all humans with the contagion. But this demon's evil purpose may be prevented by the stare of a guardian dog or by the purification ceremony known as the *Barashnum*.
References 53, 93
See also Drug, Spirit, Appendix 12, Appendix 17

NAT THAMI
See Nats

NATS
These are the malevolent nature spirits of Burmese mythology. The Nats must be constantly guarded against, especially by making offerings and sacrifices to placate them. They mostly inhabit forest areas and are ruled by up to 37 chiefs, over whom there is a supreme king. There are different groups of these demons, whose names vary according to the domain of their influence. The Akakasoh, Boomasoh, Shekkasoh, and Hmin dwell in the trees. The Jan, Shitta, Mbōn, and Mu inhabit the air. Others are the Saba-Leippya, Sinlap, Thien, Trikurat, and Upaka. The Nats use the natural elements to bring misfortune, disease, and destruction to humans, but they can also protect house, family, and property. Nat Thami, for instance, is a group of Nat maidens who guard royal property in Mandalay.
References 39, 53, 88, 110
See also Boomasoh Demon, Guardian, Hmin, Mbōn, Sinlap, Appendix 10, Appendix 17, Appendix 19, Appendix 22

NAUNHAS
See Naonhaithya

NBURU
This is the name of a forest demon mentioned as inhabiting the Congo region in reports of 1865.
References 57
See also Demon, Appendix 25

NDOGBOJUSUI
This nature spirit is a type of Dyinyinga in the folklore of the Mende people of Sierra Leone. The Ndogbojusui takes the form of a white-skinned human with a long white beard. This spirit is particularly malevolent toward human beings, but he may be outwitted and made to offer gifts instead of the usual mischief.
References 33
See also Dyinyinga, Spirit

ÑE'NVETIČÑIN
The name given to the Kalau spirits by the Reindeer Koryak people of Siberia.
References 88
See also Kala

NE-A-GO
See Ga-oh

NEBED
This is a demon of darkness in ancient Egyptian mythology. Nebed was associated with the god Set.

References 39
See also Demon

NECHISTAIA SILA
This name means Unclean Force and is a general term for evil spirits in the folklore of Russia.
References 75
See also Demon, Ia, Nechistyi Dukh, Spirit

NECHISTYI DUKH
This name, which means Unclean Spirit, is a general term for an evil spirit in the folklore of Russia.
References 75
See also Demon, Ia, Nechistyi Sila, Spirit

NECK, NECKAN, NEK
These are the variant names of a type of water spirit in the folklore of Scandinavia. The Neck may manifest as a floating log, an empty boat, or as a dog on the lakes and river banks. These spirits were most often recognized in the form of a golden-haired, green-eyed bearded man dripping with water and playing his harp on the surface of the lake. Although these spirits are said to demand a human sacrifice each year, they are also supposed to be concerned with the acquisition and redemption of a soul.
References 18, 44, 88, 95, 132
See also Näkki, Nicker, Nix, Spirit, Appendix 25

NEDA
See Hagno

NEDƏK
This is the name of a demon in the folklore of the Cheremis/Mari people of the former Soviet Republic. The Nedək's name means Toothache, and it is the personification of the toothache as an evil spirit that inflicts pains and problems of the gums.
References 118
See also Demon, Kož Nedək, Appendix 17

NEGAFOK
In the folk beliefs of the Inuit people of Canada this is said to be a spirit that brings cold weather.
References 25
See also Spirit, Appendix 26

NELLIE LONGARMS, NELLY LONG-ARMS
This is the name of a vicious female goblin in the folklore of Derbyshire, Cheshire, Lancashire, Shropshire, and Yorkshire in England. Nelly Long-arms would lurk beneath the surface of stagnant water, waiting for any unwary or naughty child to venture too close. The spirit would then catch hold of

the child and drag the unfortunate victim under the water, never to be seen again. She is, of course, a nursery bogie and a cautionary spirit used by parents to curb overadventurous behavior and prevent children from coming to harm.
References 15, 17, 123, 133
See also Goblin, Grindylow, Jenny Greenteeth, Kappa, Nursery Bogie, Peg Powler, Appendix 22, Appendix 25

NEMAN, NEAMHAIN

This is the name of a female evil spirit of conflict and death in the traditions and folklore of Ireland. She was originally a goddess, later a member of the Irish Tuatha dé Danann whose role was more in keeping with that of the Valkyries.
References 17, 105
See also Badb, Banshee, Bodua, Macha, Spirit, Tuatha dé Danann, Valkyries, Appendix 16

NEMDƏ KURƏK KUGƏ AND NEMDƏ KURƏK KUGUZA
See Čembulat

NEMISSA

This is the name of a supernatural Star Maiden in the Algonquin Native American mythology. She was so beautiful that even the Cloud Carrier was dazzled and went to live with her in the Star Country.
References 122
See also Mikak'e, Appendix 13

NENABU-SHU
See Manabozo

NENAUNIR

This is the name of a powerful evil spirit in the beliefs of the Masai of Kenya. He creates storms and threatens the earth with the rainbow, which is also considered to be evil. Legends tell how if the Masai had not beaten Nenaunir off by shooting their arrows accurately, the spirit might have succeeded in swallowing the earth.
References 102
See also Spirit, Appendix 26

NENUFAREMI

This is the name given to elementals of the air in the occultism of medieval Europe.
References 53
See also Elemental

NEPOKWA'I

This is the name of a hunter Kachina spirit in the beliefs of the Tewa Native American people.
References 88
See also Kachina, Kokopelli, Spirit

NEREID

There are two different descriptions for spirits bearing this name of ancient and modern Greece.

(1) These are the sea nymphs in classical Greek mythology whose name means the Wet Ones. The Nereids are the daughters of Nereus, the Old Man of the Sea, and the nymph Doris. They are described as beautiful young maidens with long golden hair, or in later texts as having green hair and the tail of a fish like a mermaid. They could be seen frolicking in the waves or riding white *hippo campi* (sea horses) along with the Tritons as the attendants of Neptune and his wife, Amphitrite, who was also a Nereid. Their number varies between 50 and 100, and most of their names appear in Spenser's *The Faerie Queen* (bk. IV, lxi, verses 48–51). The most famous of them are Amphitrite, Doto, Galatea, Panope, and Thetis.

(2) In modern Greek folklore these are beautiful young maidens who are nymphs of the countryside and woodlands, where they may be heard playing their *bouzoukia*. They may be mischievous toward humans, deceiving them into dancing to exhaustion or abducting and leading them astray in muddy places. They may even be malevolent if they are offended and may cause a person's face to swell or become distorted. Typical of the stories about them is one that tells of a young man who was reclining under a fig tree (traditionally a place where spirits lurk), when a beautiful young woman appeared. Later on, he told his grandfather that he would like to marry her, and the old man, recognizing a Nereid, told his grandson that the only way to do this would be to steal her scarf and keep it. This the young man did, and when a child was born his happiness was complete. She was the best wife a man could have, and he was proud when they went to the village festival together and she danced better than anyone else. He told her this, to which she replied that to do it properly all dancers need their scarves. Thinking no more of it, he gave her the scarf, whereupon she danced superbly straight into the air and was never seen again.
References (1) 20, 40, 56, 62, 92, 93, 114, 130; (2) 12
See also (1) Attendant Spirit, Amphitrite, Doris, Galatea, Mermaid, Nymph, Panope, Thetis, Tritons, Appendix 25; (2) Exotica, Melusina, Nymph, Appendix 18

NERGE KUBA AND NERGE KUGUZA

This is a keremet or devil in the folk beliefs of the Cheremis/Mari people of the former Soviet Republic. The spirit may be personified in the form of a male or female being, and these personifications are addressed as Nerge Kuba or Nerge Kuguza, Cold Old Woman or Cold Old Man. When a person has caught a cold it is said that these spirits of the sickness have invaded the body. These demons would be even more irritated if the human were to have a bath, so the only recommended way of dislodging them is to be smeared with chopped radishes.

References 118
See also Devil, Keremet, Spirit, Appendix 17

NERRIVIK
See Sedna

NESARU
In the beliefs of the Arikara Native American people, this is the name of a sky spirit. He helped humans to emerge from their underworld onto an earth prepared for their survival, and to ensure this, Nesaru taught them how to grow corn.

References 119
See also Spirit, Tutelary Spirit

NETUN
See Lutin

NEUGLE
This is the name of a fearsome water spirit in the folklore of Scalloway on the mainland of the Shetland Islands, north of Scotland. This spirit was also known by the names Nogle, Noggle, Nuggle, Nuggie, and Nygel. It inhabited Njugals Water and manifested in the shape of a horse with an odd tail like a wheel curling over its back. Like the Each Uisge, it would appear saddled and bridled, prancing on the shore. Should any human be tempted to mount and ride him, the Neugle would immediately enter the water with the human unable to dismount, and the victim might never be seen again. However, the Neugle was not always as malicious as the Cabyll-Ushtey or the Ceffyll-dŵr, and the rider would often suffer no more than an undignified drenching, whereupon the spirit would disappear into the water as a blue dancing flame. This spirit was fond of water wheels on the mills and would take great delight in causing them to stop, thereby causing immense irritation to the millers. This spirit is said to have been seen in British Columbia by Scandinavian and Shetlander immigrants and has passed into the folklore of Canada as the Nogle.

References 17, 47, 99
See also Cabyll-Ushtey, Ceffyll-dŵr, Each Uisge, Spirit, Appendix 12, Appendix 25

NGWOREKARA
This is the name of a demon king in the beliefs of the Fan people of the Congo. Like his subjects, he is described as being hideously ugly with a mouth resembling the end of an elephant's trunk, a pendu-

lous nose, and straggly hair. These spirits inhabit the tops of the mountains, where they inflict dizzy spells and panic attacks upon any human who ventures there. Ngworekara could be excessively malicious even to his own devils, who were mostly demonized souls of the wicked dead, by vindictively condemning them to another death.

References 29
See also Demon

ÑI'NVIT
This is the alternative name given to the Kalau spirits by the Reindeer Koryak people.

References 88
See also Kalau, Ñe'nvetičñin, Spirit

NIÄGRIUSAR
These are a type of brownie, elf, or goblin in the folklore of the Faröe Islands in the North Sea. Niägriusar are described as tiny Little People wearing red caps. These spirits are considered to bring good fortune wherever they dwell. The Niägriusar inhabit the tall trees that surround the homes of humans and act as guardian spirits. It is considered to be extremely reckless to remove any trees from the property, as the Niägriusar may be deprived of their residence. In this event the owner may not only cause the spirits to leave but also his good fortune as well.

References 110
See also Brownie, Elf, Goblin, Guardian, Little People, Spirit, Appendix 20

NIAMH
This is the name of a fairy member of the Tuatha dé Danann in the legends and folklore of Ireland. She married Osian and went to live in the land of Tir Nan Og.

References 18
See also Fairy, Tuatha dé Danann

NIBELUNG
This is the name of a king of the dwarfs in Scandinavian and Teutonic mythology. He dwelt in Nibelheim, the place of mist and darkness, where a great hoard of treasure was guarded by Alberich. His story was made famous in the opera *The Ring of the Nibelung* by Wagner, retelling how the treasure was stolen by Siegfried. Later, guardians of their treasure became known as the Nibelungs.

References 87, 95, 119
See also Alberich, Dwarf, Guardian

NICKAR
See Nicker

NICKEL

This name is used for two different types of spirits.

(1) This is the name of a type of goblin in the folklore of Germany. They inhabit the mines where copper was thought to be in abundance because of the color of the rocks. As no copper could ever be obtained, the mischief of the goblin was blamed for the miners' misfortune.

(2) Nickel is the local name of the Nicker in the Island of Rügen in the Baltic Sea.
References 40
See also Goblin, Haus-Schmiedlein, Kobold, Mine Spirits, Nicker

NICKER, NICKUR, NIKKE, NICOR

In the folklore of Scandinavia this is a water demon. It is known by the names of Näcken in Sweden; Nickar in the Faroe Islands; Nickur, Ninnir, and Haikur in Iceland; Nickel in Rügen Island; Nikyr in the Isle of Man, United Kingdom; and Nøkke in Denmark. This spirit is variously described as a golden-haired boy wearing a red cap, an old man with a dripping wet beard, a handsome youth to the waist with a horse's body and legs, or as a beautiful white horse with its hooves in reverse. These spirits inhabit the seas, lakes, rivers, and streams. They are generally benign toward humans if left alone to make their music; however, if anyone tries to ride one in the form of a horse, that person will be taken under the water forever. The Nicker will sometimes desire a human wife and will be a most attentive lover, but if scorned he can be as malicious and terrifying as the Scottish kelpie. A knife or metal object is placed in the bottom of a fishing boat as a precaution against the Nicker, as iron is supposed to "bind" his power.
References 28, 41, 78, 81, 88
See also Demon, Kelpie, Näcken, Näkineiu, Näkki, Neck, Nickel, Nix, Nøkke, Appendix 12, Appendix 25

NICKNEVEN

The name of a malignant spirit in the folklore of Scotland. It was variously described as an evil hag, by William Dunbar in his work *Flyting of Dunbar and Kennedy*, or as the Queen of Elfame. As Elfame was the Norse land of the Alfar, this might imply a connection with the underworld of the Dark Elves.
References 17, 40, 114
See also Alfar, Elf, Hag, Spirit

NICOLAI CHUDOVORITS

This is the name of the supernatural winter spirit of the Russian Arctic in the folklore of Russia. At the feast of Epiphany, 6 January, he travels through the freezing air in his reindeer sleigh and enters each house secretly to deliver gifts to humans and their children. Then he disappears again via the smoke ris-ing up the chimney. Nicolai Chudovorits is derived from Saint Nicholas, but was a well-established supernatural of shamanism long before the advent of Christianity throughout the Russias.
References 75
See also Father Christmas, Father Frost, Spirit

NIDHOGG, NIDHÖGGR

This is the name of the demon of the underworld in Scandinavian mythology. This evil spirit, whose name means Envy Dragon, threatens the existence of the world by gnawing constantly at the roots of the tree Yggdrasil and at the bodies of the dead.
References 78, 93
See also Demon, Spirit, Appendix 12

NIGHEAG NA H-ATH

See Ban Nighechain

NIGHTMARE

This is the medieval European fiend of the night known in Latin as the Incubus. It goes by different names in the folklore of each country; in England it is the Nightmare, from the Anglo-Saxon *mara*, meaning "crusher." This demon comes in the night and lies on top of sleeping humans, depriving them of their breath and causing them to awaken terrified and exhausted.
References 88
See also Cauchemar, Demon, Fiend, Incubus, Mara, Nightmare

NIHANSAN

See Spider

NIKYR

See Nicker

NIMBLE MEN, THE

See Fir Chlis

Nicker, a water demon, grabs the skirt of his lover.

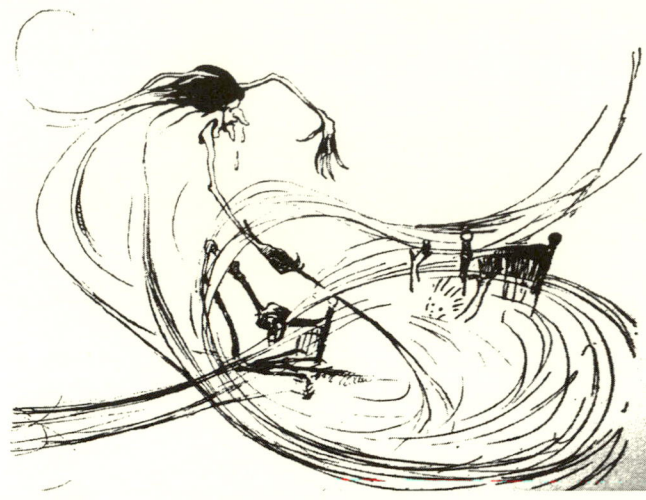

Nightmare awakens a sleeping child.

NIMÜE

This is the name often given to the Lady of the Lake in the Arthurian legends. Nimüe may also be known as Niniane or Vivienne in the northern French versions of the tales. In one tale she is described as a wood nymph in the Forest of Broceliande, where Merlin is enchanted by her. She asks him to show her how to build a crystal tower, and when he does she imprisons him in it. As the Lady of the Lake she represents the alter ego of Morgan le Fay, the enigmatic half sister of Arthur, his doom and ultimate savior combined.
References 17, 56
See also Lady of the Lake, Morgan le Fay, Nymph, Appendix 19

NINGYO

This is the term for a mermaid in the folklore of Japan. Like the European spirits, the Ningyo appears as a beautiful maiden to the waist, with a fish tail instead of legs. Unlike the water spirits of occidental folklore, the Ningyo is a benevolent protective spirit against misfortune on land and at sea.
References 88, 93
See also Mermaid, Spirit, Appendix 25

NINIANE

See Nimüe

NINNIR

See Nicker

NIS, NISSE

This is a household spirit in the folklore of Denmark and Norway. In Sweden he is called the Tomte Gubbe. The Nis is described as a little fellow dressed in gray with a pointed red cap. He dislikes noise and fuss, but during the night the Nis will work diligently on the house chores, like the English brownie, expecting only a bowl of porridge with a pat of butter as a reward.

Unlike the brownie, however, the farm where the Nis is a guardian may profit by his pilfering from neighbors in much the same way as the Aitvaras. If they are slighted or see any irregularity in the home, these spirits will exact severe punishment on offenders. In one tale an angry Nis broke the neck of a cow when he thought there was no butter in his porridge. When he found it at the bottom of the bowl, he left a chest full of treasure beside the dead cow out of remorse. Another tale tells how a Nis who was angry at a youth's constant teasing carried him outside one night naked and asleep, and placed him on two planks of wood over a deep well in the yard. The youth fortunately awoke because of the cold and escaped with no more than a fright. The same story is told of the Nis, as of the Boggart, "Ay, we're flittin'" where the Nis's words are recorded as "*I dag flytter vi.*"
References 18, 28, 34, 78, 88
See also Aitvaras, Boggart, Brownie, Gardsvor, Gobelin, Household Spirit, Julenisse, Piskey, Tomtar, Appendix 22

NITTERSING

See Gumnut Babies

NIU T'OU

This is the Ox Head Demon in the mythology of China. He is the attendant of Yen Lo, the demonic ruler of hell.
References 131
See also Attendant Spirit, Demon, Wu Ch'ang Kuei

NIVASHI, NIVASHO

In the folk beliefs of the Romany Gypsies, this is a malignant water demon. In the guise of a spirit like an incubus, its physical union with a young girl in her sleep, will turn her into a future witch.
References 31, 53
See also Demon, Incubus, Matiya, Spirit

NIX, NIXE, NIXIE

These are water spirits in the folklore of Scandinavia, Germany, and Switzerland. The females are described as being beautiful women above the waist and having the tail of a fish in the manner of a mermaid, but the Nix usually inhabits freshwater. This beautiful image was the guise by which the Nixes enticed mortals to their doom in the waters. Their more usual image was as wizened little beings with green skin, teeth, and hair, or even as a gray horse. They were said to have families and children under the water and to dwell in fine palaces, but their children were ugly. In the folklore of Germany the Nixes were said to exchange their own children for human babies, and the Changeling was known as a Wasserkopf. Sometimes they might take a human wife or lover,

but they would always have a discreet midwife who was very well paid. The Nixie women, like the Ellyllon of Wales, were fond of going to human markets in disguise as housewives, but they could be detected and avoided if one saw the water dripping from the edges of their aprons.
References 88
See also Berg People, Changeling, Ellyllon, Mermaid, Näkineiu, Näkki, Neck, Nicker, Appendix 22

NJAMBAI, NJEMBAI

This is the name of a spirit in the beliefs of the people of Nigeria, from a report of 1865. It is the guardian spirit of women, protecting them from the persecution of men and the unreasonable demands that may be made of them. Njambai would also avenge wrongs committed against women and advise them in the home. This benevolent spirit had a widespread following and was propitiated for its guidance and help.
References 81
See also Appendix 22

NOBODY, MR.

In the traditions and folklore of the English, this is a nursery spirit of the home. Although he is never visible, he may be glimpsed as a diminutive transient shadow. Whenever any misdemeanor has been effected, such as clothes left untidily on the bedroom floor, toys left scattered in the playroom, or ink spilled over important documents, one can be sure that it is the work of the prankster imp Mr. Nobody.
See also Imp, Olsen, Spirit, Appendix 22

NOČNITSA

This is a malignant demon or hag in the folklore of the Bulgarian, Czech, Polish, Russian, Serbian, and Slovak people. She is also known as Gorska Makua in Bulgaria and Krisky or Plasky in Russia. Nočnitsa was said to come in the night to torment children who had not been blessed by their parents before going to sleep. This night spirit might simply disturb the child with itching and tickling on the feet, or prodding in the stomach. When she was really malicious, Nočnitsa would inflict sickness on the child after sucking the blood from its veins. Like all such demons, the Nočnitsa would vanish when a caring parent came to investigate the cries of their child. Protection was thought to be effected if a knife were hidden beneath the cradle or an "iron circle" were drawn around it on the floor with the point of a knife.
References 88, 104
See also Demon, Hag, Polunochnitsa, Spirit, Appendix 22

NOGLE, NOGGLE
See Neugle

NØKK/E, NÖKKE, NØKKEN (pl.)

This is the water man in the folklore of Finland, where he is known as Nökke, and in Norway, where he is called Nøkke. In Finland he may manifest as a log floating on the surface of the water, but in Norway he may shape shift to the form of a horse, a grass snake, or even a haystack. Like the Nicker in its various forms in the rest of Scandinavian and Teutonic folklore, this water spirit has an ambivalent relationship with human beings and is best avoided altogether.
References 99
See also Näkineiu, Näkki, Neck, Nicker, Nix, Spirit, Appendix 12, Appendix 25

NOL JEη

The name of a keremet or demon in the folk beliefs of the Cheremis/Mari people of the former Soviet Republic. An offering of a chicken is made to placate this spirit.
References 118
See also Demon, Keremet, Spirit, Appendix 9

NONA
See Parcae

NOOTAIKOK

This is a benevolent nature spirit in the beliefs of the Inuit people. He is the spirit of the icebergs who lives in the sea and is the guardian of the seals. Nootaikok makes sure that there are enough seals for the hunters not to go hungry and that the seals breed successfully.
References 102
See also Guardian, Spirit, Appendix 12, Appendix 25

NORG

This is the name of a demon in Teutonic folklore. He inhabited the hollow trunks of trees in the forests of northern Europe.
References 110
See also Demon

NORNS, NORNIR

This is the collective name for the Fates of Nordic mythology, the daughters of Davalin the dwarf. They are also known as the Alrauns, Dises, Idises, Nornir, and Wurds. There are normally three supernatural sisters who dwell at the base of the sacred ash tree, Yggdrasil. They are Udur, who represents the past; Verdandi, who represents the present; and Skuld, who represents the future. They appear after the birth of

Nøkke surrounded by his water family.

each child to determine its destiny. These are the fairies invited to the christening party in the traditional tale of the Sleeping Beauty, although in later tales their number expanded to more than 12. They are usually depicted as wearing long gray garments with their heads covered by gray gossamer veils.
References 33, 39, 40, 41, 56, 78, 88, 95, 114
See also Alraun, Béfind, Davalin, Dis, Dwarf, Fates, Held, Moiræ, Oosood, Parcae, Skuld, Udur, Valkyries, Appendix 22, Appendix 23

NOS BONNES MÈRES AND BONNES DAMES
These are names that mean Our Good Mothers and Good Ladies, given to the fairies in the folklore of Brittany, France. They are euphemisms used when referring directly to the spirits so that they will neither be invoked nor offended enough to seek revenge.
References 87
See also Fairy, Spirit

NUALA
In some accounts of the Irish mythology, Nuala is the wife of the king of the Tuatha dé Danann, Finvarra, and is his fairy queen.
References 17, 18
See also Fairy, Finvarra, Tuatha dé Danann

NUBERO, EL
In the folklore of northwestern Spain, this is an evil weather spirit described as having a long beard and wearing animal skins. He is also called Juan Cabrito. With his wife and family, el Nubero is supposed to inhabit a mist-veiled mountain in Egypt, from which he rides out on great clouds and sends violent storms, bringing disasters to humans.
References 88
See also Spirit, Appendix 26

NUGGIES
See Noggle

NUGGLE
See Neugle

NULES-MURT
This is the nature spirit in the folk beliefs of the Finno-Ugric Votyak people of the Vyatka region of Russia. The name of this spirit means Man of the Forest and, as this implies, he is the guardian spirit of the forests in much the same way as the Leshii in the folklore of Russia. The Nules-murt must be propitiated to ensure his benevolence.
References 88
See also Ataman, Čodra Kuba, Guardian,

Keltəmaš, Laskowice, Leshii, Murt, Spirit, Appendix 19

NUMBER NIP
See Rübezahl

NUꞑUÍ
This is the name of a nature spirit or fairy in the folk beliefs of the Jívaro people in the Amazon region of Equador. Nuꞑuí whose name means Earth Mother, is said to have taught the Jívaro the art of pottery and how to hunt using a dog. Although she is always spoken of in the singular, the concept is in fact plural in that a Nuꞑuí exists in every garden, and they all gather to dance in the forest clearings. When visible she is described as being very fat, about three feet high, and wearing a black *tarací* (a woman's cloth dress). The Nuꞑuí dwells beneath the ground, where she pushes up the shoots of the plants to ensure their first growth. In this respect she is the guardian spirit of germination and emergent growth, and the Jívaro are at pains to ensure that the Nuꞑuí will come to their cleared planting site and stay to make their crops grow. This spirit will only stay where the ground has been cleared, with no weeds or full growth, as she needs room to dance at night. Therefore a well-tended garden will have the best attention from its Nuꞑuí. The spirit will go deep underground, away from any garden that is not tended, and may even leave altogether, taking the crops with her to someone else's well-tended plot. It is believed that the spirit descends deeper into the ground during the day, taking the growth with her, and for this reason the women go early in the morning to harvest the manioc. They sing placatory songs to the Nuꞑuí so that they do not frighten her away, and they provide her with "babies" in the form of treasured semi-precious jasper to keep her contented with her abode. When contented she will also protect the home of the family by sucking out, through the soles of his feet, all the blood of any stranger who goes through the garden. For this reason the children are warned not to play there in case they should anger the Nuꞑuí.
References 64
See also Fairy, Guardian, Spirit, Appendix 14, Appendix 18

NUNYUNUWI
This is a demon in the folk beliefs of the Cherokee Native American people. This evil spirit, whose name means Dressed in Stone, is said to be a destructive cannibal spirit.
References 25
See also Demon, Spirit

NUR BODƏŽ
This is a keremet or devil in the folk beliefs of the Cheremis/Mari people of the former Soviet Republic. This vegetation spirit, whose name means Field Spirit, must be placated with an offering of a cockerel and a hen to keep him from destroying the crops or animals in the fields.
References 118
See also Devil, Keremet, Spirit, Appendix 9, Appendix 18

NUR KUBA AND NUR KUGUZA
These are the female and male personification of a nature spirit in the folk beliefs of the Cheremis/Mari people of the former Soviet Republic. They are invoked for their protection in the early springtime when the cattle are released into the fields for the first time after the winter. Nur Kuba and Nur Kuguza, whose names mean Field Old Woman and Field Old Man, respectively, will then guard the cattle from harm and ensure good grazing during the summer season.
References 118
See also Gid-murt, Gunna, Kudə Ört Kuba, Lauko Sargas, Spirit, Appendix 9, Appendix 12, Appendix 18

NURSERY BOGIES
In many cultures there are spirits that never seem to have been taken too seriously by mature adults, although they are spoken of with serious expression, and even reverence, when adults address children. This class of spirit is used to threaten or caution children to pursue activities approved of by the social group in which they live. These supernaturals have, for the most part, an extremely terrifying appearance and an even worse reputation in dealing with humans who enter their domain.

The following British ones are used as a warning for bad behavior: Auld Scratty, Black Annis, Black Sow, Bodach, Bogie, Bucca Dhu, Bug, Bug-a-boo, Bugbear, Cankobobus, Cutty Dyer, Hobyah, Jack up the Orchut, Jennie of Biggersdale, Mumpoker, Old Bloody Bones, Raw Head and Bloody Bones, the Spoorn, Tanterabogus, Tod Lowery, Tom Dockin, and Tom Poker.

The following are used to protect crops from being gathered unripe by greedy children: Awd Goggie, Churnmilk Peg, Clim, the Gooseberry Wife, Lazy Lawrence, and Melsh Dick.

To keep British children from dangerous waters the following are used: Grindylow, Jenny Greenteeth, Nellie Longarms, and Peg Powler.

In other countries the following may be used by adults to warn children from danger or bad behavior: Afrit, Baba Yaga, Berchta, Bockmann, Caypór, Croquemitaine, Holle, Katzenveit, Krampus, Lamia

and Lara, Nuɲuí, Oats Goat, Père Fouettard, Poludnica, Sri, and Zwart Piet.
References 17
See also Bogie, Appendix 21, Appendix 22, Appendix 25

NYGEL
See Neugle

NYKKJEN, NYKUR
See Nicker

NYMPH
These are female nature spirits especially in the classical mythology of Greece and Rome. They were portrayed as beautiful young maidens dressed in diaphanous flowing garments, with lovely hair tied in the classical Greek fashion with golden bands around the head. Although not immortal, they were said to live for several thousand years. The Nymphs were usually the attendants of the gods, often providing musical or theatrical entertainment. They frequently played instruments, danced, educated infant gods, and delivered prophesies. There were distinct groups of Nymphs named according to where they dwelled and what they protected. They could be both benevolent and malevolent toward humans and have also been called demons or sprites. In the pantheon of the ancient mythologies of most cultures there are spirit maidens whose activities are the same as those of the Nymphs and whose roles were as the attendants of the deities and having guardianship responsibilities. They are the subject of numerous tales and legends in their own right. The following are the names of groups of Nymphs from different cultures:

Cherokee Native American: Anitsutsa
Germany: Moss Maidens
Greece and Rome: Alsaieds, Atlantides, Auloniads, Carmenæ, Crenæ, Dryads, Hamadryads, Hesperides, Hyades, Hylæoræ, Leimoniades, Limnæ, Limenia, Limonead, Meliæ, Meliades, Melissa, Muses, Naiads, Napææ, Naphæ, Nereid, Oceanids, Oriades, Pagæ, Pleiades, Sylphs, Undines
India: Apsaras, Devas, Gandharvas, Kollimalaikanniyarka, Urvasi, Vrikshakas
Ireland: Suire
Persia: Houri, Huran

References 20, 40, 56, 62, 88, 92, 93, 102, 110, 114, 129
See also Attendant Spirit, Demon, Spirit, Sprite, Appendix 11

NYYRIKKI
See Tuulikki

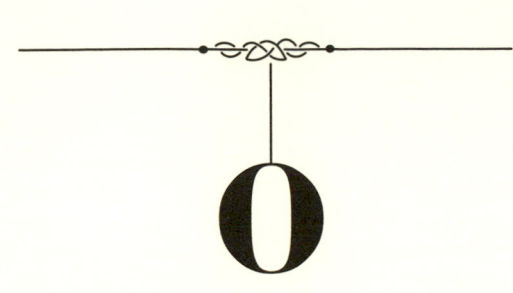

O

O'BENGH
See Beng

O-YAN-DO-NE
See Ga-oh

OAF
This word is the corruption of the word Ouphe meaning an elf or changeling. The term has come to mean a person of aged appearance and dull wit from the belief that it was a changeling and not a human being thus addressed.
References 40, 76
See also Changeling, Elf, Ouphe

OAK KING
See Erl King

OAKMEN, OAK MEN
These are a type of dwarf or wood elf in English folklore. They are described as little wizened men with red noses and caps of red toadstools. The Oakmen inhabit the copses where the saplings have been cut many times and the new shoots rise thickly from the ground. Within these copses there is abundant wildlife, and the bluebells flower profusely in the spring. These Little People were the guardians of this domain, and any human who did not respect it would be dealt with severely. Cutting or damaging any of their oaks without permission was to invite disaster. Humans would wisely avoid such places after sunset, but anyone who ventured there might be enticed by their prank of disguising fungi as a delicious feast, only to find it inedible. Details of these sinister Little People may be found in Beatrix Potter's *The Fairy Caravan*
References 17, 18, 44
See also Dryad, Dwarf, Elf, Erl King, Guardian, Little People, Appendix 19

OATS GOAT
This is the name of a field spirit in the folklore of eastern Europe. It is known in Germany as the Haferbocks. In Prussia, unlike the Kornwolf that is chased, the Oats Goat is a malicious spirit that comes behind the lazy reapers intent on doing them harm and encouraging them to work faster. The spirit is used as a nursery bogie as a warning to children not to play in an oats field or the Oats Goat will get them. Usually the last sheaf to be cut is fashioned into an effigy of the spirit, or, as in the Grenoble region of France, a live goat is turned loose in the field as the last of the reaping takes place. This goat is then killed and roasted for the harvest feast. Its hide was made into a cloak for the proprietor, but as the Oats Goat has a reputation as a curing spirit of farming ailments, the hide cloak would be given to anyone suffering from a strained back during the threshing.
References 88
See also Corn Spirit, Haferbocks, Kornwolf, Nursery Bogie, Spirit, Appendix 15, Appendix 22

OB
In the Jewish tradition and folklore this is the name of a familiar spirit, and, by association, the object in which it dwelt. These were used in ancient times by sorcerers for divination.
References 87
See also Familiar

OBDA
This is a forest spirit in the folk beliefs of the Cheremis/Mari people of the former Soviet Republic. It may also be known as Kožla Ia, Kožla Oza, Kožla Peri or Suräli. It resembles a squat, hairy, naked human with long hair and with pendulous breasts thrown over its shoulder. It tends to face backwards; its feet are turned backwards; and if it rides a horse, it does so facing backwards. It has holes in its armpits, and if it manages to catch a human, the victim should stop up these holes with the fist. This will drain the power of the spirit so that the human can escape. It is not advisable to try to injure the Obda in any way, because any drops of blood that fall to the earth will each generate another Obda. This spirit can be heard laughing and clapping its hands in the forest. Sometimes it may be seen sitting in a tree combing its long

hair. It will call any human by name, enticing them deeper into the forest where they will be lost. The demon will torment sleeping travelers by tickling their feet and, once the travelers are awake, may make them dance to exhaustion. The Obda is fond of riding and will also ride a horse all night, leaving it lathered in the stable at dawn. An Obda is said to be afraid of dogs and the old-fashioned Cheremis belt, so those who must go to the forest will take these with them as a precaution against the Obda.
References 118
See also Demon, Jer Oza, Kožla Kuba, Kulshedra, Näkinneito, Ouda, Pixy, Spirit, Appendix 19

OBE

This is the name for a witch's familiar spirit in the folk beliefs of the Basutu people of South Africa. It usually takes the form of an animal.
References 87
See also Familiar, Ob, Appendix 12

OBERON

The name of the fairy king mentioned in the French romance *Huon de Bordeaux* and introduced into English literature in Shakespeare's *A Midsummer Night's Dream* with Titania as his wife. He is described as being a dwarf with a beautiful face and kingly deportment. He is, however, capable of playing pranks and working mischief both with his fairy retinue as well as with humans. Oberon haunts the English woods and forests with his sprites led by Puck. The fairy king will attempt to deceive any human traveler through the forests and detain them in fairy time (like Rip Van Winkle). Humans who meet him are well advised to remain silent and not to address him, no matter what evil horrors, storms, and frightening visions he conjures up, for anyone who speaks to Oberon is forever in his power.
References 17, 18, 21, 40, 78, 114, 133
See also Dwarf, Fairy, Puck, Sprite, Titania

OBIN-MURT

This is a spirit whose name means Man of the Kiln in the folk beliefs of the Finno-Ugric Votyak people of the Vyatka region of Russia. He is their guardian spirit of the drying kiln in much the same way as the Gabijaujis in the folklore of Lithuania. He must be propitiated to ensure his benevolence.
References 88
See also Gabijauji, Guardian, Murt, Spirit

OCEANIDS, OCEANIDES

This is the name of a group of nymphs also known as the Okeanides and Okeaninai in the classical mythology of Greece and Rome. They were the daughters of Tethys and Oceanus and were nymphs of the seas to

The fairy king Oberon.

whom sailors made offerings. There were said to be between 50 and 3,000 Oceanids. The best known are Amphitrite, Doris, Electra, and Styx.
References 40, 92, 93
See also Amphitrite, Doris, Electra, Nymph, Appendix 25

OCH
This is an Olympian spirit in the literature of the medieval European mysticism. Och is the personification of the Sun, celebrated as Sunday, and is said to rule over 28 provinces of the Olympian Universe.
References 53
See also Olympian Spirit

OCYPETE, OCYPETA
The name—also spelled Okypete, which means Rapid—is that of one of the fiends known as the Harpies in ancient Greek mythology.
References 29, 40, 93
See also Fiend, Harpy

ODQAN
This is a spirit in the folk beliefs of the Mongolian people. Odqan, whose name means Fire King, is the guardian spirit of fire. The name has been taken from the Turkish words, since the name for his female counterpart, a more ancient spirit Mother of Fire, is in the Mongolian words *Yal-un eke*.
References 93
See also Guardian, Spirit

OEILLET
See Devil

ŒNGUS MAC OG (YOUNG SON)
See Angus Og

OENONE, ŒNONE, OINONE
This is the name of a nymph, dwelling in Mount Ida in the classical mythology of Greece and Rome. She was a Naiad, the daughter of Oneus the river god, and she was married to Paris, the son of King Priam of Troy. Oenone was a prophetic nymph and foretold the disaster that would result from her husband's journey to Sparta. When Paris abducted Helen and initiated the Trojan Wars, his fate was sealed. When he sent for Oenone to heal him of his fatal wounds, she refused to go. Later relenting, she arrived after his death and destroyed herself in grief. Her story is the subject of Tennyson's works *Oenone* and *Death of Oenone*.
References 40, 62, 88, 114
See also Naiad, Nymph, Appendix 11, Appendix 23, Appendix 25

OGU FERAI
This is a spirit in the folk beliefs of Voodoo in the island of Haiti. He is a military spirit associated with the Feast of Saint Patrick but derived from the African deity Ogun. In the cockfighting arena a cockerel may often be given the name of this spirit to ensure its success.
References 137
See also Encantado, Ogun, Spirit

OGUN
This is the name of an encantado in the Afro-Brazilian cults of Umbanda and Batuque. Ogun is derived from the warrior deity of the Yoruba in Nigeria. In the South American cults he is associated with the warrior Saint George and his feast day, 23 April (although originally he was associated with Saint Antony, the soldier saint). The Ogun family includes the spirits Ogun Beira-Mar, Ogun-iara, Ogun-mergê, Ogun de Ronda, Ogun Sete Ondas, and Rompe Mato. Only the last of these encantados has any popularity in Belém. The others figure mostly in the Umbanda cult.
References 89
See also Encantado, Ogu Ferai, Rompe Mato

OGUN BEIRA-MAR, OGUN-IARA, OGUN-MERGÊ, OGUN DE RONDA, OGUN SETE ONDAS
See Ogun

OHDOWAS
One of the three groups of dwarfs in the folk beliefs of the Iroquois Native Americans. The Ohdowas were nature spirits that dwelt beneath the earth. They were the guardians of those creatures, especially venomous ones, that lived either under the ground or in dark places such as crevices and caves.
References 102
See also Dwarf, Gahongas, Gandayaks, Guardian, Spirit, Appendix 12

OKEANIDES, OKEANINAI
See Oceanids

OKSA OROLA, OKSA SALTAK
See Ia Saltak

OKULAM
This is an evil spirit in the folk beliefs and mythology of the Chinook Native Americans. He is a spirit of the storms and is to be heard in its howling winds.
References 122
See also Spirit, Appendix 26

OKYPETE
See Ocypete

OLD BLOODY BONES
This is a version of the North of England evil spirit Raw Head and Bloody Bones. Old Bloody Bones was said to inhabit an area of Cornwall called Knockers Hole, near Baldhu. This is an ancient battle site and the kind of place that attracts these malignant imps. However, when "old" is attached to the name of a spirit, it usually indicates a diminished power, and the threat of Old Bloody Bones was frequently used as a nursery bogie.
References 17
See also Auld Hornie, Imp, Nursery Bogie, Raw Head and Bloody Bones

OLD BOOT, OLD GENTLEMAN, OLD HARRY, OLD HORNY, OLD LAD
See Auld Hornie

OLD LADY OF THE ELDER TREE
See Elder Mother

OLD MAN COYOTE
See Coyote

OLD MAN OF THE SEA
In the Arabian tales of *The Thousand and One Nights,* the story of Sindbad's fifth voyage gives details of this terrifying djinn. It is a demon or fiend of the desert that mounts the backs of men and rides them ceaselessly until they die of exhaustion. Sindbad managed to dislodge and destroy it.
References 36, 88,
See also Demon, Djinn, Fiend, Mara, Nightmare, Succubus

OLD NICK
This is a name for the Devil of diminished powers in the folklore of northern England. It is said to be derived from the Scandinavian water demon Nickur, or Nix, brought to the country by the Viking invaders. The name was certainly in use during the seventeenth century and has come to have a humorous association with wickedness and little in common with absolute evil.
References 28, 40, 41
See also Auld Hornie, Demon, Nicker, Nix

OLD PEOPLE, THE
This is a euphemism used in Cornwall, England, for the fairies and Little People. In this county it was believed that these spirits were derived from either ancient deities or the souls of ancient people who, with the coming of Christianity, were too good for Hell and inelegible for Heaven. They were, therefore, condemned to inhabit a netherworld, often invisibly affecting the lives of the present inhabitants.
References 17
See also Fairy, Spirit, Appendix 6

OLD ROGER
This is the red-faced spirit of apples and the guardian of apple trees in some areas of England. In the mythology and beliefs of the Celts, the apple was the fruit of life that gave passage to the land of the gods. It has been speculated that because of the similarity this name has to the French word *rouge,* meaning red, this spirit was envisaged as an old man with ruddy cheeks.
References 123
See also Appletree man, Colt Pixy, Guardian, Lazy Laurence, Spirit, Appendix 21

OLD SHUCK
See Black Shuck

OLD SIMMIE, OLD TEASER
See Auld Hornie

OLD WHITE HAT
See Jack the White Hat

OLD WOMAN OF THE MOUNTAIN
This hag is one of the Gwillion in the folklore of west Wales who inhabited Llanhyddal Mountain. She is described as a hideous old woman dressed in gray garments with her apron over her shoulder and wearing a four-cornered black hat. The Old Woman of the Mountain may be encountered carrying a milk pail on dark, lonely roads, and though she trudges slowly, it is impossible, and imprudent, to catch up with her. If she greeted the traveler, they were certainly going to get lost, but drawing an iron knife would dispel her and her enchantment immediately.
References 17, 123
See also Gwillion, Hag

OLE LUK ØJ, OLE LUK ÖIE
This is the Dust Man and nursery spirit of Danish and Swedish folklore described in the work of Hans Christian Andersen. He is a tiny elf or fairy dressed in a beautiful silk jacket, the color of which changes with the light, and under each arm he carries a magic umbrella. Ole Luk Øj, whose name means Ole Close Your Eyes, has many wonderful stories for children, which they may be told in their dreams. So at night this spirit tiptoes quietly up to the tiny children of the household, blowing magic dust at their eyes and necks. Their little eyes and heads become heavy and sleepy, and when they are safely tucked in bed Ole

Ole Luk Øj, a nursery spirit, holds a magic umbrella over a sleeping boy in order to ensure good dreams.

Luk Öie will open over the good children the umbrella with wonderful pictures on it, which brings them beautiful dreams. Over all the naughty children, however, he opens the other umbrella, which contains no pictures, and they will have no wonderful stories and no beautiful dreams.
References 2, 17
See also Billy Winker, Dormette, Dustman, Elf, Fairy, Sandman, Spirit, Wee Willie Winkie, Appendix 22

OLIFAT, OLAFAT, OLOFAD

These are the names of the trickster spirit who is also known as Wolphat, Yalafath, and Yelafath in the Caroline Islands of Micronesia. He was the son of the sky god Lugeilan and a human mother. Although he was usually seen in human form, Olifat could assume any shape at will. He was unaware of the identity of his father until he tipped his head back to drink from a coconut and saw him above. Olifat desired to be with his father and traveled up on a column of smoke. When he arrived there he saw some children playing with some creatures, but they wouldn't let him join them. To punish them Olifat gave these creatures spines, teeth, and stings, and that is how the scorpion fish, sharks, and stingrays became dangerous to touch. Another legend tells how Olifat outwitted the Evil One and rescued a number of beautiful women, restoring them to their future partners. This trickster spirit, although responsible for giving the secret of fire to humans, was also the cause of discord and misery through his outrageous pranks and breaking of taboos.
References 29, 33, 93, 109, 119
See also Anansi, Bamapama, Basajaun, Blue Jay, Coyote, Eshu, Manabozo, Mink, Spirit, Trickster

OLIVIER
See Devil

OLSEN

This is the name of a spirit in the folklore of Denmark that is responsible for all the minor problems of a household that seem inexplicable. Where a door is left ajar, items mislaid, toys broken, or cakes missing, he is the culprit. Like Mr. Nobody of English folklore, Olsen flits invisibly about the house able to get away with his pranks because he knows that no one will ever see him.
See also Nobody, Appendix 22

OLT
See Tündér

OLYMPIADES
See Muses

OLYMPIAN SPIRITS
These are spirits of the atmosphere and space, according to a mystical document of sixteenth-century Europe. They were said to have guardianship of 196 regions and were the means of communicating divine intervention. Magic rituals were associated with belief in these spirits. The seven main spirits were Arathron, Bethor, Hagith, Och, Ophiel, Phaleg, and Phul.
References 53
See also Arathron, Bethor, Guardian, Hagith, Och, Ophiel, Phaleg, Phul, Spirit, Appendix 13

OMBWIRI
This is a tree spirit in the beliefs of West Africa. Ombwiri dwells within the trees and groves as their guardian spirit in much the same way as the Hamadryads of ancient Greek mythology. Small token offerings are made to them by humans when passing the particular tree they are thought to inhabit.
References 110
See also Guardian, Hamadryad, Spirit, Appendix 19

ONAGH, OONAGH
Finvarra and Onagh are the supreme King and Queen of the Sídhe in Irish folklore, receiving allegiance from tributary provincial queens Cliodna, Aoibhinn, and Aine. Onagh is described by Lady Wilde as having golden hair so long that it sweeps the ground and wearing a beautiful garment spun from glittering silver gossamer. Although she is more lovely than any mortal woman, her consort is unfaithful in his philandering with the mortal women he charms with his magic music.
References 17, 18, 125
See also Aine, Aoibhinn, Cliodna, Finvarra, Sídhe

ONATAH, ONATHA
In the mythology of the Seneca and Iroquois Native American people, this is one of the vegetation spirits known as the Deohako, the daughters of the Earth Mother Eithinoa. Onatah, whose name means Corn, is the spirit of corn, and her story follows the theme of the death of vegetation in winter and its regeneration in spring (like that of the Greek legend of Persephone). One day when Onatah became thirsty, she left her place with her sisters in the field and was captured by Hahgwehdaetgah, the evil one. He trapped her underground and sent such fierce winds over the fields that her sisters fled. Onatah was rescued by the sun, but now she stays with the maize,

standing in the field in all weathers until the crop is ripe, sooner than risk leaving it again.
References 25, 87, 88, 119
See also Corn Spirit, Deohako, Spirit, Appendix 15

ONDICHAOUAN
This is an evil spirit or demon in the folk beliefs of the Huron Native American people. Ondichaouan is the demon that inhabits the Great Lakes. He appears sometimes as a flame or as a fire and sometimes as an island floating in the lake where there was none before. He will stir up great storms on the lakes in order to capsize the canoes of his victims under cover of the darkness of the tempest. When he is not taking the drowned to his lair under the water, Ondichaouan, who is also a disease demon, will spread contagious sicknesses to those humans who live by the waters.
References 99
See also Demon, Spirit, Appendix 17, Appendix 25

ONE WITH THE WHITE HAND, THE
This is a malignant wood spirit in the folklore of Somerset. It appears as a pale, gaunt young maiden darting fleetingly between the tall pale trunks of the birch tree copses that she inhabits. She waylays any young man who ventures into the copses on the lonely moors, and if she touches him, his fate is sealed. If she touches his head he will go mad, but if she touches his chest he will die instantly.
References 44
See also Spirit, Appendix 24

ONI
This is the name of a group of demons in the Shinto and Buddhist beliefs of Japan. There are two types of Oni: those that come from hell and those that inhabit the earth. The former, known as Gaki, take a somewhat human shape, but their huge-bellied bodies are red or green and have the head of either a horse or an ox with three eyes, and grotesque horns and talons. They are tortured incessantly by raging hunger and thirst. These demons pounce upon the souls of the wicked who are about to die and convey them to the torments of hell. The latter are earth demons that can shape shift to assume the form of a relative or friend of the human they wish to torment. Some of these are said to be the distorted souls of women who have died of excessive grief. These demons are responsible for bringing misfortune and spreading diseases, especially the plague. The Oni may be driven out at the Shinto Oni-yarahi ceremony, and some may lose their malicious character by being converted to Buddhism.
References 33, 56, 102, 119
See also Demon, Appendix 12, Appendix 17

ONO

A trickster spirit in the folk beliefs of Hawaii. This demon could shape shift at will to any form or size when visible. Ono was renowned for his ability to regenerate after he had been destroyed, by reassembling the pieces he had been chopped into.
References 109
See also Demon, Kapua, Trickster

OOSOOD

This is a female birth spirit in the folk beliefs of the Serbian people. She is a similar spirit to Veela, a type of fairy, but is only visible to the mother of the child that she visits. Oosood comes to the infant on the seventh night after its birth to pronounce the development of the child's destiny.
References 41
See also Béfind, Chang Hsien, Eshu, Fairy, Fates, Moiræ, Norns, Pi-Hsia Yüan-Chün, Spirit, Veela, Appendix 22, Appendix 23

OPHIEL

This is the name of an Olympian Spirit in the European literature of mysticism. Ophiel is the personification of the planet Mercury. This supernatural was celebrated as Wednesday and was said to rule over 14 provinces of the Olympian Universe.
References 53
See also Olympian Spirit, Appendix 13

OPKƏN

This is a fearsome water spirit in the folk beliefs of the Cheremis/Mari people of the former Soviet Republic. It manifests as a large, fat form with an enormous mouth. It inhabits large areas of open water such as wide rivers, lakes, and inland seas, where it appears suddenly to swallow up any boats unaware of danger.
References 118
See also Spirit, Appendix 25

ORA

This is a guardian spirit in the folklore of Albania. Each person is assigned one of these spirits from birth. In general they may take the form of a human, but they take a different appearance according to the character of their charge. They may have a white or a black appearance according to whether the person they are protecting is industrious and brave or deceitful and lazy.
References 93
See also Grine, Guardian, Ka, Appendix 23

ORANG BUNYI, ORANG BUNYIAN

These are the Little People or diminutive spirits that inhabit the forests in the folklore of the Malay people in West Malaysia. This group of fairies, whose name means Voice People, are considered so simple that they may easily be tricked by humans or other spirits. They are usually only heard, and their voices sound exactly like those of a human calling in distress deep in the forest. Lonely travelers who have thought that someone needed their help have tried to find the person, and thus been lured ever deeper into the jungle, unable to retrace their path. The searchers have called plaintively to others to help them find their way, and eventually only their voices remain to witness their transformation into an Orang Bunyi spirit.
References 110
See also Echo, Fairy, Hantu, Leshii, Little People, Spirit, Will o' the Wisp

ORC

This is the name given by J. R. R. Tolkien to the goblins that people his works *The Hobbit* (1937) and *The Lord of the Rings* (1955), which feature his other supernatural creation, the Hobbit. (Orc was originally the name of a sea monster described by Ariosto and also applied as a name for the whale.)
References 5, 40
See also Goblin, Hobbit

OREAD

The Oreads are a type of nymph in the classical mythology of Greece and Rome. They inhabited the mountains and the caves there and were in the retinue of Diana, the goddess of the hunt. They are described in the work of Percy Bysshe Shelley, *The Witch of Atlas.*
References 40, 92, 93
See also Echo, Nymph, Appendix 11

OREANDE LA FÉE

This is the name of a benevolent spirit or fairy who figures in a European legend and romance from the fifteenth century.
References 18
See also Fairy, Spirit

ORISHA

This is the name of a group of spirits from the folk beliefs of the Yoruba people of Nigeria. These spirits were responsible for giving humans their different moods and personalities. The Orisha were the subjects of elaborate cults that centered on the Gelede Society, who sometimes performed public dances to honor these spirits. They were represented by humans who wore elaborate masks and long garments to conceal their normal identity. Each mask was a representation of the wearer's guiding spirit.
References 24
See also Encantado, Eshu, Kachina, Spirit, Tutalary Spirit

ORITHYIA, OREITHYIA
She was a nymph in the classical mythology of Greece and Rome. Orithyia was loved by the god of the north wind, Boreas, by whom she bore the two sons, Zetes and Calais. These sons became the winged warriors who accompanied Jason and his Argonauts on his epic voyage.
References 114
See also Nymph, Appendix 11

ORIXÁ
An important group of encantados in the Afro-Brazilian cult Batuque whose names are derived from those of Yoruban deities of West Africa. These include Ogun, Oxossi, Oxun, Inhaçan, Xangô, Imanja, and Exu.
References 89
See also Encantado, Exu, Imanja, Ogun, Oxossi, Oxun, Rainha Barba, Xangô

OROBAS
The name of a demon in European demonology considered to be a devil from Hell. He was invoked in rituals of black magic by sorcerers who considered Orobas to be loyal and helpful.
References 53
See also Demon, Devil

OŠ BUJ VANUŠKA
This name, which means White Head Vanuška, is an alternative name for Vanuška. This spirit is a keremet in the folk beliefs of the Cheremis/Mari people of the former Soviet Republic.
References 118
See also Keremet, Spirit, Vanuška

OSCHAERT
The name in Belgian folklore for the demon or bogle that has the same characteristics as the Kludde. The Oschaert was said to inhabit an area surrounding the town of Hamme near Duendemonde. It was a shape-shifting spirit that would appear as a huge horse, changing to a leaping rabbit or a padding Black Dog with fiery eyes. It would seize upon unwary travelers on dark nights, leaping upon their backs and growing heavier the more its victims tried to be free. It particularly oppressed those who were troubled by a guilty conscience, for it would dig its claws deep into their flesh and breathe fiery breath on their necks. It is said that a priest of the area finally exorcised the evil spirit and banished it over the seas for 99 years.
References 66
See also Black Dog, Bogle, Demon, Kludde, Old Man of the Sea, Padfoot, Picktree Brag, Spirit, Appendix 12, Appendix 24

OSƏR PAMAŠ
See Čembulat

OUDA
This is the name of a malignant spirit in the folklore of Finland. It inhabited the forests, where it could appear in any form, but mostly that of a naked male or female human being. The forest workers knew how to recognize the demon, which presented itself as a human, because when the feet were visible they were turned backwards. However, by the time that anyone could discern this it was usually too late. This spirit destroyed his victims by inviting them to dance or wrestle, and under its spell they either danced or were tickled to death.
References 33
See also Demon, Obda, Spirit

OUM ÇEBIANE
This is a female djinn in the folk beliefs of Morocco. Her name, Oum Çebiane, which means Mother of the Little Ones, is a euphemism used for this malicious spirit in order to avert its hostility to children. She will invisibly pinch and beat an infant, making it cry incessantly until it dies of convulsions. Mothers protect their infants from this evil spirit by placing an amulet on the child.
References 90
See also Djinn, Khadem Quemquoma, Spirit, Appendix 22

OUPHE
This used to be a common name for a mountain nymph, elf, or fairy in the folklore of Europe. The Ouphes appear in the works of Shakespeare and are especially named in *The Merry Wives of Windsor*. The Ouphes were considered not so agile or quick-witted as the Trooping Fairies, and therefore were left as changelings when human babies had been abducted. This practice led to their other name of Oaf being used for the changeling and ultimately for a person of dull wit.
References 7, 17, 28, 76, 92
See also Changeling, Elf, Fairy, Nymph, Oaf, Appendix 22

OUR MOTHER'S BROTHER
See Coyote

OVINNIK
In Russian folklore this is the spirit of the barn (*ovin* means barn). He inhabited a corner of the barn in the guise of a half-wild black cat, but could bark like a dog or laugh like a human. If displeased he would readily burn down the barn and anything else near it.

The construction of the Russian barn was effected in such a manner that a crude furnace was lit on the ground floor beneath the threshing and drying level, which stored the harvested crop. The building was sited as far as possible from the main dwellings since the malevolence of the Ovinnik could trigger a fire from the smallest draft taking a spark. In order that all should be well with the process, an offering of a cockerel was made to the spirit, who forbade the lighting of the kiln on saints' feast days, or when there was a high wind. Like the Bannik the Ovinnik was consulted on the eve of the New Year to divine each individual's fortune. A soft touch indicated a good year to come and a cold prickly touch indicated misfortune.
References 75, 87
See also Bannik, Domovik, Spirit, Appendix 12

OXOSSI
This is an encantado of the Afro-Brazilian cults Batuque and Umbanda. This spirit is derived from the spirits of West Africa, but in Brazil he is associated with Saint Sebastian and his feast day, 20 January. He is invited mostly to the ceremonies of the Umbanda cult, where his family includes the spirits Dorada Mata, Pena Verde, and Sete Flechas.
References 89
See also Encantado, Pena Verde, Rei Sebastião, Spirit

OXUN
This is the name of a spirit or encantado in the Afro-Brazilian cult Batuque. She is a type of mermaid derived from spirits of the Yoruba people of Nigeria. Oxun is a quite recent introduction to the cult in Belém and is considered to be a spirit of freshwater. In the possession of devotees, she exhibits a tendency toward inconsistency and vanity.
References 102
See also Encantado, Imanja, Jamaína, Mermaid, Orixá, Appendix 25

OYNYENA MARIA
This is a female spirit, whose name means Fiery Mary, in the folk beliefs of the Slav people. She was originally the attendant of Peroun, the ancient god of thunder, but her status has been reduced in later beliefs.
References 41
See also Attendant Spirit, Spirit

OZA
This designation, which means Master, is used when referring to the spirits in the folk beliefs of the Cheremis/Mari people. It is partly an epithet but is more usually used as a euphemism to avert the power of an offended demon. However, when the spirits are addressed directly, the more euphemistic kuba and kuguza are used.
References 118
See also Demon, Kuba, Kuguza, Spirit

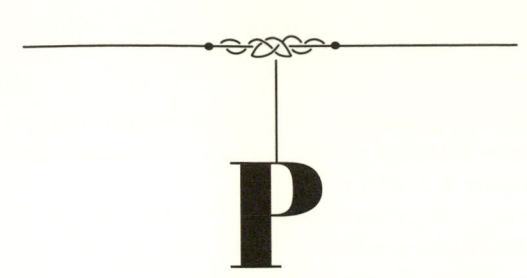

P

PACOLET

This is the name of a dwarf in the traditional French legends of Valentine and Orson. Clérimond and her brother the Green Knight also feature in these romances. These characters are the subjects of many heroic adventures. Orson, who has been separated from his twin brother Valentine, is brought up by a bear in the forests, while Valentine is taken to the royal court of their uncle King Pepin. In the final phase of one of their adventures, Orsen, Valentine, and Clérimond have been trapped in a dungeon of the castle held by the giant Ferragus. Pacolet effects their rescue by using his magic wooden horse to transport Valentine, Orson, and Clérimond back to the court of King Pepin.
References 40, 114
See also Dwarf, Green Knight

PADFOOT

A frightening spirit also known as Padfooits. It is found haunting the moors, particularly around Leeds in Yorkshire in northern England. It is described variously as taking the form of a supernatural sheep with shaggy fleece and fiery eyes, or of a bowling bundle of fleece, or of a large white dog, or even of a black donkey with huge glaring eyes. Sometimes it is reported as invisible. Whatever shape it assumes, it is the soft eerie padding behind its victim as it draws alongside them in the dark that warns of its presence. This is often accompanied by roaring or the sound of chains. Terrified victims have died of fright. Some have attempted to hit it, but anything solid goes right through it. Padfoot is a bogey beast, boggart, or bogie not unlike the Barguest, Gytrash, Skryker, and Trash, all road spirits of northern England. These are usually evil omens and must never be approached or touched.
References 15, 17, 18, 28
See also Barguest, Black Dog, Black Shuck, Boggart, Bogie, Bullbeggar, Capelthwaite, Church Grim, Freybug, Gytrash, Mauthe Dhoog, Rongeur d'Os, Skriker, Appendix 24

PAHUANUIAPITAAITERAI

In Tahitian mythology, a male sea spirit or sea demon. Pahuanuiapitaaiterai, whose name means the Great One that Opens Up the Sky, is one of the spirits personifying the dangers of the sea and is greatly feared by the Tahitian fishermen. The other sea demons are called Ahifatumoana, which means Sea Serpent; Arematapopoto, which means Short Wave; Aremataroroa, which means Long Wave; and Puatutahi, which means Coral Rock Standing Alone.
References 33
See also Demon, Spirit, Appendix 25

PAI BENEDITO, PAI JERONIMO, PAI TOMAS
See Pretos Velhos

PAIJA

This is the name of a devil in the folk beliefs of the Inuit and Ihalmiut people of Canada. She manifests in a grotesque female human form, with one leg, which emerges from the region of her genitalia, and long black hair flowing over her body. In the long winter nights she will seek men caught in the blizzards to devour them. A single look from her, or merely the sight of her, will cause instantaneous death, and therefore anyone seeing her twisted single-foot track in the snow will not venture out until it is safe.
References 101
See also Biasd Bheulach, Cacy Taperere, Devil, Dodore, Fachan, Hinky-Punk, Nashas, Shiqq

PAIL PAK

This is a particularly malicious spirit in the folk beliefs of the Cheremis/Mari people of the former Soviet Republic. It is a demon that inhabits the house and is said to look like a dwarf. Once it has gained entry, the Pail Pak causes bad dreams at night when people are asleep. It is even more dangerous for pregnant mothers and the newborn, as it may eat the babies in the womb and the hearts of young children asleep in their beds.
References 118

See also Demon, Dwarf, Penanggalan, Spirit, Zagaz, Appendix 22

PAJBERDA ŠƏRT
This is a keremet or evil spirit in the folklore of the Cheremis/Mari people of the former Soviet Republic. It is placated by the sacrifice of a calf.
References 118
See also Čort, Keremet, Spirit

PALTƏKAN
This is the name of a keremet in the folk beliefs of the Cheremis/Mari people of the former Soviet Republic. He appears in human form wearing a red cloak. This demon inhabits groves of trees and may sometimes be seen there or traveling in a golden boat on the nearby river.
References 118
See also Demon, Keremet, Appendix 9

PAMAŠ OZA
This is a fearsome water spirit in the folk beliefs of the Cheremis/Mari people of the former Soviet Republic. As its name, which means Spring Master, implies, it inhabits the freshwater springs, where it demands respectful behavior from those humans who draw their water there. If anyone uses bad language, shouts, quarrels, or uses dirty water vessels, the Pamaš Oza will punish them by inflicting them with boils, rashes, and other ailments of the skin. Any victim of the punishment may be relieved of it by the spirit if an offering of porridge is made at the edge of the spring.
References 118
See also Oza, Spirit, Appendix 25

PAMOLA
The name of an evil spirit in the legends of the Algonquian Native American people. This spirit terrorized humans at night until he was destroyed by the culture hero Glooscap.
References 41
See also Spirit

PANCHAJANA
Originally this was the name of an evil sea demon in the Hindu mythology of India. The demon inhabited a conch shell deep in the ocean. One day he grew bold and abducted the son of Sandipani and took him deep into the waters. Krishna became enraged at the audacity of Panchajana and plunged into the ocean to find him. Krishna destroyed the demon and took Panchajana's conch shell, with its magical properties, as his own. Whenever Krishna blows the shell, now known by the name of the demon Panchajana, it signals the demise of any unrighteous being, such as its former occupant.

References 88
See also Demon, Appendix 25

PANCZUMANCZI
See Rumpelstiltskin

PANOPE
The name of a Nereid who is mentioned by Milton in his work *Lycidas* (1637).
References 40
See also Nereid, Appendix 11, Appendix 25

PARA
This is the name of a household spirit in the folklore of the Finnish people. The name is derived from the Swedish *büra*, meaning bearer, and resembles the Scandinavian Smiera-Gatto. It may manifest in the form of a domestic animal, such as a cat, or an amphibian, such as a frog, and engages in the acquisition of goods for the owner. The Para may be obtained by the transformation of stolen property taken by the owner himself. Thereafter this spirit will steal butter, milk, cream, rye, and other valuable goods, usually from a neighbor, to enrich its master.
References 87, 88, 93
See also Aitvaras, Household Spirit, Kaukas, Pukis, Smiera-Gatto, Appendix 12, Appendix 22

PARALDA
See Sylph

PARAVOJ IA
This is the name, meaning Ship Devil, of a spirit in the folk beliefs of the Cheremis/Mari people of the former Soviet Republic. These demons appear in the shape of humans in the holds of ships. In the depths of the winter darkness and in the long summer nights, these spirits can be heard moving about below the decks of the ship when everyone else is asleep.
References 118
See also Klaboterman, Spirit

PARCAE
These are the spirits in the mythology of ancient Rome that correspond with the Greek Moirae. They are the three Fates who appear at the birth of each child to determine its future. Their individual names were Nona, Decuma, and Morta.
References 93, 114
See also Béfind, Moiræ, Spirit, Appendix 22, Appendix 23

PARIKAS, PAIRIKAS
See Peri

PARNASSIDES
See Muses

PASIKOLA
See Manabozo

PAŠKƏČE
A spirit or devil in the folk beliefs of the Cheremis/Mari people of the former Soviet Republic. Paškače, also known as Bashkir, is the attendant of the keremet Kugə Jen.
References 118
See also Attendant, Devil, Keremet, Kugə Jen, Spirit

PASU
This is the first part of the name of a number of field spirits within the Pasu designation in the folklore of the Cheremis/Mari people of the former Soviet Republic. The spirit names are Pasu Jər, meaning Field Offering; Pasu Kögə, meaning Field Center; Pasu Kuba and Pasu Kuguza, which mean Field Old Woman and Field Old Man, respectively. These spirits are the guardians of the agricultural fields. They are invoked at the first plowing of the season and in times of need, such as the emergence of the crops. Pasu Kögə is assisted by the Šurnə group of spirits.
References 118
See also Guardian, Izə Nur Bodəž, Nur Bodəž, Spirit, Šurnə, Appendix 18

PASUK
This is the familiar spirit in the folk beliefs of the Jívaro people of the Amazon region of Equador. It takes the form of an insect or an animal, which will remain with the victim of the shaman's sorcery to make sure that the spells succeed. If a curing shaman manages to discern the nature of the spell and remove it, the Pasuk may shoot the victim again for its master. The Pasuk itself cannot be destroyed, as it is said to have a protection of magic armor.
References 64
See also Familiar, Appendix 12

PATU-PAIAREHE
This is the name of the Trooping Fairies in the folklore of the Maori people of New Zealand. They were tiny human-shaped beings, but with pale skins and hair. They inhabited the *kowharawhara* (fairy flax) that grows in the forks of the trees high in the mountain forests, where they dwelled in much the same kind of communities as humans. On a ridge of the hills near the Waitara River, the fruit of the *kiekie* is red when everywhere else it is white. This is because it is the food of the fairies. If a human wishes to take some of these, an offering must be made first or there may be misfortune. The Patu-paiarehe always know when humans are there, and they may call the Maori greeting, *"Haere-mai e te manuhiri tuarangi."* When the person follows in the direction of the welcome greeting, he will find no one and may even lose his way. Like the Atuas the Patu-paiarehe appear on the edges of reality in mists, twilight, and dawn, when no humans are likely to see them. These fairies were particularly fond of music and dancing and would, like the European fairies, encourage humans to join them and even sometimes marry them. It is thought that albinos are the offspring of such a marriage. These charming spirits were responsible for teaching humans about magic, special chants, and charms. They also taught them the entertainment of puppets and the art of making fishing nets. The Patu-paiarehe were the guardians of some sacred places and would punish those who neglected to make offerings to the gods.
References 63, 110
See also Atua, Fairy

PAZUZU
This is a disease demon in the ancient mythology of the Assyrians. He was portrayed as a hideous creature with part-human form, two pairs of wings, and a scorpion's tail. Pazuzu was the personification of the scorching stormy winds from the desert. He was the bringer of fevers and sickness but could be thwarted by charms and special incantations.
References 93
See also Asmodeus, Demon, Appendix 17, Appendix 26

PEALLAIDH
This is the name of a Urisk in the folklore of Perthshire, Scotland. It belongs to a group of spirits called fuaths, which are evil in nature. Any human meeting with a Peallaidh will be certain to have misfortune and misery. It is known as the Shaggy One from its appearance; like most of the fuaths, it is covered in shaggy hair. This one inhabits the river-divided forested areas of Perthshire, but a lowland version of the Peallaidh is known, and this is called the Shellycoat.
References 17
See also Fuath, Shellycoat, Urisk

PEASE BLOSSOM
This is the name of one of the Flower Fairies. She is one of the attendants of Titania, the fairy queen, in Shakespeare's *A Midsummer Night's Dream*. Pease Blossom, in company with the other fairies called Cobweb, Moth, and Mustard Seed, is directed by Titania to attend the peasant Bottom, who has been given the head of an ass by Oberon, the fairy king.
References 114
See also Attendant, Fairy, Flower Fairy, Oberon, Spirit, Titania

PECHS, PECHTS, PICTS

This is the name of a group of Little People in the folklore of the Highlands of Scotland. They are described as having the appearance of elves, being squat little men with red hair, long arms, and such huge feet that when it rained heavily, they lay on their backs and took shelter under their feet. Some say that they are the ancient Picts who built the *brochs*, who with time have diminished to the spirits that now inhabit these fortifications and the ancient mounds.
References 10, 17, 18
See also Elf, Little People, Muryans, Spirit, Appendix 6

PEERIE FOLK

See Peerifool

PEERIE TROWS

See Troll

PEERIFOOL

This is the name of one of the Little People known in the Orkney Islands, north of Scotland, as Peerie Folk. He figures in a traditional tale in much the same fashion as the story of Tom Tit Tot. In the Scottish tale a young princess, the youngest of a king's three daughters, is captured by an evil ogre and imprisoned in his stronghold. She is told that she must spin, but as in the story of Habetrot, the hapless maiden has never learned this skill. In her misery she shares both her sorrows and her porridge with the Little People who have come through the cracks in the walls to investigate the sobbing. Later a flaxen-haired fairy skillfully does all the princess's spinning for her but requires her to know his name before a given time, or all will be lost. Gratefully the princess delivers the flax and is able to return home. But the time is approaching when the flaxen-haired fairy will return. She is almost at her wits' end when an old beggar lady tells the princess of how she had looked down the hole of the Little People's dwelling to hear one telling of how the princess cannot guess his curious name, Peerifool. With this the old lady is rewarded for helping to relieve the princess of the impending curse had she not got the name in time.
References 17
See also Fairy, Habetrot, Little People, Rumpelstiltskin, Troll, Appendix 14

PEG O' NELL, PEGGY O' NELL

This is the name of an evil spirit in the folklore of North Yorkshire, England. An account of this spirit first appears in a book by Roby (1831). He states that the frequent drownings in the River Ribble were attributed to the bogie known as Peggy of Peggy's Well at Waddow Hall nearby. Here the headless statue of a female had been placed after its removal from the great house, as all the servants blamed its spirit for the disasters that took place there. It was thought that this boggart was the transformed soul of a servant girl who had been drowned in the well many centuries ago for prostituting herself or as a victim of a jealous mistress. Dobson describes her in his *Rambles by the Ribble* (1864), and it is she who is deemed responsible for blights on crops, sickness of livestock and humans, and the loss or destruction of property. During the Roman occupation of Britain over a thousand years ago, the River Ribble was sacred to Minerva, and her priestesses demanded sacrifices. It is possibly as a derivation of the goddess or one of her attendant nymphs that the tradition of Peg O' Nell also demands the sacrifice of either a human or a substitute animal at least once every seven years. If no one has drowned by the end of this period, the residents are in fear of the spirit of the river taking someone for herself.
References 15, 17, 18, 69, 123
See also Bogie, Nymph, Peg Powler, Spirit, Appendix 17, Appendix 25

PEG POWLER

This is the name of an evil river spirit in the folklore of the border between Yorkshire and Durham, England. She is the evil hag that inhabits the River Tees and is described as having a hideous female form with green hair and a gaping mouth with green teeth. She lurks in the river awaiting the opportunity of dragging unwary humans to her underwater lair, where she may devour them. Peg Powler's favorite prey are the little children who defy their parents to play at the water's edge, and in this respect she is a nursery bogie. There are two indications of the presence of this spirit: One is the froth on the upper reaches of the river, which is known as Peg Powler's Suds, and the other is the green surface scum on the slower sections of the river, which is called Peg Powler's Cream.
References 15, 17, 18, 123, 132
See also Bogie, Grindylow, Hag, Jenny Greenteeth, Kappa, Nellie Longarms, Peg O' Nell, Spirit, Appendix 22, Appendix 25

PEKOI

This is a trickster spirit in the folk beliefs of Hawaii. This demon could shape shift at will to any form when visible and was renowned for his outrageous exploits.
References 29
See also Demon, Kapua, Spirit, Trickster

PƏL NER

This is a weather spirit in the folk beliefs of the Cheremis/Mari people of the former Soviet Republic.

Pəl Ner, whose name means Cloud Nose, is the demon of bad weather directed from clouds. The Cheremis will make libations to this spirit to dissuade him from sending heavy rainfalls or storms that will destroy the crops.
References 118
See also Demon, Spirit, Appendix 26

PELƏ KOLŠƏ

This is the name of a fearsome water spirit in the folklore of the Cheremis/Mari people of the former Soviet Republic. Pelə Kolšə, whose name means Half Dead, is a demon that manifests in the shape of a human corpse floating facedown in the river. Anyone who attempts to reach it, thinking to restore the dead to their family, will be pulled under the water and devoured or drowned.
References 118
See also Demon, Spirit, Appendix 25

PELISIT

This is the name of a spirit in the folk beliefs of the Malay people of West Malaysia. The Pelisit is a familiar spirit, usually taking the shape of a cricket. This spirit is sent by the human who controls it to work some mischief during the night. It may be used by its owner to disturb the sleep of other households and in particular the women and children.
References 120
See also Familiar, Hantu, Spirit, Appendix 12, Appendix 22

PELZNICKEL, PELZE NOCOL

This is the name of the Christmas spirit of northern Germany. As his name, which means Furry Nick, implies, this was the folkloric form accepted after the Lutheran reformation and the denial of the earlier Saint Nicholas. Instead of the religious title and robes, he was now a jovial winter spirit dressed in furs. He arrives at each human home by flying through the skies on the night before the original feast of Saint Nicholas to deliver gifts to all good children. Pelzenickel is also known as Weinachts Mann, which means the White Night Man, or Schimmel Reiter, which means the Rider of the White Horse. More interestingly, this last name, having been one of the epithets of Odin the Teutonic god, indicates that the debased god was probably still alive in the folk beliefs that had been suppressed by Christianity long before.
References 34
See also Knecht Ruprecht, Spirit, Appendix 22

PENA VERDE

The name of an important encantado in the Afro-Brazilian cult Batuque. Although the name means Green Macaw, the bird itself is actually blue, and its feathers are used to decorate effigies of the spirit in the Batuque *terrieros*. Pena Verde is probably derived from the local animism and shamans' spiritual beliefs.
References 89
See also Jurema, Oxossi

PENANGGALAN

These are evil spirits in the folk beliefs of the Malay people of West Malaysia. The Penanggalan preys at night on the newborn infant, bringing disease and death.
References 120
See also Abiku, Khadem Quemquoma, Langsuir, Oum Çebiane, Spirit, Appendix 17, Appendix 22

PENATES

These are household guardian spirits in the mythology and beliefs of ancient Rome. They are usually referred to in the plural, although their name is derived from *penus,* the name for the pantry or food store, which was their special responsibility. They inhabited the hearth and were propitiated by the family to ensure the spirits' benevolence in the form of health and riches.
References 29, 40, 88, 93, 114
See also Guardian, Household Spirit, Lar, Appendix 22

PEOPLE OF PEACE

See Appendix 6

PEOPLE WHO KILLED BY LIGHTNING IN THEIR EYES

This is the name of a group of evil spirits in the legends of the Native American people in the Southwest United States. These spirits inhabited a marvelous palace made of glistening precious jewels. Travelers who passed by and saw this beautiful dwelling were tempted to go in and thus sealed their fate, for the demons attacked and devoured them. These spirits were eventually defeated by Nagenatzani, the child of the sun, who tricked them with the magic of salt and fire.
References 25
See also Demon, Spirit, Appendix 24

PERCHT/A, PERCHTEN

See Berchta

PÈRE FOUETTARD

This is a Christmas spirit introduced into the folklore of France about the beginning of the eighteenth century. He is the counterpart to the generous Père Noël, for Père Fouettard, whose name means Father Spanker, is the spirit who seeks and deals with all the naughty children. In this respect he is therefore used

Pelznickel, the Christmas spirit of North Germany.

by parents as a nursery bogie to encourage their children's good behavior before the festive season.
References 34
See also Krampus, Nursery Bogie, Père Noël, Spirit, Appendix 22

PÈRE NOËL

This is the name in France for the winter spirit, or Father Christmas, who replaced the ecclesiastical tradition of Saint Nicholas. Unlike Saint Nicholas, who came on his feast day, Père Noël delivers gifts on the night before Christmas to the children who have been good throughout the year. Like most gnomes or beneficent spirits, he is dressed in red and may come on a white horse. He is not generous to all children in the tradition of the former Christian saint, since the more sinister Père Fouettard was introduced to punish those children who were naughty.
References 34
See also Berchta, Father Christmas, Father Frost, Gnome, Pelznickel, Père Fouettard, Spirit, Appendix 22

PEREŠTA

This is the name for an angel in the folk beliefs of the Cheremis/Mari people of the former Soviet Republic. Many different kinds of angel were acknowledged, in the same way as the devils, according to the region of their guardianship and protective intervention. The Kas Perešta is the Evening Angel, the Məlandə Perešta is the Earth Angel, and the Mükš Perešta is the Bee Angel.
References 118
See also Angel, Devil, Guardian Angel, Appendix 1

PERI

There are two cultures that have this name for spirits as follows:

(1) Peri was the name for diminutive spirits in the mythology and beliefs of Persia prior to the coming of the Zoroastrian religion. They were said to be a type of fairy and, like them, were both benevolent and mischievous toward humans. They were deemed responsible for catastrophes such as the appearance of comets, eclipses of the sun, and the mass ruin of crops, and they may have been earlier river or forest deities. In the later religion of Islam, the Peris were regarded as the Fallen Angels with the name spelled Piris, and Eblis was ascribed as their leader. They were said to have repented too late for their actions to be restored to heaven, and the Prophet Mohammed was sent to convert them to Islam. In this transitional phase the Peris became a type of genii benevolent to mankind.

Similarly, in the Zoroastrian religion, these beautiful, tiny, shimmering female fairies were regarded originally as the demon Parikas, who were members of the group of spirits known as the Drujes. This representation later developed to the gentler image of the Peris who became the fairies of folklore. In this guise they existed only on the choicest perfumes and were persecuted by the evil Deevs, which waged constant war on them. When caught, the Peris were locked in iron cages strung in the tops of the trees, where their own companions sustained them with perfumes. The Peris were not immortal, and could die from neglect or naturally after thousands of years.

(2) Peri is the name of an evil spirit in the folklore of the Cheremis/Mari people of the former Soviet Republic. The Peri is said to originate in the drops of blood shed by the victim of a murder or a suicide and is confined to the area in which the offense took place. It can take almost any form but most frequently takes that of a pig, a calf, a bear, a man, or a cask of liquid rolling down the road. In any of these guises it will

attempt to befuddle human travelers so that they become so confused they do not recognize anything for what it really is. At other times it will chase travelers until they are exhausted or lost. A Peri may be controlled and loses power over humans when they pray for God's help.
References (1) 40, 41, 78, 88, 92, 110
See also (1) Deev, Demon, Drug, Fairy, Fallen Angel, Iblis, Genius, Perit; (2) Hedley Kow, Kazna Peri, Spirit, Appendix 12, Appendix 24

PERIFOAL
See Peerifool

PERIT
This is a nature spirit that inhabits the mountains in the folklore of Albania. The Perit appears as a delicate female sprite wearing white garments. She is particularly annoyed with anyone who is improvident and will punish humans who are wasteful with bread by giving them the deformity of a hunchback.
References 93
See also Peri, Spirit, Sprite

PERRY DANCERS, THE
The name for the northern lights in the folklore of Suffolk, England, where they were thought to be dancing fairies in the summer night's sky.
References 17
See also Fairy, Fir Chlis

PESEIAS
This is a household spirit in the folklore of the Slav people of Europe. He was considered to be the guardian of the domestic animals in much the same way as the Kikimora of Russia.
References 102
See also Guardian, Household Spirit, Kikimora, Krukis, Appendix 12, Appendix 22

PETER PAN
This is the name of the main character in the play *Peter Pan* (1904) by J. M. Barrie (1860–1930). Peter Pan is the mischievous spirit of boyhood as the "boy who refused to grow up," leading a group of Lost Boys in Neverland. In this realm lurks the fearsome Captain Hook, but the boys' delivery comes in the shape of the fairy Tinkerbelle, with the human child Wendy, her brothers, and a dog called Nana. They were created originally as stories for the children of Sylvia Llewellyn Davies, and were so popular that they were later published as the story of *Peter and Wendy* (1911). This story achieved enduring popularity with later generations of children through the Disney film. These tales were created in the same Victorian moralizing genre, for the children of the nursery, as Charles Kingsley's The Water Babies and its fairy characters Mrs. Bedonebyasyoudid and Mrs. Doasyouwouldbedoneby.
References 56
See also Bedonebyasyoudid, Doasyouwouldbedoneby, Fairy, Spirit, Tinkerbelle, Appendix 22

PETIT HOMME ROUGE, LE
See Nain Rouge

PETIT POUCET, LE
See Tom Thumb

PEY
These are demons in the Tamil mythology of India and are also known in the female forms under the names of Alakai, Iruci, and Picacu. They are the attendants of Yama and are depicted as a type of goblin with shaggy hair. The Pey are the bringers of misfortune and misery, and they drink the blood of the wounded in battle, ensuring the victim's death. Parviti, the consort of Siva, may take the *avatar* form of one of these demons in some of the legends.
References 68, 93
See also Attendant Spirit, Bhut, Demon, Goblin, Piśācas, Pret

PHALEG
This is the name of an Olympian spirit in the European medieval literature of mysticism. Phaleg is the personification of Mars, celebrated as Tuesday, and rules over 35 provinces of the Olympian Universe.
References 53
See also Olympian Spirit, Appendix 16

PHARAILDIS
See Ben Socia

PHI
This name is used for spirits in two different cultures where the spirits have similar characteristics.

(1) In the mythology of Burma this nat is a demon of the jungles. He is considered responsible for giving fever, especially malaria, to those who venture into the jungle. In order to be cured of the fever it is thought that the person must travel back to the place where they last sheltered against a tree. The spirit has been offended and inflicted this fever as a punishment, and an offering in apology will ensure the spirit's removal of the sickness.

(2) In the beliefs of Thailand the Phi is an entire group of nature spirits equating to the group known as nats in the folk beliefs of Burma. If offended, these spirits will inflict sickness and misfortune on the human perpetrators. They inhabit the forests, specific trees, air, ground, mountains, hills, houses, freshwater rivers, waterfalls, lakes, pools, and sea. When benevolent they promote the growth of the crops and bring good weather, fishing, and fertility. To offend them is disastrous.

References (1) 110; (2) 39
See also (1) Demon, Hmin, Nats, Appendix 10, Appendix 17; (2) Nats, Phra Phum, Spirit, Appendix 18, Appendix 19, Appendix 25

PHONOS
See Acephalos

PHOOKA
See Pooka

PHRA PHUM
This is the name of the spirit of the earth in the beliefs of Thailand. Phra Phum is a household spirit and guardian of the home. He is an important member of the spirit group known as the Phi who, if not propitiated, will bring disaster and misfortune. To ensure the benevolence of Phra Phum, most households have a small house or *sam* especially built and placed by the entrance to the home. Offerings are made here daily to ensure the continued prosperity of the family.

References 39, 110
See also Guardian, Household Spirit, Penates, Phi (2), Spirit, Appendix 22

PHUL
This is an Olympian spirit in the European medieval literature on mysticism. Phul is the personification of the Moon, celebrated as Monday, and rules over seven provinces of the Olympian Universe.

References 53
See also Olympian Spirit, Appendix 13

PHYNNODDEREE
See Fenodyree

PI NERESKƏ
This is a group of evil spirits in the folk beliefs of the Cheremis/Mari people of the former Soviet Republic. Pi Nereskə means Dog Nose, and these spirits are described as being the shape of humans with only one foot and hand each, and having the nose of a dog. They are hunter spirits that use their keen sense of smell to track down the humans who travel through the Siberian forests. Because they hunt in pairs, a human may be deceived into thinking that the tracks he has seen are those of a man and not two Pi Nereskə, who will ultimately make him their victim.

References 118
See also Fachan, Fuath, Spirit, Appendix 12, Appendix 24

PIAMBAR
This is the designation of a group of spirits in the folk beliefs of the Cheremis/Mari people of the former Soviet Republic. Although translated as Prophet, there is little in common with the activities of human prophets. The spirit is usually the guardian of some feature or natural phenomenon. It may be the appellation of a keremet, its attendant, or a deity in its own right. Names of spirits within this category are Bolək Piambar, which means the Livestock Prophet; Kaba Piambar, meaning the Fate Prophet, who is the attendant of the god of fate Kaba Jumə; Kazna Piambar, which means the Treasure Prophet; Kurək Piambar, meaning the Mountain Prophet, who is a keremet; Mükš Piambar, which means Bee Prophet; and Šurnə Piambar, which means the Grain Prophet.

References 118
See also Attendant Spirit, Čembulat, Guardian, Keremet, Spirit, Appendix 9

PIASA
This is the name of a water demon in the folk beliefs of the Native Americans of Mississippi. A portrayal of this terrifying spirit was described in 1855 by a French traveler named Marquette. The image, painted on the rocks over a massive waterfall, showed a being about the size of a deer. The head had the face of a man with a beard, with red eyes. The green body was covered in scales and from it extended a long tail on the end of which was a poisonous barb. It was later considered to be the fish-man spirit of a whirlpool.

References 99
See also Demon, Spirit, Appendix 25

PICĀCU, PIÇACÂS
See Piśācas

PICKTREE BRAG

A malicious spirit in the region of Garland, Durham, England. It is well known in the folklore of northern England for its shape-shifting devilment and trickery on unwary humans. The Picktree Brag is a bogey-beast that was sometimes seen as a donkey, then as a calf with a white rag collar. It was seen once as a headless naked man and once as a white sheet held at the corners by four men. It played very much the same sorts of tricks as the Hedley Kow, either trotting in front of night-bound travelers and then making them jump with fright, or allowing the tired travelers to mount its back, giving them the worst ride of their lives before dumping them somewhere unpleasant.
References 15, 18, 66
See also Brag, Dunnie, Hedley Kow, Kelpie, Pooka, Spirit, Appendix 12, Appendix 24

PICUS

This was a forest demon in the mythology and beliefs of ancient Rome. He was believed to have been the son of the god Saturn, or an ancient hunter who spurned the love of Circe. Whatever the origins, his bright purple and golden garments gave way to the colors of the plumage characteristic of the wood-pecker into which he was transformed.
References 93, 110
See also Demon, Appendix 12, Appendix 19

PIERIDES

See Muses

PIGWIDGEON, PIGWIGGEN

The name of the fairy knight in Drayton's *Nymphidia* who fell in love with Queen Mab, the consort of the king of the fairies, Oberon.
References 40, 114
See also Fairy, Mab, Oberon, Appendix 6

PI-HSIA YÜAN-CHÜN

This is the name of the Turquoise Cloud Princess in the classical mythology of China. She was the daughter of the god of T'ai Mountain, and she was the wife of the god of the Western Sea. She is described as a gentle maiden who traveled through the skies on delicate clouds wafted by the gentlest breezes. Pi-Hsia Yüan-Chün is the guardian of women in childbirth who presides over them in their chamber at the moment of birth.
References 131
See also Béfind, Chang Hsien, Eshu, Guardian, Oosood, Appendix 22

PILLYWIGGIN

In the folklore of England this is a diminutive nature fairy. It is said to be the size of the inside of the flow-ers that are so small that only the honeybee may enter. Such flowers as the bluebell, the cowslip, the foxglove, and the wild thyme, growing at the base of the woodland oak, may harbor this tiny elf.
References 44
See also Elf, Fairy, Flower Fairies

PILOSI

See Dusii

PILWIZ

See Bilwis

PINARI

These are the Little People in the folk beliefs of the people of the Solomon Islands. These spirits are described as appearing in a human shape having long legs and hairy bodies.
References 109
See also Little People

PINKET

See Will o' the Wisp

PIRENE

This is the name of a nymph in the classical mythology of Greece and Rome. She grieved so much for the loss of her son that her tears became a fountain near Corinth.
References 102, 130
See also Nymph, Appendix 25

PIRIS

See Peri

PIŚĀCAS

These are disease demons in the classical mythology and folk beliefs of India. They are variously known as Piçacâs, Pisakas, Pishachas, or Pishashas, and the females are known as Piśāchi. In the Vedic myth they were said to be the vilest of the demons created at the same time as the Asuras and Rakshasas. In the Puranas they are described as being descended from Kashyapa and his wife Pishacha. These demons are considered to be the most malignant and offensive of all. They prey upon both the living and the dead, frequently devouring their flesh. Like the ghouls they inhabit the charnel houses, the graveyards, and deserted places, chattering in their fiendish manner as they seek humans to destroy by disease or madness. In southern India these fiends are also thought to lurk in the deep forests between the villages, and pregnant women are considered particularly vulnerable to their malice. Consequently, when making a necessary journey from one village to another, a piece of iron or leaves of the neem tree are carried as

charms against the Piśācas, and women may make propitiations along the way to ensure their safety. The forest and mountain demons known as Bhuts and Chûtâs also belong to the Piśācas, as does the female demon of Tamil folk belief Picācu.
References 29, 39, 41, 53, 68, 88, 110, 111
See also Asura, Bhut, Chûtâs, Demon, Fiend, Ghoul, Rakshasas, Appendix 17

PISCA
See Puck

PISHUMI
This is a disease spirit in the folk beliefs of the Acoma Native American people.
References 25
See also Spirit, Appendix 17

PISKEY, PISKY
This is the household spirit in the folklore of Cornwall, England. Although they are somewhat like the usual English brownie in their willingness to do work in the home or the farm, the Piskeys are extremely capricious and more given to trickery than work. The Piskeys have a fondness for riding horses to such an extent that they will leave the beasts quite lathered in their stalls in the morning, having ridden them all through the night. At other times they will delight in playing the Will o' the Wisp and lead a stranger on the road at night by their lantern until the human is totally lost, the Piskey vanishing in a gale of laughter. They are described as appearing like little wizened old men, and not at all like the neighboring earthy, strong youthful Pixies of other counties. The Piskeys are considered to bring exceptional good fortune to those they favor.
References 18, 28, 41, 87
See also Brownie, Goblin, Household Spirit, Kobold, Nis, Pixie, Tomtar, Will o' the Wisp, Appendix 22

PISUHÄND
See Kratt

PITRIS
These are a group of ancestral spirits in the Hindu mythology of India. They are regarded also in the occult philosophy as being instrumental in the evolution of human abilities. Theosophists consider that there are solar and lunar Pitris. These spirits are regarded in much the same role as the Guardian Angels.
References 53
See also Angiris, Guardian Angel, Lars, Manes, Rishis, Spirit, Appendix 13

PITYS
The name of a nymph in the classical mythology of Greece and Rome. She was loved by both Pan and

Boreas, the god of the north wind. However, because she loved Pan, the god of nature, Boreas in a fit of jealousy blew at Pitys so hard that she was lost over the edge of a precipice. On the spot where she fell, she changed into a pine tree, which thereafter was the sacred tree of Pan.
References 102, 110, 130
See also Nymph

PIXIE, PIXY
This is a type of Trooping Fairy or elf in the English folklore of the Southwestern Counties. They are described as having red hair, small, pale youthful faces with turned-up noses, and pointed ears. They usually wear green garments and often a pointed type of nightcap, but may be seen in other guises. Like most domestic spirits they will do work for the poor or the oppressed, but Pixies, like other house-hold spirits, are "laid" (compelled to depart) by the gift of new clothes. More frequently, however, they were rewarded with a bowl of cream, or by Pixy-worting (leaving the last of the harvest apples under the tree for them). If someone in the household were considered to be lazy, the Pixies would persecute them by nipping, chasing, and scaring them with objects moved invisibly, much like a poltergeist. They are not always benevolent, and like the Piskies are apt to ride a horse to a lather all night in a *gallitrap* or fairy ring, leaving it exhausted and in a lather in the morning with the mane and tail curiously knotted. They also take a delight in misleading night-bound weary travelers until they become exhausted and lost; this was called being "Pixy-led." These sprites are thought to dwell underground in the ancient mounds, in stone circles, or in caves, coming out to dance in the woods and glades at night. Any traveler who happens upon them may be compelled to dance, losing all sense of time. The usual manner of disen-chanting oneself from this situation was to remove one's jacket and put it back on inside out. Pixies were thought to be the transformed souls of unbaptized children and were frequently accused of stealing human babies and leaving changelings in their place. In the counties of Somerset and Devon, women still tied their babies into the cot as recently as Victorian times to prevent the child's being taken by the Pixies.
References 15, 18, 19, 40, 56, 76, 88, 92, 114
See also Changeling, Elf, Fairy, Household Spirit, Piskey, Poltergeist, Sprite, Appendix 22, Appendix 24

PLANT ANNWN
This is the name of the fairies of Welsh folklore. They are ruled by a king called Gwyn ap Knudd in their fairy underworld, which is reached through the depths of the Welsh lakes. Their beautiful damsels, known as the Gwragen Annwn, have white fairy cattle

and dogs. The Cwn Annwn, the Fairy Hounds, may be heard with their mistresses, like the Wild Hunt, flying through the midsummer skies in search of the souls of unrepentant sinners.
References 17
See also Cwn Annwn, Fairy, Gwyn ap Knudd, Wild Hunt, Appendix 6

PLANT RHYS DDWFN
This is the name of a particular tribe of fairies in the folklore of Wales. They were said to inhabit an island off the Dyfed coast, which was kept invisible by a herb that grew profusely there. These fairies, whose name means Children of Rhys Ddwfn, appeared in the shape of humans, although generally a little smaller, and often went to the market in Cardigan. Unfortunately they were not only honest but rich enough to pay higher prices than anyone else could afford. Therefore they made it difficult for some of the poorer humans to buy the goods after the Plant Rhys Ddwfn's purchases had inflated the prices.
References 17, 18, 59
See also Fairy, Appendix 6

PLASKY
See Nočnitsa

PLAT-EYE
This is the name of an evil spirit in the folk beliefs of the people of the West Indies and the State of Georgia in the United States. It manifests at night on dark and lonely roads in the shape of a large Black Dog with huge glowing eyes. Sometimes only the eyes may appear, seemingly growing larger by the minute. The shape will float silently about the human it encounters until it entirely envelopes its victim, who disappears.
References 87
See also Barguest, Black Dog, Oschaert, Padfoot, Shuck, Spirit, Appendix 12, Appendix 24

PLATINA
See Melusina

PLEIADES
This is the name of the nymphs in the classical mythology of Greece and Rome who were the daughters of Pleione and Atlas. They were sometimes called the Atlantides and were the sisters of the Hyades. The Pleiades were seven in number, their individual names being Alcyone, Asteropea, Celœno, Electra, Maia, Merope, Sterope, and Taygete. They were so distressed at being pursued by Orion that they implored the gods to save them, whereupon they were changed into pigeons and then into the constellation of the Pleiades. One of the Pleiades is not visible from the earth; this is said to be either Merope,

who had married the mortal Sisyphus and was too ashamed to show herself, or Electra mourning the destruction of Troy.
References 130
See also Alcyone, Anitsutsa, Electra, Hyades, Maia, Merope, Nymph, Appendix 13

POAKE
In an account by Jabez Allies of the folklore of Worcestershire in England, the name of Poake is given as that of a sprite that plays tricks on humans. This spirit seemed to be in the habit of misleading and frightening night-bound travelers on lonely roads, often leaving them struggling in bogs or pools, and vanishing in laughter. In this respect the sprite behaves in much the same way as the Will o' the Wisp or Puck.
References 110
See also Puck, Spirit, Sprite, Will o' the Wisp, Appendix 24

PODARGE
This is the name of a demon in the classical mythology of Greece and Rome. Podarge is a Harpy, the only one mentioned by Homer in the *Iliad*. By Zeus she is the mother of Balios and Xanthos, two supernatural horses.
References 88
See also Demon, Harpy

POKER BOYS
These are the spirits associated with the fire in Zuñi Native American folk belief and legends.
References 88
See also Grandmother Fire, Spirit

POKEY HOKEY
In the folklore of East Anglia, England, this bogie or goblin behaved in much the same way as a poltergeist, knocking from within the fabric of the walls of a house and scaring the occupants.
References 17
See also Bogie, Goblin, Poltergeist, Appendix 22

POKŠEM KUBA, POKŠEM KUGUZA, AND POKŠEM OBƏSKA
These are nature spirits in the folk beliefs of the Cheremis/Mari people of the former Soviet Republic. Pokšem Kuba and Pokšem Kuguza mean Frost Old Woman and Frost Old Man, respectively, but they may also be collectively called Pokšem Obəska. They are considered to be responsible for the frost damage to the crops and property. The Old Man Frost is the morning frost and the Old Woman Frost is the evening or night frost. There may be an entire family of frost spirits called Koča (Grandfather), Ača (Father),

Ərbəza (Child), and Üdər (Daughter). Each one comes consecutively, nipping at the plants and destroying them. They may be propitiated by the sacrifice of a gray or white animal to prevent the crops from being destroyed by the frosts.
References 118
See also Jack Frost, Jüštə Kuba, Spirit, Appendix 26

POLEVIK
This is a nature spirit in the folklore of Russia. The Polevik is the spirit of the field (*pole* means field); in the Slavic folklore this spirit is called Polevoi. This spirit is described variously as having a human shape, often that of a dwarf, with flax, straw, or grass for hair, with eyes of different colors and skin the color of the earth (usually black), wearing white garb. The Polevik is rarely seen because he is able to vary his height with that of the crops in the field. He could not tolerate laziness and would strangle any worker who fell into a drunken sleep in the field. He might also play tricks on travelers or farmworkers from another district, leading them astray in the vastness of unknown fields. He might be propitiated by leaving either a cockerel or a couple of eggs for him at the edge of the field.
References 102
See also Domovik, Dwarf, Poludnica, Spirit, Appendix 18

POLONG
In the folklore of the Malay people of West Malaysia, these are malicious, diminutive female spirits or bottle imps held by a person to inflict harm on others as their familiar spirit.
References 53, 120
See also Bottle Imp, Familiar, Spirit

POLTERGEIST
This is a household spirit, whose German name means Noise Spirit, in the folk beliefs of Europe. Occurrences of Poltergeist activity have been recorded since before ancient Roman times. It manifests as an unseen force that disturbs household objects by throwing or moving them, taps on walls and floors, and even throws people about. One famous instance in England was given the name of the Drummer of Tidworth (1622). A celebrated instance, which took place in Wales and was called Bwgan yr Hafod, appeared in 1751 and again in 1759. The spirit would move things that were usually required by the family in a most friendly fashion, but when it started to shift stones in the hearth and other difficult things, a priest was called. This priest unfortunately was grievously hurt by the spirit. Thereafter it manifested in all sorts of guises, from that of a pig to a human kissing the women and snatching candles from their hands. Such spirit activity is often centered around a human child or adolescent, and unexplained occurrences have been recorded even to the present day.
References 40, 53, 59, 91, 113
See also Baravashka, Bullerman, Household Spirit, Knocky-boh, Pokey Hokey, Appendix 22

POLUDNICA, POLUDNITSA
This is the female spirit of the fields in the folklore of Russia. She was also called Poludnitsa and was known as Psezpolnica in the folklore of the Serbian people. Poludnica was described as appearing in the fields like a tall, pretty, black-haired maiden dressed in white, but sometimes she manifests as a whirlwind. She was the Midday Spirit of the fields who would not allow anyone to work during the hottest hours of the day. Poludnica was responsible for pulling the hair of those who disobeyed and for leading small children astray in the fields of tall wheat. If she were offended, the spirit could drive people mad or chop off their heads with her sickle. By the nineteenth century, belief in the spirit had waned, and she had become more or less a nursery bogie to keep the children from the fields and orchards.
References 29, 75, 102
See also Nursery Bogie, Spirit, Appendix 18, Appendix 22

POLUNOCHNITSA
This is a type of night demon in the folklore of Russia. These spirits were said to be hideous hags that inhabited the swamps. At night these evil spirits came to torment sleeping children, giving them bad dreams and nightmares. The name is derived from the Russian word *polnoch*, meaning midnight.
References 75
See also Demon, Hag, Nightmare, Nočnitsa, Spirit, Appendix 22

POLYHYMNIA
See Muses

PONPHYOI
This is the name of one of the nats in the beliefs of the Kachin people of Burma.
References 87
See also Chinün Way Shun, Nats, Appendix 10

PONTIANAK
A frightening spirit in the folk beliefs of the Malay people. It is a demon associated with problems of childbirth. The Pontianak is described as appearing in the form of a hideous head with entrails attached and dangling down from it. This is an evil night spirit that sucks the blood of babies and infants, ensuring that they weaken and die.

References 120
See also Demon, Penanggalan, Spirit, Appendix 22

POOKA, POUKA

This is the name of a shape-shifting spirit in the folk-lore of Ireland. This supernatural is also known as Phooka and Púca. It most usually takes the form of a horse or a shaggy-haired colt that may be hung about with chains. He is said to haunt wild places, the edge of lakes, and streams. This is where he will try to entice small children to mount his back, and if they do, he will race off with them straight over a precipice. Curiously there is an account of a pooka doing work as a horse in the fields for a poor farmer. As a household spirit he may work like the English brownie but, as Keightley puts it, Pooka is more aligned with the English Puck in his mischievous attitude toward humans. When Pooka was rewarded by the present of a new coat, like all such spirits, he was offended and vanished. On the Celtic Feast of Samhain (1 November) the Pooka, in the shape of a horse, was said to trample the remaining blackberries and to give prophetic answers to those humans who might consult him.

References 15, 17, 18, 41, 66, 87
See also Brownie, Hedley Kow, Household Spirit, Kelpie, Picktree Brag, Puck, Spirit, Appendix 12, Appendix 22

PORESKORO

In the folk beliefs of the Romany Gypsies this is a disease demon. This evil spirit was the result of the union between Ana and the king of the demons. This happened when she had eaten the cake that her horrified Keshalyi had made from the hair of a hell hound, a cat, and powdered snake, which was intended to repulse her demon husband's advances. Poreskoro is described as having a human body with seven heads, three of which are those of cats and four of which are those of dogs, with a snake complete with a forked tongue as his tail. This demon and his children are considered to be responsible for all the worst epidemics of contagious diseases, especially those that are spread by parasites.

References 31
See also Ana, Demon, Keshalyi, Loçolico, Melalo, Spirit, Appendix 17

PORPOISE GIRL

This is the name of a water spirit in the folk beliefs and legends of Micronesia. In one of the traditional tales, much like that of the British Merrows, she came to the shore at night, leaving her porpoise tail hidden in the rocks, so that she might watch the humans dancing. One night a man, following the strange marks in the sand, discovered the hidden tail and took it away with him. The Porpoise Girl could not return to the sea without it and married the man, who kept the tail hidden from her. Some years later, when she was in the hut with just her children, she discovered the tail hidden in the roof. She took it immediately and, warning her children never to eat porpoise meat, put on her tail and, saying goodbye to them, returned forever to the sea.

References 29
See also Mermaid, Merrow, Nereid, Spirit, Appendix 25

PÖRT BODƏZ

This is the name of an evil spirit in the folk beliefs of the Cheremis/Mari people of the former Soviet Republic. Pört Bodəz, whose name means House Spirit, is a keremet and a spirit that incites fear. If it is propitiated correctly, it will protect the members of the family whose home it has invaded. But otherwise it will become dangerous. Although this spirit is usually invisible, it may also manifest in a female or male form known as Pört Kuba and Pört Kuguza. In these manifestations the spirit is much more benevolent.

References 118
See also Household Spirit, Keremet, Pört Kuba, Spirit, Appendix 22

PÖRT IA AND PÖRT OZA

See Pört Kuba

PÖRT KUBA AND PÖRT KUGUZA

These are the female and male manifestations of the guardian spirit of the home in the folk beliefs of the Cheremis/Mari people. Their names Pört Kuba and Pört Kuguza mean House Old Woman and House Old Man, respectively. They may also be referred to as Pört Ia or Pört Oza, which mean the House Devil or House Master, but the euphemistic address is used when they are believed to be present. They are the guardians of the family health, happiness, and fortune in much the same way as the Lars of ancient Rome. The Cheremis spirits are propitiated whenever the family must move and are thanked for any good fortune that occurs. To offend them in any way is to bring misfortune, disease, or death to the whole family.

References 118
See also Guardian, Household Spirit, Lar, Appendix 22

PORTUNES

This is a group of diminutive fairies in English folklore. They inhabited the farms and, like the brownies, would work at night at those tasks that had been left incomplete by the human workers. They were described by Gervaise of Tilbury in the thirteenth century as being very tiny, looking like the farm

workers with wizened faces and patched worn clothes. Although the Portunes were usually benevolent, they had the habit of catching and roasting frogs for their supper. Another of their pranks was mischievously taking the bridle of travelers' horses and leading them at night into a ditch or pond and laughing at the startled human before vanishing.
References 15, 17, 18, 133
See also Brownie, Fairy, Pixie, Appendix 22, Appendix 24

POTAN'KA OR POTAN'KA THE LAME
This is the name of a spirit in the folklore of Russia. Potan'Ka is the name of a demon or devil. But when he is referred to as Potan'Ka the Lame, it is very much in the same irreverent tone as the term Auld Hornie in Scotland and northern England, or *Le Diable boiteux* (The Devil upon Two Sticks), the derisory term for a demon that has lost most of its power.
References 75
See also Auld Hornie, Demon, Devil, Spirit

POUK/E
See Puck

POWERS
See Angel

POWRIES
See Dunters

PRAY
This is a term for evil spirits in the folk beliefs of Cambodia. They are frequently the transformed souls of those who have died an unnatural death. The Khmóc Prây are the evil spirits derived from women who have died in childbirth. These hideous demons are invisible and are said to inhabit the trees. Their presence is easily detected as they shower passersby with stones, deriding and laughing at the terrified humans and sometimes killing them.
References 53, 88
See also Cihuateteo, Demon, Langsuir, Spirit, Appendix 19

PRECHT
See Berchta

PRESSINA
See Melusina

PRET, PRETA
In the Hindu beliefs and folklore of India, these spirits may be spiteful goblins or the transformed souls of the sinful dead condemned to roam the earth without rest. They may manifest in the shape of a burnt tree,

or in human form with huge bellies and tiny mouths. They lurk near cemeteries, boundaries, and crossroads, terrifying the humans who must pass there.
References 88, 102
See also Acheri, Bhut, Goblin, Pey, Piśācas, Spirit, Yakkhas

PRETOS VELHOS
This is the term for a group of encantados in the Afro-Brazilian cults of Batuque and Umbanda. Encantados or spirits of lowly status are termed Cabaclos or Pretos Velhos, which means Old Blacks. They are usually envisaged as old humble spirits, possibly the transformed souls of those who were slaves. They are thought to be kindly, gentle spirits who figure frequently in the Umbanda curing sessions. The most well known of this group are Pai Benedito, Pai Jeronimo, Pai Tomas, and Senhora Ana.
References 89
See also Cabocolo, Encantado, Pretos Velhos, Spirit

PRIGIRSTITIS
This is the name of a household spirit in the folklore of the Slav people of Europe. It is described as being much like the Domovoi both in its appearance as a little old man and in doing work in the home. The Prigirstitis had extremely acute hearing and was able to hear the slightest whispers in the home. Because of the sensitivity of his hearing, the spirit loathed excessive noise, especially any kind of shouting, and would exact retribution on anyone who offended him.
References 102
See also Domovik, Household Spirit, Appendix 22

PRINCESA D'ALVA
One of the main encantado spirits in the Afro-Brazilian cult Batuque. She belongs to the families of both Averekete and Seu Turquia and is therefore one of the most popular spirits of the devotees. Princesa d'Alva is a spirit of high status and is therefore addressed as one of the Senhores.
References 89
See also Averekete, Encantado, Senhor, Seu Turquia, Spirit

PRINCIPALITIES
See Angel

PRIPARCHIS
This is the name of a nature spirit in the folklore of Poland. He was one of the guardian spirits of the domestic animals who made sure that they were healthy and unharmed. Priparchis was considered particularly responsible for the sows in farrow and the successful weaning of the piglets. This supernatural worked in collaboration with another spirit

called Kremara, who was also concerned with the pigs' welfare.
References 102
See also Guardian, Kremara, Spirit, Appendix 12

PSEZPOLNICA
See Poludnica

PSKÉGDEMUS
This is the name of an evil spirit in the folk beliefs of the Penobscot Native American people. She is a female demon that inhabits the swamps. She manifests as a distraught woman, like the spirit called La Llorona who wails at night outside the dwellings of humans. Pskégdemus is particularly intent on enticing men or children to her. But it is dangerous to show any form of sympathy toward this distraught woman's crying, even in thought, for then that person is unable to resist her evil power.
References 88
See also Demon, Lilith, Llorona, Spirit, Appendix 22

PSUVASHI
This is the name of a group of spirits in the folk beliefs of the Romany Gypsies of Europe. The Psuvashi are earth spirits or demons that behave like the incubus. These demons will come at night with the purpose of having intercourse with young women who are destined to become witches.
References 31
See also Demon, Incubus, Matiya, Nivashi, Spirit

PSYCHOPOMPOS, PSYCHOPOMPS
This is not a spirit in its own right, but rather the defining role of particular spirits in various cultures. The term *Psychopompos* means Conductor of Souls in Greek and is applied to those spirits that are in charge of conducting the souls of the dead to the underworld.
References 39
See also Charontes, Ker, Appendix 16

PUATUTAHI
See Pahuanuiapitaaiterai

PÚCA
See Pooka

PÚCÁ
See Pooka

PUCA
See Bucca, Puck

PUCK/E
These are the two most usual spellings of the name for the mischievous household sprite and nature

spirit of English folklore. In different parts of the country he is known as Poake, Pouke, Puckle, and Pug. He is variously described as being a hobgoblin, a fairy, a brownie, an elf, or a goblin. The fact that no two descriptions seem to be the same attests to the shape-shifting abilities of this tricksy supernatural. A generally accepted image seems to be of a small human-shaped hairy being that may have the feet of a goat, like the fauns. He appears in numerous stories and works of literature from the earliest times, the most famous perhaps being Shakespeare's *A Midsummer Night's Dream* and Rudyard Kipling's *Puck of Pooks Hill*. His character is that of a playful sprite tricking gullible humans, often as a Will o' the Wisp, leading them into discomfort or embarrassing situations. But this spirit is also credited with promoting the interests of the poor, the oppressed, and lovers. In this respect Puck is often confused with the exploits of Robin Goodfellow or the legends of Robin Hood, who was also said to be a nature spirit. The Welsh people call this spirit Pisca or Pwca. In Germany he is Pouk, in Iceland he is Púka, in Scandinavia he is Pukje, and in Estonia and Latvia he is Pukis.
References 7, 15, 17, 18, 37, 40, 56, 59, 69, 87, 92, 93, 114, 125
See also Ariel (2), Brownie, Bucca, Elf, Fairy, Faun, Goblin, Hobgoblin, Pukis, Robin Goodfellow, Spirit, Sprite, Will o' the Wisp, Appendix 6, Appendix 8, Appendix 22

PUCKLE
See Puck

PUDDLEFOOT
This is the name of the individual brownie attached to Clochfoldich Farm, near Pitlochry in Tayside, Scotland. He had the habit of splashing about in pools of the Altmor Burn, a stream close to the property. He came by his name as he was in the habit of paddling about in the burn before going to the farmhouse to do tasks there. The result was that he left his wet footprints everywhere. Consequently the inhabitants could tell who was responsible for tidying what had been left undone and making a mess of what had been tidy and clean. One evening a drunken man on his way home greeted the brownie and called out the spirit's local name. At this the horrified brownie moaned, "Oh no, I've gotten a name! T'is Puddlefoot they call me!" whereupon he disappeared forever. It is common knowledge that the naming of a supernatural is to have power to dismiss them, as with Tom Tit Tot.
References 17, 133
See also Brownie, Rumpelstiltskin, Short Hoggers of Whittinghame, Tom Tit Tot, Appendix 22

Psychopomps gently guides the departed soul.

PUG
See Puck

PUK, PÛKS AND PÜCK
See Pukis

PÚKA
See Puck

PUKIS

This is the name of a household spirit in the folklore of the Latvian people. He is also known as Pukys to the Lithuanians and Pukje or Puuk to the Estonians, which may be derived from the German regional names of Puk, Pûks, and Pück. He is a tricksy treasure-hoarding spirit that enriches its master usually to the detriment of the neighbors. It is a shape-shifting sprite that may manifest in the shape of a domestic creature such as a cat or a cockerel when on the ground, but in the air it may resemble a dragon with a fiery tail.

References 87, 88, 93

See also Aitvaras, Household Spirit, Kaukas, Para, Smiera-Gatto, Sprite, Appendix 12, Appendix 20, Appendix 22

PUKJE
See Puck

PUKKUMERIA
This is the name of a type of spirit in the folk beliefs of Jamaica. The Pukkumeria are said to inhabit the forests and are venerated in a Jamaican cult.
References 87, 88
See also Apuku, Aziza, Ijimere, Mmoatia, Spirit, Appendix 19

PULCH
This is a wood spirit in the folklore of Germany. He was the guardian of the trees in the Kammerforst and would exact retribution from any human who damaged the trees or took wood without permission.
References 110
See also Guardian, Spirit, Appendix 19

PURONGO
See Waruk

PUTANA
An evil female demon in the classical Hindu mythology of India. She was the daughter of the demon Bali. Putana tried to destroy the infant Krishna by suckling him with her poisoned milk, but instead the god drained the demon of her life's energy and rendered her powerless to harm him. Putana is still regarded as the cause of abortion in pregnancy and the bringer of infantile diseases. It is believed that her name is the derivation of the word for a prostitute in some languages.
References 88, 111
See also Bali, Demon, Appendix 17, Appendix 22

PUTAR ALI
This is the name of an angel in the Islamic beliefs of the people of West Malaysia. The name Putar Ali means Lord of the Rainbow.
References 120
See also Angel, Mala'ikat

PUTTI, PUTTO
These diminutive spirits, also known as Erotes in classical Greek and Roman mythology, were a profane version of the cherub. They were very much a feature of the arts of Renaissance Europe, in which they are also called Amoretti. They were derived from the attendant spirits of the gods and goddesses of love in the classical mythology of Greece and Rome and were their messengers. The Putti are usually portrayed as little chubby infant boys with tiny wings protruding from their shoulders hovering above earthly lovers.
References 62

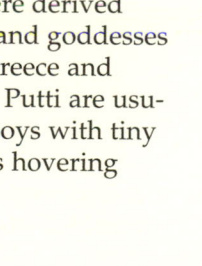

A putti sits as an imp takes aim at a butterly.

See also Attendant Spirit, Cherub, Erotes, Spirit, Appendix 22

PUUK
See Kratt

PWARONGA
See Kakamora

PWCA
See Puck

PYTHO
See Devil

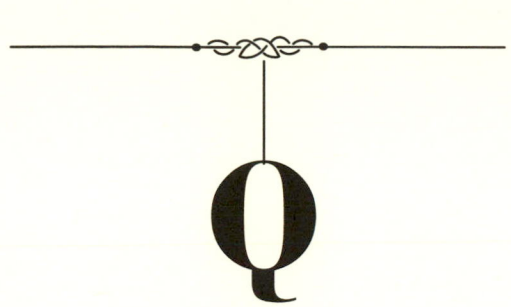

QANDIŠA

This is the name of a female demon or djinn in the folk beliefs of Morocco. Qandiša is a shape-shifter, but she usually appears in the form of an attractive young woman. She inhabits the springs and rivers where she entices young men to join her. Any who do will never regain their senses, for she will drive them mad. In one area of the country sacrifices are made to her at the time of the summer solstice. It is thought that she may be the degenerated form of an ancient goddess of love.
References 93
See also Demon, Djinn

QASAVARA

See Qat

QAT, QUAT

This is the name of a nature spirit and hero in the beliefs of the Banks Islanders in Melanesia. Qat is a Vui or spirit who, with his supernatural brothers, features in a number of creation legends. Qat and the spider spirit named Marawa often helped each other, especially when Qat's brothers laid traps for him out of jealousy for his magic powers. In one tale he hides himself in a coconut shell with all his possessions, then travels by magic in order to arrive before his brothers after they thought that they had got rid of him. In another tale a cannibal demon called Qasavara devoured Qat's brothers, but after Qat destroyed the demon, he found the bones of his brothers in the demon and restored them to their original form.
References 33
See also Anansi, Blue Jay, Demon, Spirit

QIQIRN

This is a disease spirit in the folk beliefs of the Inuit people. It manifests in a shape that resembles a large dog, but it has hair only around its mouth, feet, ears, and tail. Qiqirn is considered to be responsible for causing the affliction of convulsions in humans. This spirit like many demons and Little People may be "laid" by the mention of its name.
References 88
See also Black Dog, Demon, Little People, Appendix 17

QUEEN MAB

See Mab

QUTRUB

See Ghoul

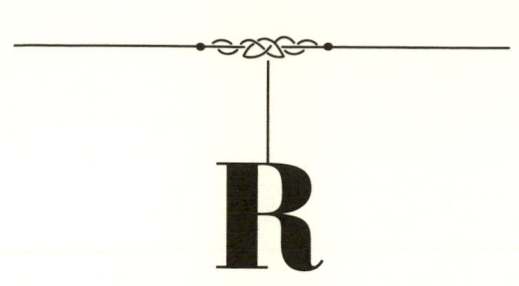

R

RÅ OR RÅDANDE

This is the name of an individual type of tree spirit known by the names of Rå or Rådande in the folklore of Sweden. They belong to a group of wood spirits known collectively as the Löfjerskor. They are perhaps the Scandinavian equivalent of the Hamadryads and the Dryads of classical Greek mythology. Each tree had its resident Rå, which inhabited the tree or sat in its shade during the hot days of summer. Although they were usually invisible, the Rådande were said to hang their washing from the branches of the tree to dry. The Rådande were their tree's guardian spirit, and they would be most benevolent to humans who respected their trees. One famous tree in Westmanland was a pine tree growing from a rock. It was believed that a mermaid was its Rå, as white fairy cattle had been seen grazing around it for many years before it fell with age.
References 110
See also Dryad, Fairy, Guardian, Hamadryad, Löfjerskor, Mermaid, Spirit, Appendix 19

RAGANA
See Laumé

RAGGED BLOSSOM
See Gumnut Babies

RAGING HOST, THE
See Wild Hunt

RAGUEL
See Archangel

RAHU

This is the name of a daitya or demon in the Hindu mythology of India. This demon stole the flask containing the elixir of immortality, and had managed to drink a little of it before being discovered by the sun and moon, who informed Vishnu. The god immediately retrieved the flask and punished Rahu by severing his head and banishing him to the stars as the constellation Draco. However, because the demon had swallowed some of the elixir, his head was immortal, and it now chases the sun and moon to punish them for denouncing his theft. Whenever Rahu catches up with either the sun or the moon, he takes a bite out of them or swallows them, until they are rescued by the gods. Thus, Rahu is deemed responsible for eclipses, which are regarded as portents of imminent disasters for humans. In the mythology of the Khmer people of Cambodia, this spirit is called Reahu.
References 40, 53, 88, 93, 114
See also Apep, Buber, Daitya, Demon, Appendix 13

RAIN PEOPLE
See Cloud People

RAINHA BARBA

This is the name of a high-ranking encantado in the Afro-Brazilian cult Batuque. She is also known as Barba Sueira and Maria Barba in Belém, and as Inhaçan in the region of the Umbanda cult. She is associated with the feast day of Santa Barbara on 4 December. Rainha Barba is considered to be able to control the thunder and lightning of violent storms.
References 89
See also Averekete, Encantado, Senhor, Seu Turquia, Appendix 26

RAINHA EOWA

An encantado in the Afro-Brazilian cult Batuque, her name means Queen Eowa. She is a high-ranking spirit associated with Saint Anne and the feast day of 26 July. Her "family" includes Toia Navéroaim, who is associated with Our Lady of Conception and the feast day of 8 December. Neither Rainha Eowa nor Toia Navéroaim is as popular with devotees now as they were a generation ago.
References 89
See also Encantado

RAINHA OYÁ

An encantado in the Afro-Brazilian cult Batuque, her name means Queen Oyá. She is a high-ranking spirit

who would be addressed by the title Senhora. Rainha Oyá is associated with two other spirits, known as Cosme and Damião. They were supposed to have been born as humans who were thrown into the sea at Baia by their human mother. They were saved by Rainha Oyá, who brought them to her *encantaria* under the sea, where they were transformed into encantados.
References 89
See also Bedonebyasyoudid, Cosme, Damião, Encantado, Senhor, Appendix 25

RAJA BRAHIL
See Jabra'il

RAKSHASAS
These are the evil demons in the Vedic myths of India. They are powerful, shape-shifting evil spirits, also known as Rakahasa or Rashas, whose strength increases with the fall of night. During the hours of darkness, these evil spirits defile humans and their food, causing sickness and death. They are shape-shifters, and may appear on the earth in the form of a creature such as an owl, a dog, or a vulture. Their real shape, however, may be like that of a human, but hideously deformed, with huge arms, multiple heads or eyes, red hair and beards, and enormous, bloated bellies. The female demons are known as Rakshasi. While the males indulge in feasting on the flesh of mortals, the females may intermarry with humans and be transformed into beautiful damsels. In the Ramayana, their king is Ravana, the demon king of Lanka. The Rakshasas display every form of vice that is deplored such as greed, lechery, and violence toward humans and gods. Toward one another, however, they are loyal and even loving. As they are not responsible for the malevolent role they are obliged to perform, the gods allowed them to have a wonderful jeweled palace as their abode.
References 29, 53, 88, 93, 114
See also Asura, Demon, Ravana, Spirit, Appendix 22

RANGAS
See Bitâbohs

RAPAHANGO
See Akuaku

RAPHAEL
This is the name of an Archangel or chief angel in Judeo-Christian scriptures. Raphael is the guardian spirit of the traveler, of pilgrims, and of the young, and is often depicted in the garments of a pilgrim. He is portrayed as a traveler in the legend of Tobias and the Angel, the frequent subject of Renaissance paintings. Raphael defeated the demon called Asmodeus.

He is known as the "healer," and in this respect may also go by the name Suriel. In the astrological calendar, he was associated with the sun in Jewish writings, but in medieval Christian astrology, he was associated with the planet Mercury.
References 40, 62, 88, 93, 114
See also Angel, Archangel, Asmodeus, Guardian, Appendix 13

RASHNU
This is the name of an angel in the mythology and beliefs of Persia. As the angel of justice, Rashnu is depicted holding the golden scales in which he will weigh the souls of the dead on the Day of Judgment.
References 88
See also Angel, Michael

RASOGONAGA
This is the name of a spirit in the folk beliefs of the Chaco peoples of Chile. He is a benevolent weather spirit that inhabited the air and provided the people with rain.
References 56, 102
See also Cherruve, Huecuvu, Spirit, Appendix 26

RATAINITSA
This is the name of a domestic spirit in the folklore of the Russian people. She was the guardian spirit of the stables and the horses resting inside.
References 102
See also Dobie, Dvorovoi, Guardian, Household Spirits, Appendix 12, Appendix 22

RAVANA
This is the name of the demon king of the Rakshasas in the Hindu mythology of India. His story forms part of the epic *Ramayana*. In his original image, Ravana has ten heads and 20 arms, which reappear each time they are cut off in battle. Ravana wears magnificent robes, but is hideous from the scars of battle. These conflicts take place as a result of his efforts to remove the Hill of Heaven to Lanka and abduct Sita, the wife of Rama. He goes through two incarnations as Hiranyakasipu and Sisupala before being defeated by Krishna.
References 29, 88, 93, 102, 114, 119
See also Bali, Demon, Rakshasas

RAVEN
See Yehl

RAVIYOYLA
This is the name of a spirit known in the folklore of Serbia as a veela. This spirit manifests as a type of female nature spirit or fairy, but could take on the appearance of a beautiful mortal woman. She has a

supreme knowledge of all the healing properties of every plant. In a Serbian folktale, Raviyoyla accidentally caused the death of Prince Marko's greatest friend, but with her herbal magic she restored him to life immediately.
References 41
See also Fairy, Spirit, Veela, Appendix 18

RAW HEAD AND BLOODY BONES
This is an evil spirit or water demon in the folklore of Lancashire, Lincolnshire, and Yorkshire in England. It is also known by the names Bloody-bones, Old Bloody-bones, and Tommy Rawhead. This demon is described as the gory semblance of a human that has blood running down its face, and is usually observed seated on a pile of bones. It is essentially a nursery bogie that is said to be lurking in stagnant ponds, marl pits, or in the understairs cupboards of a house. From these gruesome places it watches and awaits its opportunity to drag impetuous and defiant children to their demise. One reference to this spirit includes the lines: "Made children with your tones to run for't, As bad as Bloody-bones or Lunsford." Lunsford was a colonel with the earl of Bedford's militia during the English civil war in the seventeenth century. Such a reference used in conjunction with this spirit gives some evidence of the terror invoked by the colonel's reputation, which survives in this folk "memory."
References 15, 17, 28
See also Demon, Nursery Bogie, Spirit, Appendix 22

REAHU
See Rahu

RED CAP
This name is used for spirits in two different cultures:
(1) It is an alternative name for the evil spirit known as Bloody Cap of English folklore, associated with Lord Soulis.
(2) It is also the name of a household spirit in the folklore of Holland. He is an industrious spirit much like the English brownie, and will invisibly provide warmth for the whole family by lighting fires in the hearth at night. This spirit invokes his supernatural powers to use far less brushwood than a human, extending the store of wood for the family's future warmth. The Dutch Red Cap is described as shaped like a little human with green hands and face, dressed completely in red. Like most domestic spirits, the Dutch Red Cap is offended by a reward and will be "laid" by a gift of clothes.
References 66, 123
See also Bloody Cap, Brownie, Household Spirits, Spirit, Appendix 22

RED COMB
See Bloody Cap

REDJAL EL MARJA
This is a species of malevolent water djinn in the folklore of Morocco. Redjal el Marja means the Men of the Marshes, and this indicates that they originally inhabited the marshes outside Marrakech. When the marshes were drained, these djinns transferred to the canals and fountains supplying Marrakech. People light votive candles at these water sources to propitiate these spirits and ensure that the water supply remains constant and uncontaminated.
References 90
See also Djinn, Appendix 25

REGIN
He is one of the treacherous dwarfs in Scandinavian mythology. Regin is the magical smith of the *Volsung Saga* that forged the sword Branstock. By his deceit, not only was Fafnir slain, but Regin also met his demise.
References 88
See also Alberich, Dwarf, Appendix 14

REI FLORIOANO
See Dom José

REI SEBASTIÃO
This is an important encantado in the Afro-Brazilian cult Batuque. He is known by the alternate name of Xapanan, which is the name of a previous African deity of disease, but in the Batuque cult this spirit is a warrior and not involved with diseases. Rei Sebastião is said to be derived from the spirit of King Sebastian of Portugal, who was killed at the age of 24 in the battle of Alcazar-Kebir (4 August 1578). A legend developed around the death of this young monarch in similar fashion to that of the English king Arthur. In the cult of Batuque, it is also accepted that the spirits of the "sleeping" monarch and his warriors exist on the enchanted beach of Lençol in Maranhão. He is associated with the feast day of Saint Sebastian on 20 January, and also "related" to two other prominent encantados—Jarina and Sebastino—who are regarded as his "family."
References 89
See also Encantado, Jarina, Spirit

REI TURQUIA
See Seu Turquia

RI
This is a female sea spirit in the folk beliefs and legends of the Maori people of New Zealand. The Ri is a type of siren or mermaid.

References 99
See also Mermaid, Siren, Spirit, Appendix 25

RICDIN RICDON
See Rumpelstiltskin

RIESENGEBIRGE
This is the name of a group of dwarfs or demons in the folklore of Germany. They were said to inhabit the Riesengebirge Mountains, where they were ruled by a monarch whose name translates as Number Nip. These dwarfs were renowned for their evil nature, but they could only be active at night and were a menace to anyone traveling through the district during the hours of darkness. There was one way of defeating them: Should the rays of the morning sun shine on them, they would be turned to stone.
References 95
See also Demon, Dwarf, Rübezahl, Appendix 24

RIGAI
This is a nature spirit in the folk beliefs of the Witoto people of Columbia in South America. He is a spirit of the air, and the guardian of all the birds and insects that fly.
References 88
See also Guardian, Spirit, Appendix 12

RISHIS
See Angiris

RIZOS
This is a road spirit and a member of the group of evil spirits known as the Exotica in the folklore of modern Greece. It manifests in the shape of a huge dog with enormous claws that may be encountered by travelers on the highways at night. It is a frightening spirit that may offer harm, but more frequently it disappears, leaving the human in a state of terror.
References 12
See also Black Dog, Exotica, Spirit, Appendix 12, Appendix 24

ROANE
This is the Scottish Gaelic name for a seal, but also the spirit of the Seal People, who are said to be a type of fairy. These gentle supernaturals appeared in the shape of humans, but needed the sealskin to travel through the sea to their underwater abode. Once they were in their subaqueous caves, they removed the sealskin and breathed air again. The Roane come to the northern beaches around the Scottish coast and the outer islands to dance in the light of the midsummer evenings. In the Shetland Islands they may also be called Sea Trows. If a human can retain the skin of one of the beautiful Roane maidens (or Seal Maidens), then she may consent to be his wife. The clan of Mac Codum of North Uist is known as *Sliochd na Ron* (the Offspring of the Seals), as they are said to be descended from such a marriage. However, as with many such supernatural marriages the world over, any offense, or the retrieval of the magic item that binds them, will result in the wife's departure for her own kind, leaving her human family forever.
References 15, 17, 18, 47
See also Fairy, Melusina, Nereid, Porpoise Girl, Spirit, Trow, Appendix 25

ROBGOBLIN
See Hobgoblin

ROBIN GOODFELLOW
This is the name of a supernatural who features prominently in English literature and folklore. The name of Robin Goodfellow was recorded as early as 1489 in one of the Pastern Papers, where the proclamation "In the name of Mayster Hobbe Hyrste, Robyn Godfelaws brodyr he is as I trow" shows the link between the supernatural activities of this spirit and those of the hob. Robin Goodfellow is described as possibly being Puck, but certainly a type of household spirit, hobgoblin, or brownie. He was well known for helping at night with all the domestic tasks that remained unfinished, for which the maids of the household would leave him a bowl of cream. However, this spirit was equally capable of trickery and pranks. This occurred to such an extent that a saying of the sixteenth century, "Robin Goodfellow has been with you tonight," referred to the disorder his misadventures could bring. Indeed, Harsnet in 1603 gives a description of the havoc that this sprite could wreak if he was not rewarded with his bowl of curds or cream. He is the elfin servant of the king of the fairies in Shakespeare's *A Midsummer Night's Dream,* although in another work he is described as the son of Oberon and a mortal woman. In these works his shape-shifting and other powers are detailed, but the image of Robin Goodfellow on the frontispiece of *Robin Goodfellow his Mad Prankes and Merry Jests* (1628) shows him as a kind of satyr with horns, carrying a besom and a lit torch. It is perhaps this torch that associates him with the Will o' the Wisp activities, but although Robin was misleading, he was never known to leave his victims to perish. As his name implies, Robin Goodfellow was always held in some affection, as well as caution, and the many stories about him reveal a benevolent attitude toward humans in general.
References 7, 16, 17, 18, 28, 37, 40, 88, 92, 133
See also Brownie, Elf, Friar Rush, Grim, Hinzelmann, Hob, Hobgoblin, Household Spirits, Oberon, Puck, Satyr, Sprite, Will o' the Wisp, Appendix 6, Appendix 22

A medieval woodcut of Robin Goodfellow.

ROBIN HOOD
See Green Man, Kobold, Puck

ROBIN ROUND-CAP
This is the name of a household spirit in the folklore of Holderness in East Yorkshire, England. He was a type of hobgoblin or brownie that would work about the farmlands, harvesting and threshing the wheat, or doing the domestic tasks of Spaldington Hall. However, like Robin Goodfellow, the Robin Round-Cap was just as capable of causing mischief. He would remix the wheat with chaff from the winnowing, douse the fires in the kitchen, or perform some other prank if offended. This spirit appears to have been "laid," not in the usual fashion by a gift of clothes, but by exorcism delivered by a group of clergy, who are said to have banished the sprite to the bottom of Robin Round-Cap's Well.

References 17
See also Brownie, Hobgoblin, Household Spirits, Robin Goodfellow, Appendix 22

ROBIQUET
See Rumpelstiltskin

ROGGERHUNDS
See Kornwolf

ROK ŠƏRT
This is a keremet or evil spirit in the folklore of the Cheremis/Mari people of the former Soviet Republic. It is said to be placated and its malice avoided by the sacrifice of a goose.
References 118
See also Čort, Keremet, Spirit

ROMPE MATO

This is the name of an important encantado in the Afro-Brazilian cult Batuque. Rompe Mato is described as a warrior spirit who was derived from the Exus or demons. In the folk legend of this spirit, it is said that he was "adopted" and "educated" by Jurema. When in possession of a devotee, this spirit will bring many of the demon characteristics of behavior without the usual wickedness of an Exu.
References 89
See also Demon, Encantado, Exu, Jurema, Ogun, Spirit

RONGEUR D'OS

This is the name of an evil spirit in the folklore of Normandy in northern France. This demon, whose name Rongeur d'Os means the Gnawer of Bones, may manifest in the form of a dog. This fiend is said to waylay night-bound travelers on lonely roads in much the same manner as the Gytrash of English folklore.
References 17, 19, 47, 69, 133
See also Barguest, Black Dog, Black Shuck, Boggart, Bullbeggar, Capelthwaite, Church Grim, Demon, Fiend, Freybug, Gytrash, Mauthe Dhoog, Padfoot, Skriker, Spirit, Appendix 24

RONWE

This demon was described by Collin de Plancy in his *Dictionnaire Infernal* (1863). This spirit is said to imbue a human with the ability and knowledge of other languages.
References 113
See also Demon, Spirit

ROSANIA

See Rumpelstiltskin

ROSIER

See Devil

ROU SHOU

This is the name of a spirit in the folk beliefs and legends of China. This supernatural is always associated with Gou Mang. Together they are the spirit messengers of the sky god, and they manifest in the form of the double dragon. Individually, Rou Shou presages retribution, disaster, and the decay of autumn. He is associated with the western directions.
References 93
See also Gou Mang, Spirit, Appendix 23

ROWER

See Knecht Ruprecht

RUACH

These are a type of spirit in Jewish beliefs and traditions that may be described in various ways according to their form or derivation. Some of these spirits are of human origin, and others are entirely supernatural. The following Ruach belong to the latter group: Ruach Ra'ah is defined as an evil spirit or demon, Ruach Zelahta is a demon that causes headaches, and Ruach Tezarit is a disease spirit or demon that causes fevers and madness.
References 88
See also Demon, Spirit, Appendix 17

RUBBET

See Knecht Ruprecht

RÜBEZAHL

This is the name of a forest demon in the German folklore of the Riesengebirge region of Silesia, formerly Prussia, now in Poland. He is known in English as Number Nip, but his German name means Turnip Counter. Rübezahl is an unpredictable guardian of the forests and mountains. He is said to be a dwarf, but those who have met him describe him as a monk, a charcoal burner, a woodcutter, or a hunter, bearing testimony to this sprite's shape-shifting abilities. He does not seem to offer any harm to the innocent, but will delight in misleading the traveler, like a Will o' the Wisp. Rübezahl also enjoys causing sudden storms to confuse the humans who may do harm in his domain. The story of his name, however, attests to his gullibility. Rübezahl abducted a beautiful princess, whom he hoped would be his bride. He therefore set out to please her as much as possible. She expressed a passion for the taste of turnips and a plentiful supply of fresh ones, so the ardent dwarf planted a whole field of them. When the plants emerged, the princess feigned a desire to know how many had grown. In his eagerness to show his numerical ability, Rübezahl proceeded to count each one, while his clever captive escaped.
References 40, 44, 88, 95, 110
See also Demon, Dwarf, Gübich, Katzenveit, Riesengebirge, Sprite, Will o' the Wisp, Appendix 19

RUDRAS

See Haruts

RUGEKLAS

See Knecht Ruprecht

RUGINIS

This is the name of a nature spirit in the folklore of Lithuania. Ruginis is a corn spirit, and specifically the guardian spirit of the rye crop. The spirit is known as the Man of Rye, and his effigy was formed from the last sheaf of the crop to be cut. He was then propitiated with the sacrifice of a he-goat at the feast that took place on completion of the harvest. His female counterpart is known as Rugiu Boba.

References 88
See also Cailleac, Corn Spirit, Guardian, Kuršis, Rugiu Boba, Spirit, Appendix 15

RUGIU BOBA

This is the corn spirit in the folklore of Lithuania. It is known as the Old Woman of the Rye Field, and her effigy was formed from the last sheaf of the crop to be cut. Effigies of Rugiu Boba were also made from bread dough, and kept for good luck and fertility. She was then propitiated with the sacrifice of a cockerel at the feast that took place on completion of the harvest. Her male counterpart is known as Ruginis.

References 88
See also Cailleac, Corn Spirit, Kuršis, Ruginis, Sara-Mama, Appendix 15

RUMPELSTILTSKIN, RUMPELSTILTZCHEN

In the folklore of Germany, Rumpelstiltskin is a little deformed dwarf of very ugly appearance made famous in *Grimm's Fairy Tales* (#55). The story tells how the dwarf helps a miller's daughter spin straw into gold after she, or her mother, had foolishly tried to impress the king and gain his love. The dwarf's price for this help was that he should take the first-born child of the marriage. The miller's daughter readily agreed, but when the child was born and Rumpelstiltskin returned for the debt to be paid, the miller's daughter, now queen, was distraught. The dwarf was so confident in his victory that he said he would not take the child if she could tell him his name within three days. The queen had never asked the name of her benefactor, and she sent servants far and wide to find it out before the time was up. Almost at the point of despair when the morning of the third day came, a servant happened to overhear Rumpelstiltskin's triumphant chanting in the woods, and she silently hurried to tell the queen. When the dwarf came to take the child, the queen at first pretended not to know his name, then suddenly declared it. Rumpelstiltskin flew into such a rage that he stamped his feet right into the ground and tore himself apart trying to get them out.

The appearance and demise of Rumpelstiltskin have many variations throughout Europe and western Russia, where he goes by such names as Tom Tit Tot in England, Ricdin Ricdon or Robiquet in France, Kruzimügeli in Austria, Titiliture and Dancing Vargaluska in central Europe, Panczumanczi and Winterkolbe in Hungary, Gilitrutt in Iceland, Rosania in Italy, and Kinkach and Martinko in Russia. In his studies of this folktale, C. W. Sydow ultimately concluded that it had originated in the British Isles, and had spread to the Continent with traders. There are similar tales in Scandinavia of a supernatural builder who leaves churches unfinished if his identity is guessed.

References 17, 18, 40, 66, 87, 114
See also Dwarf, Girle Guairle, Gwarwyn-a-Throt, Jili Ffrwtan, Peerifool, Terrytop, Tom Tit Tot, Appendix 14, Appendix 22

RUN KUBA AND RUN KUGUZA

These are spirits in the folk beliefs of the Cheremis/Mari people of the former Soviet Republic. The names Run Kuba and Run Kuguza mean Mucus Old Woman and Mucus Old Man, and as their names imply, they are the disease or nuisance spirits that bring discomfort to the human's breathing during a cold infection. These spirits cannot tolerate the atmosphere in the bathhouse, and will leave the human temporarily so that their own noses do not become burned.

References 118
See also Moča Kuba, Spirit, Appendix 17

RUPRICH

See Knecht Ruprecht

RUSALKA, RUSALKI, RUSALKY

These are the spirits of freshwater in the folklore of Russia and eastern Europe, where they are also known by the names of Chertovka (Jokestress), Shutovka (Demon Joker), Leskotukha or Loskotukha (Tickler), and Khitka or Khitkha (Abductor). In the south of Russia, they are described as beautiful young maidens with long blond hair, sometimes wearing diaphanous white garments. In the north, the Rusalki tend to be depicted as old women with green hair, pallid faces, and ghastly, glowing green eyes above a torso endowed with overly huge breasts. Whether beautiful or ugly, their habits were the same; the Rusalki would inhabit the water during the dark months, emerging to dwell in the forests and glades during the months of summer. In this latter abode, they would entice young men to them with singing and dancing on moonlit nights. Once the human was within their spell, the evil nymphs would pull their victim into a deadly embrace under the water, never to be seen again. Sometimes the Rusalki could be capable of love. In one tale, a Rusalka married a mortal prince on his promise that he would always be faithful to her. One night he broke his promise, and she returned to her river. The prince was distraught with grief for his stupidity and his loss, and set out to find her. Arriving at her abode, he begged her forgiveness and reaffirmed his love. The prince desired only to hold her in his arms, caring for nothing else. She warned him that she was truly a Rusalka once again, although she still loved him. Knowing the consequences of holding her once more, he kissed and embraced the only one he had truly loved and then died.

References 29, 44, 56, 75, 93, 102, 110, 119
See also Beregini, Domovik, Nymph, Spirit, Appendix 25

RYE DOG
See Kornwolf

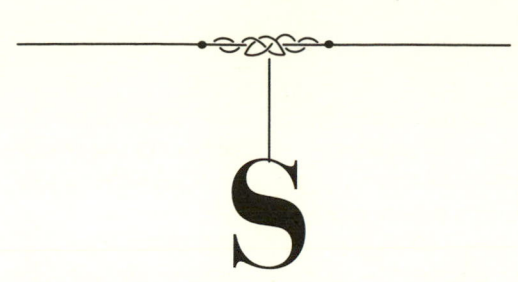

S

SABA-LEIPPYA

This is the name of a group of agricultural spirits in the folk beliefs of the Taungthus, Taungyos, and Sawngtung Karen peoples of Burma. They are a type of nat that manifests in the shape of the paddy-field butterfly. One spirit is assigned to each field. Saba-Leippya are regarded as the guardian spirits of the rice crops. When the people sell the crops after the harvest of rice, a little is kept from each container to retain the Saba-Leippya, which is then returned to each field that it protects. A libation is offered to the Saba-Leippya whenever new land is cleared for planting.
References 88
See also Corn Spirit, Guardian, Nats, Appendix 10, Appendix 12, Appendix 18

SA-BDAG

These are nature spirits in the Bon religion of Tibet. They are described as "earth movers" that inhabit the earth, houses, springs, and lakes. There is a protective spirit for each locality, and the spirit's image is portrayed at the gateway of the temple or monastery where it may be offered libations of wine.
References 88
See also dMu, Spirit, Appendix 21

SABDH

In the folklore and legend of Ireland, she is a woman of the Sidhe and the fairy mother of Oisin.
References 88
See also Fairy, Sídhe

SABUR ALI

This is the name of an angel in the Islamic beliefs of the Malay people of West Malaysia. The name Sabur Ali means Lord of the Winds.
References 120
See also Angel, Sir Ali

SACHIEL

See Zadkiel

SACI

See Cacy Taperere

SAHIRIM

See Se'irim

ŠAHRĒVAR

See Kshathra

SAHTE

This is a demon in the folk beliefs and the creation legends of the Tuleyone Native American people. This evil spirit set the world on fire, but it was saved by Coyote, who sent a great flood to put the fire out.
References 41
See also Coyote, Demon, Spirit

SAIVO-NEITA

This is the name for a mermaid in the folk beliefs of the Lapp people of northern Norway and Finland. Saivo-Neita means the Sea Maiden.
References 88
See also Čacce-haldde, Čacce-olmai, Mära-Halddo, Mermaid, Appendix 25

SAJA

Saja, which means Death Messenger, is the name of the messenger spirit from hell, in the folk beliefs of Korea. This spirit is sent to those who are ill in order to summon them to the underworld. When a human is critically ill, the *mansin* or female shaman may direct the family to prepare an effigy of the sick person. This is to fool the Saja into taking the wrong one, or to make him give up and go away when he receives no response to his summons from the substituted dummy.
References 79
See also Spirit, Appendix 16

ŠAJTAN

This is the name for a group of devils or demons in the folk beliefs of the Cheremis/Mari people of the former Soviet Republic. They were said to have been

created when the god of thunder tried to emulate the manner in which God made the angels, by striking sparks from a stone. These devils cause misery and discord among humans wherever they go, and even among the deities. As a result of their mischief, the Šajtans are pursued by the thunder god, and the devils will assume the shape of a boy or girl in order to hide among humans. People will therefore frequently carry a piece of iron with them to ward off the demons. Sometimes it may be deemed necessary to perform exorcism ceremonies in the village to remove any Šajtan, especially those that have taken the form of a wolf.
References 118
See also Demon, Devil, Shaitan

SAKHR

This is a djinn or demon that features in one of the traditional Islamic tales of the Jewish King Solomon. The legend tells how Solomon had a magic ring which he gave to the safekeeping of one of his concubines each day while he performed his ablutions. On one occasion Sakhr assumed the guise of the monarch and persuaded the concubine to give him the ring. Dispossessed of his power and his throne, the real Solomon had to exist as a fisherman before the ministers of his court discovered the deception and exorcised the demon by reading the scriptures. In his fury Sakhr threw the ring into the sea, and 40 days after this Solomon caught the fish that had swallowed it. The rightful ruler was thus returned to his throne.
References 30
See also Afrit, Ashmedai, Demon, Djinn, Karina

SAKUNTALA

The name of an Apsara, a heavenly nymph in the classical mythology of India. She is also known as Shakuntala. This nymph was the lover of King Dushyanta and the mother of King Bharta. Her story is told in the Maharbharata.
References 111
See also Apsara, Nymph

SAL

This is a term for a group of evil spirits in the folk beliefs of Korea. These spirits enter a human at a transitional period of the person's life. This may be at birth, at a wedding, at a sixty-first birthday feast, or a funeral. If the intended procedures are interrupted and do not run according to tradition, then the Sal may "shoot" any person present who has a bad "fate" for that day. A person who has been attacked in this way may display an immediate reaction or a delayed reaction. The immediate reaction would manifest as a green and blue discoloration of the face and body followed by severe sickness or even death.

The delayed reaction is experienced mostly by children, who may later have severe difficulties in their social relationships, such as the acquisition of a job or a spouse.
References 79
See also Demon, Spirit, Appendix 22

SALAMANDER

One of a group of nature spirits or elementals defined by the mystical philosopher Paracelsus (1493–1541) in terms of the natural elements from which they were supposed to be derived. The Salamanders were the spirits of fire, described as thin, red, and dry-skinned with a temperamental, wrathful character. According to the occultist Elephas Levi, the name of their emperor is Djin.
References 40, 98, 107, 136
See also Djinn, Elemental

SALGFRÄULEIN

This is a type of Wood Wife or Moss Woman in the folklore of the Tyrol region of Austria. She is a tree spirit who may sometimes be seen sitting under an old larch tree. The Salgfräulein is usually in the form of a maiden dressed completely in white, who may be heard gently singing in the woods.
References 110
See also Moss Folk, Spirit, Wood Wife, Appendix 19

SALMACIS, SALMACHIS, SALMAKIS

Salmachis was a nymph and the guardian of a spring in the classical mythology of Greece and Rome. She loved the son of Hermes, Hermaphroditos, so much that their bodies fused and became the one androgynous being.
References 29, 102, 130
See also Guardian, Nymph, Appendix 11, Appendix 25

SALT WOMAN

This is an important spirit in the beliefs of the Cochiti, Isleta, Sia, and Zuñi Pueblo Native American peoples. This spirit may also be known as Salt Old Woman or Salt Mother, but among the Hopi of Taos, the spirit is Salt Man. Only those who have been through the correct preparations may be permitted to bring the spirit to the autumn ceremony. She is particularly associated with the Corn Mother.
References 45, 87, 88
See also Awl-man, Clay Mother, Corn Mother, Grandmother Fire, Spirit, Tutelary Spirit

SALVANELLI

These are elves or wood spirits in the folklore of Italy. They inhabit the cracks in the bark of the oak trees and other cavities in the trees. The Salvanelli are

described as resembling tiny men dressed in overalls or jackets which, though bright red, appear to be worn and well used. These imps behave much as the English pixies, who love riding the horses in the stables to a lather all through the night. The Salvanelli are also given to stealing milk if it is not left for them.
References 44
See also Elf, Imp, Oakmen, Pixie, Spirit, Appendix 19

SAMAEL, SAMMAEL
This is the name of one of the Archangels in the early Judeo-Christian scriptures. Samael is a chief angel and sometimes named as the angel of death. In early Jewish writings on the astrological calendar, he was associated with the planet Mars, as well as in medieval Christian astrology. In the later teachings from the third century onwards, Samael was described as one of the Fallen Angels and regarded as a demon or devil whose liaison with Lilith gave rise to the djinns.
References 53, 93, 114
See also Angel, Archangel, Demon, Devil, Djinn, Fallen Angel, Lilith, Appendix 7, Appendix 13

SAMHANACH
The name of a spirit in the folklore of Scotland. The Samhanach is a type of goblin or bogie that is most active on the Celtic feast of Samhain (Halloween, 31 October), from which the spirit's name is derived.
References 125
See also Bogie, Goblin, Spirit

SAMHGHUBHA
See Merrow

SAMMICHLAUS
See Knecht Ruprecht

SAND ALTAR WOMAN
This is the name of an important female spirit in the legends and beliefs of the Hopi Native American people. Sand Altar Woman, also known as Child Medicine Woman, is the wife of Masauwi and the sister of Möy'ingwa, chief of the underworld and emergent growth. As the guardian spirit of childbirth, Child Medicine Woman safely bestows children to their mothers. She is also the guardian spirit of the game animals, ensuring their survival.
References 88
See also Guardian, Spirit, Appendix 12, Appendix 22

SAND YAN Y TAD
These are the names of two night spirits in the folklore of Brittany in northwestern France. The words Sand Yan y Tad mean Saint John and the Father in the Breton language of the region. They are described as a type of elf that dance together at night with candles attached to their fingertips. These candles are beguiling, for they spin independently. Consequently any mortal who comes across them in the dark may become befuddled and disoriented.
References 10
See also Elf, Spirit, Will o' the Wisp, Appendix 24

SANDALPHON
This is the name of an angel in Hebrew legend. Sandalphon is one of the three angels in the realms of heaven who receive the prayers offered by humans and weave them into crowns for the Lord.
References 114
See also Angel, Appendix 1, Appendix 13

SANDMAN, MR.
This is a nursery spirit in the folklore of England. Mr. Sandman is also known as the Dustman, and his sprinkling of magic sand or dust over the eyes of tiny children gently sends them off to sleep with pleasant dreams. He is described as a sprite dressed in brightly colored silks whose magic sand provides pictures and stories whenever it touches the eyes of a sleeping infant. This gentle spirit, known by many different names, is the subject of traditional nursery rhymes and popular songs throughout Europe and the countries in which Europeans have settled.
References 17
See also Billy Winker, Dormette, Dustman, Ole Luk Øj, Spirit, Sprite, Wee Willie Winkie, Appendix 22

SANG GADIN
See Sang Gala Raja

SANG GALA RAJA
This is the name of a king of the jinns in the beliefs of the Malay people of West Malaysia. Sang Gala Raja, also known as Sa-Raja Jin, is portrayed as a human form with a red chest, black head, and enormous fangs for teeth. He dwells in the depths of the earth with his wife, Sang Gadin. Their offspring are the 193 evil genies of various identified *badi* or mischiefs, which reside in living things. The seven main offspring are: Sa-Lakun Darah, meaning He of the Blood Pool; Sa-Halilintar, meaning He of the Thunder Bolt; Sa-Rukup Rang Bumi, World Coverer; Sa-Gertak Rang Bumi, World Pricker; Sa-Gunchang Rang Bumi, World Shaker; Sa-Tumbok Rang Bumi, World Beater; and Sa-Gempar 'Alam, Universe Terrifier. All these demons dwell in wild, lonely, and festering places such as the hollows in the hills, the deep jungle, and in parasitic growths on trees. They are subdivided according to whether they are the "faithful," known as Jin Aslam, or the "infidel," known as the Jin Kafir.

The Jin Afrit, also known as Jin Rafit, was supposed to have been the creator of the Europeans. Other jinns are the guardian spirits of state property such as the royal musical instruments (protected by Jin Nemfiri or Lempiri, Gendang, and Naubat), and the royal weapons (protected by Jin Sembuana), and their duties associate them with the jinn of the state known as Jin Karaja'an. Whatever their status, they are all intent on causing harm to humans unless propitiated.
References 120
See also Afrit, Demon, Djinn, Guardian

SANGMUN

These are evil spirits in the folk beliefs of the people of Korea. They are at large wherever a death has taken place, a corpse is laid out, or funeral rites are being observed. These spirits will attach themselves to those humans who do not observe the correct procedures for cleansing the "death pollution" from themselves before entering their home or making offerings to the household deity. An offended deity may drop the protection of the home, and the released death spirits will then wreak havoc in the household causing quarrels, drunkenness, misfortune, sickness, convulsions, or even death. The services of a *mansin* (female shaman) will be called on to exorcise the spirits as soon as their presence is observed in the unnatural behavior of the family members.
References 79
See also Spirit, Appendix 16

SANKCHINNIS

In the Hindu beliefs of India these are spirits that inhabit trees. They are described as beautiful women who appear as a shimmering white form standing beneath their tree at midnight. Unlike the Hamadryads of Greek mythology, the Sankchinnis do not seem to be benevolent toward humans. In one traditional tale concerning these spirits, the wife of a Brahmin was attacked by one of the Sankchinnis and entombed in a cavity in the trunk of the tree.
References 110
See also Con-Tinh, Hamadryad, Spirit, Appendix 19

SANSAVI
See Lilith

SANTA CLAUS

This is the name of the Christmas gift bringer for English and American children. He may usually be called Father Christmas in England and also Santa Claus in the European and American traditions. This spirit of generosity and goodwill to children was transformed from the episcopal figure of Saint Nicholas (d. A.D. 326), whose appearance was likewise transformed to the image of the fat, jolly, winter spirit reminiscent of the ancient Nordic/Teutonic god Odin. He is no longer dressed in the clothes of a sober cleric, but in bright red garments adorned with thick white fur from the Arctic. Santa Claus inhabits a cavern of diamond icicles filled with good things at the North Pole. Here he is assisted throughout the year by elves before he travels across the winter skies on Christmas Eve (24 December) in his magic sleigh pulled by supernatural reindeer, each of which also has a name in nursery lore. In English households he must be propitiated by the traditional supper of a mince pie and glass of alcohol, while in American homes children may leave him milk and cookies. This is left near the hearth of the chimney through which he enters the house. Santa Claus is also a nursery spirit as children are told that his pixy helpers gather the names of good children who will receive gifts, and that the naughty children will receive nothing.

A delightful account from 24 December 1852 tells how the naming committee of a community in Indiana was influenced by their children in the choice of the town's name. In the middle of argumentative discussion, the committee was interrupted by excited children awaiting the arrival of Santa Claus, joyfully shouting his name. The people and their committee adopted the spirit's name for their new town, which has since been the focus of mail from children at Christmastime. Happily an army of Santa Claus helpers ensures that each child receives a reply.
References 56, 75, 119
See also Befana, Berchta, Butzenbercht, Elf, Father Christmas, Nursery Bogie, Pixie, Sinter Klaas, Spirit, Zwart Piet, Appendix 22

SANTO

This is an alternative designation for the encantados of the Afro-Brazilian cult Batuque. As the term means saint or spirit, this indicates the encantados' claimed association with the saints of the Roman Catholic Church.
References 89
See also Encantado, Spirit

SANVI
See Lilith

SAO

These are disease spirits in the folk beliefs of the people of Abysinnia. There were said to be 88 of these disease spirits divided into two groups, each of which was ruled by a chief. In an account from 1865, the *Kalijas* (magicians) would be called to a sick person to drive out the demon responsible for the particular illness. This would be undertaken through a ceremony involving the fumigation of the patient with aromatic herbs and threatening the demon with physical violence if it did not leave the sufferer.

Regrettably, the victim was the recipient of the physical violence if the demon declined to depart.
References 57
See also Demon, Spirit, Appendix 17

SARA-MAMA
This is the corn spirit in the ancient beliefs of the Chimu people of Peru. The name Sara-Mama means Maize Mother, and she was said to reside in the particularly large cobs of corn, or those which showed some aberration in shape. These were gathered and placed ceremonially in a special corn bin made of maize stalks. In this receptacle the Sara-Mama was propitiated and honored at the harvest celebration. During the period after the harvest the spirit resided in this container until the next harvest to ensure the continuity of abundance. It is probable that excavated ancient vases showing maize with a human head, are representations of the Sara-Mama.
References 88
See also Cailleac, Corn Spirit, Kornmutter, Appendix 15

SARAUA
In the folklore of Native South American people of Venezuela, this is the collective name of the evil spirits or demons of the forest.
References 110
See also Demon, Gamainhas, Spirit, Appendix 19

SARIEL
See Archangel

SARKANY
This is the name of a weather spirit in the ancient beliefs of the Hungarian people. He was described as appearing like a human but with up to nine heads sprouting from his shoulders. Sarkany rode his wild horse through the thunder clouds, armed with a sword and holding the morning star. This evil spirit was capable of turning humans to stone. In today's folklore this demon's name is now that of a dragon.
References 93
See also Demon, Spirit, Appendix 26

SASABONSAM
This is the name of a group of forest spirits in the beliefs of the Tschwi and Ashanti people of West Africa. They live in the forests or under individual silk-cotton trees, around the roots of which the earth is turned red. It is said to be this color because the Sasabonsam wipes the blood of his victims off himself here before going underground. The Sasabonsam appears as a tall thin human shape with red skin, straight hair, and bloodshot eyes. When he hangs in the trees his long legs dangle down, and with his feet he hooks up unwary travelers who pass beneath. Those humans who do not escape in time will have their blood drained from them. The female counterpart of Sasabonsam is his wife, known as Shamantin.
References 41, 88, 110
See also Dyombie, Huntin, Shamantin, Spirit, Appendix 19, Appendix 24

SASY PERERE
See Cacy Taperere

SATAN
See Devil

SATYR
This is the name of a group of nature spirits or demons in the classical mythology of Greece that were equated with the fauns of Roman mythology. They were depicted in the shape of men with the legs of a goat, short horns on their heads, and hairy bodies. The Satyrs were the attendants of Dionysus (Bacchus), and their leader was Silenus. They inhabited the woods, mountains, and countryside, where they pursued the nymphs in drunken amorous play and were adept at music and dancing. These spirits were noted for their lechery, rudeness, and love of playing pranks; their attitude toward humans was unpredictable and could be harmful. The humorous and often derisory plays in which they were featured after performances of the Greek tragedies are the origin of our present satire.
References 20, 40, 56, 88, 92, 93, 114
See also Demon, Faun, Kallikantzari, Nymph, Silenus, Spirit, Appendix 12

SAURU
See Kshathra

SCANTILIE MAB
See Habetrot

SCHILALYI
This is a female disease demon in the folk beliefs of the Romany Gypsies of Europe. Schilalyi came into existence as the progeny of the queen of the Keshalyi, called Ana, who was forced into a union with the king of the demons. This occurred when she had eaten the soup he had made from spittle and a dead mouse. Ana vomited the demon Schilalyi in the shape of a white mouse. Schilalyi manifests as a creature like an insect with numerous little feet. When Schilalyi runs across the body of a human, he or she becomes infected with a fever or cold.
References 31
See also Bitoso, Demon, Keshalyi, Loçolico, Melalo, Appendix 12, Appendix 17

SCHIMMEL REITER
See Pelznickel

SCHRAT
See Elf

SCRATCH
See Auld Hornie

SCYLLA
This is the name of a water nymph in the classical mythology of ancient Greece. Scylla was very beautiful, and Glaucus became infatuated with her. Unfortunately, Glaucus was in turn loved by the sorceress Circe. There are a number of versions of the manner in which Scylla was turned into a hideous monster. The first is as a result of the insane jealousy of Circe, who cast a poison into the water where Scylla habitually bathed. Another version is as a result of Scylla's dallying with Poseidon. As the sea monster, Scylla destroyed six of Ulysses' companions before she was transformed into an equally dangerous rock.
References 20, 130
See also Amphitrite, Nymph, Appendix 25

SEAL MAIDENS
See Roane

SEBETTU
This is the name given to a group of seven demons in ancient Babylonian mythology. They are the progeny of the sky god, and they travel through the skies causing sickness and plague in the wake of the plague god Erra. The Sebettu occasionally encircle and obscure the moon and were thus said to cause eclipses. Their name is also that by which the Akkadians of ancient Babylon knew the Pleiades.
References 93
See also Demon, Pleiades, Appendix 13, Appendix 17

SEDNA
She is a female guardian spirit of the Inuit of North America and is also known as Arnaknagsak or Nerrivik. She is usually described as an old woman who lives under the sea. Sedna is the guardian spirit of all the sea creatures on which the Inuit depend. There are many stories about her origins. Some say that as a child she was abandoned by her parents when they recognized her growing mystic powers; others tell of how she was stolen by sea spirits and was transformed. Another story tells how she refused human courtship, preferring a bird (usually a fulmar), which her father killed. Taking Sedna away in his boat, he cast her overboard in terror when she raised a storm. Sedna tried to hang onto the boat, but

her horrified father hacked her fingers off. As they fell into the water each of Sedna's fingers turned into sea creatures that devoured Sedna's father. This supernatural can be both benevolent and malicious. Ceremonies to propitiate her for the season's fishing are performed by shamans wearing masks of sea creatures.
References 29, 87, 93
See also Bonito Maidens, Guardian, Spirit, Appendix 12, Appendix 25

ŠEDRA KUBA AND ŠEDRA KUGUZA
These are the disease spirits of smallpox in the folk beliefs of the Cheremis/Mari people of the former Soviet Republic. The spirits are said to take human form and wander about the countryside in order to distribute the disease. Šedra Kuba and Šedra Kuguza, whose names mean Smallpox Old Woman and Smallpox Old Man, each carry a basket on their arm, the old man's containing peas and his wife's containing hemp seeds. The epidemic will be a bad one if the spirits wander upstream, but if they go downstream, then the outbreak will be slight. Similarly, if the child receives peas from the Kuguza, then the infection will be a bad one with severe scarring of the face and body, but if the Kuba distributes hemp seeds, then the infection will be a mild one. The parents of a child with smallpox may make an offering consisting of *bliny* and porridge to placate the spirits enough to prevent them from taking or scarring their child. If the offering has diminished when the humans return to where it was left, then they are assured that the offering has been accepted and the child will be safe.
References 118
See also Alardi, Con-Ma-Dāu, Kuba, Kuguza, Minceskro, Spirit, Tou Shen, Appendix 17, Appendix 22

ŠEDU
See Lama

SEELIE COURT, SEELY COURT
In British folklore there is a subdivision of the fairies according to their character, and these groups are known as the Seelie Court and the Unseelie Court. The Seelie Court are those Trooping Fairies who are generally engaged in their own society with royalty, nobility, and a community existing relatively peacefully within the human world. They enjoy feasting, hunting, and dancing in the earth's rural idyll. They comprise such groups as the elves and the Sidhe. The Unseelie Court, however, comprises those malignant spirits whose purpose is the destruction of humans at every opportunity, and these are generally of ugly appearance, usually having a solitary existence in the wilderness areas and places associated with

bloodshed. Within this group, also known as the Slaugh, are such beings as the Brown Man of the Muirs, Shellycoat, and the Red Caps.
References 15, 17, 18, 133
See also Brown Man of the Muirs, Elf, Fairy, Red Cap, Shellycoat, Sídhe, Slaugh, Appendix 6

SEIKTHA

This is an evil spirit in the folk beliefs of Burma. It is a malignant demon that inhabits the trees.
References 53
See also Demon, Spirit, Appendix 19

SE'IRIM

A group of spirits or demons also known as Sahirim and mentioned in the Hebrew and Christian scriptures. They manifest in the form of goats, the name being derived from the word *sa'ir,* meaning hairy. It is possible that they were the origin of the Greek satyrs.
References 93
See also Demon, Satyr, Spirit, Appendix 12

SELKIES

These are the sea spirits in the folklore of the Orkney and Shetland Islands (United Kingdom), which are similar to the Roane of the Hebrides. They are the Fin Folk or Seal People who appear as beautiful doe-eyed humans but must assume the misshapen form and skin of the seal, keeping only the beauty of their eyes, in order to reach their underwater caverns. They were thought to have been Fallen Angels that were too good to be sent to Hell and fell to the earth on the coastline. Sometimes they have been persecuted by humans, and if the blood of the Selkie is shed then this will result in a fierce storm and the loss of human lives at sea. The Selkie males are flirtatious and will often marry human women, but they are unreliable, and the marriage does not usually last. Children of such a marriage are said to have webbed fingers and toes.
References 17
See also Fallen Angel, Fin Folk, Merrow, Porpoise Girl, Roane, Spirit, Appendix 25

SELU

This is the name of the Corn Mother in the beliefs and mythology of the Cherokee Native Americans. In the legends Selu is the wife of the Hunter Kanati and the mother of the Thunder Boys.
References 88
See also Corn Mother, Corn Spirit, Thunder Boys, Appendix 15

SEMANGELAF
See Lilith

The fairy king and queen sit beneath a mushroom canopy as the encircling Seely Court performs a dance.

SEMJÂZÂ
See Shemyaza

SEMNAI
This is the name used for the Erinyes in the classical mythology of ancient Greece. The name Semnai means the Venerable Ones and was used as a euphemism for these awesome spirits, who were also known as the Dirae, Eumenides, and the Furies.
References 93
See also Erinys, Eumenides, Furies, Spirit, Appendix 23

SENHOR, SENHORES
This is the designation given to an encantado of high status in the Afro-Brazilian cult Batuque. It is the title most frequently used for the main spirit to be received at a Batuque ceremony, but the title may be used inter-changeably with that of Branco or Orixá. Many of the spirits who "head" a "family" group are addressed in this manner, but there are also other spirits that have this privilege accorded them, and these are:

Male: Akossi-Sapata, Ben Boçu da Cana Verde, Dom Luiz, Rei de Nagô, Rei Noé, Rei Solomão, Rei Taculumi, Rei Toi Aduça, José Tupinambá, Urubatan Jesus, Xangô.
Female: Imanjá, Jaimína, Nan Burocô, Oxun, Princesa Sinha Bê, Rainha Barba.

References 89
See also Akossi-Sapata, Encantado, Imanjá, Orixá, Rainha Barba, Spirit, Xangô

SENHORA ANA
See Pretos Velhos

SERAFIL
See Ijrafil

SERAPHIM, SERAPH
This is the name of the highest order of angels in the Judeo-Christian scriptures. In Hebrew the word *saraph* originally meant "to burn" then "snake" (perhaps with reference to the result of its bite), and possibly this derivative refers to the zealousness of the spirits' devotion. According to the Book of Isiah they are the attendant spirits in constant adoration at the throne of God. Some of their number followed the rebellion by Lucifer and were cast out from Heaven as the Fallen Angels. The Seraphim are described in the texts as having human form with three pairs of wings. In Romanesque and Renaissance art they are more frequently portrayed just as a child's head and torso with short wings emerging from behind the neck or shoulders.
References 39, 40, 93, 114, 119

See also Angel, Attendant, Devil, Lucifer, Appendix 1, Appendix 7, Appendix 13

ŠERDƏŠ ŠƏRT
This is a keremet or evil spirit in the folklore of the Cheremis/Mari people of the former Soviet Republic. This was a particularly malevolent type of spirit, and from time to time it was thought necessary that it should be placated by the sacrifice of a bull.
References 118
See also Čort, Keremet, Spirit

SERIM
These were a group of spirits or djinns in the beliefs of the Semitic peoples of the pre-Islamic period. These supernaturals were said to appear in the form of a hairy human in the desert and other wastelands. They are mentioned as evil spirits in the Book of Leviticus (xvii:7).
References 41
See also Djinn, Spirit

ŠƏRT
See Čort

ŠERT BODƏZ
This is an evil spirit or keremet in the folk beliefs of the Cheremis/Mari people of the former Soviet Republic. The name Šert Bodəz means Devil Spirit, and this spirit's malevolence was so feared that the sacrifice of a ram may be made in times of severe distress to propitiate this demon and remove his curse.
References 118
See also Keremet, Spirit, Appendix 9

ŠERT TERKAN
This is the name of an individual keremet or evil spirit in the folk beliefs of the Cheremis/Mari people.
References 118
See also Keremet, Spirit

SEU LEGUA
See Legua Bogi da Trinidade

SEU TURQUIA
A high-ranking encantado in the Afro-Brazilian cult Batuque. He is the senior spirit of the Turcos "family" and therefore also known as Rei Turquia, which means King Turkey. The name is said to be derived from the *Mouriscas* or mock battles commemorating the expulsion of the Moors from the Iberian Peninsula. The Turcos encantados, however, are envisaged as noble warriors of Native South American, Moorish, or Turkish appearance. Seu Turquia's "family" includes the following spirits:

Sons: Basilio Bom, Caboquinho, Flechiero, Guapindaia, Guerriero, Guido, Jatórana, João Fama, Joaquimzinho, Laurencino, Mariano, Mensageiro da Roma, Mirian, Nilo Fama, Pindá, Pindaié, Rondado, Sentinella, Tabajara, Tapinaré; also fostered: Caboclo Nobre and Goiabeira.
Daughters: Ana Joaquima, Ciganina, Flechiera, Jaguarema, Juracema, Laurencina, Mariana, Menina Daleira, Noxinina, Princessa Dora, Princessa Flora, Siriaki; also fostered: Ita, Ubirajara, Ubiratan, and Zizué.
Sisters: Floriope, Flor do ceu, Flor do ouro, Flor do nuvems, Flor do mar, Flor do vinho.
Brother: Jandira.

References 89
See also Avarekete, Basilio Bom, Encantado, Guapindaia, Mariana, Princesa d'Alva, Senhor, Tapinaré, Appendix 5

SEVEN WHISTLERS, THE
This is the collective name given to a group of evil spirits in the folklore of Worcestershire, England. They manifest on stormy nights or at sunset as a shrieking, whistling noise racing across the skies. In the local folklore of the Lickey Hills near Bromsgrove, the Seven Whistlers are claimed to be seven of the Devil's demons in the form of dogs loose from the Wild Hunt, searching for lost souls. They are a portent of misfortune and disaster to any who hear them (they are rarely sighted), as they come one by one. But if all seven should come together, it is said that the world will end.
References 17, 47, 133
See also Demon, Spirit, Wild Hunt, Appendix 12, Appendix 23

SHAG FOAL
The name of a bogie or bogey beast in the folklore of Lincolnshire, England. This spirit may also be called a Tatter Foal. It is a road spirit that is adept at shape-shifting, but it usually manifests in the shape of a shaggy-haired horse or donkey with huge fiery eyes. It is mostly a frightening spirit that may chase its victims rather than do them actual harm.
References 17, 133
See also Black Dog, Bogie, Bogie Beast, Colt Pixy, Shock, Appendix 12, Appendix 24

SHAI
In the beliefs of the ancient Egyptians, this was a personal guardian spirit. The Shai was the spirit of destiny that shaped people's lives, deciding their fate, their fortune, and even the length of their lives. Like the Grine the Shai was assigned to the individual mortal at birth, but the Shai was also responsible for pleading the case of the soul after death, for its place in heaven. In this respect it was like a spiritual advocate in the court of Osiris at the judgment of the soul's worth. When the judgment had been given, the Shai accompanied the soul to its final destination.
References 119
See also Daimon, Grine, Guardian, Appendix 16, Appendix 23

SHAITAN/T
In the beliefs of Islam, this is a group of evil spirits and the third species of djinn. With the djinn Iblis these spirits, also known as Sheitan, were created from the smokeless fires of hell. They are shape-shifters and may manifest in many different forms such as voluptuous females, ogres, sprites, wild animals, disembodied voices in the desert wind, or the whirlwind itself. They lurk in the desert, the wastelands, the crossroads, and the market places, where they prey on unwary humans. The Shaitans try to ensnare humans at every opportunity with deceits and lead them into sin and everlasting torment. The name Shaitan was the derivation of the word Satan, used by Christians as the designation for the Devil.
References 41, 56
See also Djinn, Iblis, Šajtan, Spirit, Sprite

SHAKAK
The name of a spirit in the beliefs and legends of the Acoma Native American people. He is the spirit of winter.
References 25
See also Spirit, Appendix 25

SHAKUNTALA
See Sakuntala

SHAMANTIN
This is the name of the wife of the forest spirit known as Sasabonsam in the beliefs of the Tschwi and Ashanti people of West Africa. The Shamantin, also

known as Srahman, live in the forests or under individual silk-cotton trees in the same way as Sasabonsam, awaiting the unwary traveler to pass beneath the trees. These spirits are more gentle toward humans, only detaining and instructing them in the forest lore of animals and herbs.
References 41, 110
See also Dyombie, Huntin, Sasabonsam, Spirit

SHAMEFUL HOUR, THE
Although it doesn't sound like the name for a spirit, this name denotes a type of evil spirit in the modern folklore of Greece. The Shameful Hour is the alternative name used on the Island of Thera for the Bad Hour of the Greek mainland.
References 12
See also Bad Hour, Spirit

SHEDDIM
See Asmodeus

SHEDEEM
See Mazikeen

SHĒDÎM, ŠEDIM
This is the name of a group of devils or demons mentioned in both the Hebrew and Christian scriptures of Deuteronomy and Psalms. They have been referred to as goblins and were considered to be dangerous to humans and often associated with magic invocations.
References 93
See also Demon, Devil, Goblin

SHEE
See Sídhe

SHEE HOGUE, SHEEHOGUE
See Sídhe

SHEELA-NA-GIG, SHEILA-NA-GIG
In the Celtic traditions of Britain, this was a hideous female demon. The image of Sheela-na-gig was placed in sacred places throughout the United Kingdom long before the coming of the Romans. She is represented as a voluptuous yet hideous naked hag whose open display of her enlarged genitalia was used as a powerful charm against death, in the same way as Baubo, and as the assurance of fertility. Images of this demon were still portrayed on churches during the Middle Ages to ward off the powers of darkness and evil.
References 56, 93
See also Baubo, Demon, Hag, Karina

SHEFRO
This is the name of a group of Trooping Fairies that are also known as Siofra in the folklore of southern Ireland. In his work *Fairy Legends of the South of Ireland*, Crofton Croker describes them as tiny supernaturals wearing caps that resemble foxglove bells. Like most fairies inhabiting the hills and woods, they are shape-shifters, and their queen is well known for the pranks she plays on humans.
References 17
See also Fairy, Tuatha dé Danann, Appendix 6

SHEITAN
See Shaitan

SHEKKASOH
These are tree spirits or nats in Burmese folklore. These spirits are much like the Hamadryads of Greek mythology in that they inhabit the trunks of the trees.
References 110
See also Akakasoh, Boomasoh, Hamadryad, Hmin, Nats, Appendix 19

SHELLYCOAT
This is the name of a bogle or water demon, also known as Spelly Coat, in the folklore of Scotland. It was said to manifest in something of an animal shape that was draped with waterweed and shells that clattered as it moved. Although one was supposed to be able to detect the presence of this spirit from its noise, nevertheless it frequently succeeded in misleading and tricking inhabitants and travelers alike. The Shellycoat was supposed to dwell on a great rock in Leith harbor, and another of its haunts was the great tower house of Gorrenberry. However, perhaps the most famous story of the Shellycoat's pranks was told by Sir Walter Scott in his *Minstrelsy of the Scottish Border* (1802). The tale relates how two men traveling on a very dark night heard a voice on the banks of the River Ettrick exclaim, "Lost! Lost!" Thinking that a person was drowning, they followed the source of the voice, surprisingly going upstream. Eventually when the voice seemed to come from across the mountain, the exhausted and disheveled men gave up, and the Shellycoat appeared in front of them, laughing as it vanished again.
References 17, 18, 28, 123, 133
See also Bogle, Demon, Hedley Kow, Appendix 24, Appendix 25

SHEMYAZA
This is the name of a Fallen Angel also known as Semjâzâ. He was originally charged with descending to earth and guiding humans, but was persuaded by Asasel to teach the evil arts of war. Shemyaza and Asasel were condemned to be buried alive below the Valleys of Fire, where the other Fallen Angels were banished, until the Day of Judgment. Shemyaza is

one of the group of angels who repented and seeks readmittance to Heaven.
References 39, 40, 41, 53, 56, 87, 114
See also Angel, Asasel, Fallen Angel, Harut and Marut, Appendix 1

SHÊN
This is a term in the beliefs and mythology of China used to signify benevolent spirits. This term originally meant supernaturals of all forms that existed above the earth, as opposed to the Kuei that dwelled below and were malevolent. Later the use of the term included the soul and life essence of humans, and from thence to include other supernaturals, the main one for the purposes of this entry being the guardian spirit. Shen Hsien is the name of those spirits that have assumed the form of a mortal for a task and have then returned to immortality.
References 39, 111, 131
See also Angel, Daimon, Guardian, Kuei, Spirit

SHEN HSIEN
See Shên

SHEWRI
This is the name of a female road spirit in the folklore of Wales. She manifested as an elderly woman on the roads in the hills of Gwent, but she would only be seen by travelers who were unfamiliar with the roads. Shewri would call out to and beckon an unsuspecting and grateful traveler, who would then follow what he thought was his rescuer. After a long and arduous journey through the hills in pursuit of this nimble spirit, the unfortunate humans would find themselves exactly where they had first sighted her.
References 28
See also Appendix 24

SHIKO-ME
See Hisa-Me

SHINSEËN
These are diminutive spirits in the folklore of China. They may manifest as old men with long beards, or at other times as beautiful young women. They inhabit the hills and forests, where they love to gather in the glades on moonlit nights. They seem to relate to humans much like the fairies of Europe.
References 110
See also Fairy, Spirit

SHIQQ
These are a form of djinn in the pre-Islamic mythology of Yemen. They appeared in the shape of a human who had been divided longitudinally. These malevolent spirits were the creators of the Nashas by mating with humans.
References 41
See also Biasd Bheulach, Cacy Taperere, Djinn, Dodore, Fachan, Hinky-Punk, Nashas, Paija

SHISHIMORA
See Domikha

SHITTA
One of the nats in the beliefs of the Kachin people of Burma. He is the demon of the moon, but, unlike other nats, Shitta is regarded as benevolent.
References 87
See also Chinün Way Shun, Demon, Nats, Appendix 10, Appendix 13

SHIWANNA
See Cloud People

SHOCK, THE
This is the name of a bogey beast in the folklore of Suffolk, England. It is a frightening road spirit not unlike the Shag Foal of Lincolnshire. The Shock is a shape-shifting spirit that may manifest as a donkey, a dog, a foal, or a calf with shaggy hair and glowing huge saucer eyes. It will materialize at the side of travelers on lonely roads at night, transfixing and terrifying them with its supernatural gaze.
References 17, 18
See also Black Dog, Bogie, Shag Foal, Spirit, Appendix 12, Appendix 24

SHONEY, SHONY
This is an ancient sea spirit revered in the Isle of Lewis off the northwestern coast of Scotland. In a solemn ceremony on Halloween (31 October), until as late as the eighteenth century, this spirit was given an annual libation of ale to ensure an abundance of the seaweeds used for fertilizing the soil. Although there is no clear description of this spirit, it is speculated that its name may have been associated with the origin of the sea spirit Davy Jones.
References 17, 123
See also Davy Jones, Spirit, Appendix 25

SHOOPILTIE
This is the fearsome water spirit of the Shetland Islands (United Kingdom) that resembles the Cabyll-Ushtey of the Isle of Man or the Each Uisge of the Scottish Highlands. It may manifest in the shape of a handsome young man, but more usually in the form of a pretty little prancing pony on the edge of the sea. Its main object is to entice unwary humans to mount its back, whereupon it will dash into the water and devour its prey.

References 17, 18, 132
See also Cabyll-Ushtey, Kelpie, Nix, Spirit,
Appendix 12, Appendix 25

SHORT HOGGERS OF WHITTINGHAME
This is the name of a sprite that was said to haunt the
area of Whittinghame in Scotland. A local tale retold
by Chambers in his *Popular Rhymes of Scotland* (1826)
explains how the spirit was in the habit of running to
and fro, wailing and disturbing the community. It was
believed to have originated as the soul of an unbaptized child, but most of the community was terrified
by it. Eventually one jovial drunk met the sprite on
his way home and addressed it as "Short Hoggers," a
friendly name for a street urchin. This naming of the
spirit, as in the case of so many others, like
Rumpelstiltskin, was enough to dismiss it forever.
References 18, 133
See also Puddlefoot, Rumpelstiltskin, Spirit, Sprite,
Appendix 22

SHRIKER
See Skriker

SHRUISTHIA
This is the name of the spirit of autumn in the beliefs
and legends of the Acoma Native American people.
References 25
See also Spirit

SHUCK, SHUCK-MONKEY
See Black Shuck

SHUTOVKA
See Rusalka

SHVOD
This is the group name for the household spirits of
the Armenian people. These spirits act as the
guardian spirit of the home and the property. When
the last day of February arrives, the people take sticks
and other soft implements to beat the interior walls of
the home to disturb the resident Shvod. It is believed
that the spirits have become too used to the warmth
of the home over the winter and must be forced out
to do their duty in the fields for the summer.
References 88
See also Guardian, Household Spirits,
Appendix 22

SHYSHOK
The name of a supernatural resembling a dwarf in
the folklore of the region surrounding Vladimir, the
ancient capital of Russia.
References 46
See also Dwarf

SI RAYA
This is the name of a sea spirit in the folk beliefs of
the Malay people. Si Raya is said to be a particularly
dangerous spirit for humans, as it may appear to a
person in the likeness of a member of the family in
order to cause discord and distress. The human
whose image the demon has taken will be accused of
the problems the demon caused, and, if severe, the
person may be in danger of being killed.
References 120
See also Demon, Hantu Laut, Spirit, Appendix 25

SI WANG MU
This is the name of a queen of genii in the folklore
and legends of China. Si Wang Mu is the consort of
Tung Wang Kung, the king of the genii. Together they
inhabit the mountain of Kwen-Lun.
References 41
See also Genius, Spirit

SIBHREACH
In the folklore of Scotland the Changeling was known
by this Scottish Gaelic word.
References 80
See also Changeling

SICKSA
This is a spirit in the folklore of the Slav people. It is a
forest sprite that can shape shift at will and is well
known for playing pranks on travelers and people
who make their living in the woods.
References 102
See also Spirit, Sprite, Appendix 19, Appendix 24

SÍDHE, SIDHE
This is the name most often used for the fairy people
in the folklore of Ireland. The name is derived from
the mounds or ancient barrows known as *sidh* which
they are said to inhabit. These beings may also be
known as Aes Sídhe (which means: the People of the
Mounds), Shee, Si, Sidh, or Sith. These Little People
of Ireland, also sometimes referred to as the
Sheehogue, are descended from the Tuatha dé
Danann of mythology. Tradition tells how they followed their leader, the Dagda, into the ancient hill
forts and barrows after their defeat by the Milesians.
They are the Trooping Fairies of Ireland, with their
own regional kings and queens who owe allegiance
to Finvarra and Onagh.
References 17, 41, 88, 125
See also Dagda, Fairy, Finvarra, Little People, Onagh,
Tuatha dé Danann, Appendix 6

SIDI HAMOU
This is the name of a powerful leader of the djinns in
the folklore of Morocco.

References 90
See also Djinn

SIDI MIMOUM EL DJINNAOUI
This name, which means the Guest of God, is used as a euphemism for a powerful king of the djinns in the folklore of Morocco. It is prudent to use such a form of naming the djinn in order to avert any offense if he should be listening.
References 90
See also Djinn

SIDI MOUSA EL BAHARI
This name, which means the Sailor, is used as a euphemism for a powerful leader of the djinns in the folklore of Morocco. It is prudent to use such a form of naming the djinn in order to avoid invoking the spirit. It is possible that this spirit was originally concerned with the seas.
References 90
See also Djinn, Spirit

SIDNA DJEBRIL
See Gabriel

SIGRUN
The name of a Valkyrie in Nordic and Teutonic mythology. This spirit as well as, Swawa and Brunhilde were the progeny of supernaturals and humans and were particularly attracted to mortals, assisting them on the battlefields. When they intermarried with mortals all their Valkyrie power was lost.
References 95
See also Valkyries

SIHO I SALO
This is the name of a sky demon in the folklore of the people of the Solomon Islands. He is described as a rather ridiculous being appearing in the shape of a man but having such huge ears that he can wrap himself up in one and lie down on the other. One day he appeared from out of a storm and immediately devoured the catch that a group of fishermen had just landed. But he was still hungry, so the men told him to wait while they got more bait. They left the foolish spirit while they went to alert their neighbors. The demon found the fishermen in their hut and promptly ate all the food there as well. One of the neighbors was a sorcerer who put a spell on this greedy but amiable demon so that Siho I Salo henceforth guarded the vegetable plots from other spirits in return for a share of the fishermen's catch.
References 29
See also Demon, Spirit

SILAT
This is the name of a female demon or djinn in the pre-Islamic mythology of the Arabian Peninsula. She was a djinn of lightning and storms who was said to inhabit the mountains and forests. If she caught any humans in her domain she would make them dance to death.
References 41
See also Demon, Djinn, Ouda

SILENI
See Silenus

SILENUS, SILENI
This is the name of the wisest and oldest of the satyrs in classical Greek mythology. He is possibly derived from the Egyptian guardian spirit Bes. Silenus is portrayed as a drunken, fat old man riding an ass, and he is the attendant of Dionysus (Bacchus). In later myths the older satyrs were all named Sileni. Silenus was their leader, and in some legends was their father. Silenus, although essentially a comic character, is able to see both the past and the future, and any humans who could tie him up long enough could get him to tell them their destiny. Silenus and the satyrs were frequently the subjects of Renaissance paintings. Instead of being half goat like the other satyrs, the Sileni had the lower body of a horse.
References 20, 40, 56, 88, 92, 93, 119
See also Attendant Spirit, Bes, Satyr, Appendix 12

SILI FFRIT AND SILI-GO-DWT
These are the names of two fairies in the folklore of Wales. Their story is almost the same as that of Trwtyn-Tratyn and Rumpelstiltskin, wherein the supernatural provides the spinning skills for a human in return for a promise. The promise is revoked when the human succeeds in finding the name of the supernatural benefactor. In the case of Sili-go-dwt she was overheard singing: *"Bychan a wyddai hi / Maj Sili-go-dwt yw f'enw i."* (Little did she know / That Sili-go-dwt is my name.)
References 17, 59
See also Fairy, Gwarwyn-a-throt, Rumpelstiltskin, Trwtyn-Tratyn

SILINIETS
This is the name of a nature spirit in the folklore of Poland. Siliniets resides in the forests.
References 102
See also Spirit, Appendix 19

SILKY
This is a type of household spirit or boggart in the folklore of northern England. She is the equivalent of the brownie but manifests as a lady dressed in silks,

which rustle as she materializes or moves invisibly from place to place. Although she may be particularly helpful with domestic tasks in some great houses, in others she is well known for her mischievous pranks. She guards the house, observing everything from the branches of a tree known as Silky's Chair, and sometimes frightens travelers by landing behind them on their horse's back. The Silky of Black Heddon mentioned by Henderson in his *Folklore of the Northern Counties* (1866) was unusually boisterous and could only be controlled by someone wearing a cross made of rowan wood. This spirit never disturbed the household again after a part of the ceiling fell in a room, revealing a hoard of gold. Another instance of a Silky was that of the Silky of Denton Hall, who had been benevolent and industrious while two elderly ladies of the Sowerby family lived there. However, when they died and a distant male member of the family took over, the Silky's activities resembled more those of a poltergeist. Another was the Silky of Gilsland, described by Ruth Tongue. This spirit was a much more dangerous character who not only guarded the family and its property but took revenge one night on an intruder who had intended to rob the house by slowly strangling him.

References 15, 17, 47, 66
See also Boggart, Brownie, Household Spirits, Poltergeist, Spirit, Appendix 22

SILLYONG

This is a general term for lesser spirits in the folk beliefs of the Korean people.
References 79
See also Sin, Spirit

SILTIM

This is a demon or malicious Deev in the mythology of ancient Persia. It is a forest demon that manifests in the shape of a human so that it may attract and do injury to travelers in the forests.
References 110
See also Deev, Demon, Appendix 24

SIMBI

This is the name of a spirit in the Voodoo cult of Haiti. Simbi is a healing spirit invoked during curing ceremonies. He is derived from a West African deity.
References 137
See also Encantado, Spirit

SIN

This is a general term for lesser spirits or supernatural forces in the folk beliefs of the Korean people.
References 79
See also Sillyong, Spirit

SINDRI

See Brock

SINLAP

One of the benevolent nats in the beliefs of the Kachin people of Burma. Sinlap is a spirit of the air dwelling in the skies. He is the spirit of wisdom who gives insight to his devotees.
References 87, 88
See also Chinün Way Shun, Nats, Spirit, Appendix 10

SINTER KLAAS

Dressed like a bishop, this spirit of moral benevolence in the folk beliefs of Holland has his summer home in Spain (the former colonial ruler of the Low Countries). There, with his Moorish assistant Zwart Piet, he records the deeds of good and bad children. In November they sail in their galleon loaded with toys to Amsterdam. From this port Sinter Klaas tours Holland on his white horse, distributing gifts to good children and the means for the bad ones to receive punishment.

While Sinter Klaas is derived from Saint Nicholas, his environment and servants recall the time when Holland was ruled by Spain and the Moors were part of that culture, but his character and the white horse he rides are derived from the Nordic/Teutonic god Odin.
References 34
See also Father Christmas, Spirit, Zwart Piet, Appendix 22

SIO HUMIS

This is an important spirit in the beliefs and legends of the Hopi Native American people. Sio Humis is the benevolent Rain Spirit.
References 25
See also Spirit, Appendix 26

SÍOD BRAD

See Corpán síde

SIOFRA

See Shefro

SIR ALI

The name of an angel in the Islamic beliefs of the people of West Malaysia. Sir Ali is given the meaning Lord of the Waters of the Sea, and this is the region of his protection.
References 120
See also Angel, Putar Ali, Appendix 25

SIREN

These sea nymphs were malicious spirits in the mythology of ancient Greece and Rome. Their name is variously given as Sireen, Sirene, or Syrene, and they were the offspring of Phorcys. These maidens appeared as half bird and half woman and congregated on the rocks of Sicily, where they sang melodiously to attract and beguile or devour passing sailors. Their individual names are Aglaopheme, Leucosia, Ligia, Parthenope, Pisinoe, and Thelxiepia. Legend has it that Odysseus was able to pass by their island successfully by stopping up the ears of his men with wax and lashing himself to the mast of his ship. Jason and the Argonauts were said to have caused the demise of the Sirens when they heard Orpheus, Jason's passenger, singing more sweetly than they did.

In the northwestern Spanish coastal area there is a type of mermaid whose name is "la Sirena," which seems to be a derivative of the Siren. However, this spirit is not malevolent.
References 20, 40, 56, 88, 92, 93, 114, 119, 129, 130, 132
See also Hesperidos, Lorelei, Mermaid, Nymph, Appendix 25

SISI
See Faingaa

SITKONSKY
The name of a trickster spirit in the folk beliefs and legends of the Assiniboine Native American people.
References 88
See also Spirit, Trickster

SJÖRA
The name of a water spirit in the folklore of Sweden. This spirit is said to inhabit Lake Helga in the region of Småland.
References 99
See also Spirit, Appendix 25

SJÖTROLL
See Troll

SKADEGAMUTC
This is the name of a demon in the folk beliefs and legends of the Micmac Native American people. These devils inhabited the forests and would terrify solitary travelers by following them and giving an eerie shriek in the woods. Even more disturbing was their ability to blend with the shapes of the trunks of the trees, so that humans could not catch sight of them.
References 99
See also Demon, Devil, Leshii, Appendix 19

ŠKENAN ONČƏMƏ KEREMET AND ŠKE KEREMET
These are the names of demons or keremets which a family of many households will revere in much the same way as the lars and penates of ancient Rome.
References 118
See also Demon, Keremet, Lar, Penates, Appendix 9, Appendix 22

SKILLY WIDDEN
The name of an individual fairy boy said to have been found and adopted by a farmer of Terridge in Cornwall, England.
References 17, 18, 41
See also Coleman Gray, Fairy, Green Children, Undine, Appendix 6, Appendix 22

SKOGS FRU
This is a type of female wood spirit in the folklore of Scandinavia whose name means Woods Woman. She is also known as the Skogsrå. This spirit may manifest as an owl in the trees or as the violent whirlwinds, but more often she appears as a small, beautiful human woman. She seems to come in a friendly manner to the hunters' campfires at night in the forest. It is very unlucky to meet her, as she entices young men to follow her into the forest. Anyone foolish enough to do this will never be seen again, unless she can be propitiated with some of the results of the hunt.
References 44, 88, 99, 110
See also Dirne-weibl, Appendix 12, Appendix 19

SKOGSRÅ
See Skogs Fru

SKOGUL
See Valkyries

SKOVTROLDE
See Berg People

SKRIKER
This is the local name in Lancashire, England, for the goblin, boggart, or bogie beast that may also be known as Brash, Gytrash, Shriker, Striker, or Trash. The name Trash is used to describe the squelching noise it may make as it moves along behind someone. The Skriker has been described as taking the form of a huge dog or a shape with enormous glowing eyes. It appears in front of lonely travelers, drawing them irresistibly toward it, or padding along invisibly beside them. As it does this it is constantly moaning and howling, or it may be heard shrieking in the woods. To see the Skriker is a portent of misfortune; to try to hit it brings disaster or death.
References 17, 69, 123
See also Black Dog, Bogie, Boggart, Goblin, Gytrash, Skriker, Appendix 24

SKRIMSL
The name of a type of water spirit in the folklore of Iceland. It is entirely unfriendly and malevolent toward humans.
References 88
See also Nix, Spirit, Appendix 25

SKULD
See Norns

SLAUGH, THE
This is the name of the Unseelie Court or the evil fairies in the folklore of Scotland. The name means the Host, which is a euphemism to avoid invoking them with the mention of their name and deter them from inflicting harm. They are believed to be the Fallen Angels that roam the midnight skies of the earth searching for lost souls. The Slaugh are also believed to be responsible for causing sickness and death among domestic animals and to lead humans astray.
References 17, 18
See also Fairy, Fallen Angel, Fuath, Seelie Court

SLEAGH MAITH, SLEETH MA
These are names used for the fairies in the folklore of the Highlands of Scotland. Sleagh Maith means the Good People, and Sleeth Ma means the People/Men of Peace in Scottish Gaelic. These names are euphemisms for the spirits, who can have a very ambivalent attitude toward their relationship with humans. Like the Daoine Sidhe of Ireland, the Sleagh Maith inhabit the Iron Age forts, long barrows, and *brochs* of the ancient landscape. They may also be encountered among the wild mountain crags and forests.
References 15, 17, 18
See also Fairy, Daoine Sidhe

SLEIGH BEGGEY, SLEIGH VEGGEY
This is the euphemism used for the Little People or fairies in the Manx language of the Isle of Man, United Kingdom. These spirits may also be referred to as Ny Mooinjer Veggey, which means the Little Kindred. It was always considered prudent to be extremely polite when referring to them, as they were considerably malicious if offended. They were the diminutive Trooping Fairies that lived in communities in the island's woods and hills. They had the same kinds of relationships amongst themselves as the humans, and they have been known to have battles. If they were in a battle or on a hunt, it was very dangerous for a human to see or come near them. The Sleigh Beggey were very fond of making music and would use it to entice and abduct humans. There were many fiddlers in the Isle of Man who, on their way to play at feasts, might catch one of the fairy tunes, but when they arrived they could never remember it. The fairies are said to have retreated to the hills with the coming of the noise of modern machinery.
References 17, 81
See also Fairy, Little People, Spirit

SLOGUTE
This is the name for the spirit of the nightmare in Lithuanian folklore.
References 88
See also Nightmare, Spirit

SMALL PEOPLE
See Muryans

SMIERA-GATTO
This is the name of a household spirit in the folklore of the Lapp people of northern Scandinavia. It is a demon whose name means the Butter Cat, for this is the guise in which it usually appears. In the shape of a cat, the Smiera-Gatto will steal produce and especially butter for its master. It is a dangerous spirit to have as a friend, for it enriches its host family at the expense of the neighbors with all the resultant problems this would bring.
References 87, 88, 93
See also Aitvaras, Demon, Household Spirits, Kaukas, Para, Pukis, Appendix 12, Appendix 22

SMILAX
This is the name of a nymph in the classical mythology of Greece and Rome. A youth named Crocus fell in love with her, but, unable to be with her, pined until he was transformed into the saffron flower. Smilax was later changed into a yew tree.
References 130
See also Nymph

SMOLENKOS
The name of a demon in the folk beliefs of the Native American people from the Great Lakes region. Smolenkos was described as having only one eye, and, despite having no joints in its limbs, was able to run more swiftly than the deer. This fiend was said to inhabit the forests and the mountainsides.
References 110
See also Demon, Fiend

SNOW MAIDEN
See Father Frost

SNOW QUEEN
This is the name of a fairy queen in the folklore of Denmark. She is described as dazzling in her loveliness and as beautiful as the ice crystals themselves.

She is the spirit queen of the ice realm, who travels in the blizzards blown from the Arctic wastes. The Snow Queen will entice mortal men to follow her, but, like Yuki-onna of Japanese folk belief, to be loved by the Snow Queen means instant death.
References 44
See also Fairy, Spirit, Yuki-onna, Appendix 26

SNUGGLEPOT
See Gumnut Babies

ŠOKŠA KUBA AND ŠOKŠA KUGUZA
These are spirits of warmth in the folk beliefs of the Cheremis/Mari people of the former Soviet Republic. The names Šokša Kuba and Šokša Kuguza mean Warmth Old Woman and Warmth Old Man and are terms of respect and encouragement. These spirits are benevolent toward humans in that they are the adversaries of the spirits of cold, Jüštə Kuba and Jüštə Kuguza, who bring sickness and misery to the people during the winter.
References 118
See also Jüštə Kuba, Spirit

SONNEILLON
See Devil

SOUIN-SOUIN, LE
This is the name of the sleep spirit in the folklore of France. Like Mr. Sandman in England, Le Souin-souin is the nursery spirit who guides French children gently to sleep at night with pleasant dreams. His female counterpart is known in France as La Dormette.
References 17, 88
See also Dormette, Dustman, Ole Luk Øj, Sandman, Spirit, Wee Willie Winkie, Appendix 22

SPAE-WIVES
This is the name of a type of female elf also called Elf Damsels in the folklore of Iceland. Like many other of the spirits of Iceland, these are derived from the Scandinavian Little People and have their counterparts in the Wood Wives. They have been described as appearing like tiny peasant women who inhabit the ancient burial places, long barrows, and sacred mounds like the Sidhe of Ireland. The Spae-wives are experts in the lore of herbal magic and healing. A folk tale tells of a wounded man being advised by a Spae-wife to sacrifice a bull at an "Elf Mound," smearing the mound with the blood and preparing a feast of the flesh, and in return the elves would heal him of his injuries.
References 110
See also Elf, Little People, Sídhe, Wood Wives

SPANDULE
See Gremlin

SPELLY COAT
See Shellycoat

SPIDER
This is the designation of certain culture spirits in the beliefs and legends of the Native North American people. In the legends of the Navajo, the benevolent spirits that taught humans how to weave are known as Spider Man and Naste Estsan/Spider Woman. The latter also features among the Coeur d'Alene, Jacarilla, and Kiowa as a shrewd and benevolent spirit and is known among the Hopi as Kotyangwuti. Further helpful spirits are the Spider Grandmother and the Black Spider Old Woman of the Taos Pueblo and White Mountain Apache, respectively. Among the Arapaho the Spider Supernatural is a trickster spirit named Nihansan. Like Anansi in the legends of Africa and African-Americans, the supernatural manifests with all the properties and appearance of either a human or the spider, according to the situation. However, each concept of the supernatural held by the peoples who believe in the being varies widely in the type of powers, character, and behavior toward humans. These spirits inhabit the earth or the skies with equal facility, and they feature in the legends of many other cultures around the world.
References 45, 56, 88
See also Anansi, Qat, Spirit, Trickster, Appendix 12

SPIGENA
See Laumé

SPINNSTUBENFRAU
This is an epithet of the spirit called Berchta in the folklore of Germany. As the Spinnstubenfrau, which means Spinning-Room Woman, she takes the form of an old hag who may appear about the property of humans during the long winter months. In this guise she is the guardian spirit of the barns and of the spinning room. She oversees the work of these places until the coming of light nights and the return of spring.
References 87, 88, 93, 95
See also Berchta, Deive, Guardian, Hag, Holle, Appendix 14, Appendix 22

SPIRIT
This is the concept of a supernatural entity that occupies and influences the same world as that inhabited by humans. Although the term may be applied to a deity, it refers mostly to those beings that have lesser powers and limited scope in their activities. All cultures have spirits in their mythology and folklore to

The Snow Queen's beauty entices gullible humans to follow her to death in the ice.

some degree. Their character, activities, and relationship to humans and supreme deities form the rich heritage of beliefs in each society.
References 39, 88

SPOORN, THE

This is the name of a spirit in the folklore of Dorset in England. Also known as the Spurn, this is a malevolent sprite or nursery bogie whose activities may have been used to frighten small children into good behavior.
References 107
See also Nursery Bogie, Spirit, Sprite, Appendix 22

SPRET

See Sprite

SPRIGGANS

These are a type of dwarf or fairy people in the folklore of Cornwall, England. They are extremely ugly, squat little human forms that can shape shift to an enormous, terrifying size. They inhabit the cromlechs, ancient forts, and dwellings in the remote countryside, where they are said to be the guardians of treasure. The Spriggans are deemed responsible for stealing human babies and leaving their changelings and also bringing storms and blighting the crops. In a tale retold by Robert Hunt in his *Popular Romances of the West of England* (1865), a man thought that he had located the treasure hidden in one of the hills. On a moonlit night he took his spade and went to dig

there. No sooner had he started than a great storm arose, and in the flashes of lightning he saw hundreds of Spriggans emerging from the rocks around him. As they got closer they swelled menacingly, and fearing for his life, the man fled. When he reached his home he took to his bed, and even when recovered from his fright, never went back to dig there again.
References 15, 17, 18, 44, 133
See also Changeling, Dwarf, Fairy, Guardian, Knockers, Appendix 20, Appendix 22

SPRITE, SPRIGHT, SPRYTE

This is a term generally applied to a lesser spirit, such as an elf, fairy, or pixy, which usually indicates their unpredictable and mischievous characters. It is rarely used for entirely benevolent supernaturals, but is usually used for a malevolent being such as a familiar or demon in its benign state. The obsolete form of this word is *spret*, which may be found in old manuscripts.
References 17, 59, 92, 133
See also Demon, Elf, Fairy, Familiar, Pixie, Spirit

SPUNKIES, SPUNKY

This is a type of spirit that is usually spoken of in the plural in the folklore of Scotland. Spunkies manifest in the form of a malignant goblin that goes about furtively in wild places at night. It is a particularly evil being in its relationship with humans as it delights in providing lights for lost travelers to follow, in much the same manner as the Will o' the Wisp. However, Spunkies are much more demonic in their purpose, for they frequently lead the unsuspecting human either over a precipice or into a morass. In the days of sailing ships before lighthouses were established the Spunkies also signaled from the coastal cliffs to the ships at night, and were thus considered to be the cause of shipwrecks off the east coast of Scotland.
References 17, 18, 53
See also Goblin, Will o' the Wisp, Appendix 24

SPURN, THE

See Spoorn

SRAHMAN

See Shamantin

SRAOSHA, SRAOŠA

The name of a spirit in the Zoroastrian religion of Iran. He is derived from the genius of hearing in the ancient Persian mythology. Sraosha, whose name means To Harken, is a Yazata or a type of angel. It is this spirit who listens to the cries of humans who have been caused misery by the demons. Sraosha is commanded by Ahura Mazda to oppose the evil of Aeshma and comes to earth at night to pursue this

evil spirit. In the later conversion to Islam, Sraosha survived as the angel Surush, the messenger of Allah sometimes equated with the Archangel Gabriel.
References 33, 41, 88, 93
See also Aeshma, Angel, Demon, Gabriel, Genius, Spirit, Yazatas, Appendix 13

ŠRAT
This is the name of a household spirit in the folklore of the Slav people. Like the Aitvaras and the Kratt, it may manifest as a domestic creature while in the home. When it is outside the human dwelling, this spirit may fly through the air and appear to have a fiery tail. The Šrat is a fortune demon that enriches its family at the expense of the neighbors through theft of material goods.
References 93
See also Aitvaras, Demon, Household Spirits, Kratt, Smierra-Gatto, Appendix 20, Appendix 22

SREI AP
This is a malicious spirit in the folk beliefs of Cambodia. It is a demon that brings about the death of humans or hovers about the dying in order to devour their flesh.
References 53
See also Spirit, Sri, Appendix 16

SRI
These are evil spirits in the former Bon religion of Tibet. They dwell in the dark places of the earth, under rocks, in caves and tombs. Like the Srei of Cambodia, these demons lurk in places where the dead and dying humans may be laid before burial. They devour human flesh and, if not satisfied, will entice the unwary, especially little children, to follow them to their demise. To some extent these demons have been used as nursery bogies to prevent small children from venturing into unseemly places.
References 93
See also Demon, Nursery Bogie, Spirit, Srei Ap, Appendix 16, Appendix 22

STAPHYLE
This is the name of a nymph in the classical mythology of Greece and Rome. She was the lover of Dionysus.
References 102, 130
See also Nymph

STAR PEOPLE
See Mikak'e

STAR WOMAN
This is a celestial spirit in the legends of the Native South American people. The myth tells of an ugly man who yearns for love but grows old having never taken a bride as he is so unattractive. In his wistful misery he expresses his sorrow to a star shining brightly above him, and praising its beauty, says how glad he would be to make her his bride. As soon as he has finished speaking, a beautiful young woman appears at his side, and when he marries her, the years and ugliness fall away. His success is soon complete, and in his happiness, he desires to see the place where his wife has come from. The Star Woman takes her husband to her heavens, where he is soon so cold that he dies.
References 88
See also Spirit, Appendix 13

STIHI
This is an evil spirit in the folklore of southern Albania. It is a female demon that breathes fire and is supposed to be the guardian of hidden treasure.
References 93
See also Demon, Guardian, Spirit, Appendix 20

STILLE VOLK
This is an epithet given to the Little People in the folklore of Germany. They were said to resemble the dwarfs when they materialized, but the Stille Volk, which means the Silent People, rarely made an appearance, preferring to remain invisible or hidden. These spirits would work for the country folk in the fields and also in the farm buildings and the cow byres. These spirits were often implicated in mischief and pranks.
References 38
See also Dwarf, Little People, Pixie

STOLAS
The name of a demon in European demonology considered to be a devil from Hell. He was invoked in rituals for his instruction in the arts of astronomy and the qualities of precious stones.
References 53
See also Demon, Devil, Appendix 13

STOMACH-SLASHER
This is the epithet used for the spirit otherwise known as Berchta in the folklore of Germany. In this guise she is the spirit or hag that appears like an aged human during the winter season. She is a terrifying demon who, if not respectfully given her portion from the Feast of Epiphany (6 January), will rip open the stomachs of the sleeping revelers. Then she will remove her due portion and sew up the gash with a plough share for a needle and chains for thread.
References 87, 88, 93, 95
See also Berchta, Demon, Hag, Spirit

STRAKH
See Tras

STRANGERS, THE
This is a euphemism used for the fairies in the Fenlands of Lincolnshire, England. They were Trooping Fairies that were more like the pixies or brownies than the delicate woodland spirits. They inhabited the reed beds and eerie washes of the marshland in the Fens. The Strangers required propitiation and would exact revenge from anyone who forgot or offended them.
References 18
See also Brownie, Fairy, Pixie, Spirit, Appendix 6

STRÄTELLI
See Strudeli

STRIGÆ
These are evil female spirits in the beliefs of the people of ancient Rome. They manifested as birds and would steal small children who were left unattended.
References 93
See also Spirit, Appendix 22

STRINGLOS, STRINGLA (f.)
This is a shape-shifting spirit in the folklore of modern Greece. It may manifest in the shape of a human, an animal, the sound of galloping hooves on a road, or a disembodied voice in the darkness. The Stringlos inhabits lonely places in the mountains, deserted roads, and deep ravines. It will cry like a baby, imitate a relative, and cause all manner of deception. The Stringlos is deemed responsible for the unexpected deaths of animals. Although it never seems to have done any real harm to humans, it is such a frightening spirit that people have died as a result of encounters with it. A typical story tells of a man traveling late at night on the road to Spathi in the Doxorio region. In the gloom he saw a tiny baby lying in the road in front of him. Thinking aloud, what kind of mother could have left her child like this, he gently picked up the baby and, cradling it in his arms, started on his journey again. Soon his arms began to ache, and he noticed that the farther he walked, the heavier the baby became, and the larger it appeared to be. At last he could hold it no longer, and the spirit threw its arms in the air and flew off threatening to devour him. The terrified man arrived home in such a state that he died of a heart attack not long after.
References 12
See also Spirit, Appendix 12, Appendix 22, Appendix 24

STROKE LAD, THE
See Amadán,

STRÖMKARL
This is a water spirit in the folklore of Norway and Sweden. In Norway this spirit specifically inhabits the waterfalls. The Strömkarl, whose name means River Man, is a particularly musical supernatural whose playing is literally enchanting. He is reputed to have 11 melodies, of which he plays ten regularly. If any humans are within hearing distance of him when he plays the eleventh melody, then even the infirm, the cradled infants, the elderly, and any objects not bolted to the ground cannot resist dancing. Those musicians who wish to have superior ability must make a sacrifice of a black lamb to the Strömkarl by the water on a Thursday evening. As they approach the water with their eyes averted, the offering is extended in the right hand. The Strömkarl will seize the offering and fling the hand of the human to and fro until blood pours from the fingers. Thereafter the aspiring musician should be able to play like his maestro.
References 78, 88
See also Spirit, Appendix 25

STRUDELI AND STRÄTELLI
These are the names of two evil spirits in the folklore of Switzerland. They are malignant female wood sprites that are supposed to inhabit the woods surrounding Lake Lucerne. These spirits take a delight in spoiling the fertility of the local fruit trees and install themselves in the orchards and woods for this purpose. Consequently, each year on the feast of the Twelfth Night (6 January), the boys of the region form a procession which tours the area with flaming torches. They also beat gongs, ring bells, sound horns, and make as much noise as possible to ensure that the sprites are frightened away.
References 48, 110
See also Sprite, Appendix 19

STYX
See Oceanids

ŠÜČ PUNDƏŠ
See Čembulat

SUCCUBUS, SUCCUBA
This is the medieval European female fiend of the night. The name is from the Latin *sub*, under, and *cubare*, to lie down. Just like the incubus that mounts a sleeping woman for the purpose of sexual relations, this is the female form that copulates with a man in his sleep. It may take on any shape, male or female, but usually appears in the semblance of the wife or lover, or it may be entirely invisible. During the witch hunts of the sixteenth and seventeenth centuries, women were often accused of being the Succubus of the Devil, with little chance of refuting such a charge.
References 40, 53, 88, 92, 93, 98
See also Fiend, Incubus, Lilith, Nightmare

Succubus (left) taunts Saint Dunstan.

SUIRE
See Merrow

ŠUČƏ
This is the name for an angel. Šučə means Angel in the folk beliefs of the Cheremis/Mari people of the former Soviet Republic. These angels are said to have been created when God struck sparks from a stone. As with other Christian beliefs, these spirits may perform different functions as the attendants of God or as the Guardian Angel of a human being, place, creature, or phenomenon. The Guardian Angel of a person is known as Buj Šučə, Head Angel, or Bučə Ümbal Šučə, Angel on the Shoulder. This latter name is derived from the belief that an angel sits on the right shoulder of a person throughout life, recording all the good things performed, while a devil sits on the left shoulder recording and encouraging all the bad things. Whichever has the longer list at the end of the person's life claims the soul.
References 118
See also Angel, Attendant Spirit, Bes, Devil, Guardian Angel, Spirit, Appendix 1 (for individual names)

ŠÜKŠƏNDAL
This is the name of a malicious household spirit in the folk beliefs of the Cheremis/Mari people of the former Soviet Republic. It may take the form of a beautiful, diminutive young woman with long blond hair, or that of a handsome young man. It may be seen in the bathhouse at night or in the homes of humans. But this evil spirit comes from the mountains and has its abode under stones, in rocks, or in millstones. This demon usually causes harm to children left alone in the house, and it will jump upon people sleeping at night, bringing stomachache and nightmares. It might even cause the death of anyone foolish enough to go to the bathhouse alone late at night. There is a tale, however, of a Šükšəndal that took pity on a young man who could not go to his brother's wedding and transported him there invisibly. The Cheremis would often ask the Šükšəndal of their locality to keep away other evil spirits from their homes.
References 118
See also Albastor, Asmodee, Astarotte, Demon, Household Spirits, Nightmare, Spirit, Appendix 22

SULTAN
This is the name of a demon in the folk beliefs of the Cheremis/Mari people of the former Soviet Republic. It is a keremet that has been brought into the beliefs of the Cheremis by association with the Tartars. An offering is made to him in July.
References 118
See also Demon, Keremet, Appendix 9

SUMERKLAS
See Knecht Ruprecht

SUMMER
This is the name of the queen of the elves of light in the Algonquin Native American mythology. In the most famous legend, Glooscap abducts Summer and takes her to the home of Winter. Eventually the spirit of cold melts with her warmth, and as the fairies re-emerge, nature blossoms once again.
References 122
See also Elf, Fairy, Spirit

SÜNAWAVI
See Cünawabi

ŠUNDY-MUMY
See Mumy

SUPAY
These were a group of evil demons in the ancient Inca mythology of Peru. The name is used now by the Quechua people to denote the Devil.
References 88
See also Demon

SURÄLI
See Obda

SÜREM MUŽƏ
This is an evil spirit or night demon in the folk beliefs of the Cheremis/Mari people of the former Soviet Republic. Care is taken to drive this spirit away from the village or town at night to be rid of its torments.
References 118
See also Demon, Spirit

SURIEL
See Raphael

ŠUR-MUMY
See Mumy

ŠURNƏ
This is the first part of the name of a number of field spirits within the Šurnə designation in the folklore of the Cheremis/Mari people of the former Soviet Republic. The spirit names are: Šurnə Pujəršə, meaning Grain Creator; Šurnə Perke, meaning Grain Blessing; Šurnə Saus, meaning Grain Overseer; and Šurnə Šočan, meaning Grain Fructifier. These are all the attendant spirits of Pasu Kögə, and together, they are responsible for ensuring that the agricultural fields produce abundant crops. As these spirits are types of demons, they are propitiated to ensure that

they do not become offended and destroy the crops as retribution.
References 118
See also Attendant Spirit, Demon, Pasu, Spirit, Appendix 18

ŠURNƏ PIAMBAR
See Piambar

SURT MƏLANDƏ BODƏZ
This is the name of a keremet or demon in the folk beliefs of the Cheremis/Mari people of the former Soviet Republic. Surt Mǝlandǝ Bodǝz means House Earth Spirit, and this evil spirit is one that could materialize through the foundations of the property.
References 118
See also Demon, Keremet, Spirit, Appendix 22

SURUSH
See Sraosha

SUT
A djinn or demon in the beliefs associated with Islam who is the instigator of lies and the progeny of Iblis.
References 41
See also Demon, Djinn, Iblis

SVALD
See Iwaldi

SWAN MAIDEN
These are fairy spirits in the folklore of northern European countries, especially where there is a Celtic tradition. But similar themes exist in the folklore of many other cultures. The Swan Maidens usually inhabit the woods and forest surrounding desolate and beautiful lakes and occasionally inhabit the edge of the sea. These spirit maidens are able to shape shift from the form of a beautiful young woman to that of a graceful swan, by way of a magic cloak of feathers. This magic transformer may also be a ring, a crown, or a pair of wings in other traditions. In her human form, the Swan Maiden may leave her cloak while bathing, and thus it may be stolen by a prospective husband or a villain with evil intent. The Swan Maiden is then in the power of the one who has the magic garment until she retrieves it and flies away or is rescued by the hero.
References 17, 18, 40, 88, 110
See also Angus Og, Brunhilde, Fairy, Roane, Spirit, Urvashi, Valkyries, Völund

SWARTALFAR, SVARTALFAR
See Alfar

SWAWA
See Sigrun

SYEN
These are household spirits in the folklore of the Slav people of southeastern Europe. They are a type of demon or djinn that enters the home in the guise of a domestic animal. Once established and propitiated they will become the guardian spirit of the family and home.
References 41
See also Demon, Djinn, Dyavo, Guardian, Household Spirits, Appendix 22

SYLPH
One of a group of nature spirits or elementals defined by the mystical philosopher Paracelsus (1493–1541) in terms of the natural elements from which they were supposed to be derived. Sylphs are spirits of the air and winds, described as taller and stronger than humans with a volatile and unreliable temperament. Their "emperor," according to the occultist Elephas Levi, is called Paralda. They are also described as being the transformed souls of those who died as virgins, whether male or female. Humans who live a chaste life are said to expect to enjoy their company in the afterlife.
References 40, 92, 98, 107, 114, 136
See also Elemental, Fairy, Houri, Nymph, Appendix 18

SYRINX
This is the name of a Naiad or water nymph in the classical mythology of Greece. She was pursued by the overamorous god Pan, and in her terror, entered the marshes on the edge of the River Ladon. Unable to go any further, she implored her sister nymphs for help. When Pan reached out to grab her, he found that he was clutching at reeds. When the wind blew gently across them, they made the most beautiful sound. Pan therefore cut seven of the reeds and turned them into the musical Pan pipes, to which he gave the name of Syrinx.
References 40, 110, 114
See also Naiad, Nymph, Appendix 11, Appendix 25

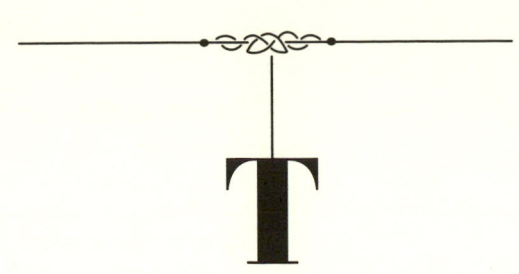

T

TABI

The familiar of Arab folklore is an attendant spirit known as a Tabi. It is not like the familiar of European folklore, but rather a "follower" or shadowy spirit that reveals secret knowledge when requested by the sorcerer who controls it.
References 87
See also Attendant Spirit, Familiar

TACHUKI

This is the name for a group of the Koyemshi fertility spirits in the beliefs of the Hopi Native American people.
References 88
See also Koyemshi, Spirit

TADEBTSY

In the folk beliefs of the Samoyed people of the Asian Arctic, the Tadebtsy are the familiar spirits of the shamans, who are known as Tadibey.
References 88
See also Familiar

TAGAMALING

This is a type of Buso in the folklore of the Bagobo Malay peoples of the Philippines. These spirits are not so malicious as the others, as they only take the form of Buso on alternate months.
References 87
See also Buso, Spirit

TAK-KENG

See Hkum Yeng

TALONHALTIJA

This is the name of the household spirit or guardian spirit in the folk beliefs of the Estonian people. It is usually attached to the home itself rather than the occupants, and is often represented in the form of the original occupant in much the same manner as the Domovoi of Russian folklore.
References 88

See also Domovik, Guardian, Haldde, Haldjas, Household Spirits, Kodinhaltia, Metsänhaltia, Spirit, Tonttu, Vedenhaltia, Appendix 22

TANGIE

This is the name of a sea spirit or demon sea horse in the folklore of the Orkney and Shetland Islands (United Kingdom). It may manifest in the shape of an old man covered in seaweed, or as a little rough-haired pony. It is not a gentle spirit, but more in keeping with the kelpie or the noggle. It is recorded that a fearsome sheep rustler named Black Eric rode a Tangie, which gave him supernatural assistance in a fight with a crofter named Sandy Breamer. Although Black Eric finally fell over a coastal cliff known as Fitful Head, the Tangie continued to terrorize the area, and particularly the young women he had been hoping to abduct.
References 17, 40, 47, 78
See also Demon, Each Uisge, Kelpie, Neugie, Spirit, Appendix 12, Appendix 25

TANGÓ DO PARÁ

This is the name of an important encantado, who is also known as Guapindaia, in the Afro-Brazilian cult Batuque. His name is derived from the songbird Tangaru-Pará. Tangó do Pará is known by other names in the Catimbó cult: Ritangó do Pará and Tangaru-Pará.
References 89
See also Encantado, Guapindaia, Pena Verde

TANKERABOGUS, TANTRABOBUS

See Cankobobus

TAPAIRU

This is the name of the fairies in the folk beliefs and legends of the Mangaia people of the Pacific. They are the four daughters of Miru, the female demon. The Tapairu, whose name means the Peerless Ones, are extremely beautiful with long silken hair. At sunset they may ascend to the human world to

dance in the festivals honoring their brother Tautiti.
References 110
See also Demon, Fairy, Miru

TAPINARÉ

This is the name of an important encantado in the Afro-Brazilian cult Batuque and a member of the Turquia "family." Tapinaré means the Jaguar, and as this implies, he is associated with the jaguar and its derivation from the shaman beliefs of the region. Tapinaré is considered by devotees to be a powerful healer and features prominently in curing ceremonies.
References 89
See also Encantado, Seu Turquia

TARANUSHI

In the beliefs and folklore of the Islamic countries of Mediterranean North Africa, Taranushi was the first djinn created from the Saharan wind, the Simoon. He was charged with controlling the activities of all the other djinns.
References 78, 90, 93
See also Djinn

TARTUGA DE AMAZONAS

This is the name of a group of encantados in the Afro-Brazilian cult Batuque. Their name, Tartuga de Amazonas, means Turtle of the Amazon, and these spirits are derived from the original shamanistic beliefs of the region.
References 89
See also Encantado, Spirit

TATANE

These are supernaturals in the folklore and legends of the Easter Islanders. To some extent, they resemble the familiar spirits of the Northern Hemisphere. The Tatane may manifest in the form of beautiful young girls or as handsome young men, in order to gain the confidence of humans. At other times they are reluctant to make themselves visible, or may manifest in the shape of a familiar animal, bird, or even an inanimate object. They are said to exist in societies much like those of the humans and to have families of their own. The Tatane are deemed responsible for giving humans skills in the preparation of food, clothing, and hunting. Other Tatane behave more like demons, and are malevolent toward humans.
References 22
See also Akuaku, Demon, Familiar

TATARIKI
See Atua

TATTER FOAL
See Shag Foal

TAURU, TAUVI

This is the name of an evil spirit or demon in the mythology of the Zoroastrian religion of Iran. In conjunction with Zairisha, also known as Zairi, the two demons were responsible for bringing about the misery of decrepitude and old age to humans. They opposed the good works of Ameretat and Haurvatat in order to bring about the downfall of mankind.
References 102
See also Ameretat, Demon, Haurvatat, Spirit

TAUS

An epithet of Iblis in pre-Islamic mythology, this name signifies the Peacock Angel, a reference to his pride and ultimate downfall.
References 41
See also Angel, Iblis

TÇARIDYI

In the folk beliefs of the Romany Gypsies, this is a female disease demon. This evil spirit was the result of the union between Ana and the king of the demons after Ana had been fed with crayfish. Tçaridyi became the wife of the demon Tçulo. She is described as having the body of a worm covered in hairs. This evil spirit tries to enter the bodies of humans, and when she enters a man, she causes burning fevers. When she enters a woman, she lies in wait until she has the opportunity to cause puerperal fever in childbirth. In order to protect themselves, women would carry a talisman made of a crayfish.
References 31
See also Ana, Demon, Loçolico, Spirit, Tçulo, Appendix 17, Appendix 22

TCHATSE-OLMAI

These are a type of water spirit in the folk beliefs of the Lapp people of the northern Baltic regions. These "watermen," or water demons, inhabited the sacred lakes and rivers of the region, which are known as *passe-javrre* and *passe-jokka*.
References 102
See also As-iga, Demon, Kul, Näkki, Spirit, Appendix 25

TÇULO

In the folk beliefs of the Romany Gypsies, this is a male disease demon. This evil spirit was the result of the union between Ana and the king of the demons after he had eaten a crayfish and a stag beetle, then lay with Ana, who was asleep. Tçulo is described as being a thick, potbellied ball of prickles that rolled itself up into a sphere to enter the body of a human. Once he had entered the body, Tçulo would cause violent pains in the lower abdomen; Tçulo specialized in torturing women in pregnancy. As with his

sibling demon wife, Tçaridyi, women might carry a talisman made of a crayfish to protect themselves from the malice of Tçulo.
References 31
See also Ana, Demon, Loçolico, Tçaridyi, Spirit, Appendix 17

TE MAKAWE
See Atua

TELCHINES
The Telchines are described variously as a type of dwarf or merman in the mythology of ancient Greece. Like the dwarfs of Scandinavian mythology, the Telchines were skilled in the arts of metalworking and magic. Legends of their skills abound, especially on the Island of Rhodes. But as diminutive mermen, they were charged with the education of the infant god Poseidon. Some authorities class these beings as an ancient race conquered by later invasions, in similar circumstances to the Formorians and the Tuatha dé Danann of Irish mythology.
References 93, 130
See also Dwarf, Formor, Merman, Tuatha dé Danann, Appendix 22

TELMAČ
See Čembulat

TEN-GU, TENGU/S
These are spirits in the Shinto traditions of Japan. They are described as having the appearance of humans, but with the wings and beaks of birds. Although they wear garments and exist in communities like those of humans, they inhabit trees in the forests and mountains. Their activities are not exactly malicious, but more in keeping with those of the trickster.
References 33, 41, 53, 88, 93, 119
See also Kappa, Spirit, Trickster, Appendix 12

TERPISCHORE
See Muses

TERRYTOP
This is the name of the Cornish variant of Tom Tit Tot in English folklore. Terrytop, however, is a demon rather than a dwarf. The Cornish story also has an unusual ending, and the full tale may be read in Hunt's *Popular Romances of the West of England*. Briefly, the girl in the tale, called Duffy, was very lazy. One day, Squire Lovel of Trewoof overheard her claims of spinning and knitting in a quarrel with her stepmother, and carried Duffy off to his house to help the housekeeper. Duffy was secretly helped by a demon with the usual expectation of reward against

the discovery of his name. As in the tale of Rumpelstiltskin, when the name was revealed the demon disappeared in a cloud of smoke, and with him all his handiwork, and the unfortunate squire found himself walking home half-naked.
References 17, 18
See also Demon, Dwarf, Rumpelstiltskin, Tom Tit Tot, Appendix 14

THALIA
See Graces, Muses

THEKKR
This is the name of a dwarf, also known as Thror, in Scandinavian mythology. The name is also used for Odin, king of the gods, and a dwarf form may have been one of his many disguises or the name was used as an implied association with them.
References 41
See also Dwarf, Appendix 4

THEMSELVES
See Appendix 6

THETIS
This is the name of a nymph in the classical mythology of Greece. She is a Nereid, the daughter of Nereus and Doris, and the mother of Achilles, the hero of the Trojan Wars. She was exceptionally beautiful, but a prophecy stated that she would bear a child more powerful than its father. On hearing this, her suitors (Zeus and Poseidon) became fearful for their superiority, and persuaded Peleus, king of Thessaly, to marry her instead. She almost managed to give immortality to Achilles, but the heels by which she held him remained mortal. Thus, knowing his most vulnerable spot, his enemies slew him in a battle of the Trojan Wars.
References 20, 40, 56, 92, 93, 114, 119, 129, 130
See also Doris, Neried, Nymph, Appendix 25

THIEN
These are nats in the folk beliefs of the people of Burma. They are rain spirits that inhabit the stars. It is said that rain falls when they emerge from their homes to stage mock battles, and that the electric storms are the flashes and noise of their weapons clashing. When the earth was parched, the Burmese enacted a village tug-of-war to arouse the spirits and get them to deliver the much-needed rain.
References 88
See also Nats, Spirit, Appendix 10, Appendix 26

THISOA
See Hagno

THRAIN
See Dain

THRONES
See Angel

THROR
See Thekkr

THRUD
See Alvis

THRUMMY CAP
This is the name of a spirit in the folklore of the Northern Counties of England, which until this century were famous for the quality of the wool and weaving produced there. Thrummy Cap was described as a type of fairy with a cap made from "thrums," the short ends of wool that are clipped off when the weaving is finished. The Thrummy Cap was supposed to inhabit the cellars of old houses. However, in the manuscripts known as the "Denham Tracts," these spirits are mentioned in association with the Thrummy Hills near Catterick in North Yorkshire.
References 17
See also Fairy, Spirit

THRUMPIN
A spirit in the folklore of the Border counties between Scotland and England, it was described as a sprite that remained with the individual throughout his or her life. Unlike the Guardian Angel, whose duties were to preserve the life of its human charge, the Thrumpin had the power to terminate the human's existence. In his *Folklore of the Northern Counties* (1866), William Henderson quotes the following:

"When the moon is in the latter fa',
When the owlets are scraughin drearie;
When the elleried are clumperin,
When the toweries hard are thrumpin,
When the bawkie bird he kisses the yud,
Then, then's the time for thrumpin.
An gif ye miss the mystic hour,
When vengeful sprites are granted power,
To thrump ilk faithless wight;" (p. 226)

References 17, 66
See also Grine, Guardian Angel, Spirit, Sprite, Appendix 16

THUMBELINA
See Tom Thumb

THUNDER BOYS
In the Native American legends of the Cherokee people, the Thunder Boys are the sons of Kanati and Selu. These spirits are the personification of the thunder and lightning associated with storms. They inhabit the skies or rock crevices, from which they emerge to play their ball games, and in doing so, create thunderstorms. The same characters appear in the legends of the Shawnee people, except they are spirit boys who use reversed word order when talking and have the power to move mountains, but show confusion over the simplest tasks.
References 88
See also Heng, Selu, Spirit, Appendix 26

THURSE
See Hob Thrush

TI MALICE, 'TI MALICE
See Anansi

TIAK
See Čembulat

**TIDDY ONES, TIDDY MEN,
TIDDY MUN, TIDDY PEOPLE**
Along with the Strangers and the Yarthkins, the Tiddy Men in their various name forms were one group of many undifferentiated lesser spirits or Little People revered by the Fen men and people of the Lincolnshire marshes in England. The Tiddy Mun was recognized more as an individual spirit than the others, and regarded with some affection. People addressed their invocation to him in times of severe flooding, as he was known to be able to withdraw the waters. However, should Tiddy Mun feel offended in any way, he would send blight to the crops and sickness to the family. Standing outside the house and addressing the spirit with a charm would ensure that the curse was lifted. This was assured if Tiddy Mun made a peewit call out across the water.
References 17
See also Little People, Yarthkins

TIGBANUA
These are particularly malicious Buso demons in the folklore of the Bagobo Malay peoples of the Philippines. These evil spirits constantly cause accidents and disease to provoke the early death of humans, whose flesh they consume.
References 87
See also Buso, Demon, Spirit

TIKDOSHE
This is the name of a malevolent spirit in the folk beliefs of the Zulu people of South Africa. The

Tikdoshe appears in the form of a wicked dwarf who gleefully challenges humans to fight him. He is almost assured of victory each time because he is immortal. In each combat, this spirit uses his magic powers, and the defeated human becomes his victim. However, some men still accept the challenge because whoever can conquer Tikdoshe will be rewarded with a great knowledge of powerful, supernatural charms.
References 33
See also Dwarf, Spirit

TIKI

This word is used in the beliefs and legends of the people of Polynesia. It denotes both a protective spirit of any status and the image or amulet that symbolizes its power. The amulets called Tikis are most frequently carved in a form of jade worn by Maoris, especially on the islands of New Zealand.
References 102
See also Guardian, Spirit, Appendix 21

TI-MIKU

See Lau

TINGOI

This nature spirit is a type of Dyinyinga in the folklore of the Mende people of Sierra Leone. The Tingoi takes the form of a beautiful young woman with soft white skin. She is usually benevolent or benign toward human beings.
References 33
See also Dyinyinga, Spirit

TINIHOWI

This is a water spirit in the folk beliefs of the Achomawis Native American people of California. Tinihowi was said to inhabit a deep lake. This spirit was benevolent toward humans, and would rescue them if they fell into the water.
References 99
See also Spirit, Appendix 25

TINKERBELLE

The name of the fairy in the story of Peter Pan. She is described as a gossamer-winged diminutive spirit, dressed in a diaphanous garment, whose presence is signaled by the tinkling sound of a silver bell. Tinkerbelle is able to materialize at will where she is needed, and can set wrongs to right by the wave of her magic wand. She is a nursery spirit with none of the vitality and ambivalent character of the fairies in folklore and mythology.
References 56
See also Fairy, Peter Pan, Spirit

TIR

This is the name of a djinn in Arabic folklore and Islamic beliefs. Tir is the progeny of Iblis and the demon responsible for causing fatal accidents.
References 40, 78, 88, 93
See also Demon, Djinn, Iblis, Appendix 16

TIRA

This is an evil spirit or demon in the folk beliefs of the Quechua people of Peru. The Tira inhabits the *qaqa*, or great cliffs of the region's mountains.
References 94
See also Demon

TISIPHONE

This is the name of a fearsome spirit in the mythology of ancient Greece and Rome. Tisiphone, whose name means Retaliation, is the spirit or genius of ultimate revenge. This spirit is described as a snake-haired woman wearing a bloodied robe who waits by the gates of hell. She is one of the Furies who exact retribution from those whose hideous crimes, especially matricide or patricide, remain unpunished by human law.
References 29, 40, 114
See also Erinys, Furies, Genius, Spirit

TITANIA

The name of the fairy queen and wife of Oberon in Shakespeare's *A Midsummer Night's Dream*. The name appears more anciently in the work of Ovid, where it is an alternate name for Diana, the goddess of the moon and the chase. Shakespeare's Titania is more regal than the more familiar Queen Mab, with a group of courtiers all equally splendidly attired. She is certainly active, weaving her magic in the moonlight with her Flower Fairy attendants, but still unwittingly enchanted and duped by Oberon. In the local folklore of the Scottish Highlands, she is the one who is supposed to have given the Fairy Flag to the Chief of the Clan MacLeod at Dunvegan Castle on the Isle of Skye in the thirteenth century. This flag was to be produced in times of extreme danger, when her magic would resolve the situation, but after the third event the flag would be reclaimed by Titania. Sadly, or happily, the third event took place quite recently, and the flag remains unclaimed by the supernatural.
References 17, 40, 114, 133
See also Attendant Spirit, Fairy, Oberon, Mab

TITIHAI

See Atua

TITILITURE

See Rumpelstiltskin

A Tiki guards the family and possessions of the Maori.

TOBADZISTSINI

This is the name of a spirit in the folk beliefs and legends of the Native Americans of the Great Desert region. It is known as the Child of the Waterfall, but is a spirit associated with war.
References 25
See also Spirit

TOD LOWERY, TOM LOWERY

This is the name of a goblin in the folklore of Lincolnshire, England. It was said to inhabit the bogs and marshes, into which it would lure the unwary. It was mostly invoked as a nursery bogie to prevent young children from coming to harm in the Fens.
References 17
See also Goblin, Nursery Bogie, Will o' the Wisp, Appendix 22

TOKTAL POŠKUDƏ

This name, which means Toktal Neighbor, is a euphemism for a keremet in the folk beliefs of the Cheremis/Mari people. A keremet is an evil spirit or devil that may do harm if inadvertently invoked.
References 118
See also Devil, Keremet, Spirit

TOM COCKLE

This is the name of a fairy or brownie attached to a family rather than the place. Tom Cockle was the domestic spirit of an Irish family. When they emigrated to America, he went with them.
References 17
See also Brownie, Fairy, Household Spirits, Spirit, Appendix 22

TOM DOCKIN, TOM DONKIN

This is the name of a nursery bogie in the folklore of Yorkshire, England. It was a terrifying fiend described as having huge iron teeth with which to devour naughty children. The name of this supernatural was used to keep children from venturing unaccompanied in places of danger.
References 17
See also Fiend, Nursery Bogie, Appendix 22

TOM PO, TOM POKER

This is the name of a nursery bogie in the folklore of East Anglia, England. He was supposed to inhabit the dark places under the stairs and in cellars, deep cupboards, and lofts, where children were not supposed to venture. Consequently, the possibility of this bogie's presence in such places was deemed sufficient to keep children away.
References 17, 107
See also Nursery Bogie, Appendix 22

TOM THUMB

This is the name of a spirit in English folklore. He first appears in a pamphlet written by Richard Johnson and printed in 1621, which details the story of how a farmer and his wife longed for a child. They asked Merlin, the sorcerer of King Arthur's court, to help them even if the child were no more than the size of the farmer's thumb. The tiny child duly came endowed with all the magic that a fairy child living with humans should have. His story is checkered with dangerous incidents from which he escapes with his fairy magic. Tom Thumb has remained a popular character in English fairy tales ever since. An equivalent diminutive supernatural is to be found in French folklore. The story of *Le Petit Poucet,* as told by Perrault, was published in 1697. The female counterpart of Tom Thumb is the fairy child called Thumbelina, whose adventures are the subject of folk songs and rhymes. A similar story is told in Danish folklore of the diminutive Tommelise.
References 2, 17, 28, 40
See also Fairy, Spirit, Appendix 22

TOM TIT TOT

This is the name of a demon in English folklore in a story similar to that of Rumpelstiltskin. The tradition comes from the county of Suffolk, and was published by Edward Clodd (1840–1930) as a monograph entitled "Tom Tit Tot." The story tells of a housewife who made some cakes that turned out too hard. She told her daughter to set them aside and they would "come again," meaning that they would soften. Her daughter took her mother literally, and being hungry, ate the lot. When the girl confessed, her mother shouted so loudly that a king riding past the house asked what the commotion was about. The embarrassed mother instead boasted of her daughter's spinning skills. The king vowed to marry the girl upon the production of a room full of finely spun skeins of linen, but if she did not, she would die. The mother agreed, and after the daughter was married to the king, the time came for the spinning to be shown. The girl was locked in a room filled with flax and a spinning wheel to do the work. She sat down and cried until she heard someone knocking at the door. When she opened it, there stood a little black thing with a tail. It inquired why she was crying, and when she told of her predicament, it promised to take the flax each morning and return with it spun into skeins. In return, if she couldn't guess its name by the end of the month, then she would be his. On the evening before the last day, she still had not learned the imp's name. While at supper with the king, he described to her how he had seen a strange black imp spinning in a chalk pit and reciting a rhyme about its name. The following day when the demon came for

Tom Thumb arrives as a fairy child to a human couple.

its prize, the girl recited "Nimmy nimmy not, my name is Tom Tit Tot," whereupon it shrieked terribly and flew away into the darkness, never to be seen again.

Variations of this tale abound throughout the British Isles, and the names of spirits in these stories are: Habetrot (Scotland), Peerifool (Orkney Islands), Terrytop (Cornwall), Trwtyn-Tratyn (Wales), and Whoopity Stoorie (Scotland).

References 17, 18, 66
See also Demon, Habetrot, Imp, Peerifool, Rumpelstiltskin, Terrytop, Trwtyn-Tratyn, Whoopity Stoorie, Appendix 14

TOM TITIVIL

This is the name of a demon, also known as Tutivillus, in English medieval folklore and ecclesiastical legend. This demon's task was to watch out for the occasions when religious duties were not performed correctly in the religious establishments. He was there, ready and waiting, to record every word that was skipped over or mumbled by lazy priests and monks. These he assembled in Hell to be used as evidence in the damnation of the offender. Tom Titivil featured in many of the English medieval morality plays, but has since declined in tradition to the name for a telltale nuisance.

References 114
See also Demon, Friar Rush

TOM TUMBLER
The old name for an imp, demon, or familiar in the folklore of England.

References 107
See also Demon, Familiar, Imp

TOMMELISE
See Tom Thumb

TOMMY RAWHEAD
See Raw Head and Bloody Bones

TOMTAR, TOMTE, TOMTE GUBBE
These are the Little People in the folklore of Sweden. They were thought to be the previous race of people displaced from the land when the Vikings invaded. Like the Tuatha dé Danann, they inhabited the ancient forts, cromlechs, and other earthworks. They were skilled in magic, the making of tools, and other crafts. The Tomtar harassed the humans who had invaded the land, and were generally very malicious. People eventually learned how to propitiate the Tomtar by leaving small gifts, for which they would do farm and domestic work during the night. Eventually each farm had its guardian Tomtar, which brought good luck and prosperity. They are said to resemble the nisse of Denmark, but are much smaller and slower. Like them, they enjoy a bowl of porridge, and some bread and tobacco, but only on Christmas morning. To give the Tomtar any better gift during the year would be sure to offend him, and he would do no more work.

References 18, 34, 66
See also Brownie, Goblin, Guardian, Household Spirits, Kobold, Nis, Piskey, Tuatha dé Danann, Appendix 22

TONGA
See Atua

TONGBŎP
These supernaturals are the evil imps of Korean folk belief. They are particularly malevolent, and will enter houses hidden in new items crossing the thresh-

old for the first time on an inauspicious day. If not detected at an early stage by the humans and banished by a *Mansin* (a female shaman), the Tongbŏp will cause family discord and illness.

References 79
See also Chisin Tongbŏp, Imp

TONT
See Kratt

TONTTU
This is the name of the household spirit in the folklore of Finland, possibly derived from the Swedish Tomte. Like the Aitvaras, he is a fortune demon, and may be obtained from the graveyard on the promise of a solemn pact with the Devil or other evil forces. The Tonttu is given the best accommodation and table in the house; in return, the spirit enriches the household with grain and gold, often at the expense of the neighbors.

References 87, 88
See also Aitvaras, Demon, Domovik, Haldde, Haldjas, Household Spirits, Kodinhaltia, Metsänhaltia, Tomtar, Vedenhaltia, Appendix 20, Appendix 22

TONX
This is a benevolent water spirit in the folklore of the Vogul people of western Siberia. The Tonx is propitiated for the good fortune he bestows on those hunting and fishing. Like the Vu-kutis, this spirit is considered to bring cures for those with sickness.

References 102
See also As-iga, Kul, Spirit, Appendix 25

TOOTEGA
This is a female water spirit in the folk beliefs of the Inuit people of Canada. She may materialize as a little old woman, and can be seen walking on the surface of the water. She is said to inhabit a little stone house on an island.

References 102
See also Spirit, Appendix 25

TOOTH FAIRY, TOOTHY FAIRY
This is the name of a nursery spirit in the folklore of most European cultures. This fairy is in charge of making sure that when a child loses a milk tooth, another will grow in its place. At some point in the evolution of this fairy tradition, it became important for the child to place the dislodged tooth beneath the pillow at night, where the fairy would pay for its retrieval with a piece of silver. The payment for the tooth now seems to take into account local currency and the rate of inflation!

References Folklore Society Documents
See also Fairy, Spirit, Appendix 22

Julenissè (left) and two Tomtars distribute gifts at Yuletide to Scandinavian children.

TOPIELEC

This is a water demon in the folklore of the Slav people. It is said to be the transformed spirit of a human who has drowned and now feeds off other humans who fall into the water.
References 99
See also Demon, Spirit, Appendix 25

TORNAK, TORNAQ, TORNAT, TORNRAK

This is the concept of a guardian spirit in the beliefs of the Inuit/Ihalmiut people of northern Canada. The shaman, or *Angakok,* achieves his status with the acquisition of a Tornak's protection and guidance. There are three types of Tornak according to the manner of their appearance: a stone, a human, and a bear; the bear is the most powerful. Through the guidance of the Tornak, the shaman can cure the sick, warn of dangers, and ensure good weather for hunting. One curious element of the relationship between the Angakok and his Tornak is that if the

spirit does not assist when required, the shaman may consider it too lazy, and will send it away weeping and out of a job.
References 41, 88, 101
See also Guardian, Tutelary Spirit

TORTO

This is a demon in the folklore of the Basque people of northwest Spain and southwest France. It appears in a human form with only one eye in the middle of its head. It waylays humans, especially the young, abducting and devouring them.
References 93
See also Demon

TOŠTƏ KOŽ JEŋ

This is a keremet in the folk beliefs of the Cheremis/Mari people of the former Soviet Republic. The name Toštə Kož Jeŋ means Old Pine Man, and this evil spirit may lurk in the forests. It may be pro-

pitiated from time to time by the sacrifice of a cockerel to prevent it from harming any humans who might venture through its domain.
References 118
See also Keremet, Kož Jeη

TOŠTOT JEη
This is the name of a keremet or demon in the folk beliefs of the Cheremis/Mari people of the former Soviet Republic to whom an offering of a hare is made to placate the spirit.
References 118
See also Demon, Keremet, Spirit, Appendix 9

TOT, TOT GRID
This is the local name in Lincolnshire, England, for a hobgoblin, also known as Tut or Tut Gut. It is mostly regarded as a harmless household spirit.
References 18, 40
See also Hobgoblin, Household Spirits, Appendix 22

TOU SHEN
This is the name of a terrifying spirit in the folk beliefs and legends of China. Tou Shen is a disease spirit, and specifically the bringer of smallpox.
References 131
See also Alardi, Con-Ma-Dāu, Minceskro, Šedra Kuba and Šedra Kuguza, Spirit, Appendix 17

TRANCA RUA
This is an encantado in the Afro-Brazilian cult Batuque. He is a member of the Exus, a demon group considered very dangerous to devotees.
References 89
See also Demon, Encantado, Exus

TRAS
The two spirits called Tras and Strakh are demons in the folk beliefs of Bohemia. Their names mean Tremor and Terror, respectively. These spirits inhabited the great forests of the region, and were regarded as a type of warrior spirit. During battles, they were said to burst out of the gloomy forests and launch at the enemy soldiers. They would grip each foe by the throat and wring out loud cries of terror from them.
References 110
See also Dain, Demon

TRASGU, EL
This is a spirit in the folklore of northwest Spain. He is a household spirit of the brownie type common in English folklore. El Trasgu appears at night in the form of a dwarf dressed in red, who will complete household tasks—or, if everything is already complete, turn it all to utter disorder, even to breaking the furniture. When the family moves, el Trasgu will go

with them, frequently turning up with some forgotten item such as a broom.
References 88
See also Boggart, Brownie, Domovik, Dwarf, Household Spirits, Spirit, Appendix 22

TRASH
See Skriker

TRICKSTER
This is a conceptual term used for categorizing the characteristics and activities of a spirit, and may be applied equally to a deity as well as to a lesser spirit. These spirits are usually amoral, lazy, unreliable, greedy, and sly, and their negative activities range from murder, theft, obscenity, and deceit to the more acceptable playing of pranks. On the more positive side, these spirits may be clowns, rescuers of the oppressed, teachers of skills, and bringers of important gifts such as fire. These interesting and ambivalent spirits are frequently the catalyst for actions between others, whether for good or evil, and as such play a very important role in mythology and folklore. Some Trickster spirits with entries in this book are: Anansi, Aunt Nancy, Bamapama, Basajaun, Blue Jay, Cin-an-ev, Coyote, Cünawabi, Eshu, Exu, Géde, Isakawuate, Iwa, Kawelo, Kwati, Legba, Lemminkäinen, Mahih-Nah-Tiehey, Manabozo, Maui, Mink, Nagas, Napi, Olifat, Ono, Pekoi, Sitkonsky, Spider, Ten-gu, and Yehl.
References 39, 56, 88
See also Spirit

TRIEE
In the beliefs of the Dayak people of Borneo, this is a group of spirits created by Tapa, the chief deity.
References 57
See also Komang, Spirit

TRIKURAT
This is the name of a nat in the folk beliefs of the people of Burma. He is a benevolent spirit who is the guardian of game animals; he ensures that there is sufficient game for the hunters to capture for food.
References 39, 53, 78, 88
See also Guardian, Nats, Spirit, Appendix 10, Appendix 12

TRITONS
These are sea spirits in the classical mythology of Greece and Rome. They are the sons of Neptune and Amphitrite and are depicted as mermen carrying a trident and blowing a conch shell horn. They are the escorts of the Nereids and the attendants of Neptune and Galatea. The Tritons were frequently portrayed in Italian art of the Renaissance period.

References 62, 114
See also Amphitrite, Attendant Spirit, Galatea, Merman, Nereid, Spirit

TROLL

This supernatural is essentially Scandinavian, but variations in description and characteristics are apparent between Trolls in Scandinavia and those of other countries. In Scandinavia, the Troll may also be referred to as Trold or Trolld. They were originally described as a large, hairy shape with a malignant character; they are now considered to appear somewhat like a gnome or dwarf, but as shape-shifters they can assume any guise. The usual description in *Denmark* is of a little old man with a long white beard, wearing a red cap and a craftsman's leather apron. In Ebletoft, the Trolls had humps on their backs, large hooked noses, and wore gray jackets and pointed red caps, but in Gudmanstrup, the Trolls were tall men in long black clothes. The Troll women in *Norway* were said to be beautiful, with long red hair. They lived in communities under the hills, long barrows, and ancient earthworks, a feature that also identified them as the Berg Folk or Hill People in *Sweden.* Their homes were said to be wonderful palaces full of treasure, which may glow at night. These supernaturals hate noise and have been driven away from places with church bells. Their attitude toward humans is sometimes benevolent, and they will endow a family they like with riches and good fortune. At other times they will be malicious, bring bad luck, and be destructive. They will also steal women, children, and property. A branch of mistletoe is used to protect humans and animals from being taken. The Trolls are considered to be expert metalworkers and expert healers with herbs and magic, but will only be seen between dusk and dawn, as they will turn to stone if the sun shines on them.

In the *Faröe Islands*, the Trolls are known as Fodden Skemaend. They are the Hollow Men, or the Underground People, who were known for abducting humans and keeping them for many years. In *Iceland*, the Trolls are malicious one-eyed giants. In *Finland*, there was a lake-dwelling malignant Troll known as the Sjötroll. It was said to be confined to the depths of the water by way of two runic stones placed at each end of the lake it inhabited at Kökar. When there was a fog or a storm and the magic of the stones was obscured, the people stayed inside and would not fish, because the Troll was released and would drown them. The Trolls of the *Shetland* and *Orkney Islands* (United Kingdom) were known as Trows or Drows, of which there were three distinct groups: Land Trows, Peerie Trows, and Sea Trows. The Trolls of *Greenland* and *Canada* in the folklore of the Inuit and Ihalmiut people resemble the more ancient concept of the Scandinavian Troll. These are described as huge malignant beings having an enormous, hairless belly that drags along the ground, and knife-sharp talons on the fingers. These Trolls inhabit the hills, where they lurk, waiting for the opportunity to attack humans and rip the flesh from their victims.

References 17, 18, 40, 47, 56, 78, 88, 92, 93, 99, 101, 110, 114, 133
See also Berg People, Duergar, Dwarf, Gnome, Henkies, Hill Folk, Hogboon, Knurre Murre, Roane, Trows, Appendix 22

TROWS

This is the name for the Trolls of the Orkney and Shetland Islands (United Kingdom). There were three different types of Trow, also known as Drows. The Land Trows are called the "guid folk" or the "guid neighbors" that inhabit the ancient earth mounds, cromlechs, and caves, the interiors of which are said to glisten with gold and precious gems. The Land Trows are usually dressed in gray, and are skilled metalworkers and healers who will bring luck to any human family to whom they take a liking. The Kunal Trows are a melancholy group that take human wives, who die upon the birth of their offspring. One Kunal Trow who married a sorceress was said to have fathered the two spirits known as the Ganfer and the Finis. A subgroup of the Land Trows is called the Peerie Trows. These are extremely small fairy trows who are dressed in green and live under toadstools. They love making music and dancing in the moonlight in magic rings. When they travel, they fly through the air on bulrushes. A further group is the Sea Trows, which inhabit caverns deep under the sea. When they come to land, they assume the appearance of an aquatic creature, and therefore resemble the mermaids and mermen or the Haaf Fish (Gray Seal). They have only one aquatic "skin" each, which they must remove to venture on dry land. Like the Fin Folk and merrows, a human who can find the skin of a beautiful Sea Trow may claim her as his bride. However, Trows can only emerge between dusk and dawn, because the rays of the sun would turn them to stone. All Trows abduct humans, and they consider young mothers and infants a particular prize, as the human mothers could nurse their young and the Trows could leave a changeling in the place of a human baby. Whenever a human fiddler or piper rested near a place inhabited by Trows, there was the strongest possibility of being abducted to make music for them. Some musicians have accounted for their musical compositions and good fortune as the result of playing for the Trows.

References 17, 18, 40, 78, 88, 133
See also Changeling, Fairy, Fin Folk, Finis, Mermaid, Merman, Merrow, Roane, Troll, Appendix 22

Trolls chase a rider as he gallops to safety.

TRWTYN-TRATYN
This is the name of a fairy woman in the folklore of Wales. Like the fairy Habetrot, Trwtyn-Tratyn is a spinster spirit who comes to the aid of a human girl. Also in this traditional tale are the same consequences of not discovering the name of her supernatural helper, as in the stories of Sili Ffrit and Sili-go-dwt.
References 15, 17, 18
See also Fairy, Gwarwyn-a-Throt, Habetrot, Perifool, Rumpelstiltskin, Sili Ffrit and Sili-go-dwt, Terrytop, Tom Tit Tot, Whoopity Stoorie, Appendix 14

TSECTS
This is the name of a benevolent female spirit in the beliefs of the Native Americans of the North Pacific coast.
References 25
See also Spirit

TSI-ZHUI
This is the name of the Sky People or sky spirits in the beliefs of the Osage Native American people.
References 25
See also Cloud People, Spirit

TUA
This is the name of the guardian spirit in the beliefs of the Iban/Sea Dayak people of Borneo. The spirit is acquired during the development of the individual as a dream, and usually manifests in the form of a snake. If the Tua is a python, the person is to be guided by his ancestors. If the Tua is a cobra, the person will be guided by Kling, the god of war. Tuas may manifest as cats, deer, or other familiar animals.
References 33
See also Familiar, Guardian, Spirit, Appendix 12

TUATHA DÉ DANANN
These are the fairy people of Ireland whose name means People of the Goddess Dana. They were a legendary race who overthrew the Fir Bholgs and Formors who had previously inhabited the land. The Tuatha dé Danann were renowned for their magical powers, beauty, grace, and intellect. They could become visible or invisible, and shape shift at will. Although generally immortal, they could be killed in battle. They consorted freely with human beings, upon whom they bestowed favors or destruction as the fancy took them. They brought wonderful treasures with them. These are now known as the four treasures: Dagda's inexhaustible cauldron, Lug's invincible spear, Nuada's infallible sword, and a sacred stone known as the Stone of Fal. When the Tuatha dé Danann were in turn defeated by the Milesians, they took refuge in the earth barrows, the grassy hill mounds known as the *sidh*, which is the name by which they themselves came to be

known. From these refuges they still practice their magic arts and are revered by their vanquishers for their supernatural powers. The areas of the previous kingdom were taken into account, and kings and queens were appointed to rule in their underworld as they had in the world above. They maintained their courts, their communities, their music, and their revelry. Humans are enticed into their underworld, where the passages of time, taste of food, sights, and sounds bear no relation to normal human experience. The Tuatha dé Danann form the subject of hundreds of Irish myths and folktales.
References 17, 29, 56, 87, 88, 93, 105
See also Aillen Mac Midhna, Aine, Angus Og, Badb, Black Annis, Bóann, Bodb, Cairpré, Cliodna, Dagda, Daoine Sidhe, Diancécht, Fairy, Fir Bholg, Formor, Gentle Annis, Goibniu, Luchtaine, Mac Cecht, Macha, Mebd, Midar, Sídhe

TUCHULCHA
This is the name of a demon of the underworld in the religion of the ancient Etruscans of Italy. It was a grotesque supernatural depicted with snakes curled around its arms.
References 93
See also Demon

TUKI
This is the name for the Little People of the Solomon Islands. The Tuki were described as about a foot in height with long black hair and talons. They inhabited the brush and wild places, where they dwelled in the cracks of rocks, hollow trees, or under stones.
References 109
See also Little People

TUKTORIAK
This is a nature spirit in the folk beliefs of the Inuit and Ihalmiut people of northern Canada. The Tuktoriak is the guardian spirit of the deer and will send game when required for the hunters to take for food.
References 101
See also Guardian, Spirit, Appendix 12

TUL BODƏZ
This is the name of a keremet in the folk beliefs of the Cheremis/Mari people of the former Soviet Republic. The name Tul Bodəz means Fire Spirit. There is a further spirit of this designation whose name is Tul Bodəz Təlmaze, which means Fire Spirit Təlmaze, denotes an association with either a place or another spirit called Təlmaze.
References 118
See also Keremet, Spirit

TULIHÄND
See Kratt

TUMA DÜŋ KEREMET
This is the name of a keremet or evil spirit in the folk beliefs of the Cheremis/Mari people of the former Soviet Republic. The name Tuma Düŋ Keremet means Keremet Under the Oak, which possibly signifies his place of abode. This spirit is, however, a powerful disease demon.
References 118
See also Keremet, Spirit, Appendix 9, Appendix 17

TÜNDÉR
This is the word used in Hungarian folklore to denote a fairy. There were both good and bad fairies who were able to enchant humans by means of magic water, milk, tears, saliva, herbs, and precious metals and gems. They loved music and dancing, and would come out into the forest glades in the moonlight. The Tündér live in the mountains in fairy castles that have beautiful gardens with golden summerhouses. They are Trooping Fairies who live in communities with an organized social life. There are numerous individual fairies in the folklore of Hungary. Most of these gentle, benevolent beings are given local names according to the area in which they are said to reside. Some of these names are: Dame Hirip, Dame Jenö, Dame Rampson (a fairy queen), Dame Vénétur, Fairy Helen, Firtos (queen of the good fairies), Maros (a water fairy), Mika (a warrior fairy), Olt (a water fairy), Tarkö, and Tartód (queen of the bad fairies).
References 77
See also Fairy

TUNG WANG KUNG
See Si Wang Mu

TUPAN
In the folk beliefs of the Tupi Guarani or Tupinamba people of Brazil, this spirit was the demon of thunder. He was portrayed as a squat human with wavy hair. When the Christian missionaries came to that part of Brazil, they took the name of Tupan to denote the Christian God, and the name has now come to mean Sacred.
References 88, 102
See also Demon, Spirit, Appendix 26

TUREK KUGUZA
This is the name of a keremet or evil spirit in the folk beliefs of the Cheremis/Mari people of the former Soviet Republic. Turek Kuguza means Turek Old Man, and although a keremet is normally a devil, this term is used in respect. This particular demon is in fact regarded as the guardian spirit of the town of Turek.

References 118
See also Devil, Guardian, Keremet, Kuguza, Spirit

TURQUOISE BOY, TURQUOISE MAN

This is a benevolent vegetation spirit in the beliefs and legends of the Zuñi Pueblo Native American people. He is a spirit of the maize and a companion of Salt Old Woman.
References 88
See also Corn Spirit, Salt Woman, Spirit, Appendix 15

TUT, TUT GUT

See Tot

TUTELARY SPIRITS

These are spirits that perform a protective, guiding, advisory, and teaching role for the individual, family unit, group of people, or some other unit associated with humans. Unlike the guardian spirit who keeps the individual from straying, the Tutelary Spirit may even admonish humans for misdeeds in the interest of showing the true path. Some Tutelary Spirits from different cultures with entries in this book are: Àràk, Agloolik, Awl-man, Chin Chia, Clay Mother, Corn Mother, Fylgir, Harut and Marut, Leib-Olmai, Nagual, and Zoa.
References 39, 107
See also Guardian, Spirit, Appendix 22

TUTIVILLUS

See Tom Titivil

TUULIKKI

This is a female forest spirit in the folk beliefs of the Finnish people. She is the daughter of the forest god Tapio and the sister of the male forest spirit Nyyrikki.
References 88
See also Spirit, Appendix 19

TYLWYTH TEG

This is the usual name, meaning the Fair Family, for the fairies in the folklore of Wales. They are also known by the euphemisms Dynon Bach Teg, which means Little Fair Folk, in Dyfed (Pembrokeshire), and Bendith y Mamau, which means Mother's Blessing, in Glamorgan, to ward off any mischievous intentions they may have if invoked. There appear to be two types of fairy in Wales, the Tylwyth Teg being the larger of the two and the Ellyllon the smaller. They live in the mountains, woodland glades, and islands in lakes, and the diminutive ones may even live in wildflowers such as the foxglove. The Tylwyth Teg live in communities and have a king called Gwyn ap Knudd. They vary in description from being about a foot in height to taller than a man, but they are very beautiful, with fair skins and golden hair, and will show themselves only to fair-haired people. They are dressed in long, silken garments that may be red, blue, white, or yellow, but are usually green. They like human children and will often abduct them, leaving changelings in their place. They will also marry mortals, but as with most fairy wives, they will vanish if some taboo or promise is broken. In general they are benevolent to humans and will bring them good fortune if the human is generous to them. This usually involves lending them baking griddles, milk pails, or other cooking implements to use for their fairy cakes. If given a fairy cake, a human must eat it in silence before cockcrow or it will turn to toadstools. Like most fairies, the Tylwyth Teg love music and dancing and are expert musicians; however, they will kidnap any human musician who strays into their fairy ring while they are dancing in the moonlight or the morning mists, and keep him indefinitely. The only way to be rescued is to have a piece of iron in a pocket, in which case the fairies will vanish, or a piece of a rowan branch to break the spell. In return for his hospitality, the fairies of Cader Idris gave the human called Morgan Rhys a fairy harp that would play for him when he touched its strings.
References 15, 17, 18, 59, 87
See also Changeling, Ellyllon, Fairy, Gofannon, Gwyn ap Knudd, Manawyddan, Appendix 6, Appendix 22

TZADKIEL

See Zadkiel

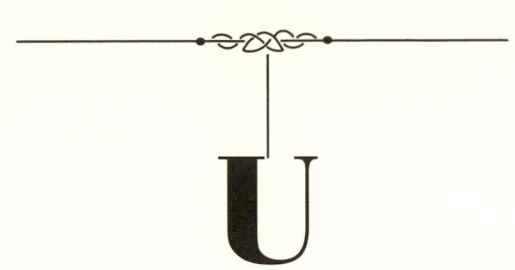

U

UACILLA

This is a weather spirit in the folk beliefs of the Ossetian people of the Caucasus. He is the spirit of rains, thunder, and lightning. The name is derived from that of the prophet Elias of Judeo-Christian scriptures, who is regarded as the lord of storms in eastern Europe.
References 93
See also Spirit, Appendix 26

UBER

See Buber

UDA

The name for a devil in the folk beliefs of the Cheremis/Mari people of the former Soviet Republic. A piece of iron is placed over a door of the home or the gate of a field to keep him out.
References 118
See also Devil

ŪDENSMĀTE

This is the name of a female nature spirit in the folk beliefs of the Latvian people. Ūdensmāte means Mother of the Water, and she is the guardian spirit of freshwater.
References 88
See also Spirit, Ūgunsmāte, Appendix 25

UDU/G

This is a term for evil spirits in the mythology of ancient Mesopotamia. The Udu are malevolent demons that equate with the Utukku of Babylon.
References 93
See also Demon, Spirit, Utukku

UDUR

This is the name of one of the Norns in Nordic and Teutonic mythology. She is also known by the following variants of the name: Urd, Urdur, Urdhr, Urth, Wurd, and Wyrd. The name Wyrd is Anglo-Saxon, and this is the name that gave rise to the later Wyrdes or Weird Sisters in English use. She is the spirit of the

past who constantly looks back and as such is associated with Hel, the goddess of death and the underworld.
References 33, 88, 95
See also Norns, Spirit, Weird Sisters, Appendix 16

UGLY HOUR, THE

Although not sounding like the name for a spirit, this name denotes a type of evil spirit in the modern folklore of Greece. The Ugly Hour is the alternative name used on the Islands of Santorini and Thera for the Bad Hour of the Greek mainland.
References 12
See also Bad Hour, Spirit

ŪGUNSMĀTE

This is the name of a female nature spirit in the folk beliefs of the Latvian people. Ūgunsmāte means Mother of the Fire, and as such she is the guardian spirit of the hearth fires in human homes.
References 88
See also Guardian, Laukumāte, Spirit, Appendix 22

UHLAKANYANA

An evil and malicious dwarf in the folklore of South Africa that was said to be the progeny of a supernatural father and a human mother. Uhlakanyana is described as being like a gnome or a little wizened old man. This spirit is a trickster whose amoral pranks tend to be malicious rather than harmless.
References 56
See also Dwarf, Gnome, Spirit, Trickster

UKULAN-TOJON

This is a powerful nature spirit in the folk beliefs of the Yakut people of Siberia. Ukulan-Tojon is the spirit of the waters. No source of water would be used or stretch of water crossed without the permission of this spirit. In order that permission may be gained, a suitable offering or libation must be made first.
References 33
See also Spirit, Appendix 25

ULLIKUMMI

This is the name of a demon in the mythology of ancient Anatolia (Asia Minor). Ullikummi was created from a stone by the deposed king of the gods, Kumarbi, to help him regain control of the other rebellious gods.
References 93
See also Demon

ÜMBAČ KOŠTŠƏ

See Čembulat

ÜMBAL KEREMET

See Čembulat

UMOT

These spirits are described in a text from 1865 as being evil supernaturals in the folk beliefs of the Land Dayaks of Borneo. These spirits are described as fierce bloodthirsty beings appearing like wild men covered entirely in hair. There are three types of these malicious and greedy beings: the Umot Sisi, the Umot Perubak, and the Umot Perusong. The Umot Sisi, although rarely seen, hover at night around the dwellings of the people, searching for meat that might have dropped through the flooring onto the earth. They are frequently heard as a munching sound from under the houses. The Umot Perubak are much more invasive, coming invisibly into the homes of the people, where they will cause starvation by eating all the rice from the pot before the humans can get to it. The Umot Perusong are much more sly. They will enter invisibly or in the form of rats, into the grain stores in the roofs of the houses and consume the entire harvest unseen. This group is responsible for causing starvation and diseases in the community and are greatly feared.
References 57
See also Spirit

UNCTOME

See Ictcinike

UNDERGROUND PEOPLE

See Troll

UNDINE

One of a group of nature spirits or elementals defined by the mystical philosopher Paracelsus (1493–1541) in terms of the natural elements from which they were supposed to be derived. The Undines were spirits of water described as looking like humans but could assume the shape of a fish or a snake. They were supposed to have a soft, cold skin and a sluggish, unreliable character. According to the occultist Elephas Levi, their emperor was called Hicks. A story of an Undine

tells of how, in a fishing village, a human couple had lost their own child but shortly after found a baby left at their door. They took her in as their own, and she grew to a most beautiful young woman with pearly skin and green eyes, both loving and fickle in her nature. Hildebrand saw and fell in love with her and took her as his wife. But he betrayed her with another named Bertalda. With this breaking of the vow, Undine was reclaimed by her Merfolk and vanished back to the sea. However, on the eve of his wedding to Bertalda, Hildebrand went to the well in the courtyard and there he saw Undine. She embraced him and took his soul with her to the waters, leaving his body by the well.
References 40, 53, 92, 132, 136
See also Coleman Gray, Elemental, Green Children, Nymph, Skilly Widden, Spirit, Appendix 12, Appendix 22, Appendix 25

UNDUR ŠƏRT

This is a keremet or evil spirit in the folklore of the Cheremis/Mari people of the former Soviet Republic, that is placated by the sacrifice of a ewe.
References 118
See also Čort, Keremet, Spirit

UNKTEHI

This is the name of a water spirit in the folk beliefs of the Dakota Native American people.
References 25
See also Spirit, Appendix 25

UNSEELIE, UNSEELIE COURT

See Seelie Court

UPAKA

See Nats

UPYRI

These are water spirits in the folklore of Russia. They are malevolent spirits that inhabit the banks of rivers and streams where the Rusalka may also be seen.
References 75
See also Rusalka, Spirit, Appendix 25

URANIA

See Muses

URCHIN

This name, and also Hurgeon (from the old French *herichon*), is the local dialect word for a hedgehog in English folklore. It was commonly believed that certain types of imp, sprite, or pixy manifest in the form of this animal. These spirits were also called Urchins or Hurgeons during the sixteenth and seventeenth centuries, and are to be found in the works of

Shakespeare and Jonson. Since that time this expression for a supernatural has gone out of use.
References 17, 18, 107
See also Imp, Pixie, Spirit, Sprite, Appendix 12

URD, URDUR, URDHR, URTH
See Udur

URIEL
The name of an Archangel, which means Flame of God. Uriel is one of the seven chief angels in Judeo-Christian scriptures. He is known as The Bringer of Light and according to the Apocrypha was sent by God to answer the questions of Esdras (2 Esd. 4). Uriel is one of the "sharpest sighted spirits" in Milton's *Paradise Lost*.
References 40, 93, 114
See also Angel, Archangel, Appendix 1, Appendix 13

URISK, URUISG
The Uruisg, whose name means Water Man, is a type of rustic brownie in the folklore of Scotland. These beings were described as being half human and half goat, like the faun or satyr of classical Greek mythology. They inhabited the wild places of the Highlands and particularly congregated at Loch Katrine in the Trossachs. Individuals of this group of spirits inhabited Glen Lyon, a waterfall near Tyndrum and Beinn Dorain. Although usually solitary beings, the Urisks would do farmwork such as herding cattle, grinding, and threshing corn and were considered very lucky to have about the homestead. However, they were also of a frolicsome nature prone to chasing a woman of their fancy and accused of killing sheep. Their ugly shape made them unwelcome companions on lonely roads when they suddenly appeared ambling beside terrified travelers at night.
References 15, 17, 18, 69, 81, 123
See also Brownie, Faun, Fuath, Killmoulis, Peallaidh, Satyr, Appendix 12, Appendix 25

URME
See Ursitory

UROBACH
A demon or devil of very limited powers, identified by Collin de Plancy in his *Dictionnaire Infernal* (1863).
References 113
See also Demon, Devil

URSITORY
These are the three fairies or spirits of fate in the folk beliefs of the Romany Gypsies of Poland, Russia, Serbia, and Romania. The Ursitory are male spirits, but as female spirits are also known as the Urme. They appear to the newborn infant on the third night after its birth to determine its future. Only the mother, the child, and the *Drabarni* (herb woman) are able to see these spirits. Once their decisions have been made they cannot be changed.
References 31, 93
See also Béfind, Chang Hsien, Eshu, Fairy, Fat, Moiræ, Oosood, Parcae, Pi-Hsia Yüan-Chün, Appendix 22

URVASI, URVASHI
The name of an Apsara or nymph in the classical Hindu mythology of India. Her story is told in the Rig Veda and Rabindranath Tagore's Bengali poem *Urvasi* (1893). The legend tells how the king Pururavas while hunting in the Himalayas heard calls for help and was able to rescue two Apsaras from demons. One of the nymphs was Urvasi, and the king was so enchanted with her that he asked her to be his wife. She consented on the promise that she should never see him unclothed. The Gandharvas, who were the consorts of the Apsaras, contrived the return of Urvasi. By taking her pet lambs by magic each night and besmirching the honor of her husband, Pururavas was made to leap naked from the bed to stop the thieves, who sent a bolt of lightning to illuminate his nakedness. The Gandhavas had effected the broken promise and Urvasi returned to Indra's heaven. Puruvaras was heartbroken and sought her everywhere. One day he saw a flock of swans on a lake, and Urvasi revealed that she was in this guise and was due to give birth to their child. She told him to return on the last day of the year to see their son. When he returned the Gandharvas took him to Urvasi in a beautiful golden palace where Urvasi met him. She told him that in the morning the Gandharvas would grant him a wish and that he must ask to become one of them. He made this request, but they told him that first he must take a sacred fire to earth and make a sacrifice. Pururavas returned home with his son and the sacred fire, but in a moment of tiredness he left the flame, and it disappeared. In its place were the *sami* tree and the *asuattha* tree. The Gandharvas advised him to cut a branch from each and to turn one against the other, which would bring back the same sacred fire. Having learned how to make fire, Pururavas made his sacrifice, and he and his son joined Urvasi forever in Indra's heaven.
References 29, 102, 111, 114
See also Angus Og, Apsaras, Demon, Devas, Fairy, Gandharvas, Nymph, Swan Maiden, Vrikshakas

ÜSTEL OROL
See Čembulat

UTHRA
In the beliefs system of the Gnostics these spirits are the equivalent of the angels in the Christian religion.

References 29
See also Angel, Spirit

UTI HIATA
This is the name for the Corn Mother in the folk beliefs and legends of the Pawnee Native American people.
References 25
See also Corn Mother, Appendix 15

UTUKKU
These are evil spirits, devils, and demons in the beliefs and mythology of the Assyrians and Babylonians. There were two types of Utukku: the souls of the dead that could not rest until they could be appeased and the truly evil spirits, which were said to emanate from the bile of an Ea (deity). These latter Utukku manifest in horrifying images of men with animal heads, claws, and horns. They dwelled in holes in rocks, caverns, and lonely ruins. These spirits brought diseases, criminal thoughts, sinful acts, and disaster upon any human with whom they came in contact.
References 93, 102
See also Demon, Devil, Spirit, Udu, Appendix 12

UŽEDƏŠ
See Čembulat

UZZIEL
The name of one of the principal angels in Hebrew mysticism and angelology. The name Uzziel means Strength of God. This angel appears in Milton's *Paradise Lost* as subordinate to Gabriel and charged by him to keep watch.
References 40, 114
See also Angel, Gabriel

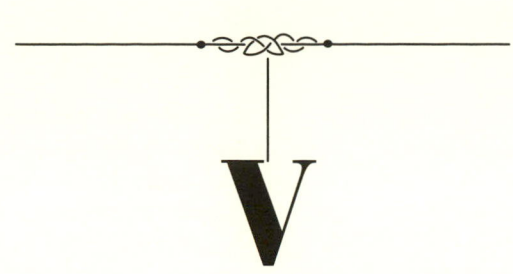

VADATJAS
This is an evil spirit in the folklore of Latvia. It may manifest in the form of a human or an animal at a crossroad where it will try to lead travelers astray.
References 93
See also Spirit, Appendix 24

VAETTRAR
These spirits, also known as Vältar, are said to be a type of nisse that enters people's houses by way of the drains. It is therefore important not to pour hot or noxious liquids down the drains for fear of causing them harm.
References 6
See also Nis

VAI-MAHSE
A powerful nature spirit in the folk beliefs of the Tukano people of the Amazon. The name Vai-Mahse means Master of the Animals. He manifests in the shape of a dwarf whose body is red, and he carries a magic red wand. He is the guardian spirit of the forest animals and river fish who controls how many are given to the hunters and fishermen. Certain small hills are sacred places for leaving offerings to him for the hunt, and care is taken not to offend him. It is believed by the women that Vai-Mahse can be particularly evil toward pregnant women and young mothers, as he will send infections and misfortune out of jealousy for not having been the father of the child himself.
References 33
See also Dwarf, Guardian, Spirit, Appendix 12

VA-KUL
See Kul

VALA
See Veela

VALKYRIES
These are the nymphs or maidens of battle, also known as the Vakkijnor or Walkyries, in Nordic and Teutonic mythology. Their name means the Choosers of the Slain. These spirits are Odin's attendants or Wish Maidens that ride the skies on the clouds or fly as Swan Maidens to the scene of battle. They hover above the fray dressed in battle armor on their mighty horses, guiding the heroes and selecting with the kiss of death, those who will be slain. Then they conduct the souls of the fallen heroes back to Valhalla in triumph, to feast with Odin and drink mead from the skulls of their enemies. Although essentially the Battle Maidens, the Valkyries often comprised members of other spirit groups such as Skuld, a member of the Norns, and Judur and Rota, who are deities. Originally the Valkyries were fearsome spirit beings of the *Prose Edda* but were later given greater prominence in the *Volsungo Saga* and Wagner's operatic work *Der Ring des Nibelungen*. Their number varies from three to 27; the named ones are Brunhilde (Brynhilde); Geirolul; Goli; Göll, meaning herald; Gondul, meaning she wolf; Held, meaning hero; Herfjotur; Hilde, meaning war; Hildur; Hlokk; Hrist, meaning storm; Judur; Mist, meaning cloud gray; Radgrid; Randgrid; Reiginlief; Rota; Sigrun; Skeggold; Skogul, meaning carrier-through; Skuld; Swawa; Thrud, meaning power; Thrudur; and Wolkenthrut, meaning cloud power.
References 20, 29, 33, 40, 41, 56, 88, 92, 93, 95, 114, 119
See also Alraun, Attendant Spirit, Badb, Ban Nighechain, Banshee, Bodua, Morrigan, Norns, Nymph, Spirit, Appendix 16

VÄLTAR
See Vaettrar

VAMANA
See Dwarf

VANADEVATAS
These are wood or tree spirits in the Vedic myth of India. Like the Dryads and Hamadryads of Greek mythology, they inhabited the trees and were their guardian spirits. If any human dares to fell one of these trees, then the Vanadevatas will take their revenge on him.

References 41, 110
See also Dryad, Guardian, Hamadryad, Spirit,
Appendix 19

VANTH

A female demon in the mythology of the ancient
Etruscans. She is depicted as a human figure with
huge eyes on her wings. She carries a flaming torch
and a key and is accompanied by a snake. She is the
portent and messenger of death who is ever present
and watchful.
References 93
See also Babd, Demon, Appendix 16

VANUŠKA

This is the name of a keremet or evil spirit in the folk
beliefs of the Cheremis/Mari people. This spirit is
also known as Oš Buj Vanuška.
References 118
See also Keremet, Spirit

VAOTERE

This is the name of the demon of the casuarina, or
ironwood tree, in the folk beliefs of the Fijian and
Tongan people. The legend tells how a man called
Oārangi had heard of the value of the ironwood tree
and was determined to defeat the demon. He went
into the jungle with four friends who, each time they
severed the main roots, died the same day, but the
roots and the tree were as though they had never
been touched. After many attempts Oārangi also
died in the attempt, and as a result the ground and
tree were then stained red. Another man called Ono,
with a special ironwood spade, came to find the tree
and do battle with Vaotere. His strategy was to
undermine all the roots and sever them at the growing tips where they were both sensitive and most
vulnerable. After this Ono revealed the major tap
root and split it, whereupon the enraged demon
became visible. Opening its terrible jaws to kill Ono,
Vaotere was smashed to death by the hero with his
magic spade. The thousands of splinters from the
body turned into the ironwood trees, which now
cover the island.
References 41, 110
See also Demon

VASA

See Kul

VASUS

This is the group of eight attendants of Indra in the
Vedic myth of India. They were possibly originally
named as Amala (fire), Anila (wind), Apu (water),
Dhruva Pole (star), Soma (moon), Dhara (earth),
Prabhasa (dawn), and Pratyusha (light). The later list

is given as Aditya, Agni, Antariksha, Chandra, Dyn,
the Nakshatras, Prithivi, and Vayu.
References 41
See also Antariksha, Archangel, Attendant Spirit,
Nakshatras

VATAK

This is the name of a female demon in the Zoroastrian religion of Iran. Vatak appears as a distorted
and ugly human and is said to be the mother of
Azidahaka. Also known as Autak or Udai, Vatak is
the fiend of incest and of indiscreet dialogue. She it is
who will encourage humans to say that which should
not be said and do that which is forbidden.
References 41, 88, 102
See also Azidahaka, Demon, Fiend

VEDENHALTIA

This is the name of a water spirit in the folk beliefs of
the Estonian people.
References 88
See also Domovik, Haldde, Haldjas, Kodinhaltia,
Metsänhaltia, Talonhaltija, Tonttu, Appendix 25

VEELA

These are the spirits or fairies of the woods, streams,
and lakes in the folk beliefs of the people of eastern
Europe. They are known variously as the Vala, Vile,
Vila, Víly or Vôlva, or Willi, especially the Balkan States.
They are like the Dryads of Greek mythology, who are
the guardians of the woods and skilled in the healing
herbs of their domain. They are described as young
beautiful maidens with long flowing hair, dressed in
white. They love to make music and dance in the forest
glades by the light of the moon. They are normally
benevolent toward humans, but if they are seen during
their dances, they may bring misfortune to the intruder.
If a man caught sight of a Veela in the woodland glades,
he would be so enchanted that he would yearn for her
until he pined to death. They live in communities, like
the Trooping Fairies, and may marry and have children
with mortals. Munya is named as a daughter of one of
these fairies. Under the name and guise of Oosood they
would define the future of the newborn child.
References 41, 44, 88, 93, 102, 110
See also Dryad, Fairy, Guardian, Oosood, Raviyoyla,
Spirit, Appendix 22, Appendix 23

VĒJASMĀTE

This is the name of a female nature spirit in the folk
beliefs of the Latvian people. Vējasmāte means
Mother of the Wind, and she is the guardian spirit of
the winds. Her male counterpart is Vejopatis, whose
name means Master of the Wind, and he is the
guardian spirit of the winds in the folk beliefs of the
Lithuanian people.

References 88
See also Guardian, Māte, Spirit, Appendix 26

VEJOPATIS
See Vējasmāte

VELES
This is the name of a demon in the folklore of the Slav people. He is the degraded version of the old god of the cattle herds.
References 41, 93
See also Demon

VELNIAS
This is a term in Lithuanian folklore for the Devil of degraded status. It is a somewhat derisory term used in much the same way as Old Hornie as a devil of diminished powers. It is a derivative of the word *vele* or *velionis*, meaning dead person. Velnias is usually portrayed as a German dandy of the nineteenth century.
References 88, 93
See also Auld Hornie

VERBTI
In the folklore of Albania this is a demon. The invocation of Verbti was said to cause blindness, as the derivation of his name *verbi* meant "the Blind One." This curse was utilized by the converting Christians to remove the cult of Verbti, who was originally the god of fire and the north wind. His status was eventually subverted to that of a debased lesser demon.
References 93
See also Demon

VERDANDI
See Norns

VERDELET
In European demonology of the sixteenth century this was the name of a familiar or demon responsible for transporting witches to their sabbat.
References 53
See also Demon, Familiar, Appendix 8

VEREKETE
See Averekete

VERRIER, VERRINE
See Devil

VETĀLA
A demon also known as Bētāla in the Tamil folklore of southern India. He is described as human shape with staring hair, hands and feet turned backwards. Vetāla is regarded as the guardian spirit of some of the villages of the Deccan, where he may reside in the

special stone painted red for him, or in the ancient stone circles of the region. He is to be encountered lurking in graveyards and lonely places, where he may terrorize late travelers as a malicious prank. The tale of Cevvi Reddi's encounter and battle with Vetāla while returning late from his fields portrays a demon that will acknowledge the bravery of a human by granting him a favor.
References 68, 88
See also Demon

VI-NUNA
See Vu-nuna

VIGONA
See Figona

VILA, VILE
See Veela

VILCANOTA
This is the name of a river spirit or Huaca in the ancient Inca religion of Peru.
References 88, 119
See also Huacas, Spirit, Appendix 25

VÍLY
In the folklore of Slavonia, this variant of the Veela or Vila is the spirit of the winds or storms. These spirits are thought to inhabit the caves in the mountains of the region, and rustic people used to leave offerings of flowers for them. They are said to be derived from the souls of virgins, who in their transformed state are now intent on enchanting men and luring them to their doom. These spirits may appear as a swan or a horse and although generally benign, they may shoot magic arrows at humans that rid them of their reason.
References 93
See also Spirit, Veela, Appendix 12, Appendix 26

VIRGINAL
This is the name of the Ice Queen, a fairy queen in the ancient German *Book of Heroes*. She is captured by a magician named Ortis, who keeps her imprisoned in one of her ice castles. Each new moon she has to surrender one of her Snow Maidens to be devoured. The hero Dietrich, who has fallen in love with Virginal, is told by Bibung of her capture. Dietrich rescues and marries her, but she is unable to survive in his lowland castle and returns to her ice home.
References 58
See also Bibung, Fairy, Snow Queen

VIRRA BIRRON
This is the whirlwind spirit, also known as the Willy Willy, of the Native Australians' Dreamtime myths.

Virra Birron is a bad-tempered traveler who in his rage uproots and despoils anything in his path. The faster he goes, the stronger and higher in the air he whirls, ignoring all pleas to calm down and go carefully. Because of this he does not have, or care for, any friendship. He only stops when he gets tired, and he then assumes a human shape. Even then he can still be seen dancing and whirling a little on his own until he is off on his travels again.

References 14
See also Big Purra, Kompagnin, Spirit, Appendix 26

VIRTUES
See Angel

VISHAPS
Originally spirits in the religion of ancient Urartu, they are now relegated to a form of trickster demon in the folklore of Armenia.

References 119
See also Demon, Spirit, Trickster

VISVAVASU
See Gandharvas

VITTORA
The name of a spirit in the folklore of modern Greece. It resembles the ancient Greek Ker in some respects. It is said to manifest as a wandering light in the darkness or as a disembodied voice sighing in the night. This spirit is the guide or luck of a person that stays with them throughout their life, but a short time before the person is due to die, the Vittora will seek another human to accompany. It is only then that any other human may see one and gain it if considered to be one that has guided its previous human well.

References 12
See also Ker, Spirit, Appendix 20

VIVIENNE
See Nimüe

VIZ-ANYA, VIZI-ANYA
This is a female water spirit in the folk beliefs and mythology of the Magyar people of Hungary that is known as Vizi-anya in other Balkan States. She was called the Water Mother, and to see her would bring misfortune. She is associated with other water spirits who were called Viz-ember, Viz-leany, and Viz-murt in Hungary and is the female counterpart of the Vizi-ember and similar to the Vizi-leany. She is a powerful demon who inhabits deep lakes and similar larger areas of freshwater. If she or the associated spirits are seen, disaster usually follows. Viz-leany is the maiden of the water, the sight of whom was also a portent of misfortune.

References 88, 102
See also Demon, Kul, Spirit, Viz-leany, Appendix 25

VIZ-EMBER, VIZI-EMBER
This is the Water Man or water demon in the folklore of the Magyar people of the Baltic States. The name Viz-ember is used in Hungary, while Vizi-ember is a variant used in other Balkan States. This spirit inhabits the deep lakes and stretches of freshwater, like his female counterpart Vizi-anya. Vizi-ember is particularly malevolent and although rarely seen, will be heard if no sacrifice has been offered. It is then that local people know someone is going to be drowned.

References 88, 102
See also Kul, Viz-anya, Vodianoi, Appendix 25

VIZ-LEANY, VIZI-LEANY
This is a female water spirit of lesser importance than the Vizi-anya in the folklore of the Magyar people of the Balkan States. She is called by the variant name Viz-leany, particularly in Hungary. Her name means Maiden of the Water. Vizi-leany is described as having a human shape with long, flowing hair. Her appearance is a portent of misfortune and disaster.

References 83, 102
See also Kul, Rusalka, Spirit, Viz-anya, Vodianikha, Appendix 25

VIZ-MURT
The Viz-murt is the Water Man in the folklore of the Magyars of the Balkan States. He is like the Viz-ember and, like him, was a water demon of the lakes and rivers who would take human victims if no sacrifice were made.

References 88, 102
See also Viz-ember, Vodianoi, Vu-murt, Appendix 25

VIZI-ANYA
See Viz-anya

VIZI-EMBER
See Viz-ember

VIZI-LEANY
See Viz-leany

VODIANIKHA
This is the name of the spirit wife of the Vodyanoi in the folklore of Russia. She is said to appear in the form of a naked woman with enormous breasts and long, tangled hair. The Vodianikha may sometimes be seen on the banks of a river, dripping with water and combing her hair. She is said to have been either the lost soul of a drowned maiden, a Rusalka, or a female Vodyanoi.

References 75
See also Rusalka, Spirit, Vodianoi, Appendix 25

VODIANOI

In Russian folklore a dangerous water spirit also called Vodyanoi, Vodyanoy, or Vodnik. This was a shape-shifting spirit that might be seen as a floating moss-covered log with wings; an old man with a blue face, white beard and green hair; an old man covered in scales or fur with huge paws, glowing eyes, horns, and a tail; or entirely as a large fish. In the appearance of humans they would seem younger or older with the phases of the moon. The Vodianoi was said to dwell in the very depths of the water, where it had either a beautiful illuminated palace that glowed on certain nights of the year, or to live in the very slime of the bottom, with which it was sometimes covered. It was to be seen lurking in rivers, mill pools and ponds, where it would lure any unwary humans to a horrible death in the water. This spirit was a threat to all humans except the millers and fishermen. It would materialize at night, very frequently in the mill race. To keep the Vodianoi from doing harm, the millers would propitiate the spirit with a cockerel. Often in the past a drunken stranger passing the water mills would also have been a sacrifice to the Vodianoi.
References 29, 44, 75, 93, 99, 102, 119
See also Jenny Greenteeth, Näkk, Nix, Viz-murt, Vu-murt, Appendix 12, Appendix 25

VOHU MANO, VOHUMANAH

One of the Amesha Spentas and the attendant genius of Ahura Mazda in the Zoroastrian religion. This spirit, whose name means Good Thought, is entirely benevolent. Vohu Mano is particularly concerned with the benign creatures of the earth, especially the cow. He is also known as Wahman in the sect of Manicheism.
References 93, 119
See also Amesha Spentas, Attendant Spirit, Genius, Spirit

VÖLUND/R

This is the name in Nordic and Teutonic mythology for the smith to the gods called Wayland Smith in English legends. He is described as the wise elf, although he is mostly linked with the dwarfs as a craftsman of metals. Völund was said to be the son of the Elf King, whose other sons were Slagfidur and Egil. Each of the three brothers married a Swan Maiden. Völund's story in the *Prose Edda* tells of how he was apprenticed to the giant Mimir, then to two dwarfs whom he killed after a quarrel. The fame of his skill spread and with it the attentions of evil beings. Völund was forced into the service of King Nithud, who had accused Völund of theft and had him hamstrung. Forced to work for the evil king, Völund first enticed the king's sons to the smithy where he decapitated them, sending their jewelled skulls to their father as drinking cups. Then he enticed and seduced Bovild, Nithud's daughter. From his prison he escaped on a flying machine built with the aid of Egil, his brother. The English tradition says that he flew to Britain for refuge, hoping to find his Swan Maiden wife Allwite.
References 41, 56, 114, 133, 135
See also Dwarf, Elf, Goibniu, Swan Maiden, Wayland Smith, Appendix 14

VÔLVA

See Veela

VOUGH

This is a type of fuath in the folklore of Scotland. The Vough are water spirits that materialize in the shape of humans but are afraid of the light. They are usually said to be female and described as having no nose on their faces, yellow hair extending as manes down their backs to an emergent tail and webbed feet and hands. When observed they have usually been dressed in green. Occasionally they have been known to intermarry with humans. One of the Vough of Beann na Caltuinn was said to be the ancestor of the Munroes, whose earlier progeny showed signs of a caudal appendage and a mane of hair on the spine.
References 123
See also Fuath, Spirit, Appendix 25

VRIKSHAKAS

These are spirits in the Hindu mythology of India. They are benevolent tree nymphs and, like the Dryads of ancient Greece, they are the spirits of the woods or forests and individual trees. They are described as appearing in the form of voluptuous women emerging from the trunks of the trees. With the Apsaras, the Vrikshakas form the retinue of Indra.
References 102
See also Apsaras, Devas, Dryad, Gandharvas, Nymph, Spirit, Urvasi, Appendix 19

VRITRA

This is the name of a demon in the Hindu mythology of India. He is the demon of drought and is one of the Asuras. The name Vritra means the Encloser. He is visualized variously as a cloud, a spider, or a snake and is often identified with Ahi. As the destructive element of nature, Vritra was the enemy of Indra who finally slew the demon and released the cloud-cattle (rains) that had been held captive in the mountains.
See also Asura, Demon, Appendix 12

VROUELDEN

See Ben Socia

VUCUB-CAQUIX

The name of a demon in the ancient mythology of the Quiché-Maya of Central America. He is mentioned in the Popul-Vuh sacred texts as being of inflated arrogance, assuming his position as sun, moon, and light. He was dealt with and overthrown by the divine brothers Hunapu and Ixbalanque.
References 93
See also Demon

VUI

See Qat

VU-KUTIS

This water spirit, whose name has been translated as the Aquatic Aggressor, is a benevolent spirit of freshwater in the folklore of the Ostyaks and Votyak people of the Vyatka region of Russia. He is described as an aggressor possibly in acknowledgment of the zeal with which he fights against the diseases and demons that afflict the people.
References 102
See also As-iga, Demon, Kul, Spirit, Appendix 25

VU-MURT

This is the malevolent water demon, whose name means Water Man, in the folklore of the Finno-Ugric Votyak people of the Vyatka region of Russia. He is described as manifesting either as a naked man or woman combing its long black hair on the river bank. Vu-murt dwelled in the rivers and lakes of the region, where he expected a human sacrifice. If none had been made, his voice would be heard booming across the water. It was then that the inhabitants knew that the spirit had selected his own victim. Fishermen and millers at water mills would frequently make offerings to this spirit to prevent his malevolence and keep the water and the fish in plentiful supply. Vu-murt corresponds with the Vizi-ember of the Magyar folklore.
References 88, 102
See also Demon, Kul, Spirit, Viz-ember, Viz-murt, Vodianoi, Appendix 25

VU-NUNA

This is a benevolent water spirit, also known as Vi-nuna, of the Votyak people of the Vyatka region of Russia. The name Vu-nuna means the Water Uncle. He is considered to be the supernatural that fights against the disease-bringing water demon Yanki-murt.
References 102
See also As-iga, Demon, Kul, Spirit, Yanki-murt, Appendix 25

VU-VOZO

This is a water demon in the folklore of the Votyak people of the Vyatka region of Russia. He is possibly the guardian of freshwater, since the Votyaks, before taking a drink from a freshwater source in a strange place, will address the Vu-vozo in order to avert any malevolent revenge he may take on them. The prayer that they were said to offer was "Do not attack me. Attack rather a Russian woman or a Cheremis."
References 88, 109
See also Demon, Guardian, Kul, Appendix 25

VYANTARAS

These spirits are said to be wood spirits in the Jain mythology of India. They may perhaps be identified with the Vrikshakas.
References 6
See also Spirit, Vrikshakas, Appendix 19

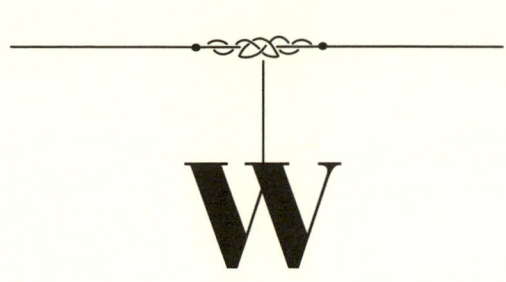

W

WACABE
See Black Bear

WAG AT THE WA'
This is the name of an individual household spirit in the folklore of the Scottish Borders. He was a spirit of the brownie type said to materialize as a little old man with crooked legs, and grizzled hair. He wore a red coat and blue breeches, or sometimes a gray coat and a woolen cap pulled over the face where his tooth ached. This spirit was distinguished by his tail, which assisted in holding him on his favorite seat, the cauldron crook in the inglenook fireplace. He loved company and could be heard laughing at any funny tales he heard beside the fire. However, he disapproved of any drink other than home brew beer and would cough angrily if anything stronger were taken. He would show even greater displeasure at untidiness or slackness in the kitchen and would torment the kitchen maids unmercifully. To prevent Wag at the Wa' from entering the kitchen, a cross was carved into the cauldron crook. Even so, people were discouraged from swinging the crook in the inglenook as the spirit took this as an invitation to haunt the home.
References 17, 18, 66
See also Brownie, Household Spirits, Appendix 22

WAHMAN
See Vohu Mano

WAKANÏ
This is the name for a familiar in the folk beliefs of the Jívaro people of the Equadorian Amazon. It manifests in the shape of a bird that the shamans use to help them put spells on their victims. The birds are sent to fly round and round the dwelling of the victim, causing sickness, insanity, and death.
References 64
See also Familiar, Appendix 12, Appendix 17

WALDGEISTER
This is the name of a group of wood or tree spirits in the folklore of Germany and Scandinavia. The forests were supposed to be the abode of numerous Waldgeister, some of whom were benevolent and others malevolent. They were thought to be healers using the herbs of the forest in their ancient medicine. The Hylde-Moer or Elder Mother is one of this group of spirits.
References 18, 88, 110
See also Hylde-Moer, Spirit, Appendix 19

WALGINO
A nature spirit in the folklore of Poland. This spirit was considered to be the guardian spirit of cattle.
References 102
See also Guardian, Spirit, Appendix 12

WALICHU
These are evil spirits in the beliefs of the Araucanian people of Chile and the Argentine Pampas. The people went to great lengths in their struggle to remove these spirits from their villages in order to avert the diseases and misfortune that they brought.
References 88
See also Spirit, Appendix 17

WALTHER
See Kobold

WALUMBE
See Balubaale

WALUTAHANGA
This is an evil spirit or demon in the mythology and folklore of Melanesia. His name, Walutahanga, means Eight Fathoms. The legend tells how this spirit was born to a mortal woman as a female snake. Her mother hid her fearing the father's reaction. When another child was born, Walutahanga was sent to look after the child, but the father saw her and chopped up the being watching his other child, not knowing it was his daughter. After eight days of rain Walutahanga became whole but in revenge ate people. Once again she was caught and chopped up. To complete her destruction she was cooked in a stew

for food. Everyone except one woman and her child ate the stew. Walutahanga reemerged and became the guardian spirit of the two who refused to eat, and brought them both good fortune.
References 29
See also Demon, Guardian, Spirit, Appendix 22

WANAGEMESWAK

These are spirits in the folk beliefs and legends of the Penobscot Native American people. They are river spirits that manifest in such a thin shape that they are only visible in profile. The Wanagemeswak inhabit the pools in river courses and sometimes leave clay effigies on the banks. The effigies are considered to be lucky if found by a human.
References 88
See also Spirit, Appendix 25

WANDERING DAME ABONDE

See Habonde

WAPAQ

This is the spirit that resides in the fly agaric toad-stool (*Amanita muscaria*) in the beliefs and folklore of the Koryak people of Siberia. The Wapaq are considered to be powerful guiding spirits that take control of those who taste the fungus. It is so powerful that if an old man should try some and the Wapaq tells him he is a child again, the old man will cry like a baby. But if the Wapaq should tell the old man "go to the afterworld," he will die immediately.
References 88
See also Spirit

WARUK

This is an evil spirit in the Dreamtime mythology of the Native Australian people. He is described as a huge bowling shape that will crush or devour anything that gets in his way, or transform anything that conflicts with him. Out of spite he changed Old Weaving Woman into a spider, and that is how she remains today. Purongo also became the victim of Waruk's evil temper. No matter how Purongo tried to get away, he was always too slow, so he transformed himself into a wallaby and went to hide in the bush. Waruk is still thrashing about there at night, looking for his intended victim.
References 14
See also Spirit

WASICONG

The name of a guardian or protective spirit in the beliefs of the Dakota Native American people.
References 25
See also Guardian, Spirit, Appendix 21

WASSERKOPF

See Nix

WASSERMANN

This is a term for a water spirit or sprite in the folk-lore of Germany. The name means Water Man. It is an alternative for the Nix or is more likely to be used when the type of water spirit is not determined.
References 18, 102
See also Nix, Spirit, Sprite, Appendix 25

WATER BABIES

A term used to denote the Little People of the waters in the beliefs and folklore of the Native American people of the Great Basin. These are diminutive water spirits that sometimes look like a dwarf and sometimes like a tiny old woman at the side of a spring. They inhabit the lakes, streams, and springs, and humans are wary of them. They are not particularly malevolent, but they will play pranks such as pulling on the fishermen's lines while fishing.

(This is also the name used by Charles Kingsley in his book of the same name, to denote the souls of drowned children. See Bedonebyasyoudid).
References 88
See also Dwarf, Little People, Spirit, Appendix 25

WATTLE BABIES

See Gumnut Babies

WĀWN

This is the name of one of the nats in the beliefs of the Kachin people of Burma.
References 87
See also Chinün Way Shun, Nats, Appendix 10

WAYLAND SMITH

In English tradition and folklore, Wayland Smith is the name given to the Germanic and Norse supernatural called Völund. The same legend is told of Wayland Smith in the Waldere Manuscript, dated to circa A.D. 1000, as is told of Völund. Prior to this manuscript, the tradition of Wayland's Smithies being of importance, and usually sited at some ancient cromlech, is demonstrated by the inclusion in a charter of Berkshire dated A.D. 855 of Weandes Smidde. On the ancient Ridgeway of Berkshire (now in Oxfordshire) referred to in that document, to this day, stands the same megalithic dolmen, which is now called Wayland's Smithy.

Wayland, also known as Weiland Smith and Weland Smith, is variously described as invisible, a giant, or an elf and belonging to the dwarfs. It is his skills that are more clearly described. King Alfred the Great (d. A.D. 899) referred to him as "that famous

and wise goldsmith Welund." Wayland is renowned as a swordsmith and armorer, especially in the Saga of Beowulf and in the twelfth-century French chronicles of the Counts of Angoulême. In later centuries in Britain, this supernatural dwelled in lonely ancient hill forts, cromlechs, and sacred sites, where his prowess as a blacksmith drew wary travelers. It was said that a horse left with a piece of money outside a Wayland Smithy would be found newly shod the following day. Francis Wise in his letter to Dr. Mead gives an account of this in 1738. Sir Walter Scott introduced the legend of Wayland Smith in his novel *Kenilworth* (1821), and Rudyard Kipling retold the tradition of the spirit smith in *Puck of Pook's Hill* (1906). Numerous sites are credited with being the workplace of this supernatural including Wayland's Pool. This is a stretch of water near Shevage Wood in Somerset, where the spirit was said to cool the metal he forged into horseshoes for the Wild Hunt. It is reported by locals that any horse will remain quietly there, even if the rider were to dismount and walk away.
References 40, 41, 56, 114, 133, 135
See also Dwarf, Elf, Gofannon, Goibniu, Ilmarinen, Völund, Wild Hunt, Appendix 14

WEE WILLIE WINKIE
This is a sleep spirit in the folklore of the British Isles. It is essentially an English nursery spirit and guardian of the young who ensures that all small children are safely tucked-up in bed and asleep at night. He is the subject of traditional nursery rhymes and popular songs. This version appears mainly in northeastern England and Scotland, but in Lancashire he is known as Billy Winker. A nursery rhyme of the name, which enjoyed great success, was created by William Miller in 1841. It is likely that it was based on an existing tradition.
References 17, 106
See also Billy Winker, Dustman, Guardian, Ole Luk Øj, Sandman, Spirit, Appendix 22

WEILAND SMITH, WELAND SMITH
See Wayland Smith

WEINACHTS MANN
See Pelznickel

WEIRD SISTERS
These spirits, also known as Wyrdes, were originally the Anglo-Saxon Fates, but later usage became restricted to a sorceress or witch, as in Shakespeare's *Macbeth*.
References 88
See also Fates, Udur, Appendix 23

WEMICUS
The name of a trickster spirit in the folk beliefs and legends of the Timigami Ojibwa Native American people.
References 88
See also Spirit, Trickster

WERDANDI
See Norns

WHIPPITY STOURIE
See Whoopity Stoorie

WHIRO
This is the evil spirit and controller of demons in the legends and beliefs of the Maori people of New Zealand. This demon is the constant adversary of the hero Tane.
References 24
See also Demon, Spirit

WHITE LADY
This is the title of a supernatural that appears as a young woman in diaphanous white robes in the folk traditions of Germany, France, and Britain. In Germany she is associated with the legends of Berchta. In France the White Ladies are a type of fairy that inhabit the crossing places of water, such as bridges and fords. Here they dance in the moonlight and enchant any passing mortal into joining them on pain of finding themselves in the water. One of these is known as la Dame Abonde, and another equally famous is la Dame d'Apigny, who is said to have appeared at the Rue St. Quentin in Bayeux. In Britain the White Ladies are associated with the fairies of foreboding such as the banshee, but are of a somewhat gentler nature. One such is featured by Sir Walter Scott in his novel *The Monastery*. She is known as the White Lady of Avenal.
References 40, 95, 114
See also Banshee, Berchta, Fairy, Habonde

WHOOPITY STOORIE
This is a spirit also known as Whippity Stourie, Whuppity Stoorie, and Fittletot in the folklore of Scotland. Usually she appears as an elderly deformed woman dressed in green. There are tales of her that reflect a Tom Tit Tot character. One of these tells how Whoopity Stoorie restored the life of a sow in farrow, but in payment for saving the pig, the sprite demanded the owner's daughter unless she could tell the fairy's name within three days. Happily the mother was able to tell the name and save her daughter. Another tale is in the same tradition of Habetrot, the spinning fairy. This relates how a young bride is asked by her

husband to spin flax into fine thread for his shirts. She confesses that she cannot spin. He insists that she may only remain as his wife if she has spun 100 hanks of linen thread by the time he returns from his journey. In despair she wanders over the braes and sits weeping on a large round stone. Suddenly she is aware of fairy music, and with a rowan twig to protect herself, she lifts the stone to reveal a green cave in the hillside. In the cave are six little ladies dressed in green with very lopsided mouths. The young woman greets them courteously and they ask why she is crying and she tells them of her plight. They tell her that if she invites them to dinner on her husband's return, all her problems will be solved. This she does. Her husband greets the little ladies dressed in green with courtesy, but begs to ask the oldest, Whoopity Stoorie, why she and her sisters have such lopsided mouths. She replies that it is because of all the spinning they do. With no more ado the husband resolves that his pretty wife should not attempt to spin ever again.

References 15, 17, 18, 80

See also Fairy, Habetrot, Spirit, Sprite, Tom Tit Tot, Appendix 14

WICHTLEIN

These are mine spirits or goblins in the folklore of the miners of Germany. They are described as little men with long hair and beards, wearing brown hooded jackets, aprons, breeches, stockings, and shoes. They have a toolbelt and carry lanterns and picks. The Wichtlein like to shower the human miners with stones, and whenever they do, there is sure to be a rich seam in that direction. However, when the spirits make a great noise of working, yet the miners see nothing done, they know that the Little People are warning them of an impending rockfall or similar disaster.

References 38

See also Cobalt, Goblin, Kobolds, Little People, Mine Spirits

WIGHT

An ancient word of Germanic origin, which meant "being," but which increasingly denoted spirits of an evil nature. The use of the word between the fourteenth and sixteenth centuries in English takes on the connotation of imp.

References 17

See also Imp, Spirit

WILD FOLK

See Moss Folk

WILD HUNT

The Wild Hunt is a feature of folklore throughout western Europe but is also found in other cultures. It is generally described as the supernatural host of spirits roaring through the skies on stormy nights in search of the souls of the damned, the unbaptized, and imprudent onlookers, to seize and convey them to Hell. This supernatural host may comprise the undead, lesser spirits in the form of hounds, goats, or horses, or the spectral armies of legendary human battles. They are led by the Wild Huntsman, who may be a demonized hero figure (Arthur), a spirit huntsman (Le Grand Vaneur), a demonized human (Wild Darrell), or the Devil himself. To hear them is a portent of physical disaster, a war, or some political or economic catastrophe. To see them usually results in the onlooker's imminent death. The earliest record is probably that of the Anglo-Saxon Chronicles of England for the year 1127, which described the appearance of huntsmen who were loathsome, huge, black beings, riding on black horses and goats, followed by horrible, wide-eyed hounds. The monks observed this phenomenon taking place between Lent and Easter above the town of Peterborough through to Stamford, prior to the installation of Henry of Poitou as abbot.

In *England* the Wild Hunt is known generally as the Furious Host, Herl's Rade, Herlethingus (an ancient legend), the Raging Host, or Woden's Hunt (from ancient mythology). The various English regional names for the Wild Hunt are Arthur's Hunt in Somerset; Dando and His Dogs and the Devil's Dandy Dogs in Cornwall; the Gabriel Hounds, Gabble Retchets, Gabriel Retchets, Gabble Rachets, and Gabblerackets in Durham, Yorkshire, and Lancashire; the Seven Whistlers in Worcestershire; the Sky Yelpers in the Eastern Counties; the Wish Hounds on Dartmoor; the Wisht Hounds in East Devon; and the Yeff (Heath) Hounds, Yeth Hounds, or Yell Hounds in North Devon.
In *Scotland* it is called Arthur's Hunt.
In *Wales* it is called Cwn Annwn, meaning Hounds of Fairyland/Hell, or Cwn Mamau, meaning Hounds of the Mothers.
In *France* it is known as L'Armée Furieuse, la Chasse d'Artu (Arthur's Hunt), Chasse de Caïn (Cain's Hunt), Chasse d'Hérode, and Mesnie Herlequin.
In *Switzerland* it is known as L'Armée Furieuse.
In *Scandinavia* it is known as Odin's Hunt.
In *Germany* it is Frau Gauden's Hunt, Holle's Hunt, or Wuotan's Hunt.

The above are described under their own or related entries.

Although the Wild Hunt as an entity seems to be confined to the folklore of western Europe, there are other spirits with many similar features throughout the world, such as the Hantu Si Buru of West Malaysia.

References 3, 17, 18, 40, 56, 69, 95, 110, 125, 133, 136
See also Fylgir, Spirit, Wild Huntsman, Appendix 12, Appendix 16, Appendix 23

WILD HUNTSMAN
This is the general term for the supernatural leader of the Wild Hunt. This being may be a demonized human (Wild Darrell), a demonized culture hero (Arthur), a spirit huntsman (Le Grand Vaneur), an ancient deity (Odin), or the Devil himself. The leader may be followed by the undead, lesser spirits in the form of hounds, goats, or horses, or the spectral armies of legendary human battles. The quarry of these spirits ranges from sinful humans, human babies, and the souls of the dead, to the other lesser spirits such as the Moss Women. As with all such traditions, there are numerous legends and folk stories about these characters, which range from the horrific and bizarre to some that show a wry sense of humor. Typical of these is a tale recounted by Baring-Gould of a farmer returning one night from the market at Widdecombe on Dartmoor. Riding past a stand of ancient stones, the farmer was overtaken by the Wild Hunt howling through the air. Showing no respect, the farmer called to ask what game the Dark Huntsman had that night and asked for a share. "Take that!" boomed the Huntsman, who tossed a bundle at the farmer as they passed. When he arrived in the light of his lamps at home the farmer opened the bundle and revealed the body of his own little child.

In *England* the Hunt may be led by Black Vaughan (a damned human), Dando (a damned human), the Devil, Dewer (a damned human), Grim, Harry-ca-Nab, Herne the Hunter, King Arthur, King Herla, Sir Francis Drake, Tregeagle (a damned human), Wild Darrell (a damned human), or Wild Edric (a Saxon hero).
In *Scotland* the hunt is led by King Arthur; in Wales by Gwyn ap Knudd, or Mallt y Nos (Matilda of the Night, a damned human).
In *France* the hunt may be led by Artu (King Arthur), Caïn (Cain of the Bible), Le Grand Vaneur de Fontainebleau (the Great Hunter of Fontainebleau), Hérode (King Herodias), Charlemagne (King), or Roland (hero).
In *Germany* the hunt may be led by Berchta, Frau Gauden or Frau Gode (a damned human), Hans von Hackelnberg (a damned human in Saxony), Hakel-Bärend (in Westphalia), Hockelblock (in Bergkirchen), Odin, Wœnsjäger (Wild Huntsman), Woenjäger (in Hanover), Woinjäger (in Saterland), or Wuotan (Woden).
In *Denmark* the hunt may be led by Waldemar (King), Christian II (King), or Grønjette.
In *Sweden* it is Odin who leads the Wild Hunt.

In *other parts of the world* the Wild Huntsman may be Hantu Pemburu or Hantu Si Buru in West Malaysia and Haruts in India.

References 17, 18, 19, 56, 69, 95, 110, 125, 133
See also Berchta, Dando and His Dogs, Fylgir, Grim, Grønjette, Gwyn ap Knudd, Hakel-Bärend, Hantu Pemburu, Hantu Si Buru, Harry-ca-nab, Haruts, Herne the Hunter, Moss Women, Sprite, Wild Hunt, Appendix 16, Appendix 22, Appendix 23

WILKIE
An obscure and ill-defined spirit said to inhabit the Wilkie Mounds, ancient burial chambers in Westray on the Orkney Islands (United Kingdom). It is conjectured that it is a fairy, since offerings of milk were said to be left at the mounds.
References 17
See also Fairy, Spirit

WILL O' THE WISP
This is the most common name of a spirit or pixy that is said to haunt the lonely roads, byways, heaths, fens, and marshes of England. It is a mischievous spirit that delights in misleading night-bound weary travelers by lighting lanterns and traveling ahead, encouraging the travelers to follow into ditches, bogs, and disaster. It is, in fact, the *ignis fatuus*, or false fire, which by spontaneous ignition of marsh gases, was supposed in local folklore to be spirits playing tricks on gullible humans. There is an account by Hentzner of a journey between Canterbury and Dover in 1598, when "there were a great many Jack-w' a-Lanthorns, so that we were quite seized with horror and amazement." The phenomenon is also known as Friar's Lanthorn, Sylham Lamp, Elf Fire, and Fire Drake. In some cases these spirits are considered to be demons or portents of misfortune; at other times they are the beguiling guardian spirits of treasure, teasing the foolish human with wealth forever just out of reach. The same traditions in folklore are to be found wherever the phenomenon occurs, and a wealth of interesting names and anecdotes exist worldwide.

The Will o' the Wisp is also known by the following names:

England: Billy wi' t' Wisp (WestYorks); Dick o' Tuesday (Eastern Counties); Gyl-burnt-tayl (Warwicks); Hinky-Punk (West Country); Hob-Lantern (East Midlands); Hobbledy's-Lantern (Warwicks, Worcs, Glos); Hobby-lantern (Worcs, Herts, East Anglia, Hants, Wilts, WestWales); Jack-a-lantern, Jacky-Lantern (Lancs); Jenny-burnt-tail (Northants, Oxon, Cornwall); Jenny-wi-t-lantern (Nthumb, NorthYorks); Joan-in-the-wad, Joan the Wad (Somerset, Cornwall); Kit-in-the-candlestick

(Hants); Kit-with-the-candlestick, Kitty-candlestick (Wilts); Kitty-wi-the-wisp (Northumb); the Lantern Man (East Anglia); Will o' the Wykes (Lincs); Peg-a-lantern (Lancs); Pinket (Worcs); Poake (Worcs); Will the Smith (Salop); Jack o' Wisp; Friar's Lantern (West Country).

Ireland: Teine Sionniic (Fox Fire), Teine Sidhe (Fairy Fire), Liam na Lasoige (William with the Little Flame); same as Will the Smith story.

Wales: Tan Ellyll, Ellylldan.

Germany: Blud, Dickepoten (human condemned to wander, e.g., Will the Smith), Irrlicht.

France: Feu Follet, Fifollet, Sand Yan y Tad.

Finland: Liekko, Liekkiö.

Penobscot Native American: Escudáit.

Cheremis/Mari: Kazna Peri, Ia Saltak.

Tupi Guarani (Amazon Basin): Baetata.

Chile: Alicanto.

Other spirits that have also played the Will o' the Wisp pranks are Buber (Cheremis/Mari), Friar Rush, Jack the White Hat, Spunkies, Piskey, Puck, and Robin Goodfellow in the British Isles; Orang Bunyi in West Malaysia.

References 15, 17, 28, 40, 88, 92, 97, 107

See also Alicanto, Buber, Demon, Elf, Ellylldan, Fire Drake, Friar Rush, Guardian, Gyl-burnt-tayl, Hinky-Punk, Hob-Lantern, Jack the White Hat, Joan the Wad, Liekkiö, Orang Bunyi, Piskey, Pixie, Poake, Puck, Robin Goodfellow, Sand Yan y Tad, Spirit, Spunkies, Will the Smith, Appendix 20, Appendix 24

WILL THE SMITH

In the folklore of Shropshire, England, this manifestation of the Will o' the Wisp was said to have been the soul of a debauched human who was given a second chance by Saint Peter so that he could redeem his soul. The smith, however, was so wicked this second time, that he was barred from entering either Heaven or Hell. So the Devil gave Will a glowing coal to warm himself while he ceaselessly wanders the marshes, luring other mortals to their doom.

References 17

See also Will o' the Wisp

WILLI

See Veela

WILLY WILY MAN

See Kompagnin

WIND OLD WOMAN

The name of a wind spirit in the folk beliefs and traditions of the Taos Pueblo Native American people. She is said to dwell in the middle of the world and is regarded as a thrifty old hag. She is revered as a healer

by those who suffer from rheumatism, who will offer her corn meal, pollen, and a turkey feather. This is also the name of a wind spirit in the traditions of the Hopi and Tewa people, while Wind Old Man is the name of a spirit in the traditions of the Taos Pueblo, the Tewa, and the Isleta peoples.

References 45, 88

See also Spirit, Appendix 26

WINTERKOLBE

See Rumpelstiltskin

WISH MAIDENS

See Valkyries

WISH WIFE

A female supernatural in the traditions and folklore of Germany who is conjured into existence to serve the mortal who invoked her. Also the name sometimes used for a succubus or for the female attendant of the Norse gods, such as the Valkyries.

References 92

See also Attendant Spirit, Succubus, Valkyries

WISHT HOUNDS

See Wild Hunt

WOKOLO

This is the name of a demon in the folk beliefs of the Baramba people of Nigeria. This diminutive devil inhabits the trees and the banks of streams and rivers. Wokolo will shoot arrows at any humans who cannot avoid him, and if they are hit will inflict misfortune on them.

References 102

See also Demon, Devil

WOLPHAT

See Olifat

WOOD FOLK

See Moss Folk

WOOD WIVES

These are diminutive female spirits or Elf Maidens that inhabited the woods in the folklore of Scandinavia and Germany. They are also known as Dirne-weibl, Elle Folk, Finz-weibl, Holz-frau, Moss Women, Spae-wives, Wild Folk, and Wish Wives. They are described as being pretty, with long blond hair, wearing a blue dress with a green bodice and a red jacket. When loud noises and steam issue from the rocks in summer, it is said that the Wood Wives are washing their clothes. Sometimes they would ask to borrow something from, or have something mended by, a human who sees them in the woods. It is

The Wish Wife is called by magic to serve the human. He must be warry for she may be a succubus.

prudent to give them assistance, for although the payment will be in wood chips, on leaving the forest these will turn to gold. Many kindly woodsmen have accepted these wood shavings without comment and discovered their reward in due course, but the mean-minded humans, having thrown away the wood chips, never knew their value. Like the Dryads and Hamadryads, the Wood Wives' existence is closely linked with that of the trees. If the trees are bent and twisted as saplings, then for each of the trees destroyed one of these spirits will cease to exist. The Wood Wives are the quarry of other spirits, especially the leader of the Wild Hunt.

References 18, 110

See also Dirne-weibl, Dryad, Elf, Elle Folk, Hamadryad, Moss Folk, Spae-wives, Spirit, Wild Hunt, Wild Huntsman, Wish Wife, Appendix 19

WRACH

This is the title given to the effigy of the corn spirit in the folklore of Pembrokeshire in Wales. It is ceremonially captured and revered at a celebration in this form and then kept until the next plowing season.

References 123

See also Cailleac, Corn Spirit

WRYNECK

The name of a spirit described by Henderson in *The Folklore of the Northern Counties* (1866) as being a malignant spirit of Lancashire and Yorkshire, England. Although said to be more evil than the Devil, reference to it was only proverbial by the middle of the nineteenth century.

References 17, 66

See also Spirit

WU CH'ANG KUEI

These are spirits in the traditions and legends of China. They are the transformed spirits of humans who have died from either grief or suicide. These Kuei now signify impermanence and are the messengers from hell. They are usually in the company of Ma Mien (the Horse-Faced Demon) and Niu T'ou (the Ox-Head Demon). There are two kinds of Wu Ch'ang Kuei, which are known as the Yang Wu-Ch'ang and the Yin Wu-Ch'ang. The Yang Wu-Ch'ang is the male Wu Ch'ang Kuei messenger from hell who is portrayed with white painted features, white garments, and hat. He is the spirit that calls to summon humans to the underworld before they have reached their fiftieth birthday. Yin Wu-Ch'ang is the female Wu Ch'ang Kuei messenger from hell who is portrayed with black painted features and black garments. She is the spirit that summons humans to the underworld after their fiftieth birthday.

References 39, 87, 88, 131

See also Kuei, Spirit, Appendix 16

WURD

See Udur

WYLL

See Yr Wyll

WYRD, WYRDES

See Udur

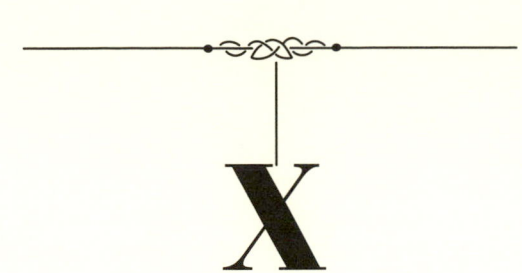

X

XANAS

These are nature spirits or nymphs in the folklore of the Asturias region of northwestern Spain. They appear as beautiful young women with long, flowing hair. They dwell in mountain caves of the region but come down into the meadows on dewy mornings to play. Sometimes they are said to be enchanted mortals who will reward the person who rescues them with gemstones. Other tales are more in keeping with the English pixies, like them the Xanas love to ride the horses in the stables at night often leaving them in a lather in the morning.

References 88
See also Nymph, Pixie, Spirit

XANGÔ

This is the name of a spirit or encantado in the Afro-Brazilian cult Batuque. He is a high-ranking spirit also known as Xangô-Badé. The name Xangô is used in the Umbanda cult, and Badé is used for this spirit in the older Mina-Nagô cult in Brazil. His name is derived from the Dahomean god of thunder and lightning, and Xangô is also said to control storms. He is thought to send the sacred stones (often prehistoric stone axe-heads), used by the mediums to "invite" spirits into the *terrieros* or cult centres. Xangô is considered to be an austere spirit that rarely possesses a devotee during ceremonies. He is associated with Saint Jerome and the feast day 30 September.

References 89
See also Encantado, Rainha Barba, Senhor

XAPANAN

See Rei Sebastião

XENÆA

See Echenais

XIAN

A general term for spirits or genii and immortals in the folk traditions and legends of China. They are usually benevolent.

References 93
See also Genius, Spirit

XIANG YAO

This is the name of an evil spirit or devil in the folk beliefs and legends of China. He manifests in a hideous form that has nine human heads on a snake's body. Xiang Yao is responsible for creating stinking swamps and diseased springs. He is the attendant of Gong Gong.

References 93
See also Devil, Gong Gong, Appendix 12, Appendix 25

XŠATRAVĒR

This is the Pahlavi version of the name for Kshathra in the Zoroastrian religion of Iran. He is one of the Amesha Spentas and attendant genius of Ahura Mazda. Xšatravēr is the guardian spirit of metals and leads Mithra, Asman, and Aniran against the evil Sauru.

References 41, 53, 119
See also Amesha Spentas, Aniran, Asman, Attendant Spirit, Genius, Guardian, Kshathra, Mithra

XUDA SILA

This is the name of an evil spirit in the folk beliefs of the Cheremis/Mari people of the former Soviet Republic. The name of this demon, Xuda Sila, means Evil Strength. It is said that it may seek to do harm to humans in company with the Keltəmaš when they appear at midday, midnight, and 6 o'clock in the morning and evening.

References 118
See also Demon, Keltəmaš, Spirit

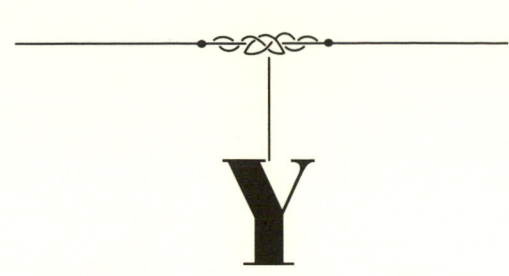

Y

Y WRACH

This is a disease spirit in the folklore of the Welsh people. It is also known as Yr hen Wrach, and is said to manifest in the guise of an old woman or hag. Like the Fad Felen of the ancient Britons, this spirit inflicted a mortal fever, in this case the ague or malaria.
References 123
See also Fad Felen, Hag, Spirit, Appendix 17

YAJUJU

See Majuju

YAKEELA

This is the name for a familiar spirit in the rituals and beliefs of the shamans and people of Siberia. It is said that when two shamans are contending with each other, the Yakeelas of each shaman will be dispatched to contend on their behalf. Should a Yakeela be destroyed, the shaman will die.
References 87
See also Familiar

YAKKHAS, YAKSHAS, YAKSHI, YAKSHINI

These are supernatural beings and demons in the beliefs and legends of India. They are shape-shifters that are sometimes benign and sometimes malevolent toward human beings. The Yakshas are the males; they may manifest as handsome youths or as hideous, potbellied, humpbacked black dwarfs. The Yakkhas are associated with Kubera in the forests of the Himalayas, guarding treasure and doing battle on the winds. They are given to bloodthirsty and hostile activities. The Yakshi or the Yakshini are female spirits, portrayed as voluptuous women, sometimes with the head of a horse. They will mislead and attack any lone traveler in the forests. The more benevolent of these supernaturals are associated with fertility and propitiated for their protection.
References 29, 39, 41, 53, 56, 88, 93, 102
See also Demon, Dwarf, Kubera, Appendix 24

YALAFATH

See Olifat

YALLERY BROWN

This is the name of an individual sprite or evil fairy in the folklore of the Fens in England. He was described in Mrs. Balfour's "Legends of the Cars" as being tiny, about the size of a year-old child, wrinkled and ugly, with long golden hair and beard. The story tells how a young farmworker called Tom Tiver, returning from work, heard a cry like a baby's coming from the side of the road. The crying appeared to be coming from under a great flat stone known as the Stranger's Stone. Lifting this up, he found that a sprite had been trapped underneath and was completely tangled up in its own hair. When Tom released the sprite, it offered him a reward of gold or a wife, but Tom preferred help with his work. The sprite agreed, and said that all Tom had to do was call Yallery Brown for the work to be done, but never to thank him or the help would cease. When Tom arrived at his work each day it had all been done, and he thought it was wonderful. But he soon discovered that the work of all the other workers was being destroyed at the same time. Soon Tom was receiving all the blame, until eventually the farmer dismissed him. Unhappy with the way things had turned out, Tom called Yallery Brown and told him what ill results had come of the work, and that Tom would thank him to be left alone. Being thanked causes offense to all fairies of the working type, and usually, as with the brownies, this is enough to dismiss them. But Yallery Brown was a malicious sprite who took revenge by troubling and bringing misfortune to Tom from that time on.
References 17, 18
See also Brownie, Fairy, Sprite

YAL-UN EKE

See Odqan

YAMA-UBA

These are nature spirits in the folk beliefs of Japan. They are the female spirits of the mountains.
References 119
See also Spirit

YAMBE-AKKA

This is a spirit in the folk beliefs of the Lapp people of the northern Baltic states. The name Yambe-akka means Old Woman of the Dead. She is the guardian of the underworld, which was conceived of as an ocean of ice supporting the upper world. Entrance to this underworld was by way of the mouth of a river. Because this underworld was peopled by the elderly departed, it was said that when their feeble hands trembled, the world above was shaken by the earth tremors.
References 33
See also Guardian, Spirit

YANG WU-CH'ANG

See Wu Ch'ang Kuei

YANKI-MURT

This is a malevolent water demon, like the Vu-vozo, in the folklore of the Votyak, a Finno-Ugric people of the Vyatka region of Russia. He is particularly danger-ous, and will inflict diseases on those who are unwary or who offend him. Vu-nuna is the benevolent spirit that defends the Votyaks against Yanki-murt.
References 88, 102
See also Darrant, Kul, Näkki, Nix, Rusalka, Spirit, Viz-ember, Vodianoi, Vu-nuna, Vu-vozo, Appendix 25

YA-O-GAH

This is the name of a spirit in the folk beliefs of the Iroquois Seneca Native American people. He is the spirit of the north wind appearing in the shape of a bear. Like the bear he is strong and powerful, and when unleashed by Ga-oh, he will bring bitterly cold storm-force winds from the north and freeze the waters with his breath.
References 17, 18
See also Ga-oh, Spirit, Appendix 12, Appendix 26

YAOTL

This is the name of a demon, which means the Enemy, in the mythology of the ancient Aztec people of Mexico. The legend tells how a human named Jappan wished to be the favorite of the gods, and so, chose a remote rock on which to become a hermit. The gods sent Yaotl to spy on Jappan and see if he was really devoted. The demon sent many volup-tuous spirit maidens to test Jappan, who refused their advances. The goddess Tlazolteotl (goddess of guilty loves, pleasure, and filth) was annoyed by this, and disguising herself as a frail but beautiful mortal, offered sympathy to Jappan if only he would help her onto his rock. The trap was sprung, and Yaotl tri-umphantly beheaded the impure Jappan, who turned into a scorpion hiding in shame under his rock.

Jappan's wife was brought to the rock, where he told her everything; she too became a scorpion. But the gods were annoyed with Yaotl, who they thought had exceeded his instructions, so they turned him into a grasshopper.
References 102
See also Spirit

YARTHKINS

This is the name of a group of nature spirits in the folklore of the Fen country of England. They may also be called the Greencoaties, the Strangers, the Tiddy Mun, or the Tiddy People. In her article Legends of the Cars, Mrs. Balfour asserts that these were fertility spirits of the earth that expected propitiation for their assistance in bringing abundance to the crops. Some-times they were benevolent like the brownies, and at other times they were malevolent like Yallery Brown.
References 17, 18
See also Brownie, Spirit, Strangers, Tiddy Ones, Yallery Brown, Appendix 18

YATUS

See Drug

YAZATAS

In the Zoroastrian religion of Persia, the celestial spir-its known as Yazatas are the divine messengers of Ahura Mazda. Their name means Worthy of Reverence. Like the angels, they have a celestial rank-ing, and the Yazatas are third in this hierarchy. The Yazatas assist the Amesha Spentas in communicating the divine will to humans. They are the personifica-tions of moral concepts and conceived of as protec-tive spirits. Among them, the following are special guardian spirits: Anahita, Apo, Asha, Atar, Daena, Drashpa, Haurvatat, Huarekhshaeta, Mah, Mithra, Rashnu, Rasun, Sraosha, Trishtrya, and Verethaghna. In the folk beliefs of modern Iran, they have come to be known as the Yazdan, who are good demons.
References 41
See also Amesha Spentas, Angel, Apo, Demon, Guardian, Haurvatat, Mithra, Spirit, Sraosha, Appendix 13

YAZDAN

See Yazatas

YECH

This is the name of a prankster demon, also known as a Yeksh, in the folk beliefs of the Native American people. Although it is said to resemble a small animal such as a cat, it is in fact a shape-shifter and can assume any form. However, it always wears its shell-shaped white cap, with which it makes itself invisi-ble. Anyone who can take the white cap from it and

put it under a millstone will have that Yech as his faithful servant. They are powerful beings that can move any large load, even mountains, but usually trap their fingers under millstones. The Yechs are mischievous spirits, and mostly delight in leading gullible human travelers astray.
References 88
See also Demon, Spirit, Will o' the Wisp, Appendix 12, Appendix 24

YEHL

This is the name of the trickster spirit of the Native American people of the North Pacific coastal region. This spirit manifests usually in the shape of a raven, by whose name he is also known. He was responsible for teaching humans many skills and giving them useful gifts, but could never resist playing pranks on gods and men alike.
References 25, 88
See also Spirit, Trickster, Appendix 12

YEITSO

This is the name of a demon in the myths and folk beliefs of the Navajo Native American people.
References 56
See also Demon

YEKSH

See Yech

YELAFATH

See Olifat

YETH HOUNDS

See Wild Hunt

YIN CHIAO

In the mythology of China, a group of ten spirits has the particular duty of presiding over periods of time. These spirits are controlled by Yin Chiao, and their "duties" are: Chiao Kun (night duty), Chou Teng (day superintendent), Fang Hsiang (a herald), Fang Pi (a guide), Han Tu-Lung (the accumulation of happiness), Hsieh O-Hu (the bearer of misfortunes), Huang Ch'eng-I (the month superintendent), Li Ping (the year superintendent), Liu Huang (the hour superintendent), and Wen Liang (the day duty). The four superintendents were said to have been destroyed in the Battle of the Ten Thousand Spirits.
References 131
See also Spirit

YIN WU-CH'ANG

See Wu Ch'ang Kuei

YN FOLDYR GASTEY

See Fenodyree

YOGINI

These are demons in the Hindu mythology of India. They are the eight female attendants of the goddess Durga, who is the consort of Siva.
References 88
See also Lamia

YR HEN WRACH

See Y Wrach

YR WYLL

This is the name of a spirit in the folklore of Wales. It is invisible, but the evidence of its presence may be seen. This supernatural, like the pixies of England, delights in riding the horses in the stables at night so that in the morning the horses are in a lather and their manes are tangled with the marks of stirrups in them.
References 59
See also Pixie, Spirit

YSBRYD DRWG

This is an evil spirit in the folklore of Wales. Ysbryd drwg is a type of devil in the Welsh language.
References 59
See also Cythraul, Devil, Spirit

YÜ NÜ

These are fairy spirits in the folk beliefs and mythology of China. They are known as the Jade Maidens. They are the five attendants of Hsi Wang Mu; each presides over a cardinal point of the compass and one over the center. They appear as beautiful young women dressed in silken traditional garments of a single color for the directions of red, yellow, white, green, or black. This name is also used for such gentle spirits as Pi-Hsia Yüan-Chün, who presides over childbirth.
References 131
See also Attendant Spirit, Fairy, Pi-Hsia Yüan-Chün, Spirit

YUKI-ONNA

This is the name of an evil spirit in the folklore and mythology of Japan. Yuki-onna is the beautiful female spirit of the snowstorms. As the Snow Woman, her beauty lures men out into her blizzards, enticing them to follow. Those who are enchanted by her charms desperately search for her until they perish from the cold.
References 119
See also Snow Queen, Spirit, Appendix 26

YUMIS

This is a corn spirit in the folklore of the Latvian people. It is the spirit of the cornfield, which inhabits the crop during its growth. Like the Kornwolf, it is

"caught" at harvest time in the last sheaf and celebrated for the continued fertility of the following year.
References 88
See also Cailleac, Corn Spirit, Kornwolf, Appendix 15

YURUPARI
This is a general term for spirits in the folk beliefs of the Tupi people of the Amazon Basin. The Yurupari include both benign and malevolent spirits. However, they are mostly dangerous demons. These evil spirits inhabit the forests and wild places, and many of these frightening spirits move into empty houses, ruins, and burial sites.
References 102
See also Demon, Spirit

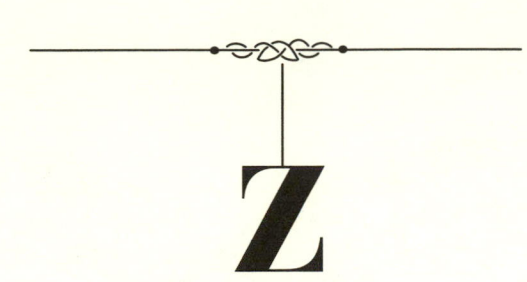

ZADKIEL, ZADEKIEL
This is the name of an Archangel or a chief angel who is also known as Sachiel or Tzadkiel in Judeo-Christian scriptures. He is said to be the angel of benevolence, piety, grace, and justice. In the Jewish mystical texts of the astrological calendar, Zadkiel was associated with the planet Jupiter, but in medieval Christian astrology, Zadkiel was associated with the same planet under his alternative name of Sachiel.
References 40, 53
See also Angel, Archangel, Appendix 13

ZAEBOS
The name of a demon in European mysticism and demonology who controls other groups of demons in the infernal empire.
References 53
See also Demon

ZA'FAR
See Ja'far

ZAGAM
This is the name of a demon in European mysticism and demonology. He rules over other groups of demons in the infernal empire.
References 53
See also Demon

ZAGAZ
This is the name of an evil spirit or djinn in the folk beliefs of Morocco. Zagaz is a disease spirit that brings death to infants and newborns in the form of infantile tetanus.
References 90
See also Djinn, Khadem Quemquoma, Spirit, Appendix 17, Appendix 22

ZAIRI, ZAIRISHA
See Tauru

ZALAMBUR
This is the name of a djinn or demon in the beliefs of Islam and the folklore of the Arab peoples. Zalambur is said to be one of the progeny of Iblis. He is the evil spirit who incites traders to commercial dishonesty.
References 41, 53, 88, 93
See also Djinn, Iblis

ZAR
This is the name of a demon in the folk beliefs of the Abyssinian people, reported in an account of 1865. This spirit is said to have the character of a leopard that takes possession of unmarried women. The possessed young girls are caused to have convulsions. During these convulsions, the girls emit the discordant growls of this demon as they writhe and stare in a hideous fashion. The remedy was said to be the expulsion of the demon either by exorcism or whipping the victim!
References 57
See also Demon, Spirit

ŽEMEPATIS
This is a nature spirit in the folk beliefs of the Lithuanian people. His name means Master of the Earth, and he is concerned with promoting the abundance of the crops. His female counterpart is Žemyna.
References 93
See also Gabijauja, Spirit, Vējasmāte, Žemyna, Appendix 18

ŽEMYNA
This is a nature spirit in the folk beliefs of the Lithuanian people. Her name means Mistress of the Earth, and she is concerned with fertility and the abundance of the crops. Her male counterpart is Žemepatis.
References 93
See also Gabijauja, Spirit, Vējasmāte, Žemepatis, Appendix 18

Zwart Piet (right) assists Sinter Klaas in recording the deeds of good and bad children.

ZEPAR
This is the name of a demon in European mysticism and demonology. He rules over other groups of demons in the infernal empire.
References 53
See also Demon

ZEPHON
This is the name of an angel named in Milton's *Paradise Lost*. Zephon accompanies Ithuriel when he is sent by the Archangel Gabriel to search out Satan in Paradise.
References 114
See also Angel, Archangel, Gabriel, Ithuriel

ZEZINHO
This is the name of an encantado in the Afro-Brazilian cult Batuque. He is said to be in the "family" of Dom José.
References 89
See also Dom José, Encantado

ZIN
This is an evil spirit or demon in the folk beliefs of the Upper Niger region of Nigeria. It is a type of water spirit that humans should be wary of seeing, because seeing one is said sometimes to be fatal. The name is possibly derived from the Arabic djinn.
References 119
See also Demon, Djinn, Spirit, Appendix 25

ZLOI DUKH
This is the name used for an evil spirit in the folklore of Russia. The name Zloi Dukh may be used for a demon or a devil.
References 75
See also Demon, Devil, Spirit

ZOA
This is the name of a tutelary spirit in the folk beliefs of the Songay people of the Upper Niger region of Nigeria. The Zoa are said to be derived from the ancient ancestors and to be protective guardian spirits similar to that of the Domovoi of Russian folk belief.
References 119
See also Domovik, Fylgir, Guardian, Household Spirits, Nagual, Tutelary Spirit

ZUIBOTSCHNIK
See Leshii

ZWART PIET
This is the sinister "Moorish" spirit in the folklore of Holland. He is the servant of Sinter Klaas, the children's gift-bringer of the Christmas season. Zwart Piet, whose name means Black Peter, is envisaged as a Moorish boy dressed in the oriental garments of Morocco or the Arab world of the sixteenth century. He keeps records during the year of all the naughty Dutch children in order to deliver punishment or carry them off in his sack to Spain; the good children receive gifts. This spirit originates in the times when the Netherlands was part of the empire of Spain (that had been ruled by the Moors until their expulsion by the Spanish hero El Cid). The folk memory of those troubled times survives over three centuries later in the punishment exacted by Zwart Piet on the naughty children of Holland.
References 34
See also Sinter Klaas, Spirit, Appendix 22

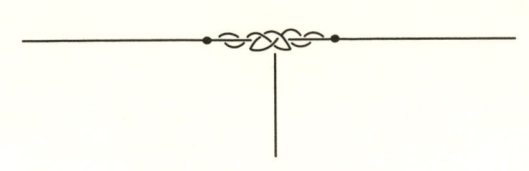

APPENDIXES

The following appendixes include additional names that are not mentioned in the text entries.
The supplementary names are provided to aid in more specific research.

1. ANGELS

Types of Angel

Amesha Spentas, Angiris, Archangels, Cherub, Cherubim, Dævas, Dominations, Dominions, Ferohers, Fravashi, Guardian Angel, Igigi, Jut Bodəž, Lamassu, Lar, Mala'ikat Puteh, Manes, Perešta, Pitris, Powers, Principalities, Seraphim, Shên, Sraosha, Šukčə, Thrones, Uthra, Virtues, Yazatas

Names of Individual Angels

Cheremis/Mari:
Arnagecen Šukčə, Friday's Angel; Azren; Biča Šukče, Pen Angel; Bol'ək Šukče, Livestock Angel; Bučə Ümbal Šukčə, Angel on the Shoulder; Buj Šukčə, Head Angel; Büt Ümbal Šukčə, Angel on the Water; Er Šukčə, Morning Angel; Jes Šukčə, Family Angel; Jumən Šukčə, God's Angel; Kaba Šukčə, Fate Angel; Kapka Šukčə, Gate Angel; Kas Šukčə, Evening Angel; Kazna Šukčə, Treasure Angel; Kində Šukčə, Grain Angel; Melandə Šukčə, Earth Angel; Mükš Šukčə, Bee Angel; Okna Šukčə, Window Angel; Pasu Šukčə, Field Angel; Šurnə Šukčə, Grain Angel; Šurt Šukčə, House Angel; Tul Šukčə, Fire Angel; Tünča Ümbal Šukčə, Angel over the World

Greek:
Charos, Ker

Hebrew:
Anpiel, Arariel, Hadarniel, Metatron, Sandalphon, Shemyaza, Uzziel

Hindu:
Angiris, Antariksha, Chitragupta

Islam:
Asasel, Futrus, Gabra'il, Harut and Marut, Israfil, Malik, Monker and Nakir

Judeo-Christian:
Abaddan, Abdiel, Angel Oliver, Ariel, Arioch, Asasel, Asmodeus, Azaziel, Azrael, Gabriel, Israfel, Ithuriel, Jophiel, Kafziel, Lucifer, Michael, Raphael, Samael, Uriel, Zadkiel, Zephon

Malaysian Islam:
Chitar Ali, Ijrafil, Ijrail, Jabra'il, Jewa-Jewa, Mala'ikat, Mika'il, Putar Ali, Sabur Ali, Sir Ali

Persia:
Apo, Rashnu

Russia:
Bes

Tupi Guarani (Brazil):
Apoiaueue

2. DEMONS (MALEVOLENT)

Class Name

Achachilas, Aerika, Afrit, Aiatar, Airi, Akaanga, Alp, Alraun, Anchancho, Anchunga, Anhanga, Asura, Asurakumāra, Ayerico, Bad Hour, Badjang, Bagul, Baka, Banksia Men, Bannaia, Baumesel, Bhut, Binaye Albani, Bodəž, Boggart, Boraro, Bottle Imp, Bouda, bTsan, Buber, Buckie, Bug-a-boo, Bugbear, Bug/g, Bull Beggar, Bullerman, Buso, Buttery Spirit, Bwcïod, Bygel nos, Cacodæmon, Caypór, Cellar Demon, Chûtâs, Cihuateteo, Citipati, Cobalt, Co-Hon, Con-Ma-Dāu, Cythraul, Daitya, Dakini, Danavas, Dasyus, Dævas, Deev, Drude, Drug, Dyavo, Exus, Familiar Spirits, Fauni Ficari, Formorian, Fylgir, Gabriel Hounds, Galley-trot, Ganas, Ghoul, gNyan, Green Women, Gremlins, Hantu, Hantu Hantuan, Hantu Hutan, Hantu Kayu, Hapiñuñu, Harpy, Hisa-Me, Hongaek, Hsien, Huecuvu, Igupiara, Illike, Iwanči, Jin Tanah, Juju, Kaia, Kajis, Kala, Kalak, Kalevanpojat, Kanaima, Kappa, Keremet, Kikiades, Kimprushas, Korybantes, Kratt, Kuei, Kurétes, La, Lahama, Langsuir, Larva, Lau, Lemur, Lu, Ma-Mo, Matabiri, Mazikeen, Nats, Oni, Paravoj Ia, People Who Killed by Lightning in Their Eyes, Pey, Piśācas, Pray,

Psuvashi, Rakshasas, Riesengebirge, Ruach, Šajtan, Sao, Saraua, Sebettu, Se'irim, Shēdîm, Škenan Ončəmə, Sri, Supay, Šurnə, Syen, Tchatse-olmai, Tigbanua, Tras, Udu, Utukku, Vishaps, Wu Ch'ang Kuei, Yakkhas, Yogini, Yurupari

Individual Names

Abaddan, Abere, Abigor, Acephalos, Addanc, Aeshma, Afanc, Aga Kurman, Agas, Agnen, Ako-Mano, Akvan, Al, Alardi, Alocer, Amaite-Rangi, Ammit, Amon, Amy, Anamelech, Andras, Aparājita, Apep, Ardat Lili, Arioch, Arzshenk, Asag, Asasel, Asəra, Ashakku, Ashmedai, Asmodeus, Astaroth, Astarotte, Astō Vidātu, Aufhocker, Ays, Az, Azidahaka, Baalberith, Baalzaphon, Babi, Bael, Balan, Bali, Barbason, Barqu, Bathym, Baubo, bDud, Beelzebub, Behemoth, Belial, Belphegor, Berith, Biasd Bheulach, Bilberry Man, Bitoso, Black Annis, Black Shuck, Black Sow, Black Vaughan, Bruder Rausch, Buckland Shag, Bushyasta, Büt Imnə, Cabyll-Ushtey, Campankitāci, Cauchemar, Ccoa, Ceffyll-dŵr, Charon, Charontes, Charos, Chertovka, Cluricaun, Colo-Colo, Culsu, Čurpan Šərt, Curupira, Cutty Dyer, Dala Kadavara, Darrant, Demon Lover, Demrush, Devil's Dandy Dogs, Dimme, Dingbelle, Durgā, Dweller on the Threshold, Dybbukim, Elel, Empusa, En, Ephialtes, Erge, Ərləgan Kuba and Ərləgan Kuguza, Erlik, Estantigua, Ezú, Falm, Fene, Flibbertigibbet, Fomagata, Forcas, Forneus, Frau Welt, Freybug, Friar Rush, Gabijauja, Galla, Galley-beggar, Gandarewa, Gaueko, Gaunab, Glykon, Gong Gong, Grant, Grim, Grindylow, Guta, Gwyn ap Knudd, Haborym, Hantu Belian, Hantu B'rok, Hantu Denai, Hantu Gaharu, Hantu Gharu, Hantu Longgok, Hantu Raya, Hantu Ribut, Hantu Rimba, Hantu Sawan, Hantu Si Buru, Hantu Songkei, Hāriti, Hayagriva, Hedammu, Herensugue, Hiranyakasipu, Hirguan, Hmin, Hotua Poro, Humbaba, Igwikalla, Ikśa Keremet, Incubus, Irdlirvirissong, Irra, Iya, Izə Nur Keremet, Jal Ümbač Kos, Jamšener, Jeršuk, Jnun, Jul Ser Kugərak, Jüštə Mužə, Kabandha, Kahausibware, Kaiamunu, Kajək Keremet, Kalu Kumāra Yaka, Kamsa, Karina, Katavi, Katzenveit, Kaukas, Kazna Peri, K'daai, Ke'lets, Ker, Kergrim, Kərtnā Bodəj, Khodumo-dumo, Khyab-pa, Kingu, Kirnis, Kiskil-lilla, Kladovik, Kmnkamtch, Kornə Bodəž, Koukoudi, Kož Jeŋ, Kož Nedək, Krampus, Kübar Kuguza, Kübar Jumal Kuguza, Kugə Aga Keremet, Kugə Jomšə, Kuge Kübar, Kugə Kurək, Kukudhi, Kul, Kulshedër, Kulshedra, Labartu, Lamaštu, Lamia, Legba, L'esak, Lha-mo, Lidérc, Lilith, Lilyi, Lioumere, Ljubi, Llamhigyn y Dwr, Llorona, Loçolico, Lolmischo, Luideag, Ma Mien, Macachera, Macardit, Mada, Mahāmāri, Mahisāsura, Malla, Malphas, Mammon, Mandarangan, Mandragora, Mani, Mara, Marchocias, Mare, Marsaba, Marsayas, Masan, Mauthe Dhoog, Mbōn, Meghamalin, Melalo, Metshaldjas, Metsik, Mimir, Mimring, Minceskro, Miru, Moros, Morozko, Mu, Munheras, Mužə, Nabaeo, Naitaka, Nalet, Namtar, Narah, Naraka, Nari, Nasu,

Nburu, Nebed, Nerge Kuba and Nerge Kuguza, Ngworekara, Nicker, Nidhöggr, Nightmare, Niu T'ou, Nivashi, Nočnitsa, Nol Jeŋ, Norg, Nunyunuwi, Obda, Old Man of the Sea, Ondichaouan, Orobas, Oschaert, Pahuanuiapitaaiterai, Paltəkan, Panchajana, Pazuzu, Pekoi, Pəl Ner, Pelə Kolšə, Phi, Piasa, Picus, Podarge, Pontianak, Poreskoro, Potan'Ka, Pskégdemus, Putana, Qandiša, Qat, Rahu, Ravana, Raw Head and Bloody Bones, Rongeur d' Os, Ronwe, Rübezahl, Sahte, Sakhr, Sarkany, Schilalyi, Seiktha, Šert Bodəz, Sheela-na-gig, Shellycoat, Shilalyi, Si Raya, Siho I Salo, Silat, Siltim, Skadegamutc, Smiera-Gatto, Smolenkos, Srei ap, Stihi, Stolas, Stomach-slasher, Šükšəndal, Sultan, Sürem Mužə, Surt Mələndə Bodəz, Sut, Tangie, Tauru, Tçaridyi, Tçulo, Terrytop, Tir, Tira, Tom Tit Tot, Tom Titivil, Tom Tumbler, Topielec, Torto, Toštot Jeŋ, Tranca Rua, Tuchulcha, Tuma Düŋ Keremet, Tupan, Ullikummi, Urobach, Vanth, Vaotere, Vatak, Veles, Verbti, Verdelet, Vetāla, Vizi-anya, Vizi-ember, Vritra, Vu-murt, Vu-vozo, Vucub-Caquix, Walutahanga, Wokolo, Xuda Sila, Yankimurt, Yaotl, Yeitso, Zaebos, Zagam, Zalambur, Zar, Zepar, Zin, Zloi Dukh

3. DEVILS
Devil: Alternative Spellings

De'el, Deevil, Deil, Del/e, Delve, Deofel, Deofel/l, Deoffel, Deofie, Deoful, Deouel, Deovel, Deul, Deuyl/le, Devel/e, Devell/e, Devill, Devle, Devyl/le, Dewelle, Dewile, Dewle, Diefel, Dievel/e, Difle, Dijevel, Diobul, Dioful, Dioul, Diowl, Diowul, Divel, Divill, Divul, Diwl, Doul, Dule, Dwylle, Dyevel, Dyevle, Dyvell

Individual Names

Aatxe, Abaddan, Abbey Lubber, Abonsam, Aërico, Agas, Aiatar, Akaanga, Ako-Mano, Amaimon, Asasel, Asmodee, Auld Clootie, Auld Hornie, Auld Scratty, Azren, Bakš Ia, Beelzebub, Belial, Belias, Belphegor, Beng, B'es, Bes, Büt Ia, Büt Ian Üdəržə, Büt Imnə, Carrean, Carrivean, Čembulat, Chert, Chertovka, Čort, Čurpan Šərt, Cythraul, Dævas, Davy Jones, Diablotin, Diavol, Diawl, Djall, Eprem Kuguza, Fallen Angels, Familiar, Fiend, Gogol, Gong Gong, Gressil, Gwr-drwgiaid, Hiisi, Hodge, Ia, Ia Kuba and Ia Kuguza, Ia Saltak, Imp, Iuvart, Izə Nur Keremet, Jabol, Jack up the Orchut, Jersey Devil, Jocoo, Joškar Ser, Juods, Kazna Peri, Keremet, Kugə Aga Keremet, Kulshedër, Kurək Ia, Leeds Devil, Leviathan, Lucifer, Lucky Devil, Makar, Mammon, Mələndə Šərt, Mephistophales, Merihim, Moča Kuba, Moča Šərt, Mükš Šərt, Nalet, Nerge Kuba, Ngworekara, Nur Bodəž, Oeillet, Old Nick, Orobas, Paija, Paravoj Ia, Paškače, Potan'Ka, Pytho, Rosier, Šajtan, Samael, Satan, Šert Bodəz, Shēdîm, Sonneillon, Stolas, Supay, Toktal Poškudə, Uda, Urobach, Utukku, Velnias, Verrier, Verrine, Wokolo, Wryneck, Xiang Yao, Ysbryd drwg, Zloi Dukh

4. DWARFS
Alternative Spellings
Dorch, Droich, Duerch/e, Duergh, Dueri, Duery, Duerz, Duorow, Durwe, Dwaeruh, Dwargh/e, Dwarw, Dwearf, Dweorh, Dweorz, Dwerf/e, Dwerff/e, Dwergh, Dwerk, Dwerowe, Dweruf, Dweruz, Dwerwe, Dwerwh/e, Dwery, Dwerz/e, Dwrf/e

Names of Groups
Alp, Apci'lnic, Apopa, Apuku, Berg People, Chanques, Coranians, Dasyus, Derricks, Duende, Duergar, Elemental, Gahongas, Ganas, Gandayaks, Gardsvor, Grig, Haus-Schmiedlein, Karliki, Korrigan, Kurək Ia, Lovar, Napfhans, Oakmen, Ohdowas, Polevik, Riesengebirge, Spriggans, Stille Volk, Troll, Water Babies, Yakshi, Yakshini

Names of Individuals
Addanc, Afanc, Alberich, Alvis, Andvari, Bali, Bes, Bibung, Biloko, Brock, Brown Man of the Muirs, Cacy taperere, Couril, Dain, Davalin, Durin, Elbgast, Erdleute, Fjalar, Hind Etin, Ilmarinen, Iwaldi, King Goldmar, Kubera, Laurin, Leprechaun, Lit, Luchtaine, Massariol, Mimring, Modsognir, Monociello, Naglfar, Nain, Nain Rouge, Nibelung, Oberon, Pacolet, Pail Pak, Regin, Rübezahl, Rumpelstiltskin, Shyshok, Telchines, Terrytop, Thekkr, Tikdoshe, el Trasgu, Uhlakanyana, Vai-Mahse, Vamana, Völund/r, Wayland Smith

5. ENCANTADOS
Groups and "Families"
Badé, Caboclos, Curupira, Exus, Falange de Bôtos, Farrista, Japetequara, João de Mata, Jurema, Ogun, Orixá, Oxossi, Pretos Velhos, Seu Gavião (Means: the Hawk), Sueira, Turcos or Turquia

Individual Names
Akosa-Sapata, Akossi-Sapata, Ana Joaquima, Angacino, Averekete, Averekitano, Barão de Goré, Basilio Bom, Belo Encanto, Ben Boçu da Cana Verde, Biranan, Boiadeiro da Visaura, Bombiero, Bôto Araçu, Bôto Branco, Bôto Castanho, Bôto Preto, Bôto Tucuxí, Bôto Vermelho, Cabocla Tartaruga de Amazonas, Cabocla Roxa, Caboclo Nobre, Caboclo Pemba, Caboquinho, Capingueiro, Capingueiro de Jurema, Cibiru, Ciganina, Codoésa da Trinidade, Conceição Sueira, Constantino, Cosme, Curupira-airara, Curupira Chica Baiana, Curupira Piriri, Damião, Dom Carlos, Dom João Sueira, Dom José, Dom Luiz, Dom Pedro Angaço, Dona Dada, Dona Ina, Dona Rosalina, Dorada Mata, Dorina, Dur Encanto, Esmerelda Edite, Exu, Exu-Mirim, Fina Joia, Flechiera, Flechiero, Flor do ceu, Flor do mar, Flor do nuvems, Flor do ouro, Flor do vinho, Floriano, Floriope, Folha Seca, Goiabeira, Gorézinho, Guapindaia, Guerriero, Guia, Guido, Imanja, Inambé, Inhaçan, Ita, Itapaquara, Itaquara, Itaquari, Jacitaria, Jaguarema, Jamaína, Jandira, Japetequara, Jarina,

Jatórana, João da Lima, João de Mata, João de Ouro, João Fama, Joãozinho, Joãozinho Sueira, Joaquimzinho Boa da Trinidade, José Raimundo Boa da Trinidade, José Tupinambá, Juçara, Junquiera, Juracema, Jurema Velha, Juremeia, Jureminha, Juruwa, Laurencina, Laurencino, Legua Bogi da Trinidade, Leovergio Sueira, Manoelzinho Boa da Trinidade, Mariana, Mariano, Menina Daleira, Menino Agudui, Mensageiro da Roma, Miguelzinho Boa da Trinidade, Mirací, Mirian, Moça da Guia, Nan Burocô, Nilo Fama, Noxinina, Ogun, Ogun Beira-Mar, Ogun de Ronda, Ogun Sete Ondas, Ogun-iara, Ogun-mergê, Oxossi, Oxun, Pai Benedito, Pai Jeronimo, Pai Tomas, Parajito, Paranguaçu, Pedro Estrelo, Pena Verde, Pindá, Pindaié, Pomba Gira, Princesa d' Alva, Princesa Sinha Bê, Princessa Dora, Princessa Flora, Principe de Espanha (Farrista) Pequenino, Rainha Barba, Rainha Eowa, Rainha Oyá, Rei de Nagô, Rei Noé, Rei Sebastião, Rei Solomão, Rei Taculumi, Rei Toi Aduça, Rei Turquia, Rompe Mato, Rondado, Sebastino, Senhora Ana, Sentinella, Sete Encruzilhados, Sete Flechas, Seu Jurema, Siriaki, Tabajara, Tanbacê, Tangó do Pará, Tapinaré, Tiriri, Toia Navéroaim, Tranca Rua, Ubirajara, Ubiratan, Urubatan Jesus, Xangô, Zezinho, Zizué

6. FAIRIES
Alternative Spellings of Fairy
Faerie, Fai, Faierie, Faiery, Fair, Fairye, Farie, Fary, Fay, Fayerie, Fayery, Fayry, Fée, Feiri, Fery, Fey Feyrie, Feyrye, Phairie, Pharie, Pherie, (From the Latin: Fata "Fates")

Individual Names by Country or Culture
Albanian:
Bukura e dheut

Australian:
Bib, Bub, Chucklebud, Cuddlepie, Narnywo, Nittersing, Ragged Blossom, Snugglepot

Chinese:
Chih Nü, Chu Pa-Chiai

Danish:
Ole Luk Øj, Snow Queen

English:
Ainsel, Ariel, Asrai, Brother Mike, Cobweb, Drop, Elaby Gathan, Gill, Godda, Green Knight, Grim, Habetrot, Habonde, Hobgoblin, Hop, Im, Lady of the Lake, Licke, Lull, Mab (Empress), Malekin, Micol, Mop, Morgan le Fée, Moth, Mrs. Bedonebyasyoudid, Mrs. Doasyouwouldbedoneby, Mustard-seed, Nanny-Button-Cap, Nit, Nymphidia, Oberon (King/Emperor), Oreande la Fée, Ouphe, Patch, Pease Blossom, Periwinckle, Perriwiggin, Pigwidgeon, Pillywiggin, Pin, Pinch, Pink, Pip, Puck, Quick, Sib, Skilly Widden, Skip, Thrummy Cap, Tib, Tick, Tit, Titania (Queen), Tomalin, Tom

Thumb, Tooth Fairy, Trip, Tryamor, Tub, Wap, Win, Yallery Brown

French:
Béfind, Ben Socia, Cannered Noz, Couril, Dormette, Mallebron, Melusine

German:
Bažaloshtsh, Frau Holle, Frau Welt, Virginal

Hungarian:
Baba, Dame Hirip, Dame Jenö, Dame Rampson, Dame Vénétur, Fairy Helen, Mika, Tündér

Irish:
Aengus, Aillen Mac Midhna, Ainé, Aine, Alp Luachra, Amadán, Angus Og, Aoibhinn, Aynia, Banshee, Cliodna, Credné, Dagda, Fear Dearc, Finvarra, Gan Ceanach, Girle Guairle, Leanan-sidhe, Macha, Mebd, Midar, Niamh, Nuala, Onagh, Sabdh

Irish-American, USA:
Tom Cockle

Italian:
Befana, Blue Fairy, Fata Morgana

Manx, Isle of Man (United Kingdom):
Lhiannan-shee

Orcadian (Orkney Islands, United Kingdom):
Peerifool

Romany Gypsy:
Ana

Scottish:
Fittletot, Glaistig, Klippie, Loireag, Peter Pan, Tinkerbelle, Whoopity Stoorie, Wilkie

Serbian:
Oosood, Raviyoyla Djins

Slav and Rumanian:
Muma Padura

Welsh:
Gofannon, Gwyn ap Nudd, Jili Ffrwtan, Sili Ffrit, Sili-go-dwt, Trwtyn-Tratyn

Euphemistic Names for Fairies
Ad-hene (Themselves, Isle of Man, United Kingdom); Bediadari (The Good People, Malaysia); Ben Socia (Good Neighbours, France); Bendith y Mamau (Mother's Blessing, Glamorgan, Wales); Bonnes Dames (Good Ladies, France); Cloan ny Moyrn (Children of Pride, Isle of Man, United Kingdom); The Crowd (Isle of Man, United Kingdom); Daoine Maite (The Good People, Ireland); Dyon Bach Teg (The Little Fair Folk, Dyfed, Wales); Feriers or Ferishers (Suffolk, England); Ferish or Ferishyn (Isle of Man, United Kingdom); Ferries (Shetland and Orkney Islands, United Kingdom); The Gentry (Ireland); The Good Neighbours (Scottish Lowlands); Green Coaties (Lincolnshire and the Fens, England); The Greenies (Lancashire, England); Guillyn Beggey, ny (The Little Boys, Isle of Man, United Kingdom); Lil Fellas (Isle of Man, United Kingdom); Mawmets (England); The Mob Beg (Isle of Man, United Kingdom); Muryans (Ants, Cornwall, England); Nos Bonnes Mèes (Our Good Mothers, France); The Old People (Cornwall, England); Orang Bunyian (Malaysia); The People of the Hills (England); Plant Rhys Ddwfn (Children of Rhys Ddwfn, Dyfed, Wales); Sleeth Ma (People of Peace, Scottish Highlands and Ireland); The Small People (Cornwall, England); The Strangers (England); The Tidy Ones (England); Tylwyth Teg (The Fair Family, Wales); The Wee Folk (Scotland and Ireland)

7. FALLEN ANGELS
Names
Abbadon, Abdiel, Adramelech, Angel Oliver, Arioch, Asasel, Asmodaios, Asmodee, Asmodeus, Astaroth, Azael, Azazel, Azazil, Baalzebub, Baalzebul, Balberith, Beelzebub, Beelzebul, Belial, Belias, Belphegor, Belsabub, Belsabubbe, Belsebub, Carrean, Carrivean, Gressil, Hares, Harut and Marut, Iblis, Iuvart, Karliki, Lucifer, Marchocias, Mastêmâ, Oeillet, Olivier, Rosier, Samael, Satan, Semjâzâ, Shemyaza, Sonneillon, Verrier, Verrine

Others Linked
Blue Men of the Minch, Cacodæmon, Devils, Djinns, Fairies, Fir Chlis, Karliki, Peri, Selkies, the Slaugh (see also Devils)

8. FAMILIARS' NAMES
Names from Reports of British Witch Trials
Elizabeth Bennet: Lizerd (red lion), Sickin (dog)
Elizabeth Clark (Matthew Hopkins 1647): Holt (kitten), Jamara (spaniel), News (polecat), Sack and Sugar (rabbit), Vinegar Tom (dog)
Elizabeth Device, Lancashire 1613: Ball (dog)
Isobel Gowdie, Scotland 1662: Makhector, Robert the Rule, Rorie, Swein
Ursula Kempe, St. Osyth 1582: Jack (cat), Pigin (toad), Tittey (cat), Tyffin (lamb)
Alice Samuel, Warboys 1593: Catch, Puck, White
Ellen Smith, Chelmsford 1597: Great Dick, Little Dick, Willet
Mother Agnes Waterhouse, Chelmsford 1597: Sathan (cat)

Other Reported Names
Abrahel, Blackman, Dunsott (dog), Elemanzer, Greedigut, Grissel, Grizzle, Ilemangar, Jezobel, Lightfoot (cat), Lizabet, Lunch (toad), Maitre Persil, Makeshift (weasel), Martinet, Pekin the Crow, Pyewacket, Pygine (mole), Russell (cat), Tissy, Verd Joli, Verdelet

9. KEREMET
Aga Kurman, Azren, Čembulat, Čopakin, Čort, Čurpan Šərt, Eprem Kuguza, Ibaśka, Ikśa Keremet, Izə Nur Keremet, Jal Ümbač Kośtśə Keremet, Jalχter Bodəz, Jamšener, Jauš Keremet, Joškar Ser, Jučuzo, Jul Ser Kugərak, Kajək Keremet, Karman Kurək Kuguza, Keremet Šərt, Kərtnā Bodəz, Kož Jeŋ, Kübar Jumal Kuguza, Kübar Kuguza, Kugə Aga Keremet, Kugə Jomšə, Kuge Kübar, Kugə Kurək, Kuplaŋgaš, Kurək Kuga Jeŋ, Kurək Kuguza, Kurək Piambar, Kurək Šərt, Lemdə Kurək Kuguza, Makar, Məlandə Bodəz, Məlandə Šərt, Moča Šərt, Mükš Šərt, Nemdə Kurək Kugə, Nemdə Kurək Kuguza, Nerge Kuba and Nerge Kuguza, Nol Jeŋ, Nur Bodəž, Oš Buj Vanuška, Pajberda Šərt, Paltəkan, Pört Bodəz, Rok Šərt, Šerdəš Šərt, Serekan Keremet, Šert Bodəz, Šert Terkan, Škenan Določəmə Keremet and Ške Keremet, Sultan, Surt Məlandə Bodəz, Toktal Poškudə, Toštə Kož Jeŋ, Toštot Jeŋ, Tul Bodəz, Tul Bodəz Təlmaze, Tuma Düŋ Keremet, Turek Kuguza, Undur Šərt, Vanuška

10. NATS
Akakasoh, Boomasoh, Chinün Way Shun, Chitōn, Eingsaung, Hkum Yeng, Hmin, Jān, Ka, La, Lu, Mbōn, Mu, Nat Thami, Phi, Ponphyoi, Saba-Leippya, Shingrawa, Shitta, Sinlap, Thein, Trikurat, Upaka, Wāwn

11. NYMPHS
Group by Domain

Air:
Sylphs

Arts:
Muses

Meadows and Valleys:
Auloniads, Limoniades, Naphæ

Mountains and Caves:
Kollimalaikanniyarka, Oreads

Paradise:
Devas, Gandharvas, Houri, Huran

Prophesy:
Carmenæ

Stars:
Anitsutsa, Atlantides, Hesperides, Hyades, Pleiades

Trees and Woods:
Alsaieds, Dryads, Hamadryads, Hylæoræ, Meliades, Moss Maidens, Napææ

Water:
Apsaras, Crenæ, Limenia, Limnæ, Naiads, Nereids, Oceanids, Pagæ, Suire, Undine

Names of Individual Nymphs
Abarbarea, Adrastea, Affric, Aganippe, Ægina, Ægle, Alcyone, Amáltheia, Ambrosia, Amphithoe, Amphitrite, Antiope, Arethusa, Argyra, Asia, Asteropea, Britomartis, Calliope, Callisto, Calypso, Carmenta, Cassotis, Castalia, Celœno, Chelone, Chih Nü, Clytie, Coronis, Corycia, Cyane, Cymodoce, Cymothoe, Cyrene, Daphne, Diuturna, Doris, Dryope, Echenais, Echo, Egeria, Electra, Erytheia, Erythesis, Eudora, Galatea, Hagno, Hesperesthusa, Huldra, Lara, Lodona, Lotis, Maia, Marica, Melobosis, Memphis, Menara, Mera, Merope, Muma Padura, Myréne, Neda, Nimüe, Oenone, Orithyia, Ouphe, Pirene, Pitys, Salmacis, Smilax, Staphyle, Sterope, Styx, Syrinx, Taygete, Thetis, Thisoa

12. SPIRITS ASSOCIATED WITH ANIMALS AND OTHER CREATURES (PROTECTING, DESTROYING, OR MANIFESTING AS CREATURES)
Benevolent Toward Creatures or Humans
Agloolik, Aiwel, Anansi, Anpiel, Aralez, Ariā, As-iga, Aumanil, Basajaun, Biča Ia, Biča Kuba, Biča Kuguza, Biča Oza, Bonito Maidens, Brown Man of the Muirs, Browney, Cailleach Bheur, Callisto, Chanques, Church Grim, Čodra Kuba and Čodra Kuguza, Coquena, Cyrene, Devil Fish People, Dobie, Falange de Bôtos, Fantine, Faun, Field Spirit, Fylgir, Gandayaks, Gandharvas, Genius, Gid-murt, Grant, Grim, Gwillion, Haferbocks, Hantu Belian, Hantu Songkei, Huasa Mallcu, Hyter Sprites, Jer Kuba and Jer Kuguza, Jūrasmāte, Kahausibware, Kajək Keremet, Kinnara, Kirkegrim, Kirkogrim, Kokopölö, Korneböcke, Kornwolf, Kremara, Krukis, Kudə Ört Kuba and Kudə Ört Kuguza, Kul-jungk, Kurinyi Bog, Kurwaichin, Laskowice, Lauko Sargas, Laukumāte, Leib-Olmai, Leshii, Liekkiö, Luot-Chozjik, Mahisāsura, Marét, Mehen, Melobosis, Merrow, Mežasmāte, Näkineiu, Näkinneito, Ningyo, Nootaikok, Nur Kuba and Nur Kuguza, Ohdowas, Pena Verde, Peseias, Priparchis, Ratainitsa, Rigai, Roane, Rye Dog, Sand Altar

Woman, Seal Maidens, Sedna, Selkies, Sileni, Swan Maiden, Syen, Tangó do Pará, Tatane, Trikurat, Trows, Tua, Tuktoriak, Undine, Vai-Mahse, Vohu Mano, Walgino

Malevolent or Tricksy

Aeshma, Asəra, Aufhocker, Bad Hour, Barguest, Black Dog, Black Shuck, Black Vaughan, Buber, Buckland Shag, Buggane, Büt Ia, Büt Imnə, Cabyll-Ushtey, Capelthwaite, Ce Sith, Cearb, Ceffyll-dŵr, Charon, Chasse d' Hérode, Cheval Bayard, Chlevnik, Chu Pa-Chiai, Colt Pixy, Cowlug Sprites, Coyote, Cu Sith, Curupira, Cwn Annwn, Dakini, Deev, Devil's Dandy Dogs, Djin, Druggen Hill Boggle, Dunnie, Eač Uisge, Empusa, Exotica, Familiar Spirit, Fiend, Foliots, Freybug, Friar Rush, Furies, Gabble Retchets, Gabriel Hounds, Galley-trot, Gaueko, Glashtin, Gytrash, Harpy, Hayagriva, Hedley Kow, Hu Hsien, Imdugud, Kaia, Kappa, Karina, Kelpie, Kimprushas, Kludde, Korrigan, Kratt, Lazy Laurence, Llamhigyn y Dwr, Lubin, Ma Mien, Maezt-Dar l' Oudou, Mauthe Dhoog, Mekala, Melalo, Mermaid, Merman, Metsik, Mink, Moros, Näkk, Nari, Neck, Neugle, Nicker, Niu T'ou, Nix, Nøkk, Oats Goat, Obe, Oni, Oschaert, Ovinnik, Padfoot, Para, Pasuk, Peri, Plat-eye, Podarge, Pooka, Poreskoro, Qiqirn, Rakshasas, Rizos, Rongeur d' Os, Satyr, Schilalyi, Se'irim, Seven Whistlers, Shag Foal, Shock, Siren, Skriker, Slaugh, Strigæ, Tangie, Ten-gu, Urchin, Urisk, Utukku, Vadatjas, Víly, Vodianoi, Wakanï, Wild Hunt, Wisht Hounds, Yakkhas, Yech, Yeth Hounds

13. SPIRITS ASSOCIATED WITH ASTRONOMY AND THE CELESTIAL WORLD

Albastor, Alcyone, Anitsutsa, Anunnaki, Apep, Apo, Arathron, Archangel, Ariā, Ariel, Asa Vahista, Asteropea, Atlantides, Azaziel, Balam, Bethor, Celœno, Cherruve, Chih Nü, Chu Pa-Chiai, Cihuateteo, Dævas, Electra, Fa, Gabriel, Hagith, Hesperides, Hyades, Ilogo, Kafziel, Le-Gerem, Lucifer, Maia, Mehen, Menara, Merope, Michael, Mikak'e, Nakshastras, Nehebkau, Nemissa, Och, Olympian Spirits, Ophiel, Phul, Pleiades, Rahu, Raphael, Sarkany, Sebettu, Shitta, Star People, Star Woman, Sylphs, Thien, Titania, Vasus, Vucub-Caquix, Yazatas

14. SPIRITS ASSOCIATED WITH THE CREATIVE ARTS

Art, Literature, Music, Poetry

Apsaras, Ariel, Bes, Cairpré, Chin Chia, Daktyloi, Erotes, Fairies, Fossegrim, Gandharvas, Gendang and Naubat (Sang Gala Raja), Graces, Houri, Israfel, Jin Nemfiri, Kingmingoarkulluk, Leanan-sidhe, Lempiri, Loireag, Marsayas, Muses, Nicker, Nuŋuí, Nymph, Patu-paiarehe, Satyr, Sleigh Beggey, Stolas, Strömkarl,

Syrinx, Trows, Tuatha dé Danann, Tündér, Tylwyth Teg, Veela

Metal Work, Pottery, Spinning, Weaving, Woodwork

Berchta, Black Spider Old Woman, Brock, Chih Nü, Clay Mother, Deive, Domikha, Fates, Girle Guairle, Gofannon, Goibhleann, Goibniu, Gwarwyn-a-Throt, Habetrot, Hag, Holle, Ilmarinen, Keshalyi, Kikimora, Kotyangwuti, Laumé, Luchtaine, Moss Folk, Naste Estsan, Nuŋuí, Peerifool, Perchta, Regin, Rumpelstiltskin, Spider Grandmother, Spider Man, Spider Woman, Spinnstubenfrau, Terrytop, Tom Tit Tot, Tomtar, Tomte Gubbe, Völund/r, Wayland Smith, Whoopity Stoorie

15. SPIRITS ASSOCIATED WITH CORN AND GRAIN

Ahren konigen, Babban ny Mheillea, Bullkater, Cailleac, Cailleach bera, Carlin, Corn Mother, Deohako, Gabijauja, The Granny, Haferbocks, Hag, Idəm Kuba and Idəm Kuguza, John Barleycorn, Kaboutermannekin, Kachina, Katcina Mana, Kerwan, Korneböcke, Kornmutter, Kornwolf, Kuršis, Morkul Kua Luan, Müy'ingwa, Nesaru, Oats Goat, Onatah, Ruginis, Rugiu Boba, Rye Dog, Saba-Leippya, Sara-Mama, Selu, Turquoise Boy, Turquoise Man, Uti Hiata, Wrach, Yumis

16. SPIRITS ASSOCIATED WITH DEATH, HADES, HELL, AND THE UNDERWORLD

Abaddan, Abigor, Akaanga, Alicanto, Amaimon, Ammit, Apollyon, Ashmedai, Astaroth, Astō Vidātu, Asurakumāra, Azrael, Azren, Baalberith, Baalzaphon, Babi, Bael, Bali, Ban Nighechain, Banshee, Barguest, Basajaun, Bathym, Bean Nighe, Ben Varrey, Black Dog, Black Shuck, Bloody Cap, Blue Men of the Minch, Bodach, Bodach Glas, Bodua, Büt Ia, Caointeach, Cauld Lad of Gilsland, Ceffyll-dŵr, Chanques, Charon, Charontes, Charos, Charun, Chasse d' Hérode, Chitragupta, Church Grim, Chutsain, Colo-Colo, Čort, Culsu, Cwn Annwn, Dain, Dando and His Dogs, Davy Jones, Demogorgon, Devil, Dis, Di-Zang, Elel, Fad Felen, Fallen Angels, Falm, Fauni Ficari, Fiend, Furies, Fylgir, Gabriel, Gabriel Hounds, Gan Ceanach, Géde, gNyan, Grim, Grindylow, Gwrach y Rhibyn, Gytrash, Hakel-Bärend, Hantu Si Buru, Havfrue, Herlethingus, Herne the Hunter, Holle, Hu Hsien, Ia, Iguma, Irā-Kewa, Jenny Greenteeth, Joint Eater, Kajis, Kamang, Kanaima, Kelpie, Ker, Keremet, Kikimora, L'esak, Lau, Lhiannan-shee, Liwa, Llorona, Lorelei, Luideag, Ma Mien, Macachera, Macha, Malik, Malphas, Manes, Mantus and Mania, Mara, Marchocias, Marsaba, Matagaigai, Matiya, Mephistophales, Mermaid, Mesnie Hellequin, Mieg Moulach, Miru, Monker and Nakir, Muileatach, Nain, Näkk, Näkki, Nalet, Namtar, Neman, Ngworekara,

Nidhogg, Niu T'ou, Nix, Oni, Orobas, Ouda, Paija, Pey, Pray, Psychopompos, Rakshasas, Raw Head and Bloody Bones, Saja, Samael, Sangmun, Seven Whistlers, Shai, Silat, Siren, Skriker, Slaugh, Snow Queen, Srei ap, Sri, Stolas, Tigbanua, Tisiphone, Tom Titivil, Tuchulcha, Udur, Valkyries, Vanth, Veela, Víly, Vodianoi, Wakanï, Walumbe, White Lady, Wild Hunt, Will the Smith, Wu Ch'ang Kuei, Yambe-akka, Zagaz

17. SPIRITS ASSOCIATED WITH DISEASE

Acheri, Aerika, Agas, Äi, Aiatar, Akhkhazzu, Akossi-Sapata, Al, Alardi, Albastor, Alfar, Alp, Amadán, Anchancho, Ariā, Asag, Asəra, Ashakku, Ayerico, Bad Hour, Badjang, Bitoso, Black Shuck, Bori, Buber, Büt Bodəž, Cauld Lad of Gilsland, Čembulat, Chanques, Chisin Tongbŏp, Cihuateteo, Colo-Colo, Con-Ma-Dāu, Coyote, Dala Kadavara, Demon, Dimme, Dogai, Elel, Elf, Elle Folk, Ərləgan Kuba and Ərləgan Kuguza, Fad Felen, Fallen Angels, gNyan, Hantu Kayu, Hantu Longgok, Hantu Si Buru, Hocereu Wahira, Hongaek, Huecuvu, Igwikalla, Imdugud, Irra, Iya, Jaljogini, Jamšener, Jer Kuba and Jer Kuguza, Jüštə Mužə, Jüštə Mužə Üdər, Kala, Kalu Kumāra Yaka, Kanaima, Karina, Ker, Keremet, Kliwa, Koukoudi, Lamaštu, Lha-mo, Lilyi, Lolmischo, Lu, Ma-Mo, Macachera, Masan, Mekala, Mekumwasuk, Melalo, Minceskro, Moksin Tongbŏp, Mužə, Nagual, Namtar, Nanggu Moksin, Nasu, Nats, Nerge Kuba and Nerge Kuguza, Nočnitsa, Ondichaouan, Oni, Pazuzu, Peg o' Nell, Penanggalan, Phi, Piśācas, Pishumi, Poreskoro, Pört Kuba and Pört Kuguza, Putana, Qiqirn, Rakshasas, Ruach, Run Kuba and Run Kuguza, Sal, Sangmun, Sao, Schilalyi, Sebettu, Šedra Kuba and Šedra Kuguza, Slaugh, Tçaridyi, Tçulo, Tiddy Ones, Tigbanua, Tongbŏp, Tou Shen, Tuma Düŋ Keremet, Umot, Utukku, Wakanï, Walichu, Y Wrach, Yanki-murt, Zagaz

18. SPIRITS ASSOCIATED WITH FIELDS AND VEGETATION
Good or Benign

Aga Kurman, Ahren Konigen, Ameretat, Appletree Man, Aramaiti, Babban ny Mheillea, Bhairon, Bullkater, Burryman, Cailleac, Carlin, Corn Spirit, Datan, Deohako, Dryad, Er Tütra, Fantine, Faun, Flower Fairy, Gabijauja, G'an, Gandharvas, Genius, Granny, Green Knight, Green Man, Grig, Gunna, Gyhldeptis, Haferbocks, Hunessai, Huntin, Idəm Kuba and Idəm Kuguza, Jack-in-the-Green, Kirnis, Korneböcke, Kornmutter, Kornwolf, Kricco, Kugə Aga Keremet, Kuršis, Lauko Sargas, Laukumāte, Lawkapatim, Liekkiö, Lilim, Limoneads, Liu-Meng Chiang-Chün, Lotis, Lugovnik, Marzanna, Müy'ingwa, Nampa, Nuŋuí, Nur Bodəž, Nur Kuba and Nur Kuguza, Oats Goat, Old Roger, Onatah, Pasu, Phi, Ruginis, Rugiu Boba, Saba-

Leippya, Sara-Mama, Shoney, Šurnə, Tachuki, Turquoise Boy, Turquoise Man, Xanas, Yarthkins, Yumis, Žemepatis, Žemyna

Cautionary

Awd Goggie, Bilberry Man, Dame Ellerhorn, Elder Mother, Gooseberry Wife, Hylde-Moer, Hyldemoder, Hylde-Vinde, Lazy Laurence, Mandragora, Polevik, Rübezahl

Destructive

Agun Kuguza, Bilwis, Cailleach Bheur, Ccoa, Curupira, Dogai, Formorian, Ia Kuba and Ia Kuguza, Izə Nur Keremet, Ljubi, Makar, Mekala, Peg o' Nell, Pəl Ner, Peri, Pokšem Kuba, Pokšem Kuguza and Pokšem Obəska, Poludnica, Spriggans, Strätelli, Strudeli, Tiddy Mun

19. SPIRITS ASSOCIATED WITH FORESTS, WOODS, TREES, AND WOOD
Forest/Woods

Abiku, Äi, Aiatar, Alan, Albastor, Alicanto, Alsaieds, Anhanga, Arapteš, Ataman, Aziza, Baba Yaga, Basajaun, Beng, Betikhân, Bhut, Bilberry Man, Bockmann, Bonga, Boraro, Caypór, Chanques, Charlot, Chûtâs, Čodra Kuba and Čodra Kuguza, Cuélebre, Curupira, Dirneweibl, Dryad, Dúc-Bà, Dziwitza, Elves, Erl King, Father Frost, Faun, Forest Folk, Gamainhas, Ghillie Dhu, Giráitis, Gorska Makua, Green Man, Grønjette, Grove Folk, Gübich, Hantu Bakal, Hantu Hutan, Hantu Rimba, Hantu Si Buru, Hea-Bani, Herecgunina, Herok'a, Hesperides, Hiisi, Hmin, Hodekin, Holz-frau, Huldra, Humbaba, Hylæoræ, Igwikalla, Jennie of Biggersdale, Jin Tanah, Kaitorak, Katzenveit, Keltəmaš, Kožla Kuba and Kožla Kuguza, Laskowice, Lau, Leib-Olmai, L'esak, Leshii, Lesovikha, Löfjerskor, Mala'ikat Puteh, Mamagwasewug, Mat Chinoi, Medeine, Mekumwasuk, Meliades, Metsänhaltia, Metsanneitsyt, Metshaldjas, Metsik, Mežasmāte, Miehts-Hozjin, Migamamesus, Mimring, Mingehe, Mmoatia, Modeina, Moss Folk, Muma Padura, Napææ, Nburu, Nimüe, Nules-murt, Obda, Oberon, One with the White Hand, Orang Bunyi, Ouda, Paltəkan, Patu-paiarehe, Phi, Picus, Piśācas, Pukkumeria, Pulch, Rüezahl, Rusalka, Salgfräulein, Salvanelli, Saraua, Sasabonsam, Satyr, Shamantin, Sicksa, Siliniets, Siltim, Skadegamutc, Skogs Fru, Smolenkos, Spae-wives, Strakh, Strätelli, Strudeli, Swan Maiden, Ten-gu, Toštə Kož Jeŋ, Tras, Tuulikki, Vyantaras, Waldgeister, Wood Folk, Wood Wives, Yakkhas

Trees

Aërico, Akakasoh, Ameretat, Appletree Man, Apsaras, Àràk, Askafroa, Awd Goggie, Bariaua, Baumesel, Biloko, Bilwis, Bisan, Bitâbohs, Boomasoh, Boruta, Co-Hon, Con-Tinh, Čurpan Šərt, Curupira, Daphne, Dewas,

(continued) **APPENDIX 19**

Dodore, Dom Carlos, Dryad, Dryope, Dyombie, Elder Mother, Elle Folk, Eschenfrau, Fa, Fauni Ficari, Frau Wachholder, gNyan, Gyhldeptis, Hamadryad, Hantu Gaharu, Hantu Gharu, Hantu Kayu, Herne the Hunter, Huntin, Hylde-Moer, Hylde-Vinde, Jarina, Jurema, Kakamora, Kakua, Kaluks, Kambuzi, Kirnis, Lilim, Lunantishee, Matagaigai, Melsh Dick, Mura Mura, Myréne, Narbrooi, Niägriusar, Norg, Oakmen, Old Lady of the Elder Tree, Old Roger, Ombwiri, Pitys, Pray, Pret, Rå, Sankchinnis, Seiktha, Shekkasoh, Smilax, Ten-gu, Vanadevatas, Vaotere, Vrikshakas, Waldgeister, Wokolo

Wood

Hantu Gaharu, Hantu Gharu, Moksin Tongbŏp, Nanggu Moksin

20. SPIRITS ASSOCIATED WITH FORTUNE, LUCK, AND TREASURE

Aitvaras, Alberich, Alicanto, Andvari, Apsaras, Bannik, Ben Varrey, Black Dog, Brownie, Cluricaun, Cuélebre, Domovik, Ekkekko, Ellyllon, Fates, Fear Dearc, Feriers, Fire Drake, Gou Mang, Guardian, Hamingja, Hinzelmann, Hu Hsien, Kaukas, Kazna Peri, Kazna Šuča, Treasure Angel, Kladovik, Kratt, Kudeiar, Landvættir, Lar, Leprechaun, Lesovikha, Macachera, Mājas gars, Monociello, Nagual, Niägriusar, Nibelung, Nis, Piambar, Piskey, Pört Kuba and Pört Kuguza, Pukis, Rugiu Boba, Silky, Spriggans, Šrat, Stihi, Tomtar, Tonttu, Tonx, Troll, Trows, Tylwyth Teg, Vittora, White Lady, Will o' the Wisp, Yakkhas

21. SPIRITS ASSOCIATED WITH GUARDIANSHIP AND PROTECTION

Abgal, Aeolus, Agathos Daimon, Agloolik, Aikren, Alan, Alardi, Ameretat, Andvari, Angiris, Anpiel, Apo, Àràk, Aramaiti, Arariel, Ariā, Ariel, Arifa, As-iga, Askafroa, Attendant Spirit, Aumanil, Awd Goggie, Axeki, Bakš Ia, Balam, Barqu, Béfind, Bes, Bethor, Bhairon, Bibung, Biča Ia, Biča Kuba and Biča Kuguza, Biča Oza, Big Water Man, Bilberry Man, Bisan, Black Bear, Black Dog, Blue Fairy, Bonito Maidens, Brown Man of the Muirs, Browney, Brownie, Bukura e dheut, Büt Bodəž, Cailleach Bheur, Chang Hsien, Chanques, Charun, Chlevnik, Chu-Uhà, Church Grim, Cluricaun, Čodra Kuba and Čodra Kuguza, Colt Pixy, Coluinn Gun Cheann, Coquena, Coventina, Cuélebre, Curupira, Cyrene, Daimon, Dakini, Davalin, Deohako, Dharmapala, Di-Zang, Dievini, Diuturna, Dobie, Domovik, Dryad, Dwarf, Eingsaung, Elder Mother, Emandwa, Emizimu, Encantado, Eshu, Essex Shuck, Falange de Bôtos, Familiar, Faun, Ferohers, Finvarra, Flower Fairy, Frau Wachholder, Fravashi, Fylgir, Gabija, Gandayaks, Gardsvor, Genius, Gid-murt,

Giráitis, Giwoitis, Glaistig, Gnome, Gooseberry Wife, Graces, Green Lady, Green Man, Grine, Grove Folk, Guardian, Guardian Angel, Haltia, Hamingja, Hantu Gaharu, Hantu Gharu, Hāriti, Haugbonde, Heitsi-Eibib, Herne the Hunter, Hesperides, Hiisi, Hkum Yeng, Hogboon, Hogboy, Holle, Honga, Hooper of Sennen Cove, Household Spirits, Howlaa, Huasa Mallcu, Humbaba, Hunessai, Hylde-Moer, Hylde-Vinde, Ia Saltak, Idun, Izeds, Jūrasmāte, Jut Bodəž, Ka, Kajək Keremet, Kakua Kambuzi, Kalfu, Kamang, Kaukas, Kazna Peri, Kirkegrim, Kirkogrim, Kirnis, Kladovik, Koduhaldjas, Korka-murt, Korneböcke, Kornmutter, Kremara, Krukis, Kshathra, Kubera, Kudeiar, Kul-jungk, Kurinyi Bog, Kurwaichin, Kyrkogrim, Lalla Mkouna Bent Mkoun, Lalla Rekya Bint el Khamar, Lama, Lamassu, Lar, Laskowice, Lauko Sargas, Laukumāte, Laumé, Lawkapatim, Lazy Laurence, Legba, Leib-Olmai, Leshii, Lhiannan-shee, Li, Liekkiö, Limenia, Limnæ, Limoneads, Liu-Meng Chiang-Chün, Llamhigyn y Dwr, Lugovnik, Lunantishee, Luot-Chozjik, Maahiset, Mahisāsura, Majahaldjas, Mājakungs, Mala'ikat Puteh, Malik, Mandarangan, Manes, Mantus and Mania, Marét, Mariana, Marica, Matergabia, Mbōn, Medeine, Mehen, Mekumwasuk, Melissa, Metsänhaltia, Mežasmāte, Michael, Mimir, Mmoatia, Modeina, Monociello, Morkul Kua Luan, Moss Folk, Mumy, Muses, Nagual, Nagumwasuk, Namtar, Napææ, Naphæ, Nats, Nemdə Kurək Kuguza, Niägriusar, Nibelung, Ningyo, Nis, Njambai, Nootaikok, Nules-murt, Nuʮuí, Nur Kuba and Nur Kuguza, Nursery Bogies, Nymph, Oakmen, Obin-murt, Odqan, Ohdowas, Old Roger, Olympian Spirits, Ombwiri, Ora, Pasu, Penates, Perešta, Peseias, Phra Phum, Piambar, Pi-Hsia Yüan-Chün, Pitris, Pört Kuba and Pört Kuguza, Priparchis, Pulch, Rådande, Raphael, Ratainitsa, Rigai, Rüezahl, Ruginis, Saba-Leippya, Sa-bDag, Salmacis, Sand Altar Woman, Sedna, Shai, Shên, Shvod, Sir Ali, Spinnstubenfrau, Spriggans, Stihi, Šukča, Syen, Talonhaltija, Tiki, Tomtar, Tornak, Trikurat, Tua, Tuktoriak, Turek Kuguza, Ūdensmāte, Ūgunsmāte, Vai-Mahse, Vanadevatas, Veela, Vējasmāte, Vetāla, Vu-vozo, Walgino, Wasicong, Wee Willie Winkie, Xšatravēr, Yambe-akka, Zoa

22. SPIRITS ASSOCIATED WITH HOUSEHOLD, DOMESTIC FAMILY, AND CHILDREN

Household and Domestic Family

Abbey Lubbar, Abiku, Abonsam, Agathos Daimon, Agun Kuguza, Aitvaras, Alastor, Albastor, Àràk, Arifa, Badjang, Bannaia, Bannik, Banshee, Baravashka, Bardha, Befana, Biersal, Billy Blin, Blue Burches, Bodach, Bodachan Sabhaill, Boggart, Bogle, Broonie, Brownie, Brownie Clod, Bruder Rausch, Buttery Spirit, Bwbach, Bwca, Cacy taperere, Caoineag, Capelthwaite, Cauld Lad of Gilsland, Cauld Lad of Hilton, Cellar Demon, Chi Lung Wang, Chu-Uhà, Cluricaun, Coluinn Gun

Cheann, Cyhiraeth, Dievini, Dobbs, Dobie, Domovik, Duende, Dugnai, Dusii, Dvorovoi, Dwarf, Eingsaung, Ekkekko, Ellyllon, Emizimu, Erinys, Familiar, Fenodyree, Feriers, Friar Rush, Gabija, Gardsvor, Genius, Gilpin Horner, Giwoitis, Glaistig, Gobelin, Goldmar, Gruagach, Guardian, Gwarwyn-a-Throt, Gwrach y Rhibyn, Hamingja, Heinzelmann, Hinzelmann, Hob, Holle, Hutkin, Jut Bodəž, Kaukas, Keltəmaš, Kikimora, Killmoulis, Knocky-boh, Kobold, Kodinhaltia, Koduhaldjas Korka-murt, Korrigan, Kratt, Krimba, Lalla Mkouna Bent Mkoun, Lar, Legba, Lhiannan-shee, Lob-Lie-by-the-Fire, Lubbar-fiend, Luridan, Lutin, Maggy Moloch, Majahaldjas, Mājakungs, Mājas gars, Massariol, Matergabia, Mieg Moulach, Moča Šərt, Nain Rouge, Napfhans, Nari, Nats, Nis, Njambai, Nobody, Olsen, Pail Pak, Para, Pelisit, Penates, Peseias, Phra Phum, Piskey, Pixie, Pokey Hokey, Poltergeist, Pooka, Pört Bodəž, Pört Kuba and Pört Kuguza, Portunes, Prigirstitis, Puck, Puddlefoot, Pukis, Ratainitsa, Raw Head and Bloody Bones, Red Cap, Robin Goodfellow, Robin Round-Cap, Shvod, Silky, Škenan Ončəmə Keremet, Smiera-Gatto, Spinnstubenfrau, Šrat, Šükšəndal, Surt Mələndə Bodəz; Šurt Šukča, House Angel; Syen, Talonhaltija, Tom Cockle, Tomtar, Tonttu, Tot, Trasgu, Tutelary Spirits, Ūgunsmāte, Wag at the Wa'

Babies, Children, and Childbirth

Abiku, Acheri, Adramelech, Adrastea, Afrit/e, Ainsel, Al, Albastor, Amáltheia, Apci'lnic, Arifa, Armée Furieuse, Auld Scratty, Awd Goggie, Baba Yaga, Badjang, Bannik, Befana, Béfind, Berchta, Billy Winker, Black Annis, Bockmann, Bodach, Bucca Dhu, Bug-a-boo, Bugbear/e, Butzenbercht, Caypór, Chang Hsien, Changeling, Cihuateteo, Clim, Coleman Gray, Con-lon, Croquemitaine, Cutty Dyer, Cwn Annwn, Daoine Sidhe, Deive, Dimme, Dogai, Domikha, Dormette, Drac, Dustman, Dwarf, Egeria, Elf/e, Ellyllon, Erl King, Fairy, Fates, Father Christmas, Father Frost, Fati, Feriers, Glaistig, Goblin, Gooseberry Wife, Green Children, Grindylow, Grine, Gull, Hagno, Hantu Sawan, Hāriti, Hobyah, Holle, Hyter Sprites, Jack up the Orchut, Jaljogini, Jenny Greenteeth, Julenisse, Jüštə Erge, Kahausibware, Kakamora, Kalu Kumāra Yaka, Karina, Kelpie, Khadem Quemquoma, Kikimora, Killimalaikanniyarka, Knecht Ruprecht, Korrigan, Krampus, Kurétes, Labartu, Lamaštu, Lamia, Langsuir, Lara, Laumé, Leshii, Lesovikha, Liekkiö, Lilith, Liu-Meng Chiang-Chün, Llorona, Lull, Lutin, Malekin, Mariana, Masan, Mebeddel, Meliæ, Melsh Dick, Moca, Moiræ, Morgan, Muma Padura, Mumpoker, Nanny-Button-Cap, Nari, Nellie Longarms, Nix, Nočnitsa, Norns, Nursery Bogies, Oats Goat, Ole Luk Øj, Oosood, Oum Çebiane, Ouphe, Pail Pak, Parcae, Peg Powler, Pelisit, Pelznickel, Penanggalan, Père Fouettard, Père Noël, Peter Pan, Pi-Hsia Yüan-Chün, Pixie, Poltergeist, Poludnica, Polunochnitsa, Pontianak, Pooka, Pskégdemus, Putana, Putti, Raw Head and Bloody

Bones, Rumpelstiltskin, Sal, Sand Altar Woman, Sandman, Santa Claus, Šedra Kuba and Šedra Kuguza, Short Hoggers of Whittinghame, Sinter Klaas, Skilly Widden, Souin-souin, Spoorn, Spriggans, Sri, Strigæ, Stringlos, Šükšəndal, Tçaridyi, Telchines, Tod Lowery, Tom Dockin, Tom Po, Tom Thumb, Tooth Fairy, Troll, Trows, Tylwyth Teg, Undine, Ursitory, Veela, Walutahanga, Wee Willie Winkie, Wild Huntsman, Zagaz, Zwart Piet

23. SPIRITS ASSOCIATED WITH PROPHESY AND FATE

Bannik, Barguest, Bean Nighe, Béfind, Bodach Glas, Carmenæ, Cassotis, Castalia, Charon, Chu-Uhà, Church Grim, Cu Sith, Cyhiraeth, Dain, Dis, Domovik, Egeria, Fa, Fates, Fati, Flagae, Fylgir, Gabriel Hounds, Genius, Gou Mang, Grine, Gwrach y Rhibyn, Gytrash, Hamingja, Hantu Si Buru, Herne the Hunter, Kelpie, Kikimora, Killmoulis, L'esak, Macachera, Mesnie Hellequin, Metshaldjas, Moiræ, Nagual, Näkk, Norns, Œnone, Oosood, Ovinnik, Parcae, Pooka, Pört Kuba and Pört Kuguza, Seven Whistlers, Shai, Silenus, Skriker, Ursitory, Vanth, Veela, Viz-anya, Vizi-leany, White Lady, Wild Hunt

24. SPIRITS ASSOCIATED WITH ROADS AND TRAVELERS

Aicha Kandida, Airi, Anchancho, Anhanga, Astarotte, Aufhocker, Ban Nighechain, Bean Nighe, Biasd Bheulach, Bilberry Man, Bitâbohs, Black Dog, Black Shuck, Bloody Cap, Boggart, Bogle, Bogyman, Boneless, Brag, Broonie, Buckie, Buggane, Bull Beggar, Capelthwaite, Ceffyll-dŵr, Charon, Cihuateteo, Colt Pixy, Coluinn Gun Cheann, Cu Sith, Curupira, Cutty Dyer, Derricks, Dirne-weibl, Dobie, Doonie, Druggen Hill Boggle, Dulachan, Ellylldan, Empusa, Erl King, Falm, Father Frost, Freybug, Galley-trot, Ghoul, Ghul-I-Beaban, Grant, Gwillion, Gytrash, Hamou Ukaiou, Hantu Denai, Hantu Raya, Headless Woman, Hedley Kow, Hinky-Punk, Hmin, Hob, Hob-Lantern, Ia, Jack-in-irons, Jeršuk, Joan the Wad, Ke'lets, Kelpie, Kludde, Kornə Bodəž, Kornovkhii, Korrigan, Kožla Kuba and Kožla Kuguza, Lamia, Lar, Leshii, Macachera, Obda, Oberon, Old Woman of the Mountain, Orang Bunyi, Oschaert, Padfoot, Paija, Patu-paiarehe, People Who Killed by Lightning in Their Eyes, Peri, Pi Nereskə, Picktree Brag, Piskey, Pixie, Plat-eye, Poake, Polevik, Portunes, Pret, Raphael, Riesengebirge, Rizos, Rongeur d' Os, Rübezahl, Sasabonsam, Shag Foal, Shamantin, Shellycoat, Shewri, Shock, Sicksa, Silky, Siltim, Skadegamutc, Skriker, Spunkies, Stringlos, Urisk, Vadatjas, Vetāla, Will o' the Wisp, Yakkhas, Yech

25. SPIRITS ASSOCIATED WITH WATER
Rivers, Streams, Brooks, Waterfalls
Affric, Afrit, Aicha Kandida, Anchancho, As-iga, Ban Nighechain, Bean Nighe, Beregini, Bia, Big Water Man, Bóann, Büt Ian Üdəržə, Cailleach Bheur, Cannered Noz, Caointeach, Charon, Cheval Bayard, Cuachag, Cutty Dyer, Darrant, Drac, Dúc-Thánh Bà, Eager, Eŋer Bodəž, Falange de Bôtos, Fossegrim, Hantu Ban Dan, Igupiara, Jul Ser Kugərak, Kappa, Kübar Kuguza also Kübar Jumal Kuguza, Kul-jungk, Llamhigyn y Dwr, Lodona, Lorelei, Marica, Marsayas, Memphis, Mi Fei, Naiad, Nemdə Kurək Kugə, Œnone, Peg o' Nell, Peg Powler, Pelə Kolšə, Qandiša, Rusalka, Strömkarl, Šur-mumy, Syrinx, Upyri, Urisk, Vilcanota, Vodianikha, Vodianoi, Vu-murt, Wanagemeswak, White Lady

Lakes, Lochs, Fens, Marshes, Swamps, Cwms, Pools, Whirlpools
Abere, Addanc, Afanc, Arawotya, Atua, Bäckahäst, Black Shuck, Bolotnyi, Chertovka, Chitar Ali, Fire Drake, Ghillie Dhu, Grindylow, Gwragedd Annwn, Jenny Greenteeth, Jer Bodəž, Jer Kuba and Jer Kuguza, Keagyihl Depguesk, Kul, Lady of the Lake, Limnæ, Liwa, Matabiri, Mhorag, Näcken, Naitaka, Näkk, Näkki, Neck, Nellie Longarms, Neugle, Nicker, Ondichaouan, Piasa, Polunochnitsa, Pooka, Pskégdemus, Raw Head and Bloody Bones, Redjal el Marja, Sjöra, Strangers, Swan Maiden, Tchatse-olmai, Tiddy Ones, Tinihowi, Tod Lowery, Veela, Vizi-anya, Vizi-ember, Vodianoi, Vu-murt, Will o' the Wisp, Will the Smith, Xiang Yao

Oceans, Seas
Adaro, Aipalookvik, Amphitrite, Aulanerk, Bar, Ben Varrey, Blue Men of the Minch, Bonito Maidens, Brounger, Calypso, Clytie, Cymothoe, Davy Jones, Devil Fish People, Dinny Mara, Doris, Fin Folk, Forneus, Galatea, Hantu Laut, Havfrue, Havmand, Hedammu, Hooper of Sennen Cove, Jamaína, Jūrasmāte, Jurua, Lamia, Lar Marini, Liban, Limenia, Mära-Halddo, Mari Morgan, Mermaid, Merman, Morgan, Muileatach, Näkineiu, Nicker, Nimüe, Ningyo, Nootaikok, Oxun, Pagæ, Pahuanuiapitaaiterai, Panchajana, Porpoise Girl, Ri, Roane, Saivo-Neita, Sea Trow, Sedna, Selkies, Shellycoat, Shoney, Si Raya, Sir Ali, Siren, Suire, Tangie, Tritons

Fountains, Springs
Aganippe, Castalia, Coventina, Cyane, Diuturna, Egeria, Ikśa Keremet, Jamaína, Mimir, Nereid, Neugle, Nickel, Pamaš Oza, Pirene, Salmacis, Water Djinns

Water (General)
Apo, Apsaras, Arariel, Asrai, Bedonebyasyoudid, Bodəž, Buckland Shag, Büt Bodəž, Büt Ia, Büt Ümbal Šukčə, Cabyll-Ushtey, Čacce-haldde, Čacce-olmai, Ceffyll-dŵr, Chahuru, Chi Lung Wang, Čort, Crenæ, Eač Uisge, Faraony, Fuath, Gahongas, Gamainhas, Gandarewa, Glashtin, Groac'h, Hakenmann, Hantu Ayer, Harun,

Haurvatat, Hunessai, Jack the White Hat, Jaljogini, Jalpari, Koti, Kulshedra, Lahama, Loireag, Maezt-Dar l' Oudou, Maros, Mauari, Melusina, Morgan le Fay, Nivashi, Nix, Nøkk, Oceanids, Olt, Opkən, Scylla, Shoopiltie, Sjötroll, Tonx, Tootega, Topielec, Üdensmāte, Ukulan-Tojon, Undines, Unktehi, Vedenhaltia, Viz-anya, Vizi-leany, Vough, Vu-kutis, Vu-nuna, Vu-vozo, Wassermann, Water Babies, Yanki-murt, Zin

26. SPIRITS ASSOCIATED WITH THE WEATHER
Achachilas, Aeolus, Anchancho, Apoiaueue, Ays, Bad, Behir, Big Purra, Brounger, Bucca, Caillagh ny Groamagh, Cailleach Bheur, Ccoa, Cloud People, Dajoji, Dinny Mara, Djin, Dongo, Dooinney-Oie, Elel, Er Tütra, Father Frost, Fomagata, Formorian, Ga-oh, Gaunab, Gentle Annis, Hantu Ribut, Harpy, Haruts, Heng, Holle, Hooper of Sennen Cove, Howlaa, Jack Frost, Jeršuk, Jombol, Jüštə Erge and Jüštə Ərbezə, Jüštə Kuba and Jüštə Kuguza, Kachina, Kasagonaga, Kliwa, Kompagnin, Kunubriar, Lei Chen-Tzu, Leshii, Marét, Mbōn, Merman, Mist, Morozko, Muileatach, Mumy, Muruwook, Nagas, Naitaka, Negafok, Nenaunir, Nubero, Okulam, Ondichaouan, Pazuzu, Pəl Ner, Pokšem Kuba, Pokšem Kuguza and Pokšem Obəska, Poludnica, Putar Ali, Rain People, Rainha Barba, Rasogonaga, Rübezahl, Sabur Ali, Sarkany, Selkies, Shaitan, Silat, Sio Humis, Skogs Fru, Snow Maiden, Snow Queen, Spriggans, Sylph, Thien, Thunder Boys, Tupan, Uacilla, Vējasmāte, Verbti, Víly, Virginal, Virra Birron, Wind Old Woman, Xangô, Ya-o-gah, Yuki-onna

27. SPIRITS BY COUNTRY, REGION, OR PEOPLE
Ancient Realms
(and Countries Whose Boundaries No Longer Exist)
Anatolia:
Ullikummi

Aram:
Mammon

Assyria:
Ardat Lili, Belphegor, Kherebu, Lama, Lamassu, Mithra, Pazuzu, Utukku

Babylon:
Adramelech, Akhkhazzu, Anunnaki, Ardat Lili, Ashakku, Gallu, Igigi, Irra, Kingu, Labartu, Lamassu, Lamaštu, Sebettu, Utukku

Chaldea:
Hea-Bani, Maskims

Mesopotamia (General to Each Culture):
Asag, Baubo, Hedammu, Humbaba, Imdugud, Labartu, Namtar, Udu

Sumer:
Abgal, Apkallu, Ardat Lili, Asag, Dimme, Dingir, Galla, Kiskil-lilla, Lahama, Lama

Modern Boundaries and Cultures

Albania:
Aërico, Bardha, Bukura e dheut, Djall, En, Fati, Kukudhi, Kulshedër, Kulshedra, Ljubi, Ora, Perit, Stihi

Argentina:
Elel, Walichu

Armenia:
Aralez, Ays, Deev, Fravashi, Javerzaharses, Kaches, Shvod, Vishaps

Australia:
Arawotya, Bamapama, Banksia Men, Big Purra, Bib and Bub, Boronia Babies, Chucklebud, Cuddlepie, Cut-Cut, Flannel Flower Babies, Gumnut Babies, Jombol, Kompagnin, Kunubriar, Kutchis, Lucky Devil, Mamandabari, Mimi, Molonga, Morkul Kua Luan, Mormo, Mura Mura, Muruwook, Narnywo, Nittersing, Ragged Blossom, Snugglepot, Virra Birron, Waruk, Wattle Babies

Austria:
Ahren Konigen, Bartel, Berchta, Bilwis, Drude, Krampus, Kruzimügeli, Lady of the Lake, Salgfräulein

Belgium:
Kludde, Oschaert

Bolivia:
Achachilas, Anchancho, Ekkekko, Hapiñuñu, Huasa Mallcu, Mekala

Brazil:
Akosa-Sapata, Akossi-Sapata, Anativa, Anchunga, Anhanga, Apoiaueue, Avarekete, Badé, Barão de Goré, Basilio Bom, Boiadeiro da Visaura, Caboclo, Cacy taperere, Caypór, Constantino, Cosme, Curupira, Curupira, Damião, Dom Carlos, Dom João Sueira, Dom José, Dom Luiz, Dom Pedro Angaço, Dona Rosalina, Encantado, Exus, Ezú, Falange de Bôtos, Farrista, Goiabeira, Guapindaia, Guia, Imanja, Jamaína, Japetequara, Jarina, João da Mata, Joãozinho, José Tupinambá, Jurema, Legua Bogi da Trinidade, Macachera, Marét, Mariana, Miguelzinho Boa da Trinidade, Ogun, Orixá, Oxossi, Oxun, Pena Verde, Pretos Velhos, Princesa d' Alva, Rainha Barba, Rainha Eowa, Rainha Oyá, Rei Sebastião, Rompe Mato, Seu Turquia, Tangó do Pará, Tapinaré, Tartuga de Amazonas, Tranca Rua, Tupan, Xangô, Zezinho

Bulgarian, Romania (Rumania), Serbian, Croatian, Slav, and Bosnian Peoples:
Djins, Dugnai, Dyavo, Giwoitis, Gorska Makua, Green George, Karliki, Kricco, Krimba, Krukis, Laskowice, Leschia, Ljeschi, Lychie Morava, Matergabia, Muma Padura, Nočnitsa, Oosood, Oynyena Maria, Peseias, Poludnitsa, Prigirstitis, Psezpolnica, Raviyoyla, Sicksa, Šrat, Syen, Topielec, Veela, Veles, Vizi-anya, Vôlva

Burma:
Akakasoh, Boomasoh, Chinün Way Shun, Chitōn, Eingsaung, Hkum Yeng, Hmin, Jān, Ka, Kaluks, Keinnara, La, Lu, Mbōn, Mu, Nagini Besandi, Nat Thami, Nats, Phi, Ponphyoi, Saba-Leippya, Seiktha, Shekkasoh, Shitta, Sinlap, Tak-Keng, Thien, Trikurat, Upaka, Wāwn

Cambodia:
Àràk, Khmóc Prây, Pray, Reahu, Srei ap, Sri

Canadian and Inuit:
Agloolik, Aipalookvik, Akselloak, Apci'lnic, Apopa, Ataksak, Aulanerk, Aumanil, Charlot, Dingbelle, Eeyeekalduk, Fifinella, Ino, Irdlirvirissong, Kaitorak, Keelut, Kingmingoarkulluk, Mamagwasewug, Negafok, Neugle, Nootaikok, Paija, Qiqirn, Sedna, Tootega, Tornak, Tuktoriak

Caribbean Islands (Including Cuba, Haiti, Jamaica, and West Indies):
Anansi, Baka, Bossu, Dyombie, Géde, Jumby, Kadja Bossu, Kalfu, Legua, Loa, Mr. Spider, Nansi, Ogu Ferai, Plat-eye, Pukkumeria, Simbi, 'Ti Malice

Central and South Africa (Including Ghana, Kenya, Madagascar, Mali, Niger, Nigeria, Tanzania, Zaire, Zambia, Zimbabwe):
Abiku, Abonsam, Afreet, Al, Anansi, Angatch, Apuku, Asuman, Aziza, Azizan, Balubaale, Bia, Biloko, Bitâbohs, Bori, Djok, Dongo, Dyombie, Efreet, Elegba, Emandwa, Emizimu, Eshu, Exu, Fa, Gaunab, Gizō, Heitsi-Eibib, Hitâbohs, Huntin, Ifa, Igwikalla, Ijimere, Ilogo, Jocoo, Juju, Kakua Kambuzi, Kamallo, Katavi, Kwaku Ananse, Legba, Liba, Loango Winti, Mingehe, Mmoatia, Mondzo, Nburu, Nenaunir, Ngworekara, Njambai, Obe, Ombwiri, Orisha, Sasabonsam, Shamantin, Srahman, Tikdoshe, Uhlakanyana, Zin, Zoa

Central America (Including El Salvador, Honduras, Mexico, Nicaragua, Yucatan):
Balam, Chanekos, Chanes, Chanques, Cihuateteo, Liwa, Llorona, Nagual, Sara-Mama, Vucub-Caquix, Yaotl

Chile (Including Tierra del Fuego):
Alicanto, Cherruve, Chonchonyi, Colo-Colo, Huecuvu, Jetaita, Kimprushas, Kinnara, Rasogonaga, Walichu

China (Including Mongolia):
Chang Hsien, Chi Lung Wang, Chih Nü, Chu Pa-Chiai, Di-Zang, Gong Gong, Gou Mang, Gui Xian, He-Li-Di, Hsien, Hu Fa, Hu Hsien, Jurong, Kishimojin, Kuei, Lei Chen-Tzu, Li, Liu-Meng Chiang-Chün, Ma Mien, Mi Fei, Nashas, Niu T'ou, Odqan, Pi-Hsia Yüan-Chün, Rou Shou, Shên, Shinseën, Si Wang Mu, Tou Shen, Wu Ch'ang Kuei, Xian, Xiang Yao, Yin Chiao, Yü Nü

Colombia:
Fomagata

Czech (Including Bohemia):
Bubák, Haus-Schmiedlein, Krimba, Murawa, Nočnitsa, Ruprich, Tras

Denmark:
See Scandinavia

Ecuador:
Iwančĭ, Nuŋuí, Pasuk

Egypt:
See North Africa

England:
Abac, Abbey Lubber, Abhac, Abundia, Adramelech, Afanc, Ainsel, Alastor, Angel, Appletree Man, Ariel, Asrai, Awd Goggie, Barbason, Barguest, Bauchan, Bedonebyasyoudid, Billy Blin, Billy Winker, Black Dog, Black Shuck, Black Sow, Black Vaughan, Bloody Cap, Blue Burches, Blue Cap, Bocan, Boggart, Bogie, Bogle, Boll, Boneless, Brag, Brother Mike, Browney, Brownie, Bucca, Buckland Shag, Bug, Bug-a-boo, Bugbear, Bull Beggar, Buttery Spirit, Cacodæmon, Cankobobus, Capelthwaite, Cauld Lad of Hilton, Cellar Demon, Church Grim, Churnmilk Peg, Clap-Cans, Clim, Clym of the Clough, Coleman Gray, Colt Pixy, Coranians, Corn Spirit, Couril, Coventina, Cowlug Sprites, Cutty Black Sow, Cutty Dyer, Dando and His Dogs, Darrant, Derricks, Devil's Dandy Dogs, Dobbs, Dobie, Drac, Dunnie, Dunters, Dustman, Dwarf, Eager, Elaby Gathan, Elder Mother, Elf, Elven, Fairy, Fat Lips, Father Christmas, Feeorin, Feriers, Fifinella, Fire Drake, Flay-boggart, Flibbertigibbet, Flower Fairy, Freybug, Friar Rush, Gabriel Hounds, Galley-beggar, Galley-trot, Garthornes, Gilpin Horner, Godda, Good Neighbours, Grant, Green Children, Green Man, Gremlins, Grig, Grim, Grime, Grindylow, Gull, Gyl-burnt-tayl, Gytrash, Habetrot, Habonde, Hag, Hairy Jack, Harry-ca-nab, Harvest Lady, Harvest Queen, Hedley Kow, Herlethingus, Herne the Hunter, Hinky-Punk, Hob, Hob Thrush, Hobany, Hobby, Hobgoblin, Hob-Lantern, Hodekin, Hodge, Hooper of Sennen Cove, Hyter Sprites, Imp, Ina Pic Winna, Jack Frost, Jack up the Orchu, Jack the White Hat, Jack-in-irons, Jack-in-the-Green, Jennie of Biggersdale, Jenny Greenteeth, Joan the Wad, John

Barleycorn, Joint Eater, Kergrim, Kirn Dolly, Knockers, Knocky-boh, Lady of the Lake, Lazy Laurence, Licke, Lob, Lob-Lie-by-the-Fire, Lodona, Lord Harry, Lubbar-fiend, Lubberkin, Mab, Malekin, Mare, Mawmets, Melsh Dick, Mephistophales, Mermaid, Merman, Mormo, Mumpoker, Muryans, Nanny-Button-Cap, Napfhans, Nellie Longarms, Nightmare, Nobody, Oakmen, Oberon, Old Bloody Bones, Old Boot, Old Nick, Old Roger, Padfoot, Peerifool, Peg o' Nell, Peg Powler, Perry Dancers, Picktree Brag, Pillywiggin, Piskey, Pixie, Poake, Pokey Hokey, Poltergeist, Pooka, Portunes, Puck, Raw Head and Bloody Bones, Red Cap, Robin Goodfellow, Robin Round-Cap, Sandman, Santa Claus, Seven Whistlers, Shag Foal, Sheela-na-gig, Shock, Silky, Skilly Widden, Skriker, Spoorn, Spriggans, Strangers, Tantrabobus, Terrytop, The Old People, Thrummy Cap, Thrumpin, Tiddy Ones, Tod Lowery, Tom Dockin, Tom Po, Tom Thumb, Tom Tit Tot, Tom Titivil, Tom Tumbler, Trash, Urchin, Wayland Smith, Wee Willie Winkie, Wild Hunt, Will o' the Wisp, Will the Smith

Estonia:
Äi, Äijo, Äijätär, Haldjas, Juods, Kodinhaltia, Koduhaldjas, Kratt, Majahaldjas, Metsänhaltia, Metshaldjas, Metsik, Näkineitsi, Näkineiu, Näkk, Pukje, Puuk, Talonhaltija, Vedenhaltia

Ethiopia (Abyssinia):
See North Africa

Faröe Islands:
See Scandinavia

Finland:
See Scandinavia

France:
Aatxe, Asmodee, Basa-Andre, Basajaun, Béfind, Ben Socia, Bodua, Bonnes Dames, Cannered Noz, Cauchemar, Chasse d' Hérode, Chasse de Caïn, Cheval Bayard, Couril, Croquemitaine, Diablotin, Dormette, Dusii, Erge, Fées, Fifollet, Follet, Gaueko, Gobelin, Groac'h, Habonde, Herensugue, Iguma, Korrigan, L' Armée Furieuse, la Chasse d' Artu, Lady of the Lake, Lamia, Le Grand Vaneur de Fontainebleau, Lubin, Lutin, Mallebron, Mari Morgan, Melusine, Mephistophales, Mesnie Herlequin, Nain, Nain Rouge, Niniane, Nos Bonnes Mères, Oats Goat, Oberon, Pacolet, Père Fouettard, Père Noël, Petit Nain Rouge, Petit Poucet, Ricdin Ricdon, Robiquet, Rongeur d' Os, Sand Yan y Tad, Souin-souin, Torto, Vivienne, White Lady

Germany:
Aelfric, Alberich, Alfar, Alferich, Alp, Alpris, Alraun, Askafroa, Aufhocker, Baumesel, Bažaloshtsh, Berchta, Berkta, Bibung, Biersal, Bilberry Man, Bilwis, Bimesschneider, Blud, Bockmann, Boggelmann, Bruder Rausch, Brunhilde, Bulleklas, Bullerman, Bullkater,

Bumann, Butzenbercht, Cobalt, Dain, Dame Ellerhorn, Dickepoten, Dirne-weibl, Dis, Döckalfar, Drude, Duergar, Durin, Dvalin, Eisenberta, Elberich, Elbgast, Erdleute, Erlkönig, Eschenfrau, Forneus, Fornjotr, Frau Berchta, Frau Gauden's Hunt, Frau Holle, Frau Wachholder, Frau Welt, Fylgir, Gübich, Haferbocks, Hakel-Bärend, Hakenmann, Hampelmann, Heinzelmann, Held, Herscheklos, Hild, Hinzelmann, Hockelblock, Hödekin, Holle, Huldra, Hutkin, Hylde-Moer, Hylde-Vinde, Irrlicht, Katzenveit, King Goldmar, Knecht Ruprecht, Kobold, Korneböcke, Kornmutter, Kornwolf, Latzman, Laurin, Liosalfar, Lorelei, Mahr, Mefistofele, Mimring, Modsognir, Moss Folk, Nibelung, Nickel, Nixe, Nökke, Norg, Pelznickel, Perchta, Pilwiz, Poltergeist, Pouk, Precht, Pück, Pûks, Pulch, Riesengebirge, Roggerhunds Rower, Rubbet, Rübezahl, Rugeklas, Rumpelstiltzchen, Schimmel Reiter, Schrat, Sigrun, Spinnstubenfrau, Stille Volk, Stomach-slasher, Sumerklas, Svartalfar, Swartalfar, Udur, Valkyries, Virginal, Völund, Waldgeister, Wassermann, Weinachts Mann, White Lady, Wichtlein, Wœsjäger, Wood Wives

Ghana:
See Central Africa

Greece:
Abarbarea, Acephalos, Adrastea, Aeolus, Aerika, Aganippe, Agathos Daimon, Ægina, Ægle, Akakasoh, Alastor, Alcyone, Alecto, Alsaieds, Amáltheia, Amphitrite, Antiope, Aœde, Aonides, Apollyon, Arethusa, Argyra, Asia, Asteropea, Atlantides, Atropos, Auloniads, Babi, Bad Hour, Baubo, Bes, Britomartis, Cacodæmon, Calliope, Callisto, Calypso, Castalia, Castalides, Cataclothes, Celœno, Charon, Charos, Chelone, Clio, Clytie, Coronis, Corycia, Crenæ, Cyane, Cymodoce, Cymothoe, Cyrene, Daimon, Daktyloi, Dæmon, Daphne, Decuma Doris, Doto, Dryad, Dryope, Echenais, Echo, Egeria, Electra, Empusa, Ephialtes, Erato, Erinyes, Erinys, Erotes, Erytheia, Eumenides, Eunice, Euphrosyne, Eurynome, Exotica, Faun, Galatea, Gratiæ, Hamadryad, Harpy, Heliconiades, Hesperides, Hyades, Hylæoræ, Iachos, Kallikantzari, Ker, Kikiades, Korybantes, Koukoudi, Kurétes, Lachesis, Lamia, Leimoniades, Leucosia, Libethrides, Limenia, Limnæ, Limoneads, Lotis, Magæra, Maia, Marica, Marsayas, Melete, Meliæ, Meliades, Melissa, Melobosis, Melpomene, Memphis, Mera, Merope, Mneme, Moiræ, Mormo, Moros, Morta, Muses, Myréne, Naiad, Napææ, Naphæ, Nereid, Nona, Nymph, Oceanids, Ocypete, Olympiades, Œnone, Oriades, Orithyia, Pagæ, Panope Parcae, Parnassides, Pierides, Pirene, Pitys, Pleiades, Podarge, Polyhymnia, Psychopompos, Rizos, Salmacis, Satyr, Scylla, Semnai, Shameful Hour, Silenus, Siren, Smilax, Staphyle, Sterope, Stringlos, Sylphs, Syrinx, Taygete, Telchines, Terpischore, Thalia, Thetis, Tisiphone, Tritons, Undine, Urania, Vittora

Greenland:
See Scandinavia

Guyana and Surinam:
Anansi, Apuku, Bakru, Dyombie, Legua, Loango Winti

Haiti:
See Caribbean

Honduras:
See Central America

Hungary:
Baba, Dame Hirip, Dame Jenö, Dame Rampson, Dame Vénétur, Fairy Helen, Fene, Firtos, Guta, Lidérc, Maros, Mika, Panczumanczi, Sarkany, Tarkö, Tartód, Tündér, Viz-anya, Winterkolbe

Iceland:
See Scandinavia

India (Including Afghanistan, Bangladesh, Bengal, Nepal, Pakistan, Sri Lanka, Tibet):
Acheri, Airi, Angiris, Antariksha, Aparājita, Apoiaueue, Apsaras, Asa Vahista, Asura, Asurakumara, Bagul, Bali, bDud, Betikhân, Bhairon, Bhut, Bonga, bTsan, Campankitāci, Chitragupta, Chûtâs, Citipati, Daitya, Dakini, Dala Kadavara, Danavas, Dasyus, Dævas, Deva, Dewas, Dharmapala, dMu, Dund, Durgā, Ganas, Gandhabbas, Gandharvas, Gara Yaka, Gauri, Gaya, Ghul, Ghul-I-Beaban, gNyan, Hāriti, Haruts, Hayagriva, Hiranyakasipu, Jaljogini, Jalpari, Kabandha, Kālanemi, Kalu Kumāra Yaka, Kamsa, Khyab-pa, Kimprushas, Kollimalaikanniyarka, Kubera, Lha-mo, Mada, Mahāmāri, Mahisāsura, Malla, Ma-Mo, Mani, Mara, Masan, Matarisvan, Meghamalin, Menara, Mitra, Muchalinda, Nagas, Nakshastras, Naonhaithya, Naraka, Panchajana, Pey, Piśācas, Pitris, Pret, Putana, Rahu, Rakshasas, Ravana, rMu, Sa-bDag, Sakuntala, Sankchinnis, Sri, Tumburu, Urvasi, Vanadevatas, Vasus, Vetāla, Visvavasu, Vrikshakas, Vritra, Vyantaras, Yakkhas, Yakshini, Yogini

Indonesia (Including Borneo and Irian Jaya):
Komang, Narbrooi, Triee, Tua, Umot

Iran (Persia):
Aeshma, Aeshma Daeva, Agas, Ako-Mano, Akvan, Ameretat, Amesa Spentas, Anahita, Aniran, Apo, Aramaiti, Arzshenk, Asa Vahista, Asha, Asman, Astō Vidātu, Asura, Atar, Az, Azidahaka, Bad, Baduh, Bushyasta, Craosa, Daena, Dævas, Deev, Demrush, Drashpa, Drug, Ferohers, Fravaši, Gandarewa, Ghul-I-Beaban, Haurvatat, Houri, Huarekhshaeta, Huran, Iblis, Indra, Izeds, Jahi, Jan-ben-Jan, Khasm, Kshathra, Mah, Mithra, Munheras, Naikiyas, Nakahet, Nakisiyya, Naonhaithya, Narah, Nasu, Peri, Rashnu, Rasun, Šahrē-var, Siltim, Sraoša, Tauru, Tauvi, Trishtrya, Vatak,

Verethaghna, Vohu Mano, Vohumanah, Xšatravēr, Yazatas Zairisha, Zairi

Ireland:
Aengus, Aillen Mac Midhna, Aine, Ainé, Alp Luachra, Amadán, Angus Og, Aoibhinn, Aynia, Badb, Banshee, Baoban Sith, Bóann, Bocan, Bodachan Sabhaill, Bodb, Breas, Cailleach bera, Cairpré, Cliodna, Cluricaun, Corpán síde, Credné, Dagda, Daoine Maite, Daoine Sidhe, Diancécht, Eochu Bres, Fachan, Fear Dearc, Fer-Sidhe, Finvarra, Fir Bholg, Formorian, Gan Ceanach, Girle Guairle, Gobhan Saer, Goibhleann, Goibniu, Granny, Gruagach, Gunna, Iubdan, Leanan-sidhe, Leprechaun, Lhiannan-shee, Liam na Lasoige, Liban, Lir, Loghery Man, Lubberkin, Lubrican, Luchorpain, Luchramán, Luchtaine, Lunantishee, Lupracan, Lúracán, Lurgadán, Luricadaune Mac Cecht, Mac Moineanta, Macha, Mebd, Mhorag, Midar, Morrigan, Moruach, Moruadh, Muir-Gheilt, Murdhuacha, Neman, Niamh, Nuala, Onagh, Pooka, Sabdh, Samhghubha, Shefro, Sídhe, Siofra, Sleagh Maith, Suire, Teine Sidhe, Teine Sionniic, Tom Cockle, Tuatha dé Danann

Isle of Man (United Kingdom):
Ad-hene, Babban ny Mheillea, Ben Varrey, Bocan, Bodachan Sabhaill, Buggane, Cabyll-Ushtey, Caillagh ny Groamagh, Dinny Mara, Dooinney Marrey, Dooinney-Oie, Fenodyree, Glashan, Glashtin, Guillyn Beggey, Hamingja, Hill-men, Howlaa, Lhiannan-shee, Lil Fellas, Mauthe Dhoog, Nikyr, Phynnodderee, Sleigh Beggey, Yn Foldyr Gastey

Israel (Including Jewish and Hebrew tradition):
Abaddan, Abdiel, Aeshma, Anpiel, Arariel, Archangel, Ardat Lili, Ariel, Asasel, Ashmedai, Asmodeus, Azael, Azazil, Baalzebul, Beelzebub, Belial, Cerubin, Cherubym, Dybbukim, Gabriel, Hadarniel, Israfel, Izra'il, Kafziel, Lilim, Lilin, Lilith, Mazikeen, Metatron, Michael, Ob, Raphael, Ruach, Samael, Sandalphon, Se'irim, Seraphim, Shēdîm, Shemyaza, Uzziel, Zadkiel

Italy (Including ancient Etruria and Rome):
Abarbarea, Acaviser, Adrastea, Aëllo, Aellopus, Aganippe, Ægina, Aglaia, Alcyone, Alecto, Alpan, Amoretti, Antiope, Aœde, Arethusa, Argyra, Asia, Asteropea, Atlantides, Atropos, Befana, Belphegor, Blue Fairy, Calliope, Calypso, Carmenæ, Carmenta, Castalia, Celeno, Charontes, Charun, Chelone, Clio, Clotho, Corycia, Culsu, Cyane, Cymodoce, Cymothoe, Cyrene, Daphne, Decuma, Dirae, Diuturna, Dryad, Dryope, Echenais, Echo, Egeria, Electra, Erato, Erotes, Erytheia, Eunice, Euphrosyne, Evan, Fata, Fata Morgana, Fata Silvanella, Fates, Fati, Foliots, Folletto, Furies, Galatea, Genius, Gratiæ, Hagno, Hamadryad, Harpy, Hyades, Incubus, Juturna, Keliano, Lachesis, Lamia, Lamiæ, Lar, Lara, Larva, Lasas, Lemur, Leucosia, Limenia, Limnæ, Limoneads, Lotis, Magæra, Maia, Manes, Mania, Mantus,

Marica, Massariol, Melete, Meliæ, Melissa, Melobosis, Melpomene, Memphis, Mera, Merope, Mithras, Mneme, Moiræ, Monociello, Mormo, Morta, Muses, Myréne, Naiad, Napææ, Naphæ, Neda, Nona, Nymph, Oceanids, Ocypete, Oinone, Oread, Orithyia, Parcae, Penates, Picus, Pirene, Pitys, Polyhymnia, Putti Podarge, Salmacis, Salvanelli, Satyr, Siren, Smilax, Staphyle, Sterope, Strigæ, Taygete, Terpischore, Thalia, Thisoa, Tisiphone, Tritons, Tuchulcha, Urania, Vanth

Japan:
Bakemono, Chih Nü, Hāriti, Hisa-Me, Hu Hsien, Kami, Kappa, Kawako, Ningyo, Oni, Ten-gu, Yama-uba, Yuki-onna

Kenya:
See Central Africa

Korea:
Chih Nü, Chisin Tongbŏp, Chudang, Hongaek, Kamang, Kami, Moksin Tongbŏp, Nanggu Moksin, Saja, Sal, Sangmun, Sin, Tongbŏp

Lapland:
See Scandinavia

Latvia:
Dievini, Juods, Jūrasmāte, Laukumāte, Laūme, Mājakungs, Mājas gars, Māte, Mežasmāte, Mežatēus, Pukis, Ragana, Spigena, Ūdensmāte, Ūgunsmāte, Vadatjas, Vējasmāte, Yumis

Lithuania:
Aitvaras, Boba, Deive, Gabieta, Gabija, Gabijaujis, Giráitis, Kaukas, Kirnis, Kotre, Kuršis, Lauko Sargas, Lauma, Laumé, Mara, Medeine, More, Pukys, Ragana, Ruginis, Rugiu Boba, Slogute, Spigena, Vejopatis, Velnias, Žemepatis, Žemyna

Madagascar:
See Central and South Africa

Malaysia (East and West):
Badi, Badjang, Bediadari, Bidadari, Bisan, Buso, Chitar Ali, Hantu, Hantu Ayer, Hantu Bakal, Hantu Ban Dan, Hantu Belian, Hantu B'rok, Hantu Denai, Hantu Gaharu, Hantu Gharu, Hantu Hantuan, Hantu Hutan, Hantu Kayu, Hantu Kopek, Hantu Laut, Hantu Longgok, Hantu Pemburu, Hantu Raya, Hantu Ribut, Hantu Rimba, Hantu Sawan, Hantu Si Buru, Hantu Songkei, Ijrafil, Ijrail, Jabra'il, Jemalang, Jewa-Jewa, Jin, Jin Tanah, Langsuir, Mala'ikat, Mala'ikat Puteh, Mika'il, Orang Bunyian, Pelisit, Polong, Pontianak, Putar Ali, Raja Brahil, Sabur Ali, Sa-Gempar 'Alam, Sa-Gertak Rang Bumi, Sa-Gunchang Rang Bumi, Sa-Halilintar, Sa-Lakun Darah, Sang Gadin, Sang Gala Raja, Sa-Rukup Rang Bumi, Sa-Tumbok Rang Bumi, Serafil, Si Raya, Sir Ali, Tagamaling, Tigbanua, Tua

Mali:
See Central and South Africa

Melanesia (Including Fiji, Papua New Guinea, New Britain, New Caledonia, New Hebrides, Solomon Islands):
Abere, Adaro, Aremha, Bariaua, Bonito Maidens, Dodore, Figona, Higona, Kaia, Kaiamunu, Kakamora, Kakangora, Karawatoniga, Marsaba, Matabiri, Matagaigai, Nabaeo, Pinari, Pwaronga, Qat, Siho I Salo, Tuki, Vaotere, Walutahanga

Micronesia (Including Caroline Islands and Yap Islands):
Le-Gerem, Lioumere, Olifat, Olofad, Porpoise Girl, Wolphat,Yalafath

Morocco:
See North Africa

Netherlands (Holland):
Kaboutermannekin, Pharaildis, Red Cap, Sinter Klaas, Vrouelden, Zwart Piet

New Zealand:
Ariā, Atua, Irā -Kewa, Korokioewe, Maui, Mokotiti, Patu-paiarehe, Ri, Tatariki, Te Makawe, Tiki, Titihai, Tonga, Whiro

Niger and Nigeria:
See Central and South Africa

North Africa and Middle East (Islamic Countries of Egypt, Ethiopia [Abssinia], Morocco, Sudan, Tunisia, Turkey, Yemen, and Arab Cultures):
Abdullah al-Kazwini, Acephalos, Afrit, Agathos Daimon, Aicha Kandida, Aiwel, Ammit, Apep, Apophis, Arifa, Awar, Azra'il, Babi, Baduh, Baghlet el Qebour, Bes, Bottle Imp, Bouda, Chaarmarouch, Dalham, Dasim, Diff Errebi, Djinn, Efrit, Gabra'il, Ghaddar, Grine, Had al' Khorine, Hadduok Ennass, Hamou Ukaiou, Harun, Hatif, Ifreet, Izra'il Jnun, Ka, Khadem Quemquoma, Lalla Mira, Lalla Mkouna Bent Mkoun, Lalla Rekya Bint el Khamar, Lalla Zouina, Macardit, Maezt-Dar l' Oudou, Malik el Abiad, Marid, Mebeddel, Medr, Mehen, Memphis, Moulay Abdelkader Djilani, Namtar, Nashas, Nass l' Akhorine, Nebed, Old Man of the Sea, Oum Çebiane, Qandiša, Redjal el Marja, Shai, Shiqq, Sidi Hamou, Sidi Mimoum el Djinnaoui, Sidi Mousa el Bahari, Sidna Djebril, Silat, Sut, Tabi, Taranushi, Tir, Zagaz, Zalambur, Zar

Norway:
See Scandinavia

Peru:
Anchancho, Apo, Apu, Auki, Awki, Ccoa, Ekkekko, Eq'eq'o, Huacas, Larilari, Sara-Mama, Supay, Tira, Vilcanota

Philippines:
Alan, Bottle Imp, Buso, Darago, Mandarangan, Tigbanua, Tagamaling

Poland:
Baba, Boruta, Datan, Dziwitza, Kremara, Kurwaichin, Lawkapatim, Marzanna, Modeina, Mora, Nočnitsa, Priparchis, Rübezahl, Siliniets, Ursitory, Walgino

Polynesia (Including Cook Islands, Easter Islands, Hawaii, Samoa, Tahiti, Tonga):
Adaro, Ahifatumoana, Akaanga, Amaite-Rangi, Arematapopoto, Aremataroroa Faingaa, Hotua Poro, Iwa, Kapua, Karaia-I-Te-Ata, Kawelo, Kumu-Tonga-I-Te-Po, Maui, Miru, Miru Kura, Ono, Pahuanuiapitaaiterai, Pekoi, Puatutahi, Tapairu, Tiki, Tonga, Vaotere

Portugal:
See Spain

Romania:
See Bulgaria

Romany Gypsies of Europe:
Ana, Beng, Bitoso, Green George, Keshalyi, Lilyi, Loçolico, Lolmischo, Matiya, Melalo, Minceskro, Nivashi, Poreskoro, Psuvashi, Schilalyi, Tçaridyi, Tçulo, Ursitory

Russia and Russian States:
Russia
Ataman, Baba Yaga, Bainikha, Bannaia, Bannik, Baravashka, Beregini, Bes, Biča Kuba, Bolotnyi, Chertovka, Chlevnik, Diavol, Domavichka, Domavikha, Domikha, Domovik, Domovoi, Dvorovoi, Faraonki, Faraonyi, Father Frost, Gid-murt, Gogol, Jezi-Baba, Khitkha, Kikimora, Kinkach, Kladovik, Kornovkhii, Kriksy, Kudeiar, Kurinyi Bog, Leshii, Leshiye, Leshonki, Leskotukha, Lesnoi, Lesovikha, Lieschi, Lisun, Ljeschi, Lugovnik, Lychie, Mājakungs, Martinko, Mora, Morozko, Nalet, Nari, Nechistaia Sila, Nechistyi Dukh, Nicolai Chudovorits, Nočnitsa, Ovinnik, Polevik, Poludnica, Polunochnitsa, Potan'Ka, Ratainitsa, Rusalka, Shishimora, Shutovka, Shyshok, Snow Maiden, Upyri, Ursitory, Vodianikha, Vodianoi

Cheremis/Mari
Aga Kurman, Agun Kuguza, Albastor, Arapteš, Asəra, Azren, Bakš Ia, B'es, Biča Kuba, Bodəž, Buber, Büt Imnə, Čembulat, Čodra Kuba, Čopakin, Čort, Čurpan Šərt, Eŋer Bodəž, Eprem Kuguza, Er Tütra, Ərləgan Kuba, Ia, Ibaśka, Idəm Kuba, Ikśa Keremet, Izə Nur Keremet, Jabol, Jal Ümbač Kośtśə Keremet, Jamšener, Jer Bodəž, Jeršuk, Joškar Ser, Jučuzo, Jul Ser Kugərak, Jüštə Kuba, Jut Bodəž, Kajək Keremet, Karman Kurək Kuguza, Kazna Peri, Keltəmaš, Keremet, Kərtnä Bodəj, Koltəšə, Kornə Bodəž, Kož Nedək, Kožla Kuba, Kuba, Kübar Kuguza, Kudə Ört Kuba, Kugə Aga Keremet, Kuguza,

Kuplaŋgaš, Kurək Ia, L'esak, Makar, Məlandə Bodəz, Moča Kuba, Mükš Šərt, Mužə, Nedək, Nerge Kuba, Nol Jeŋ, Nur Bodəž, Obda, Opkən, Oš Buj Vanuška, Oza, Pail Pak, Pajberda Šərt, Paltəkan, Pamaš Oza, Paravoj Ia, Paškəče, Pasu, Pəl Ner, Pelə Kolša, Perešta, Peri, Pi Nereskə, Piambar, Pokšem Kuba, Pört Bodəz, Rok Šərt, Run Kuba, Šajtan, Šedra Kuba, Šerdəš, Šərt, Šert Bodəz, Šokša Kuba, Šukčə, Šükšəndal, Sultan, Sürem Mužə, Šurnə, Surt Məlandə Bodəz, Toktal Poškudə, Toštə Kož Jeŋ, Tul Bodəz, Tuma Düŋ Keremet, Turek Kuguza, Uda, Undur Šərt, Vanuška, Xuda Sila

Siberia (Including Kamchatka):
As-iga, Erlik, Gid-murt, Gudyri-mumy, Ilmarinen, Kala, Kalak, Kamak, K'daai, Ke'lets, Korka-murt, Kul, Kul-jungk, Kutkinnáku, Lemminkkäinen, Mumy, Murt, Muzem-mumy, Ñe'nvetičñin, Ñi'nvit, Nules-murt, Obin-murt, Šundy-mumy, Šur-mumy, Tonx, Ukulan-Tojon, Va-kul', Vasa, Vu-kutis, Vu-murt, Vu-nuna, Vu-vozo, Yanki-murt

Ukraine:
Domovik, Nari

Scandinavia (General to All):
Alberich, Alfar, Alvíss, Alwis, Andvari, Askafroa, Bäckahäst, Bar, Brock, Brynhilde, Dain, Davalin, Döcálfar, Döckalfar, Duergar, Duneyr, Durathror, Fjalar, Fylgir, Fylgjur, Galar, Gardsvor, Harr, Haugbonde, Hill Folk, Huldra, Huldu Folk, Hylde-Moer, Idun, Iwaldi, Lit, Lovar, Mimir, Mimring, Modsognir, Näcken, Naglfar, Nain, Neck, Neckan, Nibelung, Nicker, Nickur, Nicor, Nidhöggr, Nikke, Nix, Nökk, Nornir, Pukje, Sigrun, Sindri, Skogs Fru, Skuld, Smiera-Gatto, Swawa, Thekk, Thrain, Troll, Trolld, Udur, Valkyries, Verdandi, Völund, Waldgeister, Wish Wife, Wood Wives

Denmark
Berg People, Bergfolk, Bjerg-Trolde, Elle Folk, Elle King, Ellen, Elven, Grønjette, Havfrue, Havmand, Høgfolk, Hylde-Moer, Julenisse, Kirkegrim, Knurre Murre, Nis, Nøkke, Ole Luk Øj, Olsen, Skovtrolde, Snow Queen, Tommelise, Troll

Faroe Islands (United Kingdom)
Fodden Skemaend, Nickar, Nicker

Finland
Aiatar, Haltia, Juods, Kalevanpojat, Kodinhaltia, Kratti, Liekkiö, Liekko, Luot-Chozjik, Maahiset, Maanalaiset, Mära-Halddo, Metsänhaltia, Metsanneitsyt, Näkinneito, Näkki, Nökke, Ouda, Para, Saivo-Neita, Sjötroll, Talonhaltija, Tonttu, Troll, Tuulikki, Vedenhaltia

Greenland
Havstrambe

Iceland
Gilitrutt, Haikur, Jola Sveinar, Landvættir, Nickur, Ninnir, Púka, Skrimsl, Spae-wives

Lapland (Northern Regions of Scandinavia)
Čacce-haldde, Haldde, Leib-Olmai, Luot-Chozjik, Mära-Halddo, Miehts-Hozjin, Saivo-Neita, Smiera-Gatto, Tchatse-olmai, Yambe-akka

Norway
Fossegrim, Hamingja, Julenisse, Landvættir, Nisse, Nøkke, Strömkarl

Sweden
Elvor, Grove Folk, Grove Damsels, Jule Tomte, Kirkegrim, Kyrkogrim, Löfjerskor, Näcken, Ole Luk Öie, Rå, Rådande, Sjöra, Skogsrå, Strömkarl, Tomtar, Tomte Gubbe

Scotland (Including Hebrides, Orkney, and Shetland Islands):
Affric, Aiken Drum, Alriche, Arthur's Hunt, Auld Clootie, Auld Hornie, Ban Nighechain, Baoban Sith, Bean Nighe, Behir, Ben Baynac, Biasd Bheulach, Billy Blin, Bloody Cap, Blue Men of the Minch, Bodach, Bodachan Sabhaill, Bogil, Booman, Brollachan, Broonie, Brounger, Brown Man of the Muirs, Brownie, Brownie Clod, Buckie, Burryman, Cailleac, Cailleach Bheur, Caoineag, Caointeach, Carlin, Ce Sith, Cearb, Ceasg, Clashnichd Aulniac, Coluinn Gun Cheann, Cu Sith, Cuachag, Cughtagh, Demon Lover, Dobie, Doonie, Drows, Eač Uisge, Eldrich, Fachan, Falm, Fideal, Fin Folk, Finis, Fir Chlis, Frid, Fuath, Gentle Annis, Ghillie Dhu, Glaistig, Glashtin, Good Neighbours, Green Lady, Green Man, Green Women, Gruagach, Gyre-Carling, Henkies, Hind Etin, Hogboon, It, John Barleycorn, Kelpie, Killmoulis, Klippie, Loireag, Luideag, Luridan, Maggy Moloch, Mhorag, Mieg Moulach, Muileatach, Neugle, Nickneven, Nigheag na h-ath, Peallaidh, Pechs, Peerifool, Peter Pan, Puddlefoot, Roane, Samhanach, Selkies, Shellycoat, Shoney, Shoopiltie, Short Hoggers of Whittinghame, Sibhreach, Slaugh, Sleagh Maith, Spunkies, Tangie, Titania, Trows, Urisk, Vough, Wag at the Wa', Wee Willie Winkie

Spain, Portugal (Including Basque Region and Canary Islands):
Aatxe, Basa-Andre, Basajaun, Cuélebre, Duende, Erge, Estantigua, Fada, Güestia, Herensugue, Hirguan, Iguma, Lamia, Laminak, Nubero, Sirena, Torto, Trasgu, Xanas

Surinam:
See Guyana

Sweden:
See Scandinavia

Switzerland:
Armée Furieuse, Bottle Imp, Fantine, Napfhans, Nixie, Sammichlaus, Strätelli, Strudeli

Tanzania:
See Central and South Africa

Thailand (Including Andaman Islands):
Čauga, Erem Čauga, Jurua, Juruwin, Kaluks, Lau, Phi, Phra Phum, Ti-miku

Turkey:
See North Africa and Middle East

United States of America:
Anitsutsa, Ash Boys, Ashes Man, Aunt Nancy, Awl-man, Axeki, Big Water Man, Binaye Albani, Black Bear, Black Tamanous, Blue Jay, Chahuru, Child Medicine Woman, Chutsain, Cin-an-ev, Clay Mother, Cloud People, Corn Mother, Coyote, Cünawabi, Dajoji, De Hi No, Deohako, Devil Fish People, Dingbelle, Elves of Light, Escudáit, Father Koyemshi, Fifinella, Flint Boys, Gahe, Gahongas, G'an, Gandayaks, Ga-oh, Grandmother Fire, Gremlin, Gyhldeptis, Hactci, Hactcin, Heng, Heno, Herecgunina, Herok'a, Hocereu Wahira, Hoita, Honga, Honochenokeh, H'uraru, Ictcinike, Ictinike, Ikto, Iktomi, Isakawuate, Italapas, Italapate, Iya, Jersey Devil, John Barleycorn, Kachina, Kannuk, Katcina Mana, Keagyihl Depguesk, Kerwan, Kliwa, Kmnkamtch, Kokopelli, Kokopölö, Komokyatsiky, Koti, Koyemshi, Koyimshi, Koyote, Kwati, Leeds Devil, Mahih-Nah-Tiehey, Manabozo, Maninga, Masauwi, Mayochina, Mekumwasuk, Migamamesus, Mikak'e, Mikamwes, Mink, Miss Nancy, Molanhakto, Morityama, Müy'ingwa, Nagumwasuk, Naitaka, Nantena, Napi, Ne-a-go, Nemissa, Nenabushu, Nepokwa'i, Nesaru, Nunyunuwi, Ohdowas, Okulam, Old Man, Old Man Coyote, Onatah, Ondichaouan, Our Mother's Brother, O-yan-do-ne, Pamola, Pasikola, People Who Killed by Lightning in Their Eyes, Piasa, Pishumi, Plat-eye, Poker Boys, Pskégdemus, Rain People, Sahte, Salt Woman, Sand Altar Woman, Santa Claus, Selu, Shakak, Shiwanna, Shruisthia, Sio Humis, Sitkonsky, Skadegamutc, Smolenkos, Summer, Sünawavi, Tachuki, Thunder Boys, Tinihowi, Tobadzistsini, Tom Cockle, Tsects, Tsi-Zhui, Turquoise Boy, Turquoise Man, Unctome, Unktehi, Uti Hiata, Wanagemeswak, Wasicong, Water Babies, Wemicus, Wind Old Man, Wind Old Woman, Ya-o-gah, Yech, Yehl, Yeitso

Venezuela:
Gamainhas, Mauari, Máurari, Saraua

Vietnam:
Bà-Dúc-Chúa, Chu-Uhà, Co-Hon, Con-Ion, Con-Ma-Dāu, Con-Tinh, Dúc-Bà, Dúc-Thánh Bà

Wales (United Kingdom):
Addanc, Afanc, Bendith y Mamau, Black Sow, Bo-lol, Bwbach, Bwca, Bwcïod, Bwgan, Bwgan yr Hafod, Bwgwl, Bygel nos, Ceffyll-dŵr, Coblyn, Cwn Annwn, Cwn Mamau, Cyhiraeth, Cythraul, Diawl, Dynon Bach Teg, Ellylldan, Ellyllon, Gofannon, Gwarwyn-a-Throt, Gwenhidwy, Gwillion, Gwrach y Rhibyn, Gwragedd Annwn, Gwr-drwgiaid, Gŵyll, Gwyn ap Knudd, Hobby-lantern, Jili Ffrwtan, Lady of Little Van Lake, Llamhigyn y Dwr, Mab, Manawyddan, Morgan, Old Woman of the Mountain, Pisca, Plant Annwn, Plant Rhys Ddwfn, Pwca, Shewri, Sili Ffrit, Sili-go-dwt, Trwtyn Tratyn, Tylwyth Teg, Wrach, Ysbryd drwg

West Indies:
See Caribbean

Zaire and Zambia:
See Central and South Africa

BIBLIOGRAPHY

1. *About Us: A Catalogue of the Works of May Gibbs.* From May Gibbs and Her Fantasy World by R. Holden. Sydney, Australia: Royal Botanic Gardens, 1994.
2. Anderson, Hans Christian. *Danish Fairy Legends & Tales.* London: George Bell & Sons, 1891.
3. *The Anglo-Saxon Chronicles.* Collected and translated by Anne Savage. Published by arrangement with Phoebe Phillips Editions in association with Heinemann, London, 1983.
4. Ashton, J. *Chapbooks of the Eighteenth Century.* London: Chatto & Windus 1882. Reprinted by Skoob Books, London 1992.
5. Bamberg, R. W. *Haunted Dartmoor, A Ghost-hunter's Guide.* Newton Abbot, Devon: Peninsular Press, 1993.
6. Barber, R., and A. Riches. *A Dictionary of Fabulous Beasts.* Ipswich, England: Boydell Press, 1971.
7. Barclay, James. *Barclay's Universal Dictionary.* London: James Virtue, 1848.
8. Baring-Gould, S. *A Book of Folklore.* London: Collins, 1890.
9. Baum, L. Frank. *The Wizard of Oz.* London: Hutchinson & Co., 1900.
10. Bayley, H. *Archaic England.* London: Chapman & Hall, 1919.
11. Bett, Henry. *English Legends.* London: B. T. Batsford Ltd., 1950.
12. Blum, R., and E. Blum. *The Dangerous Hour: The Lore of Crisis & Mystery in Rural Greece.* London: Chatto & Windus, 1970.
13. Burland, Cottie A. *The Gods of Mexico.* London: Eyre & Spottiswood, 1967.
14. Bozic, S., and A. Marshall. *Aboriginal Myths.* Melbourne, Australia: Gold Star Publications, 1972.
15. Briggs, K. M. *The Anatomy of Puck.* London: Routledge & Keegan Paul, 1959.
16. ———. *British Folktales & Legends: A Sampler.* London: Paladin, 1977.
17. ———. *An Encyclopaedia of Fairies (Hobgoblins, Brownies, Bogies & Other Supernatural Creatures).* New York: Pantheon Books, 1976.
18. ———. *The Vanishing People.* London: B. T. Batsford Ltd., 1978.
19. Brown, Theo. *Devon Ghosts.* Norwich: Jarrold, 1982.
20. Bullfinch, Thomas. *The Age of Fable.* London, Everyman, 1910.
21. ———. *Bulfinch's Complete Mythology.* London: Hamlyn, 1964.
22. Bullock, M. *Easter Island.* London: The Scientific Book Club, 1957.
23. Bunyan, John. *The Pilgrim's Progress.* Glasgow, London, and Edinburgh: William Mackenzie, 1861.
24. Burland, C. A. *Myths of Life & Death.* London: MacMillan, 1972.
25. ———. *North American Indian Mythology.* London: Hamlyn, 1965.
26. Burland, C., Nicholson, I., Osborne, H. *Mythology of the Americas.* London: Hamlyn, 1970.
27. Burne, C. S. *The Handbook of Folklore.* London: Sidgwick & Jackson, 1914.
28. Carew-Hazlitt, W. *Faiths & Folklore, A Dictionary.* Reeves & Turner, 1905.
29. Carlyon, Richard. *A Guide to the Gods.* London: Heinemann/Quixote, 1981.
30. Cavendish, R., ed. *Legends of the World.* London: Orbis Publishing, 1982.
31. Clébert, J. P. *The Gypsies.* Translated by C. Duff. London: Readers' Union, 1964.
32. Cliffe, S. *Shadows: A Northern Investigation of the Unknown.* Wilmslow, Cheshire, England: Sigma Press, 1993.
33. Cotterell, A. *A Dictionary of World Mythology.* London: Windward, 1979.
34. Crichton, Robin. *Who Is Santa Claus?* Edinburgh, Scotland: Canongate Publishing, 1987.
35. Dickson, M. *The Saga of the Sea Swallow.* London: H. D. Innes, 1896.
36. Dixon, E., ed. *Fairy Tales from the Arabian Nights.* London: Dent, 1893.
37. Duffy, M. *The Erotic World of Fairy.* London: Cardinal, 1989.
38. *Dwarfs.* The Enchanted World Series. Amsterdam: Time-Life Books, 1985.
39. *The Encyclopaedia of Comparative Religion.* London: Everyman, 1965.
40. Evans, I. ed. *Brewer's Dictionary of Phrase & Fable.* London: Centenary Edition, Cassell, 1978.
41. *Everyman's Dictionary of Non-Classical Mythology.* London: Everyman Reference, 1965.
42. Ewing, J. H. *Lob-Lie-by-the-Fire.* London: SPCK, 1888.

43. Eyre, K. *Lancashire Ghosts.* Yorkshire, England: Dalesman Books, 1979.

44. *Fairies & Elves.* The Enchanted World Series. Amsterdam: Time-Life Books, 1985.

45. Fewkes, J. W. *Designs on Hopi Pottery.* New York: Dover Publications, 1973.

46. "Folklore and Superstition. " Subject folder in the Library of Vladimir Pedagogical Institute, Vladimir, Russia.

47. *Folklore Myths & Legends of Britain.* London: Reader's Digest, 1973.

48. Frazer, J. G. *The Golden Bough.* London: Papermac, 1987.

49. Gainsford, J., ed. *The Atlas of Man.* London: Omega Books, 1987.

50. Galsworthy, John. *The Awakening.* London: Heinemann.

51. Gaselee, Stephen. *Stories from the Christian East.* London: Sidgwick & Jackson, 1918.

52. Gaskell, D. S. *Dictionary of Scripture & Myth.* Dorset Press, 1883.

53. Gaynor, F., ed. *Dictionary of Mysticism.* London: Wildwood House Publishers, 1974.

54. Gibbs, May. *The Complete Adventures of Snugglepot & Cuddlepie.* London: Angus Robertson, 1946. Reprinted by Bluegum Publishers, 1984.

55. ———. *Gumnut Town.* Sydney, Australia: Royal Botanic Gardens, 1992.

56. Gordon, Stuart. *The Encyclopaedia of Myths & Legends.* London: Headline, 1993.

57. Greenwood, J. *Savage Habits & Customs.* London: S. O. Beeton, 1865.

58. Guerber, H. *Myths & Legends of the Middle Ages.* London: Harrap, 1948.

59. Gwynn Jones, T. *Welsh Folklore & Folk Custom.* London: Methuen, 1930.

60. Hall, S. C. *The Book of British Ballads.* London: Jeremiah How, 1847.

61. ———, ed. *The Book of British Ballads.* Rev ed. London: Jeremiah How, 1848.

62. *Hall's Dictionary of Subjects & Symbols in Art.* London: Murray, 1979.

63. Hanson, A., and L. Hanson. *Counterpoint in Maori Culture.* London: Routledge & Kegan Paul, 1983.

64. Harner, M. J. *The Jívaro, People of the Sacred Waterfalls.* London: Robert Hale, 1973.

65. Hawthorne, N. *A Wonder Book for Boys & Girls & Tanglewood Tales.* London: Dent, 1910.

66. Henderson, W. *Folklore of the Northern Counties of England & the Borders.* London: Longmans Green, 1866.

67. Hill, D., and P. Williams. *The Supernatural.* London: Aldus Books, 1965.

68. Hiltebeitel, A., ed. *Criminal Gods & Demon Devotees.* Albany: State University of New York, 1989.

69. Hippisley-Coxe, Anthony D. *Haunted Britain.* London: Pan Books Ltd., 1973.

70. Hole, C. *A Dictionary of British Folk Custom.* London: Paladin/Collins, 1986.

71. Housman, L. *All-Fellows.* London: Kegan Paul Trench Trübner, 1896.

72. ———. *The Field of Clover.* London: Kegan Paul Trench Trübner, 1898.

73. Hyslop, Robert, ed. *Echoes from the Border Hills.* Durham: Pentland Press, 1992.

74. Irving, Washington. *Rip Van Winkle.* London: Heinemann, 1917.

75. Ivanits, Linda J. *Russian Folk Belief.* New York: M. E. Sharpe, 1989.

76. Jacobs, Joseph, ed. *Celtic Fairy Tales.* London: David Nutt, 1895.

77. Jones, Henry, and Lewis L. Kropp. *The Folk Tales of the Magyars.* London: The Folklore Society, 1889.

78. Keightley, Thomas. *The Fairy Mythology.* London: Whittacker-Treacher, 1833.

79. Kendall, L. *Shamans, Housewives & Other Restless Spirits.* Honolulu: University of Hawaii Press, 1985.

80. Ker Wilson, B. *Scottish Folktales & Legends.* Oxford: Oxford University Press, 1954.

81. Killip, M. *Folklore of the Isle of Man.* London: B. T. Batsford Ltd., 1975.

82. Knatchbull-Huggeson, E. *River Legends.* London: Daldy, Ibister & Co., 1875.

83. Lang, A. *Custom & Myth.* London: Longmans Green, 1898.

84. ———, ed. *The Elf Maiden & Other Stories.* London: Longmans Green, 1906.

85. ———, ed. *The Snow Queen & Other Stories.* London: Longmans Green , 1906.

86. Langer, William L., ed. *The Encyclopaedia of World History.* London: Harrap/Galley Press, 1987.

87. Leach, M. ed. *The Dictionary of Folklore.* Chicago: Funk & Wagnall, 1985.

88. ———, ed. *The Standard Dictionary of Folklore.* Chicago: Funk & Wagnall, 1972.

89. Leacock, S., and R. Leacock. *Spirits of the Deep.* New York: Doubleday, 1972.

90. Legey, F. *The Folklore of Morocco.* Translated from the 1926 French edition by L. Hotz. London: Allen & Unwin, 1935.

91. Litvinoff, ed. *The Illustrated Guide to the Supernatural.* Marshall-Cavendish, 1990.

92. *Lloyd's Encyclopaedic Dictionary.* London: Edward Lloyd, 1895.

93. Lurker, Manfred. *Dictionary of Gods & Goddesses, Devils & Demons.* Translated by G. L. Campbell. London: Routledge, 1989.

94. Lyon, P. J. *Native South Americans.* Boston: Little Brown, 1974.

95. Macdowall, M. W. *Asgard & the Gods: Tales & Traditions of Our Northern Ancestors.* Adapted from the work of W. Wägner. London: Swan Sonnenschein, 1902.

96. MacKinnon, J. *Scottish Folk Tales in Gaelic & English.* Edinburgh, Scotland: JMK Consultancy Publishing, 1991.

97. Maple, Eric. *Superstition & the Superstitious.* London, New York: W. H. Allen, 1971.

98. Martin, B. W. *The Dictionary of the Occult.* London: Rider, 1979.

99. Menger, M., and C. Gagnon. *Lake Monster Traditions, A Cross-Cultural Analysis.* London: Fortean Tomes, 1988.

100. Mollet, J. W. *An Illustrated Dictionary of Antique Art & Archaeology.* London: Omega, 1927.

101. Mowat, F. *People of the Deer.* London: Readers' Union, Michael Joseph, 1954.

102. *New Larousse Encyclopaedia of Mythology.* London: Book Club Associates, 1973.

103. Newman, P. *Gods & Graven Images.* London: Robert Hale, 1987.

104. *Night Creatures.* The Enchanted World Series. Amsterdam: Time-Life Books, 1985.

105. O'hOgain, D. *Myth Legend & Romance: An Encyclopaedia of the Irish Folk Tradition.* New York: Prentice Hall, 1991.

106. Opie, I., and P. Opie, eds. *The Oxford Dictionary of Nursery Rhymes.* Oxford: Oxford University Press, 1977.

107. *The Oxford English Dictionary.* Compact ed. Oxford: Oxford University Press, 1971.

108. Parry-Jones, D. *Welsh Legends & Fairy Folk Lore.* London: B. T. Batsford Ltd., 1953.

109. Poignant, R. *Myths & Legends of the South Seas.* London: Hamlyn, 1970.

110. Porteous, A. *Forest Folklore.* London: G. Allen & Unwin, 1928.

111. *The Rider Encyclopaedia of Eastern Philosophy & Religion.* London: Rider, 1986.

112. Risdon, J., A. Stevens, and B. Whitworth. *A Glympse of Dartmoor: Villages, Folklore, Tors, & Place Names.* Newton Abbot, Devon: Peninsular Press, 1992.

113. Robbins, R. H. *The Encyclopaedia of Witchcraft & Demonology.* London: Bookplan/Hamlyn, 1959.

114. Rose-Benét, W., ed. *The Reader's Encyclopaedia.* London: Book Club, 1974.

115. *Royal Pageantry, Customs & Festivals of Great Britain & Northern Ireland.* London: Purnell & Sons, 1967.

116. Ryan, J., and G. Bardon. *Mythscapes: Aboriginal Art of the Desert.* National Heart Foundation, National Gallery, Melbourne, Australia, 1989.

117. Saggs, H. W. F. *Civilization Before Greece & Rome.* London: B. T. Batsford Ltd., 1989.

118. Seebok, T. A., and F. J. Ingemann. *Studies in Cheremis: The Supernatural.* Viking Fund Publications in Anthropology No. 22. New York: Werner-Gren Foundation for Anthropological Research, 1956.

119. Senior, Michael. *The Illustrated Who's Who in Mythology.* Edited by G. Paminder. London: MacDonald Illustrated, 1985.

120. Skeat, W. W. *Malay Magic.* Oxford, England: Oxford University Press, 1889. Reprinted by Singapore: Oxford University Press, 1984.

121. *Spells & Bindings.* The Enchanted World Series. Amsterdam, Time-Life Books, 1985.

122. Spence, Lewis. *North American Indians, Myths & Legends.* Studio Editions Ltd., 1993, Copyright Bracken Books, 1985.

123. ———. *The Minor Traditions of British Mythology.* London: Rider & Co., 1948.

124. Squire, C. *Celtic Myth & Legend Poetry & Romance.* London: Gresham Publishing Co., 1889.

125. ———. *Celtic Myth & Legend Poetry & Romance.* London: Gresham Publishing Co., 1910.

126. Stow, John. *Stow's Annales.* London, 1600.

127. *Strange Scottish Stories.* Retold by W. Owen. Norwich, England: Jarrold Press, 1983.

128. Summers, Montague. *The History of Witchcraft.* London: Mystic Press, 1925.

129. Swinburne-Carr, T. *A New Classical Lexicon of Biography, Mythology & Geography.* London: Simpkins Marshall, 1858.

130. Vale, E. *Pixie Pool.* London: Heffer, 1911.

131. Walters, D. *Chinese Mythology: An Encyclopaedia of Myth & Legend.* Aquarian/Thorsons, 1992.

132. *Water Spirits.* The Enchanted World Series. Amsterdam: Time-Life Books, 1985.

133. Westwood, Jennifer. *Albion, A Guide to Lagendary Britain.* London: Grafton, 1992.

134. *William Cashen's Manx Folklore.* Ed. S. Morrisson, Douglas, Isle of Man: G. L. Johnson, 1912.

135. Williams-Ellis, A. *Fairies & Enchanters.* London: Nelson.

136. Yeats, W. B., ed. *Fairy & Folk Tales of the Irish Peasantry.* London: W. Scott Ltd.

137. Voodoo in New York. Documentary televised Oct. 22, 1995.